The Law of Higher Education

*A Comprehensive Guide
to Legal Implications
of Administrative Decision Making*

SECOND EDITION

William A. Kaplin

The Law of
Higher Education

*A Comprehensive Guide
to Legal Implications
of Administrative Decision Making*

SECOND EDITION

Jossey-Bass Publishers
San Francisco • London • 1985

THE LAW OF HIGHER EDUCATION
A Comprehensive Guide to Legal Implications
of Administrative Decision Making
   by William A. Kaplin

Copyright © 1985 by: Jossey-Bass Inc., Publishers
                      433 California Street
                      San Francisco, California 94104
                                &
                      Jossey-Bass Limited
                      28 Banner Street
                      London EC1Y 8QE

Library of Congress Cataloging in Publication Data

Kaplin, William A.
      The law of higher education.

      (The Jossey-Bass higher education series)
      Includes bibliographies and indexes.
      1. Universities and colleges—Law and legislation—
United States.   I. Title.   II. Series.
KF4225.K36   1985   344.73′074   85-47987
ISBN 0-87589-619-7 (alk. paper)   347.30474

Manufactured in the United States of America

The paper in this book meets the guidelines for
permanence and durability of the Committee on
Production Guidelines for Book Longevity of the
Council on Library Resources.

JACKET DESIGN BY WILLI BAUM

SECOND EDITION

Code 8524

The Jossey-Bass Higher Education Series

Preface

This book is the revised and expanded second edition of a volume first published in 1978 and later updated with a companion volume (*The Law of Higher Education 1980*). This new edition retains all material of continuing currency from the first edition and the update volume, reedited to maximize clarity and to accommodate the deletion and addition of materials. Considerable new material is added to this base: over half of the material in this second edition did not appear in either the first edition or the update. The new material extends the discussion of matters that (in hindsight) are given insufficient attention in the first edition; integrates pertinent new developments regarding topics in the first edition and update; and introduces numerous new topics not covered in the first edition or update.

The second edition retains the organization, format, and objectives of the first edition and reflects the same perspective on the intersection of law and education. All these matters are addressed in the preface to the first edition, portions of which bear repeating:

> The law has arrived on the campus. Sometimes it has been a beacon, other times a blanket of ground fog. But even in its murkiness, the law has not come "on little cat feet," like Carl Sandburg's "Fog"; nor has it sat silently on its haunches; nor will it soon move on. It has come noisily and sometimes has stumbled. And even in its imperfections, the law has spoken forcefully and meaningfully to the higher education community and will continue to do so.

The Law of Higher Education is written for administrators and legal counsel who deal with the multitudes of new challenges and complexities that arise from the law's presence on campus and for students and observers of higher education and law who desire to explore the intersection of these two disciplines. In this book *higher education* is considered broadly and covers all *postsecondary* education—from the large state university to the small private liberal arts college, from the graduate and professional school to the community college and vocational and technical institution, from the traditional campus-based program to the innovative off-campus or multistate program. For persons dealing with all or part of this universe, as specialists or as generalists, this book is intended to provide an analytical text, a practical guide, a ready reference, and a research resource. To be equally usable by administrators and legal counsel, the text avoids legal jargon and technicalities when possible and explains them when used. Footnotes throughout the book are designed primarily to provide additional technical analysis and research resources for legal counsel.

Chapter One provides a framework for understanding and integrating what is presented in subsequent chapters and a perspective for dealing with future legal developments. Chapters Two through Four discuss legal concepts and issues affecting the internal relationships among the various members of the campus community and address the law's impact on particular roles, functions, and responsibilities of postsecondary administrators. Chapters Five through Seven are concerned with the postsecondary institution's external relationships with local, state, and federal government and examine broad questions of governmental power and process that cut across all the internal relationships and administrative functions considered in Chapters Two through Four. These chapters also discuss particular legal issues arising from the institution's dealings with government agencies and identify connections to the issues explored in the earlier chapters. In each instance, the issues in Chapters Five through Seven involve a particular level of government, while the issues in Chapters Two through Four involve a particular institutional relationship or administrative function regardless of what level(s) of government may have an impact on it. Chapter Eight also deals with the institution's external relationships—not to government but to the private educational accrediting agencies. Although these agencies are part of the larger academic community and are themselves monitored by government, the institution's relationships with them in some respects parallel those with government agencies. The mixture creates an interesting, concluding perspective from which to view the developing relationship between education and law.

Each chapter ends with a selected annotated bibliography. Readers can use the sources listed to extend the discussion of particular issues presented in the chapter, to explore issues not treated in the chapter, to obtain additional practical guidance in dealing with the chapter's issues, to keep up to date on later developments, or to discover resources for research. Other sources pertaining to particular questions are cited occasionally in the text, and footnotes contain additional legal resources, primarily for lawyers. Court decisions, statutes, and administrative regulations are cited throughout the text. The citation form generally follows *A Uniform System of Citation* [13th ed. (Harvard Law Review Association, 1981)], and the legal resources that the citations refer to are explained in Chapter One, Sections 1.3.2 to 1.3.5. The appendix contains an abridged version of the United States Constitution.

Much has happened since publication of the first edition and the update. New problems, policy initiatives, and legal issues affecting higher education have continued to arise. In response, courts, legislatures, and administrative agencies have continued to fashion new law. And commentators on law and educational policy have continued to generate reports, articles, symposia, and books that enlarge our perspective of events. The second edition captures these developments by analyzing the major new court opinions, statutes, and administrative regulations; citing or annotating the major new commentaries; and providing practical guidance for dealing with the emerging issues. For the most important of the recent court opinions, and occasionally for the statues and administrative regulations, substantial excerpts from the primary source material are included. Cases and other authorities cited in the excerpts from court opinions are sometimes deleted without indication, and the courts' footnotes to these excerpts are routinely deleted without indication.

In the light cast by recent developments, some new topics of concern have emerged on stage and some older topics that were bit players have assumed major roles. To cover these topics, the second edition adds entirely new sections on: organizing the postsecondary institution's legal affairs (Section 1.6); bargaining unit eligibility of full-time faculty (including the U.S. Supreme Court's decision in *NLRB* v. *Yeshiva University*) (Section 3.2.3); sexual harassment, sex discrimination in pay (including the ''comparable worth'' theory), confidentiality of faculty votes on personnel decisions (including the case of *In re Dinnan*), and discrimination against white professors—all unnumbered subsections at the end of Section 3.3.2.1; protection of confidential academic information (Section 3.6.6); religious activities of student organizations (including the case of *Widmar* v. *Vincent*) (Section 4.8.4); protection against violent campus crime (Section 4.14.2); reapportionment and student voting (Section 5.4.4); chartering and licensure of church-related institutions (Section 6.3.2); state administrative procedure, unemployment compensation, and workers' compensation laws (Sections 6.5.2 to 6.5.4); applicability of employment discrimination laws to religious institutions (Section 7.2.5.2); immigration laws (Section 7.2.6); laws governing research on human subjects (Section 7.2.7); patent laws (Section 7.2.9); federal Social Security and unemployment compensation tax laws (Sections 7.3.2 and 7.3.3); and application of defamation law to accreditation (Section 8.2.4).

Other sections appearing in the first edition or added by the update volume have been considerably expanded to account for more recent developments. These include institutional federal civil rights liability (Section 2.3.3); status of part-time faculty members (Section 3.1.5); tenure termination for cause (Section 3.4.2); student bankruptcies (Section 4.3.6.1); grades, credits, and degrees (Section 4.5); local taxation of property used for educational purposes (Section 5.3.2); trespass laws (including the *Princeton University* case) (Section 5.6.3); soliciting and canvassing on campus (including the various decisions in the *American Future Systems* v. *Penn State* litigation) (Section 5.6.4.1); federal antitrust law's application to postsecondary education (Section 7.2.10); federal income taxation of postsecondary education (including the *Bob Jones University* case) (Section 7.3.1); and the scope of nondiscrimination requirements applicable to federal funding programs (Section 7.5.7).

Most of the remaining sections from the first edition or update have also been revised to accommodate some specific new development. For example, *Rendell-Baker* v. *Kohn*, the U.S. Supreme Court's decision on the state action doctrine, is inserted into Section 1.4.2; *Bradshaw* v. *Rawlings*, the case on an institution's negligence liability for injuries arising from student use of alcoholic beverages, into Section 2.3.1.1; *Kunda* v. *Muhlenberg College*, the case on judicial authority to award conditional tenure as a remedy for sex discrimination, into Section 3.3.2.1; *Valentine* v. *Smith*, the case on affirmative action plans for faculty hiring, into Section 3.3.4; *Jimenez* v. *Almodovar*, the case on faculty dismissals due to program termination, into Section 3.7.1; *Mississippi University for Women* v. *Hogan*, the case on sex discrimination in student admissions, into Section 4.2.4.2; the *DeRonde* and *McDonald* cases, on affirmative action plans for student admissions, into Section 4.2.5; *Mazart* v. *State*, the New York case on libel claims against student newspapers, into Section 4.9.4; the federal Privacy Protection Act of 1980, on police searches of files of persons preparing materials for publication, into Section 5.5; the *Nova University* case, on state regulation of out-of-state schools, into Section 6.4; the *Adams* v. *Bell* litigation, on federal guidelines for desegregating public systems of higher education, into Sections 7.5.2 and 7.5.8; the Regulatory Flexibility Act, on federal regulation of "small" entities, into Section 7.6.1; and the *Sherman College of Straight Chiropractic* case, on the secretary of education's authority to recognize accrediting agencies, into Section 8.3.

As with the first edition, some precautions on using this second edition are in order:

> The legal analyses and suggestions, of necessity, are general; they are not adapted to the law of any particular state or to the circumstances prevailing at any particular postsecondary institution. Thus, the book is not a substitute for the advice of legal counsel, for further research into primary legal resources, or for individualized study of each legal problem's specific circumstances. Nor is the book necessarily the latest word on the law. There is a saying among lawyers that "the law must be stable and yet it cannot stand still" [R. Pound, *Interpretations of Legal History*, p. 1 (1923)], and the law is moving especially fast in its applications to postsecondary education. Thus, administrators and counsel will want to keep abreast of ongoing developments concerning the issues in this book. Various aids exist for this purpose. The selected annotated bibliographies in this book list various loose-leaf services and newsletters that report periodically on legal developments in particular areas. Footnotes to the text cite *American Law Reports* (A.L.R.) annotations—lawyers' research tools on particular subjects—which are updated periodically with recent cases.

Keeping abreast of developments is just as much a necessity—and a challenge—as it was when the first edition was published. Thankfully, two new legal reporters now provide substantial help: *Specialty Law Digest: Education*, published monthly by the Bureau of National Affairs, Washington, D.C.; and *West's Educa-*

tion Law Reporter, published monthly by West Publishing Company, St. Paul, Minnesota. Both resources are included in the Selected Annotated Bibliography for Chapter One, Section 1.1. Also helpful are various periodicals providing information on current legal developments. The *School Law News*, for example, is a biweekly publication of Capitol Publications, Arlington, Virginia, providing journalistic coverage of legal events. The *College Law Digest*, published biweekly for its members by the National Association of College and University Attorneys (NACUA) in cooperation with West Publishing Company, reports on recent court decisions (unpublished as well as published), journal articles and other publications, and acquisitions by NACUA's Exchange of Legal Information program; it also contains original commentary on current topics. *Lex Collegii*, a newsletter published quarterly by College Legal Information, Inc., Nashville, Tennessee, analyzes selected legal issues and provides preventive legal planning information especially for private institutions. *Business Officer*, a monthly magazine published for its members by the National Association of College and University Business Officers, emphasizes federal legislative and administrative agency developments. And the *School Law Reporter*, published bimonthly by the National Organization on Legal Problems of Education (NOLPE), Topeka, Kansas, digests recent court decisions.

For news reporting of current events in higher education generally, but including substantial coverage of legal developments, one may wish to consult the *Chronicle of Higher Education*, published weekly by Editorial Projects for Education, Washington, D.C.; or *Higher Education Daily*, published every weekday by Capitol Publications. For extended analytical commentary of recent developments, these two journals should be helpful: the *Journal of College and University Law*, published quarterly by NACUA and focusing exclusively on postsecondary education; and the *Journal of Law and Education*, covering elementary and secondary as well as postsecondary education and published quarterly by Jefferson Lawbook Company, Cincinnati, Ohio. Most of these sources and others are described, and their uses are examined, in R. Schaffer, *Legal Resources for Higher Education Law: A Review Essay* (Monograph 84-3, Institute for Higher Education Law and Governance, University of Houston, 1984), reprinted in 7 *Review of Higher Education* 443 (1984) and to be reprinted in 12 *J. of College and University Law* no.1 (in press).

Overall, the goal for this second edition is the same as for the first edition:

> The hope of this book is to provide a base for the debate concerning law's role on campus; for improved understanding between law and academia; and for effective relationships between administrators and counsel. The challenge of our age is not to get the law off the campus; it is there to stay. The challenge is to make law more a beacon and less a fog. The challenge is for law and higher education to accommodate one another, preserving the best values of each for the mutual benefit of both. Just as academia benefits from the understanding and respect of the legal community, so law benefits from the understanding and respect of academia.

Washington, D.C.   WILLIAM A. KAPLIN
July 1985

Acknowledgments

Numerous people have helped in the preparation of this second edition, and I owe many debts of gratitude.

There would never have been a second edition had there not been a first. The contributions of the many people who helped make the first edition and the update volume a reality—and whose names appear in the acknowledgments for those volumes—continue to be reflected in this new edition.

Many people have commented on the first edition and the update volume, either in published reviews or in conversation or correspondence with me. Their comments have helped me to affirm (and thus expand) the strengths of the earlier volumes and to identify (and thus rectify) their weaknesses.

The American Council on Education and the Borden Foundation recognized the first edition as the year's outstanding book on higher education. In presenting me the Borden Award, the council and foundation provided an impetus for continuing the work that has now resulted in this new edition.

Many colleagues at the Columbus School of Law, Catholic University of America, reviewed portions of the second edition manuscript, providing helpful feedback on matters within their expertise and cheerful good wishes for the project: Leroy Clark, Robert Destro, Clifford Fishman, George Garvey, Roger Hartley, Urban Lester, David Lipton, Craig Parker (who is also assistant general counsel for Catholic University), Ralph Rohner, Samantha Sanchez, George Smith, William Taylor, and Harvey Zuckman. Ralph Rohner and Harvey Zuckman also assisted with the first edition, and Roger Hartley and William Taylor assisted with both the first edition and the update.

Various colleagues from outside my faculty also reviewed sections of the manuscript and gave helpful advice: Nancy Duff Campbell of the National Women's Law Center; Charles Chambers, counsel to the Council on Postsecondary Accreditation; Barbara Lee, a professor at the Institute of Management and Labor Relations, Rutgers; Elliott Lichtman, private practitioner in Washington, D.C.; John Murnane, private practitioner in New York City; David Pollen, chairman of the Education Appeal Board, U.S. Department of Education; and Theodore Sky, associate general counsel, U.S. Department of Education. In addition, Carol Clifford, a labor lawyer in Washington, D.C., kept me posted on current developments in labor and employment law; and Michael Olivas, director of the Institute for Higher Education Law and Governance, University of Houston, provided me a week's quiet haven at his institute to work on the latter stages of manuscript preparation.

Steven Frankino, dean of my law school, was always understanding when the pressures of this book drew my attention from other faculty obligations; he also provided for support services to meet all my needs. Gayle Campbell, law faculty office manager, organized and oversaw my support services with great skill and efficiency. Rhonda Lawrence and Alice Bush, faculty secretaries, were responsible for preparing (and frequently revising) the manuscript and maintaining the files—both displaying mastery of word processing and a sensitivity to my needs and time schedules. John Valeri, director of the law library, found every resource that I asked him to locate.

My law student research assistants provided valuable aid at every stage of this project: Lawrence Brenner, Susan Hafey, Karen Johnson, Kathleen Heenan McGuan, Charles Reid, and Thomas Scheuermann (who served as assistant to the director for resident life, University of Maryland, while studying law part time). Charles Reid won the longevity and loyalty award, having served as my research assistant for over four years, up to and including the review of page proofs—a feat he accomplished by staying at the university to obtain a degree in canon law after graduating from the law school.

Dorothy Conway, manuscript editor for this volume (as for the 1980 update), helped devise the editorial plans and then stuck with me through every page, sentence, and citation—offering constructive suggestions and technical improvements with as much precision, commitment, and patience as any author could want.

My family accepted the more than four years of intrusion that this second edition imposed on our lives. My wife, Barbara Ann, encouraged me with assurances that the ''book party'' we would have after publication would be even livelier than the one we had had for the first edition. Our children, Colleen, Keith, Lynn, and Carole, routinely accepted my protestations that ''I have to work on the book''—but nevertheless provided joys and crises that kept me from becoming too engrossed in my project. My parents, Al and Joan Kaplin of Tonawanda, New York, to whom I owe a lifetime of gratitude, were constant as ever in their support. To my family, I dedicate this book.

Table of Contents

The Author

WILLIAM A. KAPLIN is professor of law at the Catholic University of America, Washington, D.C., where he is also consultant to the university legal counsel. He was the first director of his law school's Law and Public Policy Program and has been a visiting professor at Cornell Law School. He is the former editor of the *Journal of College and University Law* and a former member of the Education Appeal Board, U.S. Department of Education.

In recognition of the first edition of his book *The Law of Higher Education*, Kaplin received the American Council on Education's Borden Award. He is also the author of numerous articles and reports in the field of education law and policy, and coauthor (with M. Sorgen, P. Duffy, and E. Margolin) of *State, School, and Family: Cases and Materials on Law and Education* (2nd ed. 1979).

William Kaplin received his bachelor's degree in political science from the University of Rochester (1964) and the Doctor of Law degree with distinction from Cornell University (1967), where he was editor-in-chief of the *Cornell Law Review*. He then worked with a Washington, D.C., law firm, served as a law clerk at the U.S. Court of Appeals for the District of Columbia Circuit, and was an attorney in the education division of the U.S. Department of Health, Education and Welfare before joining the Catholic University law faculty. He now lives in the Maryland suburbs of Washington with his wife, Barbara Ann, and children, Colleen, Keith, Lynn, and Carole.

The Law of
Higher Education

A Comprehensive Guide
to Legal Implications
of Administrative Decision Making

SECOND EDITION

I

Overview
of Postsecondary
Education Law

Sec. 1.1. How Far the Law Reaches and How Loud It Speaks: Some Illustrative Cases

Since the first edition of this volume was published, law's presence on the campus—its impact on the daily affairs of postsecondary institutions—has not diminished. Whether one is responding to campus disputes, planning to avoid future disputes, or charting the institution's policies and priorities, law remains an indispensable consideration. Issues arising on campuses across America continue to be aired outside the groves of academia. Students, faculty members, and their institutions are all frequently litigants in the courts. As this trend continues, more and more questions of educational policy become converted into legal questions as well. Cases recently filed in court indicate the extent of attempts to spread the law into every corner of campus activity. In New England a student sued his university for a million dollars in damages after he was accused of plagiarism on a take-home examination and suspended for a semester. In a Great Lakes state, a college basketball player sought an injunction ordering his institution to admit him to a bachelor's degree program so that he could maintain eligibility for intercollegiate sports. Handicapped students at various institutions have filed suits against their institutions or state rehabilitation agencies, seeking sign language interpreters or other auxiliary services to support their educations. All across the country, postsecondary institutions have been involved in bankruptcy proceedings in which former students seek discharge of student loan debts. And on the Pacific Coast, in a lawsuit surely deserv-

1

ing an award of some kind, a student sued her institution for $125,000 after an instructor gave her a B+ grade which she claimed should have been an A-.

Faculty members have been similarly active. In the Southwest a tenured professor sought an injunction after his institution reduced his laboratory space from 1,000 to 300 square feet. In the Southeast faculty members challenged their institution's plan to build a new basketball arena because they feared that construction costs would create a drain on funds available for academic programs. On the Pacific Coast, faculty members alleging sex discrimination and violation of free speech challenged their institution's decision to terminate several women's studies courses. In a number of states, female faculty members sued their institutions and the Teachers Insurance and Annuity Association–College Retirement Equities Fund (TIAA-CREF), claiming that college retirement programs illegally discriminated on the basis of sex. Across the country suits brought by faculty members who have been denied tenure—once one of the most closely guarded and sacrosanct of all institutional judgments—are now commonplace.

Outside parties also have been increasingly involved in postsecondary education disputes. In the handicapped student cases above, state rehabilitation agencies were sometimes defendants; and in the cases on faculty retirement programs, the program sponsor, TIAA-CREF, was also sued. In other recent suits, a West Coast and an East Coast university both sued a prominent charitable organization that had unilaterally terminated contracts to subsidize research centers on the two campuses; an eastern university sued a sporting goods company for trademark infringement because the company allegedly appropriated the university's insignia and emblems for use on sporting goods; a broadcasting company sued the National Collegiate Athletic Association (NCAA) over rights to control television broadcasts of intercollegiate football games; the Association for Intercollegiate Athletics for Women (AIAW) sued the NCAA for alleged violation of federal antitrust laws after the NCAA established women's championship competitions; an institution with branch campuses in a number of states sued a state licensing official for declaring a moratorium on recognizing degrees that the institution awarded to students at its branch campuses in the state; and a Pacific Coast university and a drug company sued each other in a dispute over patent rights to a discovery stemming from genetic research in which they were separately engaged.

As such judicial business has expanded, so has the use of administrative agencies as alternative forums for airing legal disputes. Since government deregulation is more talk than action thus far, government regulations still apply to many aspects of college operations, and new regulations still issue forth, though at a slower pace. Thus, postsecondary institutions may find themselves before the federal Equal Employment Opportunity Commission, the National Labor Relations Board, the administrative law judges of the U.S. Department of Education, state licensing or approval boards, state public employment commissions and civil service commissions, state or local human relations commissions, local zoning boards, and other quasi-judicial bodies at all levels of government. Proceedings can be complex, and the legal sanctions that these agencies may invoke can be substantial.

Paralleling these developments has been an increase in the forums for dispute resolution created by private organizations and associations involved in postsecondary governance. Thus, besides appearing before courts and administrative agencies, postsecondary institutions may become involved in grievance procedures of faculty and staff unions, hearings of accrediting agencies on the accreditation status of institutional programs, probation hearings of athletic conferences, and censure proceedings of the American Association of University Professors. Similarly, postsecondary institutions are themselves creating new internal processes, such as faculty grievance committees and student judiciaries for resolving legal disputes and reviewing discrimination claims.

Law's role on the campuses has been subject to much recent criticism. It is said that the law reaches too far and speaks too loudly. Especially because of the courts' and federal government's involvement, it is said that legal proceedings and compliance with legal requirements are too costly, in money, talents, and energies; that they divert higher education from its primary mission of teaching and scholarship; and that they erode the integrity of campus decision making by bending it to real or perceived legal technicalities that are not always in the campus community's best interests. Such criticisms highlight pressing issues for higher education's future, but they do not reveal all sides of these issues. We cannot evaluate the role of law on campus by looking only at dollars expended, hours of time logged, pages of compliance reports completed, or numbers of legal proceedings participated in. We must also consider a number of less quantifiable questions: Are legal claims made against institutions, faculty, or staff usually frivolous or unimportant, or are they often justified? Are institutions providing adequate mechanisms for dealing with claims and complaints internally, thus helping themselves avoid any negative effects of outside legal proceedings? Are courts and college counsel doing an adequate job of sorting out frivolous from justifiable claims, and of developing means for summary disposition of frivolous claims, where appropriate, and settlement of justifiable ones? Are courts being sensitive to the mission of higher education when they apply legal rules to campuses or devise remedies in suits lost by institutions? Do government regulations for the campus implement worthy policy goals, and are they adequately sensitive to higher education's mission? In situations where law's message has appeared to conflict with the best interests of the campus community, what have been education's responses: to kill the messenger, or to develop more positive remedies; to hide behind rhetoric, or to forthrightly document and defend its interests?

We do not yet know all we should about these questions. But they are clearly a critical counterpoint to questions about dollars, time, and pages. We must have insight into *both* sets of questions before we can fully judge law's impact on the campus—before we can know, in particular situations, whether law is more a beacon or a blanket of ground fog.

Sec. 1.2. Evolution of the Law Relating to Postsecondary Education

Traditionally, the law's relationship to postsecondary (or higher) education was much different from what it is now. There were few legal requirements relating to the educational administrator's functions, and they were not a major factor in most administrative decisions. The higher education world, moreover, tended to think of itself as removed from and perhaps above the world of law and lawyers. The roots of this traditional separation between academia and law are several.

Higher education (particularly private education) was often viewed as a unique enterprise that could regulate itself through reliance on tradition and consensual agreement. It operated best by operating autonomously, and it thrived on the privacy afforded by autonomy. Academia, in short, was like a Victorian gentlemen's club whose sacred precincts were not to be profaned by the involvement of outside agents in its internal governance.

Not only was the academic environment perceived as private; it was also thought to be delicate and complex. An outsider would, almost by definition, be ignorant of the special arrangements and sensitivities underpinning this environment. And lawyers and judges as a group, at least in the early days, were clearly outsiders. Law schools did not become an established part of American higher education until the early twentieth century, and the older tradition of "reading law" (studying and working in a practitioner's office) persisted for many years afterward. Lawyers, moreover, were often perceived as representatives of the crass world of business and industry, or as representatives of the political world, or as mere pettifoggers scratching for a fee. Interference by such "outsiders" would destroy the understanding and mutual trust that must prevail in academia.

The special higher education environment was also thought to support a special virtue and ability in its personnel. The faculties and administrators (often themselves respected scholars) had knowledge and training far beyond that of the general populace, and they were charged with the guardianship of knowledge for future generations. Theirs was a special mission pursued with special expertise— and often at a considerable financial sacrifice. The combination spawned the perception that ill will and personal bias were strangers to academia and that outside monitoring of its affairs was therefore largely unnecessary.

The law to a remarkable extent reflected and reinforced such attitudes. Federal and state governments generally avoided extensive regulation of higher education. Legislatures and administrative agencies imposed few legal obligations on institutions and provided few official channels through which their activities could be legally challenged. What legal oversight existed was generally centered in the courts.

The judiciary also was deferential to higher education. In matters concerning students, courts found refuge in the *in loco parentis* doctrine borrowed from early English common law. In placing the educational institution in the parents' shoes, the doctrine permitted the institution to exert almost untrammeled authority over students' lives:

> College authorities stand *in loco parentis* concerning the physical and moral welfare and mental training of the pupils, and we are unable to see why, to that end, they may not make any rule or regulation for the government or betterment of their pupils that a parent could for the same purpose. Whether the rules or regulations are wise or their aims worthy is a matter left solely to the discretion of the authorities or parents, as the case may be, and, in the exercise of that discretion, the courts are not disposed to interfere, unless the rules and aims are unlawful or against public policy [*Gott* v. *Berea College,* 156 Ky. 376, 161 S.W. 204, 206 (1913)].

Nor could students lay claim to constitutional rights in the higher education environment. In private education the U.S. Constitution had no application; and in the public realm—in cases such as *Hamilton* v. *Regents of the University of California,* 293 U.S. 245 (1934), which upheld an order that student conscientious objectors must take military training as a condition of attending the institution—courts accepted the proposition that attendance at a public postsecondary institution was a privilege and not a right. Being a "privilege," attendance could constitutionally be extended and was subject to termination on whatever conditions the institution determined were in its and the students' best interests. Occasionally courts did hold that students have some contract rights under an express or implied contractual relation with the institution. But—as in *Anthony* v. *Syracuse University,* 224 A.D. 487, 231 N.Y.S. 435 (1928), where the institution was upheld in dismissing a student without assigning a reason but apparently because she was not "a typical Syracuse girl"—contract law provided little meaningful recourse for students. The institution was given virtually unlimited power to dictate the contract terms, and the contract, once made, was construed heavily in the institution's favor.

Similar judicial deference prevailed in the institution's relationship with faculty members. While an employment relationship substituted here for *in loco parentis,* it focused far more on judgments of senior faculty members and experienced administrators than on the formalities of written employment contracts. Courts considered academic judgments regarding appointment, promotion, and tenure to be expert judgments suitably governed by the complex traditions of the academic world. Judges did not possess the special skill needed to review such judgments, nor, without glaring evidence to the contrary, could they presume that nonacademic considerations might play a part in such processes. Furthermore, in private institutions faculty members, like students, could assert no constitutional rights against the institution, since the Constitution had no application to private activity. And in public institutions, the judicial view was that employment, somewhat like student attendance, was a privilege and not a right. Thus, as far as the Constitution was concerned, employment could also be extended or terminated on whatever grounds the institution considered appropriate.

As further support for these judicial hands-off attitudes, higher education institutions also enjoyed immunity from a broad range of lawsuits alleging negligence or other torts. For public institutions this protection arose from the governmental immunity doctrine, which shielded state and local governments and their instrumentalities from legal liability for their sovereign acts. For private institutions a comparable result was reached under the charitable immunity doctrine, which shielded charitable organizations from legal liability that would divert their funds from the purposes for which they were intended.

Traditionally, then, the immunity doctrines substantially limited the range of suits maintainable against higher education institutions. And because of the judicial attitudes discussed above, the chances of victory in suits against either the institution or its officers and employees were slim. Reinforcing these legal limitations was a practical limitation on litigation: Before free legal services were available, few of the likely plaintiffs—faculty members, administrators, and students—had enough money to sue.

Since the mid-twentieth century, however, events and changing circumstances have worked a revolution in the relationship between academia and the law. The federal government and state governments have become heavily involved in postsecondary education, creating many new legal requirements and new forums for raising legal challenges. (See generally Carnegie Foundation for the Advancement of Teaching, *The Control of the Campus: A Report on the Governance of Higher Education* (Princeton University Press, 1982).) Students, teachers, other employees, and outsiders have become more willing and more able to sue postsecondary institutions and their officials. Courts have become more willing to entertain such suits on their merits and to offer relief from certain institutional actions. (See generally R. O'Neil,

The Courts, Government, and Higher Education (Committee for Economic Development, 1972) (Supplementary Paper No. 37).)

The most obvious and perhaps most significant change to occur since World War II has been the dramatic increase in the number, size, and diversity of postsecondary institutions. But beyond the obvious point that more people and institutions produce more litigation is the crucial fact of the changed character of the academic population itself (see, for example, K. P. Cross, *Beyond the Open Door: New Students to Higher Education* (Jossey-Bass, 1971)). The GI Bill expansions of the late 1940s and early 1950s, and the "baby-boom" expansion of the 1960s, brought large numbers of new students, faculty members, and administrative personnel into the educational process. In 1940 there were approximately 1.5 million degree students enrolled in institutions of higher education; by 1955 the figure had grown to more than 2.5 million and by 1965 to more than 5.5 million. The expanding pool of persons seeking postsecondary education prompted the growth of new educational institutions and programs, as well as new methods for delivering educational services. Great increases in federal aid for both students and institutions further stimulated these developments.

As new social, economic, and ethnic groups entered this broadened world of postsecondary education, the traditional processes of selection, admission, and academic acculturation began to break down. Because of the changed job opportunities and rapid promotion processes occasioned by rapid growth, many of the new academics did not have sufficient time to learn the old rules. Others were hostile to traditional attitudes and values because they perceived them as part of a process that had excluded their group or race or sex from access to academic success in earlier days. For others in new settings—such as junior and community colleges, technical institutes, and experiential learning programs—the traditional trappings of academia simply did not fit.

For many of the new students as well, older patterns of deference to tradition and authority became a thing of the past—perhaps an irrelevant or even consciously repudiated past. The emergence of the student-veteran; the loosening of the "lock-step" pattern of educational preparation, which led students directly from high school to college to graduate work; and, finally, the lowered age of majority—all combined to make the *in loco parentis* relationship between institution and student less and less tenable. The notion that attendance was a privilege seemed an irrelevant nicety in an increasingly credentialized society. To many students higher education became an economic or professional necessity, and some, such as the GI Bill veterans, had cause to view it as an earned right.

As a broader and larger cross section of the world passed through postsecondary education's gates, institutions became more tied to the outside world. Government allocations and foundation support covered a larger share of institutional budgets, making it more difficult to maintain the autonomy and self-sufficiency afforded by large endowments. Competition for money, students, and outstanding faculty members focused institutional attentions outward. As institutions engaged increasingly in government research projects, as large state universities grew and became more dependent on annual state legislative appropriations, and as federal and state governments increasingly paid tuition bills through scholarship and loan programs, postsecondary education lost much of its isolation from the political process. Social and political movements—notably the civil rights movement and the movement against the Vietnam War—became a more integral part of campus life. And when these movements and other outside influences converged on postsecondary institutions, the law came also.

In the 1980s the development of higher education law continues to reflect, and be reflected in, social movements in higher education and in the world outside the campus. Various trends and movements begun in the 1970s are further altering higher education's relationship to the outside world and carving new features into the face of higher education law.

One major trend is student (or educational) consumerism (see, for example, D. Riesman, *On Higher Education: The Academic Enterprise in an Era of Rising Student Consumerism* (Jossey-Bass, 1981)). A shift from a seller's to a buyer's market has spurred competition among institutions in the search for students and introduced marketing techniques and attitudes into postsecondary education. These developments, like many others in the post–World War II era, have helped turn institutional attentions outward—to competitor institutions, to the world of business, to government agencies concerned with regulating the education "marketplace." A new emphasis on students as consumers of education with attendant rights, to whom institutions owe corresponding responsibilities, has further undermined the traditional concept of education as a privilege. Student litigation on matters such as tuition and financial aid, course offerings, award of degrees, campus security, and support services has become more common, as have governmental efforts at consumer protection regulation on behalf of students.

Institutional self-regulation, partly a response to student consumerism, is another important trend (see, for example, Carnegie Council on Policy Studies in Higher Education, *Fair Practices in Higher Education: Rights and Responsibilities of Students and Their Colleges in a Period of Intensified Competition for Enrollments* (Jossey-Bass, 1979)). The movement is not back to the old days of "self-regulation," when institutions governed their cloistered worlds by tradition and consensus. Rather, the new movement is spawning an increase in institutional guidelines and regulations on matters concerning students and faculty and in grievance processes for airing complaints. On the one hand, by creating new rights and responsibilities or making existing ones explicit, this movement can give members of campus communities more claims to press against one another. On the other hand, the new self-regulation can facilitate the internal and more collegial resolution of claims, forestalling the intervention of courts, legislatures, and administrative agencies in campus matters.

Federal government deregulation of education, another nascent trend, is the flip side of institutional self-regulation: success at the latter is urged as justification for the former and vice versa. Substantial deregulation would, of course, reduce the numbers and types of federal requirements applicable to campuses; it would also reduce the potential for lawsuits and administrative agency proceedings concerning federal requirements. But the deregulation flame has not yet set fire to any forests. How far it will progress—or how much federal regulation, if removed, would be replaced by comparable state regulation or self-regulation—is not clear; nor is it clear that deregulation as currently envisioned would inevitably benefit education. (See W. Clune, *The Deregulation Critique of the Federal Role in Education* (Project Rpt. No. 82-All, Institute for Research on Educational Finance and Governance, Stanford University, 1982).)

Closely related to government regulation of postsecondary education is the issue of government financial support. Where once the trend was toward increasing aid—both for students and institutions, at federal and state levels—now the trend is reversing. In the scramble for funds, postsecondary education is drawn even further into the political process. Issues arise concerning equitable allocation of funds among and within institutions and among various categories of needy students. As the burden of diminishing support is perceived to fall on minority and low-income students, whose numbers will decrease if government aid is not forthcoming, or on the minority and women faculty newcomers most subject to layoffs prompted by budget cuts, new civil rights issues are emerging.

Government budget cutting, in turn, adds new impetus to yet another prominent trend: institutional response to tighter financial times. Because of the combined pressures of inflation, new types of institutional costs (such as computer equipment), declining enrollments, and, now, government aid reduction, financial belt tightening has become a fact of life affecting many aspects of institutional operation. Many legal questions have arisen concerning standards and procedures for faculty and staff layoffs, termination of tenured faculty, and reduction or termination of programs. As some institutions are strained to their financial limits, other questions concerning closures, mergers, and bankruptcies have arisen. Moreover, there has been renewed attention to statewide planning for postsecondary education in financial hard times. Legal, as well as political and policy, issues have emerged concerning program review and elimination in state public systems and concerning state authority to issue or refuse licenses for new programs of private (particularly out-of-state) institutions.

In a different vein, the technological revolution on campus is yet another trend with critical legal ramifications. The use of computers creates new issues of privacy. Biotechnological research raises issues concerning use of human subjects as well as patentability and licensing of discoveries. Devising and enforcing specifications for the lease or purchase of technology for office support, laboratories, or innovative learning systems can create complex contract/commercial law problems.

Similarly, as a result of private industry's interest in university research and the universities' interest in private funding of research efforts, a new alliance has been forged between the campus and the corporate world (see, for example, M. Bach and R. Thornton, "Academic-Industrial Partnerships in Biomedical Research: Inevitability and Desirability," 64 *Educational Record* 26 (1983)). As new ties with the outside world are discussed, questions of institutional autonomy and academic freedom are being raised. The legal and policy implications for postsecondary education are enormous. There are complex problems concerning the structuring of research agreements, patent and licensing arrangements, and trade secrets (see D. Fowler, "University-Industry Research Relationships: The Research Agreement," 9 *J. of College and University Law* 515 (1982-83)). The specter of conflicts of interest, for both faculty researchers and the institution as a corporate entity, arises (see Comment, "Ties That Bind: Conflicts of Interest in University-Industry Links," 17 *University of California/Davis L. Rev.* 895 (1984)). And federal government support for university-industrial cooperative research has become an issue, as has federal regulation in sensitive areas such as genetic engineering.

In addition to these new trends, the post–World War II movement toward diversity in postsecondary education has continued in important ways. Although the 1970s brought some moderation in the birth and growth of institutions and expansion of student bodies, the diversity of students and of special educational programs to serve their needs has nevertheless increased. The percentage of women enrolled as students is greater than ever before; women, in fact, are now a majority (see R. Cowan, "Higher Education Has Obligations to a New Majority," *Chronicle of Higher Education,* June 23, 1980, p. 48, col. 1). The proportion of blacks also increased in the 1970s, with black student enrollment increasing more rapidly than white student enrollment, especially in community colleges (see G. Thomas (Ed.), *Black Students in Higher Education: Conditions and Experiences in the 1970s* (Greenwood Press, 1981)). The proportion of postsecondary students who are "adult learners," beyond the traditional college-age group of eighteen to twenty-four years old, has also increased markedly (see K. P. Cross, *Adults as Learners: Increasing Participation and Facilitating Learning* (Jossey-Bass, 1981)). The proportion of part-time students (many of whom are also women and/or adult learners) has similarly increased, with part-time enrollments rising much faster than full-time enrollments in the 1970s (see A. Ostar, "Part-Time Students: The New Majority for the 1980's," *Chronicle of Higher Education,* Oct. 7, 1981, p. 56, col. 1). Military personnel also have become a significant component of the burgeoning adult learner and part-time populations.

One further category of students, standing apart from the interlocking categories above, has also begun substantial growth: foreign students. These students are making a particularly important contribution to campus diversity and are also having a direct impact on law. The application of immigration law to foreign students has become a major concern for federal officials who must balance shifting political and educational concerns as they devise and enforce regulations, and for postsecondary administrators who must work within these complex regulations on their own campuses (see Committee on Foreign Students and Institutional Policy, *Foreign Students and Institutional Policy: Toward an Agenda for Action* (American Council on Education, 1982)).

These changes in the student population have been reflected, as expected, in changes in the universe of postsecondary institutions and programs. Community colleges and private two-year institutions have become more prominent, as their student enrollments and the numbers of new institutions grew at a faster rate than four-year and graduate institutions (see A. M. Cohen and F. B. Brawer, *The American Community College* (Jossey-Bass, 1982)). Postsecondary education programs sponsored by private industry have increased, creating a new context for questions about state degree-granting authority and private accreditation, as well as academic freedom and other faculty/student rights and obligations. Work-study programs, internships, and other forms of experiential education are increasing in numbers and importance (see M. T. Keeton and P. J. Tate (Eds.), *New Directions for Experiential Learning: Learning by Experience—What, Why, How,* no. 1 (Jossey-Bass, 1978)). The movement raises new questions on matters such as institutional liability for off-campus acts; the use of affiliation agreements with outside entities; and coverage of experiential learners under workers' compensation, unemployment compensation, and minimum wage laws.

Other new initiatives have been fueled by the lifelong learning movement, which has promoted diversity in delivery mechanisms and innovations in learning models (see R. E. Peterson and Associates, *Lifelong Learning in America: An Overview of Current Practices, Available Resources, and Future Prospects* (Jossey-Bass, 1979)). Thus, continuing education programs; correspondence, television, and computer home-study courses; and off-campus and external degree programs, such as those on military bases, have all grown in recent years and are having significant impact on postsecondary education.

In all, while some individual institutions may have waned, postsecondary education as a whole has been a dynamic enterprise through the 1970s and into the 1980s. The challenge for law is to keep pace with education by maintaining a dynamism of its own which is sensitive to education's evolving mission.

Sec. 1.3. Sources of Postsecondary Education Law

The modern law of postsecondary education is no longer simply a product of what the courts say, or refuse to say, about educational problems. The modern law comes from a variety of sources, as set out in this section.

1.3.1. Federal and state constitutions. Constitutions are the fundamental source for determining the nature and extent of governmental powers. Constitutions are also the fundamental source of the individual rights guarantees that limit the powers of governments and protect citizens generally, including members of the academic community. The federal Constitution, set forth in abridged form in the Appendix, is by far the most prominent and important source of individual liberties. The First Amendment protections for speech, press, and religion are often litigated in major court cases involving postsecondary institutions, as are the Fourth Amendment protections against unreasonable searches and seizures and the Fourteenth Amendment guarantees of due process and equal protection. As explained in Section 1.4, these federal constitutional provisions apply differently to public and private institutions.

The federal Constitution has no provision that specifically refers to education. State constitutions, however, often have specific provisions establishing state colleges and universities or state college and university systems, and occasionally community college systems; state constitutions may also have provisions establishing a state department of education or other governing authority with some responsibility for postsecondary education (see Section 6.2.2).

The federal Constitution is the highest legal authority that exists. No other law, either state or federal, may conflict with its provisions. Thus, although a state constitution is the highest state law authority, and all state statutes and other state laws must be consistent with it, any of its provisions that conflict with the federal Constitution will be subject to invalidation by the courts. It is not considered to be a conflict, however, if state constitutions establish more expansive individual rights than those guaranteed by parallel provisions of the federal Constitution (see the discussion of state constitutions in Section 1.4.3).

1.3.2. Statutes. Statutes are enacted both by states and by the federal government. Ordinances, which are in effect local statutes, are enacted by local legislative bodies, such as county and city councils. While laws at all three levels may refer specifically to postsecondary education or postsecondary institutions, the greatest amount of such specific legislation is written by the states. Examples include laws establishing and regulating state postsecondary institutions or systems, laws creating statewide coordinating councils for postsecondary education, and laws providing for the licensure of postsecondary institutions (see Sections 6.2.1 and 6.3). At the federal level, the major examples of such specific legislation are the federal grant-in-aid statutes, such as the Higher Education Act of 1965 (see Section 7.4). At all three levels, there is also a considerable amount of legislation that applies to postsecondary institutions in common with other entities in the jurisdiction. Examples are the federal tax laws and civil rights laws (see Sections 7.3 and 7.5), state unemployment compensation and workers' compensation laws (see Sections 6.5.3 and 6.5.4), and local zoning and tax laws (see Sections 5.2 and 5.3). All these state and federal statutes and local ordinances are subject to the higher constitutional authorities.

Federal statutes, for the most part, are collected and codified in the *United States Code* (U.S.C.) or *United States Code Annotated* (U.S.C.A.). State statutes are similarly gathered in state codifications, such as the *Minnesota Statutes Annotated* (Minn. Stat. Ann.) or the *Annotated Code of Maryland* (Md. Ann. Code). These codifications are available in many law libraries. Local ordinances are usually collected in local ordinance books, but those may be difficult to find and may not be organized as systematically as state and federal codifications are. Moreover, local ordinance books—and state codes as well—may be considerably out of date. In order to be sure that the statutory law on a particular point is up to date, one must check what are called the session or slip laws of the jurisdiction for the current year or sometimes the preceding year. These laws are usually issued by a designated state or local office in the order in which the laws are passed; many law libraries maintain current session laws of individual states in loose-leaf volumes and may maintain similar collections of current local ordinances for area jurisdictions.

1.3.3. Administrative rules and regulations. The most rapidly expanding sources of postsecondary education law are the directives of state and federal administrative agencies. The number and size of these bodies are increasing, and the number and complexity of their directives are easily keeping pace. In recent years the rules applicable to postsecondary institutions, especially those issued at the federal level, have often generated controversy in the education world, which must negotiate a substantial regulatory maze in order to receive federal grants or contracts or to comply with federal employment laws and other requirements in areas of federal concern (see Chapter Seven).

Administrative agency directives are often published as regulations that have the status of law and are as binding as a statute would be. But agency directives do not always have such status. Thus, in order to determine their exact status, administrators must check with legal counsel when problems arise. Every rule or regulation issued by an administrative agency, whether state or federal, must be within the scope of the authority delegated to that agency by its enabling statutes. Any rule or regulation that is not authorized by the relevant statutes is subject to invalidation by a court. And, like the statutes and ordinances referred to earlier, administrative rules and regulations must also comply with and be consistent with applicable state and federal constitutional provisions.

Federal administrative agencies publish both proposed regulations, which are issued to elicit public comment, and final regulations, which have the status of law. These agencies also publish other types of documents, such as policy interpretations of statutes or regulations, notices of meetings, and invitations to submit grant proposals. Such regulations and documents appear upon issuance in the *Federal Register* (Fed. Reg.), a daily government publication. Final regulations appearing in the *Federal Register* are eventually republished—without the agency's explanatory commentary, which sometimes accompanies the *Federal Register* version—in the *Code of Federal Regulations* (C.F.R.).

State administrative agencies have various ways of publicizing their rules and regulations, sometimes in government publications comparable to the *Federal Register* or the *Code of Federal Regulations*. Generally speaking, however, administrative rules and regulations are harder to find and less likely to be codified at the state level than at the federal level.

1.3.4. Administrative adjudications. Besides promulgating rules and regulations (called rule making), administrative agencies often also have the authority to consider and make decisions in particular disputes involving particular parties (called adjudication). The extent of an administrative agency's adjudicatory authority, as well as its rule-making powers, depends on the relevant statutes that establish and empower the agency. An agency's adjudicatory decisions must be consistent with its own rules and regulations and with any applicable statutory or constitutional provision. Legal questions concerning the validity of an adjudicatory decision are usually reviewable in the courts. Examples of such decisions at the federal level would include a National Labor Relations Board decision on an unfair labor practice charge or, in another area, a Department of Education decision on whether to terminate funds to a federal grantee for noncompliance with statutory or regulatory requirements. Examples at the state level would include the determination of a state human relations commission on a complaint charging violation of individual rights, or the decision of a state workers' compensation board in a workers' compensation benefit case. Administrative agencies may or may not officially publish compilations of their adjudicatory decisions. Agencies without official compilations may informally compile and issue their opinions; other agencies may simply file opinions in their internal files or distribute them in a limited way. It can often be a difficult problem for counsel to determine what all the relevant adjudicatory precedents are within an agency.

1.3.5. Case law. Every year the state and federal courts reach decisions in hundreds of cases involving postsecondary education. Opinions are issued and published for many of these decisions. Many more decisions are reached and opinions rendered each year in cases that do not involve postsecondary education but do elucidate important established legal principles with potential application to postsecondary education. In this latter group is a large body of elementary and secondary education cases (see, for example, the *Wood* v. *Strickland* case in Section 2.4.3 and the *Goss* v. *Lopez* case in Section 4.6.2). But elementary/secondary precedents cannot be applied uncritically to postsecondary education. Differences in the structures, missions, and clienteles of these levels of education may make precedents from one level inapplicable to the other or may require that the precedent's application be modified to account for the differences. In *Lansdale* v. *Tyler Junior College,* 470 F.2d 659 (5th Cir. 1972), for instance, the court considered the applicability to postsecondary education of a prior precedent permitting high schools to regulate the length of students' hair. The court refused to extend the precedent. As one judge explained:

The college campus marks the appropriate boundary where the public institution can no longer assert that the regulation of . . . [hair length] is reasonably related to the fostering or encouraging of education. . . .

There are a number of factors which support the proposition that the point between high school and college is the place where the line should be drawn. . . . That place is the point in the student's process of maturity where he usually comes within the ambit of the Twenty-Sixth Amendment and the Selective Service Act, where he often leaves home for dormitory life, and where the educational institution ceases to deal with him through parents and guardians. . . .

The majority holds today that as a matter of law the college campus is the line of demarcation where the weight of the student's maturity, as compared with the institution's modified role in his education, tips the scales in favor of the individual and marks the boundary of the area within which a student's hirsute adornment becomes constitutionally irrelevant to the pursuit of educational activities [470 F.2d at 662–64].

Conversely, in *Cary* v. *Adams-Arapahoe School Board,* 427 F. Supp. 945 (D. Colo. 1977), the court considered whether academic freedom precedents from postsecondary education were applicable to high school education. After exploring "the role of elementary and secondary public education in the United States" and finding parallels between the missions of high school and postsecondary education, the court decided that "it would be inappropriate to conclude that academic freedom is required only in the colleges and universities."

A court's decision has the effect of binding precedent only within its own jurisdiction. Thus, at the state level, a particular decision may be binding either on the entire state or only on a subdivision of the state, depending on the court's jurisdiction. At the federal level, decisions are binding by United States District Courts and United States Courts of Appeals within a particular district or region of the country, while decisions of the United States Supreme Court are binding precedent throughout the country. Since the Supreme Court's decisions are the supreme law of the land, they bind all lower federal courts as well as all state courts, even the highest court of the state.

Court decisions may interpret state or federal statutes or the rules or regulations of state or federal administrative agencies. In order to understand the meaning of such statutes, rules, and regulations, one must understand the case law that has construed them. Court decisions may also construe the meaning of federal or state constitutional provisions, and sometimes determine the constitutionality of particular statutes or rules and regulations under particular provisions of state or federal constitutions. A statute or rule or regulation that is found to be unconstitutional because it conflicts with a constitutional provision is void and no longer enforceable by the courts. Sometimes courts issue opinions that interpret neither a statute, nor an administrative rule or regulation, nor a constitutional provision. In breach-of-contract disputes or tort litigation, for instance, the only precedents the court utilizes are those the courts have created themselves. These decisions create what is called American "common law." Common law, in short, is judge-made law rather than law that originates from constitutions or from legislatures or administrative agencies.

The important opinions of state and federal courts are published periodically and collected in bound volumes available in most law libraries. For state court decisions, besides each state's official reports, there is the National Reporter System, a series of regional case reports comprising the (1) *Atlantic Reporter* (cited A. or A.2d), (2) *Northeastern Reporter* (N.E. or N.E.2d), (3) *Northwestern Reporter* (N.W. or N.W.2d), (4) *Pacific Reporter* (P. or P.2d), (5) *Southeastern Reporter* (S.E. or S.E.2d), (6) *Southwestern Reporter* (S.W. or S.W.2d), and (7) *Southern Reporter* (So. or So. 2d). Each regional reporter publishes opinions of the courts in that particular region. There are also special reporters in the National Reporter System for the states of New York (*New York Supplement,* cited N.Y.S. or N.Y.S.2d) and California (*California Reporter,* cited Cal. Rptr.).

In the federal system, United States Supreme Court opinions are published in the *United States Supreme Court Reports* (U.S.), the official reporter, as well as in two unofficial reporters, the *Supreme Court Reporter* (S. Ct.) and the *United States Supreme Court Reports—Lawyers' Edition* (L. Ed. or L. Ed. 2d). Supreme Court opinions are also available, shortly after issuance, in the loose-leaf format of *United States Law Week* (U.S.L.W.)—which also contains digests of other recent selected opinions from federal and state courts. Opinions of the United States Courts of Appeals are published in the *Federal Reporter* (F. or F.2d). United States District Court opinions are published in the *Federal Supplement* (F. Supp.) or, for decisions regarding federal rules of judicial procedure, in *Federal Rules Decisions* (F.R.D.).

1.3.6. Institutional rules and regulations. The rules and regulations promulgated by individual institutions are also a source of postsecondary education law. These rules and regulations are subject to all the other sources of law listed above and must be consistent with all the legal requirements of those other sources that apply to the particular institution and to the subject matter of the rule or regulation. Courts may consider some institutional rules and regulations to be part of the faculty-institution contract or the student-institution contract (see Section 1.3.7), in which case these rules and regulations are enforceable by contract actions in the courts. Some rules and regulations of public institutions may also be legally enforceable as administrative regulations (see Section 1.3.3) of a government agency. Even where such rules are not legally enforceable by courts or outside agencies, a postsecondary institution will likely want to follow and enforce them internally to achieve fairness and consistency in its dealings with the campus community.

Institutions may establish adjudicatory bodies with authority to interpret and enforce institutional rules and regulations. When such decision-making bodies operate within the scope of their authority under institutional rules and regulations, their decisions also become part of the governing law in the institution; and courts may regard these decisions as part of the faculty-institution or student-institution contract, at least in the sense that they become part of the applicable custom and usage (see Section 1.3.8) in the institution.

1.3.7. Institutional contracts. Postsecondary institutions have contractual relationships of various kinds with faculties (see Section 3.1); staffs; students (Section 4.1.3); and outside parties, such as government agencies, construction firms, or other institutions. These contracts create binding legal arrangements between the contracting parties, enforceable by either party in case of the other's breach. In this sense a contract is a source of law governing a particular subject matter and relationship. When a question arises concerning a subject matter or relationship covered by a contract, the first legal source to consult is usually the contract terms.

Contracts, especially with faculty members and students, may incorporate some institutional rules and regulations (see Section 1.3.6), so that they become part of the contract terms. Contracts are interpreted and enforced according to the common law of contracts (Section 1.3.5) and any applicable statute or administrative rule or regulation (Sections 1.3.2 and 1.3.3). They may also be interpreted with reference to academic custom and usage (Section 1.3.8).

1.3.8. Academic custom and usage. This category, by far the most amorphous source of postsecondary education law, comprises the particular established practices and understandings within particular institutions. It differs from institutional rules and regulations (see Section 1.3.6) in that it is not necessarily a written source of law and, even if written, is far more informal; custom and usage may be found, for instance, in policy statements from speeches, internal memoranda, and other such documentation within the institution.

This source of postsecondary education law, sometimes called "campus common law," is important in particular institutions because it helps define what the various members of the academic community expect of each other as well as of the institution itself. Whenever the institution has internal decision-making processes, such as a faculty grievance process or a student disciplinary procedure, campus common law can be an important guide for decision making. In this sense campus common law does not displace formal institutional rules and regulations but supplements them, helping the decision maker and the parties in situations where rules and regulations are ambiguous or do not exist for the particular point at issue. Academic custom and usage is also important in another, and broader, sense: It can supplement contractual understandings between the institution and its faculty and between the institution and its students. Whenever the terms of such contractual relationship are unclear, courts may look to academic custom and usage in order to interpret the terms of the contract. In *Perry* v. *Sindermann,* 408 U.S. 593 (1972), the U.S. Supreme Court placed its imprimatur on this concept of academic custom and usage when it analyzed a professor's claim that he was entitled to tenure at Odessa College:

> The law of contracts in most, if not all, jurisdictions long has employed a process by which agreements, though not formalized in writing, may be "implied" (3 *Corbin on Contracts,* secs. 561–672A). Explicit contractual provisions may be supplemented by other agreements implied from "the promisor's words and conduct in the light of the surrounding circumstances" (sec. 562). And "the meaning of [the promisor's] words and acts is found by relating them to the usage of the past" (sec. 562).
>
> A teacher, like the respondent, who has held his position for a number of years might be able to show from the circumstances of this service—and from other relevant facts—that he has a legitimate claim of entitlement to job tenure. Just as this Court has found there to be a "common law of a particular industry or of a particular plant" that may supplement a collective bargaining agreement (*United Steelworks* v. *Warrior & Gulf Nav. Co.,* 363 U.S. 574, 579, 80 S. Ct. 1347, 1351, 4 L. Ed. 2d 1409 (1960)), so

there may be an unwritten "common law" in a particular university that certain employees shall have the equivalent of tenure [408 U.S. at 602].

Sindermann was a constitutional due process case, and academic custom and usage was relevant to determining whether the professor had a "property interest" in continued employment, which would entitle him to a hearing prior to nonrenewal (see Section 3.5.2). Academic custom and usage is also important in contract cases where courts, arbitrators, or grievance committees must interpret provisions of the faculty-institution contract (see Sections 3.1 and 3.2) or the student-institution contract (see Section 4.1). In *Strank* v. *Mercy Hospital of Johnstown,* 383 Pa. 54, 117 A.2d 697 (1955), a student nurse who had been dismissed from nursing school sought to require the school to award her transfer credits for the two years' work she had successfully completed. The student alleged that she had "oral arrangements with the school at the time she entered, later confirmed in part by writing and carried out by both parties for a period of two years, . . . [and] that these arrangements and understandings imposed upon defendant the legal duty to give her proper credits for work completed." When the school argued that the court had no jurisdiction over such a claim, the court responded: "[Courts] have jurisdiction . . . for the enforcement of obligations whether arising under express contracts, written or oral, or implied contracts, including those in which a duty may have resulted from long recognized and established customs and usages, as in this case, perhaps, between an educational institution and its students" (117 A.2d at 698). Faculty members may make similar contract claims relying on academic custom and usage. For example, in *Lewis* v. *Salem Academy and College,* 23 N.C. App. 122, 208 S.E.2d 404 (1974), the court considered but rejected the plaintiff's claim that, by campus custom and usage, the college's retirement age of sixty-five had been raised to seventy, thus entitling him to teach to that age. And in *Krotkoff* v. *Goucher College,* 585 F.2d 675 (4th Cir. 1978), discussed in this volume, Section 3.7.1, the court rejected another professor's claim that "national" academic custom and usage protected her from termination of tenure due to financial exigency. Custom and usage is also relevant in implementing faculty collective bargaining agreements (see the *Sindermann* quotation above), and such agreements may explicitly provide that they are not intended to override "past practices" of the institution.

Sec. 1.4. The Public-Private Dichotomy

1.4.1. Background. Historically, higher education has roots in both the public and private sectors, although the strength of each one's influence has varied over time. Sometimes following and sometimes leading this historical development, the law has tended to support and reflect the fundamental dichotomy between public and private education.

A forerunner of the present university was the Christian seminary. Yale was an early example. Dartmouth began as a school to teach Christianity to the Indians. Similar schools sprang up throughout the colonies. Though often established through private charitable trusts, they were also chartered by the colony, received some financial support from the colony, and were subject to its regulation. Thus, colonial colleges were often a mixture of public and private activity. The nineteenth century witnessed a gradual decline in governmental involvement with sectarian schools.

As states began to establish their own institutions, the public-private dichotomy emerged. (See D. Tewksbury, *The Founding of American Colleges and Universities Before the Civil War* (Anchor Books, 1965).) In recent years this dichotomy has again faded as state and federal governments have provided larger amounts of financial support to private institutions, many of which are now secular.

Although private institutions have always been more expensive to attend than public institutions, private higher education has been a vital and influential force in American intellectual history. The private school can cater to special interests that a public one often cannot serve because of legal or political constraints. Private education thus draws strength from "the very possibility of doing something different than government can do, of creating an institution free to make choices government cannot—even seemingly arbitrary ones—without having to provide a justification that will be examined in a court of law" (H. Friendly, *The Dartmouth College Case and the Public-Private Penumbra,* p. 30 (Humanities Research Center, University of Texas, 1969)).

Though modern-day private institutions are not always free from examination "in a court of law," the law often does treat public and private institutions differently. These differences will underlie much of the discussion in this book. They are critically important in assessing the law's impact on the roles of particular institutions and the duties of their administrators.

Although public institutions are usually subject to the plenary authority of the government that creates them, the law protects private institutions from such extensive governmental control. Government can usually alter, enlarge, or completely abolish its public institutions (see Section 6.2); private institutions, however, can obtain their own perpetual charters of incorporation, and, since the famous *Dartmouth College* case (*Trustees of Dartmouth College* v. *Woodward,* 17 U.S. 518 (1819)), government has been prohibited from impairing such charters. In that case the U.S. Supreme Court turned back New Hampshire's attempt to assume control of Dartmouth by finding that such action would violate the Constitution's contract clause (see B. Campbell, "*Dartmouth College* as a Civil Liberties Case: The Formation of Constitutional Policy," 70 *Kentucky L.J.* 643 (1981–82)). Subsequently, in three other landmark cases—*Meyer* v. *Nebraska,* 262 U.S. 390 (1923), *Pierce* v. *Society of Sisters,* 268 U.S. 510 (1925), and *Farrington* v. *Tokushige,* 273 U.S. 284 (1927)—the Supreme Court used the due process clause to strike down unreasonable governmental interference with teaching and learning in private schools.

Nonetheless, government does retain substantial authority to regulate private education. But—whether for legal, political, or policy reasons—state governments usually regulate private institutions less than they regulate public institutions. The federal government, on the other hand, has tended to apply its regulations comparably to both public and private institutions or, bowing to considerations of federalism, has regulated private institutions while leaving public institutions to the states.

In addition to these differences in regulatory patterns, the law makes a second and more pervasive distinction between public and private institutions: Public institutions and their officers are fully subject to the constraints of the federal Constitution, whereas private institutions and their officers are not. Because the Constitution was designed to limit only the exercise of government power, it does not prohibit private individuals or corporations from impinging on such freedoms as free speech, equal protection, and due process. Thus, *insofar as the federal Constitution is concerned,* a private university can engage in private acts of discrimination, prohibit student protests, or expel a student without affording the procedural safeguards that a public university is constitutionally required to provide.

Indeed, this distinction can be crucial even within a single university. In *Powe* v. *Miles,* 407 F.2d 73 (2d Cir. 1968), seven Alfred University students had been suspended for engaging in protest activities that disrupted an ROTC ceremony. Four of the students attended Alfred's liberal arts college, while the remaining three were students at the ceramics college. The state of New York had contracted with Alfred to establish the ceramics college, and a New York statute specifically stated that the university's disciplinary acts with respect to students at the ceramics college were considered to be taken on behalf of the state. The court found that the dean's action suspending the ceramics students was "state action" but the suspension of the liberal arts students was not. Thus, the court ruled that the dean was required to afford the ceramics students due process but was not required to follow any constitutional dictates in suspending the liberal arts students, even though both groups of students had engaged in the same course of conduct.

1.4.2. The state action doctrine. As *Powe* makes clear, before a court will apply constitutional guarantees of individual rights to a postsecondary institution, it must first determine that the institution's action is "state (governmental) action." Although this determination is essentially a matter of distinguishing public from private institutions, or the public part of an institution from the private part, these distinctions do not necessarily depend on traditional notions of public or private. Because of varying patterns of government assistance and involvement, a continuum exists, ranging from the obvious public school (such as the tax-supported state university) to the obvious private school (such as the religious seminary). The large gray area between these extremes provides a continuing source of debate about how far the government must be involved before a "private" institution may be considered "public" under the Constitution. Since the early 1970s, however, the trend of the U.S. Supreme Court's opinions has been to trim back the state action concept, making it less likely that courts will find state action to exist in particular cases. The leading case in this line involving educational institutions is *Rendell-Baker* v. *Kohn,* 102 S. Ct. 2764 (1982), discussed below.

Though government funding is often a central consideration, much more than money is involved in a state action determination. Courts and commentators have dissected the state action concept in many different ways, but at heart essentially three approaches have emerged for attributing state action to an ostensibly private entity. When the private entity (1) acts as an agent of government in performing a particular task delegated to it by government (the delegated power theory), or (2) performs a function that is generally considered the responsibility of government (the public function theory), or (3) obtains substantial resources, prestige, or encouragement from its contacts with government (the government contacts theory), its actions may be considered state action subject to constitutional constraints.

The first theory, delegated power, was relied on in the *Powe* v. *Miles* case (discussed in Section 1.4.1), where the court found that New York State had delegated authority to Alfred to operate a state ceramics school at the university. This same court also considered the delegated power theory in *Wahba* v. *New York University,* 492 F.2d 96 (2d Cir. 1974), in which a research professor had been fired from a government-funded research project. But here the court refused to find that the firing was state action, since the government did not exercise any managerial control over the project. This focus on state involvement *in addition to funding* has assumed increasing importance in state action law. In *Greenya* v. *George Washington University,* 512 F.2d 556 (D.C. Cir. 1975), for instance, the university had a contract with the Navy to provide instruction at the U.S. Naval School of Hospital Administration. When the university fired a teacher assigned to teach in this program, he argued state action on the basis that he had been teaching government employees at government facilities—essentially a delegated power theory. But the court rejected the argument on grounds similar to those in *Wahba:*

> [Plaintiff] was always under the supervision and control of university officials, and . . . he maintained no contractual relations with the Navy. Nothing in the record indicates that the Navy had any right to say who would be hired to teach the English course. Neither does the record indicate that the Navy had anything whatsoever to do with the failure to renew appellant's contract. Appellant was merely the employee of an independent contractor who was providing educational services to the Navy [512 F.2d at 561–62].

The second theory, the public function theory, has generally not been a basis for finding state action in education cases. Though the issue has often been raised, courts have recognized that education has substantial roots in the private sector and cannot be considered a solely public function. In the *Greenya* case, for instance, the court simply remarked: "We have considered whether higher education constitutes 'state action' because it is a 'public function' as that term has been developed . . . and have concluded that it is not. . . . Education . . . has never been a state monopoly in the United States." In the later case of *State* v. *Schmid,* 423 A.2d 615 (N.J. 1980) (this volume, Section 5.6.3), however, the court was unwilling to accord the public function theory such a summary rejection. The case concerned the applicability of the First Amendment to Princeton University's removal from campus of a nonstudent who was distributing political leaflets. After refusing to find state action under the government contacts theory, the court set out the most comprehensive analysis to date of the application of the public function theory to private college campuses. But because of the absence of decisional authority and "strong cross-currents of policy" regarding the question, the court deferred any final determination on the public function theory, deciding the case instead under the New Jersey state constitution.

It is the third theory, the government contacts theory, that has had the greatest workout in postsecondary education cases. Although this theory is closely related to the delegated power theory, it focuses on less formal and particularized relationships between government and private entities. As the U.S. Supreme Court noted in the landmark *Burton* v. *Wilmington Parking Authority* case, 365 U.S. 715, 722 (1961), "Only by sifting facts and weighing circumstances can the nonobvious involvement of the state in private conduct be attributed its true significance." The search is not for state involvement with the private institution generally but involvement in the particular activity that gives rise to the lawsuit.[1]

---

[1]The U.S. Supreme Court nailed down this point in *Jackson* v. *Metropolitan Edison Co.,* 419 U.S. 345 (1974), where it rejected the petitioner's state action argument because "there was

The *Greenya* case also illustrates the government contacts theory. In challenging his termination by George Washington University, the plaintiff sought to base state action not only on the government's contract with the university but also on the government's general support for the university. The court quickly affirmed that neither the grant of a corporate charter nor the grant of tax-exempt status is sufficient to constitute state action. It then reached the same conclusion regarding federal funding of certain university programs and capital expenditures. Government funding, in the court's view, would not amount to state action unless and until the conditions placed on such funding "become so all-pervasive that the government has become, in effect, a joint venturer in the recipient's enterprise" (*Greenya* at 561).[2]

In contrast, in *Benner* v. *Oswald*, 592 F.2d 174 (3d Cir. 1979), the court found state action by applying the government contacts theory. The plaintiffs in the case, students at Pennsylvania State University, challenged the process for selecting members of the university's board of trustees. Relying on numerous contacts between the university and the state, the court used the *Burton* joint venturer test to hold that selection of the trustees constituted state action.

Under each of the three state action theories, courts appear more likely to find state action in race discrimination cases than in any other kind of case. In the *Wahba* and *Greenya* cases above, the courts specifically noted as part of their reasoning processes that race discrimination was not involved. In *Williams* v. *Howard University*, 528 F.2d 658 (D.C. Cir. 1976), which did involve race discrimination, the plaintiff also raised a second claim, involving deprivation of due process; and the court distinguished between the two claims. It held that the defendant's receipt of substantial federal funding was not a sufficient basis for finding government (state) action as to the due process claim but that "the allegation of substantial federal funding would be enough to demonstrate governmental action as to . . . [the] claim of racial discrimination."

In *Weise* v. *Syracuse University*, 522 F.2d 397 (2d Cir. 1975), the court recognized this same "double standard" in state action cases and extended it in part to claims of sex discrimination. The plaintiffs were two women, one a rejected faculty applicant and the other a terminated faculty member, who claimed that the university had discriminated against them solely on the basis of sex. In remanding the case to the trial court, the U.S. Court of Appeals for the Second Circuit explained the significance of both race and sex discrimination in state action cases:

> If our concern in this case were with discipline and the First Amend-
> ment, the alleged indicia of state action—funding and regulation—would

---

no . . . [state] imprimatur placed on the practice of . . . [the private entity] about which petitioner complains," and the state "has not put its own weight on the side of the . . . practice by ordering it" (419 U.S. at 357). Such a showing of state involvement in the precise activity challenged may not be required, however, in race discrimination cases (see *Norwood* v. *Harrison*, 413 U.S. 455 (1973), and the cases discussed later in this section; see also note 2).

[2]The "joint venturer" concept comes from the *Burton* case, cited above, where the Court concluded that "the state has so far insinuated itself into a position of interdependence with . . . [defendant] that it must be recognized as a joint participant in the challenged activity" (365 U.S. at 725; see also *Moose Lodge* v. *Irvis*, 407 U.S. 163, at 176-77 (1972)). When the state is so substantially involved in the whole of the private entity's activities as to be considered a joint venturer, courts will normally not require proof that it was involved in the particular activity challenged in the lawsuit. Compare note 1 earlier.

most likely be insufficient. . . . [But as the] conduct complained of becomes more offensive, and as the nature of the dispute becomes more amenable to resolution by a court, the more appropriate it is to subject the issue to judicial scrutiny. . . . Class-based discrimination is perhaps the practice most fundamentally opposed to the stuff of which our national heritage is composed, and by far the most evil form of discrimination has been that based on race. It should hardly be surprising, then, that in race discrimination cases courts have been particularly vigilant in requiring the states to avoid support of otherwise private discrimination, and that where the conduct has been less offensive, a greater degree of tolerance has been shown. . . . It is not necessary to put sex discrimination into the same hole as race discrimination. . . . It is enough to note that the conduct here alleged—invidious class-based discrimination on account of sex—would appear . . . to be more offensive than the disciplinary steps taken in prior cases [522 F.2d at 405–06].[3]

Most state action cases, like those above, are concerned with whether government is so involved in the activities of a private institution as to render those activities state action. But state action issues may also arise with respect to public institutions. In that context, the basic question is whether the public institution is so involved with the activity of some private entity as to render the latter's activity state action. In *Shapiro* v. *Columbia Union National Bank and Trust Co.*, 576 S.W.2d 310 (Mo. 1978), for example, the question was whether the University of Missouri at Kansas City (a public institution) was so entwined with the administration of a private scholarship trust fund that the fund's activities became state action. The plaintiff, a female student, sued the school and the bank which was the fund's trustee. The fund had been established as a trust by a private individual, who had stipulated that all scholarship recipients be male. Shapiro alleged that, although the Columbia Union National Bank was named as trustee, the university in fact administered the scholarship fund; that she was ineligible for the scholarship solely because of her sex; and that the university's conduct in administering the trust therefore was unconstitutional. She further claimed that the trust constituted three fourths of the scholarship money available at the university and that the school's entire scholarship program was thereby discriminatory.

The trial court twice dismissed the complaint for failure to state a cause of action, reasoning that the trust was private and the plaintiff had not stated facts sufficient to demonstrate state action. On appeal the Supreme Court of Missouri reviewed the university's involvement in the administration of the trust, applying the government contacts theory:

> We cannot conclude that by sifting all the facts and circumstances there was state action involved here. Mr. Victor Wilson established a private trust for the benefit of deserving Kansas City "boys." He was a private

---

[3](Author's footnote.) After the appellate court remanded *Weise* to the trial court, that court did not rule on the state action issue until 1982. By then, the U.S. Supreme Court had decided *Rendell-Baker* v. *Kohn*, (see next page). In light of that case, the *Weise* trial court held, "with disappointment," that the plaintiffs could not "establish state action under any view of the instant matter" (*Weise* v. *Syracuse University*, 553 F. Supp. 675 (N.D.N.Y. 1982)).

individual; he established a trust with his private funds; he appointed a
bank as trustee; he established a procedure by which recipients of the trust
fund would be selected. The trustee was to approve the selections. Under
the terms of the will, no public agency or state action is involved. Discrimination on the basis of sex results from Mr. Wilson's personal predeliction.
That is clearly not unlawful.

     The dissemination of information by the university in a catalogue
and by other means, the accepting and processing of applications by the
financial aid office, the determining of academic standards and financial
needs, the making of a tentative award or nomination and forwarding the
names of qualified male students to the private trustee . . . does not in our
opinion rise to the level of state action [576 S.W.2d at 320].

Disagreeing with this conclusion, one member of the appellate court wrote in a
dissenting opinion:

     The university accepts the applications, makes a tentative award,
and in effect ''selects'' the male applicants who are to receive the benefits
of the scholarship fund. The acts of the university are more than ministerial.
The trust as it has been administered has shed its purely private character
and has become a public one. The involvement of the public university
is . . . of such a prevailing nature that there is governmental entwinement
constituting state action [576 S.W.2d at 323].

Having declined to find state action, thus denying the plaintiff a basis for applying
the Constitution to the trust fund, the appellate court majority affirmed the dismissal
of the case. (For a discussion on how the problem of sex-restricted scholarships is
treated under Title IX, see this volume, Section 4.3.3.)

     A major U.S. Supreme Court case has now added more fire power to the
postsecondary arsenal for thwarting state action challenges. *Rendell-Baker* v. *Kohn,*
102 S. Ct. 2764 (1982), was a suit brought by teachers at a private school who
had been discharged as a result of their opposition to school policies. They sued
the school and its director, Kohn, alleging that the discharges violated their federal
constitutional rights to free speech and due process. The issue before the Court
was whether the private school's discharge of the teachers was ''state action,'' subjecting it to the constraints of the Constitution.

     The defendant school specializes in dealing with students who have drug,
alcohol, or behavioral problems or other special needs. Nearly all students are referred
by local public schools or by the drug rehabilitation division of the state's department of health. The school receives funds for student tuition from the local public
school boards and is reimbursed by the state department of health for services provided to students referred by the department. The school also receives funds from
other state and federal agencies. Virtually all the school's income, therefore, is derived
from government funding. The school is also subject to state regulations on various
matters, such as record keeping and student/teacher ratios, and to requirements
concerning services provided under its contracts with the local school boards and
the state health department. Few of these requirements, however, relate to personnel
policy.

     Using an analysis based on the government contacts theory, the Supreme

Court held that neither the government funding nor the government regulation was sufficient to make the school's discharge decisions state action. As to funding, the Court determined:

> The school . . . is not fundamentally different from many private corporations whose business depends primarily on contracts to build roads, bridges, dams, ships, or submarines for the government. Acts of such private contractors do not become acts of the government by reason of their significant or even total engagement in performing public contracts.
>
> The school is also analogous to the public defender found not to be a state actor in *Polk County* v. *Dodson*, 454 U.S. 312 (1982). There we concluded that, although the state paid the public defender, her relationship with her client was "identical to that existing between any other lawyer and client" (454 U.S. at 318). Here the relationship between the school and its teachers and counselors is not changed because the state pays the tuition of the students [102 S. Ct. at 2771].

And as to regulation:

> Here the decisions to discharge the petitioners were not compelled or even influenced by any state regulation. Indeed, in contrast to the extensive regulation of the school generally, the various regulators showed relatively little interest in the school's personnel matters. The most intrusive personnel regulation promulgated by the various government agencies was the requirement that the Committee on Criminal Justice had the power to approve persons hired as vocational counselors. Such a regulation is not sufficient to make a decision to discharge, made by private management, state action [102 S. Ct. at 2772].

The Court also considered and rejected two other arguments of the teachers: that the school was engaged in state action because it performs a "public function" and that the school had a "symbiotic relationship" with—that is, was engaged in a "joint venture" with—government, which constitutes state action under *Burton* v. *Wilmington Parking Authority*, discussed above. As to the former argument, the Court reasoned:

> The relevant question is not simply whether a private group is serving a "public function." We have held that the question is whether the function performed has been "traditionally the *exclusive* prerogative of the state" (*Jackson* v. *Metropolitan Edison Co.*, 419 U.S. at 353). There can be no doubt that the education of maladjusted high school students is a public function, but that is only the beginning of the inquiry. [Massachusetts law] demonstrates that the state intends to provide services for such students at public expense. That legislative policy choice in no way makes these services the exclusive province of the state. Indeed, the Court of Appeals noted that until recently the state had not undertaken to provide education for students who could not be served by traditional public schools (641 F.2d at 26). That a private entity performs a function which serves the public does not make its acts state action [102 S. Ct. at 2772].

As to the latter argument, the Court concluded simply that "the school's fiscal relationship with the state is not different from that of many contractors performing services for the government. No symbiotic relationship such as existed in *Burton* exists here."

Having rejected all the teachers' arguments, the Court, by a 7-to-2 vote, concluded that the school's discharge decisions did not constitute state action; and it affirmed the lower court's dismissal of the lawsuit.

As part of the narrowing trend evident in the Court's state action opinions since the early 1970s, *Rendell-Baker* illustrates the trend's application to private education. The case appears to confirm the validity of many earlier cases where the court refused to find state action respecting activities of postsecondary institutions, and to cast doubt on some other cases where state action has been found.[4] *Rendell-Baker* thus may serve to insulate postsecondary institutions further from state action findings and the resultant application of federal constitutional constraints to their activities.

Rendell-Baker, however, does not create an impenetrable protective barrier for postsecondary institutions. In particular, there may be situations in which government is directly involved in the challenged activity—in contrast to the absence of government involvement in the personnel actions challenged in *Rendell-Baker*. Such involvement may supply the "nexus" missing in the Supreme Court case (see *Milonas* v. *Williams,* 691 F.2d 931 (10th Cir. 1982)). Moreover, there may be situations, unlike *Rendell-Baker,* in which government officials by virtue of their offices sit on or nominate others for an institution's board of trustees. Such involvement, perhaps in combination with other "contacts," may create the "symbiotic relationship" that did not exist in the Supreme Court case (see *Krynicky* v. *Univ. of Pittsburgh* and *Schier* v. *Temple Univ.,* 742 F.2d 94 (3d Cir. 1984)). Because these and other such circumstances continue to pose complex issues, administrators in private institutions should keep the state action concept in mind in major dealings with government. They should also rely heavily on legal counsel for guidance in this technical area. And, most important, administrators should confront the policy issue that the state action cases leave squarely on their doorsteps: When the law does not impose constitutional constraints on your action, to what extent and in what manner will your institution undertake on its own initiative to protect freedom of speech and press, equality of opportunity, due process, and other such values on your campus?

1.4.3. Other bases for legal rights in private institutions. The inapplicability of the federal Constitution to private schools does not necessarily mean that students, faculty members, and other members of the private school community have no legal rights assertable against the school. There are other sources for individual rights which may resemble those found in the Constitution.

The federal government and, to a lesser extent, state governments have increasingly created statutory rights enforceable against private institutions, particularly in the discrimination area. The federal Title VII prohibition on employment discrimination (42 U.S.C. sec. 2000e *et seq.,* discussed in Section 3.3.2.1), applicable generally to public and private employment relationships, is a prominent example.

---

[4]The cases and authorities are collected in Annot., "Action of Private Institution of Higher Education as Constituting State Action, or Action Under Color of Law, for Purposes of Fourteenth Amendment and 42 U.S.C. Section 1983," 37 A.L.R. Fed. 601 (1978 plus periodic supp.).

The Title VI race discrimination law (42 U.S.C. sec. 2000d *et seq.*) and the Title IX sex discrimination law (20 U.S.C. sec. 1681 *et seq.*) (see Sections 7.5.2 and 7.5.3), applicable to federal aid recipients, are other major examples. Such sources provide a large body of nondiscrimination law, which parallels and in some ways is more protective than the equal protection principles derived from the Fourteenth Amendment.

Beyond such statutory rights, several common law theories for protecting individual rights in private postsecondary institutions have been advanced. Most prominent by far is the contract theory, under which students and faculty members are said to have a contractual relationship with the private school. Express or implied contract terms establish legal rights that can be enforced in court if the contract is breached. Although the theory is a useful one that has been referred to in a number of cases (see Sections 3.1 and 4.1), most courts agree that the contract law of the commercial world cannot be imported wholesale into the academic environment. The theory must thus be applied with sensitivity to academic customs and usages. Moreover, the theory's usefulness may be quite limited. The "terms" of the "contract" may be difficult to identify, particularly in the case of students. (To what extent, for instance, is the college catalogue a source of contract terms?) The terms, once identified, may be too vague or ambiguous to enforce. Or the contract may be so barren of content or so one-sided in favor of the institution as to be an insignificant source of individual rights.

Despite its shortcomings, the contract theory is gaining in importance. As it becomes clearer that the bulk of private institutions can escape the tentacles of the state action doctrine, alternative theories for establishing individual rights are increasingly tested. With the lowering of the age of majority, postsecondary students have a capacity to contract under state law—a capacity that many previously did not have. In what has become the age of the consumer, students are encouraged to import consumer rights into postsecondary education. And, in an age of collective negotiation, faculties often seek to rely on a contract model for ordering employment relationships on campus (see Section 3.2).

Such developments can affect both public and private institutions, although state law may place additional restrictions on contract authority in the public sphere. While contract concepts can of course limit the authority of the institution, they should not be seen only as a burr in the administrator's side. They can also be used creatively to provide order and fairness in institutional affairs and to create internal grievance procedures that encourage in-house rather than judicial resolution of problems. Administrators thus should be sensitive to both the problems and the potentials of contract concepts in the postsecondary environment.

State constitutions have also assumed critical importance as a source of legal rights for individuals to assert against private institutions. Several recent cases—two involving private universities—have relied on state constitutions to create individual rights of speech, petition, and assembly on private property. The key case is *Prune Yard Shopping Center* v. *Robins,* 593 P.2d 341 (Cal. 1979), affirmed, 447 U.S. 74 (1980). In this case a group of high school students who were distributing political material and soliciting petition signatures had been excluded from a private shopping center. The students sought an injunction in state court to prevent further exclusions. The California Supreme Court sided with the students, holding that they had a state constitutional right of access to the shopping center to engage in expressive activity. In the U.S. Supreme Court, the shopping center argued that the California court's ruling was inconsistent with an earlier U.S. Supreme Court precedent, *Lloyd* v. *Tanner,* 407 U.S. 551 (1972), which held that the First Amendment of the federal Constitution does not guarantee individuals a right to free expression on the premises of a private shopping center. The Court rejected the argument, emphasizing that the state had a "sovereign right to adopt in its own constitution individual liberties more expansive than those conferred by the federal Constitution."

The shopping center also argued that the California court's decision, in denying it the right to exclude others from its premises, violated its property rights under the Fifth and Fourteenth Amendments of the federal Constitution. The Supreme Court rejected this argument as well:

> It is true that one of the essential sticks in the bundle of property rights is the right to exclude others (*Kaiser Aetna* v. *United States,* 444 U.S. 164, 179–80, 100 S. Ct. 383, 391–92, 62 L. Ed. 2d 332 (1979)). And here there has literally been a "taking" of that right to the extent that the California Supreme Court has interpreted the state constitution to entitle its citizens to exercise free expression and petition rights on shopping center property. But it is well established that "not every destruction or injury to property by governmental action has been held to be a 'taking' in the constitutional sense" (*Armstrong* v. *United States,* 364 U.S. 40, 48, 80 S. Ct. 1563, 1568, 4 L. Ed. 2d 1554 (1960)). . . .
>
> Here the requirement that appellants permit appellees to exercise state-protected rights of free expression and petition on shopping center property clearly does not amount to an unconstitutional infringement of appellants' property rights under the taking clause. There is nothing to suggest that preventing appellants from prohibiting this sort of activity will unreasonably impair the value or use of their property as a shopping center. The Prune Yard is a large commercial complex that covers several city blocks, contains numerous separate business establishments, and is open to the public at large. The decision of the California Supreme Court makes it clear that the Prune Yard may restrict expressive activity by adopting time, place, and manner regulations that will minimize any interference with its commercial functions. Appellees were orderly, and they limited their activity to the common areas of the shopping center. In these circumstances, the fact that they may have "physically invaded" appellants' property cannot be viewed as determinative [447 U.S. at 82–84].

Prune Yard has gained significance in educational settings with the New Jersey Supreme Court's decision in *State* v. *Schmid,* 423 A.2d 615 (N.J. 1980) (this volume, Section 5.6.3). The defendant, who was not a student, had been charged with criminal trespass for distributing political material on the Princeton University campus in violation of Princeton regulations. The New Jersey court declined to rely on the federal First Amendment, instead deciding the case on state constitutional grounds. It held that, even without a finding of state action (a prerequisite to applying the federal First Amendment), Princeton had a state constitutional obligation to protect Schmid's expressional rights (N.J. Const. (1947), Art. I, para. 6 and para. 18).

In justifying its authority to construe the state constitution in this expansive manner, the court relied on *Prune Yard.* A subsequent case involving Muhlenberg College, *Pennsylvania* v. *Tate,* 432 A.2d 1382 (Pa. 1981), follows the *Schmid* reasoning in holding that the Pennsylvania state constitution protected the defendant's rights.

Sec. 1.5. *Religion and the Public-Private Dichotomy*

Under the establishment clause of the First Amendment, public institutions must maintain a neutral stance regarding religious beliefs and activities; they must, in other words, maintain religious neutrality. Public institutions cannot favor or support one religion over another, and they cannot favor or support religion over nonreligion. Thus, for instance, public schools have been prohibited from using an official nondenominational prayer (*Engel* v. *Vitale,* 370 U.S. 421 (1962)) and from prescribing the reading of verses from the Bible at the opening of each school day (*Abington School District* v. *Schempp,* 374 U.S. 203 (1963)).

The First Amendment contains two "religion" clauses. The first prohibits government from "establishing" religion; the second protects individuals' "free exercise" of religion from governmental interference. Although the two clauses have a common objective of ensuring governmental "neutrality," they pursue it in different ways. As the Supreme Court explained in *Abington School District* v. *Schempp:*

> The wholesome "neutrality" of which this Court's cases speak thus stems from a recognition of the teaching of history that powerful sects or groups might bring about a fusion of governmental and religious functions or a concert or dependency of one upon the other to the end that official support of the state or federal government would be placed behind the tenets of one or of all orthodoxies. This the establishment clause prohibits. And a further reason for neutrality is found in the free exercise clause, which recognizes the value of religious training, teaching, and observance and, more particularly, the right of every person to freely choose his own course with reference thereto, free of any compulsion from the state. This the free exercise clause guarantees. . . . The distinction between the two clauses is apparent—a violation of the free exercise clause is predicated on coercion, whereas the establishment clause violation need not be so attended [374 U.S. at 222–23].

Neutrality, however, does not necessarily require a public institution to prohibit all religious activity on campus. If a rigidly observed policy of neutrality would discriminate against campus organizations with religious purposes or impinge on an individual's right to "free exercise" of religion, the institution may be permitted—sometimes required—to allow some religion on campus. The difficulty of delineating neutrality in such contexts is illustrated by *Keegan* v. *University of Delaware,* 349 A.2d 14 (Del. 1975). The university had banned all religious worship services from campus facilities. The plaintiffs contended that this policy was unconstitutional as applied to students' religious services in the commons areas of campus dormitories. The court first asked whether the university could permit religious worship in the commons area without violating the establishment clause:

> We hold that the university cannot support its absolute ban of all religious worship on the theory that, without such a ban, university policy allowing all student groups, including religious groups, free access to dormitory commons areas would necessarily violate the establishment clause. The establishment cases decided by the United State Supreme Court indicate that neutrality is the safe harbor in which to avoid First Amendment violations: neutral "accommodation" of religion is permitted, . . . while "promotion" and "advancement" of religion are not. . . . University policy without the worship ban could be neutral towards religion and could have the primary effect of advancing education by allowing students to meet together in the commons room of their dormitory to exchange ideas and share mutual interests. If any religious group or religion is accommodated or benefited thereby, such accommodation or benefit is purely incidental, and would not, in our judgment, violate the establishment clause. . . . The commons room is already provided for the benefits of students. It is not a dedication of the space to promote religious interests [349 A.2d at 16].

Then the court asked whether the university was constitutionally *required* by the free exercise clause to make the commons area available for students' religious worship:

> The only activity proscribed by the regulation is worship. . . . The commons area is already provided for student use and there is no request here that separate religious facilities be established. The area in question is a residence hall where students naturally assemble with their friends for many purposes. Religion, at least in part, is historically a communal exercise. . . .
>
> It can be argued, as it has been, that the question is whether the university must permit the students to worship on university property. But, in terms of religious liberty, the question is better put, in our judgment, from the perspective of the individual student. Can the university prohibit student worship in a commons area of a university dormitory which is provided for student use and in which the university permits every other student activity? It is apparent to us that such a regulation impedes the observance of religion [349 A.2d at 17, 18].

The court in *Keegan* thus held not only that the university could permit the religious services but also that the university was required to do so by the free exercise clause.[5]

A U.S. Supreme Court case decided eight years after *Keegan* provides additional insight and perspective on maintaining governmental "neutrality" toward religion on the campuses of public institutions. In *Widmar* v. *Vincent*, 102 S. Ct. 269 (1981)

---

[5]The starting point for the court's establishment clause analysis in *Keegan* was the three-pronged test set out in *Lemon* v. *Kurtzman*, 403 U.S. 602 (1971), and discussed later in this section. This test applies both to situations where public institutions support allegedly religious activity and to situations, as described later, where government supports allegedly religious activity in private institutions.

(this volume, Section 4.8.4), the Court determined that student religious activities on public campuses may be protected by the First Amendment's free speech clause; and it indicated a preference for using the free speech clause, rather than the free exercise of religion clause, whenever the institution has created a "public forum" generally open for student use. The Court also concluded that the First Amendment's establishment clause would not be violated by an "open forum" or "equal access" policy permitting student use of campus facilities for both nonreligious and religious purposes. Using this analysis, the Court reached, by a different and now preferred route, the same conclusion as the Delaware court in *Keegan:* that the Constitution requires public postsecondary institutions to allow religious activities on campus in areas generally open to other student uses.

A private institution's position under the establishment and free exercise clauses differs markedly from that of a public institution. Private institutions have no obligation of neutrality under the establishment clause. Moreover, the religious beliefs and practices of private institutions are affirmatively protected from government interference by the free exercise clause. This free exercise protection, however, is not absolute. Its limits are illustrated by *Bob Jones University* v. *United States,* 103 S. Ct. 2017 (1983) (this volume, Section 7.3.1). Because the university maintained racially restrictive policies on dating and marriage, the Internal Revenue Service had denied it tax-exempt status under federal tax laws. The university argued that its racial practices were religiously based and that the denial abridged its right to free exercise of religion. The U.S. Supreme Court, rejecting this argument, emphasized that the federal government has a "compelling" interest in "eradicating racial discrimination in education" and that that interest "substantially outweighs whatever burden denial of tax benefits places on [the university's] exercise of . . . religious beliefs."

Although the establishment clause itself imposes no neutrality obligation on private institutions, this clause does have another kind of importance for private institutions that are church related. When government—federal, state, or local— undertakes to provide financial or other support for private postsecondary education, the question arises whether this support, insofar as it benefits church-related education, constitutes government support for religion. If it does, such support would violate the establishment clause because government would have departed from its position of neutrality.

Two 1971 cases decided by the Supreme Court provide the basis for the modern law on government support for church-related schools. *Lemon* v. *Kurtzman,* 403 U.S. 602 (1971), invalidated two state programs providing aid for church-related elementary and secondary schools. *Tilton* v. *Richardson,* 403 U.S. 672 (1971), held constitutional a federal aid program providing construction grants to higher education institutions, including those that are church related. In deciding the cases, the Court developed a three-pronged test for determining when a government support program passes muster under the establishment clause:

> First, the statute must have a secular legislative purpose; second, its principal or primary effect must be one that neither advances nor inhibits religion . . . ; finally, the statute must not foster "an excessive government entanglement with religion" (*Walz* v. *Tax Commission,* 397 U.S. 664, 674 (1970))[403 U.S. at 612–13].

The first prong (purpose) has proved easy to meet and has not been of major significance in subsequent cases. But the other two prongs (effect and entanglement) have been both very important and very difficult to apply in particular cases. The Court's major explanation of "effect" came in *Hunt* v. *McNair,* 413 U.S. 734 (1973):

> Aid normally may be thought to have a primary effect of advancing religion when it flows to an institution in which religion is so pervasive that a substantial portion of its functions are subsumed in the religious mission or when it funds a specifically religious activity in an otherwise substantially secular setting [413 U.S. at 753].

Its major explanation of "entanglement" appeared in the *Lemon* case:

> In order to determine whether the government entanglement with religion is excessive, we must examine (1) the character and purposes of the institutions which are benefited, (2) the nature of the aid that the state provides, and (3) the resulting relationship between the government and the religious authority [403 U.S. at 615].

Three Supreme Court cases have applied this complex three-pronged test to church-related postsecondary institutions. In each case the aid program passed the test. In *Tilton* the Court approved the federal construction grant program, and the grants to the particular colleges involved in that case, by a narrow 5-to-4 vote. In *Hunt* v. *McNair,* the Court, by a 6-to-3 vote, sustained a state program that assisted colleges, including church-related colleges, by issuing revenue bonds for their construction projects. The third case is *Roemer* v. *Board of Public Works,* 426 U.S. 736 (1976), where the Court, by a 5-to-4 vote, upheld Maryland's program of general support grants to private, including church-related, colleges. Though there were strong dissents in each case, and though a majority of the Court could agree on an opinion only in *Hunt,* the cases nevertheless suggest that a wide range of postsecondary support programs can be devised compatibly with the establishment clause and that a wide range of church-related institutions can be eligible to receive government support. The *Roemer* case is the most revealing. There the Court refused to find that the grants given a group of church-related schools constituted support for religion—even though the funds were granted annually and could be put to a wide range of uses, and even though the schools had church representatives on their governing boards, employed Roman Catholic chaplains, held Roman Catholic religious exercises, required students to take religion or theology classes taught primarily by Roman Catholic clerics, made some hiring decisions for theology departments partly on the basis of religious considerations, and began some classes with prayers.

Though the cases have been quite hospitable to government support programs for postsecondary education, administrators of church-related institutions should still be most sensitive to establishment clause issues. Since the cases have been decided by close votes, with great disagreement among the justices in their reasoning, the law has not yet settled. Thus, administrators should exercise great care in using government funds and should keep in mind that, at some point, religious influences within the institution can still jeopardize government funding. In addition, state constitutions or the statutes creating the funding programs may contain clauses that restrict government support for church-related institutions more vigorously than the establishment clause does.

Sec. 1.6. Organizing the Postsecondary Institution's Legal Affairs

There are numerous organizational arrangements by which postsecondary institutions can obtain legal counsel. State institutions are often served by the state attorney general's office. Working relationships may vary with the state and the campus. In general, administrators should seek to have services centralized in one or a small number of assistant attorney generals who devote the bulk of their time to the institution or the system of which it is a part and become thoroughly familiar with its operations.

Many larger colleges and universities now employ their own in-house staff counsel. Such an arrangement has the advantage of providing daily coordinated services of resident counsel acclimated to the particular needs and problems of the institution. Though staff counsel can become specialists in postsecondary education law, they normally will not have the time or exposure to become expert in all the specialty areas (such as labor law, tax law, patent law, or litigation) with which institutions must deal. Thus, these institutions may sometimes retain private law firms for special problems.

Other institutions, large and small, may arrange for all their legal services to be provided by one or more private law firms. This arrangement has the advantage of increasing the number of attorneys with particular expertise available for the variety of problems that confront institutions. A potential disadvantage is that no one attorney will be conversant with the full range of the institution's needs and problems nor be on call daily for early participation in administrative decision making. Administrators of institutions depending on private firms may thus want to ensure that at least one lawyer is generally familiar with and involved in the institution's affairs and regularly available for consultation even on routine matters.

With each of these organizational arrangements, serious consideration should be given to the particular functions that counsel will perform and to the relationships that will be fostered between counsel and administrators. Broadly stated, counsel's role is to identify, define, and provide options for resolving legal problems. But there are two basic, and different, ways to fulfill this role: through *treatment* law or through *preventive* law. To analogize to another profession, the former involves curing legal diseases; the latter involves maintaining legal health.

Treatment law is the more traditional of the two approaches. It focuses on actual challenges to institutional practices and on affirmative legal steps by the institution to protect its interests when they are threatened. When suit is filed against the institution, or litigation is threatened; when a government agency cites the institution for noncompliance with its regulations; when the institution needs formal permission of a government agency to undertake a proposed course of action; when the institution wishes to sue some other party—then treatment law operates. The goal is to resolve the specific legal problem at hand. Treatment law today is indispensable to the functioning of a postsecondary institution, and virtually all institutions have such legal service.

Preventive law, in contrast, focuses on initiatives that the institution can take before actual legal disputes arise. Preventive law involves administrator and counsel in a continual process of setting the legal parameters within which the institution will operate to avoid litigation or other legal disputes. Counsel identifies the legal consequences of proposed actions; pinpoints the range of alternatives for avoiding problems and the legal risk of each alternative; sensitizes administrators to legal issues and the importance of recognizing them early; and determines the impact of new or proposed laws and regulations, and new court decisions, on institutional operations.

Preventive law has not been a general practice of postsecondary institutions in the past. But the concept has become increasingly valuable as the presence of law on the campus has increased, and acceptance of preventive law within post-secondary education has grown substantially. Today it may fairly be said that preventive law is as indispensable as treatment law and provides the more constructive posture from which to conduct institutional legal affairs.

Institutions using or considering the use of preventive law face some difficult questions. To what extent will administrators and counsel give priority to the practice of preventive law? Which institutional administrators will have direct access to counsel? Will counsel advise only administrators, or will he or she also be available to recognized faculty or student organizations or committees, or perhaps to other members of the university community on certain matters? What working arrangements will assure that administrators are alert to incipient legal problems and that counsel is involved in institutional decision making at an early stage? What degree of autonomy will counsel have to influence institutional decision making, and what authority will counsel have to halt legally unwise institutional action?

The following steps are suggested for administrators and counsel seeking to implement a preventive law system:

1. Review the institution's current organizational arrangement for obtaining legal counsel. Determine whether changes—for example, from part-time to full-time counsel or from outside firm to house counsel—are appropriate and feasible to facilitate preventive lawyering.

2. Develop a teamwork relationship between administrator and counsel; both should be substantially involved in legal affairs, cooperating with one another on a regular basis, for preventive law to work best. Since the dividing line between the administrator's and the lawyer's functions is not always self-evident, roles should be developed through mutual interchange between the two sets of professionals. While considerable flexibility is possible, institutions should be careful to maintain a distinction between the two roles. The purpose of preventive law is not to make the administrator into a lawyer or the lawyer into an administrator. It is the lawyer's job to resolve doubts about the interpretation of statutes, regulations, and court decisions; to stay informed of legal developments and predict the directions in which law is evolving; and to suggest legal options and advise on their relative effectiveness in achieving the institution's goals. But it is for the administrator (along with boards of trustees) to stay informed of developments in the theory and practice of administration; to devise policy options within the constraints imposed by law and determine their relative effectiveness in achieving institutional goals; and ultimately, at the appropriate level of the institutional hierarchy, to make the policy decisions that give life to the institution.

3. Have the lawyer-administrator team perform legal audits periodically.

A legal audit is a legal "checkup" to determine the legal "health" of the institution. A complete audit would include a survey of every office and function in the institution. For each office and function, the lawyer-administrator team would develop the information and analysis necessary to determine whether that office or function is in compliance with the full range of legal constraints to which it is subject.

4. To supplement legal audits, develop an early-warning system that will apprise counsel and adminstrators of potential legal problems in their incipiency. The early-warning system should be based on a list of situations which the institution will likely encounter *and* which are likely to create some significant legal risk. For instance, such a list might include situations where an administrator is revising a standard form contract used by the institution or creating a new standard form contract to cover a type of transaction for which the institution has not previously used such a contract. Other examples might include situations where administrators are reviewing the institution's student code of conduct, student bill of rights, or similar documents; a school or department is seeking to terminate a faculty member's tenure; a committee is drafting or modifying an affirmative action plan; administrators are preparing policies to implement a new set of federal administrative regulations; or administrators are proposing a new security system for the campus or temporary security measures for a particular emergency. Under an early-warning system, all such circumstances, or others that the institution may specify, would trigger a consultative process between administrator and counsel aimed at resolving legal problems before they erupt into disputes.

5. Based on the data obtained through legal audits, an early-warning system, and other means the institution may employ, engage in a continuing course of legal planning. If audits and other means provide detection and diagnosis, legal planning provides measures for legal health maintenance. Legal planning establishes the process and the individual steps by which the institution determines the degree of legal risk exposure it is willing to assume in particular situations, and avoids or resolves legal risks it is unwilling to assume. Successful legal planning depends on a careful sorting out and interrelating of legal and policy issues. Teamwork between administrator and laywer is therefore a critical ingredient in legal planning. Sensitivity to the authority structure of the institution is also a critical ingredient, so that legal planning decisions are made at the prescribed levels of authority.

6. For the inevitable percentage of potential legal problems that do develop into actual disputes, establish internal grievance mechanisms. These mechanisms may utilize various techniques for dispute resolution, from informal consultation, to mediation or arbitration, to hearings before panels drawn from the academic community. Whatever techniques are adopted should be generally available to students, faculty, and staff members who have complaints concerning actions taken against them by other members of the academic community. Some summary procedure should be devised for dismissing complaints that are frivolous or that contest general academic policy rather than a particular action that has harmed the complainant. Not every dispute, of course, is amenable to internal solution, since many disputes involve outside parties (such as business firms, government agencies, or professional associations). But for disputes among members of the campus community, grievance mechanisms provide an on-campus forum that can be attuned to the particular characteristics of academic institutions. Grievance mechanisms can encourage collegial resolution of disputes, thus forestalling the complainant's resort to courts or other external bodies.

Selected Annotated Bibliography

General

Bickel, R., and Brechner, J., *The College Administrator and the Courts* (College Administration Pub., 1977, plus periodic supp.) is a basic casebook written for administrators that briefs and discusses leading court cases. Topics include the legal system, sources of law, the role of counsel, distinctions between public and private colleges, and the state action concept. Updated quarterly.

Sec. 1.1 (How Far the Law Reaches and How Loud It Speaks)

1. Edwards, H. T., *Higher Education and the Unholy Crusade Against Governmental Regulation* (Institute for Educational Management, Harvard University, 1980), reviews and evaluates the federal regulatory presence on the campus. Author concludes that much of the criticism directed by postsecondary administrators at federal regulation of higher education is either unwarranted or premature.

2. Edwards, H. T., and Nordin, V. D., *Higher Education and the Law* (Institute for Educational Management, Harvard University, 1979, with periodic supplementation), is a casebook covering a range of issues in higher education law. Divided into four general parts—"The College or University as a Legal Entity," "Faculty Rights," "Student Rights," and "Federal Regulation of Higher Education"—each containing edited texts of leading court opinions, other source materials and citations, and the authors' questions and notes.

3. Gouldner, H., "The Social Impact of Campus Litigation," 51 *J. of Higher Education* 328 (1980), explores the detrimental effects on the postsecondary community of "the tidal wave of litigation . . . awash in the country"; identifies "increased secrecy on campus," "fragile friendships among colleagues," a "crisis in confidence" in decision making, and "domination by legal norms" as major effects to be dealt with.

4. Hobbs, W. C., "The Courts," in P. G. Altbach and R. O. Berdahl (Eds.), *Higher Education in American Society* 181–198 (Prometheus Books, 1981), reviews the concept of judicial deference to academic expertise and analyzes the impact of courts on postsecondary institutions. Includes illustrative cases. Author concludes that, despite complaints to the contrary from academics, the tradition of judicial deference to academic judgments is still alive and well.

5. *Specialty Law Digest: Education* (Bureau of National Affairs) is a monthly publication focusing on recent developments in the law of education, both elementary/secondary and postsecondary. Contains an "Education Law Digest" with summaries of cases arranged conceptually; a "Case Survey" with education law cases arranged by jurisdiction; "The Education Law Article," a monograph selected and reprinted by the publishers from among recent commentary; and a selected bibliography of other recent articles.

6. Weeks, K. M. (Ed.), *Legal Deskbook for Administrators of Independent Colleges and Universities* (Center for Constitutional Studies, Mercer University, 1982), with annual updates, provides a practical overview of higher education law topics most important to private institutions. Includes chapters on "Preventive Planning," "Governance," "Employment," "Students," "Physical Facilities,"

"Liability," "Taxation," "Church Related Colleges and Universities," and a collection of "Special Topics." Chapters are divided into numerous sub-chapters, most of which include summary "Planning Steps" and a list of "Sources and Resources" useful in dealing with the topic addressed.

7. *West's Education Law Reporter* (West Publishing Co.) is a monthly publication covering education-related case law on both elementary/secondary and postsecondary education. Includes complete texts of opinions, summaries written for the layperson, articles and case comments, and a cumulative table of cases and index of legal principles from the cases.

Sec. 1.2 (Evolution of the Law Relating to Postsecondary Education)

1. Astin, A., *Minorities in American Higher Education: Recent Trends, Prospects, and Recommendations* (Jossey-Bass, 1982), comprehensively examines the status of Blacks, Chicanos, Puerto Ricans, and American Indians in contemporary higher education. Using sociological data, author explains the realities of the equal access principle and analyzes such issues as the impact of government programs and the differences among colleges in their suitability for minority students. Includes sixty-six recommendations, by the Higher Education Research Institute for the Commission on the Higher Education of Minorities, for redressing inequalities.

2. Bok, D., *Beyond the Ivory Tower: Social Responsibilities of the Modern University* (Harvard University Press, 1982), analyzes the role of modern universities and the complex issues that universities now face. Divided into three parts: "Basic Academic Values," "Academic Responses to Social Problems," and "Addressing Social Problems by Nonacademic Means." Of particular relevance, part I includes discussions of academic freedom and of institutional autonomy; and part II includes discussions of racial inequality and of technological innovation.

3. Finkin, M., "On 'Institutional' Academic Freedom," 61 *Texas L. Rev.* 817 (1983), explores the history and theoretical basis of academic freedom and analyzes the constitutional basis for academic freedom claims. Throughout, author distinguishes between the freedom of private institutions from government interference (institutional autonomy) and the freedom of individual members of the academic community from interference by government or by the institution. Includes analysis of leading U.S. Supreme Court precedents from 1819 (the *Dartmouth College* case) through the 1970s, as well as copious citations to legal and nonlegal sources.

4. Lautsch, J. C., "Computers and the University Attorney: An Overview of Computer Law on Campus," 5 *J. of College and University Law* 217 (1978–79), explores the developing relationship between computers and the law and the impact of this relationship on the campus. Includes analysis of the role of contract law as it affects computers; the impact of computers on labor questions; the relationship of patent, copyright, and trade secret law to computers; and other areas.

5. Metzger, W., and others, *Dimensions of Academic Freedom* (University of Illinois Press, 1969), is a series of papers presenting historical, legal, and administrative perspectives on academic freedom. Considers how the concept has evolved

in light of changes in the character of faculties and student bodies and in the university's internal and external commitments.

6. Stark, J. S., and others, *The Many Faces of Educational Consumerism* (Lexington Books, 1977), is a collection of essays on the history and status of the educational consumerism movement. Discusses the roles of the federal government, state government, accrediting agencies, and the courts in protecting the consumers of education; the place of institutional self-regulation; and suggestions for the future. Provides a broad perspective on the impact of consumerism on postsecondary education.

7. Tatel, D., and Guthrie, R. C., "The Legal Ins and Outs of University-Industry Collaboration," 64 *Educational Record* 19 (Spring 1983), examines the complex legal and business issues that arise when universities and businesses seek to join forces to develop new technologies. Reviews various legal arrangements already effectuated, such as the Harvard University–Monsanto Company joint venture; outlines issues, such as conflict of interest, confidentiality, and patent rights, that arise in such arrangements; and discusses the federal government's role in encouraging university-industry relationships.

8. Van Alstyne, W., "The Demise of the Right-Privilege Distinction in Constitutional Law," 81 *Harvard L. Rev.* 1439 (1968), provides a historical and analytical review of the rise and fall of the right-privilege distinction; includes discussion of several postsecondary education cases to demonstrate that the pursuit of state postsecondary education opportunities and jobs is no longer a "privilege" to which constitutional rights do not attach.

Sec. 1.3 (Sources of Postsecondary Education Law)

1. Bakken, G., "Campus Common Law," 5 *J. of Law and Education* 201 (1976), is a theoretical overview of custom and usage as a source of postsecondary education law; emphasizes the impact of custom and usage on faculty rights and responsibilities.

2. Brennan, W. J., "State Constitutions and the Protection of Individual Rights," 90 *Harvard L. Rev.* 489 (1977), discusses the trend, in some states, toward expansive construction of state constitutional provisions protecting individual rights. The author, an associate justice of the U.S. Supreme Court, finds that "the very premise of the [U.S. Supreme Court] cases that foreclose federal remedies constitutes a clear call to state courts to step into the breach."

3. Edwards, H. T., and Nordin, V. D., *An Introduction to the American Legal System: A Supplement to Higher Education and the Law* (Institute for Educational Management, Harvard University, 1980), provides "a brief description of the American legal system for scholars, students, and administrators in the field of higher education who have had little or no legal training." Chapters include summary overviews of "The United States Courts," "The Process of Judicial Review," "Reading and Understanding Judicial Opinions," "State Court Systems," "Legislative and Statutory Sources of Law," and "Administrative Rules and Regulations as Sources of Law."

4. Farnsworth, E. A., *An Introduction to the Legal System of the United States,* 2nd ed. (Oceana, 1983), is an introductory text emphasizing the fundamentals of the American legal system. Written for the layperson.

Sec. 1.4 (The Public-Private Dichotomy)

1. Faccenda, P., and Ross, K., "Constitutional and Statutory Regulations of Private Colleges and Universities, 9 *Valparaiso University L. Rev.* 539 (1975), is an overview of the ways in which private institutions are subjected to federal constitutional and regulatory requirements; draws distinctions between public and private institutions. Written primarily for administrators, with footnotes designed for counsel.

2. Howard, A. E. D., *State Aid to Private Higher Education* (Michie, 1977), is a comprehensive treatment of state aid programs in each of the fifty states, as well as a general national overview. Provides legal analysis of state and federal constitutional law, historical developments, and descriptive information on aid programs; emphasizes church-state issues, such as those discussed in Section 1.5 of this chapter.

3. Phillips, M. J., "The Inevitable Incoherence of Modern State Action Doctrine," 28 *St. Louis University L. J.* 683 (1984), traces the historical development of the state action doctrine through the U.S. Supreme Court's 1982 decision in *Rendell-Baker* v. *Kohn* and analyzes the political and social forces that have contributed to the doctrine's current condition.

4. Thigpen, R., "The Application of Fourteenth Amendment Norms to Private Colleges and Universities," 11 *J. of Law and Education* 171 (1982), reviews the development of various theories of state action, particularly the public function and government contacts theories, and their applications to private postsecondary institutions. Also examines theories other than traditional state action for subjecting private institutions to requirements comparable to those that the Constitution places on public institutions. Author concludes: "It seems desirable to have a public policy of protecting basic norms of fair and equal treatment in nonpublic institutions of higher learning."

5. See entry no. 3 in bibliography for Section 1.2.

Sec. 1.5 (Religion and the Public-Private Dichotomy)

1. Greenawalt, K., "Constitutional Limits on Aid to Sectarian Universities," 4 *J. of College and University Law* 177 (1977), examines the establishment clause ramifications of public subsidies for church-related postsecondary institutions. Analyzes the *Tilton, Hunt,* and *Roemer* decisions and extracts a composite of operative legal principles from them. Also includes historical perspective and comparison of federal establishment clause interpretations with interpretations reached under parallel clauses of state constitutions.

2. Moots, P. R., and Gaffney, E. M., *Church and Campus: Legal Issues in Religiously Affiliated Higher Education* (University of Notre Dame Press, 1979), is directed primarily to administrators and other leaders of religiously affiliated colleges and universities. Chapters deal with the legal relationship between colleges and affiliated religious bodies, conditions under which liability might be imposed on an affiliated religious group, the effect that the relationship between a college and a religious group may have on the college's eligibility for governmental financial assistance, the "exercise of religious preference in employment policies," questions of academic freedom, the influence of religion on student admissions

and discipline, the use of federally funded buildings by religiously affiliated
colleges, and the determination of property relationships when a college and
a religious body alter their affiliation. Ends with a set of conclusions and recommendations and three appendices discussing the relationships between three
religious denominations and their affiliated colleges.

3. See entry no. 2 for Section 1.4.

Sec. 1.6 (Organizing the Postsecondary Institution's Legal Affairs)

1. Bickel, R., "The Role of College or University Legal Counsel," 3 *J. of Law
    and Education* 73 (1974), explores the various roles that an institution's legal
    counsel should fill. Roles include representing the university in formal legal
    proceedings, rendering preventive legal advice by identifying the legal aspects
    of management decisions, and preventing unnecessary extensions of technical
    legal factors into institutional administration. Should be read in conjunction
    with article written in response: Orentlicher, H., "The Role of College or
    University Legal Counsel: An Added Dimension," 4 *J. of Law and Education*
    511 (1975). Latter article emphasizes that counsel's role should be shaped
    by the particular character of colleges and universities as institutions designed
    to foster "free search for truth and free exposition," made up of "several
    integral components, each with its own special functions and contributions
    to make," and within which diversity should be encouraged.

2. Brown, L., and Dauer, E., *Planning by Lawyers: Materials on a Nonadversarial
    Legal Process* (Foundation Press, 1978), is a comprehensive set of materials
    presenting various perspectives on legal planning. Includes chapters on
    "Thinking About Planning" and "Techniques and Devices," with a par-
    ticularly helpful section on "Legal Audit and Periodic Checkup."

3. Block, D., and others (Eds.), *Controlling Legal Costs Deskbook* (Harcourt Brace
    Jovanovich, 1983), is a sourcebook in loose-leaf binder format. Provides prac-
    tical information and analysis, checklists, and sample documents on select-
    ing counsel, controlling costs of services, and managing litigation and other
    work assignments. Designed for administrators and counsel of nonprofit institu-
    tions, including colleges and universities. Periodic supplements planned.

4. Committee on Member Services, *Delivery of Legal Services to Higher Education
    Institutions: A Survey* (National Association of College and University Attorneys,
    1984) (monograph), is the report of NACUA's legal services survey. Presents
    and analyzes data, collected from the principal attorneys of public and private
    institutions, on "the personnel providing legal service, their level of experience,
    the type and relative amount of service provided, the equipment and publica-
    tions used, and the cost of such service." Includes summaries of data for institu-
    tions relying primarily on house counsel, institutions relying on outside counsel,
    and institutions using a combination of the two. A more detailed version of
    this report appears at 15 *College Law Digest* 7, printed in *West's Education Law
    Reporter,* NACUA Special Pamphlet (Sept. 20, 1984).

5. McCarthy, J. (Ed.), *New Directions for Higher Education: Resolving Conflict in
    Higher Education,* no. 32 (Jossey-Bass, 1980), describes and discusses
    mechanisms (such as mediation) that can be used by postsecondary institutions

to resolve internal disputes without the necessity of lawsuits. Includes both legal and policy perspectives on alternative dispute resolution techniques.

6. Symposium, 2 *J. of College and University Law* 1 (1974–75), is a series of three papers discussing the role and functions of legal counsel: J. Corbally, Jr., "University Counsel—Scope and Mission"; J. R. Beale, "Delivery of Legal Service to Institutions of Higher Education"; and R. Sensenbrenner, "University Counselor: Lore, Logic and Logistics." First paper is by a university president; latter two are by practicing university attorneys.

7. Weeks, K. M. (Ed.), *A Legal Inventory for Independent Colleges and Universities* (Center for Constitutional Studies, Mercer University, 1981), is a short monograph presenting a checklist of questions to use in conducting a legal audit of a private institution.

✤ II ✤

The College
and Trustees,
Administrators,
and Agents

✤   ✤   ✤   ✤   ✤

Sec. 2.1. The Question of Authority

Trustees, officers, and administrators of postsecondary institutions—public or private—can take only those actions and make only those decisions that they have authority to take or make. Acting or deciding without authority to do so can have legal consequences, both for the responsible individual and for the institution. It is thus critical, from a legal standpoint, for administrators to understand and adhere to the scope and limits of their authority and that of other institutional functionaries with whom they deal. Such sensitivity to authority questions will also normally be good administrative practice, since it can contribute order and structure to institutional governance and make the governance system more understandable, accessible, and accountable to those who deal with it.

Authority generally originates from some fundamental legal source that establishes the institution as a legal entity. For public institutions the source is usually the constitution or statutes of the state (see Section 6.2); for private institutions it is usually articles of incorporation, sometimes in combination with some form of state license (see Section 6.3). This source, though fundamental, is only the starting point for legal analysis of authority questions. To be fully understood and utilized, an institution's fundamental authority must be construed and implemented in light of all the sources of law described in Section 1.3. For public institutions state administrative law (administrative procedure acts or similar statutes, as well as court decisions) and agency law (court decisions) provide the backdrop against which authority is construed and implemented; for private institutions state corporation or trust law (statutes and court decisions) and agency law (court decisions) are the bases. Authority is particularized and dispersed (delegated) to institutional officers, employees, and organizations by institutional rules and regulations and the institution's employment contracts and, for public institutions, by administrative regulations of the state education boards or agencies. Gaps and ambiguities in authority may be filled in by resort to custom and usage at the institution. And authority may be limited by individual rights guarantees of federal and state constitutions (see especially Sections 3.5 and 3.6 and Sections 4.4 through 4.10) and by federal and state statutes and administrative regulations or adjudications (see especially Sections 6.3 and 6.5 and Sections 7.2 and 7.5).

There are several generic types of authority. As explained in *Brown* v. *Wichita State University* (Section 2.3.2), authority may be either *express, implied,* or *apparent.* Express authority is that which is found within the plain meaning of a written grant of authority. Implied authority is that which is necessary or appropriate for exercising express authority and can therefore be inferred from the express authority. Apparent authority is not actual authority at all; the term is used to describe the situation where someone acting for the institution induces a belief in other persons that authority exists when in fact it does not. Administrators should avoid this appearance of authority and should not rely on apparent authority as a basis for acting, because the institution may be held liable, under the doctrine of "estoppel," for resultant harm to persons who rely to their detriment on an appearance of authority (see Section 2.2.2). When an institutional officer or employee does mistakenly act without authority, the action can sometimes be corrected through "ratification" by the board of trustees or other officer or employee who does have authority to undertake the act in question (see Section 2.2.2).

One other type of authority is occasionally referred to in the postsecondary context: *inherent* authority. In *Morris* v. *Nowotny,* 323 S.W.2d 301 (Tex. 1959), for instance, the court remarked that the statutes establishing the University of Texas "imply the power, and, if they do not so imply, then the power is inherent in university officials to maintain proper order and decorum on the premises of the university." And in *Esteban* v. *Central Missouri State College,* 415 F.2d 1077 (8th Cir. 1969), the court held that the college had "inherent authority to maintain order and to discipline students." The inherent authority concept is often loosely used in judicial opinions and has no clear definition. Sometimes courts appear to apply the phrase to what is really a very broad construction of the institution's implied powers. In *Goldberg* v. *Regents of the University of California,* 57 Cal. Rptr. 463 (Ct. App. 1967), the court found broad disciplinary authority over students to be implicit in the state constitution's grant of power to the university, but then called that authority "inherent." At other times the inherent authority concept is more clearly distinguished from implied authority; inherent authority then is said to exist not because of any written words but because it would not be sensible, as measured by the norms of postsecondary education, for an institution to be without authority over the particular matter at issue. In all, inherent authority is an elusive concept of uncertain stature and questionable value, and it is a slender reed to rely on to justify actions and decisions. If administrators need broader authority, they should, with counsel's help, seek to expand their express authority or to justify a broader construction of their implied authority.

The law is not clear on how broadly or narrowly authority should be con-

strued in the postsecondary context. To some extent, the answer will vary from
state to state and, within a state, may depend on whether the institution is established
by the state constitution, by state statutes, or by articles of incorporation. Although
authority issues have been addressed in judicial opinions, such as those discussed
in Section 2.2, analysis is sometimes cursory, and authority problems are sometimes
overlooked. There is debate among courts and commentators about whether
postsecondary institutions should be subject to traditional legal principles for construing authority or whether such principles should be applied in a more flexible,
less demanding, way that takes into account the unique characteristics of postsecondary education. Given the uncertainty, administrators should rely when possible
on express rather than implied or inherent authority and should seek clarity in
statements of express authority, in order to avoid leaving authority questions to
the vagaries of judicial interpretation. If institutional needs require greater flexibility and generality in statements of authority, administrators should consult legal
counsel to determine how much breadth and flexibility the courts of the state would
permit in construing the various types of authority.

Miscalculations of the institution's authority, or the authority of particular
officers or employees, can have various adverse legal consequences. The institution's ability to enforce or accept the fruits of its actions may depend on its authority
to act. For public institutions, for instance, unauthorized acts may be invalidated
in courts or administrative agencies under the *ultra vires* doctrine of administrative
law (a doctrine applied to acts that are beyond the delegated authority of a public
body or official). For private institutions a similar result occasionally can be reached
under corporation law.

When the unauthorized act is a failure to follow institutional regulations and
the institution is public (see Section 1.4.2), courts will sometimes hold that the act
violated procedural due process. In *Escobar* v. *State University of New York/College at
Old Westbury*, 427 F. Supp. 850 (E.D.N.Y. 1977), a student sought to enjoin the
college from suspending him or taking any further disciplinary action against him.
The student had been disciplined by the judicial review committee, acting under
the college's ''Code of Community Conduct.'' After the college president learned
of the disciplinary action, he rejected it and imposed more severe penalties on the
student. The president purported to act under the ''Rules of Public Order'' adopted
by the board of trustees of the State University of New York rather than under
the college code. The court found that the president had violated the rules and enjoined enforcement of his decision:

> Even if we assume the president had power to belatedly invoke the
> Rules, it is clear that he did not properly exercise that power, since he did
> not follow the requirements of the Rules themselves. The charges he made
> against the plaintiff were included in the same document which set forth
> the plaintiff's suspension and the terms for his possible readmission. Con-
> trary to the Rules, the president did not convene the hearing committee,
> did not give notice of any hearing, and received no report from the hear-
> ing committee. There is no authority in either the Rules or the Code for
> substituting the hearing before the Code's judicial review committee for
> the one required to be held before the Rule's hearing committee. . . .

Of course, not every deviation from a university's regulations constitutes a deprivation of due process. . . . But where, as here, an offending student has been formally charged under the college's disciplinary code, has been subjected to a hearing, has been officially sentenced, and has commenced compliance with that sentence, it is a denial of due process of law for the chief administrative officer to step in, conduct his own in camera review of the student's record, and impose a different punishment without complying with any of the procedures which have been formally established for the college. Here the president simply brushed aside the college's formal regulations and procedures and, without specific authority, imposed a punishment of greater severity than determined by the hearing panel, a result directly contrary to the Code's appeal provisions [427 F. Supp. at 858].

For both public and private institutions, an unauthorized act violating institutional regulations may also be invalidated as a breach of an express or implied contract with students or the faculty. *Lyons* v. *Salve Regina College,* 422 F. Supp. 1354 (D.R.I. 1976), reversed, 565 F.2d 200 (1st Cir. 1977), involved a student who had received an F grade in a required nursing course because she had been absent from several classes and clinical sessions. After the student appealed the grade under the college's published "Grade Appeal Process," the grade appeal committee voted that the student receive an Incomplete rather than an F. Characterizing the committee's action as a recommendation rather than a final decision, the associate dean overruled the committee, and the student was dismissed from the nursing program.

The parties agreed that the "Grade Appeal Process" was part of the terms of a contract between them. Though the grade appeal committee's determination was termed a "recommendation" in the college's publications, the lower court found that, as the parties understood the process, the recommendation was to be binding on the associate dean. The associate dean's overruling of the committee was therefore unauthorized and constituted a breach of contract. The lower court ordered the college to change the student's grade to an Incomplete and reinstate her in the nursing program. The appellate court reversed but did not disavow the contract theory of authority. Instead, it found that the committee's determination was not intended to be binding on the associate dean and that the dean therefore had not exceeded his authority in overruling the committee.

Authority questions are also central to a determination of various questions concerning liability for harm to third parties. The institution's tort liability may depend on whether the officer or employee committing the tort was acting within the scope of his authority (see Section 2.3.1). The institution's contract liability may depend on whether the officer or employee entering the contract was authorized to do so (Section 2.3.2). And under the estoppel doctrine, both the institution and the individual may be liable where the institution or individual had apparent authority to act (Section 2.2.2).

Because of these various legal ramifications, a postsecondary institution should carefully organize and document its authority and the delegation of this authority among institutional officers, employees, and organizations. Counsel should be involved in this process. Organizational statements or charts should be generally available to the campus community, so that persons with questions or grievances can know where to turn for assistance. Delegations should be reviewed periodically, to determine whether they accurately reflect actual practice within the institution and maintain an appropriate balance of specificity and flexibility. Where a gap in authority is found, or an unnecessary overlap or ambiguity, it should be corrected. Where questions concerning the permissible scope of authority are uncovered, they should be resolved.

Similarly, administrators should understand the scope of their own authority and that of the officers, employees, and organizations with whom they deal. They should understand where their authority comes from and which higher-level administrators may review or modify their acts and decisions. They should attempt to resolve unnecessary gaps or ambiguities in their authority. They should consider what part of their authority may and should be subdelegated to lower-level administrators and what checks or limitations should be placed on those delegations. And they should attempt to ensure that their authority is adequately understood by the members of the campus community with whom they deal.

Sec. 2.2. Sources and Scope of Authority

The following discussion illustrates particular kinds of legal challenges that may be made to the authority of various functionaries in postsecondary institutions. Although the discussion reflects general concepts and issues critical to an understanding of authority in the postsecondary context, the specific legal principles that courts apply to particular challenges to authority may vary from state to state.

2.2.1. Trustees. In public institutions the authority of trustees is defined and limited by the state statutes, and sometimes constitutional provisions, which create trustee boards for individual institutions. Such laws generally confer power on the board itself as an entity separate from its individual members. Individual trustees generally have authority to act only on behalf of the board, pursuant to some board bylaw, resolution, or other delegation of authority from the board. Other state laws, such as conflict of interest laws or ethics codes, may place obligations on individual board members as well as on the board itself.

In *First Equity Corporation of Florida* v. *Utah State University,* 544 P.2d 887 (Utah 1975), the plaintiff, a stock brokerage company, sued the university over its failure to pay for common stocks ordered by the university's assistant president of finance. The university defended itself by asserting that its board of trustees lacked the authority to authorize the assistant president to invest in common stocks. The board had general control and supervision "of all appropriations made by the territory [state] for the support" of the school (Compiled Laws of Utah sec. 1855 (1888)), and the university had authority to handle its own financial affairs under the supervision of the board (Higher Education Act of 1969, Utah Code Ann. sec. 53-48-10(5)). The court (544 P.2d at 890) held, however, that these provisions did not give the university unlimited authority to encumber public funds:

> Whether or not the grant of a "general control" of "all appropriations" and the right to "handle its own financial affairs" grant unrestricted power to invest is answered by the *University of Utah* v. *Board of Examiners of the State of Utah* [4 Utah 2d 408, 295 P.2d 348 (1956)] case. After quoting Sections 1 and 2 of Article X of the [state] constitution, which mandates the legislature to provide for the maintenance of the University of Utah and USU, the court states:

Would it be contended by the university that under Article X, Section 1, it might compel the legislature to appropriate money the university considers essential? Is it contended that the demands of the university are not subject to constitutional debt limits? If so, respondent would have the power to destroy the solvency of the state and all other institutions by demands beyond the power of the state to meet.

The court then quotes in full Sections 5 and 7 of Article X of the constitution, which provides, respectively, that the proceeds of the sale of land reserved by Congress for the University of Utah shall constitute permanent funds of the state, and that all public school funds shall be guaranteed by the state against loss or diversion. Then the court concludes:

It is inconceivable that the framers of the constitution, in light of the provisions of Sections 1, 5, and 7 of Article X and the provisions as to debt limitations, intended to place the university above the only controls available for the people of this state as to the property, management, and government of the university. We are unable to reconcile respondent's position that the university has a blank check as to all its funds with no preaudit and no restraint under the provisions of the constitution requiring the state to safely invest and hold the dedicated funds and making the state guarantor of the public school funds against loss or diversion. To hold that respondent has free and uncontrolled custody and use of its property and funds while making the state guarantee said funds against loss or diversion is inconceivable. We believe the framers of the constitution intended no such result.

Because of this state constitutional limitation regarding finances, and the absence of any "specific authorizing grant" of investment power under the state statutes, the court held that the board did not have authority to purchase the particular type of stock involved. The board therefore could not authorize the assistant vice-president or any other agent to make the purchases.

In *Feldman* v. *Regents of the University of New Mexico,* 88 N.M. 392, 540 P.2d 872 (1975), the head football coach at the university sued the regents for discharging him during the term of his contract. According to New Mexico law, the regents had "power to remove any officer connected with the university when in their judgment the interests require it" (N.M. Stat. Ann. sec. 73-25-9). The regents relied on the statute as sufficient authority for dismissing the coach. In ruling on the regents' motion for summary judgment, the state courts refused to approve the dismissal under this statute. The courts reasoned that additional information was needed to determine whether the coach was an "officer" or an "employee" of the institution, since the statute would not authorize his discharge if he were an employee.

In private institutions the authority of institutional trustees is defined and limited by the institution's corporate charter (articles of incorporation) and the state corporation laws under which charters are issued. As in public institutions, the power generally lodges in the board of trustees as an entity separate from its individual members. But charter provisions, corporate bylaws, or board resolutions may delegate authority to individual trustees or trustee committees to act for the board in certain situations. Moreover, general state corporate law or trust law may place affirmative obligations on individual board members to act fairly and responsibly in protecting the institution's resources and interests. (For an argument favoring an increased obligation to the public on the part of private colleges and universities, see P. Haskell, "The University as Trustee," 17 *Georgia L. Rev.* 1 (1982).)

The Missouri case of *Burnett* v. *Barnes,* 546 S.W.2d 744 (Mo. 1977), illustrates how the authority of a private institution's board of trustees may be limited by the institution's articles of incorporation. The institution in this case, the Kansas City College of Osteopathic Medicine, was a "membership" corporation; graduates of the college had the status of members of the corporation. When the college's board of trustees sought to amend the corporate bylaws to eliminate this membership status, the Missouri state courts determined that the trustees had no authority to make such a change. The Missouri General Not-for-Profit Corporation Law gave the trustees power "to make and alter bylaws not inconsistent with its articles of incorporation or with the laws of this state" (Mo. Rev. Stat. sec. 355.090). The institution's original articles of agreement and its subsequent articles of acceptance each referred to the admission of new members to the corporation. On the basis of these two references, the courts concluded that the board's power to amend the bylaws was limited by the institution's articles of incorporation to matters that did not eliminate membership.

Stern v. *Lucy Webb Hayes National Training School for Deaconnesses and Missionaries,* 381 F. Supp. 1003 (D.D.C. 1974) (the "Sibley Hospital Case"), is the first reported opinion to comprehensively review the obligations of the trustees of private charitable corporations and to set out guidelines for trustee involvement in financial dealings. Although the case concerns a hospital, the court's analysis is clearly transferable to private educational institutions. The court's decision to analyze the trustees' standard of duty in terms of corporate law, rather than trust law, apparently reflects the evolving trend in the law.

The plaintiffs represented patients of Sibley Hospital, a nonprofit charitable corporation in the District of Columbia and the principal concern of the Lucy Webb Hayes National Training School. Nine members of the hospital's board of trustees were among the named defendants. The plaintiffs charged that the defendant trustees had "conspired to enrich themselves and certain financial institutions with which they were affiliated [and which were also named as defendants] by favoring those institutions in financial dealings with the hospital, and that they breached their fiduciary duties of care and loyalty in the management of Sibley's funds." The court examined evidence of the relationships between the defendant trustees and the defendant institutions. Although most of the hospital's funds were deposited in the defendant institutions, the funds were controlled and managed almost exclusively from the early 1950s until 1972 by a deceased trustee, without the active involvement of any of the defendant trustees.

The court concluded that the plaintiffs had not established a conspiracy but had established serious breaches of duty by the trustees. According to the court, the trustees owed a duty to the institution comparable to that owed by the directors of a business corporation:

1. Mismanagement

Both trustees and corporate directors are liable for losses occasioned by their negligent mismanagement of investments. However, the degree of care required appears to differ in many jurisdictions. A trustee is uniformly held to a high standard of care and will be held liable for simple negligence, while a director must often have committed ''gross negligence'' or otherwise be guilty of more than mere mistakes of judgment.

This distinction may amount to little more than a recognition of the fact that corporate directors have many areas of responsibility, while the traditional trustee is often charged only with the management of the trust funds and can therefore be expected to devote more time and expertise to that task. Since the board members of most large charitable corporations fall within the corporate rather than the trust model, being charged with the operation of ongoing businesses, it has been said that they should only be held to the less stringent corporate standard of care. More specifically, directors of charitable corporations are required to exercise ordinary and reasonable care in the performance of their duties, exhibiting honesty and good faith.

2. Nonmanagement

Plaintiffs allege that the individual defendants failed to supervise the management of hospital investments or even to attend meetings of the committees charged with such supervision. Trustees are particularly vulnerable to such a charge, because they not only have an affirmative duty to ''maximize the trust income by prudent investment,'' but they may not delegate that duty, even to a committee of their fellow trustees. A corporate director, on the other hand, may delegate his investment responsibility to fellow directors, corporate officers, or even outsiders, but he must continue to exercise general supervision over the activities of his delegates. Once again, the rule for charitable corporations is closer to the traditional corporate rule: directors should at least be permitted to delegate investment decisions to a committee of board members, so long as all directors assume the responsibility for supervising such committees by periodically scrutinizing their work.

Total abdication of the supervisory role, however, is improper even under traditional corporate principles. A director who fails to acquire the information necessary to supervise investment policy or consistently fails even to attend the meetings at which such policies are considered has violated his fiduciary duty to the corporation. . . .

3. Self-Dealing

Under District of Columbia law, neither trustees nor corporate directors are absolutely barred from placing funds under their control into a bank having an interlocking directorship with their own institution. In both cases, however, such transactions will be subjected to the closest scrutiny to determine whether or not the duty of loyalty has been violated. A deliberate conspiracy among trustees or board members to enrich the interlocking bank at the expense of the trust or corporation would, for example, constitute such a breach and render the conspirators liable for any losses. In the absence of clear evidence of wrongdoing, however, the courts appear to have used different standards to determine whether or not relief is appropriate, depending again on the legal relationship involved. Trustees may be found guilty of a breach of trust even for mere negligence in the maintenance of accounts in banks with which they are associated, while corporate directors are generally only required to show "entire fairness" to the corporation and "full disclosure" of the potential conflict of interest to the board.

Most courts apply the less stringent corporate rule to charitable corporations in this area as well [381 F. Supp. at 1013–15 (footnotes omitted)].

On the basis of these principles, the court created explicit guidelines for the future conduct of trustees in financial matters:

The court holds that a director or so-called trustee of a charitable hospital organized under the Non-Profit Corporation Act of the District of Columbia (D.C. Code sec. 29-1001 *et seq.*) is in default of his fiduciary duty to manage the fiscal and investment affairs of the hospital if it has been shown by a preponderance of the evidence that:

(1) While assigned to a particular committee of the board having general financial or investment responsibility under the bylaws of the corporation, he has failed to use due diligence in supervising the actions of those officers, employees, or outside experts to whom the responsibility for making day-to-day financial or investment decisions has been delegated; or

(2) he knowingly permitted the hospital to enter into a business transaction with himself or with any corporation, partnership, or association in which he then had a substantial interest or held a position as trustee, director, general manager, or principal officer without having previously informed the persons charged with approving that transaction of his interest or position and of any significant reasons, unknown to or not fully appreciated by such persons, why the transaction might not be in the best interests of the hospital; or

(3) except as required by the preceding paragraph, he actively participated in or voted in favor of a decision by the board or any committee or subcommittee thereof to transact business with himself or with any corporation, partnership, or association in which he then had a substantial interest or held a position as trustee, director, general manager, or principal officer; or

(4) he otherwise failed to perform his duties honestly, in good faith, and with a reasonable amount of diligence and care [381 F. Supp. at 1015].

In re Antioch University, 418 A.2d 105 (D.C. App. 1980), illustrates the delineation of authority between the board of trustees and the institution's constituent units. The case arose as a dispute between the university, located in Ohio, and a law school that it operated in Washington, D.C. The dispute concerned the extent to which the law school could operate autonomously from the university. According to the court:

Because of asserted university financial problems, the law school authorities fear that its existence as an accredited institution is threatened if funds paid by its students and grants for education and clinic programs are not administered by the law school officers. The university urges that its accountability as a trustee of all university funds and its ability to administer such funds for the welfare of the entire institution will be severely impaired unless its proper officers have full and unilateral control over all funds coming into the university. This dispute mushroomed into a claim by the . . . co-deans of the law school that the university had contractually relinquished its control over the fiscal and administrative affairs of the law school and that the university was in breach of its fiduciary duties to the students of the law school and clients of its clinic. The university counters that the co-deans of the law school breached their fiduciary obligations to the university by refusing to follow its direction in the handling of the funds [418 A.2d at 106].

The law school officials sought a preliminary injunction that would enable the law school to administer its funds independently. When the trial court denied this relief, the officials appealed. The appellate court considered the officials' contract claim in the context of the law governing private boards of trustees:

[The law school officials] argue that "commitments," which are asserted to be actual contractual agreements between the university and the law school, provide for an independent administration of the law school. They argue that a resolution passed by the board of trustees of Antioch University on December 5 and 6, 1975, established the basis for this conclusion. This resolution reaffirmed the board of trustees' commitment to a law school "built around a teaching law firm" and established an "*interim governing structure* pending a determination by the board of trustees of *ultimate governance* relationship between the school of law and the college" [emphasis added by court]. The resolution goes on to name a board of governors of the law school and to delineate its authority. The resolution specifies those matters over which the board of trustees of the university specifically reserves authority unto itself. And finally, the resolution "expressly charges the law school board of governors to develop recommendations respecting the *ultimate structure* of relationship between the law school and the college" [emphasis added by court]. . . .

Upon the basis of this record, we conclude that the trial court was amply justified in impliedly rejecting appellants' contractual argument based upon this resolution. The university is a not-for-profit corporation organized under the law of the state of Ohio. The university, [like] any corporation, is governed by the statutes of the state of its incorporation, its articles of incorporation, and its bylaws. The law school "is not organized as a corporation or other judicial entity." Concededly, it "was established pursuant to a resolution of the board of trustees of Antioch College (the predecessor in name to Antioch University) dated December 3 and 4, 1971." Resolutions adopted by the university in accordance with its articles of incorporation and bylaws effectuate the will of the corporation (see generally

Brown v. *National Loan & Investment Co.,* 139 S.W.2d 364 (Tex. Civ. App. 1940)). However, the plain meaning of this resolution bespeaks a delegation of power for the establishment of an "interim governing structure" of the law school as it relates to the university. It cannot be concluded that such a delegation deprived the board of trustees of the power given to them in Article III of the university's Articles of Incorporation, to wit: "All of the rights and powers of the corporation and the entire control and management of its college, property, and affairs shall be vested in and exercised by a board of trustees composed of twenty-five (25) persons." In fact, a contract conveying such plenary power vested by corporation charter in the trustees would be void [418 A.2d at 111–12].

In thus affirming the denial of preliminary relief, the court determined that the board of trustees had acted in accordance with its fiduciary obligations under Ohio law and its charter and bylaws.[1] The court further cautioned that, had the board granted to the law school the administrative power it sought, the board's action would have been void. This conclusion is supported by the university's charter, which apparently precludes the trustees from delegating their management powers. It may also find support in the legal principle, recognized in varying degrees by the corporation laws of the states, that excessive delegation of management powers by a corporate board violates state law even if not precluded by the charter.

With a little muscle, a framework for analyzing the power relationship between private universities and their constituent units can be squeezed from the opinion in *In re Antioch University*. First, the university is the legal entity that derives power from the state; the constituent unit usually has no separate corporate status and thus derives its authority exclusively from the university. Second, the extent to which the board of trustees may delegate authority to a constituent unit is determined initially by the relevant provisions of the corporate charter; the trustees may delegate management powers only to the extent, and in the manner, authorized by the charter. Third, charter provisions, in turn, may authorize delegation of management powers only to the extent, and in the manner, that the state's corporation statutes and case law permit; charter provisions that conflict with state law on excessive delegation are invalid. Fourth, the extent to which the university has actually delegated authority to a constituent unit is determined by construing the trustees' resolutions, the university's bylaws, and other official acts of the university. Any claimed authority that is not found in these sources, construed consistently with the charter and state law, does not exist.

2.2.2. Other officers and administrators. The authority of the highest-ranking officers and administrators of postsecondary institutions may occasionally be set out in statutes or state board regulations (for public institutions) or in corporate charters (for private institutions). But more often even the highest-ranking officers and employees, and almost always the lower-ranking ones, derive their authority

---

[1]A later case between the same parties, *Cahn* v. *Antioch University,* 482 A.2d 120 (D.C. Ct. App. 1984), dealt with the law school officials' fiduciary obligations to the university. See also *In re Antioch University,* 482 A.2d 133 (D.C. Ct. App. 1984), which rejected the law school officials' request that the university pay their attorney's fees for the litigation.

not directly from statute, state board regulation, or charter but rather from subdelegation by the institution's board of trustees. The lower the administrator in the administrative hierarchy, the greater the likelihood of subsubdelegation—that is, subdelegation
of authority from the board of trustees to an officer or administrator, who in turn
subdelegates part of this authority to some other administrator or employee.

   Silverman v. *University of Colorado,* 555 P.2d 1155 (Colo. 1976), illustrates the
subdelegation of authority. A terminated assistant professor claimed that her termination constituted a breach of contract. In December 1972 the associate dean of
the professor's school wrote the professor that she would be reappointed for 1973–74
if certain federal funding was renewed and if the professor's peers recommended
reappointment. The professor claimed that, although both conditions were fulfilled,
the school did not renew her contract, thus violating the terms of the December
1972 letter. The trial court held for the university, reasoning that the associate dean's
letter could not create a contract because, by statute, only the board of regents had
authority to appoint faculty members. The intermediate appellate court reversed,
reasoning that the associate dean could have created a contract because he could
have been acting under authority subdelegated to him by the board. The Supreme
Court of Colorado then reversed the intermediate court and reinstated the trial court's
decision, holding that hiring authority is not delegable unless "expressly authorized
by the legislature."

   In *People* v. *Ware,* 368 N.Y.S.2d 797 (App. Div. 1975), however, an appellate
court upheld a delegation of power from a system-wide board of trustees to the
president of an individual institution and thence to campus police officers employed
by that institution. The trial court had dismissed a prosecution against an illegal
trespasser at the State University of New York (SUNY) at Buffalo because the officer
making the arrest did not have authority to do so. According to this court, the New
York Education Law (sec. 355(2)(m)) designated the SUNY board of trustees to
appoint peace officers, whereas the arresting officer had been appointed by the president of the university. In reversing, the appellate court reasoned that the board
had authority under the Education Law to promulgate rules and regulations, and
the rules and regulations promulgated by the board provided for the delegation
of power to SUNY's executive and administrative officers. By resolution passed
under these rules and regulations, the board had authorized administrative officers
of each state institution to appoint peace officers for their campuses. Since the SUNY
president had properly appointed the arresting officer pursuant to this resolution,
the officer had authority to make the arrest.

   Even when an institutional officer or administrator acts beyond the scope
of his delegated power, so that the act is unauthorized, the board of trustees
may subsequently "ratify" the act if that act was within the scope of the board's
own authority. "Ratification" converts the initially unauthorized act into an
authorized act. In *Silverman* v. *University of Colorado* (above), for instance, the intermediate appellate court held that, even if the associate dean did not have authority
to reappoint the professor, the professor was entitled to prove that the offer of reappointment had been ratified by the board of regents (541 P.2d 93, 96 (1975)). Similarly, in *Tuskegee Institute* v. *May Refrigeration Co.,* 344 So. 2d 156 (Ala. 1977), two
employees of a special program operated by Tuskegee had ordered an air condi-
tioning unit from the May Company. May delivered and installed the unit but

was not paid the agreed-upon price. An intermediate appellate court reversed a damages award for May on the theory that the Tuskegee employers who ordered the unit had no authority to do so. The highest state court then reversed the intermediate court. It reasoned that, even though the employees had no actual or apparent authority, Tuskegee had kept and used the unit that the employees ordered and therefore could have ratified their unauthorized acts.

Even when an officer or administrator acts without authority and a higher officer or administrator or the board of trustees has not ratified the act, a court will occasionally estop the institution from denying the validity of the act. Under this doctrine of estoppel, courts may—in order to prevent injustice to persons who had justifiably relied on an unauthorized act—treat the unauthorized act as if it had been authorized. In the *Silverman* case, the plaintiff professor argued that various officials of the school had "advised her that her position was secure for the coming academic year" and that she had "reasonably relied on these representations to her detriment in that she did not seek other employment." The intermediate appellate court ruled that, if plaintiff's allegations regarding the assurances, the reasonableness of her reliance, and the detriment were true, then "the doctrine of estoppel may be invoked if necessary to prevent manifest injustice." The Colorado Supreme Court reversed, recognizing the estoppel doctrine but holding that the facts did not justify its application in this case. The court reasoned that, since the professor had received adequate notice of nonrenewal, there was no "manifest injustice" necessitating estoppel and that, since the *Faculty Handbook* clearly stated that the board of regents makes all faculty appointments, the professor's "reliance on statements made by university officials was misplaced."

Another illustration of estoppel is provided by *Blank* v. *Board of Higher Education of the City of New York,* 51 Misc. 2d 724, 273 N.Y.S.2d 796 (1966). The plaintiff student sought to compel the defendant board to award him a Bachelor of Arts degree. The question about the student's degree developed after he was advised that he could take advantage of a Professional Option Plan allowing him to complete a certain minimum amount of course work without attending any classes. This arrangement enabled him to begin law school in Syracuse before he had finished all his course work at Brooklyn College. The student had been advised by faculty members, the head of the department of psychology, and a member of the counseling and guidance staff, and the arrangement had been approved by the professors of the psychology courses involved, each of whom gave him the necessary assignments. At the time of his expected graduation, however, the student was denied his degree because he had not completed the courses "in attendance."

In defending its refusal to grant the degree, the college argued that only the dean of the faculty had the authority to determine a student's eligibility for the Professional Option Plan and that the dean had not exercised such authority regarding the plaintiff. The college further argued that the dean had devised regulations concerning the Professional Option Plan and that these regulations contained residence requirements which the student had not met. While the court did not dispute these facts, it emphasized, as a contrary consideration, that the plaintiff had "acted in obvious reliance upon the counsel and advice of members of the staff of the college administration to whom he was referred and who were authorized to give him such counsel and advice." Moreover:

"The authority of an agent is not only that conferred upon him by his commission, but also as to third persons that which he is held out as possessing. The principal is often bound by the act of his agent in excess or abuse of his authority, but this is only true between the principal and third persons who, believing and having a right to believe that the agent was acting within and not exceeding his authority, would sustain loss if the act was not considered that of the principal" (*Walsh* v. *Hartford Fire Insurance Co.*, 73 N.Y. 5, 10).

The dean of faculty may not escape the binding effect of the acts of his agents performed within the scope of their apparent authority, and the consequences that must equitably follow therefrom. Having given permission to take the subject courses in the manner prescribed, through his agents . . . , he cannot, in the circumstances, later assert that the courses should have been taken in another manner [273 N.Y.S.2d at 802–03].

Thus, "all of the elements of an estoppel exist" and the "doctrine should be invoked" against the college. The court ordered the college to award the plaintiff the A.B. degree.

2.2.3. Campus organizations. Authority in postsecondary institutions may be delegated not only to individual officers or administrators but also to various campus organizations which are accorded some role in governance. Common examples include academic senates, faculty assemblies, departmental faculties, and student or university judicial systems. (See Section 4.13.3 for a discussion of the last-named organization.)

Searle v. *Regents of the University of California*, 23 Cal. App. 2d 448, 100 Cal. Rptr. 194 (1972), is a leading case. By a standing order of the regents, the academic senate was given authority to "authorize and supervise all courses and curricula." Pursuant to this authority, the senate approved a course in which 50 percent of the lectures would be taught by a nonfaculty member (Eldridge Cleaver). Subsequent to the senate's approval of the course, the regents adopted two pertinent resolutions. One resolution provided that a person without an appropriate faculty appointment could not lecture more than once during a university quarter in a course offering university credit; the other provided that the course to be taught by Cleaver could not be offered for credit if it could not be restructured.

The course was taught as originally planned. When the regents resolved that the course not be given academic credit, sixteen students who took the course and six faculty members sued to compel the regents to grant the credit and to rescind its first two resolutions. The plaintiffs argued that the standing order granting the academic senate authority over courses and curricula deprived the regents of power to act. The court, however, found that the regents had specifically retained the power to appoint faculty members and concluded that the situation in this case involved an appointment to the faculty rather than just the supervisory power over courses provided by the standing order: "To designate a lecturer for a university course is to name the person to conduct the course, at least to the extent of the lectures to be given by him. When the designation is of one to conduct a full half of the course, it appears to be a matter of appointment to the faculty, which is clearly reserved to the regents." Moreover, the court indicated that the authority of the academic senate was subject to further diminishment by the regents:

In any event, the power granted to the senate is neither exclusive nor irrevocable. The bylaws specifically provide that neither they nor the standing orders "shall be construed, operate as, or have the effect of an abridgment or limitation of any rights, powers, or privileges of the regents." This limitation not only is authorized but seems required by the overriding constitutional mandate which vests the regents with "full powers of organization and government" of the university, and grants to them as a corporation "all the powers necessary or convenient for the effective administration of its trust" (Cal. Const. Art. IX, sec. 9). To accept appellants' argument would be to hold that a delegation of authority, even though specifically limited, amounts to a surrender of authority [100 Cal. Rptr. at 195–96].

The court therefore determined that the regents, and not the senate, had authority over the structuring of the course in question.

Another case illustrating delegation of authority to a campus organization—this time a student rather than a faculty group—is *Student Association of the University of Wisconsin-Milwaukee* v. *Baum,* 74 Wis. 2d 283, 246 N.W.2d 622 (1976). The Wisconsin legislature had passed a statute which accorded specific organizational and governance rights to students in the University of Wisconsin system:

The students of each institution or campus subject to the responsibilities and powers of the board [of regents], the president, the chancellor, and the faculty shall be active participants in the immediate governance of and policy development for such institutions. As such, students shall have primary responsibility for the formulation and review of policies concerning student life, services, and interests. Students, in consultation with the chancellor and subject to the final confirmation of the board, shall have the responsibility for the disposition of those student fees which constitute substantial support for campus student activities. The students of each institution or campus shall have the right to organize themselves in a manner they determine and to select their representatives to participate in institutional governance [Wis. Stat. sec. 36.09(5)].

The chancellor of the Milwaukee campus asserted that, despite the statute's passage, he retained the right to make student appointments to the Physical Environment Committee and the Segregated Fee Advisory Committee. The Student Association, the campus-wide student government, argued that the chancellor no longer had this authority because the statute had delegated it to the association. Applying traditional techniques of statutory interpretation, the court agreed with the students. Concerning the student appointments to the Physical Environment Committee, the court held:

When sec. 36.09(5), Stats., became effective in July 1974, the chancellor lost his authority to make these appointments. The statute gave this authority to the students as of that time. It is well settled that if a rule or directive of an administrative body or officer is in conflict with a newly enacted statute, the statute must take precedence. The students had the right to select their representatives on the Physical Environment Committee [246 N.W.2d at 626].

Using a similar analysis, the court reached the same result with respect to the Segregated Fee Advisory Committee.

Sec. 2.3. Institutional Liability for Acts of Trustees, Administrators, and Other Agents

  2.3.1. Institutional tort liability. A tort is broadly defined as a civil wrong, other than a breach of contract, for which the courts will allow a damage remedy. While any act fitting this definition may be considered a tort, there are certain classic torts for which the essential elements of the plaintiff's prima facie case and the defendant's acceptable defenses are already established. The two classic torts that most frequently arise in the setting of postsecondary education are negligence[2] and defamation, both of which are discussed later in this section. Various techniques are available to postsecondary institutions for managing the risks of tort liability, as discussed in Section 2.5.

  A postsecondary institution is not subject to liability for every tortious act of its trustees, administrators, or other agents. But the institution will generally be liable, lacking immunity or some other recognized defense, for tortious acts committed within the scope of the actor's employment or otherwise authorized by the institution or subject to its control. In the *Lumbard* case discussed in Section 2.3.1.1, for instance, the institution was liable for the acts of its janitors committed in the course of their building maintenance duties. And in *Butler* v. *Louisiana State Board of Education,* 331 So. 2d 192 (La. 1976), after finding that a professor had been negligent in allowing a biology experiment to be conducted without appropriate safeguards, the court asserted that the professor's "negligence must be attributed to the defendant university and to the state board of education."

  In some circumstances a postsecondary institution may also be liable for the acts of its student organizations. In *Wallace* v. *Weiss,* 372 N.Y.S.2d 416 (Sup. Ct. 1975), a libel action based on material printed in a student publication, the University of Rochester moved for judgment in its favor on the ground that it was not responsible for the acts of a student organization. The court denied the motion because "the question of the university's responsibility should not be determined until all the facts are presented at the trial." According to this court:

> [A university] may be in a position to take precautions against the publication of libelous matter in its student publications. . . .
>   The university, by furnishing and providing to the organization

---

  [2]The relevant cases and authorities are collected in an extensive series of annotations on the tort liability of elementary/secondary schools and postsecondary institutions in particular circumstances: 34 A.L.R.3d 1166 (1970) (accidents due to condition of buildings or equipment); 34 A.L.R.3d 1210 (1970) (accidents associated with the transportation of students); 35 A.L.R.3d 725 (1970) (accidents occurring during school athletic events); 35 A.L.R.3d 758 (1970) (accidents associated with chemistry experiments, shopwork, and manual or vocational training); 35 A.L.R.3d 975 (1970) (accidents due to condition of buildings, equipment, or outside premises); 36 A.L.R.3d 330 (1970) (injuries caused by acts of fellow students); 36 A.L.R.3d 361 (1970) (accidents occurring in physical education classes); 37 A.L.R.3d 712 (1971) (accidents occurring during use of premises and equipment for other than school purposes); 37 A.L.R.3d 738 (1971) (injuries due to condition of grounds, walks, and playgrounds); 38 A.L.R.3d 830 (1971) (injuries resulting from lack or insufficiency of supervision); 38 A.L.R.3d 908 (1971) (negligence of, or lack of supervision by, teachers and other employees or agents). All annotations are supplemented periodically with recent cases.

money, space, and in lending its name, may well be responsible for the acts of the organization at least insofar as the university has the power to exercise control. By assisting the organization in its activities, it cannot avoid responsibility by refusing to exercise control or by delegating that control to another student organization [372 N.Y.S.2d at 422].

A 1981 New York State Court of Claims case, *Mazart* v. *State,* 441 N.Y.S.2d 600 (Ct. Cl. 1981) (this volume, Section 4.9.4), contains a valuable analysis of an institution's liability for the tortious acts of its student organizations. The case concerned a libelous letter to the editor, published by the student newspaper at SUNY-Binghamton. The court's opinion addresses the liability theories proposed in *Wallace* v. *Weiss.* The court notes two possible theories for holding postsecondary institutions liable: (1) that the student organization was acting as an agent of the institution, and the institution, as principal, is vicariously liable for its agents' torts (the *respondeat superior* doctrine); and (2) that the institution had a legal duty to supervise the student organization, even if it was not acting as the institution's agent, because the institution supported or provided the environment for the organization's operation. In a lengthy analysis, the court refused to apply either theory against the institution, holding that (1) the institution did not exercise sufficient control over the newspaper to establish an agency relationship; and (2) given the relative maturity of college students and the rudimentary need and generally understood procedure for verifying information, the institution had no legal duty to supervise the newspaper's editorial process.

Public institutions can sometimes escape tort liability by asserting sovereign or governmental immunity. The availability of this defense varies greatly from state to state. While the sovereign immunity doctrine was generally recognized in early American common law, the doctrine has been abrogated or modified in many states by judicial decisions, state legislation, or a combination of the two.[3] In *Brown* v. *Wichita State University,* 217 Kan. 279, 540 P.2d 66 (1975), vacated in part, 219 Kan. 2, 547 P.2d 1015 (1976), the university faced both tort and contract claims for damages arising from the crash of an airplane carrying the university's football team. In Kansas, the university's home state, the common law doctrine of immunity had been partly abrogated by judicial decision in 1969, the court holding that the state and its agencies could be liable for negligence in the conduct of "proprietary" (as opposed to "governmental") activities. But in 1970 the Kansas legislature had passed a statute reinstituting the immunity abrogated by the court. The university in *Brown* relied on this statute to assert immunity to the tort claim. The court, after reconsidering the issue, vacated its prior judgment to the contrary and rejected plaintiffs' arguments that the statute was unconstitutional, thus allowing the university's immunity defense.

Although private institutions can make no claim to sovereign immunity, nonprofit schools may sometimes be able to assert a limited "charitable" immunity

---

[3]The cases and authorities are collected in Annot., "Modern Status of Doctrine of Sovereign Immunity as Applied to Public Schools and Institutions of Higher Learning," 33 A.L.R.3d 703 (1970 and periodic supp.).

defense to certain tort actions.[4] The availability of this defense also varies considerably from state to state. Overall, the charitable immunity defense appears to be more limited and less recognized than sovereign immunity. In a leading precedent, *President and Directors of Georgetown College* v. *Hughes,* 130 F.2d 810 (D.C. Cir. 1942), the court struck a common note by heavily criticizing charitable immunity and refusing to apply it to a tort suit brought by a special nurse injured on the premises of the college's hospital.

2.3.1.1. Negligence. When the postsecondary institution is not immune from negligence suits under either sovereign or charitable immunity, liability depends, first, on whether the institution's actions fit the legal definition of the tort with which it is charged; and, second, on whether the institution's actions are covered by one of the recognized defenses that protect against liability for the tort with which it is charged. For the tort of negligence, the legal definition will be met if the institution owed a duty to the injured party but failed to exercise due care to avoid the injury. In *Lumbard* v. *Fireman's Fund Insurance Company,* 302 So. 2d 394 (Ct. App. La. 1974), the duty was found to depend on the plaintiff's status while on the institution's property. The plaintiff was a student going to a class held on the second floor of a Southern University building. When the student reached the second floor, she noticed that it was slippery but continued to walk the fifteen feet to her classroom. The student slipped and fell, injuring her back. The slipperiness was caused by an excess amount of oil which janitors had placed on the floors. In holding the university liable, the court determined that the plaintiff was an "invitee" on the university's property, as opposed to a trespasser, and applied the general tort law principle "that the owner of property owes to invitees . . . the duty of exercising reasonable care to keep the premises in a safe condition, or of warning invitees of hidden or concealed perils of which he knows or should have known in the exercise of reasonable care."

Once a legal duty is found to exist, the next question is what standard of care the defendant will be held to under the circumstances. This issue was considered in *Mortiboys* v. *St. Michael's College,* 478 F.2d 196 (2d Cir. 1973). A student sued the institution for injuries sustained while he was skating on an outdoor ice rink maintained by the college for student pleasure skating. The student had fallen when his skate hit a one-inch-high lump of ice. The court refused to hold the college liable and articulated the standard of care owed by the college as "reasonable care under all the circumstances." For the college to be held liable, the dangerous condition would either have to be "known . . . or [to] have existed for such a time that it was [the college's] duty to know it." The court concluded that it was "a matter of speculation what caused the lump to be formed and whether it had been there for any substantial length of time." Expensive maintenance equipment, which would be used for indoor intercollegiate hockey rinks, "cannot reasonably be required of a college providing an outdoor rink for the kind of use contemplated and to which this rink was actually being put at the time of the accident."

[4]The cases and authorities are collected in Annot., "Immunity of Private Schools and Institutions of Higher Learning from Liability in Tort," 38 A.L.R.3d 480 (1971 and periodic supp.), and Annot., "Tort Immunity of Nongovernmental Charities—Modern Status," 25 A.L.R.4th 517 (1983 and periodic supp.).

Before the postsecondary institution will be found negligent, the plaintiff must be able to prove that the institution's breach of duty was the proximate cause of the injury. In *Mintz* v. *State,* 362 N.Y.S.2d 619 (App. Div. 1975), the State University at New Paltz was found not liable for the deaths of two students who drowned on a canoe trip sponsored by an outing club. The court held that "it was the terrible, severe, and unforeseen weather conditions on the lake, and not any negligence on the part of the university, which were the proximate cause of the deaths herein."

Even when the plaintiff establishes all the elements for a prima facie case of negligence, the postsecondary institution may avoid liability by asserting and proving the defense of "contributory negligence" by the plaintiff or of the "assumption of the risk" of injury by the plaintiff.

While failing to find the plaintiff contributorily negligent, the court in the *Lumbard* case, discussed earlier in this section, acknowledged the acceptability of such a defense: "The invitee in a slip and fall case is under a duty to see dangers which are obvious and can be detected and avoided by the degree of care exercised by a reasonably prudent person"; under the facts presented, however, "it was not unreasonable for plaintiff to traverse the slippery floor [for only a few feet] after she discovered its slippery condition."

Liability will not be imposed where the plaintiff is found to have assumed the risk of the injury that occurred. This "assumption of risk" doctrine was applied in *Rubtchinsky* v. *State University of New York at Albany,* 260 N.Y.S.2d 256 (Ct. Cl. 1965), where a student was injured in a pushball game between freshmen and sophomores conducted by the student association as part of an orientation program. The court found that the student voluntarily assumed the risks of the game, since the student, who was offered various orientation activities, chose to play pushball.

Contemporary problems concerning the consumption of alcohol by college students provide a particularly useful illustration of negligence law's operation on campus. For postsecondary administrators, student drinking is an issue growing in importance. Recent surveys suggest that drinkers comprise at least 75 percent of the total student population (see Z. Ingalls, "Higher Education's Drinking Problem," *Chronicle of Higher Education,* July 21, 1982, p. 1, col. 2). Vandalism of campus property is one consequence of alcohol-related student activity. Of more serious concern, however, are the injuries and deaths that result from accidents caused by student drinking, and the potential tort liability of postsecondary institutions for such occurrences.

Two cases from Pennsylvania and California consider the responsibility of postsecondary institutions to control drinking of alcoholic beverages by students on campus and at college-sponsored activities off campus. The cases also add generally to an understanding of negligence liability by analyzing the relationship between the institution and its students, and the ensuing legal duty of care arising from this relationship.

In *Bradshaw* v. *Rawlings,* 612 F.2d 135 (3d Cir. 1979), a sophomore at Delaware Valley College in Doylestown, Pennsylvania, was seriously injured in an automobile accident following the annual sophomore class picnic, which had been held off campus. The injured student was a passenger in a car driven by another student, who had become intoxicated at the picnic. Flyers announcing the picnic were mimeographed by the college duplicating facility. They featured drawings of beer mugs and were prominently displayed across the campus. The sophomore class faculty adviser, who did not attend the picnic, cosigned the check that was used to purchase beer. The injured student brought his action against the college as well as the beer distributor and the municipality, alleging that the former owed him a duty of care to protect him from harm resulting from the beer drinking at the picnic. The jury in the trial court awarded the student, who was rendered quadriplegic, damages in the amount of $1,108,067 against all defendants, and each appealed on separate grounds.

The college argued on appeal that the plaintiff had failed to establish that the college owed him a legal duty of care. The appellate court agreed with this argument. Its opinion began with a discussion of the custodial character of postsecondary institutions. Changes that have taken place on college campuses in recent decades lessen the duty of protection that institutions once owed to their students:

> There was a time when college administrators and faculties assumed a role *in loco parentis*. . . . A special relationship was created between college and student that imposed a duty on the college to exercise control over students' conduct and, reciprocally, gave the students certain rights of protection by the college. . . . A dramatic reapportionment of responsibilities and social interests [has taken] place. . . . College administrators no longer control the broad arena of general morals. At one time exercising their rights and duties *in loco parentis,* colleges were able to impose strict regulations. But today students vigorously claim the right to define and regulate their own lives [612 F.2d at 139].

The concept of legal duty is neither rigid nor static. A court can create a new duty if, after evaluating the interests of the parties, it decides that a plaintiff should be entitled to legal protection against a defendant's conduct. According to the *Bradshaw* court, "The plaintiff in this case possessed an important interest in remaining free from bodily injury, and thus the law protects his right to recover compensation from those who negligently cause his injury. The college, on the other hand, has an interest in the nature of its relationship with its adult students, as well as an interest in avoiding responsibilities that it is incapable of performing."

The student had the burden of proving the existence of a legal duty by identifying specific interests that arose from his relationship with the college. Concentrating on the college's regulation prohibiting the possession or consumption of alcoholic beverages on campus or at off-campus college-sponsored functions, he argued that this regulation created a custodial relationship between the college and its students. A basic principle of law holds that one who voluntarily takes custody of another is under a duty to protect that person. The plaintiff reasoned that he was entitled to the protection voluntarily assumed by the college when it promulgated the regulation. The court dismissed this argument on the ground that the college regulation merely tracks state law, which prohibits persons under the age of twenty-one from drinking intoxicants.[5] By promulgating the regulation, then, the college

[5]In actuality the regulation went beyond the statute because it applied to every student regardless of age—a point that could have favored the plaintiff had the court been sensitive to it. Lawyers will thus want to exercise caution in relying on the court's analysis of this particular issue.

did not voluntarily assume a custodial relationship but only reaffirmed the necessity of student compliance with Pennsylvania law.

Besides creating new legal duties, courts may rely on existing case or statutory law that recognizes a legal duty arising from the particular relationship at issue. Some states impose a legal duty on a provider of intoxicants to an intoxicated person, making the provider responsible to third parties for the negligent acts of the intoxicated person. The plaintiff argued that this duty, already existing in some states, also existed in Pennsylvania. By analogy, the college would then have a duty to protect third persons from the negligent acts of intoxicated student drivers because it had furnished, or condoned the furnishing of, the alcoholic beverages. Pennsylvania does establish by statute a duty of care to third persons if the provider has a liquor license, but the Pennsylvania Supreme Court has held that a private host who supplies intoxicants to a visibly intoxicated guest may not be held civilly liable for injuries to third persons caused by the intoxicated guest's negligence. The *Bradshaw* court predicted that, since the Pennsylvania courts had refused to impose a legal duty on the private host, "it would be even less willing to find a relationship between a college and its student under the circumstances of this case."

Consequently, unable to find a legal duty based on a special relationship existing as a matter of law, and unwilling to obligate the college by creating a new duty, the appellate court reversed the trial court's judgment of liability.

The *Bradshaw* case was quoted with approval in a California case, *Baldwin* v. *Zoradi,* 123 Cal. App. 3d 275, 176 Cal. Rptr. 809 (1981). In *Baldwin* the drinking occurred on campus in a dormitory room, and the plaintiff student was injured by an intoxicated student driver involved in a drag-racing contest. The plaintiff alleged that her dormitory room agreement, which prohibited alcoholic beverages in the residence halls, created a special relationship between her and the dormitory advisers and that the advisers therefore owed her a duty to enforce the provisions of the agreement. Although California courts are particularly willing to find a duty of protection where the defendant stands in a special relationship to both the victim and the person causing the harm, as was argued here, the *Baldwin* court determined that practicality prevented the imposition of a legal duty on the college to control student drinking. The prevalence of alcohol consumption on the modern college campus would make compliance with such a duty almost impossible, and the use of alcohol by college students is not so harshly judged by contemporary standards as to require special efforts to eradicate it.

College administrators, in all probability, may safely rely on *Bradshaw* and *Baldwin* insofar as they reject the notion of a general custodial relationship between the postsecondary institution and its students. Colleges with drinking regulations that do not merely track state law, however, could still be held liable, despite *Bradshaw,* if the regulations can be interpreted as a voluntary assumption of a specific custodial duty regarding alcoholic beverages. Although many college communities are responding to alcohol abuse by establishing task forces for responsible student drinking and by operating alcohol education clinics, there is also a trend toward initiating or strengthening institutional regulations on alcohol use (see "Higher Education's Drinking Problem," above). Since courts could construe such regulations to constitute voluntary assumption of custodial duty, institutions should have counsel review all drinking regulations.

Moreover, student alcohol abuse is increasingly recognized as a serious campus problem, and special efforts are being made to eradicate it (see "Higher Education's Drinking Problem," above). These developments may undermine the reasoning of *Baldwin* and increase the likelihood that other courts, unlike the *Baldwin* court, will impose a new legal duty on institutions to protect students and others from injuries resulting from student alcohol abuse on campus or at college-sponsored activities off campus.

Some states other than Pennsylvania (the state involved in *Bradshaw*) may also have case or statute law that establishes civil liability for private hosts who furnish intoxicating beverages (see *Kelly* v. *Gwinnell*, 96 N.J. 538, 476 A.2d 1219 (1984)). A court in such a jurisdiction could rely on this law to impose a legal duty on the institution when alcohol is served at college-sponsored activities. Many states also have Dram Shop Acts, which strictly regulate licensed establishments engaged in the sale of intoxicants and impose civil liability for dispensing intoxicants to an intoxicated patron. A college or university that holds a liquor license, or contracts with a concessionaire who holds one, may wish to enlist the aid of legal counsel to assess its legal obligations as a license holder.

2.3.1.2. Defamation. The second typical tort asserted against a postsecondary institution, defamation, is committed by the oral or written publication of matter that tends to injure a person's reputation. The matter must have been published to some third person and must have been capable of defamatory meaning and understood as referring to the plaintiff in a defamatory sense. (See Sections 4.9.4 and 4.9.5 for a further discussion of defamation.)

One of the most important defenses against a defamation action is the conditional privilege of fair comment and criticism. An application of this privilege occurred in *Greenya* v. *George Washington University*, 512 F.2d 556 (D.C. Cir. 1975). A part-time off-campus instructor with George Washington University brought suit against the university, alleging a common law claim of defamation. The alleged defamatory statement was the comment "Do not staff" written on an index card in the office of academic staffing. The plaintiff claimed that "the phrase carries an innuendo of either incompetence or dishonesty." The court applied general tort law and found the following:

> It is well accepted that officers and faculty members of educational organizations enjoy a qualified privilege to discuss the qualifications and character of fellow officers and faculty members if the matter communicated is pertinent to the functioning of the educational institution. . . . Concomitantly we believe the privilege extends to internal records in which such matters are discussed or recorded. For a plaintiff to overcome the privilege, he must prove [that] the publication occurred outside normal channels or that the normal manner of handling such information resulted in an unreasonable degree of publication in light of the purposes of the privilege or that publication was made with malicious intent [512 F.2d at 563].

Another conditional privilege that is important for administrators in state institutions is the privilege afforded to executive and administrative officers of government. In *Shearer* v. *Lambert*, 547 P.2d 98 (Or. 1976), an assistant professor at Oregon State University brought a libel action against the head of her department. While admitting that the statement was defamatory, the defendant argued that the privilege of government officers should be extended to lesser executive or administrative officers, such as the head of a department. The court agreed, reasoning that, since "the privilege is designed to free public officials from intimidation in the discharge of their duties, we are unable to explain why this policy would not apply equally to inferior as well as to high-ranking officers." This qualified privilege is available, however, only where the defendant "publishes the defamatory matter in the performance of his official duties."

A constitutional privilege based on the First Amendment is also sometimes assertable as a defense in a defamation action. Under this privilege, certain defamations of "public figures" are considered to be protected speech under the First Amendment. To determine this privilege's impact on postsecondary education, it is necessary to ask whether and when an administrator, faculty member, or other member of the academic community may be considered a "public figure." In *Avins* v. *White*, 627 F.2d 637 (3d Cir. 1980) (discussed more fully in Section 8.2.4), for example, the question was whether the dean of the Delaware Law School was a public figure. After examining his role "as creator, chief architect, and the first dean" of the school, and his active involvement in the school's efforts to achieve accreditation, the court answered the question affirmatively.

If a person is a public figure, another person will not be held liable for defaming him unless that other person's comment "was made with knowledge of its falsity or in reckless disregard of whether it was false or true" (*Garrison* v. *Louisiana*, 379 U.S. 64, 74 (1964)). Thus, to the extent that members of the academic community are placeable in the public figure category, the institution's potential liability for defamation is reduced. Under factors such as those considered by the court in *Avins* v. *White*, however, it is unlikely on any given campus at any particular time that a substantial proportion of the community would be considered public figures.

    2.3.2. Institutional contract liability. The institution may be characterized as a "principal" and its trustees, administrators, and other employees as "agents" for purposes of discussing the potential liability of each on contracts transacted by an agent for, or on behalf of, the institution. The fact that an agent acts with the principal in mind does not necessarily excuse the agent from personal liability (see Section 2.4.2), nor does it automatically make the principal liable. The key to the institution's liability is authorization; that is, the institution may be held liable if it authorized the agent's action before it occurred or subsequently ratified it. However, even when an agent's acts were properly authorized, an institution may be able to escape liability by raising a legally recognized defense, such as sovereign immunity.

    Although the principles of agency law generally apply to both public and private institutions, for one purpose it is important to distinguish the two. A public institution may have more defenses against liability than a private institution in the same state. The primary example is the sovereign immunity defense. As with tort liability (see Section 2.3.1), the existence and scope of sovereign immunity from contract liability vary from state to state. In *Charles E. Brohawn & Bros., Inc.* v. *Board of Trustees of Chesapeake College*, 304 A.2d 819 (Md. 1973), the court recognized a very broad immunity defense. The plaintiffs had sued the board to compel them to pay the agreed-upon price for work and materials provided under the contract, including the construction of buildings for the college. In considering the college's defense, the court reasoned:

The doctrine of sovereign immunity exists under the common law of Maryland. By this doctrine, a litigant is precluded from asserting an otherwise meritorious cause of action against this sovereign state or one of its agencies which has inherited its sovereign attributes, unless [sovereign immunity has been] expressly waived by statute or by a necessary inference from such a legislative enactment. . . . The doctrine of sovereign immunity or, as it is often alternatively referred to, governmental immunity was before this court in *University of Maryland* v. *Maas,* 173 Md. 554, 197 A. 123 (1938), where our predecessors reversed a judgment recovered against the university for breach of contract in connection with the construction of a dormitory at College Park. That opinion, after extensively reviewing the prior decisions of this court, succinctly summed up [our predecessors'] holdings . . . : "So it is established that neither in contract nor tort can a suit be maintained against a governmental agency, first, where specific legislative authority has not been given, second, even though such authority is given, if there are no funds available for the satisfaction of the judgment, or no power reposed in the agency for the raising of funds necessary to satisfy a recovery against it" (173 Md. at 559, 197 A. at 125) [304 A.2d at 820 (notes and citations omitted)].

Finding that the cloak of the sovereign's immunity was inherited by the community college and had not been waived, the court rejected the plaintiff's contract claim.

Regarding contract liability, there is little distinction to be made among trustees, administrators, employees, and other agents of the institution. Whether the actor is a member of the board of trustees or its equivalent, the president, the athletic director, the dean of arts and sciences, or some other functionary, the critical question is whether his action was authorized by the institution.

The issue of authorization can become very complex. In *Brown* v. *Wichita State University,* 217 Kan. 279, 540 P.2d 66 (1975),[6] the court discussed the issue at length:

To determine whether the record establishes an agency by agreement, it must be examined to ascertain if the party sought to be charged as principal had delegated authority to the alleged agent by words which expressly authorize the agent to do the delegated act. If there is evidence of that character, the authority of the agent is express. If no express authorization is found, then the evidence must be considered to determine whether the alleged agent possesses implied powers. The test utilized by this court to determine if the alleged agent possesses implied powers is whether, from the facts and circumstances of the particular case, it appears there was an implied intention to create an agency, in which event the relation may be held to exist, notwithstanding either a denial by the alleged principal, or whether the parties understood it to be an agency.

[6]This decision reverses and remands a summary judgment in favor of the university by the trial court. In a second opinion in this case, 219 Kan. 2, 547 P.2d 1015 (1976), the court reaffirmed (without discussion) the portion of its first opinion dealing with authorization. The tort liability aspects of these two opinions are discussed in Section 2.3.1.

"On the question of implied agency, it is the manifestation of the alleged principal and agent as between themselves that is decisive, and not the appearance to a third party or what the third party should have known. An agency will not be inferred because a third person assumed that it existed, or because the alleged agent assumed to act as such, or because the conditions and circumstances were such as to make such an agency seem natural and probable and to the advantage of the supposed principal, or from facts which show that the alleged agent was a mere instrumentality" [quoting *Corpus Juris Secundum*, a leading legal encyclopedia]. . . .

The doctrine of apparent or ostensible authority is predicated upon the theory of estoppel. An ostensible or apparent agent is one whom the principal has intentionally or by want of ordinary care induced and permitted third persons to believe to be his agent even though no authority, either express or implied, has been conferred upon him.

Ratification is the adoption or confirmation by a principal of an act performed on his behalf by an agent, which act was performed without authority. The doctrine of ratification is based upon the assumption there has been no prior authority, and ratification by the principal of the agent's unauthorized act is equivalent to an original grant of authority. Upon acquiring knowledge of his agent's unauthorized act, the principal should promptly repudiate the act; otherwise it will be presumed he has ratified and affirmed the act [540 P.2d at 74–75].

As mentioned in Section 2.3.1, the *Brown* case arose after the crash of a plane carrying the Wichita State football team. The survivors and personal representatives of the deceased passengers sued Wichita State University (WSU) and the Physical Education Corporation (PEC) at the school for breaching their Aviation Service Agreement by failing to provide passenger liability insurance for the football team and other passengers. The plaintiffs claimed that they were third-party beneficiaries of the service agreement entered into by WSU, the PEC, and the aviation company. The service agreement was signed by the athletic director of WSU and by an agent of the aviation company. The university asserted that it did not have the authority to enter the agreement without the board of regents' approval, which it did not have; that it did not grant the athletic director the authority to enter the agreement on its behalf; that the athletic director only had authority to act as the agent of the PEC; that WSU could not ratify the agreement because it lacked authority to enter it initially; and that, as a state agency, it could not be estopped from denying the validity of the agreement.

The court held that the PEC was the agent of the university and that the athletic director, "as an officer of the corporate agent [PEC], had the implied power and authority to bind the principal—Wichita State University." The court further held that failure to obtain the board of regents' approval did not invalidate the contract:

The legislature has delegated to the board of regents the authority to control, operate, manage, and supervise the universities and colleges of this state. "For such control, operation, management, or supervision, the the board of regents may make contracts and adopt orders, policies, or rules and regulations and do or perform such other acts as are authorized by law or are appropriate for such purposes'' (K.S.A. 1974 Supp. 76-712). . . . However, no policy, rule, or regulation of the board of regents has been cited or furnished to this court regarding contract matters, and none can be found in the Kansas Administrative Regulations. . . . Absent any such rules or regulations, Wichita State cannot use the statute to deny the validity of the Aviation Service Agreement following execution and partial performance. Common honesty forbids repudiation now [540 P.2d at 76-77].[7]

The fact that the agreement had been partly performed was particularly persuasive to the court:

Today, the use of separate corporate entities in collegiate athletics appears to be common, perhaps widespread, but indeed shadowy as to involvement and responsibility. Whether such arrangements should continue is not a question for this court. But when the involvement is such as presented in the instant case, then it begs logic to hold [that] no agency relations exist and that the principles thereof do not apply. Performance under the contract had begun and payments [were] made; this constituted tacit, effective approval of the Aviation Agreement Contract [540 P.2d at 77].

Besides asserting that the purported agent lacked authority or that the institution lacked authority in its own right, an institution sued on a contract can raise defenses arising from the contract itself or from some circumstance unique to the institution. Defenses that arise from the contract include the other party's fraud, the other party's breach of the contract, and the absence of one of the requisite elements (offer, acceptance, consideration) in the formation of a contract (see J. Calamari and J. Perillo, *The Law of Contracts*, 2nd ed. (West, 1977)). Defenses unique to the institution may include a counterclaim against the other party, the other party's previous collection of damages from the agent, or, for public institutions, the sovereign immunity defense discussed earlier. Even if one of these defenses— for instance, that the agent or institution lacked authority or that a contract element was absent—is successfully asserted, a private institution may be held liable for any benefit it received as a result of the other party's performance. But public institutions may sometimes not even be required to pay for benefits received under such circumstances.

The variety of contract and agency law principles that may bear on contract liability makes the area a complex one, calling for frequent involvement of legal counsel. The postsecondary institution's main concern in managing liability should be the delineation of the contracting authority of each of its agents. By carefully defining such authority, and by repudiating any unauthorized contracts of which

[7]Not all courts will be so willing to find institutional authority in cases concerning public institutions. Other courts in other circumstances may assert that a person who deals with a public institution "does so at his peril," as in *First Equity Corp.* v. *Utah State University*, 544 P.2d 887 (Utah 1975), where the court upheld the university's refusal to pay for stocks ordered by one of its employees.

they become aware, postsecondary administrators can protect the institution from unwanted liability. While protection may also be found in other defenses to contract actions, such as sovereign immunity, advance planning of authority is the surest way to limit contract liability and the fairest to the parties with whom the institution's agents may deal.

   2.3.3. Institutional federal civil rights liability. The tort and contract liabilities of postsecondary institutions (discussed in Sections 2.3.1 and 2.3.2) are based in state law and, for the most part, are relatively well settled. The institution's potential civil rights liability, in contrast, is primarily a matter of federal law, which has undergone a complex evolutionary development.[8] The key statute, commonly known as "Section 1983," reads:

> Every person who, under color of any statute, ordinance, regulation, custom, or usage, of any state or territory or the District of Columbia, subjects, or causes to be subjected, any citizen of the United States or other person within the jurisdiction thereof to the deprivation of any rights, privileges, or immunities secured by the Constitution and laws, shall be liable to the party injured in an action at law, suit in equity, or other proper proceeding for redress [42 U.S.C. sec. 1983].

Section 1983's coverage is limited in two major ways. First, it imposes liability only for actions carried out "under color of" state law, custom, or usage. Under this language the statute applies only to actions attributable to the state in much the same way that, under the state action doctrine (see Section 1.4.2), the U.S. Constitution applies only to actions attributable to the state. While public institutions clearly meet this statutory test, private postsecondary institutions cannot be subjected to Section 1983 liability unless the action complained of was so connected with the state that it can be said to have been done under color of state law, custom, or usage.

   Second, Section 1983 imposes liability only on a "person"—a term not defined in the statute. Thus, Section 1983's application to postsecondary institutions also depends on whether the particular institution being sued is considered to be a person, as the courts construe that term. Although private institutions would usually meet this test because they are corporations, which are considered to be legal persons under state law, most private institutions would be excluded from Section 1983 anyway under the color-of-law test. Thus, the crucial coverage issue under Section 1983 is one that primarily concerns administrators of public institutions: whether a public postsecondary institution is a person for purposes of Section 1983 and thus subject to civil rights liability under that statute.

   A related issue, which also helps shape a public institution's liability under federal civil rights laws, is whether the institution is immune from suit in federal courts under Article III and the Eleventh Amendment of the U.S. Constitution.[9]

---

[8]Legal analyses of the various federal civil rights laws and extensive citations to important cases can be found in C. Antieau, *Federal Civil Rights Acts,* 2nd ed. (Lawyers' Cooperative, (1980 and periodic supp.)).

[9]The U.S. Supreme Court cases are collected in Annot., "Supreme Court's Construction of Eleventh Amendment Restricting Federal Judicial Power to Entertain Suits Against a State," 50 L. Ed. 2d 928 (1978 and periodic supp.).

If money damages is the remedy sought by the plaintiff, and the money to pay a judgment against the institution would come from the state treasury, the institution will be immune from federal court suit unless the state has expressly or implicitly consented to suit, thus waiving its immunity. (Compare *Soni* v. *Board of Trustees of University of Tennessee*, 513 F.2d 347 (6th Cir. 1975) (waiver) with *Martin* v. *University of Louisville*, 541 F.2d 1171 (6th Cir. 1976) (no waiver).) As discussed below, the U.S. Supreme Court has used Eleventh Amendment immunity law as a backdrop against which to fashion a definition of "person" under Section 1983.

In a series of cases beginning in 1978, the U.S. Supreme Court has dramatically expanded the potential liability of governmental entities under Section 1983. As a result of these cases, it is now clear that any political subdivision of a state may be sued under this statute; that such governmental defendants may not assert a qualified immunity from liability based on the reasonableness or good faith of their actions; that they may be liable not only for violations of an individual's federal civil rights but also for violations of other rights of individuals secured by federal law; and that they may not require claimants to resort to state administrative forums before seeking redress in court.

The first, and key, case in this series is the U.S. Supreme Court's decision in *Monell* v. *Department of Social Services of the City of New York*, 436 U.S. 658 (1978). Overruling prior precedents which had held the contrary, the Court decided that local government units, such as school boards and municipal corporations, are "persons" under Section 1983 and thus subject to liability for violating civil rights protected by that statute. Since the definition of "person" is central to Section 1983's applicability, the decision requires consideration of whether the Court's new definition is broad enough to encompass postsecondary institutions. The question is: Are all or some public postsecondary institutions sufficiently like local government units that they will be considered "persons" subject to Section 1983 liability?

The answer depends not only on a close analysis of *Monell* but also on an analysis of the particular institution's organization and structure under state law (see Section 6.2). Locally based institutions, such as community colleges established as an arm of a county or a community college district, are the most likely candidates for "person" status. At the other end of the spectrum, institutions established as state agencies under the direct control of the state are apparently the least likely candidates. This distinction between local agencies and state agencies is appropriate because the Eleventh Amendment immunizes states, but not local governments, from certain suits in federal courts. In *Monell* the Court limited its "person" definition "to local government units which are not considered part of the state for Eleventh Amendment purposes." And in a subsequent case, *Quern* v. *Jordan*, 440 U.S. 332 (1979), the Court emphasized this limitation in *Monell* and asserted that neither the language nor the history of Section 1983 evidences any congressional intention to abrogate the states' Eleventh Amendment immunity.

The clear implication, reading *Monell* and *Quern* together, is that local governments—such as school boards, cities, and counties—are persons suable under Section 1983 and are not immune from suit under the Eleventh Amendment, whereas state governments and state agencies controlled by the state are not persons under Section 1983 and are immune under the Eleventh Amendment. The issue in any particular case, then, as phrased by the Court in another case decided the same day as *Quern*, is whether the entity in question "is to be regarded as a political subdivision" of the state (not immune) or as "an arm of the state subject to its control" (immune) (*Lake Country Estates* v. *Tahoe Regional Planning Agency,* 440 U.S. 391, 401–02 (1979)).

This case law adds some clarity to what has been the confusing and uncertain status of postsecondary institutions under Section 1983 and the Eleventh Amendment. But many institutions may still have difficulty in determining which side of the liability line they fall on. A 1982 U.S. Court of Appeals case, *United Carolina Bank* v. *Board of Regents of Stephen F. Austin State University,* 665 F.2d 553 (5th Cir. 1982), provides an extended, instructive illustration of the analysis to be used in making this determination.

The plaintiff in *United Carolina Bank* was a professor who had been dismissed from his position. He brought a Section 1983 suit against the board of regents and president of the university and four university administrators, alleging violations of his First Amendment free speech and Fourteenth Amendment due process rights. When the professor died during the course of the action, the bank, as administrator of his estate, became the plaintiff. The threshold question was whether the Eleventh Amendment barred the federal court from taking jurisdiction over the Section 1983 claims against the university, as opposed to the claims against the four administrators sued in their individual capacities (see this volume, Section 2.4.3). To answer this question, the court had to "decide whether the board of regents of SFA is to be treated as an arm of the state, partaking of the state's Eleventh Amendment immunity, or is instead to be treated as a municipal corporation or other political subdivision, to which the Eleventh Amendment does not extend.

Overruling the district court, the appellate court characterized the university as an arm of the state and not subject to Section 1983 suits in federal courts:

> Our analysis will first examine the status of the board of regents of SFA under Texas law. In *Mt. Healthy* [*City School District Board of Education* v. *Doyle,* 429 U.S. 274, 97 S. Ct. 568 (1977)], the Supreme Court first considered the definitions provided under Ohio law for "state" and "political subdivision": "Under Ohio law the 'state' does not include 'political subdivision,' and 'political subdivisions' do include local school districts (429 U.S. at 280, 97 S. Ct. at 572). The district court omitted this particularly illuminating inquiry. Texas law provides: "'State agency' means a university system or an institution of higher education as defined in section 61.003 Texas Education Code, other than a public junior college" (Tex. Rev. Civ. Stat. Ann. art. 6252-9b(8)(B) (Vernon)). By contrast, Texas statutory definitions of "political subdivision" typically exclude universities in the category of SFA. For example, Tex. Rev. Civ. Stat. Ann. art. 8309h states: "Political subdivision means a county, home-rule city, a city, town, or village organized under the general laws of this state, a special district, a junior college district, or any other legally constituted political subdivision of the state."
>
> Tracking *Mt. Healthy,* 429 U.S. at 280, 97 S. Ct. at 572, we next examine the state's degree of control over SFA, and SFA's fiscal autonomy. SFA was created by the legislature in 1921, and in 1969 was placed under the control of its own board of regents. Texas' statutes authorizing the operation of SFA and providing for its governance are codified at Tex. Educ.

Code Ann. sec. 95.01 *et seq.* and sec. 101.01 *et seq.* These statutes provide that members of the board of regents are to be appointed by the governor with the advice and consent of the senate (Tex. Educ. Code Ann. sec. 101.11). Texas also subjects SFA to some control by the Coordinating Board, Texas College and University System, which exercises broad managerial powers over all of the public institutions of higher learning in Texas. This board consists of eighteen members appointed by the governor with the advice and consent of the senate (Tex. Educ. Code Ann. sec. 61.001 *et seq.*).

SFA's board has the power of eminent domain, but "the taking of the land is for the use of the state" (Tex. Educ. Code Ann. sec. 95.30). The university's real property is state property (Tex. Rev. Civ. Stat. Ann. art. 601b sec. 1.02; cf. *Walsh* v. *Univ. of Texas,* 169 S.W.2d 993 (Tex. Civ. App. 1942)), and the funds used to purchase it were appropriated by the legislature from the general revenues of the state (cf. *Texas Tech College* v. *Fry,* 278 S.W.2d 480 (Tex. Civ. App. 1954)). State law is the source of the university's authority to purchase, sell, or lease real and personal property (see Tex. Rev. Civ. Stat. Ann. art. 601b). The university's operating expenses come largely through legislative appropriation (1981 Tex. Sess. Law Serv. ch. 875 at 3695). Even those public funds which do not originate with the state are reappropriated to the university (ch. 875 at 3720) and become subject to rigid control by the state when received (ch. 875 at 3719-21). The source and use of the university's monies is governed comprehensively (ch. 875 at 3716-28), and all funds are subject to extensive reporting requirements and state audits (ch. 875 at 3721).

In addition to the functions cited above, because SFA is a state agency it is subject to state regulation in every other substantial aspect of its existence, such as employee conduct standards, promotions, disclosure of information, liability for tort claims, workers' compensation, inventory reports, meetings, posting of state job opportunities, private consultants, travel rules, and legal proceedings (see generally 1981 Tex. Sess. Law Serv. ch. 875 at 3790-3824). Also, Texas courts have held repeatedly that suits against universities within SFA's classification are suits against the state for sovereign immunity purposes (*Martine* v. *Board of Regents, State Senior Colleges of Texas,* 578 S.W.2d 465, 469-70 (Tex. Civ. App. 1979); *Lowe* v. *Texas Tech University,* 540 S.W.2d 297, 298 (Tex. 1976)). In short, under Texas law SFA is more an arm of the state than a political subdivision [665 F.2d at 557-58].

The court carefully noted that its conclusion concerning Stephen F. Austin University would not necessarily apply to state universities in other states, nor to all other postsecondary institutions in Texas: "Each situation must be addressed individually because the states have adopted different schemes, both intra and interstate, in constituting their institutions of higher learning." As an example, the court noted the distinction between Texas institutions such as SFA, on the one hand, and Texas junior colleges, on the other. Relying on Texas statutes, the court reaffirmed its earlier decisions in *Hander* v. *San Jacinto Junior College,* 519 F.2d 273 (5th Cir. 1975), and *Goss* v. *San Jacinto Junior College,* 588 F.2d 96 (5th Cir. 1979), that Texas junior colleges are not arms of the state and are thus suable under Section 1983:

Junior colleges, rather than being established by the legislature, are created by local initiative (Tex. Educ. Code Ann. sec. 130.031). Their governing bodies are elected by local voters rather than being appointed by the governor with the advice and consent of the senate (sec. 130.083(e)). Most telling is the power of junior colleges to levy *ad valorem* taxes (sec. 130.122), a power which the board of SFA lacks. Under Texas law, political subdivisions are sometimes defined as entities authorized to levy taxes (Tex. Rev. Civ. Stat. Ann. art. 2351b–3; see generally *Hander,* 519 F.2d at 279) [665 F.2d at 558].[10]

Even if the institution is characterized as a Section 1983 "person" with no Eleventh Amendment immunity, it may still be able in particular cases to avoid liability. According to *Monell:*

Local governing bodies . . . can be sued directly under 1983 . . . [where] the action that is alleged to be unconstitutional implements or executes a policy statement, ordinance, regulation, or decision officially adopted and promulgated by the body's officers. Moreover, although the touchstone of the Section 1983 action against a government body is an allegation that official policy is responsible for a deprivation of rights protected by the Constitution, local governments, like every other Section 1983 "person," by the very terms of the statute, may be sued for constitutional deprivations visited pursuant to governmental "custom" even though such a custom has not received formal approval through the body's official decision-making channels. . . .

On the other hand, the language of Section 1983 . . . compels the conclusion that Congress did not intend municipalities to be held liable unless action pursuant to official municipal policy of some nature caused a constitutional tort. In particular, we conclude that a municipality cannot be held liable solely because it employs a tortfeasor—or, in other words, a municipality cannot be held liable under Section 1983 on a *respondeat superior* theory [436 U.S. at 690–91].

Thus, along with its expansion of the "persons" suable under Section 1983, *Monell* also clarifies and limits the types of governmental actions for which newly suable entities can be held liable.

The predictable reaction of local governments to the *Monell* decision, aside from general criticism of their inclusion within Section 1983, was to assert that they had a "qualified immunity" from monetary liability whenever their actions had been taken in "good faith." In effect, local governments sought to assume for themselves the kind of immunity that their officers and employees would have if sued personally (see this volume, Section 2.4.3). This argument was rejected by the U.S. Supreme Court in *Owen* v. *City of Independence,* 100 S. Ct. 1398 (1980).

[10]Two other arguments presented by the plaintiff and considered by the court will be of interest to attorneys: (1) that the state had waived its Eleventh Amendment immunity to suit and (2) that the claim against SFA was not really a claim against the state because damages could be paid from an independent fund rather than from the state treasury. After addressing their technical nuances, the court rejected both arguments (665 F.2d at 559–61).

The *Owen* case involved a former police chief's claim that the city had violated his constitutional rights to a notice of reasons for discharge and a hearing. The city claimed that the officials who decided to terminate the chief's employment had acted in good faith, since they had no knowledge that notice and a hearing were required; the Supreme Court decisions crystallizing the need for the procedural protection Owen sought had not been decided until several months after his discharge. The city claimed that it was entitled to qualified immunity because its officials had believed in good faith that their acts were constitutional. The U.S. Court of Appeals agreed.

Reversing, the Supreme Court responded:

> There is no tradition of immunity for municipal corporations, and neither history nor policy supports a construction of Section 1983 that would justify the qualified immunity accorded the city of Independence by the Court of Appeals. We hold, therefore, that the municipality may not assert the good faith of its officers or agents as a defense to liability under Section 1983. . . .

> A damages remedy against the offending party is a vital component of any scheme for vindicating cherished constitutional guarantees, and the importance of assuring its efficacy is only accentuated when the wrongdoer is the institution that has been established to protect the very rights it has transgressed. Yet owing to the qualified immunity enjoyed by most government officials (see *Scheuer* v. *Rhodes,* 416 U.S. 232, 94 S. Ct. 1683, 40 L. Ed. 2d 90 (1974)), many victims of municipal malfeasance would be left remediless if the city were also allowed to assert a good-faith defense. Unless countervailing considerations counsel otherwise, the injustice of such a result should not be tolerated [100 S. Ct. at 1409, 1415].

In further support of its decision in *Owen,* the Court set out this synthesis of, and justification for, its modern Section 1983 precedents:

> Doctrines of tort law have changed significantly over the past century, and our notions of governmental responsibility should properly reflect that evolution. No longer is individual ''blameworthiness'' the acid test of liability; the principle of equitable loss-spreading has joined fault as a factor in distributing the costs of official misconduct.

> We believe that today's decision, together with prior precedents in this area, properly allocates these costs among the three principals in the scenario of the Section 1983 cause of action: the victim of the constitutional deprivation; the officer whose conduct caused the injury; and the public, as represented by the municipal entity. The innocent individual who is harmed by an abuse of governmental authority is assured that he will be compensated for his injury. The offending official, so long as he conducts himself in good faith, may go about his business secure in the knowledge that a qualified immunity will protect him from personal liability for damages that are more appropriately chargeable to the populace as a whole. And the public will be forced to bear only the costs of injury inflicted by the ''execution of a government's policy or custom, whether made by its lawmakers or by those whose edicts or acts may fairly be said to represent

official policy'' (*Monell* v. *New York City Dept. of Social Services,* 436 U.S. at 694, 98 S. Ct. at 2038) [100 S. Ct. at 1419].

Although *Monell* and *Owen* made clear that political subdivisions could be held liable under Section 1983 for monetary damages, the case did not determine whether political subdivisions could be liable for *punitive* as well as compensatory damages. In an earlier case, *Carey* v. *Piphus,* 435 U.S. 247 (1978), the Supreme Court had held that punitive damages could be assessed in an appropriate case against a governmental employee ''with the specific purpose of deterring or punishing violations of constitutional rights.'' But in *City of Newport* v. *Fact Concerts, Inc.,* 101 S. Ct. 2748 (1981), the Court refused to extend this concept to local governments. The Court held that local governments do not share in liability for punitive damages, although they may be liable for compensatory damages. The Court also found that the goal of deterrence would not be served by awards of punitive damages against local governments, since it was far from clear that policy-making officials would be deterred from wrongdoing by the knowledge that awards could be assessed against their governments.

In yet another leading case, *State of Maine* v. *Thiboutot,* 100 S. Ct. 2502 (1980), the U.S. Supreme Court expanded the types of claims that plaintiffs may bring under Section 1983. The plaintiffs in *Thiboutot* did not claim a violation of their constitutional or civil rights, as Section 1983 plaintiffs typically had done up to that time; instead, they claimed that Maine had incorrectly computed their benefits under the Aid to Families with Dependent Children program and that this error violated their rights under the Social Security Act. Maine argued that this claim was not a civil rights claim and therefore could not be brought under Section 1983.

In its opinion rejecting Maine's argument, the Court focused on the language of the statute, which permits redress for ''the deprivation of any rights, privileges, or immunities secured by the Constitution *and laws*'' (emphasis added):

The question before us is whether the phrase ''and laws,'' as used in Section 1983, means what it says, or whether it should be limited to some subset of laws. Given that Congress attached no modifiers to the phrase, the plain language of the statute undoubtedly embraces respondents' claim that petitioners violated the Social Security Act [100 S. Ct. at 2504].

Three justices vigorously dissented, asserting that the majority's reading of the statute was inconsistent with Section 1983's legislative history, which (according to the dissenters) reveals ''an intention to protect enduring civil rights rather than the virtually limitless entitlements created by federal statutes'' (100 S. Ct. at 2515 n.15).

A year after *Thiboutot,* the Supreme Court engrafted a major qualification to the decision. In *Pennhurst State School and Hospital* v. *Halderman,* 101 S. Ct. 1531 (1981), the Court noted that, even if a plaintiff seeks to enforce a right secured by federal law, as indicated in *Thiboutot,* Section 1983 will not be available if the statute relied on provides some other remedy as the exclusive remedy for violations of that particular statute. Then, in *Middlesex County Sewage Authority* v. *National Sea Clammers Association,* 101 S. Ct. 2615 (1981), the Court denied the plaintiffs relief under Section 1983 even though their claims were based on federal law. Reasoning that the statutes invoked by the plaintiffs (a marine life protection act and the Federal Water Pollution Control Act) contained comprehensive enforcement mechanisms and that plaintiffs had no "private cause of action" (see Section 7.5.9) under these statutes, the Court concluded that the statutory remedies were exclusive within the meaning of *Pennhurst* and that a *Thiboutot* type of suit was therefore not available to enforce these laws.

The latest of the major Section 1983 cases is *Patsy* v. *Board of Regents of the State of Florida,* 102 S. Ct. 2557 (1982), a suit by a staff employee of Florida International University alleging race and sex discrimination. The case addressed a critical procedural issue: whether a Section 1983 plaintiff must "exhaust" available state administrative remedies before a court may consider her claim (see Section 3.5.3). Invoking such an exhaustion requirement would be yet another way for governmental defendants to ameliorate the impact of the recent decisions expanding Section 1983 liability. For many years preceding these cases, however, the U.S. Supreme Court had refused to impose an exhaustion requirement on Section 1983 suits, and in *Patsy* the Court declined the Florida board of regents' invitation to overrule this line of decisions.[11]

The board had argued that exhaustion "should be required because it would . . . lessen the perceived burden that Section 1983 actions impose on federal courts; . . . improve federal-state relations by postponing federal court review until after the state administrative agency had passed on the issue; and . . . enable the agency, which presumably has expertise in the area at issue, to enlighten the federal court's ultimate decision." But the Supreme Court rejoined:

> Policy considerations alone cannot justify judicially imposed exhaustion unless exhaustion is consistent with congressional intent. Furthermore, . . . the relevant policy considerations do not invariably point in one direction, and there is vehement disagreement over the validity of the assumptions underlying many of them. The very difficulty of these policy considerations, and Congress's superior institutional competence to pursue this debate, suggest that legislative not judicial solutions are preferable [102 S. Ct. at 2566-67].

The premises supporting this rejoinder are that "Congress is vested with the power to prescribe the basic procedural scheme under which claims may be heard in federal courts" and that "a court should not defer the exercise of jurisdiction under a federal statute unless it is consistent with . . . [Congress's] intent." After canvassing the legislative history of Section 1983 and related statutes, the

---

[11]In a case subsequent to *Patsy, Burnett* v. *Grattan,* 104 S. Ct. 2924 (1984), the Court rejected yet another procedural device for limiting the impact of Section 1983. The defendant in *Burnett,* a state university, had argued that a six-month statute of limitations applied to the case—the same time period as applied to the filing of discrimination complaints with the state human rights commission—and that the plaintiffs' complaint should be dismissed because it was not filed within six months of the harm (employment discrimination) that the plaintiffs alleged. The Court concluded that, in order to accomplish the goals of Section 1983, it was necessary to allow a longer, three-year, time period for bringing this particular suit, the same period generally allowed for civil actions under the law of the state in which the plaintiffs had sued.

Court found that Congress's intent was consistent with a "no-exhaustion rule," subject only to narrow exceptions carved out by Congress itself. The Court therefore reaffirmed that exhaustion of state administrative remedies is not a prerequisite to bringing a Section 1983 action.[12]

The combined impact of these Supreme Court decisions on Section 1983 is clearly substantial. *Monell, Owen,* and *Thiboutot* expand governmental defendants' potential liability in two directions at once: (1) local governments and other "political subdivisions" of states are now suable for both compensatory damages and injunctive relief, thus expanding the "persons" that are subject to Section 1983; and (2) suits may now be brought to enforce rights under all federal laws for which Congress has not provided some other exclusive remedy, thus expanding the "laws" that are subject to Section 1983. Moreover, *Patsy* makes clear that defendants cannot neutralize the impact of these developments by demanding exhaustion of state remedies as a prerequisite to suit. The applicability of these new Section 1983 interpretations to public postsecondary institutions, however, is still not clear. Each institution's potential liability turns on whether it is to be considered a "person" within the meaning of *Monell.* While the letter of the law remains uncertain, administrators should be encouraged to foster full and fair enjoyment of federal civil rights and federal entitlements within their institutions in order to comply with the spirit of Section 1983, which compels that where officials "may harbor doubt about the lawfulness of their intended actions . . . [they should] err on the side of protecting citizens' . . . rights" (*Owen,* 100 S. Ct. at 1416).

Even if the courts ultimately determine that particular public institutions are not Section 1983 persons, these institutions will still be suable under some other federal civil rights laws (see, for example, Section 3.3.2 of this volume). They may also be suable under state civil rights laws or individual rights guarantees of the state constitution (see Section 1.3.1). And, under developing trends in the law, public institutions may sometimes be suable in *state* court on *federal* constitutional claims that would be barred from the *federal* courts by the Eleventh Amendment (see L. Wolcher, "Sovereign Immunity and the Supremacy Clause: Damages Against States in Their Own Courts for Constitutional Violations," 69 *California L. Rev.* 189 (1981)). Moreover, trustees and administrators of public institutions are sometimes suable in their individual capacities under Section 1983 even where the institution could not be sued (see Section 2.4.3). The constitutional immunity under Article III and the Eleventh Amendment will not protect institutions from such suits in federal courts where the plaintiffs seek injunctive relief or other relief that would not require a monetary award from state funds.

Sec. 2.4. Personal Liability of Trustees, Administrators, and Other Agents

2.4.1. Personal tort liability. A trustee, administrator, or other agent of a

---

[12]Another potential issue—the board of regents' amenability to suit under the Eleventh Amendment—was not addressed by the Court's majority opinion (see 102 S. Ct. at 2568 n.19). In dissent, however, Justice Powell argued that the Court should have held the suit to be barred by the Eleventh Amendment (102 S. Ct. at 2570–76). In a separate opinion concurring with the majority, Justice White disagreed with Justice Powell and argued that Florida law waived the board's immunity (102 S. Ct. at 2569–70).

postsecondary institution may be liable for his torts even if they are committed while he is conducting the institution's affairs. The individual must actually have committed the tortious act, directed it, or otherwise participated in its commission, however, before personal liability will attach. He will not be personally liable for torts of other institutional agents merely because he represents the institution for whom the other agents were acting. The elements of a tort and the defenses against a tort claim (see Section 2.3.1) in suits against the individual personally are generally the same as those in suits against the institution. An individual sued in his personal capacity, however, is usually not shielded by the sovereign immunity and charitable immunity defenses that sometimes protect the institution.

If a trustee, administrator, or other institutional agent commits a tort while acting on behalf of the institution and within the scope of the authority delegated to him, both he and the institution may be liable for the harm caused by the tort. But the institution's potential liability does not relieve the individual of any measure of liability; the injured party could choose to collect a judgment solely from the individual, and the individual would have no claim against the institution for any part of the judgment he was required to pay. However, where individual and institution are both potentially liable, the individual may receive practical relief from liability if the injured party squeezes the entire judgment from the institution or the institution chooses to pay the entire amount.

If a trustee, administrator, or other institutional agent commits a tort while acting outside the scope of authority delegated to him, he may be personally liable but the institution would not be liable (Section 2.3.1). Thus, the injured party could obtain a judgment only against the individual, and only the individual would be responsible for satisfying the judgment. The institution, however, may affirm the individual's unauthorized action (''affirmance'' is similar to the ''ratification'' discussed in connection with contract liability in Section 2.3.2), in which case the individual will be deemed to have acted within his authority, and both institution and individual will be potentially liable.

Officers and employees of public institutions can sometimes escape tort liability by proving the defense of ''official immunity.'' For this defense to apply, the individual's act must have been within the scope of his authority and must have been a discretionary act involving policy judgment. Because it involves this element of discretion and policy judgment, official immunity is more likely to apply to a particular individual the higher in the authority hierarchy he is.

In *Tarasoff* v. *Regents of the University of California,* 551 P.2d 334 (Cal. 1976), the parents of a girl murdered by a psychiatric patient at the university hospital sued the university regents, four psychotherapists employed by the hospital, and the campus police. The patient had confided his intention to kill the daughter to a staff psychotherapist. Though the patient was briefly detained by the campus police at the psychotherapist's request, no further action was taken to protect the daughter. The parents alleged that this constituted a tortious failure to confine a dangerous patient and a tortious failure to warn them or their daughter of a dangerous patient. The psychotherapists and campus police claimed official immunity under a California statute freeing ''public employee(s)'' from liability for acts or omissions resulting from ''the exercise of discretion vested in [them]'' (Cal. Gov't Code sec. 820.2). The court accepted the official immunity defense in relation to the failure to confine, because that failure involved a ''basic policy decision'' sufficient to constitute discretion under the statute. But regarding the failure to warn, the court refused to accept the psychotherapists' official immunity claim because the decision whether to warn was not a basic policy decision. The campus police needed no official immunity from their failure to warn, because the court held that they had no legal duty (see Section 2.3.1) to warn in light of the facts in the complaint.

The Supreme Court of Virginia in *James* v. *Jane,* 221 Va. 43, 267 S.E.2d 108 (1980), rejected a defense of sovereign immunity asserted by physicians who were full-time faculty members at the state university medical center and members of the hospital staff. The defendants had argued that, as state employees, they were immune from a suit charging them with negligence in their treatment of certain patients at the university's hospital. The trial court accepted the physicians' defense. Although agreeing that under Virginia law certain state employees and agents could share the state's own sovereign immunity, the Virginia Supreme Court reversed the trial court and refused to extend this immunity to these particular employees.

In reaching its decision, the appellate court analyzed the current status of the immunity defense and the circumstances in which its assertion is appropriate:

> The Commonwealth of Virginia functions only through its elected and appointed officials and its employees. If, because of the threat of litigation, or for any other reason, they cannot act, or refuse to act, the state also ceases to act. Although a valid reason exists for state employee immunity, the argument for such immunity does not have the same strength it had in past years. This is because of the intrusion of government into areas formerly private, and because of the thousandfold increase in the number of government employees. We find no justification for treating a present-day government employee as absolutely immune from tort liability, just as if he were an employee of an eighteenth-century sovereign. It is proper that a distinction be made between the state, whose immunity is absolute unless waived, and the employees and officials of the state, whose immunity is qualified, depending upon the function they perform and the manner of performance. Certain state officials and state employees must of necessity enjoy immunity in the performance of their duties. These officers are inclusive of, but not limited to, the governor, state officials, and judges. They are required by the Constitution and by general law to exercise broad discretionary powers, often involving both the determination and implementation of state policy.
>
> Admittedly, no single all-inclusive rule can be enunciated or applied in determining entitlements to sovereign immunity. . . . A state employee who acts wantonly, or in a culpable or grossly negligent manner, is not protected. And neither is the employee who acts beyond the scope of his employment, who exceeds his authority and discretion, and who acts individually.
>
> The difficulty in application comes when a state employee is charged with simple negligence, a failure to use ordinary or reasonable care in the performance of some duty, and then claims the immunity of the state. Under such circumstances we examine the function this employee was performing and the extent of the state's interest and involvement in that function. Whether the act performed involves the use of judgment and discretion

is a consideration, but it is not always determinative. Virtually every act performed by a person involves the exercise of some discretion. Of equal importance is the degree of control and direction exercised by the state over the employee whose negligence is involved. . . .

In the case under review, the paramount interest of the Commonwealth of Virginia is that the University of Virginia operate a good medical school and that it be staffed with efficient and competent administrators and professors. The state is of course interested and concerned that patients who are treated at the university hospital receive proper medical care. However, the state has this same concern for every patient who is treated in any private hospital or by any doctor throughout the commonwealth. This is evidenced by the numerous statutes enacted by the General Assembly of Virginia designed to assure adequate medical care and medical facilities for the people of the state. The state's interest and the state's involvement, in its sovereign capacity, in the treatment of a specific patient by an attending physician in the university hospital are slight: equally slight is the control exercised by the state over the physician in the treatment accorded that patient. This interest and involvement is not of such moment and value to the commonwealth as to entitle [the defendants] to the immunity enjoyed by the state [267 S.E.2d at 113–14].

The "sovereign" or "state employee" immunity thus created by the Virginia court is potentially broader than the "official immunity" recognized in some other jurisdictions. In states recognizing "official immunity," the likelihood of successfully invoking the defense is, as mentioned, proportional to the officer's or employee's level in the authority hierarchy. This official immunity doctrine seeks to protect the discretionary and policy-making functions of higher-level decision makers, a goal that the *James* v. *Jane* opinion also recognizes. The sovereign immunity defense articulated in *James,* however, encompasses an additional consideration: the degree of state control over the employee's job functions. In weighing this additional factor, the Virginia sovereign immunity doctrine also seeks to protect state employees who are so closely directed by the state that they should not bear individual responsibility for negligent acts committed within the scope of this controlled employment. Sovereign immunity Virginia-style may thus extend to lower-echelon employees not reached by official immunity. Although *James* held that this theory does not apply to physicians treating patients in a state university medical center, there are other postsecondary employees—such as middle- or low-level administrative personnel (*Messina* v. *Burden,* 321 S.E.2d 657 (Va. 1984), concerning the superintendent of buildings at a community college), support staff, or even medical interns at a state university hospital (*Lawhorne* v. *Harlan,* 214 Va. 405, 200 S.E.2d 569 (1973))—who may share the state's immunity under the court's approach.

Although *James* is binding law only in Virginia, it illustrates nuances in the doctrine of personal tort immunity that may also exist, or may now develop, in other states. When contrasted with the cases relying on the official immunity doctrine, *James* also illustrates the state-by-state variations that can exist in this area of the law.

The official immunity and state employee immunity defenses are not available to officers and employees of private institutions. But it appears that at least the trustees of private nonprofit institutions will be leniently treated by some courts out of deference to the trustees' special discretionary functions (see W. C. Porth, "Personal Liability of Trustees of Higher Educational Institutions," 2 *J. of College and University Law* 143 (1974–75)). As a result, the personal liability of such trustees may be limited in a way somewhat akin to the official immunity limitation available to officers and employees of public institutions.

Institutions should consider whether or not they wish to protect their personnel from the financial consequences of personal tort liability. Insurance coverage and indemnification agreements, discussed in Section 2.5.2, may be utilized for this purpose.

2.4.2. Personal contract liability. A trustee, administrator, or other agent who signs a contract on behalf of an institution may be personally liable for its performance if the institution breaches. The extent of personal liability depends on whether his participation on behalf of the institution was authorized—either by a grant of express authority, an implied authority, an apparent authority, or a subsequent ratification by the institution. (See the discussion of authority in Section 2.3.2.) If the individual's participation was properly authorized, and if he signed the contract only in the capacity of an institutional agent, he will not be personally liable for performance of the contract. If, however, the individual's participation was not properly authorized, or if he signed in an individual capacity rather than as an institutional agent, he may be personally liable.

In some cases the other contracting party may be able to sue both the institution and the agent or to choose between them. This option is presented when the contracting party did not know at the time of contracting that the individual participated in an agency capacity, but later learns that was the case. The option is also presented when the contracting party knows that the individual is acting as an institutional agent, but the individual also gives a personal promise that the contract will be performed. In such situations, if the contracting party obtains a judgment against both the institution and the agent, the judgment may be satisfied against either or against both, but the contracting party may receive no more than the total amount of the judgment. Where the contracting party satisfies the judgment against only one of the two liable parties, the paying party may have a claim against the nonpayor for part of the judgment amount.

If the agent is a party to the contract in his personal capacity and thus potentially liable on it, he can assert the same defenses that are available to any contracting party. These defenses may arise from the contract—such as the absence of some formality necessary to complete the contract or fraud or inadequate performance by the other party—or may be personal to the agent, such as a particular counterclaim against the other party.

2.4.3. Personal federal civil rights liability. The federal civil rights liability of trustees, administrators, and other employees of postsecondary institutions is determined under the same body of law that determines the liability of the institutions themselves, and presents many of the same legal issues (see Section 2.3.3). As with institutional liability, an individual's action must usually be done "under color of" state law, or must be characterizable as "state action," before federal civil rights liability will attach. Like tort and contract liability, the civil rights liability of individual trustees, administrators, and other employees is not coterminous with the institution's liability.

Defenses that may be available to the institution (such as the constitutional immunity defense) may not be available to individuals sued in their individual capacities; but, conversely, defenses that may be available to individuals (such as the qualified immunity discussed later in this section) may not be available to the institution.

The federal statute referred to as Section 1983, quoted in Section 2.3.3 of this chapter, is again the key civil rights statute. An individual trustee, administrator, or employee is clearly a "person" under Section 1983 and thus subject to its provisions whenever he has acted under color of state law. But courts have long recognized a qualified immunity from Section 1983 liability for certain public officers and employees. In 1974 and again in 1975, the U.S. Supreme Court attempted to explain the scope of this immunity as it applies to school officials.

In *Scheuer* v. *Rhodes,* 416 U.S. 232 (1974), the Court considered a suit for damages brought on behalf of three students killed in the May 1970 disturbances at Kent State University. The Court rejected the contention that the president of Kent State and other state officials had an absolute "official immunity" protecting them from personal liability. The Court instead accorded the president and officials a "qualified immunity" under Section 1983:

> In varying scope, a qualified immunity is available to officers of the executive branch of government, the variation being dependent upon the scope of discretion and responsibilities of the office and all the circumstances as they reasonably appeared at the time of the action on which liability is sought to be based. It is the existence of reasonable grounds for the belief formed at the time and in light of all the circumstances, coupled with good-faith belief, that affords a basis for qualified immunity of executive officers for acts performed in the course of official conduct [416 U.S. at 247–48].

Because the availability of this immunity depended on facts not yet in the record, the Supreme Court remanded the case to the trial court for further proceedings.[13]

In *Wood* v. *Strickland,* 420 U.S. 308 (1975), the Supreme Court extended, and added enigma to, its discussion of Section 1983 immunity in the institutional context. After the school board in this case had expelled some students from high school for violating a school disciplinary regulation, several of them sued the members of the school board. In a controversial decision with strong dissents, the Court held that school board members, as public school officials, are entitled to a qualified immunity from such suits:

> We think there must be a degree of immunity if the work of the schools is to go forward; and, however worded, the immunity must be such that public school officials understand that action taken in the good-faith fulfillment of their responsibilities and within the bounds of reason under all the circum-

---

[13]On remand the case proceeded to trial against all defendants. No defendant was held immune from suit. The president of Kent State was eventually dismissed as a defendant, however, because the facts indicated that he had not personally violated any of the plaintiffs' rights (see *Krause* v. *Rhodes,* 570 F.2d 563 (6th Cir. 1977)). Eventually the case was settled and an award of $600,000 plus attorney's fees made to the plaintiffs (see *Krause* v. *Rhodes,* 640 F.2d 214 (6th Cir. 1981)).

stances will not be punished and that they need not exercise their discretion with undue timidity. . . .

The official must himself be acting sincerely and with a belief that he is doing right, but an act violating a student's constitutional rights can be no more justified by *ignorance or disregard of settled, indisputable law* on the part of one entrusted with supervision of students' daily lives than by the presence of actual malice. To be entitled to a special exemption from the categorical remedial language of Section 1983 in a case in which his action violated a student's constitutional rights, a school board member, who has voluntarily undertaken the task of supervising the operation of the school and the activities of the students, must be held to a standard of conduct based not only on permissible intentions, but also on *knowledge of the basic, unquestioned constitutional rights* of his charges. Such a standard neither imposes an unfair burden upon a person assuming a responsible public office requiring a high degree of intelligence and judgment for the proper fulfillment of its duties, nor an unwarranted burden in light of the value which civil rights have in our legal system. Any lesser standard would deny much of the promise of Section 1983. Therefore, in the specific context of school discipline, we hold that a school board member *is not immune from liability for damages under Section 1983 if he knew or reasonably should have known that the action he took within his sphere of official responsibility would violate the constitutional rights of the student affected, or if he took the action with the malicious intention to cause a deprivation of constitutional rights or other injury to the student.* That is not to say that school board members are "charged with predicting the future course of constitutional law" (*Pierson* v. *Ray,* 386 U.S. at 557). A compensatory award will be appropriate only if the school board member has acted with such an impermissible motivation or with such disregard of the student's clearly established constitutional rights that his action cannot reasonably be characterized as being in good faith [420 U.S. at 321–22 (emphasis added)].

The Court's reliance on the *Scheuer* case at several points in its *Wood* opinion indicates that the *Wood* liability standard applies to public officials in postsecondary education as well. Clearly, the qualified immunity would be available to trustees and executive heads of public postsecondary institutions. The immunity of lower-level administrators and faculty members is less clear; for, as the Court noted in *Scheuer* and reaffirmed in *Wood,* the immunity's existence and application would depend in each case on the "scope of discretion and responsibilities of the office."

In 1982 the Court modified its *Wood* analysis in ruling on a suit brought against two senior aides in the Nixon administration. The immunity test developed in *Wood* had two parts. One part was *subjective;* it focused on the defendant's "permissible intentions," asking whether he had acted "with the malicious intention to cause a deprivation of constitutional rights or other injury" to the plaintiff (420 U.S. at 322). The other part was *objective;* it focused on the defendant's "knowledge of . . . basic, unquestioned constitutional rights," asking whether he "knew or reasonably should have known that the action he took . . . would violate the constitutional rights" of the plaintiff (420 U.S. at 322). The 1982 case, *Harlow* v. *Fitzgerald,* 102 S. Ct. 2727, deleted the subjective part of the test because it had inhibited courts from dismissing insubstantial lawsuits prior to trial:

An official's subjective good faith has been considered to be a question of fact that some courts have regarded as inherently requiring resolution by a jury. . . . It now is clear that substantial costs attend the litigation of the subjective good faith of government officials. Not only are there the general costs of subjecting officials to the risks of trial—distraction of officials from their governmental duties, inhibition of discretionary action, and deterrence of able people from public service. There are special costs to "subjective" inquiries of this kind. Immunity generally is available only to officials performing discretionary functions. In contrast with the thought processes accompanying "ministerial" tasks, the judgments surrounding discretionary action almost inevitably are influenced by the decision maker's experiences, values, and emotions. These variables explain in part why questions of subjective intent so rarely can be decided by summary judgment. Yet they also frame a background in which there often is no clear end to the relevant evidence. Judicial inquiry into subjective motivation therefore may entail broad-ranging discovery and the deposing of numerous persons, including an official's professional colleagues. Inquiries of this kind can be peculiarly disruptive of effective government. . . .

We conclude today that bare allegations of malice should not suffice to subject government officials either to the costs of trial or to the burdens of broad-reaching discovery. We therefore hold that government officials performing discretionary functions generally are shielded from liability for civil damages insofar as their conduct does not violate clearly established statutory or constitutional rights of which a reasonable person would have known (see *Procunier* v. *Navarette*, 434 U.S. 555, 565 (1978); *Wood* v. *Strickland*, 420 U.S. at 321).

Reliance on the objective reasonableness of an official's conduct, as measured by reference to clearly established law, should avoid excessive disruption of government and permit the resolution of many insubstantial claims on summary judgment. On summary judgment, the judge appropriately may determine not only the currently applicable law but whether that law was clearly established at the time an action occurred. If the law at that time was not clearly established, an official could not reasonably be expected to anticipate subsequent legal developments, nor could he fairly be said to "know" that the law forbade conduct not previously identified as unlawful. Until this threshold immunity question is resolved, discovery should not be allowed. If the law was clearly established, the immunity defense ordinarily should fail, since a reasonably competent public official should know the law governing his conduct. Nevertheless, if the official pleading the defense claims extraordinary circumstances and can prove that he neither knew nor should have known of the relevant legal standard, the defense should be sustained. But again, the defense would turn primarily on objective factors [102 S. Ct. at 2737–39].

The application of the "reasonably should have known" standard to postsecondary education is illustrated by *Perez* v. *Rodriguez Bou*, 575 F.2d 21 (1st Cir. 1978). Although *Perez* was decided prior to *Harlow*, it relies on the objective part of the *Wood* immunity test, which was reaffirmed in *Harlow*. The case arose from a protest at the University of Puerto Rico in which approximately one hundred students marched to the office of the university chancellor. The chancellor, the defendant in this case, suspended several students without according them hearings or any other opportunity to defend themselves. After holding the suspensions unconstitutional, the court rejected the chancellor's assertion of immunity to plaintiffs' claim for damages:

> Although the question is close, we believe it could properly be found that Dr. Rodriguez Bou should have known his action was unconstitutional. One week before he ordered the suspension of these students, the Supreme Court had ruled in *Goss* v. *Lopez,* 419 U.S. 565, 95 S. Ct. 729, 42 L. Ed. 2d 725 (1975) (regarding suspensions), that "as a general rule, notice and hearing should precede removal of the student from school" and that only those "students whose presence poses a continuing danger to persons or property or an ongoing threat of disrupting the academic process may be immediately removed from school" [see this volume, Section 4.6.2]. Nor was this teaching unanticipated by prior federal court holdings in Puerto Rico. In *Marin* v. *University of Puerto Rico,* 377 F. Supp. 613, 623 (D.C.P.R. 1974), a three-judge court held that in cases "when the university has reasonable cause to believe that imminent danger to persons or property will exist if the student is permitted to remain on campus pending the full hearing," temporary suspension in advance of the required full hearing would be permitted. That case signaled even more stringent hearing requirements than the Supreme Court later required in *Goss* [575 F.2d at 23].

A second case that illustrates the objective portion of the immunity test is *United Carolina Bank* v. *Board of Regents of Stephen F. Austin State University,* 665 F.2d 553 (5th Cir. 1982) (this volume, Section 2.3.3). Having been denied tenure, a professor sued several administrators at his institution. He argued that the tenure denial had been precipitated by allegations he had made concerning the misuse of funds and that these allegations were an exercise of free speech, for which he should not be punished. The defendants claimed immunity; based on an analysis of the events leading to the tenure denial, they argued that they neither knew nor should have known that their actions would violate the professor's First Amendment rights. After a detailed review of the facts in the record, the court rejected the defendants' argument and held them liable. The opinion illustrates that, even under the objective immunity test approved by *Harlow,* a court may have to sort out a tangled web of facts in disposing of immunity claims.

As a result of this line of cases beginning with *Scheuer,* personnel of public institutions are charged with responsibility for knowing "clearly established law" (*Harlow,* 102 S. Ct. at 2739). Unless extraordinary circumstances prevent an individual from gaining such knowledge, the disregard of clearly established law is considered unreasonable and thus unprotected by the cloak of immunity. It will often be debatable whether particular points of law are sufficiently "clear" to fall within the Court's characterization. Moreover, the availability of immunity will depend on the particular facts of each case, as *Perez* and *United Carolina Bank* well illustrate. Since it is therefore extremely difficult to predict what actions would fall within the qualified immunity, institutional efforts will be better spent taking preventive measures to assure that Section 1983 violations do not occur, rather than making weak predictions about whether immunity would exist if violations did occur.

When individuals are sued under Section 1983, they have the responsibility of pleading and proving any immunity claim they may wish to assert. In *Gomez* v. *Toledo,* 100 S. Ct. 1920 (1980), the U.S. Supreme Court held that qualified immunity is an affirmative defense to be pleaded by the defendant, and the plaintiff's complaint therefore need not allege any facts to demonstrate that the defendant is not immune from suit. Although *Gomez* did not determine who carries the ultimate burden of proving the existence or absence of immunity, the later *Harlow* case indicates that a court should sustain the immunity defense only if the defendant "*can prove* that he neither knew nor should have known of the relevant legal standard" (102 S. Ct. at 2739; emphasis added).

Individuals who cannot successfully claim immunity may be held liable under Section 1983 for a wide range of federal law violations. *State of Maine* v. *Thiboutot,* 100 S. Ct. 2502 (1980), the case that expanded the types of violations for which Section 1983 provides redress (see Section 2.3.3), enlarges the potential liability of individual as well as governmental defendants. Under *Thiboutot* individuals may now be liable for violating not only constitutional and statutory "civil" rights but other federally secured rights as well. However, traditional civil rights—such as discrimination, due process, and freedom of speech—continue to be the focus for most Section 1983 cases against either institutions or their personnel.

Individuals found personally liable under Section 1983 are subject to both court injunctions and money damage awards in favor of the prevailing plaintiff(s). Unlike governmental defendants (see *City of Newport* v. *Fact Concerts, Inc.,* Section 2.3.3 of this volume), individual defendants may be held liable for punitive as well as compensatory damages. To collect compensatory damages, a plaintiff must prove "actual injury," tangible or intangible; courts usually will not presume that damage occurred from a violation of civil rights and will award compensatory damages only to the extent of proven injury (*Carey* v. *Piphus,* 435 U.S. 247 (1978)). To collect punitive damages, a plaintiff must show that the defendant's actions either manifested "reckless or callous disregard for the plaintiff's rights" or constituted "intentional violations of federal law" (*Smith* v. *Wade,* 103 S. Ct. 1625, 1637 (1983)).

Besides having a potentially broad scope of liability and a limited, unpredictable immunity under Section 1983, institutional personnel are also generally unprotected by the Eleventh Amendment immunity that sometimes protects their institutions from federal court suits (see Section 2.3.3). In the *Scheuer* case (discussed earlier in this section) for example, the Court held that the president of Kent State had no such immunity:

> The Eleventh Amendment provides no shield for a state official confronted by a claim that he had deprived another of a federal right under the color of state law. . . . When a state officer acts under a state law in a manner violative of the federal Constitution, he "comes into conflict with the superior authority of that Constitution, and he is in that case stripped of his official or representative character and is subjected *in his person* to the consequences of his individual conduct" [quoting *Ex parte Young,* 209 U.S. 123, 159 (1908)] [416 U.S. at 237].

If a state university president has no immunity under the Constitution, it follows that lower-level administrators, faculty members, and probably trustees would have no immunity either. The *Scheuer* case notes one circumstance, however, under which

such persons would enjoy the constitutional immunity: when they are sued only
as titular parties in a suit that is actually seeking money damages from the state
treasury. Only in this case would the suit be considered to be against the state itself
and thus barred by the Eleventh Amendment.

The state of the law under Section 1983 and the Eleventh Amendment, taken
together, gives administrators of public postsecondary institutions no cause to feel
confident that either they or other institutional officers or employees are insulated
from personal civil rights liability. To minimize the liability risk in this critical area
of law and social responsibility, administrators should make legal counsel available
to institutional personnel for consultation, encourage review by counsel of institutional policies that may affect civil rights, and provide personnel with information
on or training in basic civil rights law and other legal principles. To absolve personnel of the financial drain of any liability that does occur, administrators may
wish to consider the purchase of special insurance coverage or the development
of indemnity plans. As discussed in Section 2.5.2, public policy in some states may
limit the use of these techniques in the civil rights area.

Sec. 2.5. Institutional Management of Liability Risk

The risk of financial liability for injury to another party has increased
dramatically since the early 1960s for postsecondary institutions as well as their
governing board members and personnel. This section examines some methods
for purposefully controlling the risks of such exposure to liability and thus minimizing
the detrimental effect of liability on the institution and its personnel.[14] Such risk
management may be advisable not only because it helps stabilize the institution's
financial condition over time but also because it can improve the morale and performance of institutional personnel by alleviating their concerns about potential
personal liability. In addition, risk management can implement the institution's
humanistic concern for minimizing and compensating any potential injuries that
its operations may cause to innocent third parties.

The major methods of risk management may be called risk avoidance, risk
control, risk transfer, and risk retention.

2.5.1. Risk avoidance and risk control. The most certain method for managing
a known exposure to liability is risk avoidance—the elimination of the behavior,
condition, or program that is the source of the risk. This method is often not realistic,
however, since it could require institutions to forgo activities important to their
educational missions. It might also require greater knowledge of the details of myriad
campus activities than administrators typically can acquire and greater certainty
regarding the legal principles of liability (see Section 2.3) than the law typically
affords.

Risk control is less drastic than risk avoidance. The goal is to reduce, rather
than eliminate entirely, the frequency or severity of potential exposures to liability—
mainly by improving the physical environment or modifying hazardous behavior or

---

[14]Much of this section relies heavily on the 1976 monograph by R. Aiken, J. F. Adams,
and J. W. Hall, *Legal Liabilities in Higher Education: Their Scope and Management,* which is noted
in the Selected Annotated Bibliography at the end of this chapter and cited occasionally in the
text of this section.

activities in ways that reduce the recognized risks. Although this method may have less impact on an institution's educational mission than risk avoidance, it may similarly require considerable detailed knowledge of campus facilities and functions and of legal liability principles.

2.5.2. Risk transfer. By purchasing commercial insurance or entering a "hold harmless" or "indemnification" agreement, an institution can transfer its own liability risks to another or transfer to itself the liability risks of its officers and other personnel. A commercial insurance policy shifts potential future financial losses (up to a maximum amount) to the insurance company in exchange for payment of a specified premium. The institution can insure against liability for its own acts, as well as liability transferred to it by a "hold harmless" agreement with its personnel. With the advice of insurance experts, the institution can determine the kinds and amounts of liability protection it needs and provide for the necessary premium expenditures in its budgeting process.

Generally, liability insurance policies cover accidentally caused bodily injury and property damage. Intentionally or maliciously caused damage and damage caused by acts that violate penal laws are usually excluded from coverage because protecting an individual from responsibility for such damage would contravene public policy (see Section 2.5.4). Financial liability arising from the violation of an individual's constitutional or civil rights is also commonly excluded from standard insurance coverage—an exclusion that can pose considerable problems for administrators and institutions, whose exposure to such liability has been greatly increasing in recent years. To cover such risks effectively, the institution may need to combine a standard policy with one or more specialty endorsements or companion policies. When even this arrangement does not provide coverage meeting the institution's needs, the institution may request a "manuscript" policy tailored to its specific needs. Such policies, however, are expensive.

A second method of risk transfer is a "hold harmless" or indemnification agreement. In a broad sense, the term *indemnification* refers to any compensation for loss or damage. Insurance is thus one method of indemnifying someone. But in the narrow sense used here, an indemnification agreement refers to an arrangement whereby one party (for example, the institution) agrees to "hold" another party (for example, an individual officer or employee) "harmless" from financial liability for certain acts or omissions of that party which cause damage to another:

> In brief synopsis, the mechanism of a typical indemnification will shift to the institution the responsibility for defense and discharge of claims asserted against institutional personnel individually by reason of their acts or omissions on behalf of the institution, if the individual believed in good faith that his actions were lawful and within his institutional authority and responsibility. That standard of conduct is, of course, very broadly stated; and the question of whether or not it is satisfied must be determined on a case-by-case basis [R. Aiken, *Legal Liabilities in Higher Education: Their Scope and Management,* Part I, p. 193 (Association of American Colleges, 1976)].

Although, with respect to its own personnel, the institution would typically be the "indemnitor"—that is, the party with ultimate financial liability—the institution can sometimes also be an "indemnitee," the party protected from liability loss. The institution could negotiate for "hold harmless" protection for itself, for instance, in contracts it enters with outside contractors or lessees. In an illustrative case, *Bridston* v. *Dover Corp.* and *University of North Dakota* v. *Young Men's Christian Association,* 352 N.W.2d 194 (N.D. 1984), the university had leased a campus auditorium to a dance group. One of the group's members was injured during practice, allegedly due to the negligence of a university employee, and sued the university for damages. The university invoked an indemnity clause in the lease agreement and successfully avoided liability by arguing that the clause required the lessee to hold the university harmless even for negligent acts of the university's own employees.

Like an insurance policy, an indemnification agreement often does not cover liability resulting from intentional or malicious action or from action violating the state's penal laws, because such actions are considered contrary to public policy. Just as public policy may limit the types of acts or omissions that may be insured against, it may also limit those for which indemnification may be received.

Both public and private institutions may enter indemnification agreements. A public institution, however, may need specific authorizing legislation (see, for example, Mich. Stat. Ann. sec. 15-2108(1) *et seq.*), whereas private institutions usually can rely on the general laws of their states for sufficient authority. Some states provide for indemnification of all state employees for injuries caused by their acts or omissions on behalf of the state (see Cal. Govt. Code sec. 825 *et seq.* (West, 1980)).

2.5.3. Risk retention. The most practical option for the institution in some circumstances may be to retain the risk of financial liability. Adams and Hall note eight situations under which risk retention may be appropriate, including situations where commercial insurance is unavailable or too costly, the expected losses are so small that they can be considered normal operating expenses, or the probability of loss is so remote that it does not justify any insurance expense (J. F. Adams and J. W. Hall, *Legal Liabilities in Higher Education: Their Scope and Management,* Part II, pp. 241–242 (Association of American Colleges, 1976)). Both insurance policy deductibles and methods of self-insurance are examples of risk retention. The deductible amounts in an insurance policy allocate the first dollar coverage of liability, up to the amount of the deductible, to the institution. The institution becomes a self-insurer by maintaining a separate bank account to pay appropriate claims. The institution's risk managers must determine the amount to be available in the account and the frequency and amount of regular payments to the account. This approach is distinguished from simple noninsurance by the planning and actuarial calculations that it involves.

2.5.4. Legal limits on authority to transfer risk. An institution's ability to transfer risk is limited by the law to situations that do not contravene "public policy." When financial liability is incurred as a result of willful wrongdoing, it is generally considered contrary to public policy to protect the institution or individual from responsibility for such behavior through insurance or indemnity. Wrongdoing that is malicious, fraudulent, immoral, or criminal will often fall within this category; thus, insurance companies may decline to cover such action, or provisions in insurance policies or indemnification agreements that do cover it may be void and unenforceable under state law. Common actions to which this public policy may apply include assault and battery, abuse of process, defamation, and invasion of privacy. This public policy may also apply to intentional deprivations of constitutional or civil rights; when the deprivation is unintentional, however, public policy may not operate to prohibit risk transfer (see, for example, *Solo Cup Co.* v. *Federal Insurance Co.,* 619 F.2d 1178 (7th Cir. 1980)).

Public policy may also prohibit agreements insuring against financial loss from punitive damage awards. Jurisdictions differ on whether such insurance coverage is proscribed. Some courts have prohibited coverage because it would defeat the two purposes served by punitive damages: punishment for egregious wrongdoing and deterrence of future misconduct (see, for example, *Hartford Accident and Indemnity Co.* v. *Village of Hempstead,* 48 N.Y.2d 218, 397 N.E.2d 737 (1979)). Other courts have permitted coverage at least when punitive damages are awarded as the result of gross negligence or wanton and reckless conduct rather than intentional wrong-doing (see, for example, *Hensley* v. *Erie Insurance Co.,* 283 S.E.2d 227 (W. Va. 1981)).[15]

Depending on their state's public policy, institutions may also be prohibited from using contractual agreements to transfer the risk of negligence to the potential victims of negligence. In *Emory University* v. *Porubiansky,* 248 Ga. 391, 282 S.E.2d 903 (1981), for example, the Emory University School of Dentistry Clinic sought to insulate itself from negligence suits by inserting into its consent form a clause indicating that the patient waived all claims against the university or its agents. The Georgia Supreme Court voided the agreement as offensive to public policy because it purported to relieve state-licensed professional practitioners of a duty to exercise reasonable care in dealing with patients.

A different kind of legal problem may exist for postsecondary institutions that enjoy some degree of sovereign or charitable immunity from financial liability (see Section 2.3.1). Public institutions may not have authority to purchase liability insurance covering acts within the scope of their immunity. Where such authority does exist, however, and the institution does purchase insurance, its sovereign or charitable immunity may thereby be affected. Sometimes a statute authorizing insurance coverage may itself waive sovereign immunity to the extent of coverage. When such a waiver is lacking, in most states the purchase of insurance appears not to affect immunity, and the insurance protection is operable only for acts found to be outside the scope of immunity. In some states, however, courts appear to treat the authorized purchase of insurance as a waiver or narrowing of the institution's immunity, to the extent of the insurance coverage.[16]

Selected Annotated Bibliography

Sec. 2.1. (The Question of Authority)

1. Hornby, D. B., "Delegating Authority to the Community of Scholars," 1975 *Duke L.J.* 279, provides excellent legal and policy analysis regarding delegations of authority in public systems of postsecondary education; considers

---

[15]The cases are collected in Annot., "Liability Insurance Coverage as Extending to Liability for Punitive or Exemplary Damages," 16 A.L.R.4th 11 (1982 and periodic supp.).

[16]Relevant cases are collected in Annot., "Liability or Indemnity Insurance Carried by Governmental Unit as Affecting Immunity from Tort Liability," 68 A.L.R.2d 1438 (1959 and periodic supp.); and Annot., "Immunity of Private Schools and Institutions of Higher Learning from Liability in Tort," 38 A.L.R.3d 480, 501–02 (1971 and periodic supp.).

constitutional and statutory delegations to statewide governing boards and individual boards of trustees, and subdelegations of that authority to officials, employees, and other bodies in individual institutions; contains many useful citations to legal and policy materials.

2.   Mortimer, K. P., and McConnell, T. R., *Sharing Authority Effectively: Participation, Interaction, and Discretion* (Jossey-Bass, 1978), provides a new analysis of how to distribute and implement authority within postsecondary institutions.

3.   Reuschlein, H., and Gregory, W., *Handbook of Agency and Partnership* (West, 1979), provides a thorough explanation of the principles of agency law, with copious citations to cases; includes discussion of kinds of authority, estoppel, ratification, and tort and contract liabilities among principals, agents, and third parties.

Sec. 2.2 (Sources and Scope of Authority)

1.   Berry, C. R., and Buchwald, G. J., "Enforcement of College Trustees' Fiduciary Duties: Students and the Problem of Standing," 9 *University of San Francisco L. Rev.* 1 (1974), discusses the history, present status and effectiveness, and future direction of the law regarding trustee responsibilities and potential liability, particularly with respect to university finances; emphasis on the question of who, besides the state attorney general, can sue to enforce fiduciary responsibilities.

2.   Christie, G. C., "Legal Aspects of Changing University Investment Strategies," 58 *North Carolina L. Rev.* 189 (1980), examines legal aspects of the effort, currently undertaken by most postsecondary institutions, to increase the rate of return from existing endowments. Although focusing on North Carolina law, the article is also valuable for institutions in other states because of its discussions of the Uniform Management of Institutional Funds Act, Treasury Regulations issued under the Internal Revenue Code, and various other sources of federal guidance.

3.   Ingram, R. T., and Associates, *Handbook of College and University Trusteeship: A Practical Guide for Trustees, Chief Executives, and Other Leaders Responsible for Developing Effective Governing Boards* (Jossey-Bass, 1980), is described in the Foreword as a "comprehensive resource of authoritative information on all aspects of trusteeship" (p. ix). The book is divided into five parts: "Significance of Trusteeship," "Effective Board Management," "Effective Institutional Oversight," "Resource Development and Management," and "Performance Assessment." Each part is subdivided into chapters and topics, many of which address legal considerations. A sixth part collects resources, including model "Bylaws for Independent Colleges," a "Statement on Conflicts of Interest," and an extensive annotated list of recommended readings.

4.   King, H. M., "The Voluntary Closing of a Private College: A Decision for the Board of Trustees?," 32 *South Carolina L. Rev.* 547 (1981), reviews the legal problems inherent in any decision of a board of trustees to close a private postsecondary institution. The article focuses on questions of trust law, especially the application of the doctrine of *cy pres,* an equitable doctrine permitting the assets of a charity to be used for a purpose other than that specified in the trust instrument when the original purpose can no longer be carried out.

5. Langbein, J. H., and Posner, R., "Social Investing and the Law of Trusts," 79 *Michigan L. Rev.* 72 (1980), defines "social investing" as the exclusion of "securities of certain otherwise attractive companies from an investor's portfolio because the companies are judged to be socially irresponsible" and the inclusion of "securities of certain otherwise unattractive companies because they are judged to be behaving in a socially laudable way." Authors demonstrate that social investing invites a number of legal risks under the law of trusts. Despite such risks, authors are unwilling "to say that the law does, or should, absolutely forbid social investing by charitable trustees." Contains a section dealing with risks unique to investment of university endowments.

6. Marsh, G. H., "Governance of Non-Profit Organizations: An Appropriate Standard of Conduct for Trustees and Directors of Museums and Other Cultural Institutions," 85 *Dickinson L. Rev.* 607 (1981), compares the different standards of care applied by courts respectively to the common law trustee and the corporate director, and considers the applicability of these standards to trustees of nonprofit organizations. The article includes a section that relates the discussion to nonprofit cultural institutions. While of particular interest to institutions responsible for the management of museums or other cultural exhibits, the discussion of standards of care and the state of the case law defining a good-faith standard for trustees is of general interest for postsecondary institutions.

7. Porth, W. C., "Personal Liability of Trustees of Educational Institutions," 1 *J. of College and University Law* 84 (1973) and 2 *J. of College and University Law* 143 (1974–75), collects and discusses the small number of cases on trustee liability and suggests approaches that future courts may take to the problem; emphasis is on the *Stern* case.

8. Weiler, J. J., "Fiduciary Provisions of the Employee Retirement Income Security Act of 1974," 36 *Louisiana L. Rev.* 897 (1976), discusses ERISA (see Section 7.2.4) provisions on fiduciary responsibilities, prohibited transactions, fiduciary liability, and delegation of investment responsibility.

9. Zwingle, J. L., and Mayville, W. V., *College Trustees: A Question of Legitimacy* (ERIC Clearinghouse on Higher Education, Research Rpt. No. 10, 1974), provides a policy-oriented discussion and a review of the literature on the structure, role, and functions of trustee boards; includes discussions of authority, delegation of authority, academic tenure, and collective bargaining.

Sec. 2.3 (*Institutional Liability for Acts of Trustees, Administrators, and Other Agents*)

1. Aiken, R., Adams, J. F., and Hall, J. W., *Legal Liabilities in Higher Education: Their Scope and Management* (Association of American Colleges, 1976), printed simultaneously in 3 *J. of College and University Law* 127 (1976), provides an in-depth examination of legal and policy issues of institutional liability and the problems of protecting institutions and their personnel against liability by insurance and risk management.

2. Nahmod, S. H., *Civil Rights and Civil Liberties Litigation* (Shepard's/McGraw-Hill, 1979, with annual supplementation), is a guide to litigation brought under 42 U.S.C. sec. 1983. Primarily for legal counsel. Focuses on the positions

the courts have taken on the procedural and technical questions common to all Section 1983 litigation.

3.   Prosser, W. L., and Keeton, W. P., *Handbook on the Law of Torts,* 5th ed. (West, 1984), is a comprehensive survey of tort doctrines and concepts, with discussion of leading cases and relevant statutes; includes discussion of sovereign and charitable immunity, defamation, negligence, and the contributory negligence and assumption of risk defenses.

4.   Stevens, G., "Evaluation of Faculty Competence as a 'Privileged Occasion,'" 4 *J. of College and University Law* 281 (1979), discusses the law of defamation as it applies to institutional evaluations of professional competence.

5.   See entry no. 3 for Section 2.1.

Sec. 2.4 (Personal Liability of Trustees, Administrators, and Other Agents)

1.   Crandall, D., *The Personal Liability of Community College Officials* (ERIC Clearinghouse for Junior Colleges, Topical Paper No. 61, 1977), is a guide for administrators that "illustrates the kinds of actions taking place in the courts and provides useful background information on personal liability"; though written for community college administrators, usable by other postsecondary administrators as well.

2.   See entry no. 3 for Section 2.1.

3.   See entry no. 7 for Section 2.2.

4.   See entries no. 3 and 4 for Section 2.3.

Sec. 2.5 (Institutional Management of Liability Risks)

1.   Ad Hoc Committee on Trustee Liability Insurance, *Trustee Liability Insurance* (Association of Governing Boards, 1982), is a booklet providing guidance on the selection of liability insurance coverage for trustees of postsecondary institutions.

2.   Hollander, P., *Computers in Education: Legal Liabilities Concerning Their Use and Abuse* (College Administration Publications, 1985), is a monograph cataloging negligence, contract, criminal, and other problems in one of the newest areas of potential liability. Provides practical guidance for identifying potential liabilities and avoiding or resolving the problems.

3.   See entry no. 1 for Section 2.3.

✤ III ✤

The College
and the Faculty

The legal relationship between a college and its faculty is defined by an increasingly complex web of principles and authorities. The core of the relationship is contract law (see especially Section 3.1), but that core is encircled by expanding layers of labor relations law (Section 3.2), employment discrimination law (Section 3.3), and, in public institutions, constitutional law (see especially Sections 3.5 and 3.6) and public employment statutes and regulations.

Most of the legal principles and laws discussed in this chapter also apply generally to the institution's employment relationship with its nonfaculty employees. Administrators will thus be constrained by these legal sources with respect to administration and staff as well as faculty. The particular applications of these sources to faculty will often differ from their applications to other employees, however, because courts and administrative agencies often take account of the unique characteristics of institutional customs and practices regarding faculty and of academic freedom principles that protect faculty but not all other employers.

Sec. 3.1. The Contract of Employment

3.1.1. Scope and terms of the contract. There is considerable variety among institutions in the contracts they make with their faculties. The written contract may range from a brief notice of appointment on a standard form, with blanks to be filled in for each faculty member, to a lengthy collective bargaining agreement negotiated under state or federal labor laws. As the discussion below explains, the formal writing does not necessarily include all the terms of the contract.

A contract's meaning is ascertained primarily by reference to its express terms. Where the contract language is unambiguous, it will govern any factual situation to which it clearly applies. *Billmyre* v. *Sacred Heart Hospital of Sisters of Charity,* 331 A.2d 313 (Md. Ct. App. 1975), illustrates this principle of contract interpretation. A nurse was employed as a coordinator-instructor at the hospital's nursing school under a contract specifying that either the employer or the employee could terminate the contract "at the end of the school year by giving notice in writing to the other not later than May 1 of such school year." On May 18 the nurse received a letter terminating her employment as a teacher. The court held that the hospital had breached the contract, since the contract language unambiguously provided for teacher notification before May 1 to effectuate a termination of the contract.

Some contracts clearly state that another document has been incorporated into the terms of employment. For a postsecondary institution, such typical documents as the faculty handbook, institutional bylaws, or guidelines of the American Association of University Professors (AAUP) may be referred to in the contract. The extent to which the terms of such outside writings become part of the faculty employment contract is discussed in *Brady* v. *Board of Trustees of Nebraska State Colleges,* 242 N.W.2d 616 (Neb. 1976), where the contract of a tenured professor at Wayne State College incorporated "the college bylaws, policies, and practices relating to academic tenure and faculty dismissal procedures." When the institution dismissed the professor using procedures that violated a section of the bylaws, the court held that the termination was ineffective: "There can be no serious question but that the bylaws of the governing body with respect to termination and conditions of the employment became a part of the employment contract between the college and [the professor]. At the time of the offer and acceptance of initial appointment . . . [the professor] was advised in writing that the offer and acceptance . . . constituted a contract honoring the policies and practices set forth in the faculty handbook, which was furnished to him at that time."

Even where such outside documents are not specifically referred to in the contract language, a court, as in *Greene* v. *Howard University,* 412 F.2d 1128 (D.C. Cir. 1969), may look to outside writings to determine the customs and usual practices of the institution and interpret the contract in light of such custom and usage (see Section 1.3.8). The plaintiffs in *Greene* were five nontenured professors who had been fired after a university investigation purported to find that they had been involved in disorders on campus. When the university terminated the professors as of the close of the academic year, the professors asserted that the university had breached a contractual obligation to give appropriate advance notice of nonrenewal or to provide a hearing prior to nonrenewal. The court concluded: "The contractual relationship existing here, when viewed against the regulations provided for, and the practices customarily followed in, their administration, required the university in the special circumstances here involved to afford the teachers an opportunity to be heard."

The court derived the institution's customary practices from the faculty handbook, buttressed by testimony in court, even though the handbook was not specifically incorporated by reference and even though it stated that the university did not have a contractual obligation to follow the notice of nonreappointment procedures. The professors were found to be relying "not only on personal assurances from university officials and on their recognition of the common practice of the university, but also on the written statements of university policy contained in the faculty handbook under whose terms they were employed.'' The court reasoned:

> Contracts are written, and are to be read, by reference to the norms of conduct and expectations founded upon them. This is especially true of contracts in and among a community of scholars, which is what a university is. The readings of the marketplace are not invariably apt in this noncommercial context. . . .
>
> The employment contracts of [the professors] here comprehend as essential parts of themselves the hiring policies and practices of the university as embodied in its employment regulations and customs [412 F.2d at 1135].

Although academic custom and usage can fill in gaps in the employment contract, it cannot be used to contradict the contract's express terms. In *Lewis* v. *Salem Academy and College*, 208 S.E.2d 404 (N.C. 1974), a professor had been employed from 1950 to 1973 under a series of successive one-year contracts. The college had renewed the contract the last two years, even though the professor had reached age sixty-five, but did not renew the contract for the 1973–74 academic year. The professor argued that he had a right to continue teaching until seventy because that was a usual and customary practice of the college and an implied benefit used to attract and retain faculty. The college's faculty guide, however, which was incorporated into all faculty contracts, had an explicit retirement policy providing for continued service beyond sixty-five to age seventy on a year-to-year basis at the discretion of the board of trustees. The court held that custom and usage could not modify this clear contract provision:

> Here . . . plaintiff had his own individual written contracts of employment, and the faculty guide, which was expressly incorporated into each of these contracts, specifically covered in clear and unambiguous language the conditions under which his employment after age 65 might be continued. ''A custom or usage may be proved in explanation and qualification of the terms of a contract which otherwise would be ambiguous, or to show that the words in which the contract is expressed are used in a particular sense different from that which they usually impart, and, in some cases, to annex incidents to the contract in matters upon which it is silent; but evidence of a usage or custom is never admitted to make a new contract or to add a new element to one previously made'' (55 Am. Jur., Usages and Customs sec. 31, 292) [208 S.E.2d at 408].

Administrators should continually be sensitive to the question of what institutional documents or practices are, or should be, part of the faculty contract. Where ambiguity exists, administrators should determine whether there is some good policy reason for maintaining the ambiguity. If not, the contracts should be clarified.

3.1.2. Amendment of the contract. The terms of the original employment contract need not remain static through the entire life of the contract. Courts have accepted the proposition that employment contracts may be amended. In *Rehor* v. *Case Western Reserve University*, 331 N.E.2d 416 (Ohio 1975), the court found amendments to be valid either where the right to amend was reserved in the original contract or where there was mutual consent of the parties to amend and adequate consideration was given in return for the changed terms. The plaintiff in *Rehor* was a tenured professor employed under contract at Western Reserve University from 1942 to 1967. Throughout this period the retirement age was always seventy. After Case Institute of Technology joined with Western Reserve to form Case Western Reserve University, Case Western, which took over the faculty contracts, adopted a resolution requiring faculty members over sixty-eight to petition to be reappointed. The university bylaws provided that "the board of trustees shall from time to time adopt such rules and regulations governing the appointment and tenure of the members of the faculty as the board of trustees deems necessary." The court held that this bylaw language "includes a reservation of the right to change the retirement age of the faculty" and thus defeats the plaintiff's claim that the university was in breach of contract. Since the retirement policy is part of tenure, "the reserved right to change rules of tenure includes the right to change the retirement policy." The court also approved of the university's assertion that "an employment contract between a university and a tenured faculty member may be amended by the parties in writing when supported by adequate consideration." These considerations were satisfied in *Rehor* by the professor's execution of reappointment forms and acceptance of an increased salary after the new retirement policy was put into effect. (For a criticism of the case, see M. Finkin, "Contract, Tenure, and Retirement: A Comment on *Rehor* v. *Case Western Reserve University*," 4 *Human Rights* 343 (1975).)

Occasionally contracts may also be amended unilaterally by subsequent state legislation. But the state's power to legislatively modify its own contracts or to regulate contracts between private parties is circumscribed by Article I, Section 10(1), of the United States Constitution, known as the contract clause: "No state shall . . . pass any . . . law impairing the obligation of contracts." In *Indiana ex rel. Anderson* v. *Brand*, 303 U.S. 95 (1938) (discussed in Section 3.1.4), for instance, the U.S. Supreme Court held that an Indiana law which had the effect of canceling the tenure rights of certain public school teachers was an unconstitutional impairment of their employment contracts. Under this and subsequent contract clause precedents, a state may not impair either its own or private contracts unless such impairment is both "reasonable and necessary to serve an important public purpose," with "necessary" meaning that the impairment is essential and no viable alternative for serving the state's purpose exists (*United States Trust Company of New York* v. *New Jersey*, 431 U.S. 1 (1977)).

3.1.3. Waiver of contract rights. Once a contract has been formed, the parties may sometimes waive their contract rights, either intentionally by a written agreement or unintentionally by their actions. *Chung* v. *Park*, 514 F.2d 382 (3d Cir. 1975), concerned a professor who after teaching at Mansfield State College for five years was notified that his contract would not be renewed. Through his counsel, the professor negotiated with the state attorney general and agreed to submit the issue of the termination's validity to an arbitration panel. When the panel upheld the termination, the professor brought suit, alleging that the college did not follow the termination procedures set out in the tenure regulations and was therefore in breach of contract. The court, after pointing out that under the state law contract rights may be waived by subsequent agreement between the parties, upheld the district court's finding "that the parties had reached such a subsequent agreement when, after extensive negotiations, they specifically stipulated to the hearing procedures actually employed."

Public policy considerations may, however, preclude the waiver of certain contract terms. In *McLachlan* v. *Tacoma Community College District No. 22*, 541 P.2d

1010 (Wash. 1975), the court addressed this issue but found the rights in question to be properly waivable. The two plaintiffs were employed by the college district under contracts that specifically stated, ''The employee waives all rights normally provided by the tenure laws of the state of Washington.'' The plaintiffs, who were aware that they were employed to replace people on one-year sabbaticals, contended that the contracts should not be enforced for reasons of public policy. While avoiding the broad issue of whether a blanket waiver of tenure rights contravenes public policy, the court said, ''We envision no serious public policy considerations which would prohibit a teacher from waiving the statutory nonrenewal notice provisions in advance of the notice date, provided he knows the purpose of his employment is to replace the regular occupant of that position who is on a one-year sabbatical leave.''

    3.1.4. Statutory rights versus contract rights in public institutions. A public institution's legal relationship with faculty members may be defined by statute and administrative regulation as well as by written employment contract. Tenure rights, for instance, may be created by a state tenure statute rather than by the terms of the employment contract; or pay scales may be established by board of regents or Civil Service Commission rules rather than by the employment contract. The distinction between statutory rights and contract rights can be critical. A right created by statute or by administrative rule can be revoked or modified by a subsequent statute or rule, with the result that the public institution has no further obligation to recognize that right. A contract right, however, usually cannot be revoked or modified by subsequent statute or rule unless the parties have made provision for such changes in the contract itself.

    The case of *Busbee* v. *Georgia Conference, AAUP,* 221 S.E.2d 437 (Ga. 1975), arose after the Georgia legislature had passed an appropriations act on the basis of which faculty members in the University System of Georgia had received contracts with salary increases. The legislature subsequently reduced the appropriations, and the regents revoked the salary increases. When the faculty members sued to enforce their contracts, the regents argued that (1) the various state budgeting and fiscal laws were part of the faculty contract, and the pattern of such laws, taken together, permitted the salary revocation; and (2) even if the revocation breached the faculty contracts, the state had the power to so impair contracts if it acted out of economic necessity. The court found that (1) although the law existing when the contract is signed may be made part of the contract, the state budgetary and fiscal laws could not be read to permit the salary revocation; and (2) the state had no power to impair the faculty contracts in this case because no economic necessity for such action existed. The court therefore held that the increased salary contracts were valid and binding on the regents and that failure to pay faculty members the increased salary would be an illegal breach of contract.

    Even if particular rights emanate from statute or regulation, they may become embodied in contracts and thus be enforceable as contract rights. The contract may provide that certain statutory rights become part of the contract. Or the statute or regulation may itself be so written or interpreted that the rights it creates become enforceable as contract rights. This latter approach has twice been dealt with by the U.S. Supreme Court in cases concerning statutory tenure laws. *Phelps* v. *Board of Education of West New York,* 300 U.S. 319 (1937), concerned a New Jersey Act of 1909, which provided that teachers employed by local school boards could only be dismissed or subject to reduced salary for cause. By an Act of 1933, the state enabled the school boards to fix and determine salaries. When one board invoked this authority to reduce salaries without cause, teachers claimed that this action impaired their contracts in violation of the Constitution's contract clause (see Section 3.1.2). The Court held that there was no constitutional impairment, since the Act of 1909 did not create a contract between the state and the teachers. The Court agreed with the New Jersey court that the statute established "a legislative status for teachers" but failed to establish "a contractual one that the legislature may not modify." Thus, "although the Act of 1909 prohibited the board, a creature of the state, from reducing the teacher's salary or discharging him without cause, . . . this was but a regulation of the conduct of the board and not a continuing contract of indefinite duration with the individual teacher."

A year after *Phelps,* the Supreme Court came to a contrary conclusion in a similar impairment case. *Indiana ex rel. Anderson* v. *Brand,* 303 U.S. 95 (1938), dealt with Indiana's Teachers Tenure Act, adopted in 1927. The Act provided that, once a teacher had tenure, his contract "shall be deemed to be in effect for an indefinite period." Sometime after the Act was amended in 1933 to omit township school corporations, the job of the plaintiff, a tenured teacher, was terminated. The Court found that the Act of 1927 created a contract with the teacher because the title of the Act was "couched in terms of contract," the "tenor of the Act indicates that the word 'contract' was not used inadvertently or in other than its usual legal meaning," and the state courts had previously viewed the Act of 1927 as creating a contract. The Court then held that the 1933 amendment unconstitutionally impaired the contracts created by the Act of 1927.

Given the fundamental distinction between contract and statutory rights, and the sometimes subtle relationships between them, administrators of public institutions should pay particular attention to the source of faculty members' legal rights and should consult counsel whenever attempting to define or change a faculty member's legal status.

3.1.5. Status of part-time faculty members. The status of part-time faculty members in postsecondary institutions is receiving increasing consideration within and outside the postsecondary community (see, for example, D. Leslie, S. Kellams, and G. M. Gunne, *Part-Time Faculty in American Higher Education* (Praeger, 1982); T. A. Emmet and others, *Part-Time Faculty* (Current Issues in Higher Education, No. 4, American Association for Higher Education, 1981)). The number and percentage of part-time faculty members in the academic work force increased substantially during the 1970s. While data vary from year to year, as well as by discipline and type of institution, a rough guideline would be that approximately one third of the total number of postsecondary faculty are part-timers, with the percentage being highest in community colleges. Legal issues concerning this large and important faculty group are likely to demand special attention.

The questions being raised about part-time faculty involve such matters as pay scales, eligibility for fringe benefits (life insurance, health insurance, sick leave, sabbaticals, retirement contributions), access to tenure, rights upon dismissal or nonrenewal, and status for collective bargaining purposes. Each of these questions may be affected by two more general questions: (1) How is the distinction between a part-time and a full-time faculty member defined? (2) Are distinctions made between (or among) categories of part-time faculty members? The initial and primary source for answering these questions is the faculty contract (see Section 3.1.1). State and federal statutes and administrative rulings on such matters as defining bargaining units for collective bargaining (see *University of San Francisco and University of San Francisco Faculty Association,* 225 NLRB 1221 (1982), approving part-time faculty unit, and see also Section 3.2.4), retirement plans, civil service classifications, faculty tenure, wage-and-hour requirements, and unemployment compensation may also be important and may substantially affect what can and cannot be provided for in faculty contracts.

The leading recent controversy has concerned the application of state statutes to part-time faculty in public institutions. Most of the reported court decisions are from California, which has a complex statutory scheme with special provisions applicable to community colleges. This statutory scheme provides the framework for part-time faculty contracts with public institutions. The California experience merits study not only to understand that state's law but also to develop insights on approaches to take and problems to avoid in other states, where the law is less developed.

Generally, California has three classes of community college faculty members: permanent (also known as regular or tenured), probationary (also known as contract), and temporary. In *Balen* v. *Peralta Junior College District,* 11 Cal. 3d 821, 523 P.2d 629 (1974), the California Supreme Court explained the statutory classifications of community college teachers:

> The essence of the statutory classification system is that continuity of service restricts the power to terminate employment which the institution's governing body would normally possess. Thus, the legislature has prevented the arbitrary dismissal of employees with positions of a settled and continuing nature—that is, permanent and probationary teachers—by requiring notice and hearing before termination. . . . Substitute and temporary teachers, on the other hand, fill the short-range needs of a school district, and may be summarily released absent an infringement of constitutional or contractual rights. . . . Because the substitute and temporary classifications are not guaranteed procedural due process by statute, they are narrowly defined by the legislature and should be strictly interpreted [523 P.2d at 631–32; citations and footnotes omitted].

The most extensively litigated section of California's statutes, Cal. Educ. Code sec. 13337.5, has been recodified as Cal. Educ. Code sec. 87482 (West, 1978):

> Notwithstanding the provisions of Section 13337, the governing board of a school district maintaining a community college may employ as a teacher in grade 13 or grade 14, for a complete school year but not less than a complete semester or quarter during a school year, any person holding appropriate certification documents and may classify such person as a temporary employee. The employment of such persons shall be based upon the need for additional certificated employees for grades 13 and 14 during a particular semester or quarter because of the higher enrollment of students in those grades during that semester or quarter as compared to the other semester or quarter in the academic year, or because a certificated employee has been granted leave for a semester, quarter, or year or is experiencing long-term illness, and shall be limited, in number of persons so employed, to that need, as determined by the governing board.

Such employment may be pursuant to contract fixing a salary for the entire semester or quarter.

No person shall be so employed by any one district for more than two semesters or quarters within any period of three consecutive years.

Notwithstanding any other provision to the contrary, any person who is employed to teach adult or community college classes for not more than 60 percent of the hours per week considered a full-time assignment for permanent employees having comparable duties shall be classified as a temporary employee and shall not become a probationary employee under the provisions of Section 13446.

The first two paragraphs define temporary appointees who replace permanent teachers on leave or are employed in response to increased student enrollment. The third paragraph limits the duration of temporary employment under the first two paragraphs to no more than two semesters or quarters within a consecutive three-year period. Faculty members with a work load less than 60 percent of the full-time assignment for permanent faculty are designated as temporary by the fourth paragraph of Section 13337.5; temporary employees as defined by this paragraph can never achieve permanent status. The relationship of this fourth paragraph to the other paragraphs is the key issue confronted in the court decisions.

The *Balen* case, above, concerned a part-time hourly instructor whose employment was terminated without notice or hearing after four and a half years of service. Since Balen taught less than 40 percent of the hours of a full-time load, the college argued he was a temporary employee under the fourth paragraph of Section 13337.5. But that paragraph had not been enacted when Balen was initially hired, and the court refused to apply it retroactively. Since the plaintiff had attained probationary status under other provisions of the California Education Code, and Section 13337.5 could not be used to divest him of that status, he could be dismissed only for cause after notice and opportunity for a hearing.

In *California Teachers Association* v. *Santa Monica Community College District,* 79 Cal. App. 3d 836, 144 Cal. Rptr. 620 (1978), the association sought reclassification and back pay for teachers whom the district had classified as temporary. The association argued that the paragraphs of Section 13337.5 are not disjunctive and that the fourth paragraph (the 60 percent rule) is qualified by the third paragraph and thus limited in effect. The court disagreed, concluding that the fourth paragraph stands as independent authority for long-term classification of employees as temporary. Thus, under this case, community colleges could continue hiring their faculty members as temporary employees paid at lower rates of pay and without procedural rights upon dismissal.

The analysis of the *California Teachers Association* opinion was adopted and expanded by the Supreme Court of California in *Peralta Federation of Teachers (AFL-CIO)* v. *Peralta Community College,* 24 Cal. 3d 364, 595 P.2d 113 (1979). The plaintiffs, all employed for less than 60 percent of a full-time load, were separated into two categories—those hired before and those hired after November 8, 1967, the effective date of Section 13337.5. Both groups sought tenure, higher compensation, and back pay. Those hired after November 8 asserted that their status was unaffected by the fourth paragraph of Section 13337.5 because their employment did not meet the conditions of the first three paragraphs. The court disagreed, thus confirming the independent status of the fourth paragraph as construed in *California Teachers*. These plaintiffs therefore obtained no relief bcause they were within the fourth paragraph's definition of temporary. Those hired before November 8, 1967, however, were not subject to the fourth paragraph because, under *Balen* (above), Section 13337.5 did not apply retroactively. Construing other statutory provisions defining permanent status, the court held that faculty members in this group were permanent (tenured) employees and awarded them that status along with back pay.

The *Peralta* decision was applied and explained by a lower court in *Warner* v. *North Orange County Community College District,* 99 Cal. App. 3d 617, 161 Cal. Rptr. 1 (Ct. App. 4th Dist. 1979). A subsequent California Supreme Court opinion in *California Teachers Association* v. *San Diego Community College District,* 28 Cal. 3d 692, 621 P.2d 856 (1981), reaffirmed *Peralta* and analyzed the issue of computing pro rata pay for part-time faculty under the California statutes.

To respond effectively to issues like those in California, and the many other legal and policy issues that are arising, administrators should understand the differences in legal status of part-time and full-time faculty members at their institutions. In consultation with counsel, they should make sure that the existing differences in status and any future changes are adequately expressed in faculty contracts and institutional rules and regulations. Administrators should also consider the extent and clarity of their institution's legal authority to maintain the existing differences if they are challenged or to change the legal status of part-timers if changes are advisable to effectuate new educational policy.

Sec. 3.2. Collective Bargaining

Collective bargaining presents administrators with a complex mixture of the familiar and the foreign. Many faculty demands, such as for lighter teaching loads, smaller class sizes, and larger salaries, may be familiar on many campuses; but other demands, such as for standardized pay scales rather than individualized "merit" salary determinations, may present new situations. If a shift in emphasis from "academic" to "economic" issues occurs, it may prompt a reorganization of institutional budgetary priorities and governance procedures. Legal, policy, and political issues may arise concerning the extent to which collective bargaining and the bargained agreement ("the contract"; see Section 3.1 above) preempt or circumscribe not merely traditional administrative elbow room but also the customary forms of faculty and student self-government. Reconciliation of traditional collective bargaining features such as seniority with academic standbys such as tenure similarly remains an issue. And potential tension for academia clearly exists in the participation in campus affairs of the "outsiders" involved in bargaining agent certification elections, negotiation of agreements, fact finding, mediation, conciliation, arbitration, and ultimate resolution of internal disputes through state or federal administrative agencies and courts.

The mix of factors involved, the importance of the policy questions, and the complexity of the law make collective bargaining a most difficult area for administrators. Heavy involvement of legal counsel is clearly called for. Use of professional negotiators, or of administrators experienced in the art of negotiation, is also usually appropriate—particularly when the faculty has such professional expertise on its side of the bargaining table.[1]

   3.2.1. The public-private dichotomy in collective bargaining. Theoretically, the legal aspects of collective bargaining divide into two distinct categories: public and private. However, these categories are not necessarily defined in the same way as they are for constitutional state action purposes (see Section 1.4.2). In relation to collective bargaining, "public" and "private" are defined by the collective bargaining legislation and interpretive precedents. Privately chartered institutions (see Section 6.3) are likely to be considered private for collective bargaining purposes even if they receive substantial government support. In *University of Vermont and State Agricultural College,* 223 NLRB 423 (1976), for instance, the National Labor Relations Board (NLRB) asserted jurisdiction over an institution receiving 25 percent of its support directly from the state, because the institution was chartered as private and nonprofit and was not a political subdivision of the state.

   Private-sector bargaining is governed by the National Labor Relations Act of 1935 (the Wagner Act) as amended by the Labor-Management Relations Act of 1947 (the Taft-Hartley Act), 29 U.S.C. sec. 141 *et seq.* (see Section 7.2.2). The NLRB first asserted jurisdiction over private nonprofit postsecondary institutions in *Cornell University,* 183 NLRB 329 (1970), and made clear that its jurisdiction extended to faculty members in *C. W. Post Center of Long Island University,* 189 NLRB 904 (1971). The board's jurisdiction was judicially confirmed in *NLRB* v. *Wentworth Institute,* 515 F.2d 550 (1st Cir. 1975), where the court enforced an NLRB order finding that Wentworth had engaged in an unfair labor practice in refusing to bargain with the certified faculty bargaining representative. Today all private postsecondary institutions, at least all those large enough to have a significant effect on interstate commerce, are included within the federal sphere. Disputes about collective bargaining in private institutions are thus subject to the limited body of statutory authority and the vast body of administrative and judicial precedent regarding the Taft-Hartley Act.

   Legal authority and precedent provide few easy answers, however, for collective bargaining issues in postsecondary education. The uniqueness of academic institutions, procedures, and customs poses new problems not previously encountered in the NLRB's administration of the national labor law in other employment contexts. There are, moreover, many ambiguities and unsettled areas in the national labor law even in nonacademic contexts. They derive in part from the intentionally broad language of the federal legislation and in part from the NLRB's historic insistence on proceeding case by case rather than under a policy of systematic rule making (see K. Kahn, "The NLRB and Higher Education: The Failure of Policy Making Through Adjudication," 21 *UCLA L. Rev.* 63 (1973); and A. P. Menard and N. DiGiovanni, Jr., "NLRB Jurisdiction over Colleges and Universities: a Plea for Rulemaking," 16 *William and Mary L. Rev.* 599 (1975)). Administrators will find working with the NLRB's body of piecemeal precedential authority to be a very

---

[1]The major issues concerning postsecondary education bargaining have been frequently discussed in articles, books, and speeches. This section will cite the literature extensively, in order to provide a broad range of sources for pursuing the many complexities in this area. Other sources are included in the Selected Annotated Bibliography at the end of this chapter.

different experience from working with the detailed regulations of other agencies, such as the U.S. Department of Education.

Public postsecondary education, on the other hand, is exempt from NLRB jurisdiction (see 29 U.S.C. sec. 152(2)) and subject only to state authority. Approximately half of the states have some type of legislation permitting at least some form of collective bargaining in public postsecondary education (see Academic Collective Bargaining Information Service, *Analysis of Legislation in Twenty-Four States Enabling Faculty Collective Bargaining in Postsecondary Education* (Special Report No. 17, Update May 1976)). In 1983 Illinois and Ohio became the two most recent states to authorize collective bargaining for faculty members (Ohio Rev. Code Ann. sec. 4117.01 *et seq.;* Ill. Ann. Stat. ch. 48, sec. 1701 *et seq.*). Such legislation is often limited in coverage or in the extent to which it authorizes or mandates the full panoply of collective bargaining rights and services. A statute may grant employees rights as narrow as the right to "meet and confer" with administration representatives. In *Lipow* v. *Regents of University of California,* 54 Cal. App. 3d 215, 126 Cal. Rptr. 515 (1976), for instance, the defendant had only the obligation to "meet and confer" with the organization representing the University of California faculty regarding revisions in the defendant's administrative manual—an obligation which the court held was met. The permissibility of strikes is also a major variable among state statutes.

Frequently, state legislation is designed to cover public employees generally and makes little, if any, special provision for the unique circumstances of postsecondary education. (For analyses of what a state statute should contain, see Comment, "The Legislation Necessary to Effectively Govern Collective Bargaining in Public Higher Education," 1971 *Wisconsin L. Rev.* 275; and R. Sensenbrenner, "Collective Bargaining Legislation for Public Higher Education from the Management Side of the Table," 4 *J. of College and University Law* 27 (1977)). State labor law may be as unsettled as the federal labor law, providing few easy answers for postsecondary education, and may also have a smaller body of administrative and judicial precedents. State agencies and courts often fill in the gaps by relying on federal labor law precedents. State legislatures may also conceivably become directly involved (see J. Henkel and N. Wood, "Legislative Power to Veto Collective Bargaining Agreements by Faculty Unions: An Overlooked Reality?" 11 *J. of Law and Education* 79 (1982)).

Even where state collective bargaining legislation does not cover public postsecondary institutions, some "extralegal" bargaining may still take place. A public institution's faculty members, like other public employees, have a constitutional right, under First Amendment freedom of speech and association, "to organize collectively and select representatives to engage in collective bargaining" (*University of New Hampshire Chapter AAUP* v. *Haselton,* 397 F. Supp. 107 (D.N.H. 1975)). But faculty members do not have a constitutional right to require the public institution "to respond to . . . [faculty] demands or to enter into a contract with them." The right to require the employer to bargain in good faith must be created by statute. Even if the public institution desires to bargain with faculty representatives, it may not have the authority to do so under state law. The employment powers of public institutions may be vested by law in the sole discretion of institutional governing boards; sharing such powers with collective bargaining representatives or arbitrators appointed under collective bargaining agreements may therefore be construed as an improper delegation of authority. In *Board of Trustees of Junior College District No. 508* v. *Cook County College Teachers Union*, 62 Ill. 2d 470, 343 N.E.2d 473 (1976), the court held that the board's powers to decide which faculty members to employ and promote were "nondelegable" and thus not subject to binding arbitration under the collective bargaining agreement. (See generally G. M. Alley and V. J. Facciolo, "Concerted Public Employee Activity in the Absence of State Authorization," 2 *J. of Law and Education* 401 (1973); E. Green, "Concerted Public Employer Collective Bargaining in the Absence of Explicit Legislative Authorization," 2 *J. of Law and Education* 419 (1973).)

An additional distinction may have been built into the public-private dichotomy by the U.S. Supreme Court's decision in *NLRB* v. *Catholic Bishop of Chicago*, 440 U.S. 490 (1979). If the principles of this elementary/secondary education case are extended to higher education, it will be necessary to subdivide the private side of the dichotomy into "private nonreligious" and "private religious" institutions.

The *Catholic Bishop* case arose after teachers at two groups of Catholic high schools voted for union representation in NLRB-sponsored elections. Although the NLRB certified the unions as the teachers' collective bargaining representatives, the schools refused to negotiate and the unions filed unfair labor practice charges against them. In response, the schools claimed that the First Amendment precluded the NLRB from exercising jurisdiction over them. After the board upheld its authority to order the elections and ordered the schools to bargain with the unions, the U.S. Court of Appeals for the Seventh Circuit denied enforcement of the NLRB's order. By exercising jurisdiction over "church-operated" schools, the court said, the board was interfering with the freedom of church officials to operate their schools in accord with their religious tenets, thus violating both the free exercise clause and the establishment clause of the First Amendment (see Section 1.5).

The U.S. Supreme Court affirmed the appellate court's decision, by a 5-to-4 vote, but it did so on somewhat different grounds. Rather than addressing the First Amendment issue directly, as did the appeals court, the Supreme Court focused on a question of statutory interpretation: whether Congress intended that the Labor-Management Relations Act would give the board jurisdiction over church-operated schools. In deciding that issue, the Court considered the constitutional problem indirectly by positing that an Act of Congress should be construed, whenever possible, in such a way that serious constitutional issues are avoided. Emphasizing the key role played by teachers in religious schools, the Court found that grave First Amendment questions would result if the Act were construed to allow the board jurisdiction over such teachers:

> It is already clear that the board's action will go beyond resolving factual issues. The Court of Appeals opinion refers to charges of unfair labor practices filed against religious schools. The court observed that in those cases the schools had responded that their challenged actions were mandated by their religious creeds. The resolution of such charges by the board, in many instances, will necessarily involve inquiry into the good faith of the position asserted by the clergy-administrators and its relationship to the school's religious mission. It is not only the conclusions that may be reached by the board which may impinge on rights guaranteed by

the religion clauses, but the very process of inquiry leading to findings and conclusions.

The board's exercise of jurisdiction will have at least one other impact on church-operated schools. The board will be called upon to decide what are "terms and conditions of employment" and therefore mandatory subjects of bargaining. . . .

Inevitably the board's inquiry will implicate sensitive issues that open the door to conflicts between clergy-administrators and the board, or conflicts with negotiators for unions. . . .

The church-teacher relationship in a church-operated school differs from the employment relationship in a public or other nonreligious school. We see no escape from conflicts flowing from the board's exercise of jurisdiction over teachers in church-operated schools and the consequent serious First Amendment questions that would follow. We therefore turn to an examination of the National Labor Relations Act [now the Labor-Management Relations Act] to decide whether it must be read to confer [such] jurisdiction [440 U.S. at 502–04].

A survey of the Act's legislative history convinced the Court that Congress had not manifested any "affirmative intention" that teachers in church-operated schools be covered by the Act. Since "Congress did not contemplate that the board would require church-operated schools to grant recognition to unions," and since such a construction of the Act would require the Court "to resolve difficult and sensitive questions" under the First Amendment, the Court held that the board's jurisdiction does not extend to teachers in church-operated schools.

The impact of the *Catholic Bishop* case on postsecondary education is debatable. Since the schools in the case were elementary and secondary schools, and the U.S. Supreme Court relied only on First Amendment precedents dealing with elementary and secondary schools, the case does not directly apply to postsecondary institutions. Moreover, the First Amendment decisions since *Lemon* and *Tilton* in 1971 (see Section 1.5) indicate that greater First Amendment dangers arise from involvement with elementary and secondary education than with higher education; the courts may therefore be less hesitant to permit NLRB jurisdiction over postsecondary church-operated schools. However, the Supreme Court in its opinion gives short shrift to the possible distinction between elementary/secondary and higher education. It asserts generally that, whenever extension of NLRB jurisdiction over teachers in "church-operated schools" would raise "serious constitutional questions," a court can uphold the NLRB only if it finds a "clear expression of Congress's intent" to authorize jurisdiction. Thus, the extension of *Catholic Bishop* to higher education apparently hinges on two questions: (1) whether NLRB jurisdiction would raise "serious constitutional questions" in light of the First Amendment case law distinguishing between elementary/secondary and higher education; and (2) whether the legislative history of the NLRA and its amendments can be construed differently for higher education, so as to reveal a clearly expressed congressional intent to include higher education teachers within the board's jurisdiction. Only if a court holds that (1) "serious constitutional questions" *would* be raised and (2) Congress did *not* clearly express an intention to include higher education teachers will *Catholic Bishop* be extended to church-operated colleges and universities.

The NLRB has not been inclined to consider an extension of *Catholic Bishop* to higher education. In *College of Notre Dame* (Calif.), 245 NLRB 386 (1979), and *Barber-Scotia College*, 245 NLRB 906 (1979), the board curtly rejected the colleges' arguments for an extension. In *Lewis University*, 265 NLRB 1239 (1982), the board reiterated its position: "as we have stated before, *Catholic Bishop* applies only to parochial elementary and secondary schools." The issue, therefore, clearly rests with the courts.

If the courts were to extend *Catholic Bishop* to higher education, questions would still remain concerning what institutions are "church operated" and thus within the opinion's coverage. In each of the three NLRB rulings above, the board asserted an alternative reason for holding that *Catholic Bishop* did not apply: because the college "is not church operated as contemplated by *Catholic Bishop*." In *Lewis University*, for instance, the board asserted jurisdiction over a historically church-related institution because operating authority had been transferred to a private board of trustees and the local diocese "does not exercise administrative or other secular control" over, and does not perform any services for, the institution. The courts, however, may have a different view of this issue. In *NLRB v. Bishop Ford Central Catholic High School*, 623 F.2d 818 (2d Cir. 1980), a U.S. Court of Appeals denied enforcement of an NLRB order asserting jurisdiction over lay teachers in a Catholic school severed from ownership and control of the local diocese and operated instead by a predominantly lay board of trustees. According to the appellate court, the critical question in determining whether a school is "church operated" under *Catholic Bishop* is not whether a church holds legal title or controls management; it is whether the school has a "religious mission" that could give rise to "entanglement" problems under the establishment clause. Since the school's history and "present religious characteristics" indicated that its religious mission continued after separation from the diocese, the court held the school to be exempt from NLRB jurisdiction.

3.2.2. Organization, recognition, and certification. Once a faculty or a substantial portion of it decides that it wants to bargain collectively with the institution, its representatives can ask the administration to recognize them for collective bargaining purposes. A private institution has two choices at this point. It can voluntarily recognize the faculty representatives and commence negotiations, or it can withhold recognition and insist that the faculty representatives seeking recognition petition the NLRB for a certification election (see *Linden Lumber Division v. NLRB*, 419 U.S. 817 (1974)). Public institutions that have authority to bargain under state law usually have the same two choices, although elections and certification would be handled by the state labor board.

Administrators should consider two related legal implications of choosing the first alternative. First, it is a violation of the Taft-Hartley Act (and most state acts) for an employer to voluntarily recognize a minority union—that is, a union supported by less than 50 percent of the faculty in the bargaining unit (see 29 U.S.C. sec. 158(a)(1) and (2); and *International Ladies Garment Workers Union v. NLRB*, 366 U.S. 731 (1961)). Second, it is also a violation of Taft-Hartley (and most state acts) to recognize any union (even one with apparent majority support) when a rival union makes a "substantial claim of support," which the NLRB interprets to mean a claim "not . . . clearly unsupportable and lacking in substance" (*American Can Co.*, 218 NLRB 102, 103 (1975)). Thus, unless a union seeking recognition can prove the clear support of the majority of the members of the proposed bargaining unit (usually through "authentication cards" or a secret ballot poll), and the administration has no reason to believe that a rival union with a "substantial claim of support" is also seeking recognition, it is usually not wise to recognize any union without a certification election.

In the interim between the beginning of organizational activity and the actual certification of a union, the institution is in a delicate position. In the private sector, the Taft-Hartley Act prohibits the employer from doing anything that would appear to favor any of the contenders for recognition (29 U.S.C. sec. 158(a)(2)) or that would "interfere with, restrain, or coerce employees in the exercise of their rights" to self-organize, form or join a union, or bargain collectively (29 U.S.C. sec. 158(a)(1)). This would include promises of benefits, threats of reprisals, coercive interrogation, or surveillance. Furthermore, the institution may not take any action that could be construed as a discrimination against union organizers or supporters because of their exercise of rights under the Act (29 U.S.C. sec. 158(a)(3)). In the public sector, state laws generally contain comparable prohibitions on certain kinds of employer activities.

Another crucial aspect of the organizational phase is the definition of the "bargaining unit"—that is, the portion of the institution's employees that will be represented by the particular bargaining agent seeking certification. Again, most state laws parallel the federal law. Generally, the NLRB or its state equivalent has considerable discretion to determine the appropriate unit (see 29 U.S.C. sec. 159(b)). The traditional rule has been that there must be a basic "community of interest" among the individuals included in the unit, so that the union will represent the interests of everyone in the unit when it negotiates with the employer. Moreover, under the Taft-Hartley Act (see 29 U.S.C. sec. 152(3) and (11)) and most state laws, supervisory personnel are excluded from any bargaining unit. Individual determinations must be made, in light of the applicable statutory definition, of whether particular personnel are excluded from the unit as supervisors.

Generally, several factors have traditionally been used to determine a "community of interest," including the history of past bargaining (if any), the extent of organization, the skills and duties of the employees, and common supervision. But these factors are difficult to apply in postsecondary education's complex world of collegially shared decision making. To define the proposed unit as "all faculty members" does not resolve the issue. For example, does the unit include all faculty of the institution, or only the faculty of a particular school, such as the law school? Part-time as well as full-time faculty members? Researchers and librarians as well as teachers? Graduate teaching assistants? Chairpersons of small departments whose administrative duties are incidental to their primary teaching and research functions? The problems are compounded in multicampus institutions, especially if the programs offered by the individual campuses vary significantly from one another. (See, for example, R. Head and D. Leslie, "Bargaining Unit Status of Part-Time Faculty," 8 *J. of Law and Education* 361 (1979); E. Moore, "The Determination of Bargaining Units for College Faculties," 37 *University of Pittsburgh L. Rev.* 43 (1975); M. W. Finkin, "The NLRB in Higher Education," 5 *University of Toledo L. Rev.* 608, 612–45 (1974); Comment, "The Bargaining Unit Status of Academic Department Chairmen," 40 *University of Chicago L. Rev.* 442 (1973).)

Once the bargaining unit is defined and the union recognized or certified, the union becomes the exclusive bargaining agent of all employees in the unit, whether or not they become union members and whether or not they are willing to be represented (see *J. I. Case Co.* v. *NLRB*, 321 U.S. 332 (1944)). Courts have generally upheld the constitutionality of such exclusive representation systems. The leading case for higher education, *Minnesota State Board for Community Colleges* v. *Knight*, 104 S. Ct. 1058 (1984), examines (but is not particularly sensitive to) the special concerns that exclusive systems may create for higher education governance.

The *Knight* case upheld a Minnesota law that requires public employers to "meet and negotiate" with exclusive bargaining representatives of public employees over mandatory subjects of bargaining and, when the employees are professional, to also "meet and confer" with their exclusive representatives regarding nonmandatory subjects. (Subjects of bargaining are discussed in Section 3.2.4.) Pursuant to this law, the Minnesota Community College Faculty Association was designated the exclusive bargaining agent for state community college faculty members. The association and the state board established statewide meet-and-confer committees as well as local committees on each campus. These committees discussed various policy matters, such as curriculum, fiscal planning, and student affairs. Only members of the association served on the committees.

This arrangement was challenged by a group of faculty members who were not members of the association and thus could not participate in the meet-and-negotiate or meet-and-confer processes. The faculty members argued that their exclusion deprived them of their First Amendment rights to express their views and also discriminated against them in violation of the Fourteenth Amendment's equal protection clause. The lower court (1) rejected these arguments as applied to the negotiation of mandatory bargaining subjects but (2) agreed with the faculty members that exclusion from the meet-and-confer committees violated the First Amendment (571 F. Supp. 1 (D. Minn. 1982)). On the faculty members' appeal from the first ruling, the U.S. Supreme Court summarily affirmed the lower court (*Knight* v. *Minnesota Community College Faculty Association*, 103 S. Ct. 1493 (1983)). On the state board's and association's appeal from the second ruling, in an opinion joined by only five members, the U.S. Supreme Court overruled the lower court. According to the Court majority, the faculty members' free speech challenge to their exclusion from meet-and-confer committees was unavailing:

> Appellees have no constitutional right to force the government to listen to their views. They have no such right as members of the public, as government employees, or as instructors in an institution of higher education. . . . The academic setting of the policy making at issue in this case does not alter this conclusion. To be sure, there is a strong, if not universal or uniform, tradition of faculty participation in school governance, and there are numerous policy arguments to support such participation. But this Court has never recognized a constitutional right of faculty to participate in policy making in academic institutions. . . . Even assuming that speech rights guaranteed by the First Amendment take on a special meaning in an academic setting, they do not require government to allow teachers employed by it to participate in institutional policy making. Faculty involvement in academic governance has much to recommend it as a matter of academic policy, but it finds no basis in the Constitution [104 S. Ct. at 1065, 1067–68].

The equal protection claim similarly failed:

> The interest of appellees that is affected—the interest in a government audience for their policy views—finds no special protection in the Constitution. . . . The state has a legitimate interest in insuring that its public employers hear one, and only one, voice presenting the majority view of its professional employees on employment-related policy questions, whatever other advice they may receive on those questions. Permitting selection of the ''meet-and-confer'' representatives to be made by the exclusive representative, which has its unique status by virtue of majority support within the bargaining unit, is a rational means of serving that interest. . . . Similarly, the goal of basing policy decisions on consideration of the majority view of its employees makes it reasonable for an employer to give only the exclusive representative a particular formal setting in which to offer advice on policy [104 S. Ct. at 1069–70].

3.2.3. Bargaining unit eligibility of full-time faculty. In *NLRB* v. *Yeshiva University,* 100 S. Ct. 856 (1980), the U.S. Supreme Court considered, for the first time, how federal collective bargaining principles developed to deal with industrial labor-management relations apply to private academic institutions. Adopting a view of academic employment relationships very different from that of the dissenting justices, a bare majority of the Court denied enforcement of an NLRB order requiring Yeshiva University to bargain collectively with a union certified as the representative of its faculty. The Court held that Yeshiva's full-time faculty members were ''managerial employees'' and thus excluded from the coverage of the Taft-Hartley Act.

In 1975 a three-member panel of the NLRB had reviewed the Yeshiva University Faculty Association's petition seeking certification as bargaining agent for the full-time faculty members of certain of Yeshiva's schools. The university opposed the petition on the grounds that its faculty members were managerial or supervisory personnel and hence not covered by the Act. After accepting the petition and sponsoring an election, the board certified the Faculty Association as exclusive bargaining representative. The university refused to bargain, maintaining its position that its faculty members' extensive involvement in university governance excluded them from the Act. When the Faculty Association charged that the refusal was an unfair labor practice, the board ordered the university to bargain and sought enforcement of its order in federal court. The U.S. Court of Appeals for the Second Circuit denied enforcement, holding that Yeshiva's faculty were endowed with ''managerial status'' sufficient to remove them from the coverage of the Act (*NLRB* v. *Yeshiva University,* 582 F.2d 686 (2d Cir. 1978)).

In affirming the appellate court's decision, Justice Powell's majority opinion recognized two distinct exemptions that could support the university's position but focused its analysis on only one:

> Professionals, like other employees, may be exempted from coverage under the Act's exclusion for ''supervisors'' who use independent judgment in overseeing other employees in the interest of the employer, or under the judicially implied exclusion for ''managerial employees'' who are involved in developing and enforcing employer policy. Both exemptions grow

out of the same concern: that an employer is entitled to the undivided loyalty of its representatives (*Beasley* v. *Food Fair of North Carolina*, 416 U.S. 653, 661–62 (1974); see *NLRB* v. *Bell Aerospace Co.*, 416 U.S. 267, 281–82 (1974)). Because the Court of Appeals found the faculty to be managerial employees, it did not decide the question of their supervisory status. In view of our agreement with that court's application of the managerial exclusion, we also need not resolve that issue of statutory interpretation [100 S. Ct. at 862].

The Court looked to previous NLRB decisions and Supreme Court opinions to formulate a definition of managerial employee:

Managerial employees are defined as those who " 'formulate and effectuate management policies by expressing and making operative the decisions of their employer.' " . . . Managerial employees must exercise discretion within or even independently of established employer policy and must be aligned with management. Although the board has established no firm criteria for determining when an employee is so aligned, normally an employee may be excluded as managerial only if he represents management interests by taking or recommending discretionary actions that effectively control or implement employer policy [100 S. Ct. at 862].

Applying this standard to the Yeshiva faculty, the Court concluded:

The controlling consideration in this case is that the faculty of Yeshiva University exercise authority which in any other context unquestionably would be managerial. Their authority in academic matters is absolute. They decide what courses will be offered, when they will be scheduled, and to whom they will be taught. They debate and determine teaching methods, grading policies, and matriculation standards. They effectively decide which students will be admitted, retained, and graduated. On occasion their views have determined the size of the student body, the tuition to be charged, and the location of a school. When one considers the function of a university, it is difficult to imagine decisions more managerial than these. To the extent the industrial analogy applies, the faculty determines within each school the product to be produced, the terms upon which it will be offered, and the customers who will be served [100 S. Ct. at 864].

The board had acknowledged this decision-making function of the Yeshiva faculty but argued that "alignment with management" was the proper criterion for assessing management status:

The board argues that the Yeshiva faculty are not aligned with management because they are expected to exercise "independent professional judgment" while participating in academic governance, and because they are neither "expected to conform to management policies [nor] judged according to their effectiveness in carrying out those policies." Because of this independence, the board contends there is no danger of divided loyalty and no need for the managerial exclusion. In its view, union pressure cannot divert the faculty from adhering to the interests of the university, because the university itself expects its faculty to pursue professional values rather than institutional interests. The board concludes that application of the managerial exclusion to such employees would frustrate the national labor policy in favor of collective bargaining [100 S. Ct. at 863].

In reaching its conclusion, the Court explicitly rejected the board's approach:

We are not persuaded by this argument. There may be some tension between the Act's exclusion of managerial employees and its inclusion of professionals, since most professionals in managerial positions continue to draw on their special skills and training. But we have been directed to no authority suggesting that that tension can be resolved by reference to the "independent professional judgment" criterion proposed in this case. Outside the university context, the board routinely has applied the managerial and supervisory exclusions to professionals in executive positions without inquiring whether their decisions were based on management policy rather than professional expertise. . . .

Moreover, the board's approach would undermine the goal it purports to serve: to ensure that employees who exercise discretionary authority on behalf of the employer will not divide their loyalty between employer and union. In arguing that a faculty member exercising independent judgment acts primarily in his own interest and therefore does not represent the interest of his employer, the board assumes that the professional interests of the faculty and the interests of the institution are distinct, separable entities with which a faculty member could not simultaneously be aligned. The Court of Appeals found no justification for this distinction, and we perceive none. In fact, the faculty's professional interests—as applied to governance at a university like Yeshiva—cannot be separated from those of the institution [100 S. Ct. at 864].

Four members of the Court dissented. In a perceptive opinion for these dissenters, Justice Brennan argued that the NLRB's decision should be upheld:

Unlike the purely hierarchical decision-making structure that prevails in the typical industrial organization, the bureaucratic foundation of most "mature" universities is characterized by dual authority systems. The primary decisional network is hierarchical in nature: Authority is lodged in the administration, and a formal chain of command runs from a lay governing board down through university officers to individual faculty members and students. At the same time, there exists a parallel professional network, in which formal mechanisms have been created to bring the expertise of the faculty into the decision-making process. (See J. Baldridge, *Power and Conflict in the University* 114 (1971); M. Finkin, "The NLRB in Higher Education," 5 *U. of Toledo L. Rev.* 608, 614–18 (1974).)

What the board realized—and what the Court fails to apprehend—is that whatever influence the faculty wields in university decision making is attributable solely to its collective expertise as professional educators, and not to any managerial or supervisory prerogatives. Although the administration may look to the faculty for advice on matters of professional and academic concern, the faculty offers its recommendations in order to serve its own independent interest in creating the most effective environment for learning, teaching, and scholarship. And while the administration may attempt to defer to the faculty's competence whenever possible, it must and does apply its own distinct perspective to those recommendations, a perspective that is based on fiscal and other managerial policies which the faculty has no part in developing. The university always retains the ultimate decision-making authority, and the administration gives what weight and import to the faculty's collective judgment as it chooses and deems consistent with its own perception of the institution's needs and objectives.

The premise of a finding of managerial status is a determination that the excluded employee is acting on behalf of management and is answerable to a higher authority in the exercise of his responsibilities. The board has consistently implemented this requirement—both for professional and nonprofessional employees—by conferring managerial status only upon those employees "whose interests are closely aligned with management *as true representatives of management*" (emphasis added). (See, for example, *Sutter Community Hospitals of Sacramento,* 227 NLRB 181, 193 (1976); *Bell Aerospace,* 219 NLRB 384, 385 (1975); *General Dynamics Corp.,* 213 NLRB 851, 857 (1974).) Only if the employee is expected to conform to management policies and is judged by his effectiveness in executing those policies does the danger of divided loyalties exist.

Yeshiva's faculty, however, is not accountable to the administration in its governance function, nor is any individual faculty member subject to personal sanction or control based on the administration's assessment of the worth of his recommendations. When the faculty, through the schools' advisory committees, participates in university decision making on subjects of academic policy, it does not serve as the "representative of management." Unlike industrial supervisors and managers, university professors are not hired to "make operative" the policies and decisions of their employer. Nor are they retained on the condition that their interests will correspond to those of the university administration. Indeed, the notion that a faculty member's professional competence could depend on his undivided loyalty to management is antithetical to the whole concept of academic freedom. Faculty members are judged by their employer on the quality of their teaching and scholarship, not on the compatibility of their advice with administration policy. . . .

It is no answer to say, as does the Court, that Yeshiva's faculty and administration are one and the same because their interests tend to coincide. In the first place, the National Labor Relations Act does not condition its coverage on an antagonism of interests between the employer and the employees. The mere coincidence of interests on many issues has never been thought to abrogate the right to collective bargaining on those topics as to which that coincidence is absent. Ultimately, the performance of an employee's duties will always further the interests of the employer, for in no institution do the interests of labor and management totally diverge.

Both desire to maintain stable and profitable operations, and both are committed to creating the best possible product within existing financial constraints. Differences of opinion and emphasis may develop, however, on exactly how to devote the institution's resources to achieve those goals. When these disagreements surface, the national labor laws contemplate their resolution through the peaceful process of collective bargaining. And in this regard, Yeshiva University stands on the same footing as any other employer. . . .

Finally, the Court's perception of the Yeshiva faculty's status is distorted by the rose-colored lens through which it views the governance structure of the modern-day university. The Court's conclusion that the faculty's professional interests are indistinguishable from those of the administration is bottomed on an idealized model of collegial decision making that is a vestige of the great medieval university. But the university of today bears little resemblance to the "community of scholars" of yesteryear. Education has become "big business," and the task of operating the university enterprise has been transferred from the faculty to an autonomous administration, which faces the same pressures to cut costs and increase efficiencies that confront any large industrial organization. The past decade of budgetary cutbacks, declining enrollments, reductions in faculty appointments, curtailment of academic programs, and increasing calls for accountability to alumni and other special interest groups has only added to the erosion of the faculty's role in the institution's decision-making process [100 S. Ct. at 869–73].

Just as the *Yeshiva* case sparked sharp debate within the Court, it has generated much dialogue and disagreement among commentators (see, for example, G. Bodner, "The Implications of the *Yeshiva University* Decision for Collective Bargaining Rights of Faculty at Private and Public Institutions of Higher Education," 7 *J. of College and University Law* 78 (1980–81); and the response in M. Finkin, "The *Yeshiva* Decision: A Somewhat Different View," 7 *J. of College and University Law* 321 (1980–81)). The debate has developed on two levels. The first is whether the Court majority's view of academic governance and its adaptation of labor law principles to that context are justifiable—an issue well framed by Justice Brennan's dissenting opinion. The second level concerns the extent to which the "management exclusion" fashioned by the Court should be applied to university settings and faculty governance systems different from Yeshiva's.

On the latter issue, it is important to take account of the Court's close attention to the specific circumstances of Yeshiva University. The majority opinion described the institution and the faculty's governance role at length:

The individual schools within the university are substantially autonomous. Each is headed by a dean or director, and faculty members at each school meet formally and informally to discuss and decide matters of institutional and professional concern. At four schools, formal meetings are convened regularly pursuant to written bylaws. The remaining faculties meet when convened by the dean or director. Most of the schools also have faculty committees concerned with special areas of educational policy. Faculty welfare committees negotiate with administrators concerning salary and conditions of employment. Through these meetings and committees, the faculty at each school effectively determine its curriculum, grading system, admission and matriculation standards, academic calendars, and course schedules.

Faculty power at Yeshiva's schools extends beyond strictly academic concerns. The faculty at each school make recommendations to the dean or director in every case of faculty hiring, tenure, sabbaticals, termination, and promotion. Although the final decision is reached by the central administration on the advice of the dean or director, the overwhelming majority of faculty recommendations are implemented. Even when financial problems in the early 1970s restricted Yeshiva's budget, faculty recommendations still largely controlled personnel decisions made within the constraints imposed by the administration. Indeed, the faculty of one school recently drew up new and binding policies expanding their own role in these matters. In addition, some faculties make final decisions regarding the admission, expulsion, and graduation of individual students. Others have decided questions involving teaching loads, student absence policies, tuition and enrollment levels, and in one case the location of a school [100 S. Ct. at 859–60].

The Court relied on these facts throughout its opinion, focusing on the faculty role at Yeshiva or "a university like Yeshiva." In a final footnote, the majority emphasized the narrowness of its holding that faculty are managers:

> Other factors not present here may enter into the analysis in other contexts. It is plain, for example, that professors may not be excluded merely because they determine the content of their own courses, evaluate their own students, and supervise their own research. There thus may be institutions of higher learning unlike Yeshiva where the faculty are entirely or predominantly nonmanagerial. There also may be faculty members at Yeshiva and like universities who properly could be included in a bargaining unit. It may be that a rational line could be drawn between tenured and untenured faculty members, depending upon how a faculty is structured and operates. But we express no opinion on these questions, for it is clear that the unit approved by the board was far too broad [100 S. Ct. at 866–67 n.31].

Thus, the *Yeshiva* decision appears to create a managerial exclusion only for faculty at "Yeshiva-like," or what the Court called "mature," universities. Even at such universities, it is unlikely that all faculty would be excluded from bargaining under federal law. Most part-time faculty, for instance, would not be considered managers and would thus remain eligible to bargain. Legitimate questions also exist concerning faculty with "soft-money" research appointments, instructors and lecturers not on a tenure track, visiting professors, and even nontenured faculty generally, at mature universities.

At institutions that are not "Yeshiva-like," the managerial exclusion may not apply at all. In a post-*Yeshiva* case, *NLRB* v. *Stephens Institute*, 620 F.2d 720 (9th Cir. 1980), a U.S. Court of Appeals refused to apply the managerial exclusion to the faculty of an art academy on the opposite end of the spectrum from Yeshiva. The academy was a corporation whose principal shareholder was also chief executive officer. Faculty members, except department heads, were paid according to the number of courses they taught each semester. According to the court, "The instructors at the academy . . . have no input into policy decisions and do not engage in management-level decision making. They are simply employees. Also, the academy bears little resemblance to the nonprofit 'mature' university discussed in *Yeshiva*."

Later, another U.S. Court of Appeals refused to apply the managerial exclusion to the faculty of a liberal arts college that was closer to Yeshiva on the spectrum than was the art academy. In *Loretto Heights College* v. *NLRB*, 742 F.2d 1245 (10th Cir. 1984), the court determined that "faculty participation in college governance occurs largely through committees and other such groups" and that, outside such committees, faculty members' governance roles were limited to participation in decision making "within or concerning particular program areas" in matters such as hiring and curriculum development. After carefully examining all these facts, the court concluded:

> It is evident from these facts that faculty members at Loretto Heights play a substantial role in college governance, participating in decision making and implementation in a wide range of areas. It is equally clear, however, that the faculty's authority in most aspects of college governance is severely circumscribed. . . . Thus, while [the faculty] committees may in fact perform important functions, the extent of faculty involvement in the committees' work is so limited as to be only incidental to, or in addition to, their primary function of teaching, research, and writing, rather than truly managerial in nature. . . . In light of the infrequent or insignificant nature of some committee work, the mixed membership of many committees, the faculty's limited decision-making authority, and the layers of administrative approval required for many decisions, the impact of faculty participation in college governance falls far short of the "effective recommendation or control" contemplated by *Yeshiva*. Outside the committee structure, as in the hiring and budget processes for example, faculty participation is similarly limited in authority and ultimately subject to one or more levels of administrative approval [742 F.2d at 1252–54; cites to *Yeshiva* omitted].

Moreover, said the court, since the college's governance structure limited the administration's need to rely on faculty members' professional judgment, it was unnecessary for faculty to be aligned with management as they had been in *Yeshiva*.

At other institutions that are not "Yeshiva-like," the managerial exclusion could apply to individual faculty members who have special governing responsibilities. Deans, for example, would likely be excluded from bargaining units. Depending on circumstances, the same result could apply to faculty serving as assistant or associate deans, department heads, members of academic senates, or members of grievance committees or other institutional bodies with governance functions. But the numbers involved are not likely to be so large as to preclude formation and recognition of a substantial bargaining unit.

Given the many possible variations from the circumstances in *Yeshiva*, administrators and counsel can estimate the case's application to their campus only by comprehensively analyzing the institution's governance structure, the faculty's governance role in this structure, and the resulting decision-making experience.

The task will be eased by additional law being fashioned not only by the courts but also by the NLRB as it deals on a case-by-case basis with management structures differing from Yeshiva's. The board issued its first group of post-*Yeshiva* cases on April 30, 1982. In three of these cases, the faculty members were held to be managerial employees excluded from bargaining (*Ithaca College and Ithaca College Faculty Association,* 261 NLRB 577 (1982); *Thiel College and Thiel College Chapter, AAUP,* 261 NLRB 580 (1982); *Duquesne University of the Holy Ghost and Duquesne University Law School Faculty Association,* 261 NLRB 587 (1982)). In the other two cases, faculty members were held to be nonmanagerial and thus eligible to bargain (*Bradford College and Milk Wagon Drivers and Creamery Workers Union, Local 380,* 261 NLRB 565 (1982); *Montefiore Hospital and Medical Center and New York State Federation of Physicians and Dentists,* 261 NLRB 569 (1982)). Subsequent board opinions have maintained this same split in results (see B. Lee and J. Begin, "Criteria for Evaluating the Managerial Status of College Faculty: Applications of *Yeshiva University* by the NLRB," 10 *J. of College and University Law* 515 (1983–84)).

On campuses with faculty members who would be considered "managers," bargaining does not become unlawful as a result of *Yeshiva.* The remaining faculty members not subject to exclusion may still form bargaining units under the protection of federal law. And even faculty members subject to the managerial exclusion may still agree among themselves to organize, and the institution may still voluntarily choose to bargain with them. But this process would lose the protection of federal law. Thus, for instance, faculty managers would have no federally enforceable right to be included in a certified bargaining unit or to demand good-faith bargaining over mandatory bargaining subjects (see Section 3.2.4). Conversely, the institution would have no federally enforceable right to file an unfair labor practice charge against a union representing only faculty managers for engaging in recognitional picketing, secondary boycotts, or other activity that would violate Section 8(b) of the LMRA (29 U.S.C. sec. 158(b)) if the federal law applied.

For public institutions *Yeshiva* has no direct application, since the case interprets a federal statute regulating only the private sector (see Section 3.2.1). But *Yeshiva* may nevertheless have persuasive impact on state labor board and state court decisions in some states. If a state customarily relies on federal labor law precedents, for instance, or has developed its own concept of managerial employee, it may choose to apply the *Yeshiva* reasoning to faculties of public institutions subject to its bargaining laws. Labor boards and courts would be precluded from this approach, however, to the extent that their state's labor laws explicitly recognize the right of faculty members to bargain. (See generally C. A. Clarke, "The *Yeshiva* Case: An Analysis and an Assessment of Its Potential Impact on Public Universities," 52 *J. of Higher Education* 449 (1981).)

In addition to questions concerning the legal status of their faculties under *Yeshiva,* administrators should also consider the more subtle impacts the decision may have on relationships between faculty and administration (see generally J. V. Baldridge, F. Kemerer, and Associates, *Assessing the Impact of Faculty Collective Bargaining* (ERIC/Higher Education Research Report no. 8, American Association for Higher Education, 1982)). The Court's opinion in *Yeshiva* raises numerous policy issues and sociological questions about faculty power on campus, and such matters may now merit a healthy reconsideration. Faculty at "mature" institutions may press for new mechanisms for exercising authority the Supreme Court has characterized as "managerial." At "nonmature" institutions administrators may wish to accord greater authority to faculty in order to forestall their resort to the bargaining process highlighted by *Yeshiva*. And at all types of institutions—mature or not, public or private—all affected constituencies may wish to better define and implement faculty's role in academic governance, not as a legal matter but as an exercise of sound policy judgment.

3.2.4. Bargainable subjects. Once the unit has been defined and the agent certified, the parties must proceed to negotiations. In the private sector, under Taft-Hartley, the parties may negotiate on any subject they wish, although other laws (such as federal employment discrimination laws) may make some subjects illegal. In the public sector, the parties may negotiate on any subject that is not specifically excluded from the state's collective bargaining statute or preempted by other state law, such as a tenure statute. Those terms that may be raised by either party and that are negotiable with the consent of the other are referred to as "permissive" subjects for negotiation. Academic collective bargaining can range, and has ranged, over a wide variety of such permissive subjects (see M. Moskow, "The Scope of Collective Bargaining in Higher Education," 1971 *Wisconsin L. Rev.* 33). A refusal to negotiate on a permissive subject of bargaining is not an unfair labor practice; on the contrary, it may be an unfair labor practice to insist that a permissive subject be covered by the bargaining agreement.

The heart of the collective bargaining process, however, is found in those terms over which the parties *must* negotiate. These "mandatory" subjects of bargaining are defined in the Taft-Hartley Act as "wages, hours, and other terms and conditions of employment" (29 U.S.C. sec. 158(d)). Most state laws use similar or identical language but often exclude particular subjects from the scope of that language or add particular subjects to it (see Academic Collective Bargaining Information Service, *Scope of Public Sector Bargaining in Fourteen Selected States* (Special Report no. 25, Nov. 1975)). The parties must bargain in good faith over mandatory subjects of bargaining; failure to do so is an unfair labor practice under the Taft-Hartley Act (see 29 U.S.C. secs. 158(a)(5) and 158(b)(3)) and most state statutes.

The statutory language regarding the mandatory subjects is often vague (for example, "terms and conditions of employment") and subject to broad construction by labor boards and courts. Thus, the distinction between mandatory and permissive subjects is difficult to draw, particularly in postsecondary education, where faculties have traditionally participated in shaping their jobs to a much greater degree than have employees in industry. Internal governance and policy issues that may never arise in industrial bargaining may thus be critical in postsecondary education. There are few court or labor board precedents in either federal or state law to help administrators determine whether educational governance and educational policy issues are mandatorily or permissibly bargainable. Nor in the states, where some subjects may be impermissible, are there many precedents to help administrators determine when particular subjects fall into that category. One court case, *Association of New Jersey State College Faculties* v. *Dungan*, 64 N.J. 338, 316 A.2d 425 (1974), concerned a state statute that gave public employees the right to bargain over the "terms and conditions of employment" and "working conditions." The court held that rules for granting tenure are not "mandatorily negotiable" under the statute because such rules "represent major educational policy pronouncements entrusted by the legislature [under the state Education Law] to the board . . . [of higher education's] educational expertise and objective judgment.'' Under such reasoning, tenure rules could also be beyond the scope of permissible bargaining, as "inherent managerial policy" (*University Education Association* v. *Regents of University of Minnesota*, 353 N.W.2d 534 (Minn. 1984)) or as a nondelegable function of the board (see the *Cook County College Teachers Union* case in Section 3.2.1) or a function preempted by other state laws or administrative agency regulations (see *New Jersey State College Locals* v. *State Board of Higher Education*, 91 N.J. 18, 449 A.2d 1244 (1982)). Other courts or agencies, however, particularly when dealing with private institutions under the Taft-Hartley Act, may reason that tenure is a mandatory, or at least permissive, bargaining subject because it concerns job security (see A. Menard, "May Tenure Rights of Faculty Be Bargained Away?" 2 *J. of College and University Law* 256 (1975)). In *Hackel* v. *Vermont State Colleges*, 438 A.2d 1119 (Vt. 1981), for example, the court determined that faculty promotion and tenure are "properly bargainable" under that state's Employee Labor Relations Act and upheld a provision on tenure and promotion in a collective bargaining agreement.

When the parties are unable to reach agreement on an item subject to mandatory bargaining (called *impasse*), a number of resolution techniques may be available to them. It is critical to distinguish between bargaining impasse in the private sector and in the public sector. In the private sector, the Taft-Hartley Act specifically recognizes that employees have the right to strike under certain circumstances (see 29 U.S.C. sec. 163). The basic premise of the Act is that, given the free play of economic forces, employer and union can and will bargain collectively and reach agreement, and the ultimate economic force available to a union is the strike. In the public sector, however, it is almost unanimously regarded as unlawful, either by state statute or state judicial decision, for an employee to strike. The rationale is that states have a vital interest in assuring that government services remain available to the public without interruption that would be created by a strike.[2]

Consequently, almost all state statutes prescribe impasse resolution techniques to take the place of strikes. Depending on the statute, these techniques include mediation, fact finding, and interest arbitration. Mediation—the appointment of a third party who may make recommendations to the disputing parties but does not dictate any terms of settlement—is the most commmonly prescribed impasse procedure. Fact finding usually involves the appointment of an independent panel to review the dispute and make findings regarding the critical facts underlying it. This process is sometimes mandatory if the parties fail to reach agreement within a specified time period; at other times a fact finder is appointed by order of a labor board or agreement of the parties (see J. Stern, "The Wisconsin Public Employee Fact-Finding Procedure," 20 *Industrial and Labor Relations Rev.* 3 (1966)). Interest arbitration (as distinguished from grievance arbitration, discussed below) utilizes a third party to settle the contract terms on which the negotiating parties cannot agree. Interest arbitration can be either compulsory (in which case the statute requires the submission of unresolved issues to an arbitrator, who makes a final decision) or voluntary (in which case the parties decide for themselves whether to resort to binding arbitration).

The same techniques used to resolve an impasse in bargaining may also be

---

[2]The statutes and cases are collected in Annot., "Labor Law: Right of Public Employees to Strike or Engage in Work Stoppage," 37 A.L.R.3d 1147 (1971 and periodic supp.).

used in the public sector to resolve disputes concerning the application or inter-
pretation of the bargaining agreement after it has gone into force. The most common
technique for resolving such disputes is grievance arbitration (see M. Finkin, "The
Arbitration of Faculty Status Disputes in Higher Education," 30 *Southwestern L. J.*
389 (1976); B. Mintz and A. Golden, "In Defense of Academic Judgment: Settling
Faculty Collective Bargaining Agreement Grievances Through Arbitration," 22
Buffalo L. Rev. 523 (1973); J. Douglas, "An Analysis of the Arbitration Clause in
Collective Bargaining Agreements in Higher Education," 39 *Arbitration J.* 38 (1984)).

   In the private sector, there are only two techniques for resolving an impasse
in negotiating an agreement—mediation and interest arbitration—and the latter
is rarely used. Mediation is available through the Federal Mediation and Conciliation Service, which may "proffer its services in any labor dispute . . . either upon
its own motion or upon the request of one or more of the parties" (29 U.S.C. sec.
173(b)). Interest arbitration may be used when the parties already have a collective bargaining agreement in effect, due to expire, in which they have agreed to
submit to arbitration terms they cannot agree upon when negotiating their new
agreement. Interest arbitration has no statutory basis and is entirely the creature
of an existing agreement between the parties. Negotiated agreements in the private
sector usually provide for grievance arbitration to resolve disputes concerning the
application or interpretation of the agreement. In an illustrative case, *Trustees of
Boston University* v. *Boston University Chapter, AAUP,* 746 F.2d 924 (1st Cir. 1984),
the court upheld an arbitrator's interpretation of his powers under an arbitration
clause of a bargaining agreement and affirmed the arbitrator's award of equity and
merit raises to three professors who had filed grievances.

   3.2.5. Coexistence of collective bargaining and traditional academic practices.
Collective bargaining contracts traditionally come in two kinds, those with a "zipper"
clause and those with a "past practices" clause. A zipper clause usually states that
the union agrees to forgo its rights to bargain about any employment term or condition not contained in the contract; prior relationships between the parties thus
become irrelevant. A past practices clause incorporates previous customary relationships between the parties in the agreement, at least insofar as they are not already
inconsistent with its specific terms. Administrators faced with collective bargaining should carefully weigh the relative merit of each clause. A contract without either
clause will likely be interpreted consistently with past practice when there are gaps
or ambiguities in the contract terms. (See Sections 1.3.8 and 3.1.1.)

   The availability of the past practices clause, however, by no means assures
that such traditional academic practices as tenure and faculty participation will endure
under collective bargaining. Many commentators argue that such academic practices
will steadily and inevitably disappear (for example, see D. Fellers, "General Theory
of the Collective Bargaining Agreement," 61 *California L. Rev.* 663, 718–856 (1973)).
The theory is that collective bargaining brings with it the economic warfare of the
industrial bargaining model, forcing the two parties into much more clearly defined
employee and management roles and diminishing the collegial characteristics of
higher education. The opposing view is that collective bargaining can be domesticated
in the postsecondary environment with minimal disruption of academic practices
(see M. Finkin, "Collective Bargaining and University Government," 1971 *Wisconsin
L. Rev.* 125; and M. Finkin, "Faculty Collective Bargaining in Higher Education:
An Independent Perspective," 3 *J. of Law and Education* 439 (1974)). Thus, a critical

issue for administrators is the extent to which faculty involvement in institutional governance should and can be maintained by incorporating such arrangements in the bargaining agreement, through either a past practices clause or a more detailed description of forms and functions (see F. R. Kemerer and J. V. Baldridge, *Unions on Campus: A National Study of the Consequences of Faculty Bargaining* (Jossey-Bass, 1975); B. Lee, "Contractually Protected Governance Systems at Unionized Colleges," 5 *Rev. of Higher Education* 69 (1982)).

    3.2.6. Students and collective bargaining. During the 1970s students became increasingly concerned with collective bargaining's potential impact on their interests. The questions are basically whether faculty and student interests are potentially, or necessarily, inconsistent and whether collective bargaining will reduce student power by reducing the policy issues in which students participate or the internal remedies they can utilize. If either of these effects flows from collective bargaining, another question then arises: Should students have a formal role in bargaining— and, if so, what kind? Several state legislatures have provided such a role for students in public institutions. In 1975 Oregon passed a law providing an independent observer-participant role for students (Or. Rev. Stat. ch. 679(1), secs. 243.650–243.782), and Montana passed a law allowing students to be part of the administration bargaining team (Rev. Code Mont. sec. 59-1602(1)). In 1976 Maine passed a law giving students the formal opportunity to consult with both administrators and faculty members before bargaining begins and with administrators at reasonable intervals during negotiations (Me. Rev. Stat. Ann. vol. 26, sec. 1024-A.6). In states without such statutes, some formal student participation has been provided by institutional or state governing board regulations or by agreement of the bargaining parties. Such action, however, may raise legal questions concerning institutional authority, particularly if students are authorized to postpone or veto the resolution of issues by the faculty and administration bargaining teams.

    Some students may have interests in collective bargaining not only as students but also as employees of the institution. Graduate students, for instance, may also be lecturers or laboratory or teaching assistants. If the latter duties would legally be characterized as employment, these students (as employees) would be eligible to participate in organizational efforts or collective negotiations covering positions of the type that they hold. It is sometimes difficult, however, to determine whether instructional, research, or clinical duties create an employment relationship or, instead, are part of an educational program which the student undertakes as student rather than employee. In *Physicians National House Staff Association* v. *Fanning,* 642 F.2d 492 (D.C. Cir. 1980), for example, the court held that interns, residents, and clinical fellows on staffs belonging to the association were "primarily students" and thus not covered by federal collective bargaining law.

    3.2.7. Collective bargaining and antidiscrimination laws. A body of case law is developing on the applicability of federal and state laws prohibiting discrimination in employment (see Section 3.3) to the collective bargaining process. Courts have interpreted federal labor relations law (Section 3.2.1) to impose on unions a duty to represent each employee fairly—without arbitrariness, discrimination, or bad faith (see *Vaca* v. *Sipes,* 386 U.S. 171 (1967)). In addition, some antidiscrimination statutes, such as Title VII and the Age Discrimination in Employment Act, apply directly to unions as well as employers. But these laws have left open several questions concerning the relationships between collective bargaining and antidiscrimination statutes. For instance, when employment discrimination problems are covered in the bargaining contract, can such coverage be construed to preclude faculty members from seeking other remedies under antidiscrimination statutes? If a faculty member resorts to a negotiated grievance procedure to resolve a discrimination dispute, can that faculty member then be precluded from using remedies provided under antidiscrimination statutes?

Most cases presenting such issues have arisen under Title VII of the Civil Rights Act of 1964 (see Section 3.3.2.1). The leading case is *Alexander* v. *Gardner-Denver Co.,* 415 U.S. 36 (1974). A discharged black employee had contested his discharge in a grievance proceeding provided under a collective bargaining contract. He claimed that his discharge was a result of racial discrimination. Having lost before an arbitrator in the grievance proceeding, and having had a complaint to the federal Equal Employment Opportunity Commission dismissed, the employee filed a Title VII action in federal district court. After the district court had held that the employee was bound by the arbitration decision and thus had no right to sue under Title VII, the U.S. Supreme Court reversed. The Court held that the employee could still sue under Title VII, which creates statutory rights "distinctly separate" from the contractual right to arbitration under the collective bargaining agreement. Such independent rights "are not waived either by inclusion of discrimination disputes within the collective bargaining agreement or by submitting the nondiscrimination claim to arbitration."

More recently, in *McDonald* v. *City of West Branch,* 104 S. Ct. 1799 (1984), the Court relied on *Gardner-Denver* in holding that a dismissed employee's resort to a union arbitration proceeding did not preclude him from seeking judicial relief under the Section 1983 civil rights statute (see Section 2.3.3). In an opinion that would cover employees who file Section 1983 claims alleging discrimination as well as Section 1983 claims alleging other violations of constitutional and statutory rights, the Court concluded that arbitration "cannot provide an adequate substitute for a judicial proceeding in protecting the federal statutory and constitutional rights that Section 1983 is designed to safeguard."

Thus, collective bargaining does not provide an occasion for postsecondary administrators to lessen their attention to the institution's Title VII responsibilities or its responsibilities under other antidiscrimination and civil rights laws. Faculty members can avail themselves of rights and remedies both under the bargaining agreement and under civil rights statutes. There is one exception, however, noted by the Court in the *Garden-Denver* case: It may be possible to waive a Title VII cause of action (and presumably actions under other statutes) "as part of a voluntary settlement" of a discrimination claim. The employee's consent to such a settlement would have to be "voluntary and knowing," however, and "mere resort to the arbitral forum to enforce contractual rights" could not constitute such a waiver (see 415 U.S. at 52).

Sec. 3.3. Nondiscrimination in Employment

3.3.1. The statutory, regulatory, and constitutional thicket. The problem of employment discrimination is probably more heavily blanketed with overlapping statutory and regulatory requirements than any other area of postsecondary education law. The federal government has no less than eight major employment discrimination

statutes and one major executive order applicable to postsecondary education, each
with its own comprehensive set of administrative regulations or guidelines (see Sections 3.3.2 and 3.3.4). Many states also have fair employment practices statutes,
some of which may exclude educational institutions (such as Md. Ann. Code art.
49B, sec. 18), and others of which may apply to educational institutions and overlap
federal statutes. New York has a statute, for instance, that was the basis of extended
proceedings, culminating in *State Division of Human Rights* v. *Columbia University,*
39 N.Y.2d 612, 350 N.E.2d 396 (1976). In that case a rejected faculty applicant
filed a sex discrimination complaint, as provided by the statute, with the State
Division of Human Rights. The division conducted an investigation and hearing
and found no discrimination; the Human Rights Appeal Board reversed and held
that the applicant had been discriminated against; and the New York Court of
Appeals reversed the appeal board, holding that the applicant had been rejected
for legitimate staffing and financial reasons rather than on grounds of sex.

Because of their national scope and comprehensive coverage of problems
and remedies, and because they take precedence over any conflicting state law,
the federal antidiscrimination statutes have assumed greater importance than the
state statutes. The federal statutes, moreover, supplemented by those of the states,
have outstripped the importance of the federal Constitution (see Sections 3.3.3 and
3.3.4) as a remedy for employment discrimination. The statutes cover almost all
major categories of discrimination and tend to impose more affirmative and stringent
requirements on employers than does the Constitution.

Race discrimination in employment is covered by Title VII of the Civil Rights
Act of 1964 as amended, by 42 U.S.C. sec. 1981, and by Executive Order 11246
as amended. Sex discrimination is covered by Title VII, by Title IX of the Education Amendments of 1972, by the Equal Pay Act, and by Executive Order 11246.
Age discrimination is covered, in part, by the Age Discrimination in Employment
Act. Discrimination against the handicapped is covered by the Rehabilitation Act
of 1973. Discrimination on the basis of religion is covered by Title VII and Executive Order 11246. Discrimination on the basis of national origin is covered by
Title VII and by Executive Order 11246. Discrimination against aliens is covered
indirectly under Title VII (see Section 3.3.2.1 under "National Origin Discrimination") and directly by 42 U.S.C. sec. 1981. Discrimination against veterans is
covered in part by 38 U.S.C. sec. 2012.

The nondiscrimination aspects of the statutes and Executive Order 11246
are discussed in Section 3.3.2. The affirmative action aspects of the statutes and
Executive Order 11246 are discussed in Section 3.3.4. And the interstitial importance of the federal Constitution is discussed in Sections 3.3.3 and 3.3.4.

3.3.2. Nondiscrimination under federal statutes and executive orders. Employment discrimination law continues to develop at such a rapid pace that keeping
abreast is a formidable challenge even for highly experienced administrators and
counsel. The major issues, U.S. Supreme Court cases, and other judicial and administrative agency developments are discussed in the subsections below. Since Title
VII of the Civil Rights Act of 1964 has been the primary focus of recent
developments, it receives the most extensive treatment. Most of the issues being
addressed under Title VII, however, have parallels under other federal employment discrimination statutes. The teachings of the Title VII developments should
therefore provide guidance in dealing with other statutes as well.

3.3.2.1. Title VII. Title VII of the Civil Rights Act of 1964, 42 U.S.C. sec. 2000e *et seq.,* is the most comprehensive and most litigated of the federal employment discrimination laws. It was extended in 1972 to cover educational institutions both public and private. According to the statute's basic prohibition, 42 U.S.C. sec. 2000e-2(a):

> It shall be an unlawful employment practice for an employer—
> (1) to fail or refuse to hire or to discharge any individual, or otherwise to discriminate against any individual with respect to his compensation, terms, conditions, or privileges of employment, because of such individual's race, color, religion, sex, or national origin; or
> (2) to limit, segregate, or classify his employees or applicants for employment in any way which would deprive or tend to deprive any individual of employment opportunities or otherwise adversely affect his status as an employee, because of such individual's race, color, religion, sex, or national origin.

The major exception to this general prohibition is the "BFOQ" exception, which permits hiring and employing based on "religion, sex, or national origin" when such a characteristic is a "bona fide occupational qualification necessary to the normal operation of that particular business or enterprise" (42 U.S.C. sec. 2000e-2(e)(1)).

Title VII is administered by the Equal Employment Opportunity Commission (EEOC), which has implemented the statute with a series of regulations and guidelines published at 29 C.F.R. Parts 1600 through 1610. The EEOC may receive, investigate, and conciliate complaints of unlawful employment discrimination and may sue violators in court or issue right-to-sue letters to complainants (29 C.F.R. Part 1601).

Though Title VII broadly prohibits employment discrimination, it does not hamstring postsecondary institutions in hiring faculty members on the basis of job-related qualifications or distinguishing among faculty members on the basis of seniority or merit in pay, promotion, and tenure policies. Institutions retain discretion to hire, promote, reward, and terminate faculty as they choose, as long as they do not make distinctions based on "race, color, religion, sex, or national origin." If, however, an institution does distinguish among faculty on one of these bases, courts have broad powers to remedy the Title VII violation by "making persons whole for injuries suffered through past discrimination" (*Albemarle Paper Co.* v. *Moody,* 422 U.S. 405 (1975)). Remedies may include back-pay awards (*Albemarle*), awards of retroactive seniority (*Franks* v. *Bowman Transportation Co.,* 424 U.S. 747 (1976)), and various affirmative action measures to benefit the group whose members were the subject of the discrimination (see this chapter, Section 3.3.4).

There are two basic types of Title VII claims: the "disparate treatment" claim and the "disparate impact" or "adverse impact" claim. In the former type of suit, an individual denied a job, promotion, or tenure, or subjected to a detrimental employment condition claims to have been treated less favorably than other applicants or employees because of her race, sex, national origin, or religion (see, for example, *Lynn* v. *Regents of University of California,* 656 F.2d 1337 (9th Cir. 1981) (alleged sex discrimination in denial of tenure)). In the latter type of suit, the claim is that some ostensibly neutral policy of the employer has a discriminatory impact on the claimants or the class of persons they represent (see, for example, *Scott* v. *University of Delaware*, 455 F. Supp. 1102, 1123–32 (D. Del. 1978), affirmed on other grounds, 601 F.2d 76 (3d Cir. 1979) (alleged race discrimination in hiring, promotions, and tenure); and *Zahorik* v. *Cornell University*, 729 F.2d 85, 95–96 (2d Cir. 1984) (alleged sex discrimination in denial of tenure)). Of the two types of suits, disparate treatment is the more common for postsecondary education.

The paradigm for disparate treatment suits is *McDonnell Douglas Corp.* v. *Green*, 411 U.S. 792 (1973). Under that decision:

> The complainant in a Title VII trial must carry the initial burden under the statute of establishing a prima facie case of racial discrimination. This may be done by showing (i) that he belongs to a racial minority; (ii) that he applied and was qualified for a job for which the employer was seeking applicants; (iii) that, despite his qualifications, he was rejected; and (iv) that, after his rejection, the position remained open and the employer continued to seek applicants from persons of complainant's qualifications. . . .
>
> The burden then must shift to the employer to articulate some legitimate, nondiscriminatory reason for the employee's rejection [411 U.S. at 802].

Although *McDonnell Douglas* concerned only racial discrimination, its methodology has been applied to other types of discriminatory treatment prohibited by Title VII; likewise, though the case concerned only job applications, courts have adapted its methodology to faculty hiring, promotion, and tenure situations. A subsequent Supreme Court case adds important gloss to *McDonnell Douglas* by noting that, in a disparate treatment (as opposed to disparate impact) case, "proof of discriminatory motive is critical [to complainant's case], although it can in some situations be inferred from the mere fact of difference in treatment" (*International Brotherhood of Teamsters* v. *United States*, 431 U.S. 324, 355 n.12 (1977)).

The paradigm for disparate impact suits is *Griggs* v. *Duke Power Co.*, 401 U.S. 424 (1971). As the U.S. Supreme Court explained in that case:

> Under [Title VII,] practices, procedures, or tests neutral on their face, and even neutral in terms of intent, cannot be maintained if they operate to "freeze" the status quo of prior discriminatory employment practices. . . .
>
> Congress has now provided that tests or criteria for employment or promotion may not provide equality of opportunity merely in the sense of the fabled offer of milk to the stork and the fox. On the contrary, Congress has now required that the posture and condition of the job seeker be taken into account. It has—to resort again to the fable—provided that the vessel in which the milk is proffered be one all seekers can use. The Act proscribes not only overt discrimination but also practices that are fair in form but discriminatory in operation. The touchstone is business necessity. If an employment practice which operates to exclude Negroes cannot be shown to be related to job performance, the practice is prohibited [401 U.S. at 429–31].

In its unanimous opinion in *Griggs,* the Court interpreted Title VII to prohibit employment practices that (1) operate to exclude or otherwise discriminate against employees or prospective employees on grounds of race, color, religion, sex, or national origin, and (2) are unrelated to job performance. Both requirements must be met before Title VII is violated. Under the first requirement, it need not be shown that the employer intended to discriminate; it is the *effect* of the employment practice, not the *intent* behind it, that controls. Under the second requirement, the employer, not the employee, has the burden of showing the job relatedness of the employment practice in question.

Two well-publicized cases provide excellent examples of the issues and controversy spawned by Title VII litigation against colleges and universities. The first, *Board of Trustees of Keene State College* v. *Sweeney,* 439 U.S. 25 (1978), on remand, 604 F.2d 106 (1st Cir. 1979), concerns the respective burdens of proof borne by the parties in disparate treatment litigation. The second, *Kunda* v. *Muhlenberg College,* 621 F.2d 532 (3d Cir. 1980), concerns the question of the remedies (or relief) a court may order once it has found an institution liable for a Title VII violation. These two cases are discussed at length in this section; following this discussion, a number of other current Title VII issues, such as sexual harassment, are noted in briefer fashion.

Sweeney involved a claim that Keene State College's refusal to promote the plaintiff, a female faculty member, constituted sex discrimination. Both the trial court and the appellate court had upheld the plaintiff's claim. But the U.S. Supreme Court vacated the appellate court's affirmance of the trial court because the appellate court had imposed too heavy a burden on the defendant college to rebut the plaintiff's initial showing of discrimination:

> In *Furnco Construction Co.* v. *Waters,* 438 U.S. 567, 98 S. Ct. 2943, 57 L. Ed. 2d 957 (1978), we stated that "to dispel the adverse inference from a prima facie showing under *McDonnell Douglas,* the employer need only 'articulate some legitimate, nondiscriminatory reason for the employee's rejection'" (98 S. Ct. at 2950, quoting *McDonnell Douglas Corp.* v. *Green,* 411 U.S. 792, 802, 93 S. Ct. 1817, 1824, 36 L. Ed. 2d 668 (1973)). We stated in *McDonnell Douglas* that the plaintiff "must . . . be afforded a fair opportunity to show that [the employer's] stated reason for [the plaintiff's] rejection was in fact pretext." The Court of Appeals in the present case, however, referring to *McDonnell Douglas,* stated that "in requiring the defendant to *prove absence of discriminatory motive,* the Supreme Court placed the burden squarely on the party with the greater access to such evidence" (emphasis added).
>
> While words such as "articulate," "show," and "prove" may have more or less similar meanings depending upon the context in which they are used, we think that there is a significant distinction between merely "articulat[ing] some legitimate, nondiscriminatory reason" and "prov[ing] absence of discriminatory motive." By reaffirming and emphasizing the *McDonnell Douglas* analysis in *Furnco Construction Co.* v. *Waters,* we made it clear that the former will suffice to meet the employee's prima facie case of discrimination. Because the Court of Appeals appears to have imposed a heavier burden on the employer than *Furnco* warrants, its judgment is vacated and the case is remanded for reconsideration in the light of *Furnco.*

The Court's opinion in *Sweeney* is confusing. Four justices joined in a strong dissent, criticizing the majority for drawing "illusory" distinctions inconsistent with prior law. By suggesting that the defendant employer need only "articulate," not "prove," some "legitimate" reason for its decision, the Court also fostered speculation that it had lightened the employer's burden.[3]

Fortunately, a later U.S. Supreme Court case has dispelled the uncertainty left by *Sweeney*. This case, *Texas Department of Community Affairs* v. *Burdine*, 101 S. Ct. 1089 (1981), was brought by a state agency employee whose position had been abolished in a staff reorganization. Speaking for a unanimous court, Justice Powell gave this explanation of burdens of proof in Title VII disparate treatment cases:

> The burden of establishing a prima facie case of disparate treatment is not onerous. The plaintiff must prove by a preponderance of the evidence that she applied for an available position, for which she was qualified, but was rejected under circumstances which give rise to an inference of unlawful discrimination. The prima facie case serves an important function in the litigation; it eliminates the most common nondiscriminatory reasons for the plaintiff's rejection (see *Teamsters* v. *United States,* 431 U.S. 324, 358, and n.44 (1977)). As the Court explained in *Furnco Construction Co.* v. *Waters,* 438 U.S. 567, 577 (1978), the prima facie case "raises an inference of discrimination only because we presume these acts, if otherwise unexplained, are more likely than not based on the consideration of impermissible factors." Establishment of the prima facie case in effect creates a presumption that the employer unlawfully discriminated against the employee. . . .
>
> The burden that shifts to the defendant, therefore, is to rebut the presumption of discrimination by producing evidence that the plaintiff was rejected, or someone else was preferred, for a legitimate, nondiscriminatory reason. The defendant need not persuade the court that it was actually motivated by the proffered reasons (see *Sweeney,* 439 U.S. at 25). It is sufficient if the defendant's evidence raises a genuine issue of fact as to whether it discriminated against the plaintiff. To accomplish this, the defendant must clearly set forth, through the introduction of admissible evidence, the reasons for the plaintiff's rejection. The explanation provided must be legally sufficient to justify a judgment for the defendant. If the defendant carries this burden of production, the presumption raised by the prima facie case is rebutted, and the factual inquiry proceeds to a new level of specificity. . . .
>
> The plaintiff retains the burden of persuasion. She now must have the opportunity to demonstrate that the proffered reason was not the true reason for the employment decision. This burden now merges with the ultimate burden of persuading the court that she has been the victim of intentional discrimination. She may succeed in this either directly by persuading the court that a discriminatory reason more likely motivated the employer or indirectly by showing that the employer's proffered explanation is unworthy of credence (see *McDonnell Douglas,* 411 U.S. at 804–05). . . .

---

[3]The uncertainty, however, did not alter the lower court's conclusion that the plaintiff had been the victim of sex discrimination. On remand from the Supreme Court, the trial court and then the appellate court reaffirmed their prior decisions (604 F.2d 106 (1st Cir. 1979)).

The court [of appeals] placed the burden of persuasion on the defendant apparently because it feared that "if an employer need only articulate not prove a legitimate, nondiscriminatory reason for his action, he may compose fictitious, but legitimate, reasons for his actions" (*Turner* v. *Texas Instruments, Inc.,* 555 F.2d 1251, 1255 (5th Cir. 1977)). We do not believe, however, that limiting the defendant's evidentiary obligation to a burden of production will unduly hinder the plaintiff. First, as noted above, the defendant's explanation of its legitimate reasons must be clear and reasonably specific. . . . Second, although the defendant does not bear a formal burden of persuasion, the defendant nevertheless retains an incentive to persuade the trier of fact that the employment decision was lawful. Thus, the defendant normally will attempt to prove the factual basis for its explanation. Third, the liberal discovery rules applicable to any civil suit in federal court are supplemented in a Title VII suit by the plaintiff's access to the Equal Employment Opportunity Commission's investigatory files concerning her complaint (see *EEOC* v. *Associated Dry Goods Corp.,* 449 U.S. 590 (1981)) [101 S. Ct. at 1094–96; footnotes omitted].

After *Burdine* the *Sweeney* division of burdens of proof can be understood in light of the distinction between *burden of production* (of producing evidence on a particular fact) and *burden of persuasion* (of convincing the trier of fact that illegal discrimination occurred). The plaintiff always carries the ultimate burden of persuasion; it is only the burden of production that shifts from plaintiff to defendant and back to plaintiff again. Requiring that the defendant "articulate" rather than "prove" a nondiscriminatory reason thus does not relieve the defendant of the need to introduce probative evidence; it merely frees the defendant from any obligation to carry the ultimate burden of persuasion on that issue. The *Burdine* Court, apparently sensitive to criticism of the majority opinion in *Sweeney,* sets out three reasons why this allocation of burdens does not "unduly hinder the plaintiff" in Title VII litigation.

The second Title VII case, *Kunda* v. *Muhlenberg College,* 621 F.2d 532 (3d Cir. 1980), also involved burdens of proof; the court discusses *Sweeney,* but not *Burdine,* which was decided subsequently. The primary importance of the *Kunda* opinion, however, is its analysis of a question that arises only when the plaintiff does prove discrimination: What remedy shall the court order to redress the harm to the plaintiff? The plaintiff in *Kunda,* a physical education instructor, brought suit after the college had denied her applications for promotion and tenure. The trial court (463 F. Supp. 294 (E.D. Pa. 1978)), holding that the college had intentionally discriminated against Kunda because of her sex, awarded her (1) reinstatement to her position; (2) back pay from the date her employment terminated, less amounts earned in the interim; (3) promotion to the rank of assistant professor, back-dated to the time her application was denied; and (4) the opportunity to complete the requirements for a master's degree within two full school years from the date of the court's decree, in which case she would be granted tenure.

In affirming the trial court's award of relief, the appellate court carefully analyzed the particular facts of the case. These facts, as set out below, played a vital role in supporting and limiting the precedent set by this opinion.

When Kunda was appointed an instructor in the physical education department in September 1966, she held a Bachelor of Arts degree in physical education.

Although the department's terminal degree requirement, for tenure purposes, was the master's, Kunda was never informed that a master's was needed for advancement. Kunda was first recommended for promotion in the academic year 1971–72. The department forwarded its recommendation to the Faculty Personnel and Policies Committee (FPPC) of the college, which rejected the recommendation. The dean of the college, Dean Secor, who seldom attended FPPC deliberations on promotions, spoke against the recommendation. In order to determine the reasons for the denial, Kunda met individually with her department chairman; Dean Secor; and the college's president, President Morey. The court found that none of these persons told her that she had been denied promotion "because she lacked a master's degree" or stated that "a master's would be mandatory" in any future consideration for promotion or for tenure.

Again in 1972–73 Kunda's department chairman initiated the recommendation process. Because of an "egregious oversight," Dean Secor did not present the recommendation to the FPPC until after it had sent all other recommendations to President Morey and the board of trustees. Nonetheless, the FPPC voted unanimously to recommend Kunda for promotion. Dean Secor then wrote the president, arguing against Kunda's promotion; he did note her contributions to the college, however, and suggested that an alternative be devised which would allow the college to retain her services. President Morey did not recommend Kunda, and her promotion was denied.

Finally, in academic year 1973–74, Kunda's department chairman, now joined by all senior department members, recommended Kunda's promotion and, for the first time, a grant of tenure. The FPPC concurred, noting that the usual advanced degree requirement should not apply to Kunda and that her qualifications should instead be measured by her other contributions to her profession and the community. Again, Dean Secor sent a negative recommendation to the president. His memorandum did not refer to Kunda's lack of a terminal degree, instead citing the high number of tenured faculty in the department and the department's uncertain status at the college. When the president did not recommend Kunda's appointment, Kunda was notified that tenure had been denied and that she would be given a terminal contract for 1974–75.

Kunda appealed the tenure denial to the Faculty Board of Appeals (FBA). A three-member subcommittee of the FBA unanimously recommended that she be granted tenure and promoted to the rank of assistant professor. The full committee then adopted the recommendation and notified the president that it had done so because Kunda displayed the scholarly equivalent of a master's degree, the policy of granting promotions only to faculty possessing the terminal degree had been bypassed frequently by the physical education department, and no significant financial considerations mandated a denial of tenure. Despite the FBA recommendation, the board of trustees voted to deny tenure.

After reviewing these facts, the Court of Appeals examined other facts comparing Kunda's situation with that of similarly situated males at Muhlenberg. With respect to promotion, three male members of the physical education department had been promoted during the period of Kunda's employment, notwithstanding their lack of master's degrees. In another department of the college, a male instructor had been promoted without a terminal degree. There was also a difference between the counseling offered Kunda and that offered similarly situated males; while Kunda was not told that the master's would be a prerequisite for a grant of tenure, male members had been so advised.

Based on its analysis of these facts found by the trial court, and its approval of the trial court's allocation of burdens of proof, the appellate court agreed that Kunda had been discriminated against in both the denial of promotion and the denial of tenure. Concerning promotion, the appellate court affirmed the finding that the defendant's reason for denial articulated at trial, lack of the terminal degree, was a pretext for discrimination. Concerning tenure, the appellate court affirmed the trial court's determination that the articulated reason (lack of terminal degree) was not pretextual but that Kunda had been subjected to intentional disparate treatment with respect to counseling on the need for the degree.

Having held the college in violation of Title VII, the court proceeded to what it considered the most provocative issue raised on appeal: the propriety of the remedy fashioned by the trial court. Awards of back pay and reinstatement are not unusual in employment discrimination litigation; awards of promotion or conditional tenure are. The appellate court therefore treated the latter issues extensively, emphasizing the special academic freedom context in which they arose:

> Academic freedom, the wellspring of education, is entitled to maximum protection.
>
> It does not follow that because academic freedom is inextricably related to the educational process it is implicated in every employment decision of an educational institution. Colleges may fail to promote or to grant tenure for a variety of reasons, such as anticipated decline in enrollment, retrenchment for budgetary reasons, termination of some departments, or determination that there are higher priorities elsewhere. These are decisions which may affect the quality of education but do not necessarily intrude upon the nature of the educational process itself.
>
> On the other hand, it is beyond cavil that generally faculty employment decisions comprehend discretionary academic determinations which do entail review of the intellectual work product of the candidate. That decision is most effectively made within the university and although there may be tension between the faculty and the administration on their relative roles and responsibilities, it is generally acknowledged that the faculty has at least the initial, if not the primary, responsibility for judging candidates. "The peer review system has evolved as the most reliable method for assuring promotion of the candidates best qualified to serve the needs of the institution" (*Johnson* v. *University of Pittsburgh,* 435 F. Supp. 1328, 1346 (W.D. Pa. 1977)).
>
> Wherever the responsibility lies within the institution, it is clear that courts must be vigilant not to intrude into that determination, and should not substitute their judgment for that of the college with respect to the qualifications of faculty members for promotion and tenure. Determinations about such matters as teaching ability, research scholarship, and professional stature are subjective, and unless they can be shown to have been used as the mechanism to obscure discrimination, they must be left for evaluation by the professionals, particularly since they often involve inquiry into aspects of arcane scholarship beyond the competence of individual

judges. In the cases cited by appellant in support of the independence of
the institution, an adverse judgment about the qualifications of the individual
involved for the position in question had been made by the professionals—
faculty, administration, or both. It was those adverse judgments that the
courts refused to reexamine. (See, for example, *Johnson* v. *University of Pittsburgh,* above; *Huang* v. *College of the Holy Cross,* 436 F. Supp. 639 (D. Mass.
1977); *EEOC* v. *Tufts Institution of Learning,* 421 F. Supp. 152 (D. Mass.
1975). But see *Sweeney* v. *Board of Trustees of Keene State College,* 604 F.2d
106 (1st Cir. 1979), on remand from 439 U.S. 24, 99 S. Ct. 295, 58 L.
Ed. 2d 216 (1978).)

The distinguishing feature in this case is that Kunda's achievements,
qualifications, and prospects were not in dispute. She was considered
qualified by the unanimous vote of both faculty committees which evaluated
her teaching, research and creative work, and college and public service.
Her department chairman consistently evaluated her as qualified. Even Dean
Secor, who did not affirmatively recommend Kunda, commented favorably
on her performance, which he rated as "justify[ing] a permanent
appointment." . . .

The district court made a specific finding of fact (No. 30) that President Morey did not recommend tenure for Kunda "because of her lack
of an advanced degree." The record is manifest that if President Morey
had recommended Kunda for tenure, the board of trustees would have
ratified that decision. The college had ample opportunity during the trial
to present testimony as to any other factor on which the decision to deny
tenure was based and failed to do so. Thus, the trial judge's finding that
plaintiff "had satisfied both alternatives to the terminal degree requirement
for promotion and tenure" was based not on his independent judgment,
but on the judgment of the university community itself. In the line of cases
challenging university decisions not to promote or grant tenure, this case
may therefore be *sui generis* or, at least, substantially distinguishable.

Nor can the court's order be construed as appellant does—as a judicial
grant of tenure. Underlying the court's order was its finding of fact that
"had Mrs. Kunda been counseled in the same manner as male members
of the physical education department, we find that she would have done
everything possible to obtain a master's degree in order to further enhance
her chances of obtaining tenure." The court did not *award* Kunda tenure.
The court instead attempted to place plaintiff in the position she should
have been "but for" the unlawful discrimination. Having found she was
denied tenure because she did not have a terminal degree, the court gave
her the opportunity to secure one within two full school years, the period
between the time she should have been counseled in 1972 and the tenure
decision in 1974. The direction by the court to the college to grant her tenure
after she secured the one missing link upon which her rejection by the college
had been based is consistent with the line of Title VII cases awarding seniority and other employment perquisites to those found to have been victims
of discrimination (*International Brotherhood of Teamsters* v. *United States,* 431
U.S. 324, 97 S. Ct. 1843, 52 L. Ed. 2d 1843 (1977); *Franks* v. *Bowman*

Transportation Co., 424 U.S. 747, 96 S. Ct. 1251, 47 L. Ed. 2d 444 (1976)).The court could have reasonably decided that there would be no purpose to be served to require that the board of trustees reconsider plaintiff's tenure after she achieved a master's degree because of the impossibility of asking the board to ignore changes such as the financial situation, student enrollment, and faculty hiring which may have occurred in the intervening five-year period, as well as the intangible effect upon that decision because the candidate being considered was the successful party to a Title VII suit.

     The touchstone of Title VII remedies is "to make persons whole for injuries suffered on account of unlawful employment discrimination" (*Albemarle Paper Co.* v. *Moody,* 422 U.S. 405, 418, 95 S. Ct. 2362, 2372, 45 L. Ed. 2d 280 (1975)). In directing the award of competitive-type seniority, the Court noted the broad scope of the courts' equitable discretion in Title VII cases:

> To effectuate this "make-whole" objective, Congress in Section 706(g) vested broad equitable discretion in the federal courts to "order such affirmative action as may be appropriate, which may include, but is not limited to, reinstatement or hiring of employees, with or without back pay . . . , or any other equitable relief as the court deems appropriate." The legislative history supporting the 1972 amendments of Section 706(g) of Title VII affirms the breadth of this discretion. "The provisions of [Section 706(g)] are intended to give the courts wide discretion exercising their equitable powers to fashion the most complete relief possible. . . . The Act is intended to make the victims of unlawful employment discrimination whole, and . . . the attainment of this objective . . . requires that persons aggrieved by the consequences and effects of the unlawful employment practice be, so far as possible, restored to a position where they would have been were it not for the unlawful discrimination" . . . (*Franks* v. *Bowman Transportation Co.,* 424 U.S. 747, 763–64, 96 S. Ct. 1251, 1264, 47 L. Ed. 2d 444 (1976) (citations omitted)).

     The fact that the discrimination in this case took place in an academic rather than commercial setting does not permit the court to abdicate its responsibility to insure the award of a meaningful remedy. Congress did not intend that those institutions which employ persons who work primarily with their mental faculties should enjoy a different status under Title VII than those which employ persons who work primarily with their hands.

     The legislative history of Title VII is unmistakable as to the legislative intent to subject academic institutions to its requirements. When originally enacted, Title VII exempted from the equal employment requirements educational institution employees connected with educational activities. This exemption was removed in 1972. The need for coverage is amply set forth in the Report of the House Committee on Education and Labor:

> There is nothing in the legislative background of Title VII, nor does any national policy suggest itself, to support the exemption of the educational institution employees—primarily teachers—from Title VII

coverage. Discrimination against minorities and women in the field of education is as pervasive as discrimination in any other area of employment. In the field of higher education, the fact that black scholars have been generally relegated to all-black institutions, or have been restricted to lesser academic positions when they have been permitted entry into white institutions, is common knowledge. Similarly, in the area of sex discrimination, women have long been invited to participate as students in the academic process, but without the prospect of gaining employment as serious scholars.

When they have been hired into educational institutions, particularly in institutions of higher education, women have been relegated to positions of lesser standing than their male counterparts. In a study conducted by Theodore Kaplow and Reece J. McGee, it was found that the primary factors determining the hiring of male faculty members were prestige and compatibility, but that women were generally considered to be outside of the prestige system altogether.

The committee feels that discrimination in educational institutions is especially critical. The committee cannot imagine a more sensitive area than educational institutions, where the nation's youth are exposed to a multitude of ideas that will strongly influence their future development. To permit discrimination here would, more than in any other area, tend to promote misconceptions leading to future patterns of discrimination. . . . (Equal Employment Opportunity Act of 1972, H. Rep. No. 92-238, 92nd Cong., 2d Sess. (1972), reprinted in [1972] U.S. Code Cong. & Admin. News, pp. 2137, 2155). . . .

The lack of success of women and minorities in Title VII suits alleging discrimination against academic institutions can, in large part, be attributed to the subjective factors upon which employment decisions are made, previously discussed. The danger that judicial abnegation may nullify the congressional policy to rectify employment bias in an academic setting has been noted:

This anti-interventionist policy has rendered colleges and universities virtually immune to charges of employment bias, at least when that bias is not expressed overtly. We fear, however, that the common-sense position we took in [*Faro* v. *New York University,* 502 F.2d 1229 (2d Cir. 1974)], namely that courts must be ever mindful of relative institutional competence, has been pressed beyond all reasonable limits and may be employed to undercut the explicit legislative intent of the Civil Rights Act of 1964 (*Powell* v. *Syracuse University,* 580 F.2d 1150, 1153 (2d Cir.), certiorari denied, 439 U.S. 984, 99 S. Ct. 576, 58 L. Ed. 2d 656 (1978)).

When a case is presented such as this, in which the discrimination has been proven and the required remedy is clear, we cannot shirk the responsibility placed on us by Congress [621 F.2d at 547–51; footnotes omitted].

Kunda is a ground-breaking case because the court in effect awarded a promotion and conditional tenure as the remedy for the discrimination against the plaintiff. The case is also controversial because the remedy is subject to the charge that it interferes with institutional autonomy in areas (promotion and tenure) where autonomy is most important to postsecondary education. Yet, as a careful reading of the opinion indicates, the court's holding is actually narrow and its reasoning sensitive to the academic community's needs and the relative competencies of college and court. The court emphasizes that "in the line of cases challenging university decisions not to promote or grant tenure, this case may . . . be *sui generis* [the only one of its kind] or, at least, substantially distinguishable." Thus, the case's significance is tied tightly to its facts. According to those facts, the plaintiff had, by the consensus of her peers, met all requirements for promotion and tenure but one: the terminal degree; and since that requirement had been tainted by the discrimination, the defendant could not rely on it. The court thus made an independent judgment about the existence of discrimination, not about the plaintiff's qualifications. The court's remedy puts the plaintiff in the position she would have been in, by the institution's own determination, had the discrimination not occurred. Since she would have been promoted had the administration not discriminatorily imposed the degree requirement, the court ordered the promotion; since she would have had two more years to obtain the degree had she not been the subject of discriminatory counseling, the court ordered that she receive tenure *if* she earned the degree within two years.

Both the *Kunda* and the *Sweeney* v. *Keene State College* opinions are built on the same premise: that postsecondary institutions have no special dispensation from the requirements of federal antidiscrimination legislation. Courts will defer to institutions' expert judgments concerning scholarship, teaching, and other educational qualifications, but courts will not subject institutions to a lesser standard of discrimination or a lesser obligation to repair the adverse effects of discrimination. This point is the most important lesson of the cases. In *Kunda* the court's lengthy discussion made the point emphatically. In *Sweeney* the Supreme Court opinion did not directly address the point; but its reliance on precedents (such as *Furnco*) that did not involve education and its later discussion of *Sweeney* in *Burdine,* another noneducation case, demonstrate that the *Sweeney* ruling is not especially tailored for the academic world. Moreover, the appellate court in *Sweeney* did expressly reject the college's argument that courts should not second-guess faculty employment decisions. Although some other courts had taken such a "hands-off" approach, the appellate court said:

> This reluctance no doubt arises from the courts' recognition that hiring, promotion, and tenure decisions require subjective evaluation most appropriately made by persons thoroughly familiar with the academic setting. Nevertheless, we caution against permitting judicial deference to result in judicial abdication of a responsibility entrusted to the courts by Congress. That responsibility is simply to provide a forum for the litigation of complaints of sex discrimination in institutions of higher learning as readily as for other Title VII suits [569 F.2d at 169, 176 (1st Cir. 1978)].

Besides the burden of proof and remedies issues discussed above, a number of other important developments have arisen under Title VII. Each is treated summarily below.

1. *Sexual harassment.* Employee claims of sexual harassment at the work place are a new development in employment law. Typically, sexual harassment claims are

brought by female employees who allege that they suffer sexual discrimination when their refusal to submit to a male's sexual advances results in tangible loss of job benefits or more intangible emotional and psychological pain (see, for example, *Bundy* v. *Jackson*, 641 F.2d 934 (D.C. Cir. 1981)). The current focus for these claims is Section 703(a) of Title VII and the Title VII guidelines issued by the Equal Employment Opportunity Commission (EEOC). Such claims may also be brought under Title IX of the Education Amendments of 1972, which applies to sex discrimination against students as well as employees (see Sections 7.5.3 and 7.5.7.1).

On November 10, 1980, the EEOC issued its final guidelines prohibiting sexual harassment (see 29 C.F.R. sec. 1604.11). The guidelines expansively define sexual harassment and establish standards under which an employer can be liable for harassment occasioned by its own acts as well as the acts of its agents and supervisory employees:

(a) Harassment on the basis of sex is a violation of Sec. 703 of Title VII. Unwelcome sexual advances, requests for sexual favors, and other verbal or physical conduct of a sexual nature constitute sexual harassment when (1) submission to such conduct is made either explicitly or implicitly a term or condition of an individual's employment, (2) submission to or rejection of such conduct by an individual is used as the basis for employment decisions affecting such individual, or (3) such conduct has the purpose or effect of unreasonably interfering with an individual's work performance or creating an intimidating, hostile, or offensive working environment.

(b) In determining whether alleged conduct constitutes sexual harassment, the commission will look at the record as a whole and the totality of the circumstances, such as the nature of the sexual advances and the context in which the alleged incidents occurred. The determination of the legality of a particular action will be made from the facts, on a case-by-case basis.

(c) Applying general Title VII principles, an employer, employment agency, joint apprenticeship committee, or labor organization (hereinafter collectively referred to as "employer") is responsible for its acts and those of its agents and supervisory employees with respect to sexual harassment regardless of whether the specific acts complained of were authorized or even forbidden by the employer and regardless of whether the employer knew or should have known of their occurrence. The commission will examine the circumstances of the particular employment relationship and the job functions performed by the individual in determining whether an individual acts in either a supervisory or agency capacity.

(d) With respect to conduct between fellow employees, an employer is responsible for acts of sexual harassment in the work place where the employer, its agents or supervisory employees, knows or should have known of the conduct, unless it can show that it took immediate and appropriate corrective action.

(e) An employer may also be responsible for the acts of nonemployees, with respect to sexual harassment of employees in the work place, where the employer, its agents or supervisory employees, knows or should have known of the conduct and fails to take immediate and appropriate corrective action. In reviewing these cases the commission will consider the extent of the employer's control and other legal responsibility which the employer may have with respect to the conduct of such nonemployees.

(f) Prevention is the best tool for the elimination of sexual harassment. An employer should take all steps necessary to prevent sexual harassment from occurring, such as affirmatively raising the subject, expressing strong disapproval, developing appropriate sanctions, informing employees of their right to raise and how to raise the issue of harassment under Title VII, and developing methods to sensitize all concerned.

(g) Other related practices: Where employment opportunities or benefits are granted because of an individual's submission to the employer's sexual advances or requests for sexual favors, the employer may be held liable for unlawful sex discrimination against other persons who were qualified for but denied that employment opportunity or benefit.

Subsection (f) of the EEOC guidelines emphasizes the advisability of implementing clear internal guidelines and sensitive grievance procedures for resolving sexual harassment complaints. The EEOC guidelines' emphasis on prevention suggests that the use of such internal activities may alleviate the postsecondary institution's liability under subsections (d) and (e) and diminish the likelihood of occurrences occasioning liability under subsections (c) and (g).

In light of the social and legal developments, postsecondary institutions should give serious attention and sensitive treatment to sexual harassment issues. Sexual harassment on campus can be not only an employment issue but, for affected faculty and students, an academic freedom issue as well. Advance preventive planning is the key to successful management of these issues, as the EEOC guidelines indicate. Institutions should involve the academic community in developing specific written policies and information on what the community will consider to be sexual harassment. Institutions should also establish processes for receiving, investigating, and resolving complaints and for preserving the privacy of the complainants and charged parties to the maximum practical extent. (For specific recommendations on steps to take in developing a preventive program, see N. Deane and D. Tillar, *Sexual Harassment: An Employment Issue* (College and University Personnel Association, 1981), pp. 31–50, 55–59; and E. Fishbein, "Sexual Harassment: Practical Guidance for Handling a New Issue on Campus," 13 *College Law Digest* at 19–20, printed in *West's Education Law Reporter* (NACUA Special Pamphlet) (Sept. 28, 1982).

2. Sex-based retirement plans. In a number of Title VII cases, plaintiffs have challenged the use of sex-based mortality tables to calculate the contributions to be made or the benefits to be received by employees under employer-sponsored retirement plans. In *City of Los Angeles* v. *Manhart,* 435 U.S. 702 (1978), the U.S. Supreme Court held that employers cannot require women to make larger contributions than males when the benefits to be paid women are the same as those to be paid men. The Court applied its decision only prospectively, to contributions made to the defendant's plan after the Court's ruling, so that previous contributions and benefits based on them were not affected. Five years later, in *Arizona Governing Committee* v. *Norris,* 103 S. Ct. 3492 (1983), the Court applied its *Manhart* ruling to plans under which contributions are equal but women are paid lower monthly retirement benefits than men. Refusing to make fine distinctions based on the type of plan involved, the Court broadly reaffirmed its statement in *Manhart* that "the use of sex-segregated retirement benefits violates Title VII whether or not the tables are an accurate prediction of the longevity of women as a class." Six justices concurred in this ruling. A separate majority of five justices again refused to apply the ruling retroactively, instead holding that the prohibition of sex-based tables would apply only to those retirement benefits under the defendant's plan that were based on contributions made on or after August 1, 1983 (the beginning of the month following the ruling).

On the same day that it decided *Norris*, the Court also vacated the judgments in two U.S. Court of Appeals cases involving the Teachers' Insurance and Annuity Association–College Retirement Equities Fund (TIAA-CREF), the retirement plan widely used at colleges and universities across the country. In the first case, *Spirt* v. *TIAA & CREF*, 691 F.2d 1054 (2d Cir. 1982), the Second Circuit had held that both TIAA's and CREF's use of sex-based tables to determine retirement benefits violates Title VII. In the second case, *Peters* v. *Wayne State University*, 691 F.2d 235 (6th Cir. 1982), the Sixth Circuit had held that neither plan's use of sex-based tables violates Title VII. The Supreme Court remanded both cases to the lower courts for further consideration in light of *Norris*. Subsequently, in the second *Spirt* v. *TIAA & CREF*, 735 F.2d 23 (2d Cir. 1984), the Second Circuit affirmed its earlier ruling as consistent with *Norris*. The court did not agree to apply its ruling only prospectively, however, as the Supreme Court had done in *Norris*. Emphasizing that the TIAA-CREF system for calculating benefits differs fundamentally from that of the Arizona plan in *Norris*, the *Spirt* court determined that retroactive relief would not impose added financial burdens on employers or on the plan. Accordingly, the court ordered TIAA-CREF to use unisex (gender-neutral) tables to calculate benefits for all persons retiring after May 1, 1980 (a date shortly after the trial court's original decision), including benefits based on contributions made prior to that date. The U.S. Supreme Court declined to review the Second Circuit's decision (105 S. Ct. 247 (1984)).

It is clear, after *Manhart* and *Norris*, that the law now prohibits the use of sex-segregated tables by all types of retirement plans sponsored by postsecondary employers. After *Spirt*, it is also clear that TIAA-CREF, in particular, must use unisex tables for *all* contributions of *all* annuitants retiring any time after May 1, 1980.

3. *Sex discrimination in pay*. In *County of Washington* v. *Gunther*, 101 S. Ct. 2241 (1981), the U.S. Supreme Court differentiated Title VII from the Equal Pay Act, 29 U.S.C. sec. 206 *et seq.* (see this volume, Section 3.3.2.4), with respect to their applicability to sex-based claims of wage or salary discrimination. Since the Equal Pay Act embodies an "equal pay for equal work" principle, a plaintiff can assert only claims based on pay disparities between males and females holding *the same jobs*. The *Gunther* Court decided by a 5-to-4 vote that Title VII is not so limited. Rather, under Title VII, a plaintiff can assert a claim based on pay disparities between males and females holding *different jobs*. To prevail, however, the Title VII plaintiff would have to prove that the pay disparity is attributable to intentional sex discrimination rather than to market supply and demand or to seniority, merit, or other neutral factors.

Although the *Gunther* decision broadens the avenues that aggrieved employees have for challenging sex-based pay discrimination, the Court's opinion does not adopt the "comparable worth" theory that some forecasters had hoped the case would establish. According to the majority:

We emphasize at the outset the narrowness of the question before us in this case. Respondents' claim is not based on the controversial concept of "comparable worth," under which plaintiffs might claim increased compensation on the basis of a comparison of the intrinsic worth or difficulty of their job with that of other jobs in the same organization or community. Rather, respondents seek to prove, by direct evidence, that their wages were depressed because of intentional sex discrimination, consisting of setting the wage scale for female guards, but not for male guards, at a level lower than its own survey of outside markets and the worth of the jobs warranted. The narrow question in this case is whether such a claim is precluded by [Title VII] [101 S. Ct. at 2246].

Although the *Gunther* opinion neither rejects nor accepts the comparable worth theory, the Court's application of Title VII to pay disparity claims did provide impetus for further attempts to establish the theory. A number of new lawsuits were filed in the wake of the Court's decision. In the first faculty case to reach the appellate courts, *Spaulding* v. *University of Washington,* 740 F.2d 686 (9th Cir. 1984), members of the university's nursing faculty raised both discriminatory treatment and disparate impact claims to challenge disparities in salary levels between their department and others on campus. The court rejected both claims. As to the former claim, the plaintiffs had not shown that the university acted with discriminatory intent in establishing the salary levels. According to the court, the direct evidence did not indicate such intent, and "we will not infer intent merely from the existence of wage differences between jobs that are only similar." As to the latter claim (which does not require a showing of intent), the court held that the law does not permit use of the disparate impact approach in cases, such as this one, that "involve wide-ranging allegations challenging general wage policies" for jobs that are "only comparable" rather than equal. In particular, said the court, an employer's mere reliance on market forces in setting wages cannot itself constitute a disparate impact violation.

While *Spaulding* is clearly not receptive to comparable worth claims, further enlightenment from other courts and from economic experts can be expected before the debate is finally resolved. See generally *Comparable Worth: Issue for the '80's* (U.S. Commission on Civil Rights, 1984) (a series of papers from outside consultants); and for an analysis of postsecondary education's particular interests in such developments, see J. Koch, "The *Gunther* case, Comparable Worth, and Implications for Academe," 13 *College Law Digest* 312, printed in *West's Education Law Reporter* (NACUA Special Pamphlet) (July 28, 1983).

4. *Pregnancy disability benefits.* Regulations issued by the Equal Employment Opportunity Commission (EEOC) pursuant to the Pregnancy Discrimination Act of 1978 make it a violation of Title VII for an employer to discriminate on the basis of pregnancy, childbirth, or related illnesses in either employment opportunities, health or disability insurance programs, or sick leave plans (29 C.F.R. sec. 1604.10 and appendix "Questions and Answers on the Pregnancy Discrimination Act"). Pregnancy-related conditions must be treated the same as any other disabilities, and health insurance for pregnancy-related conditions must extend not only to female employees but also to wives of male employees (*Newport News Shipbuilding and Dry Dock Co.* v. *EEOC,* 103 S. Ct. 2622 (1983)).

5. *Confidentiality of faculty votes on personnel decisions.* A highly publicized decision

holding a university professor in contempt of court and sending him to jail vividly portrays the issue whether faculty members must reveal and explain their votes on appointment, promotion, or tenure decisions when these decisions are challenged as sex biased. The issue arose in the context of a Title VII suit against the University of Georgia brought by a female assistant professor who had been denied a promotion and tenure. The jailed professor, James Dinnan, served on the College of Education's promotion review committee, which had considered and rejected the plaintiff's application. During a pretrial deposition of Dinnan by the plaintiff's counsel, Dinnan refused to answer any questions regarding his vote. Upon plaintiff's motions to compel an answer and to impose the contempt sanction, the trial court ordered Dinnan to pay a fine and serve a ninety-day jail term if he did not answer counsel's questions. In *In re Dinnan*, 661 F.2d 426 (11th Cir. 1981), a U.S. Court of Appeals affirmed the order:

> The appellant basically contends that he has the privilege not to testify in the proceedings below because he is sheltered by an "academic freedom privilege." . . .
> Unquestionably, academic freedom is one of the paramount values of this republic. However, if the concept is expanded too far it can cause other important societal goals (such as the elimination of discrimination in employment decisions) to be frustrated. Indeed, if the concept were extended as far as the appellant argues, it would rapidly become a double-edged sword threatening the very core of values that it now protects. . . .
> Though we recognize the importance of academic freedom, we must also recognize its limits. The public policy of the United States prohibits discrimination; Professor Dinnan and the University of Georgia are not above that policy. To rule otherwise would mean that the concept of academic freedom would give any institution of higher learning a *carte blanche* to practice discrimination of all types [661 F.2d at 427, 430–31].

A week before the appellate court decision in *Dinnan*, a New York federal district court judge reached the opposite result in *Gray* v. *Board of Higher Education*, 92 F.R.D. 87 (S.D.N.Y. 1981), a similar case in which a faculty member at La Guardia Community College of the City University of New York alleged race discrimination in the denial of tenure. The district court's decision was reversed by the U.S. Court of Appeals for the Second Circuit, however, which ordered that the plaintiff be given the votes of members of the tenure review committee (692 F.2d 901 (2d Cir. 1982)). The appellate court's holding was narrow; the opinion did not spurn the concept of an "academic freedom privilege" as had the Eleventh Circuit's opinion in *Dinnan*. In *Gray* the college had never given the plaintiff a statement of reasons for his denial of tenure. Since the college had not done so, according to the Second Circuit, the plaintiff had a right to request information about why his application had been denied. Had the faculty member been given a statement of reasons, the court implied (but declined to state unequivocally) that it would have treated the information sought by the plaintiff (the individual votes) as privileged.

In other Title VII cases presenting related issues, the U.S. Court of Appeals for the Ninth Circuit has ruled in favor of a plaintiff seeking access to her tenure review file, which included confidential peer evaluations (*Lynn* v. *Regents of Univer-*

sity of California, 656 F.2d 1337 (9th Cir. 1981)); the First Circuit has ruled against a plaintiff who argued that the college had to articulate the specific reasons behind the votes of each tenure committee member (*Banerjee* v. *Board of Trustees of Smith College,* 648 F.2d 61 (1st Cir. 1981)); and the Seventh Circuit has ruled that a government agency, investigating a discrimination claim on behalf of a black professor, could obtain tenure evaluations from the institution's personnel files but that the institution's ''qualified academic privilege'' protects the confidentiality of the evaluators' identities unless the agency makes ''a substantial showing of particularized need'' (*EEOC* v. *University of Notre Dame du Lac,* 715 F.2d 331 (7th Cir. 1983)).

6. *Discrimination against white professors.* In *McDonald* v. *Santa Fe Trail Transportation Co.,* 427 U.S. 273 (1976), the U.S. Supreme Court made clear that Title VII's prohibition against race discrimination protects white persons as well as minorities. Several subsequent cases against postsecondary institutions illustrate how Title VII, as well as the equal protection clause (Section 3.3.3) and the civil rights statute ''Section 1981'' (Section 3.3.2.7), can ''cut both ways'' to protect white as well as black faculty members from discrimination. In *Craig* v. *Alabama State University,* 451 F. Supp. 1207 (M.D. Ala. 1978), a class action brought on behalf of white faculty and other white employees and former employees at a predominantly black institution, the court concluded on the basis of evidence presented at trial that ''in the hiring of its administrative, teaching, and clerical and support staff and the promotion and tenure of its faculty, A.S.U. has . . . engaged in a pattern and practice of discrimination against whites.'' The U.S. Court of Appeals for the Fifth Circuit affirmed (614 F.2d 1295 (5th Cir. 1980)).

Shortly after *Craig,* the Fifth Circuit reached a similar result in a case brought by a single faculty member. In *Whiting* v. *Jackson State University,* 616 F.2d 116 (5th Cir. 1980), a white psychometry professor working at a predominantly black university claimed that his discharge was motivated by racial discrimination. The court outlined the burdens of proof applicable to the professor's claim, using the same standards applicable to other Title VII ''disparate treatment'' claims (see above discussion of the *Sweeney* and *Kunda* cases). Finding that the university's articulated reason for the discharge was a pretext and that the discharge had been motivated by racial considerations, the court affirmed the trial court's judgment for the professor: ''Our traditional reluctance to intervene in university affairs cannot be allowed to undermine our statutory duty to remedy the wrong.''

The *Whiting* standards were followed in *Fisher* v. *Dillard University,* 499 F. Supp. 525 (E.D. La. 1980), in which a predominantly black university had discharged a white Ph.D. psychologist and hired a black psychologist instead at a higher salary. The court entered judgment for the white professor. And in another similar case, *Lincoln* v. *Board of Regents of the University System of Georgia,* 697 F.2d 928 (11th Cir. 1983), the court affirmed the lower court's ruling that a white professor would have had her contract renewed but for her race.

7. *Time limitations on filing Title VII claims.* Under Title VII, an individual claiming discrimination must file a complaint with the EEOC within 180 days ''after the alleged unlawful employment practice occurred'' (42 U.S.C. sec. 2000e-5(e)). The claim lapses if the individual does not comply with this time limit. In *Delaware State College* v. *Ricks,* 449 U.S. 250 (1980), the U.S. Supreme Court interpreted this time requirement as it applies to faculty members making claims against postsecondary institutions. Overruling the appellate court, the Supreme Court held

that the time period commences when an institution officially announces its employment decision and not when the employment relationship itself terminates.

In a 5-to-4 decision, the Court dismissed the claim of Ricks, a black Liberian professor who had been denied tenure, because he had not filed his claim of national origin discrimination within 180 days of the date the college notified him of its decision. Ricks had claimed that his terminal year of employment, after the tenure denial, constituted a "continuing violation" of Title VII, which allowed him to file within 180 days of his last day of employment. The Court rejected this view:

> Mere continuity of employment, without more, is insufficient to prolong the life of a cause of action for employment discrimination. If Ricks intended to complain of a discriminatory discharge, he should have identified the alleged discriminatory acts that continued until, or occurred at the time of, the actual termination of his employment. . . .
>
> In sum, the only alleged discrimination occurred—and the filing limitations period therefore commenced—at the time the tenure decision was made and communicated to Ricks. That is so even though one of the *effects* of the denial of tenure—the eventual loss of a teaching position—did not occur until later [449 U.S. at 257–58].

The Court also rejected an intermediate position, adopted by three of the dissenters, that the limitations period should not have begun until after the final decision of the college grievance committee, which had held hearings on Ricks's complaint.

In *Chardon* v. *Fernandez,* 102 S. Ct. 28 (1981), a *per curiam* opinion from which three justices dissented, the Court extended the reasoning of *Ricks* to cover nonrenewal or termination of term appointments (as opposed to tenure denials). Unless there are allegations that discriminatory acts continued to occur after official notice of the decision, the 180-day time period for nonrenewal or termination claims also begins to run from the date the complainant is notified.

8. *Religious discrimination under Title VII.* As noted above, discrimination "because of [an] individual's . . . religion" is one of the prohibited forms of discrimination under Title VII (42 U.S.C. sec. 2000e-2(a)), subject to an exception for situations where a particular religious characteristic is a "bona fide occupational qualification" for the job (42 U.S.C. sec. 2000e-2(e)(1)). A related exception, applicable specifically to educational institutions, permits the employment of persons "of a particular religion" if the institution is "owned, supported, controlled, or managed" by a particular religion or if the institution's curriculum "is directed toward the propagation of a particular religion" (42 U.S.C. sec. 2000e-2(e)(2)).

Title VII defines religion to include "all aspects of religious observance and practice, as well as belief" (42 U.S.C. sec. 2000e(j)). The same section of the statute requires that an employer "reasonably accommodate to" an employee's religion unless the employer can demonstrate an inability to do so "without undue hardship." In *Trans World Airlines* v. *Hardison,* 432 U.S. 63 (1977), the U.S. Supreme Court narrowly construed this provision, holding that it would be an undue hardship to require an employer to bear more than *de minimus* costs in accommodating an employee's religious beliefs. To further explicate the statute and case law, the EEOC has issued revised guidelines on the employer's Title VII duty to reasonably accommodate the religious practices of employees and applicants (29 C.F.R. Part 1605).

For related developments on the applicability of Title VII to church-related postsecondary institutions, see this volume, Section 7.2.5.2.

9. *National origin discrimination under Title VII.* Title VII also prohibits discrimination "because of [an] individual's . . . national origin" (42 U.S.C. sec. 2000e-2(a))—that is, discrimination based on the employee's nationality. In *Briseno* v. *Central Technical Community College Area,* 739 F.2d 344 (8th Cir. 1984), for example, the court held that the defendant had intentionally discriminated against the plaintiff, a Mexican-American, because of his national origin.

The U.S. Supreme Court has ruled that the statutory term "national origin" does not cover discrimination on the basis of alienage—that is, discrimination against employees who are not citizens of the United States (*Espinoza* v. *Farah Manufacturing Co.,* 414 U.S. 86 (1973)). But the Court cautioned in *Espinoza* that a citizenship requirement may sometimes be part of a scheme of, or a pretext for, national origin discrimination and that "Title VII prohibits discrimination on the basis of citizenship [alienage] whenever it has the purpose or effect of discriminating on the basis of national origin." The Court also made clear that aliens, as individuals, are covered by Title VII if they have been discriminated against on the basis of race, color, religion, or sex, as well as national origin.

To implement the statute and case law, the EEOC has issued guidelines barring discrimination on the basis of national origin (29 C.F.R. Part 1606).

3.3.2.2. Executive Orders 11246 and 11375. Executive Order 11246, 30 Fed. Reg. 12319, as amended by Executive Order 11375, 32 Fed. Reg. 14303 (adding sex to the list of prohibited discriminations), prohibits discrimination "because of race, color, religion, sex, or national origin," thus paralleling Title VII (Section 3.3.2.1). Unlike Title VII, the executive orders apply only to contractors and subcontractors under federal government contracts and federally assisted construction contracts. Contracts with each such contractor must include an equal opportunity clause (41 C.F.R. sec. 60-1.4) and contractors must file post-award compliance reports and annual compliance reports thereafter (41 C.F.R. sec. 60-1.7(a)) with the federal contracting agency. In addition to their equal opportunity provisions, the executive orders and regulations place heavy emphasis on affirmative action by federal contractors, as discussed in Section 3.3.4.

The regulations implementing these executive orders contain exemptions for various contracts and contractors (41 C.F.R. sec. 60-1.5), including an exemption for church-related educational institutions which is the same as Title VII's (41 C.F.R. sec. 60-1.5(a)(5)). While the regulations contain a partial exemption for state and local government contractors, "educational institutions and medical facilities" are specifically excluded from this exemption (41 C.F.R. sec. 60-1.5(a)(4)). The enforcing agency may hold compliance reviews (41 C.F.R. sec. 60-1.20), receive and investigate complaints from employees and applicants (41 C.F.R. secs. 60-1.21 to 60-1.24), and initiate administrative or judicial enforcement proceedings (41 C.F.R. sec. 60-1.26(a)(1)). It may seek orders enjoining violations and providing other relief, as well as orders terminating, canceling, or suspending contracts (41 C.F.R. sec. 60-1.26(a)(2)). The enforcing agency may also seek to debar contractors from further contract awards (41 C.F.R. sec. 60-1.26(a)(2)).

On October 8, 1978, all authority for enforcing compliance with Executive Orders 11246 and 11375 was centralized in the Department of Labor (Executive Order 12086). In 1981 the department issued new proposals for modifying (some commentators would say weakening) the regulations implementing these executive orders (see 46 Fed. Reg. 42968 (Aug. 25, 1981)). Although they met with heavy criticism, these proposals and other suggested modifications of the regulations continue to be discussed. As of early 1985, no final action had been taken.

3.3.2.3. Title IX. Title IX of the Education Amendments of 1972, 20 U.S.C. sec. 1681 *et seq.,* prohibits sex discrimination by public and private educational institutions receiving federal funds (see Section 7.5.3). The statute is administered by the Office for Civil Rights (OCR) of the Department of Education. The department's regulations contain provisions on employment (34 C.F.R. secs. 106.51 through 106.61) which are similar in many respects to the EEOC's sex discrimination guidelines under Title VII. Like Title VII, the Title IX regulations contain a provision permitting sex-based distinctions in employment where sex is a "bona fide occupational qualification" (34 C.F.R. sec. 106.61). Also like Title VII, Title IX contains an exemption applicable to some religious institutions. Title IX's is differently worded, however, to exempt "an educational institution which is controlled by a religious organization" if Title IX's requirements "would not be consistent with the religious tenets of such organization" (20 U.S.C. sec. 1681(a)(3); 34 C.F.R. sec. 106.12).

The applicability of Title IX to employment discrimination was hotly contested in a series of cases beginning in the mid-1970s. The U.S. Supreme Court has resolved the dispute, holding that Title IX does apply to and prohibit sex discrimination in employment (see *North Haven Board of Education* v. *Bell,* 102 S. Ct. 1912 (1982) (discussed in Section 7.5.7.1)).

3.3.2.4. Equal Pay Act. The Equal Pay Act of 1963, as amended, 29 U.S.C. sec. 206 *et seq.,* covers only sex discrimination in the context of wage rates. The basic prohibition, in 29 U.S.C. sec. 206(d)(1), is applicable to both public and private institutions:

> No employer having employees subject to any provisions of this section shall discriminate, within any establishment in which such employees are employed, between employees on the basis of sex by paying wages to employees in such establishment at a rate less than the rate at which he pays wages to employees of the opposite sex in such establishment for equal work on jobs the performance of which requires equal skill, effort, and responsibility, and which are performed under similar working conditions, except where such payment is made pursuant to (i) a seniority system; (ii) a merit system; (iii) a system which measures earnings by quantity or quality of production; or (iv) a differential based on any other factor other than sex: *Provided,* That an employer who is paying a wage rate differential in violation of this subsection shall not, in order to comply with the provisions of this subsection, reduce the wage of any employee.

Congress's purpose in enacting this provision was to combat the "ancient but outmoded belief that a man, because of his role in society, should be paid more than a woman" and establish, in its place, the principle that "'equal work will be rewarded by equal wages'" (*Corning Glass Workers* v. *Brennan,* 417 U.S. 188 (1974)).

The Equal Pay Act has been applied to discrimination against men as well as against women. In *Board of Regents of University of Nebraska* v. *Dawes,* 522 F.2d 380 (8th Cir. 1975), the university had, under pressure of a threatened federal fund cutoff, developed a complicated numerical formula for computing the average salary of male faculty members. The university used this average as the minimum salary for female faculty members. In a declaratory judgment action by the university, the court held that the practice violated the Equal Pay Act because ninety-two male faculty members received less than the female minimum even though they had substantially equal qualifications. (For an overview of Equal Pay Act issues in higher education, see D. Green, ''Application of the Equal Pay Act to Higher Education,'' 8 *J. of College and University Law* 203 (1981–82).)

In *County of Washington* v. *Gunther* (this volume, Section 3.3.2.1), the U.S. Supreme Court sorted out the relationships between the Equal Pay Act and Title VII as they apply to claims of sex discrimination in pay. In the first major post-*Gunther* case involving faculty pay scales, the U.S. Court of Appeals for the Ninth Circuit rejected the claim of University of Washington nursing faculty members that their jobs were equal to those of faculty members in other departments who had higher salaries (*Spaulding* v. *University of Washington*, 740 F.2d 686 (9th Cir. 1984)). The court emphasized, however, that:

> A plaintiff may show that the jobs are substantially equal, not necessarily that they are identical. Actual job performance and content, rather than job descriptions, titles, or classifications, is determinative. Thus, each claim that jobs are substantially equal necessarily must be determined on a case-by-case basis. . . . We disagree therefore, with the university's contention that jobs from different academic disciplines can never be substantially equal [740 F.2d at 697].

On July 1, 1979, the Equal Employment Opportunity Commission assumed responsibility for the administration of the Equal Pay Act from the U.S. Department of Labor (Reorganization Plan No. 1 of 1978, 3 C.F.R., 1978 Compilation, p. 321). The EEOC's procedural regulations on the Act are codified in 29 C.F.R. Part 1620. The EEOC has also proposed new interpretations of the Equal Pay Act (see 46 Fed. Reg. 43848 (Sept. 1, 1981)) to replace the Department of Labor interpretations (29 C.F.R. Part 800). Among other matters, the new EEOC interpretations address sex-based differentials in retirement benefits and other employee fringe benefits.

3.3.2.5. Age Discrimination in Employment Act (ADEA). This Act, 29 U.S.C. sec. 621 *et seq.,* prohibits age discrimination only with respect to persons who are at least forty years of age. Prior to the Act's amendment in 1978, the upper age limit was sixty-five (29 U.S.C. sec. 631). The 1978 amendments raised that limit to seventy, effective January 1, 1979. Until July 1, 1982, however, postsecondary institutions could continue to require mandatory retirement of tenured faculty members at age sixty-five. July 1, 1982, marked the expiration of this temporary faculty exemption from ADEA's increase of the retirement age to seventy. Now colleges and universities, like other employees, may not require their faculty members or other employees to retire before that age. The 1978 amendments make clear that the provisions of seniority systems or pension plans cannot serve to justify such involuntary retirements.

Within the forty to seventy age limits, the Act's basic provision, applicable to both public and private institutions, makes it unlawful for an employer:

(1) to fail or refuse to hire or to discharge any individual with respect to his compensation, terms, conditions, or privileges of employment, because of such individual's age;

(2) to limit, segregate, or classify his employees in any way which would deprive or tend to deprive any individual of employment opportunities or otherwise adversely affect his status as an employee, because of such individual's age; or

(3) to reduce the wage rate of any employee in order to comply with this chapter.[4]

On July 1, 1979, the authority to enforce ADEA was transferred from the U.S. Department of Labor to the Equal Employment Opportunity Commission (EEOC) (Reorganization Plan No. 1 of 1978, 3 C.F.R. p. 321). On September 29, 1981, the EEOC issued its own interpretations of ADEA (29 C.F.R. Part 1625), replacing previous interpretations of the Department of Labor. Among other matters, the interpretations specify the criteria an employer must meet to establish age as a bona fide job qualification.

As under other statutes, the burden of proof has been an issue in court litigation. Generally, the plaintiff must make a prima facie showing of age discrimination, at which point the burden shifts to the employer to show that "age is a bona fide occupational qualification reasonably necessary to the normal operation of the particular business" at issue (29 U.S.C. sec. 623(f)(1)); or that distinctions among employees or applicants were "based on reasonable factors other than age" (29 U.S.C. sec. 623(f)(1)); or that, in the case of discipline or discharge, the action was taken "for good cause" (29 U.S.C. sec. 623(f)(3)). (See *Laugeson* v. *Anaconda Co.,* 510 F.2d 307 (6th Cir. 1975), and *Hodgson* v. *First Federal Savings and Loan,* 455 F.2d 818 (5th Cir. 1972).) The case of *Leftwich* v. *Harris-Stowe College,* 702 F.2d 686 (8th Cir. 1983), illustrates the application of these principles to postsecondary education.

The plaintiff in *Leftwich* had lost his position as a tenured biology professor when the state legislature transferred control of the college from a local board of education to the state college system. After the governor appointed a board of regents for the "new" college, the board decided to hire a "new" faculty of substantially smaller size. Under the regents' plan, a certain number of tenured and a certain number of nontenured positions from the "old" college were retained. Faculty members were invited to apply for these positions in the "new" college, and those not hired were sent termination letters and offered the opportunity to have their applications reviewed in a hearing with the regents. Of the two biology positions at the "new" college, one was to be filled by a nontenured and the other by a tenured faculty member. Even though Leftwich had scored higher than either of his two competitors on the regents' evaluation measure, these other two men were retained and Leftwich was terminated. Leftwich filed suit, contending (among other things) that the regents' specification of the numbers of new college positions to be filled by tenured and by nontenured faculty members had the effect of discriminating by age. The plaintiff's expert witness testified that tenured faculty at the "old" college

---

[4]Relevant authorities construing the Act are collected in Annot., "Construction and Application of Age Discrimination in Employment Act of 1967," 24 A.L.R. Fed. 808 (1975 and periodic supp.).

were older and higher paid as a group than nontenured faculty and that the regents' reservation of a specified number of positions for nontenured faculty (and their use of salary as a selection factor) therefore had an adverse impact on the employment of older faculty members. The regents did not refute this expert testimony. Instead, they argued that "business necessity" justified this adverse impact of their selection plan—in other words, that they could consider nontenured status to be a bona fide occupational qualification under Section 623(f)(1) of the ADEA statute. The regents asserted that their needs to cut costs and to promote innovation and quality created the "business necessity" to hire the specified number of nontenured faculty.

After the district court rejected the regents' contentions and determined that they had discriminated against Leftwich in violation of the ADEA, the U.S. Court of Appeals for the Eighth Circuit affirmed:

> To establish a prima facie case of age discrimination under a disparate impact theory, a plaintiff need not show that the employer was motivated by a discriminatory intent; he or she need only demonstrate that a facially neutral employment practice actually operates to exclude from a job a disproportionate number of persons protected by the ADEA. . . .
>
> Statistical evidence such as that presented by [the plaintiff's expert] is clearly an appropriate method to establish disparate impact (see, for example, *Hazelwood School District* v. *United States,* 433 U.S. 299, 306–09, 97 S. Ct. 2736, 2740–42, 53 L. Ed. 2d 768 (1977); *International Brotherhood of Teamsters* v. *United States,* 431 U.S. 324, 337–40, 97 S. Ct. 1843, 1855–57, 52 L. Ed. 2d 396 (1977)).
>
> Once the plaintiff established his prima facie case, the burden of persuasion shifted to the defendants to prove that their selection plan was justified by business necessity (see, for example, *Albemarle Paper Co.* v. *Moody,* 422 U.S. 405, 425, 95 S. Ct. 2362, 2375, 45 L. Ed. 2d 280 (1975); *Geller* v. *Markham,* 635 F.2d 1027, 1032 (2d Cir. 1980)).
>
> The defendants' primary justification is that they adopted their selection plan as a cost-saving measure. Quite simply, the plan was intended to reduce costs by eliminating some positions at the college for tenured faculty, who were generally higher paid than the nontenured faculty. The district court held that this cost justification did not establish a business necessity defense. We agree. . . .
>
> Here, the defendants' selection plan was based on tenure status rather than explicitly on age. Nonetheless, because of the close relationship between tenure status and age, the plain intent and effect of the defendants' practice was to eliminate older workers who had built up, through years of satisfactory service, higher salaries than their younger counterparts. If the existence of such higher salaries can be used to justify discharging older employees, then the purpose of the ADEA will be defeated. . . .
>
> The other justification offered by the defendants for their selection plan is that it promotes innovation and quality among the faculty by giving the college flexibility to hire nontenured faculty. The district court also rejected this justification. We again affirm that finding.
>
> First, the record makes it clear that the defendants' principal, if not only, purpose in adopting their selection plan was to eliminate some tenure

positions in order to effectuate cost savings. Second, to the extent that the
defendants in fact utilized their selection plan in an attempt to increase
the quality of the college's faculty, they have failed to establish that the
plan was necessary to achieve their goal. . . .

The defendants failed to demonstrate that reserving nontenured slots
was necessary to bring new ideas to the college. Instead, their assertion
that younger nontenured faculty would have new ideas apparently assumes
that older tenured faculty members would cause the college to "stagnate."
Such assumptions are precisely the kind of stereotypical thinking about older
workers that the ADEA was designed to eliminate [702 F.2d at 690–92].

Having affirmed the lower court's decision for the professor, the appellate
court reviewed the relief the lower court had awarded to him. After making several
modifications in the lower court's order, the appellate court awarded the professor
a position on the "new" college faculty, retroactive seniority for the years missed
due to his discriminatory termination, back pay, attorney's fees, and court costs.

In *Oscar Mayer & Co.* v. *Evans,* 441 U.S. 750 (1979), the U.S. Supreme Court
considered whether an employee or a former employee claiming age discrimination must seek relief from appropriate state agencies in his state before bringing
an ADEA suit in the federal courts. The Court held that such resort to state agencies
is mandatory under Section 14(b) of ADEA (29 U.S.C. sec. 633(b)) whenever there
is a state agency authorized to grant relief against age discrimination in employment, but that the employee need not commence state proceedings within the time
limit specified by state law. If the state agency rejects the employee's complaint
as untimely or does not resolve the complaint within sixty days, the employee can
then turn to the federal courts.

*3.3.2.6. Rehabilitation Act of 1973, as amended by the Rehabilitation Act Amend-
ments of 1974 (handicapped).* Section 504 of the Rehabilitation Act, 29 U.S.C. sec.
794 (also discussed in Section 7.5.4), is patterned after the Title VI and Title IX
provisions (see Sections 7.5.2 and 7.5.3), which prohibit, respectively, race and
sex discrimination in federally funded programs and activities. Each federal funding
agency enforces the statute with respect to its own funding programs. The regulations of the U.S. Department of Education (ED), the funding agency of primary
importance to postsecondary institutions, are discussed below.

Regarding employment, the ED regulations implementing Section 504 have
the following provisions:

(a) *General.* (1) No qualified handicapped person shall, on the basis
of handicap, be subjected to discrimination in employment under any program or activity. . . .

(2) A recipient that receives assistance under the Education of the
Handicapped Act shall take positive steps to employ and advance in employment qualified handicapped persons in programs assisted under that Act.

(3) A recipient shall make all decisions concerning employment under
any program or activity to which this part applies in a manner which ensures
that discrimination on the basis of handicap does not occur and may not
limit, segregate, or classify applicants or employees in any way that adversely
affects their opportunities or status because of handicap.

(4) A recipient may not participate in a contractual or other relationship that has the effect of subjecting qualified handicapped applicants or employees to discrimination prohibited by this subpart. The relationships referred to in this subparagraph include relationships with employment and referral agencies, with labor unions, with organizations providing or administering fringe benefits to employees of the recipient, and with organizations providing training and apprenticeship programs.

(b) *Specific activities.* The provisions of this subpart apply to:

(1) Recruitment, advertising, and the processing of applications for employment;

(2) Hiring, upgrading, promotion, award of tenure, demotion, transfer, layoff, termination, right of return from layoff, and rehiring;

(3) Rates of pay or any other form of compensation and changes in compensation;

(4) Job assignments, job classifications, organizational structure, position descriptions, lines of progression, and seniority lists;

(5) Leaves of absence, sick leave, or any other leave;

(6) Fringe benefits available by virtue of employment, whether or not administered by the recipient;

(7) Selection and financial support for training, including apprenticeship, professional meetings, conferences, and other related activities, and selection for leaves of absence to pursue training;

(8) Employer-sponsored activities, including social or recreational programs; and

(9) Any other term, condition, or privilege of employment.

(c) A recipient's obligation to comply with this subpart is not affected by any inconsistent term of any collective bargaining agreement to which it is a party [34 C.F.R. sec. 104.11].

For purposes of this section, a qualified handicapped person is defined as one who "with reasonable accommodation can perform the essential functions" of the job in question (34 C.F.R. sec. 104.3(k)(1)). The regulations impose an affirmative obligation on the recipient to make "reasonable accommodation to the known physical or mental limitations of an otherwise qualified handicapped applicant or employee unless the recipient can demonstrate that the accommodation would impose an undue hardship on the operation of its program" (34 C.F.R. sec. 104.12(a)). Reasonable accommodations can take the form of modification of the job site, of equipment, or of a position itself. What hardship would relieve a recipient of the obligation to make reasonable accommodation depends on the facts of each case. As a related affirmative requirement, the recipient must adapt its employment tests to accommodate an applicant's sensory, manual, or speaking handicap unless the tests are intended to measure those types of skills (34 C.F.R. sec. 104.13(b)).

The regulations include explicit prohibitions regarding employee selection procedures and preemployment questioning. As a general rule, the fund recipient cannot make any preemployment inquiry or require a preemployment medical examination to determine whether an applicant is handicapped or to determine the nature or severity of a handicap (34 C.F.R. sec. 104.14(a)). Nor can a recipient use any employment criterion, such as a test, which has the effect of eliminating qualified handicapped applicants, unless the criterion is job related and there is no alternative job-related criterion which does not have the same effect (34 C.F.R. sec. 104.13(a)).

In *Southeastern Community College* v. *Davis,* 442 U.S. 397 (1979), discussed in Sections 4.2.4.3 and 7.5.4, the U.S. Supreme Court addressed for the first time the extent of the obligation that Section 504 imposes on colleges and universities. The case involved the admission of a handicapped applicant to a clinical nursing program, but the Court's opinion also sheds light on the law's application to employment of the handicapped.

According to the Court, an "otherwise qualified handicapped individual" protected by Section 504 is one who is qualified *in spite of* his or her handicap, and the institution need not make major program modifications to accommodate the handicapped. In contrast, the Department of Education's regulations implementing Section 504 define a "qualified handicapped individual" for employment purposes as one who, "with reasonable accommodation," can perform the job's essential functions (34 C.F.R. secs. 104.3(k)(1), 104.12(a)). Thus, the Court's opinion in *Davis* raises questions concerning the extent of federal agencies' authority to require "accommodation" under their Section 504 regulations:

> The language and structure of the Rehabilitation Act of 1973 reflect a recognition by Congress of the distinction between the evenhanded treatment of qualified handicapped persons and affirmative efforts to overcome the disabilities caused by handicaps. Section 501(b), governing the employment of handicapped individuals by the federal government, requires each federal agency to submit "an affirmative action program plan for the hiring, placement, and advancement of handicapped individuals." These plans "shall include a description of the extent to which and methods whereby the special needs of handicapped employees are being met." Similarly, Section 503(a), governing hiring by federal contractors, requires employers to "take affirmative action to employ and advance in employment qualified handicapped individuals." . . .
>
> Under Section 501(c) of the Act, by contrast, state agencies . . . are only "encourage[d] . . . to adopt such policies and procedures." Section 504 does not refer at all to affirmative action, and except as it applies to federal employers it does not provide for implementation by administrative action. A comparison of these provisions demonstrates that Congress understood [that] accommodation of the needs of handicapped individuals may require affirmative action and knew how to provide for it in those instances where it wished to do so [442 U.S. at 410–11].

The implication from this and other language in the *Davis* opinion is that the courts will narrowly construe the "reasonable accommodation" obligations that the ED handicap regulations impose on federal fund recipients.

For many postsecondary institutions, however, even a narrow reading of these regulations will have little effect on their obligations regarding employment of the handicapped. As the quote above indicates, Section 503 of the Rehabilitation Act requires all institutions holding contracts with the federal government in excess of $2,500 to "take affirmative action to employ and advance in employment qualified handicapped individuals.'' While the Court in *Davis* emphatically rejected an affirmative action obligation under Section 504, its decision in no way affects the express obligation imposed on federal contractors by Section 503 (see Section 3.3.4). Moreover, even those institutions *not* subject to Section 503 should be cautious in reacting to *Davis*'s approach to accommodation. The Court stopped far short of saying that accommodation is *never* required:

> We do not suggest that the line between a lawful refusal to extend affirmative action and illegal discrimination against handicapped persons always will be clear. It is possible to envision situations where an insistence on continuing past requirements and practices might arbitrarily deprive genuinely qualified handicapped persons of the opportunity to participate in a covered program. Technological advances can be expected to enhance opportunities to rehabilitate the handicapped or otherwise to qualify them for some useful employment. Such advances also may enable attainment of these goals without imposing undue financial and administrative burdens upon a state. Thus, situations may arise where a refusal to modify an existing program might become unreasonable and discriminatory. Identification of those instances where a refusal to accommodate the needs of a disabled person amounts to discrimination against the handicapped continues to be an important responsibility of HEW [442 U.S. at 412–13].

Administrators and counsel should watch for future litigation interpreting the *Davis* precedent in the employment context and for interpretation by ED and other funding agencies regarding the effect of *Davis* or later litigation on their regulations.

3.3.2.7. Section 1981 (Race and Alienage). A post–Civil War civil rights statute, 42 U.S.C. sec. 1981, commonly known as ''Section 1981'' (''equal rights under the law''), states:

> All persons within the jurisdiction of the United States shall have the same right in every state and territory to make and enforce contracts, to sue, be parties, give evidence, and to the full and equal benefit of all laws and proceedings for the security of persons and property as is enjoyed by white citizens, and shall be subject to like punishment, pains, penalties, taxes, licences, and exactions of every kind, and to no other.

Section 1981 is enforced through court litigation by persons denied the equality that the statute guarantees.

Section 1981 covers racially based employment discrimination against white persons as well as racial minorities (*McDonald* v. *Sante Fe Trail Transportation Co.*, 427 U.S. 273 (1976)). It also has been held to apply to employment discrimination against aliens (*Guerra* v. *Manchester Terminal Corp.*, 498 F.2d 641 (5th Cir. 1974)). Section 1981 prohibits discrimination in both public and private employment, as the U.S. Supreme Court affirmed in *Johnson* v. *Railway Express Agency,* 421 U.S. 454 (1975).

While Section 1981 overlaps Title VII (see Section 3.3.2.1) in its coverage of racial discrimination in employment, a back-pay award is not restricted to two years of back pay under Section 1981 as it is under Title VII (see *Johnson* v. *Railway Express Agency*). Moreover, Section 1981 directly covers discrimination against aliens, which Title VII does not (see Section 3.3.2.1 under "National Origin Discrimination"); and Title VII covers religion, sex, and national origin discrimination, whereas Section 1981 does not.

In *General Contractors Association* v. *Pennsylvania,* 102 S. Ct. 3141 (1982), the U.S. Supreme Court engrafted an intent requirement onto the Section 1981 statute. To prevail on a Section 1981 claim, therefore, a plaintiff must prove that the defendant intentionally or purposefully engaged in discriminatory acts. This requirement is the same as the Court previously applied to discrimination claims brought under the equal protection clause (see this volume, Section 3.3.3).

3.3.3. Constitutional prohibitions against employment discrimination. While the Fourteenth Amendment's equal protection clause applies to employment discrimination by public institutions (see Section 1.4.2), the constitutional standards for justifying discrimination are generally more lenient than the various federal statutory standards. (See the discussions of constitutional equal protection standards in Sections 4.2.4 and 4.2.5.) Even where constitutional standards are very strong, as for race discrimination, the courts usually strike down only discrimination found to be intentional; the federal statutes, on the other hand, often do not require a showing of discriminatory intent. In *Washington* v. *Davis,* 426 U.S. 229 (1976), for instance, the U.S. Supreme Court distinguished between disparate impact cases brought under Title VII (see Section 3.3.2.1) and those brought under the equal protection clause, noting that the equal protection cases "have not embraced the proposition that a law or other official act, without regard to whether it reflects a racially discriminatory purpose, is unconstitutional solely because it has a racially disproportionate impact." Under Title VII, in contrast, "discriminatory purpose need not be proved." Title VII thus "involves a more probing judicial review of, and less deference to, the seemingly reasonable acts of administrators and executives than is appropriate under the Constitution where special racial impact, without discriminatory purpose, is claimed."

In *Personnel Administrator of Massachusetts* v. *Feeney,* 442 U.S. 256 (1979), the Court elaborated on the requirement of discriminatory intent, which must be met to establish a violation of the equal protection clause. *Feeney* concerned a female civil servant who challenged the constitutionality of a state law providing that all veterans who qualify for civil service positions must be considered ahead of any qualified nonveteran. The statute's language was gender neutral—its benefits extended to "any person" who had served in official United States military units or unofficial auxiliary units during wartime. The veterans' preference law had a disproportionate impact on women, however, because 98 percent of the veterans in Massachusetts were men. Consequently, nonveteran women who received high scores on competitive examinations were repeatedly displaced by lower-scoring male veterans. Feeney claimed that the preference law discriminated against women in violation of the Fourteenth Amendment. The Court summarized the general approach it would take in ruling on such constitutional challenges of state statutes:

> The equal protection guarantee of the Fourteenth Amendment does
> not take from the states all the power of classification. Most laws classify,
> and many affect certain groups unevenly, even though the law itself treats

them no differently from all other members of the class described by the law. When the basic classification is rationally based, uneven effects upon particular groups within a class are ordinarily of no constitutional concern. The calculus of effects, the manner in which a particular law reverberates in society, is a legislative and not a judicial responsibility. In assessing an equal protection challenge, a court is called upon only to measure the basic validity of the . . . classification. When some other independent right is not at stake . . . and when there is no "reason to infer antipathy," it is presumed that "even improvident decisions will eventually be rectified by the democratic process" (*Vance* v. *Bradley,* 99 S. Ct. 939, 59 L. Ed. 2d 171) [442 U.S. at 271–72; citations omitted].

The Supreme Court agreed with the district court's finding that the law was not enacted for the purpose of preferring males, but rather to give a competitive advantage to veterans. Since the classification "nonveterans" includes both men and women, both sexes could be disadvantaged by the laws. The Court concluded that too many men were disadvantaged to permit the inference that the classification was a pretext for discrimination against women.

Feeney argued that, although the legislation assisted only veterans, the curtailing of job opportunities for women was an inevitable, foreseeable concomitant of the veterans' preference policy and that where "a law's consequences are *that* inevitable they cannot meaningfully be described as unintended." The Court disagreed:

Discriminatory purpose . . . implies more than intent as volition or intent as awareness of consequences. . . . It implies that the decision maker, in this case the state legislature, selected or reaffirmed a particular course of action at least in part "because of," not merely "in spite of," its adverse effects upon an identifiable group [442 U.S. at 279].

Since neither the statute's language nor the facts concerning its passage demonstrated that the preference was designed to deny women opportunity for employment or advancement in the Massachusetts civil service, the Supreme Court, with two justices dissenting, upheld the statute.

Feeney extends the reasoning in *Washington* v. *Davis* by stating unequivocally that a statute which has a disproportionate impact on a particular group will withstand an equal protection challenge unless the plaintiff can show that it was enacted in order to affect that group adversely. Thus, a statute neutral on its face will be upheld unless the disparate impact of the law "could not plausibly be explained on neutral grounds," in which case "impact itself would signal that the classification made by the law was in fact not neutral." The effect of this reasoning—controversial especially among civil rights advocates—is to increase the difficulty of proving equal protection violations.

Besides its less vigorous standards, the equal protection clause also lacks the administrative implementation and enforcement mechanisms that exist for most federal statutes. Consequently, postsecondary administrators will have more guidance, via regulations and interpretive bulletins, but will also be subject to more detailed rules and a broader range of remedies for ensuring compliance, under the statutes than under the Constitution.

In employment discrimination the Constitution assumes its greatest importance in areas not covered by any federal statute. Age discrimination against persons
seventy or more years old or less than forty years old is one such area, since the
Age Discrimination in Employment Act does not cover those ages (see Section
3.3.2.5). A second example is discrimination against aliens. Although courts have
also reached such discrimination under the statute called Section 1981 (this volume,
Section 3.3.2.7), they have devised standards under the statute comparable to those
under the Constitution; alienage discrimination suits are thus often treated as equal
protection suits. Another important uncovered area is discrimination on the basis
of sexual preference (such as discrimination against homosexuals)[5] (see G. Siniscalso,
"Homosexual Discrimination in Employment," 16 *Santa Clara L. Rev.* 495 (1976)).
Discrimination on the basis of residence is a fourth important example.[6]

Although the Constitution restrains public institutions in areas such as the
four mentioned above, the restraints may be more lax than those under federal
statutes. In an age discrimination case, *Weiss* v. *Walsh,* 324 F. Supp. 75 (S.D.N.Y.
1971), for instance, the plaintiff was denied the Schweitzer Chair at Fordham University allegedly because of his age, which at that time was seventy. The court broadly
rejected the plaintiff's equal protection argument:

> I am constrained to hold that Professor Weiss is not the victim of
> an invidious and impermissible discrimination. Notwithstanding great ad-
> vances in gerontology, the era when advanced age ceases to bear some
> reasonable statistical relationship to diminished capacity or longevity is still
> future. It cannot be said, therefore, that age ceilings upon eligibility for
> employment are inherently suspect, although their application will inevitably
> fall unjustly in the individual case. If the precision of the law is impugnable
> by the stricture of general applicability, vindication of the exceptional indi-
> vidual may have to attend the wise discretion of the administrator. On its
> face, therefore, the denial of a teaching position to a man approaching seventy
> years of age is not constitutionally infirm [324 F. Supp. at 77, affirmed,
> 461 F.2d 846 (2d Cir. 1972)].

Similarly, in *Ambach* v. *Norwick,* 441 U.S. 68 (1979), the U.S. Supreme Court
considered the constitutionality of a New York statute that discriminated against
aliens by prohibiting their employment as public school teachers. The Court determined that "the Constitution requires only that a citizenship requirement applicable

---

[5]Such discrimination is often challenged on freedom of speech or association grounds
rather than equal protection. See *Aumiller* v. *University of Delaware,* 434 F. Supp. 1273 (D. Del.
1977), where the court ordered reinstatement and $15,000 damages for a lecturer whose freedom
of speech was violated when the university refused to renew his contract because of statements
he had made on homosexuality.
[6]See, for example, *McCarthy* v. *Philadelphia Civil Service Commission,* 424 U.S. 645 (1976),
upholding a continuing residency requirement for city employees; and *Cook County College Teachers
Union* v. *Taylor,* 432 F. Supp. 270 (N.D. Ill. 1977), upholding a similar requirement for college
faculty members. Compare *United Building and Construction Trades Council* v. *Camden,* 104 S. Ct.
1020 (1984), suggesting that discrimination in employment on the basis of state or local residency
may violate the privileges and immunities clause in Article IV, Section 2, of the Constitution.
Also compare the student residency cases discussed in Section 4.3.4.

to teaching in the public schools bear a rational relationship to a legitimate state interest.'' Applying this principle, the Court held that the state's citizenship requirement did not violate equal protection because it was a rational means of furthering the teaching of citizenship in public schools. The Court focused specifically on elementary and secondary education, however, and it is not clear that its reasoning would also permit states to refuse to employ aliens as teachers in postsecondary education, where the interest in citizenship education may be less.

And in *Naragon* v. *Wharton,* 737 F.2d 1403 (5th Cir. 1984), the court rejected an instructor's claim that Louisiana State University had reassigned her to nonteaching duties because of her homosexual orientation. The instructor had had an intimate relationship with a female undergraduate student who was not in her classes. Over a strong dissent, the court concluded that university officials had transferred the instructor because they considered any intimate relationship between an instructor and a student to be unprofessional, rather than because this particular relationship was homosexual rather than heterosexual. Thus, in the court's view, the university's action did not constitute discrimination based on sexual orientation.

3.3.4. Affirmative action in employment. Affirmative action has been an intensely controversial concept in many areas of American life. While the ongoing debate on affirmative action in student admissions (Section 4.2.5) parallels the affirmative action debate on faculty employment in its intensity, the latter has been even more controversial because it is more crowded with federal regulations and requirements. The future character and mission of postsecondary education continue to depend, in part, on the outcome of the debates.

Affirmative action became a major issue because the federal government's initiatives regarding discrimination have a dual aim: the goal is not only to ''bar like discrimination in the future'' but also to ''eliminate the discriminatory effects of the past'' (*Albemarle Paper Co.* v. *Moody,* 422 U.S. 405 (1975)). Addressing this latter objective under Title VII, courts may ''order such affirmative action as may be appropriate'' (*Franks* v. *Bowman Transportation Co.,* 424 U.S. 747 (1976), quoting *Albemarle*). Affirmative action can be appropriate under *Franks* even though it may adversely affect other employees, since ''a sharing of the burden of the past discrimination is presumptively necessary.'' Under statutes other than Title VII, and under Executive Orders 11246 and 11375, courts or administrative agencies may similarly require employers, including public and private postsecondary institutions, to engage in affirmative action to eliminate the effects of past discrimination.

Executive Orders 11246 and 11375 (see Section 3.3.2.2) have been the major focus of federal affirmative action initiatives. Aside from their basic prohibition of race, color, religion, sex, and national origin discrimination, these executive orders require federal nonconstruction contractors and subcontractors with specified amounts of contracts and numbers of employees to develop affirmative action plans. Under Section 60-2.10 of the Department of Labor's implementing order, known as ''Revised Order No. 4'' (41 C.F.R. Part 60-2, as amended in 1977 by 42 Fed. Reg. 3454):

> An acceptable affirmative action program must include an analysis of areas within which the contractor is deficient in the utilization of minority groups and women, and further goals and timetables to which the contractor's good-faith efforts must be directed to correct the deficiencies, and thus

to achieve prompt and full utilization of minorities and women, at all levels and in all segments of his work force where deficiencies exist.

Section 60-2.12 of the implementing order requires that a contractor's affirmative action program include affirmative action goals and timetables. There has been considerable confusion and controversy over the concept of goals. While the order states that "goals should be specific for planned results, with timetables for completion" (sec. 60-2.12(d)), it also states that "goals may not be rigid and inflexible quotas which must be met, but must be targets reasonably attainable by means of applying every good-faith effort to make all aspects of the entire affirmative action program work" (sec. 60-2.12(e)).

Since the obligation that this requirement places on postsecondary institutions has been somewhat unclear, administrators should be prepared to push for clarification and support from each agency with which their institution has federal contracts. The order does not make clear, however, that an institution cannot achieve compliance by having a disproportionately high number of minorities or women in one or a few schools or departments. Section 60-2.13 provides for the establishment of goals and timetables by "organizational units and job groups."

Postsecondary institutions contracting with the federal government are also subject to federal affirmative action requirements regarding handicapped persons, disabled veterans, and Vietnam veterans. Handicapped persons are covered by Section 503 of the Rehabilitation Act of 1973, 29 U.S.C. sec. 793:

> Any contract in excess of $2,500 entered into by any federal department or agency for the procurement of personal property and nonpersonal services (including construction) for the United States shall contain a provision requiring that, in employing persons to carry out such contract, the party contracting with the United States shall take affirmative action to employ and advance in employment qualified handicapped individuals.

Section 402 of the Vietnam Era Veterans' Readjustment Assistance Act of 1974, 38 U.S.C. sec. 2012, contains similar language covering disabled veterans as well as Vietnam veterans whether or not disabled. Section 402, however, applies to contracts "of $10,000 or more" rather than the lower figure specified in Section 503. Section 402, moreover, deletes the language in Section 503 which requires affirmative action only "in employing persons to carry out such contract," thus suggesting that Section 402 has a broader scope than Section 503.[7]

---

[7]This language distinction between Section 402 (veterans) and Section 503 (handicapped) does not appear to be reflected in the Department of Labor regulations implementing the two statutes. Both sets of regulations, as well as the regulations under Executive Orders 11246 and 11375, contemplate affirmative action for a wider group of employees than those working directly on the contract. All three sets of regulations, however, permit contractors to request waivers of affirmative action requirements concerning facilities not connected with the contract. Under 41 C.F.R. secs. 60-1.5(b)(2), 60-250.3(a)(5), and 60-741.3(a)(5), the Department of Labor may grant waivers "with respect to any of a prime contractor's or subcontractor's facilities which [it] finds to be in all respects separate and distinct from activities of the prime contractor or subcontractor related to the performance of the contract or subcontract, provided that . . . [it] also finds that such a waiver will not interfere with or impede the effectuation of the Act."

The Department of Labor has issued regulations to implement both Section 503 (41 C.F.R. Part 60-741) and Section 402 (41 C.F.R. Part 60-250). Both sets of regulations provide that any job qualification which tends to screen out members of the covered groups must be job related and consistent with business necessity (41 C.F.R. sec. 60-741.6(c)(1); 41 C.F.R. sec. 60-250.6(c)(1)). The regulations also require contractors to accommodate the physical and mental limitations of handicapped persons and disabled veterans "unless the contractor can demonstrate that such an accommodation would impose an undue hardship on the conduct of the contractor's business" (41 C.F.R. sec. 60-741.6(d); 41 C.F.R. sec. 60-250.6(d)).

Under the various affirmative action provisions in federal law, the most sensitive nerves are hit when affirmative action creates "reverse discrimination"; that is, when the employer eradicates the effects of past discrimination by granting employment preferences to members of the class subject to past discrimination, thus discriminating "in reverse" against other employees or applicants.[8] Besides creating policy issues of the highest order, such affirmative action measures create two sets of complex legal issues: (1) To what extent does the applicable statute, executive order, or implementing regulation require or permit the employer to utilize such employment preferences? (2) What limitations does the Constitution place on the federal government's authority to require or permit, or the employer's authority to utilize, such employment preferences?

The response to the first question depends on a close analysis of the particular legal authority involved. The answer is not necessarily the same under each authority. In general, however, federal law is more likely to require or permit hiring preferences when necessary to overcome the effects of the employer's own past discrimination than it is when no such past discrimination is shown or when preferences are not necessary to eliminate its effects. Section 703(j) of Title VII, for instance, relieves employers of any obligation to give "preferential treatment" to an individual or group merely because of an "imbalance" in the number or percentage of employed persons from that group compared with the number or percentage of persons from that group in the "community, state, section, or other area" (42 U.S.C. sec. 2000e-2(j)). But where an imbalance does not arise innocently but rather arises because of the employer's discriminatory practices, courts in Title VII suits have sometimes required the use of hiring preferences or goals to remedy the effects of such discrimination (see, for example, *United States* v. *International Union of Elevator Constructors*, 538 F.2d 1012 (3d Cir. 1976)).

Constitutional limitations on the use of employment preferences stem from the Fourteenth Amendment's equal protection clause. (See the discussion of equal protection's application to admissions preferences in Section 4.2.5.) Even if the applicable statute, executive order, or regulation is construed to require or permit employment preferences, such preferences may still be invalid under the federal Constitution. Courts have usually held hiring preferences to be constitutional where necessary to eradicate the effects of the employer's past discrimination, as in *Carter* v. *Gallagher*, 452 F.2d 315 (8th Cir. 1971). Where there is no such showing of past discrimination, the constitutionality of employment preferences is more in doubt.

---

[8]The relevant authorities are collected in Annot., "What Constitutes Reverse or Majority Discrimination on Basis of Sex or Race Violative of Federal Constitution or Statutes," 26 A.L.R. Fed. 13 (1976 and periodic supp.).

Strong new support for affirmative action was provided by the U.S. Supreme Court in the highly publicized case of *Weber* v. *Kaiser Aluminum Co.,* 443 U.S. 193 (1979), and, subsequent to *Weber,* by the U.S. Court of Appeals for the Eighth Circuit in *Valentine* v. *Smith,* 645 F.2d 503 (8th Cir. 1981).

In *Weber* the court considered a white steelworker's challenge to an affirmative action plan negotiated by his union and employer. The plan provided for a new craft training program, with admission to be on the basis of one black worker for every white worker selected. The district court ruled (415 F. Supp. 761 (E.D. La. 1976)) that the plan unlawfully discriminated against white employees in violation of Title VII of the Civil Rights Act, and the U.S. Court of Appeals for the Fifth Circuit affirmed (563 F.2d 216 (5th Cir. 1978)). In a 5-to-2 decision written by Justice Brennan, the Supreme Court reversed, ruling that employers and unions in the private sector may take race-conscious steps to eliminate "manifest racial imbalance" in "traditionally segregated job categories." Such action, the Court said, does not run afoul of Title VII's prohibition on racial discrimination (see Section 3.3.2.1).

The Court described the factual setting of the *Weber* case as follows:

> In 1974 petitioner United Steelworkers of America (USWA) and petitioner Kaiser Aluminum & Chemical Corporation (Kaiser) entered into a master collective bargaining agreement covering terms and conditions of employment at fifteen Kaiser plants. The agreement contained, *inter alia,* an affirmative action plan designed to eliminate conspicuous racial imbalances in Kaiser's then almost exclusively white craft work forces. . . .
>
> This case arose from the operation of the plan at Kaiser's plant in Gramercy, La. Until 1974 Kaiser hired as craft workers for that plant only persons who had had prior craft experience. Because blacks had long been excluded from craft unions, few were able to present such credentials. As a consequence, prior to 1974 only 1.83 percent (five out of 273) of the skilled craft workers at the Gramercy plant were black, even though the work force in the Gramercy area was approximately 39 percent black.
>
> Pursuant to the national agreement Kaiser altered its craft hiring practice in the Gramercy plant. Rather than hiring already trained outsiders, Kaiser established a training program to train its production workers to fill craft openings. Selection of craft trainees was made on the basis of seniority, with the proviso that at least 50 percent of the new trainees were to be black until the percentage of black skilled craft workers in the Gramercy plant approximated the percentage of blacks in the local labor force.
>
> During 1974, the first year of the operation of the Kaiser-USWA affirmative action plan, thirteen craft trainees were selected from Gramercy's production work force. Of these, seven were black and six white. The most junior black selected into the program had less seniority than several white production workers whose bids for admission were rejected. Thereafter one of those white production workers, respondent Brian Weber, instituted this class action in the United States District Court for the Eastern District of Louisiana [443 U.S. at 197–99].

The Court then considered Weber's claim that, by giving preference to junior black employees over more senior whites, the training program discriminated against white employees in violation of the 1964 Civil Rights Act (Court's footnotes and some of Court's citations omitted):

> We emphasize at the outset the narrowness of our inquiry. Since the Kaiser-USWA plan does not involve state action, this case does not present an alleged violation of the equal protection clause of the Constitution. Further, since the Kaiser-USWA plan was adopted voluntarily, we are not concerned with what Title VII requires or with what a court might order to remedy a past proven violation of the Act. The only question before us is the narrow statutory issue of whether Title VII *forbids* private employers and unions from voluntarily agreeing upon bona fide affirmative action plans that accord racial preferences in the manner and for the purpose provided in the Kaiser-USWA plan. . . .
>
> Respondent argues that Congress intended in Title VII to prohibit all race-conscious affirmative actions plans. Respondent's argument rests upon a literal interpretation of Sections 703(a) and (d) of the Act. Those sections make it unlawful to "discriminate . . . because of . . . race" in hiring and in the selection of apprentices for training programs. . . .
>
> The prohibition against racial discrimination in Sections 703(a) and (d) of Title VII must . . . be read against the background of the legislative history of Title VII and the historical context from which the Act arose. . . . Examination of those sources makes clear that an interpretation of the sections that forbade all race-conscious affirmative action would "bring about an end completely at variance with the purpose of the statute" and must be rejected (*United States* v. *Public Utilities Commission,* 345 U.S. 295, 315 (1953)) [443 U.S. at 200–02].

After reviewing the legislative history describing the concerns that led Congress to pass Title VII, the Court reasoned:

> Accordingly, it was clear to Congress that "the crux of the problem [was] to open employment opportunities for Negroes in occupations which have been traditionally closed to them" (110 Cong. Rec. at 6548 (remarks of Sen. Humphrey)), and it was to this problem that Title VII's prohibition against racial discrimination in employment was primarily addressed.
>
> It plainly appears from the House Report accompanying the Civil Rights Act that Congress did not intend wholly to prohibit private and voluntary affirmative action efforts as one method of solving this problem. The report provides: "No bill can or should lay claim to eliminating all of the causes and consequences of racial and other types of discrimination against minorities. There is reason to believe, however, that national leadership provided by the enactment of federal legislation dealing with the most troublesome problems *will create an atmosphere conducive to voluntary or local resolution of other forms of discrimination*" (H.R. Rep. No. 914, 88th Cong., 1st Sess. (1963), at 18; emphasis supplied).
>
> Given this legislative history, we cannot agree with respondent that Congress intended to prohibit the private sector from taking effective steps

to accomplish the goal that Congress designed Title VII to achieve. The very statutory words intended as a spur or catalyst to cause "employers and unions to self-examine and to self-evaluate their employment practices and to endeavor to eliminate, so far as possible, the last vestiges of an unfortunate and ignominious page in this country's history" (*Albemarle* v. *Moody*, 422 U.S. 405, 418 (1975)) cannot be interpreted as an absolute prohibition against all private, voluntary, race-conscious affirmative action efforts to hasten the elimination of such vestiges. It would be ironic indeed if a law triggered by a nation's concern over centuries of racial injustice and intended to improve the lot of those who had "been excluded from the American dream for so long" (110 Cong. Rec. at 6552 (remarks of Sen. Humphrey)) constituted the first legislative prohibition of all voluntary, private, race-conscious efforts to abolish traditional patterns of racial segregation and hierarchy.

Our conclusion is further reinforced by examination of the language and legislative history of [Section] 703(j) of Title VII. . . . The section provides that nothing contained in Title VII "shall be interpreted to *require* any employer . . . to grant preferential treatment . . . to any group because of the race . . . of such . . . group on account of" a de facto racial imbalance in the employer's work force. The section does *not* state that "nothing in Title VII shall be interpreted to *permit*" voluntary affirmative efforts to correct racial imbalances. The natural inference is that Congress chose not to forbid all voluntary, race-conscious affirmative action.

The reasons for this choice are evident from the legislative record. Title VII could not have been enacted into law without substantial support from legislators in both houses who traditionally resisted federal regulation of private business. . . . [Section 703(j)] was designed to prevent Section 703 of Title VII from being interpreted in such a way as to lead to undue "federal government interference with private businesses because of some federal employee's ideas about racial balance or imbalance" (110 Cong. Rec. at 14314 (remarks of Sen. Miller)). Clearly, a prohibition against all voluntary, race-conscious affirmative action efforts would disserve these ends. Such a prohibition would augment the powers of the federal government and diminish traditional management prerogatives while at the same time impeding attainment of the ultimate statutory goals [443 U.S. at 200–07].

Thus concluding that the use of racial preferences in hiring is sometimes permissible, the Court went on to uphold the Kaiser plan in particular. In doing so, the Court found it unnecessary to set forth detailed guidelines for employers and unions:

We need not today define in detail the line of demarcation between permissible and impermissible affirmative action plans. It suffices to hold that the challenged Kaiser-USWA affirmative action plan falls on the permissible side of the line. The purposes of the plan mirror those of the statute. Both were designed to break down old patterns of racial segregation and hierarchy. Both were structured to "open employment opportunities for

Negroes in occupations which have been traditionally closed to them'' (110 Cong. Rec. at 6548 (remarks of Sen. Humphrey)).

At the same time, the plan does not unnecessarily trammel the interests of the white employees. The plan does not require the discharge of white workers and their replacement with new black hires. Nor does the plan create an absolute bar to the advancement of white employees; half of those trained in the program will be white. Moreover, the plan is a temporary measure; it is not intended to maintain racial balance, but simply to eliminate a manifest racial imbalance. Preferential selection of craft trainees at the Gramercy plant will end as soon as the percentage of black skilled craft workers in the Gramercy plant approximates the percentage of blacks in the local labor force.

We conclude, therefore, that the adoption of the Kaiser-USWA plan for the Gramercy plant falls within the area of discretion left by Title VII to the private sector voluntarily to adopt affirmative action plans designed to eliminate conspicuous racial imbalance in traditionally segregated job categories [443 U.S. at 208-09].

Several factors were critical to the Court's holding in *Weber*. First, there was a "manifest racial imbalance" in the job categories for which Kaiser had established the special training program. While the percentage of blacks in the area work force was approximately 39 percent, less than 2 percent of the craft jobs at Kaiser were filled by blacks. Second, as the Court noted in a footnote to its opinion, these crafts had been "traditionally segregated"; rampant discrimination in the past had contributed to the present imbalance at Kaiser. Third, the Court emphasized that the plan in *Weber* did not "unnecessarily trammel" the interests of white employees; it did not operate as a total bar to whites, and it was temporary, designed to bring minority representation up to that of the area's work force rather than to maintain racial balance permanently.

These factors cited by the Court leave several questions open: How great a racial imbalance must there be before it will be considered "manifest"? What kind of showing must be made before a job category will be considered "traditionally segregated"? At what point will the effects of a plan on white workers be so great as to be considered "unnecessary trammeling"? But the absence of specific elaborations on these points should not be allowed to obscure the overall thrust and spirit of the *Weber* opinion. The Court emphasizes the broad remedial objectives of Title VII and the compatibility of affirmative action with these objectives. In describing when an employer may utilize racial preferences, the Court establishes broad and hospitable prerequisites: While traditional underrepresentation of minorities in the work force must exist, it is not necessary that the employer had itself engaged in discriminatory practices which helped create the imbalance. Rather, alleviating the effects of past societal discrimination is a sufficient basis for utilizing racial preferences. This approach is even broader than that urged in *Weber* by the employer, whose position was that racial preferences are permissible when used to alleviate an *arguable violation* of Title VII by the employer and/or union involved (see 443 U.S. at 209-16 (Blackmun, concurring)).

Moreover, the Kaiser affirmative action plan is far reaching, utilizing explicit racial quotas that continue in effect over an extended time period. The Court's approval of this particular plan suggests that employers can go quite far in providing special consideration to minorities without being guilty of "unnecessarily trammeling" the interests of white employees.

While *Weber* thus constitutes a broad affirmance of the permissibility of affirmative action, administrators and counsel should keep two limiting considerations especially in mind in applying the decision to the particular context of postsecondary education:

1. The effect of an affirmative action plan on existing and prospective white faculty members should be carefully analyzed to assure that racial preferences are not implemented in a way that would "unnecessarily trammel" their interests. Two of the factors relied on in *Weber*—that the plan did not require the discharge of any white workers and that the plan was temporary—appear to be easily transferable to and easily met in the postsecondary context. But the third factor—that the plan did not "create an absolute bar to the advancement of white employees"—bears careful watching in postsecondary education. The special training programs at issue in *Weber* benefited both black and white employees. Thirteen workers were selected, seven black and six white. At postsecondary institutions, however, faculty vacancies or special opportunities such as department chairmanships generally occur one at a time and on an irregular basis. A decision that a particular opening will be filled by a minority may, in effect, serve as a complete bar to whites, especially in a small department where there is little turnover and where the date of the next opening cannot be predicted.

2. *Weber* directly applies only to affirmative action plans adopted by *private* employers. While state and local government entities are subject to Title VII, they are also bound by the requirements of the U.S. Constitution. This means that *public* postsecondary institutions have an additional hurdle to clear in devising affirmative action plans: the Constitution's equal protection clause. In the past, courts have applied different standards when evaluating an employer's action under Title VII than under the equal protection clause. In a footnote in the *Weber* decision, Justice Brennan reaffirmed this distinction, pointing out that Title VII was enacted "to regulate purely private decision making and was not intended to incorporate and particularize the commands of the Fifth and Fourteenth Amendments."

Before *Weber* the *Bakke* case (438 U.S. 265 (1978)) (see Section 4.2.5), which involved admissions rather than employment, was the only Supreme Court precedent to consider constitutional standards regarding affirmative action. After *Weber* the Court shed further light on these constitutional standards in *Fullilove* v. *Klutznick,* 448 U.S. 448 (1980), which upheld a remedial program Congress had fashioned to eliminate traditional barriers to minority participation in public contracting opportunities. The program was implemented in the Minority Business Enterprise (MBE) provision of the Public Works Employment Act of 1977, which allocates federal funds to state and local governments for public works projects. This provision requires that state and local grantees use at least 10 percent of the funds they receive under the Act to procure services from minority-owned business. Although six opinions were written, and six justices voted to uphold the MBE provision, no opinion gathered a majority vote. For this reason, and because the opinions emphasize the unique power and competence of Congress to combat discrimination, the case's significance for postsecondary education is limited. The case makes clear for employment, however, as *Bakke* did for admissions, that the Constitution does permit some affirmative action even when it has adverse effects on nonminority persons. The *Fullilove* opinions also set out the apparent choices that courts have for establishing standards to determine how much affirmative action the Constitution permits. The Burger opinion does not adopt any of the standards used in the *Bakke* opinions; instead, it requires that an affirmative action program be "narrowly tailored" to achieve the objective of "remedying the present effects of past discrimination" and that the program not be "underinclusive" or "overinclusive" (that is, benefit neither fewer nor more individuals than is required in order to accomplish its objective). The Powell opinion adopts the standards that Justice Powell used in his separate opinion in *Bakke:* whether a "competent" decision maker had made appropriate findings of past discrimination and whether use of racial preferences is "necessary" to achieve a "compelling" government interest in remedying the past discrimination identified in the findings. The Marshall opinion relies on the test articulated in the *Bakke* opinion jointly written by Brennan, White, Marshall, and Blackmun: "whether racial classifications designed to further remedial purposes serve important governmental objectives and are substantially related to achievement of those objectives."

Principles from the Supreme Court's affirmative action cases were applied to postsecondary education, and in particular to a *public* postsecondary institution, in *Valentine* v. *Smith,* 654 F.2d 503 (8th Cir. 1981). Valentine, a disappointed white job applicant, challenged an affirmative action plan in place at Arkansas State University (ASU). The plaintiff had taught on ASU's business education faculty from 1967 until she resigned in 1974. In 1976 Valentine's replacement, the only black member of the department, resigned. Valentine then applied for her former position and was rated first on a list of applicants that the head of the division submitted to the university's vice-president for instruction. Following a meeting of the division head, the vice-president, and ASU's affirmative action officer, Valentine's name was deleted from the list, and a new list, containing only the names of two black applicants, was submitted. ASU hired one of these applicants.

At the time Valentine sought to be rehired, ASU had an affirmative action program for faculty hiring that was implemented as part of an effort to desegregate the Arkansas state college and university system. In 1973 a federal court, in *Adams* v. *Richardson,* 356 F. Supp. 92 (D.D.C. 1973) (Section 7.5.8), ordered HEW to bring Arkansas and other southern states into compliance with Title VI of the Civil Rights Act of 1964. ASU submitted an affirmative action hiring program to HEW in 1975; it was this program, implemented to remedy the past effects of racial discrimination, that ASU relied on when it deleted Valentine from the applicant list.

Valentine challenged that the ASU program was unconstitutional as applied to her because it constituted reverse discrimination, violating the Constitution's equal protection clause. In rejecting Valentine's challenge, the appellate court first determined that findings of past discrimination had been made by an appropriate decision-making body:

> The constitutional guarantee of equal protection does not prohibit states from taking appropriate measures to remedy the effects of past discrimination. The Supreme Court has not yet defined guidelines for permissible affirmative action for employing state university faculty. Because the justification for race-conscious affirmative action is remedying the effects

of past discrimination, a predicate for the remedy is that qualified persons make findings of past discrimination before the plan is implemented. Absent findings of past discrimination, courts cannot ascertain that the purpose of the affirmative action program is legitimate. Such findings enable courts to ensure that new forms of invidious discrimination are not approved in the guise of remedial affirmative action. Likewise, a court can determine that the remedy substantially relates to its purpose only if it is certain that the persons shaping and implementing the plan understood the nature and extent of the past discriminatory practices (see *Setser* v. *Novack Investment Co.*, 638 F.2d 1137 (8th Cir. 1981)).

The Supreme Court has determined that the Congress, federal courts, and, in some instances, the states have the competency to make such findings of past discrimination as are sufficient to justify a race-conscious remedy. The record reflects that HEW and the District Court for the District of Columbia [in *Adams* v. *Richardson,* above] found that Arkansas's colleges and universities did not comply with Title VI. Because of these findings and the action taken by OCR [HEW's Office for Civil Rights], ASU developed its affirmative action program. HEW and the district court are competent to make findings of past discrimination sufficient to justify the remedial purpose of an affirmative action program.

There is no consensus on what findings of past discrimination justify remedial affirmative action. Nevertheless, the issue of whether the findings of past discrimination made by the District of Columbia District Court and HEW were adequate to justify a race-conscious remedy is not even close. Findings of previous statutory violations of Title VI by a district court and OCR justify the use of some type of race-conscious remedy by a state to serve its constitutionally permissible objective of remedying past discrimination [654 F.2d at 507–09].

The court next determined that racial preferences may be used to remedy the effects of past employment discrimination:

We now turn to the question of whether, as a means to accomplish the plainly constitutional objective of remedying past discrimination, the state of Arkansas can prefer a black applicant over a white for a particular faculty vacancy. Arkansas could not practically achieve its constitutionally permissible ends in the foreseeable future without the use of race-conscious remedies. We examine the means used by Arkansas without any bright line distinction between permissible and impermissible affirmative action plans. Any racial preference must receive a searching examination to make certain that it does not conflict with constitutional guarantees ([*Fullilove,*] 448 U.S. at 491). Until we know more about the long-term effects of affirmative action, however, we are reluctant to discourage states from acting voluntarily to remedy past racial discrimination. A flexible evaluation of the means adopted by Arkansas is all the more appropriate in this case because, on the one hand, the state faced termination of federal benefits and liability for past discrimination against blacks if it failed to institute an affirmative action plan and, on the other hand, it faced liability to whites for any voluntary preferences adopted to mitigate the effects of prior discrimination against blacks (see generally *United Steelworkers* v. *Weber*, 443 U.S. 193, 210, 99 S. Ct. 2721, 2731, 61 L. Ed. 2d 480 (1979) (Blackmun, concurring); *Setser*, 638 F.2d at 1143–44; *Hunter* v. *St. Louis–San Francisco Railway*, 639 F.2d 424, 425 n.2 (8th Cir. 1981)). The test for determining whether Arkansas has adopted constitutionally permissible means is whether the affirmative action plan is "substantially related" to the objective of remedying prior discrimination. A race-conscious affirmative action program is substantially related to remedying past discrimination if (1) its implementation results or is designed to result in the hiring of a sufficient number of minority applicants so that the racial balance of the employer's work force approximates roughly, but does not unreasonably exceed, the balance that would have been achieved absent the past discrimination; (2) the plan endures only so long as is reasonably necessary to achieve its legitimate goals; (3) the plan does not result in hiring unqualified applicants; and (4) the plan does not completely bar whites from all vacancies or otherwise unnecessarily or invidiously trammel their interests [654 F.2d at 509–10].

Finally, the court determined that the ASU affirmative action program was itself a constitutionally permissible use of racial preferences to remedy past discrimination:

ASU's affirmative action plan set a goal of raising the percentage of blacks on the faculty to a total of 5 percent by 1979. To reach this goal, ASU planned that 25 percent of the faculty hired between 1976 and 1979 would be black. These goals do not exceed reasonable efforts to remedy ASU's past discrimination. In 1976, when Valentine was not hired for the position, ASU had 10 black faculty members among a total faculty of 296 (3.4 percent of faculty was black). Upon [the] retirement [of Valentine's replacement], the business college had no black faculty members. If Valentine had been rehired, the business college would have continued to have no black faculty members at least until the next vacancy occurred. ASU attracts students from an area which has a population which is approximately 23.6 percent black. We find that the plaintiff has failed to show that ASU's goals exceed those which would be substantially related to ASU's legitimate purpose.

ASU's 25 percent hiring goal is neither permanent nor even long lasting. Instead, ASU's plan extends over a four-year period and contemplates the achievement of a modest increase in black faculty members. Nothing about the duration of the plan suggests any purpose other than a remedial one, and Valentine has not shown that the period of the plan exceeds the time substantially necessary for achieving the plan's remedial purpose.

An affirmative action plan may be constitutionally infirm if it unduly stigmatizes either the beneficiaries or the persons disadvantaged by the plan (*Bakke*, 438 U.S. at 374–75, 98 S. Ct. at 2791–92). But a plan designed to eliminate past racial discrimination is not invalid merely because some innocent persons bear the brunt of the racial preference (*Fullilove*, 448 U.S. at 484, 100 S. Ct. at 2777–78). So long as a plan does not result in the hiring of unqualified persons, we conclude that any stigma caused by the plan is constitutionally acceptable. Members of the majority group are rarely, if ever, stigmatized by operation of a racial preference; it is hard for us to believe that people will treat Bonnie Valentine as a second-class person because a black person was hired instead of her. The more serious risk of stigma is with the successful minority applicant. The absence—not the presence—of affirmative action stigmatizes minority groups, by perpetuating the disadvantages of minorities. When an institution remedies its past wrongs by providing opportunities for members of previously victimized groups, it does not stigmatize those groups. Where the applicant is qualified, the risk of stigma is considerably less because presumably the person can perform the task adequately. The evidence in this case shows not only that Georgia Mitchell was fully qualified for the job but also [that] she performed very well as a teacher. We cannot invalidate ASU's affirmative action plan, or its application to the facts here, on the supposition that someone might be stigmatized.

ASU's affirmative action plan does not require firing any employees to make room for minority applicants. Nor does the plan deprive innocent persons of employment rights or benefits they already enjoyed. The plan contemplates that only 25 percent of new faculty over a four-year period will be black; we cannot say that this plan completely bars whites from faculty positions.

In summary, because we find ASU's affirmative action goals substantially related to the legitimate goal of ending and remedying previous racial discrimination, because the plan does not require the hiring of unqualified persons, because it is temporary, and because it does not completely bar whites or otherwise invidiously trammel their interests, we conclude that ASU's plan, on its face, is a constitutionally permissible solution to a difficult problem (*United States* v. *City of Miami,* 614 F.2d at 1338–40; *Detroit Police Officers Ass'n.* v. *Young,* 608 F.2d at 696) [654 F.2d at 510–11].

Although *Valentine,* unlike *Weber,* is an equal protection case, the court's equal protection analysis of affirmative action plans is similar to the *Weber* Title VII analysis. The court's opinion focuses, for example, on the existence of racial imbalance in the relevant job categories, on the temporary character of the affirmative action plan, and on the absence of unnecessary "trammeling" on white employees' interests—the same factors emphasized in *Weber.*

The major difference between the equal protection *(Valentine)* and Title VII *(Weber)* approaches is apparently the need, under the former, for explicit findings that past discrimination existed and is responsible for the present employment imbalance. Unlike the "racial imbalance" data in *Weber,* these findings must be made by a "competent" or "qualified" governmental authority, and must be made before the affirmative action plan is implemented. In *Valentine* the findings substantiated that the Arkansas state college system had itself discriminated in the past. *Fullilove* appears to support the position, however, that findings of general societal discrimination in the relevant employment category are sufficient.

Once such findings are made, a public college or university apparently has much the same authority as a private institution to implement an affirmative action plan. There is still some question whether the public institution can use explicit racial or sexual *quotas.* *Weber* allows private employers to use explicit quotas. But of the public institution cases, *Valentine* involved goals rather than quotas, and the majority of justices in *Bakke* prohibited the use of explicit quotas for admissions. Even if such a difference between public and private authority is ultimately recognized, it would likely be more a difference of form than substance (see *Valentine* v. *Smith*, 654 F.2d at 510 n.15) and would not substantially intrude on public institutions' broad authority (given appropriate findings) to implement affirmative action plans.

3.3.5. Coping with the equal employment thicket. There is no magic machete that postsecondary administrators can use to cut through the equal employment thicket. Though they embody critical social goals, the complex range of statutes, executive orders, regulations, and court cases create a formidable administrative challenge under the best of circumstances. The challenge is not one for amateurs. Postsecondary institutions need equal employment officers and other administrators who are qualified specialists on the subject. Postsecondary institutions also need legal counsel in the formation of equal employment policies and should encourage a smooth working relationship between equal opportunity officers and legal advisers.

The various laws provide many channels for challenging alleged discrimination in an institution's employment decisions. Administrators should be attentive to the increased possibilities for such challenges from faculty members, applicants, or government agencies. In order to avoid or overcome charges of employment discrimination, administrators should be prepared to do more than provide nondiscriminatory reasons, after the fact, for the institution's employment decisions. Instead, administrators should endeavor to assure that legitimate, nondiscriminatory reasons are the actual basis for each employment decision at the time it is made. As the court noted in an age discrimination case, *Laugeson* v. *Anaconda Co.,* 510 F.2d 307, 317 (6th Cir. 1975): "There could be more than one factor in the decision to discharge . . . [the employee] and . . . he was nevertheless entitled to recover if one such factor was his age and if in fact it made a difference in determining whether he was to be retained or discharged." (See also the discussion of the *Mt. Healthy* case in Section 3.6.5.)

Sec. 3.4. Standards and Criteria for Faculty Personnel Decisions

3.4.1. General principles. Postsecondary institutions commonly have written and published standards or criteria to guide decision making regarding faculty appointments, contract renewals, promotions, and tenure. Since they will often constitute part of the contract between the institution and the faculty members (see Section 3.1) and thus be binding on the institution, such evaluative standards and criteria should receive the careful attention of administrators and faculty members alike. If particular standards are not intended to be legally binding or are not intended to apply to certain kinds of personnel decisions, those limitations should be made clear in the standards themselves.

While courts will enforce standards or criteria found to be part of the faculty contract, the law accords postsecondary institutions wide discretion in determining the content and specificity of those standards and criteria. Courts are less likely to become involved in disputes concerning the *substance* of standards and criteria than in disputes over *procedures* for enforcing standards and criteria. (Courts draw the same distinction in cases concerning students; see the discussion in Sections 4.4 through 4.6.) In rejecting the claims of a nontenured professor, for example, the court in *Stebbins* v. *Weaver*, 537 F.2d 939 (7th Cir. 1976), emphasized that it would not review the merits or wisdom of denying tenure or refusing to rehire. And the court in *Brouillette* v. *Board of Directors of Merged Area IX*, 519 F.2d 126 (8th Cir. 1975), rejecting the claims of a community college faculty member, quoted an earlier case to note that "such matters as the competence of teachers and the standards of its measurement are not, without more, matters of constitutional dimensions. They are peculiarly appropriate to state and local administration."

Despite a generally deferential judicial attitude, there are several bases on which an institution's evaluative standards and criteria may be legally scrutinized. When standards or criteria are part of the faculty contract, both public and private institutions' disputes over interpretation may wind up in court or in the institution's internal grievance process. The "financial exigency" and program discontinuance disputes discussed in Section 3.7.1 are an example. For public institutions, standards or criteria may also be embodied in state statutes or administrative regulations subject to interpretation by courts, state administrative agencies (such as boards of regents or civil service commissions), or the institution's internal grievance process. Cases on attaining tenure and on dismissal from tenured positions for "just cause" are prominent examples.[9] And under the various federal nondiscrimination statutes discussed in Section 3.3.2, public and private institutions' standards and criteria may be scrutinized for their discriminatory impact by courts or federal administrative agencies or in an internal grievance process when one is required by federal regulations.

In public institutions, standards and criteria may also be subjected to constitutional scrutiny under the First and Fourteenth Amendments. Under the First Amendment, a standard or criterion can be challenged as "overbroad" if it is so broadly worded that it can be used to penalize a faculty member for having exercised constitutionally protected rights of free expression. Under the Fourteenth Amendment, a standard or criterion can be challenged as "vague" if it is so unclear that institutional personnel cannot understand its meaning. (The overbreadth and vagueness doctrines are discussed further in Sections 4.4.1 and 4.7.2.) The leading U.S. Supreme Court case on overbreadth and vagueness in public employment standards is *Arnett* v. *Kennedy*, 416 U.S. 134 (1974). A federal civil servant had been dismissed under a statute authorizing dismissal "for such cause as will promote the efficiency of the service." A majority of the Court held that this standard, as applied in the federal service, was neither overbroad nor vague.

While the result in *Arnett* suggests that the overbreadth and vagueness doctrines do not substantially restrict the standard-setting process, it does not necessarily mean that public postsecondary institutions can use the standard approved in *Arnett*. Employment standards should be adapted to the characteristics and functions of the group to which the standards apply. A standard acceptable for a large heterogeneous group such as the federal civil service may not be acceptable for a smaller, more homogeneous group such as a college faculty. (See, for example, *Bence* v. *Breier*, 501 F.2d 1185 (7th Cir. 1974), which held that the discharge standard of a local police force must be more stringently scrutinized under the overbreadth

---

[9]The cases and authorities for both statutes and contract clauses are collected in Annot., "Construction and Effect of Tenure Provisions of Contract or Statute Governing Employment of College or University Faculty Member," 66 A.L.R.3d 1018 (1975 plus periodic supp.).

and vagueness doctrines than was the federal discharge standard in *Arnett.*) Courts may thus require somewhat more of a postsecondary institution's standards than of those of the federal government. This is particularly so for the overbreadth doctrine, which, in connection with the academic freedom principles discussed in Section 3.6, is likely to remain an important limit on institutional discretion in devising employment standards.

3.4.2. Terminations of tenure for cause. Perhaps the most sensitive issues concerning standards arise in situations where institutions attempt to dismiss a tenured faculty member "for cause" (see T. Lovain, "Grounds for Dismissing Tenured Postsecondary Faculty for Cause," 10 *J. of College and University Law* 419 (1983–84)). Such dismissals should be distinguished from dismissals due to financial exigency or program discontinuance, discussed in Section 3.7. For-cause dismissals—being more personal, potentially more subjective, and more debilitating to the individual concerned—may be even more troublesome and agonizing for administrators than financial exigency or program discontinuance dismissals. Similarly, they may pose even greater legal complexities. Along with the issue of adequate procedures for effecting dismissal (see Section 3.5.2), the critical issue is the adequacy of standards for defining and determining "cause."

The American Association of University Professors' 1976 "Recommended Institutional Regulations on Academic Freedom and Tenure" (62 *AAUP Bulletin* 184) acknowledge "adequate cause" as an appropriate standard for dismissal of tenured faculty. These guidelines caution, however, that "adequate cause for a dismissal will be related, directly and substantially, to the fitness of the faculty member in his professional capacity as a teacher or researcher." Since the guidelines do not further define the concept, institutions are left to devise cause standards on their own or, occasionally for public institutions, to find standards in state statutes or agency regulations.

In *Garrett* v. *Matthews,* 625 F.2d 658 (5th Cir. 1980), the University of Alabama had dismissed the plaintiff, a tenured professor, for "insubordination and dereliction of duty." The charges had been brought pursuant to a faculty handbook provision permitting dismissal for "adequate cause" as found after a hearing. The plaintiff argued in court that the handbook's "adequate cause" standard was so vague that it violated constitutional due process. Although recent due process precedents suggest that this argument is one to be taken seriously,[10] the court rejected it in one incredible sentence that contains no analysis and relies on a prior opinion in *Bowling* v. *Scott,* 587 F.2d 229 (5th Cir. 1979) (this volume, Section 3.5.2.3), that does not even address the argument. *Garrett* is thus authority for the constitutionality of a bare "adequate cause" standard, but it is anemic authority indeed.

A more instructive example of a dismissal for cause of a tenured professor is provided by *Adamian* v. *Jacobson,* 523 F.2d 929 (9th Cir. 1975). The professor, from the University of Nevada (Reno), had allegedly led a disruptive demonstration on campus. Charges were brought against him under a university code provision requiring faculty members "to exercise appropriate restraint [and] to show respect for the opinions of others," and the board of regents determined that violation

---

[10]See, for example, *Tuma* v. *Board of Nursing,* 593 P.2d 711 (Idaho 1979) (suspension under standard of "unprofessional conduct" invalidated); *Davis* v. *Williams,* 598 F.2d 916 (5th Cir. 1979) (regulation prohibiting "conduct prejudicial to good order" invalidated).

of this provision was adequate cause for dismissal. In court the professor argued that this standard was both unconstitutionally vague, in violation of due process, and "overbroad," in violation of the First Amendment. The appellate court held that the standard would violate the First Amendment if interpreted broadly but could be constitutional if interpreted narrowly, as prescribed by AAUP academic freedom guidelines, so as not to refer to the content of the professor's remarks. The court therefore remanded the case to the trial court for further findings on how the university interpreted its code provision. On a second appeal, the court confined itself to the narrow issue of the construction of the code provision. In holding that the university's construction was sufficiently narrow to avoid a vagueness or overbreadth challenge, the court determined that this construction was consistent with the AAUP guidelines and reflected a limitation on the *manner,* rather than the *content,* of expression.

In another instructive case, *Korf* v. *Ball State University,* 726 F.2d 1222 (7th Cir. 1984), the university had adopted the AAUP "Statement on Professional Ethics" and published it in the faculty handbook. Subsequently, the university applied the statement's ethical standards to a tenured professor who, according to the findings of a university hearing committee, had made sexual advances toward and exploited male students. Specifically, the university relied on the portions of the statement that prohibit "exploitation of students . . . for private advantage" and require that a professor "demonstrates respect for the student as an individual and adheres to his proper role as intellectual guide and counsellor." When the university dismissed the professor for violating these standards, the professor sued, claiming that the dismissal violated due process because the statement did not specifically mention sexual conduct and therefore did not provide him adequate notice of the standard to which he had been held. The court rejected this claim (which was essentially a claim of unconstitutional vagueness):

> It is unreasonable to assume that the drafters of the "Statement on Professional Ethics" could and must specifically delineate each and every type of conduct (including deviant conduct) constituting a violation. . . . We agree with [the professor's] academic peers on the hearing committee and the board of trustees in their application of [the statement]. . . . They were well qualified to interpret the AAUP "Statement on Professional Ethics" as well as to determine what is and is not acceptable faculty conduct within an academic setting. . . . The facts and circumstances clearly demonstrate that [the professor] should have understood both the standards to which he was being held and the consequences of his conduct [726 F.2d at 1227–28].

Despite the summary approval in *Garrett,* institutions should not comfortably settle for a bald adequate cause standard. Good policy and (especially for public institutions) good law should demand more. Since incompetency, insubordination, immorality, unethical conduct, and medical disability are the most commonly asserted grounds for cause dismissals, institutions may wish to include in their dismissal policies definitions of these concepts and criteria for applying them to particular cases. Such definitions or criteria should be sufficiently clear to guide the decision makers who will apply them and to forewarn the faculty members who will be subject to them. As in *Adamian,* they should be sufficiently specific to preclude dismissal of faculty members because of the content of their expression. They should also conform to the AAUP's caution that cause standards must have a direct and substantial relationship to the faculty member's professional fitness. Hand in hand with such standards, if it chooses to adopt them, the institution will want to develop periodic faculty review policies and record-keeping policies that will provide the facts necessary to make reliable termination decisions.

Administrators will also want to keep in mind that *involuntary* terminations of tenured faculty, because of their coercive and stigmatizing effect on the individuals involved, usually create far more legal problems than voluntary means for dissolving tenured faculty members' employment relationship with the institution. Thus, another way to minimize legal vulnerability is to rely on voluntary alternatives to dismissals for cause. Suggestions that have been made include increased incentives for early retirement, development of opportunities for phased or partial retirement, and sponsorship of retraining for mid-career shifts to underpopulated teaching or research fields. Other suggestions—with potentially different consequences for the institution—focus on maintaining flexibility in faculty development by increased use of fixed-term contracts, visiting professorships, and other non-tenure-track appointments. All these alternatives have one thing in common with involuntary termination: their success depends on thorough review of personnel policies, coordinated planning for future contingencies, and careful articulation into written institutional policies.

Sec. 3.5. *Procedures for Faculty Personnel Decisions*

3.5.1. *General principles.* Postsecondary educational institutions have established varying procedural requirements for making and internally reviewing faculty personnel decisions. These requirements are the first place administrators should look in attempting to resolve procedural issues concerning appointment, retention, promotion, and tenure. Whenever such requirements can reasonably be construed as part of the faculty member's contract with the institution (see Section 3.1), the law will usually require both public and private institutions to comply with their own procedures. In *Skehan* v. *Board of Trustees of Bloomsburg State College,* 501 F.2d 31 (3d Cir. 1976), for instance, a nonrenewed professor alleged that the institution had not complied with a college policy statement providing for hearings in academic freedom cases. The appellate court held that the college would have to follow the policy statement if, on remand, the lower court found that the statement granted a contractual right under state law and that the professor's case involved academic freedom within the meaning of the statement. Upon remand and a second appeal, the court held that the professor did have a contractual right to the procedures specified in the statement and that the college had violated this right (590 F.2d 470 (3d Cir. 1978)).

Public institutions will also often be subject to state statutes or administrative regulations that establish procedures applicable to faculty personnel decisions. In *Brouillette* v. *Board of Directors of Merged Area IX,* 519 F.2d 126 (8th Cir. 1975), for example, the court applied a public hearing statute for terminated teachers to a community college faculty member, concluding that the institution had complied with the statute. In a "turnabout" case, *Rutcosky* v. *Board of Trustees of Community College District No. 18,* 14 Wash. App. 786, 545 P.2d 567 (1976), the court found that the plaintiff faculty member had not complied with a state procedural requirement applicable to termination-of-employment hearings and therefore refused to grant him any relief.

The procedures used by a state institution or other institution whose personnel decision is considered state action (see Section 1.4.2) are also subject to constitutional requirements of procedural due process. These requirements are discussed in Section 3.5.2.

Since private institutions are not subject to these constitutional requirements, or to state procedural statutes and regulations, contract law may be the primary or sole basis for establishing and testing the scope of their procedural obligation to faculty members. In *Johnson* v. *Christian Brothers College,* 565 S.W.2d 872 (Tenn. 1978), for example, an associate professor instituted suit for breach of his employment contract when the college did not grant him tenure. The college, a religiously affiliated institution in Memphis, had a formal tenure program detailed in its faculty handbook. The program included a seven-year probationary period, during which the faculty member worked under a series of one-year contracts. After seven years, on the prior recommendation of the tenure committee and approval of the president, the faculty member either received tenure along with the award of the eighth contract or was dismissed. The plaintiff claimed that, once he had reached the final probationary year and was being considered for tenure, he was entitled to the formal notice and hearing procedures utilized by the college in terminating tenured faculty. The Supreme Court of Tennessee held that nothing in the terms of the one-year contracts, the published tenure program, or the commonly used procedure of the college evidenced an agreement or practice of treating teachers in their final probationary year as equivalent to tenured faculty. The college therefore had no express or implied contractual obligation to afford the professor notice and an opportunity to be heard.

3.5.2. The public faculty member's right to constitutional due process. In two landmark cases, *Board of Regents* v. *Roth,* 408 U.S. 564 (1972), and *Perry* v. *Sindermann,* 408 U.S. 593 (1972), the U.S. Supreme Court established that faculty members have a right to a fair hearing whenever a personnel decision deprives them of a "property interest" or a "liberty interest" under the Fourteenth Amendment's due process clause. The "property" and "liberty" terminology is derived from the wording of the Fourteenth Amendment itself, which provides that states shall not "deprive any person of life, liberty, or property, without due process of law." (The identification of property and liberty interests is also important to many procedural due process questions concerning students; see Sections 4.3.1, 4.3.6.2, 4.6.3, and 4.11.1.)

In identifying these property and liberty interests, one must make the critical distinction between faculty members who are under continuing contracts and those whose contracts have expired. It is clear, as *Roth* notes, that "a public college professor dismissed from an office held under tenure provisions . . . and college professors and staff members dismissed during the terms of their contracts . . . have interests in continued employment that are safeguarded by due process." But the situation is not clear with respect to faculty members whose contracts are expiring and are up for renewal or a tenure review. Moreover, when a personnel decision would infringe a property or liberty interest, as in tenure termination, other questions then arise concerning the particular procedures that the institution must follow.

   3.5.2.1. Nonrenewal of contracts. Roth and *Perry* (above) are the leading cases on the nonrenewal of faculty contracts. The respondent in *Roth* had been hired as an assistant professor at Wisconsin State University for a fixed term of one year. A state statute provided that all state university teachers would be employed for one-year terms and would be eligible for tenure only after four years of continuous service. The professor was notified before February 1 that he would not be rehired. No reason for the decision was given, nor was there an opportunity for a hearing or an appeal.

   The issue addressed by the Supreme Court was "whether the [professor] had a constitutional right to a statement of reasons and a hearing on the university's decision not to rehire him for another year." The Court ruled that he had no such right because neither a "liberty" nor a "property" interest had been violated by the nonrenewal. Concerning liberty interests, the Court reasoned:

> The state, in declining to rehire the respondent, did not make any charge against him that might seriously damage his standing and associations in his community. It did not base the nonrenewal of his contract on a charge, for example, that he had been guilty of dishonesty or immorality. Had it done so, this would be a different case. For "where a person's good name, reputation, honor, or integrity is at stake because of what the government is doing to him, notice and an opportunity to be heard is essential" [citations omitted]. In such a case, due process would accord an opportunity to refute the charge before university officials. In the present case, however, there is no suggestion whatever that the respondent's "good name, reputation, honor, or integrity" is at stake.
>
>   Similarly, there is no suggestion that the state, in declining to reemploy the respondent, imposed on him a stigma or other disability that foreclosed his freedom to take advantage of other employment opportunities. The state, for example, did not invoke any regulations to bar the respondent from all other public employment in state universities. Had it done so, this, again, would be a different case. . . .
>
>   Hence, on the record before us, all that clearly appears is that the respondent was not rehired for one year at one university. It stretches the concept too far to suggest that a person is deprived of "liberty" when he simply is not rehired in one job but remains as free as before to seek another [408 U.S. at 573–74, 575].

   The Court also held that the respondent had not been deprived of any property interest in future employment:

> The Fourteenth Amendment's procedural protection of property is a safeguard of the security of interests that a person has already acquired in specific benefits. . . . To have a property interest in a benefit, a person clearly must have more than an abstract need or desire for it. He must have more than a unilateral expectation of it. He must, instead, have a legitimate claim of entitlement to it. . . .

Property interests, of course, are not created by the Constitution.
Rather, they are created and their dimensions are defined by existing rules
or understandings that stem from an independent source such as state law—
rules or understandings that secure certain benefits and that support claims
of entitlement to those benefits. . . . Respondent's "property" interest in
employment at Wisconsin State University–Oshkosh was created and defined
by the terms of his appointment, [which] specifically provided that the
respondent's employment was to terminate on June 30. They did not provide
for contract renewal absent "sufficient cause." Indeed, they made no provision for renewal whatsoever.

. . . In these circumstances, the respondent surely had an abstract
concern in being rehired, but he did not have a *property* interest sufficient
to require the university authorities to give him a hearing when they declined
to renew his contract of employment [408 U.S. at 578].

Since the professor had no protected liberty or property interest, his Fourteenth Amendment rights had not been violated, and the university was not required
to provide a reason for its nonrenewal of the contract or to afford the professor
a hearing on the nonrenewal.

In the *Perry* case, the respondent had been employed as a professor by the
Texas state college system for ten consecutive years. While employed, he was actively
involved in public disagreements with the board of regents. He was employed on
a series of one-year contracts, and at the end of his tenth year the board elected
not to rehire him. The professor was given neither an official reason nor the opportunity for a hearing. Like Roth, Perry argued that the board's action violated his
Fourteenth Amendment right to procedural due process.

But in the *Perry* case, unlike the *Roth* case, the Supreme Court ruled that
the professor had raised a genuine claim to "de facto" tenure, which would create
a constitutionally protected property interest in continued employment. The professor relied on tenure guidelines promulgated by the coordinating board of the
Texas College and University System and on an official faculty guide's statement
that "Odessa College has no tenure system. The administration of the college wishes
the faculty member to feel that he has permanent tenure as long as his teaching
services are satisfactory and as long as he displays a cooperative attitude toward
his co-workers and his superiors, and as long as he is happy in his work."

According to the Court:

The respondent [professor] offered to prove that a teacher with his
long period of service at this particular state college had no less a "property"
interest in continued employment than a formally tenured teacher at other
colleges, and had no less a procedural due process right to a statement of
reasons and a hearing before college officials upon their decision not to retain
him.

We have made clear in *Roth* . . . that "property" interests subject
to procedural due process protection are not limited by a few rigid technical
forms. Rather, "property" denotes a broad range of interests that are
secured by "existing rules or understandings." A person's interest in a

benefit is a "property" interest for due process purposes if there are such rules or mutually explicit understandings that support his claim of entitlement to the benefit and that he may invoke at a hearing.

A written contract with an explicit tenure provision clearly is evidence of a formal understanding that supports a teacher's claim of entitlement to continued employment unless sufficient "cause" is shown. Yet absence of such an explicit contractual provision may not always foreclose the possibility that a teacher has a "property" interest in reemployment. . . .

In this case, the respondent has alleged the existence of rules and understandings, promulgated and fostered by state officials, that may justify his legitimate claim of entitlement to continued employment absent "sufficient cause." We disagree with the court of appeals insofar as it held that a mere subjective "expectancy" is protected by procedural due process, but we agree that the respondent must be given an opportunity to prove the legitimacy of his claim of such entitlement in light of "the policies and practices of the institution" [citation omitted]. Proof of such a property interest would not, of course, entitle him to reinstatement. But such proof would obligate officials to grant a hearing at his request, where he could be informed of the grounds for his nonretention and challenge their sufficiency [408 U.S. at 603].

One other Supreme Court case should be read together with *Roth* and *Perry* for a fuller understanding of the Court's due process analysis. *Bishop* v. *Wood,* 426 U.S. 341 (1976), concerned a policeman who had been discharged, allegedly on the basis of incorrect information, and orally informed of the reasons in a private conference. With four judges strongly dissenting, the Court held that the discharge infringed neither property nor liberty interests of the policeman. Regarding property, the Court, adopting a stilted lower court interpretation of the ordinance governing employment of policemen, held that the ordinance created no expectation of continued employment but only conditioned dismissal on compliance with certain procedures, all of which had been provided in this case. Regarding liberty, the Court held that the charges against an employee cannot form the basis for a deprivation-of-liberty claim if they are privately communicated to the employee and not made public. The Court also held that the truth or falsity of the charges is irrelevant to the question of whether a liberty interest has been infringed.

Under *Roth, Perry,* and *Bishop,* there are three basic situations in which courts will require that a nonrenewal decision be accompanied by appropriate procedural safeguards:

1. The existing rules, policies, or practices of the institution, or "mutually explicit understandings" between the faculty member and the institution, support the faculty member's claim of entitlement to continued employment. Such circumstances would create a property interest. In *Soni* v. *Board of Trustees of University of Tennessee,* 513 F.2d 347 (6th Cir. 1975), for example, the court held that a nonrenewed, nontenured mathematics professor had such a property interest based on the voting and retirement plan privileges extended to him and the representations made to him concerning his status.

2. The institution, in the course of nonrenewal, makes charges against the

faculty member that could seriously damage his or her reputation, standing, or associations in the community. Such circumstances would create a liberty interest.[11] *Roth*, for instance, suggests that charges of dishonesty or immorality accompanying nonrenewal could infringe a faculty member's liberty interest. And in *Wellner* v. *Minnesota State Junior College Board*, 487 F.2d 153 (8th Cir. 1973), the court held that charges of racism deprived the faculty member of a liberty interest.

The *Bishop* case makes clear that such charges must in some way be made public before they can form the basis of a liberty claim. Although *Bishop* did not involve faculty members, a pre-*Bishop* case, *Ortwein* v. *Mackey*, 511 F.2d 696 (5th Cir. 1975), applies essentially the same principle in the university setting. Under *Ortwein* the institution must have made, or be likely to make, the stigmatizing charges "public 'in any official or intentional manner, other than in connection with the defense of [related legal] action'" (511 F.2d at 699; quoting *Kaprelian* v. *Texas Woman's University*, 509 F.2d 133, 139 (5th Cir. 1975)). Thus, there are still questions to be resolved concerning when a charge has become sufficiently "public" to fall within *Ortwein* and *Bishop*.

3. The nonrenewal imposes a "stigma or other disability" on the faculty member that "foreclose[s] his freedom to take advantage of other employment opportunities." Such circumstances would create a liberty interest. *Roth*, for instance, suggests that a nonrenewal which bars the faculty member from other employment in the state higher education system would infringe a liberty interest. Presumably, charges impugning the faculty member's professional competence or integrity could also infringe a liberty interest if the institution keeps records of the charges, and the contents of these records could be divulged to potential future employers of the faculty member.

A liberty or property interest might also be infringed when the nonrenewal is based on, and thus would penalize, the faculty member's exercise of freedom of expression. The Supreme Court dealt with this issue briefly in a footnote in the *Roth* case (408 U.S. at 575 n.14), appearing to suggest that a hearing may be required in some circumstances where the nonrenewal "would directly impinge upon interests in free speech or free press." Whenever a nonrenewed faculty member has a basis for making such a claim (see Sections 3.6.1 to 3.6.4), administrators should consider providing a hearing. Properly conducted (see Section 3.5.2.3), a hearing may not only vitiate any subsequent procedural due process litigation by the faculty member but may also resolve or defuse First Amendment claims that otherwise might be taken to court.

3.5.2.2. Denial of tenure. Denials of tenure, like contract renewals, must be distinguished analytically from terminations of tenure. Whereas a tenure termination always infringes the faculty member's property interests, a tenure denial may or may not infringe a property or liberty interest, triggering due process protections. The answer in any particular case will depend on application of the teachings

---

[11]In *Paul* v. *Davis*, 424 U.S. 693 (1976), the U.S. Supreme Court held that "defamation, standing alone," does not infringe a liberty interest. But defamation can still create a liberty infringement when combined with some "alteration of legal status" under state law, and termination or nonrenewal of public employment is such a change in status. Defamation "in the course of declining to rehire" would therefore infringe a faculty member's liberty interest even under *Paul* v. *Davis*.

from *Roth* and *Perry* (Section 3.5.2.1) and their progeny. Denials of promotions, for due process purposes, are generally analogous to denials of tenure and thus are subject to the general principles developed in the tenure denial cases below. For a leading illustration, see *Clark* v. *Whiting*, 607 F.2d 634 (4th Cir. 1979), where the court held that an associate professor had no right to an evidentiary hearing upon denial of promotion to full professor.

In 1978 a West Virginia court determined that a faculty member denied tenure had been deprived of a property interest (*McLendon* v. *Morton*, 249 S.E.2d 919 (W. Va. 1978)). Parkersburg Community College published eligibility criteria for tenure, which included six years as a teaching member of the full-time faculty and attainment of the rank of assistant professor. Having fulfilled both requirements, McLendon applied for tenure. After her tenure application was rejected on grounds of competence, McLendon filed suit, claiming that the institution's failure to provide her a hearing abridged her due process rights. The court held that (1) satisfying "objective eligibility standards gave McLendon a sufficient entitlement, so that she could not be denied tenure on the basis of her competence without some procedural due process"; and (2) minimal due process necessitates notice of the reasons for denial and a hearing before an unbiased tribunal, at which the professor can refute the issues raised in the notice. This decision thus extends the *Roth* doctrine to include, among persons who have a property interest in continued employment, faculty members who teach at public institutions having objective eligibility criteria for tenure and who have met those criteria. In West Virginia and any other jurisdiction that may accept the *McLendon* reasoning, institutions must give such faculty members notice and an opportunity for a hearing before any final decision to deny tenure.

In contrast to *McLendon*, the court in *Beitzel* v. *Jeffrey*, 643 F.2d 870 (1st Cir. 1981), held that a professor hired as a "probationary employee" did not have a sufficient property interest at stake under *Roth* to challenge his denial of tenure on due process grounds. The standards for the granting or denial of tenure were outlined in the university handbook; but, unlike those in *McLendon*, these standards were subjective. The court determined that the professor had no basis for the expectation that he would be granted tenure automatically. Similarly, in *Goodisman* v. *Lytle*, 724 F.2d 818 (9th Cir. 1984), the court rejected a professor's claim that he had a property interest in the university's procedures and guidelines for making tenure decisions. The court concluded that the procedures and guidelines "do not significantly limit university officials' discretion in making tenure decisions. They provide only an outline of relevant considerations. They do not enhance a candidate's expectation of obtaining tenure enough to establish a constitutionally protected interest."

In *Davis* v. *Oregon State University*, 591 F.2d 493 (9th Cir. 1978), the same court that later decided *Goodisman* rejected a different type of professorial claim to a hearing prior to tenure denial. The plaintiff had been an associate professor in the university's department of physics. He alleged that the department chairman had assured him at the time of his appointment that he would be granted tenure "as a matter of course." In 1972 and again in 1973, under the university's published tenure policy, the university tenure committee reviewed Davis's case and on both occasions obtained insufficient votes to either grant or deny tenure. Davis was thereafter terminated at the end of the 1973–74 academic year and brought suit, contending that he had de facto tenure arising from an oral contract with the department chairman. The court ruled that the university's written tenure policy defeated any claim to a contractual tenure agreement, since the policy vested no authority to grant tenure in department chairmen, and Davis was fully aware of this fact. The court thus held that Davis had no property interest that would support his claim to a hearing.

The court in *Kilcoyne* v. *Morgan*, 664 F.2d 940 (4th Cir. 1981), rejected yet another argument for procedural protections prior to denial of tenure. The plaintiff, a nontenured faculty member at East Carolina University, argued that his employment contract incorporated a provision of the faculty manual requiring department chairmen to apprise nontenured faculty of their progress toward tenure both by personal conference and written evaluation. Although Kilcoyne received a letter from the department chairman and had a follow-up conference toward the end of each of his first two years at the university, he argued that these procedures did not conform to the faculty manual. University guidelines also mandated a tenure decision following a three-year probationary period. At the beginning of his third year, Kilcoyne was notified that he would be rehired for a fourth year; later in the third year, however, he was informed that he would not be granted tenure or employed beyond the fourth year. After his claim of "de facto tenure" was summarily dismissed by the courts (405 F. Supp. 828 (E.D.N.C. 1975), affirmed, 530 F.2d 968 (4th Cir. 1975)), Kilcoyne argued that the alleged failure of the university to conform precisely to the faculty manual procedures incorporated into his contract deprived him of procedural due process. The court held that Kilcoyne lacked any *Roth* property interest in further employment at the university; denial of tenure would thus have been constitutionally permissible even if accompanied by *no* procedural safeguards. According to the court, if a state university *gratuitously* provides procedural safeguards that are not constitutionally mandated, deviations from such procedures will not violate due process even if the procedures are enumerated in the faculty contract. Although the contract may provide a basis for a breach of contract action, the mere fact that the state is a contracting party does not raise the contract problem to the status of a constitutional issue.

3.5.2.3. Termination of tenure. Whenever an institution's personnel decision would infringe a property or liberty interest, constitutional due process requires that the institution offer the faculty member procedural safeguards before the decision becomes final. The crux of these safeguards is notice and opportunity for a hearing. In other words, the institution must notify the faculty member of the reasons for the decision and provide a fair opportunity for him to challenge these reasons in a hearing before an impartial body.

Decisions to terminate tenured faculty members must always be accompanied by notice and opportunity for a hearing, since such decisions always infringe property interests. The cases in this section provide specific illustrations of the procedural due process requirements applicable to tenure termination cases. Decisions to terminate a nontenured faculty member during the contract term are generally analogous to tenure terminations and thus subject to principles similar to those in the cases below; the same is true for nonrenewal and denial of tenure decisions when they would infringe property or liberty interests.

In *Poterma* v. *Ping*, 462 F. Supp. 388 (E.D. Ohio 1978), a tenured member of the economics department at Ohio University claimed that he was denied due process when the university dismissed him for failure to perform his faculty duties and inability to communicate with students. The court ruled that the teacher's minimum due process safeguards included (1) a written statement of the reasons for the proposed termination prior to final action, (2) adequate notice of a hearing, (3) a hearing at which the teacher has an opportunity to submit evidence to controvert the grounds for dismissal, (4) a final statement of the grounds for dismissal if it does occur. The court held that the university had complied with these requirements and had not infringed the faculty member's due process rights.

In a similar case, *Bowling* v. *Scott*, 587 F.2d 229 (5th Cir. 1979), a tenured English professor at the University of Alabama filed suit after the university terminated his tenure. The court enunciated a minimum due process standard similar to that used in *Poterma* and ruled that no deprivation of procedural due process had occurred, since the university had served Bowling with a list of charges; informed him that formal proceedings would commence; given advance notice of each of fourteen hearing sessions, all of which the faculty member had attended with his lawyer; and subsequently issued a twelve-page report stating the grounds for dismissal.

In another decision, *Frumkin* v. *Board of Trustees, Kent State*, 626 F.2d 19 (6th Cir. 1980), the court focused particularly on the type of hearing an institution must provide prior to a decision to terminate tenure. The university had slated the professor for dismissal after federal funding for his position was cut. In support of the recommendation for dismissal, the university charged the professor with "unsatisfactory performance as grant director, recurring unproven charges against faculty members, unprofessional conduct, false charges against the department, and violation of university policy." When the professor chose to contest his dismissal, the university scheduled a hearing. The professor was permitted to have a lawyer present at the hearing, but the lawyer's role was limited. He was permitted to consult and advise his client and to make closing arguments in his client's behalf. But he was prohibited from conducting any cross-examination or direct examination of witnesses or from raising objections.

Reasoning that this limited hearing was well suited to the type of decision to be made, the court held that the university had not violated the professor's due process rights:

> The criteria which determine the parameters of procedural due process are set out in *Mathews* v. *Eldridge*, 424 U.S. 319, 334, 96 S. Ct. 893, 903, 47 L. Ed. 2d 18 (1976):
>
>> Identification of the specific dictates of due process generally requires consideration of three distinct factors: first, the private interest that will be affected by the official action; second, the risk of an erroneous deprivation of such interest through the procedures used, and the probable value, if any, of additional or substitute procedural safeguards; and finally, the government's interest, including the function involved and the fiscal and administrative burdens that the additional or substitute procedural requirement would entail.
>
> The Supreme Court has consistently rejected a concept of due process which would afford all complaining parties, whatever the context of the dispute, an inflexible "checklist" of legal rights. On the contrary, procedural

due process issues, originating as they may in diverse situations, demand a more sensitive judicial approach. Thus, we find in *Mathews, supra,* an analysis designed to balance competing interests in lieu of imposing rigid legal formulae. . . .

The narrow issue is . . . whether procedural due process required the university to permit Dr. Frumkin's retained counsel to conduct direct and cross-examination of witnesses at the pretermination hearing. The second *Mathews* criterion requires us to assess the "risk of erroneous deprivation" and the "value of the additional procedural safeguards" at issue. Under certain circumstances, the active participation of a legal representative is likely to mitigate an otherwise considerable risk of "erroneous deprivation." The Supreme Court has, for example, recognized the potential importance of counsel's role in welfare benefits pretermination hearings (see *Goldberg* v. *Kelly,* 397 U.S. 254, 90 S. Ct. 1011, 25 L. Ed. 2d 287 (1970)). . . .

We cannot, however, accept appellant's contention that we should rule in his favor on the basis of an analogy between the problems which beset an unrepresented welfare recipient confronted with an administrative court and the position of a professional academic who, under the direction of his attorney, presents his case to a panel of fellow faculty members. As the *Mathews* court noted:

> The judicial model of an evidentiary hearing is neither a required nor even the most effective method of decision making in all circumstances. . . . All that is necessary is that the procedures be tailored, in light of the decision to be made, to the "capacities and circumstances of those who are to be heard" to insure that they are given a meaningful opportunity to present their case (424 U.S. at 348, 96 S. Ct. at 909; see also *Toney* v. *Reagan,* 467 F.2d 953, 958 (9th Cir. 1972)).

We believe that Dr. Frumkin had ample opportunity to present his case to the hearing committee in a manner calculated to achieve a fair result. . . .

The third guideline set out in *Mathews* requires an analysis of "the government's interest, *including the function involved,* and the fiscal and administrative burden that the additional . . . procedure would entail" (emphasis added). The administrative burden, in this instance, of permitting appellant's counsel to examine witnesses would have been comparatively slight. However, we are persuaded that the university has a legitimate argument in its expressed reluctance to transform the type of inquiry involved here into a full-fledged adversary trial. Because universities have traditionally been afforded broad discretion in their administration of internal affairs (see *Downing* v. *Le Britton,* 550 F.2d 689, 692 (1st Cir. 1977)), we do not deem it necessary to interfere where, as here, there is no showing that the overall procedure was prejudicial to the rights [of the] terminated employee [626 F.2d at 21–22].

Another case, *Clarke* v. *West Virginia Board of Regents,* 279 S.E.2d 169 (W. Va.

1981), also focuses on one specific part of the termination process but is not as deferential to institutions as *Frumkin* is. In this case the court considered the reasons and evidence an institution must provide to support a decision terminating tenure. Clarke, a tenured professor at Fairmont State College, had been dismissed following a hearing before a hearing examiner. The hearing examiner made a written report, which merely cited the testimony of witnesses who supported dismissal and did not state any specific reasons or factual basis for affirming the dismissal. The professor argued in court that this report did not comply with due process requirements. Although the court's analysis is based on the *state* constitution, the opinion relied on federal constitutional precedents and is indicative of federal constitutional analysis as well.

As a starting point for determining what a hearing examiner's report must contain, the court consulted a policy bulletin of the West Virginia board of regents:

> The hearing examiner is not required by statute to make written findings of fact and conclusions of law, nor does the bulletin specifically require him to state on the record the reasons for his decision or to specify the evidence which supports those reasons. The bulletin does, however, require the hearing examiner to "enter such recommendations *as the facts justify and the circumstances may require*" (emphasis added). Clearly, the bulletin contemplates that the hearing examiner will make a reasoned determination which is supported by the evidence adduced at the hearing. At the very least, the hearing examiner should make some sort of findings on the record and indicate the evidence supporting those findings in order to demonstrate that he has fulfilled his obligations as a fact finder and has not acted arbitrarily and capriciously in reaching his conclusions. "The decision maker should state the reasons for his determination and indicate the evidence he relied on, though his statements need not amount to a full opinion or even formal findings of fact and conclusions of law" (*Goldberg v. Kelly*, 397 U.S. 254, 271, 90 S. Ct. 1011, 1022, 25 L. Ed. 2d 287, 301 (1970)) [279 S.E.2d at 177].

The court then stressed the importance of an adequate report to give a reviewing court a basis for review and to give the affected individual a basis for identifying grounds for review:

> The need for an adequate statement of the hearing examiner's reasons for his determination and the evidence supporting them is obvious. Our function as a reviewing court is to review the record to determine if the evidence adduced at the hearing supports the findings of the hearing examiner and whether his conclusions follow from those findings. We must rely on the facts and logic upon which the hearing examiner ruled . . . and determine whether he erroneously applied them in reaching his final determination. If the record of the administrative proceeding does not reveal those facts which were determinative of the ruling or the logic behind the ruling, we are powerless to review the administrative action. We are thrust into the position of a trier of fact and are asked to substitute our judgment for that of the hearing examiner. That we cannot do.
> Equally important is the burden placed on the individual seeking

review of the administrative action. Where the hearing examiner fails to make adequate findings on the record to support his conclusions, the appellant cannot assert his grounds for review. He cannot allege error with particularity because he is unable to determine where the error was committed. Where, as here, the proceeding involves more than one ground for dismissal, the party seeking review is unable to discuss which of those charges the hearing examiner found to be supported by the evidence. The failure of the hearing examiner to state on the record adequate reasons for his determination and the evidence he relied upon infringes upon the right of the party to have an effective and meaningful review of the administrative action taken against him in violation of due process (see *Specht* v. *Patterson,* 386 U.S. 605, 87 S. Ct. 1209, 18 L. Ed. 2d 326 (1967); *Gardner* v. *Louisiana,* 368 U.S. 157, 82 S. Ct. 248, 7 L. Ed. 2d 207 (1961)) [279 S.E.2d at 178].

Based on its review of the regents' bulletin and applicable constitutional principles, the court held that the hearing examiner's report did not meet due process standards:

The only statement made by the hearing examiner here was his conclusion that, in view of the ''particularly impressive'' testimony of other faculty members, Dr. Clarke's dismissal was for cause and pursuant to the procedures of the board of regents. This comment is nothing more than a conclusory pronouncement of the hearing examiner's decision on the ultimate question before him. Neither this court nor Dr. Clarke is informed of the reasons for the conclusion nor the specific evidence relied on. A proper statement of the hearing examiner's reasons and a clear indication of the evidence on which he relied is especially important where there are myriad charges and hundreds of pages of testimony. In the report of findings and recommendations, a hearing examiner should list the specific charges found to be supported by the evidence adduced at the hearing and provide some reference to the evidence supporting those findings. In view of our discussion above, we conclude that the failure of the hearing examiner to state on the record the charges against Dr. Clarke which were found to be supported by the evidence constitutes reversible error [279 S.E.2d at 178].

Taken together, these cases provide a helpful picture of how courts will craft procedural requirements for tenure termination decisions. When reviewing such decisions, courts will generally look for compliance with basic elements of due process, as set out in *Poterma.* When an institution fails to accord the faculty member one or more of these basic elements, *Clarke* indicates that courts will invalidate the institution's decision. But *Bowling* and *Frumkin* illustrate judicial reluctance to provide more specific checklists of procedures mandated by due process. Beyond the minimum requirements, such as those in *Poterma,* courts will usually defer to institutional procedures that appear suited to the needs and expectations of the faculty member and the institution.

3.5.3. Implementing procedural requirements. An institution's procedures for making and internally reviewing the various kinds of faculty personnel decisions should be in writing and made generally available. Public institutions (see

Section 1.4.2) must, at a minimum, comply with the constitutional due process requirements in Section 3.5.2 and may choose to provide additional procedures beyond those required by the Constitution. Private institutions are not required to comply with constitutional requirements but may wish to use these requirements as a guide in establishing their own procedures.

Though personnel procedures can be administratively burdensome, that is not the whole story. They can also help the institution avoid or rectify mistaken assessments, protect the academic freedom of the faculty, foster faculty confidence in the institution, and encourage the resolution of nonrenewal and termination disputes in-house rather than in the courts. When effective personnel procedures do exist, courts may require, under the "exhaustion of remedies" doctrine, that the faculty member "exhaust" those procedures before filing suit. In *Rieder* v. *State University of New York,* 47 A.D.2d 865, 366 N.Y.S.2d 37 (1975), affirmed, 39 N.Y.2d 845, 351 N.E.2d 747 (1976), for instance, employees at a state institution were covered by a collective bargaining agreement containing a four-step grievance procedure. When some employees filed suit while awaiting a determination at step two, the appellate courts ordered the suit dismissed for failure to exhaust administrative remedies. Similarly, in *Beck* v. *Board of Trustees of State Colleges,* 32 Conn. Supp. 153, 344 A.2d 273 (1975), faculty members sought to enjoin the board of trustees of the state colleges from implementing proposed new personnel policies that allegedly threatened the rights of tenured faculty. The court dismissed the suit under the exhaustion doctrine because the state's administrative procedure act "provides a comprehensive, potentially inexpensive, and completely adequate method of resolving the issues raised in the present . . . [suit]."[12]

In cases such as *Rieder* and *Beck,* where public institutions are involved, the administrative law of the state provides the source of the exhaustion doctrine. Such administrative law principles do not apply to private institutions, since they are not agencies of the state. Private institutions may be subject to a comparable exhaustion doctrine, however, which stems from the common law of "private associations" (see Section 4.11.4, note 13 and accompanying text). For an overview of this common law exhaustion doctrine, see "Developments in the Law—Judicial Control of Actions of Private Associations," *76 Harvard L. Rev.* 983, 1069–80 (1963).

In devising or reviewing procedures, administrators should carefully consider what procedural safeguards they should provide *before* making a personnel decision or *before* suspending or terminating job benefits, as opposed to *after.* In public institutions, for example, a full-scale hearing need not be provided before the personnel decision is tentatively made. Some courts, however, require a hearing before the decision is actually implemented by terminating the faculty member's pay or other substantial employment benefits. *Skehan* v. *Board of Trustees of Bloomsburg State College,* 501 F.2d 31 (3d Cir. 1974), for instance, involved a faculty member who had been relieved of his duties, dismissed, and removed from the payroll for almost three months before he was afforded a hearing. The court held that the hearing, because of its timing, did not meet due process requirements. In *Peacock* v. *Board of Regents of University and State Colleges of Arizona,* 510 F.2d 1324 (9th Cir. 1975),

---

[12]Plaintiffs filing civil rights claims under "Section 1983," the federal civil rights statute, need not exhaust state administrative remedies (see *Patsy* v. *Board of Regents of the State of Florida,* 102 S. Ct. 2557 (1982), discussed in Section 2.3.3).

however, the court upheld a posttermination hearing where the faculty member had been removed only from a nonpaying position as department head; and in *Chung v. Park,* 514 F.2d 382 (3d Cir. 1975), the court upheld a hearing that had been provided after the decision to terminate was made but before job benefits were actually terminated.[13]

The question of when and in what detail statements of reasons for personnel decisions are to be given must also be carefully considered. The question of who shall preside over hearings is likewise important, with impartiality being the key consideration. Other critical issues are the confidentiality of the statements of reason—and of any proceedings in which the faculty member challenges these reasons—and the question of what permanent records should be kept of adverse personnel decisions and who should have access to them. While the legal principles in Sections 3.5.1 and 3.5.2 create some limits on administrative discretion in these areas, considerable flexibility remains for administrators to make wise policy choices.

Sec. 3.6. Faculty Academic Freedom

3.6.1. Background and general principles. The concept of academic freedom eludes precise definition. It is a concept that draws meaning from both the world of education and the world of law. Courts have increasingly used academic freedom as the catch-all term to describe the legal rights and responsibilities of the teaching profession. This judicial conception of academic freedom is essentially an attempt to reconcile basic constitutional principles with the prevailing views of academic freedom's social and intellectual role in American life.

Though courts usually discuss academic freedom in cases concerning the constitutional rights of faculty members, the legal boundaries of academic freedom are initially defined by contract law. Faculty members possess whatever academic freedom is guaranteed them under the faculty contract (see Section 3.1). The AAUP's 1940 "Statement of Principles on Academic Freedom and Tenure," its 1970 "Interpretive Comments" (60 *AAUP Bulletin* 269 (1974)), and its 1976 "Recommended Institutional Regulations on Academic Freedom and Tenure" (62 *AAUP Bulletin* 184 (1976)) are often looked to as the prevailing policy statements on academic freedom, and it is crucial for administrators to determine whether either document has been—or should be—incorporated in the faculty contract. Courts will interpret and enforce the terms of the AAUP documents, by reference to contract law principles, to the extent that those terms have become a part of the faculty contract. Even when the documents have not been incorporated into the contract, they may be an important source of academic "custom and usage," which courts will consider in interpreting unclear contract terms (see Sections 1.3.8 and 3.1).

In private institutions the faculty contract may be the only legal restriction on the administrator's authority to regulate academic freedom. But in public institutions (see Section 1.4), administrators are also limited by state statutes or adminis-

---

[13]The closest Supreme Court case is *Cleveland Board of Education* v. *Loudermill,* 105 S. Ct. 1487 (1985), decided as this book went to press. Resolving cases brought by two discharged state civil servants, the Court held that "some form of pretermination hearing" is constitutionally required, its extent dependent on various factors including the kind of post-termination hearing that would also be available.

trative regulations and by constitutional concepts of academic freedom. (The same constitutional concepts would limit legislatures and other government officials whose regulatory actions affected academic freedom, whether in public or private institutions.) Whereas contract and statutory provisions may distinguish between tenured and nontenured faculty, tenure and job status are immaterial to most constitutionally based academic freedom claims. In *Perry* v. *Sindermann,* 408 U.S. 593 (1972), discussed in Section 3.5.2.1, the U.S. Supreme Court held that a nonrenewed faculty member's "lack of a contractual or tenure right to reemployment . . . is immaterial to his free speech claim" and that "regardless of the . . . [teacher's] contractual or other claim to a job," government cannot "deny a benefit to a person because of his constitutionally protected speech or associations."[14]

In a series of leading cases in the 1950s and 1960s, the U.S. Supreme Court gave academic freedom constitutional status under the First Amendment freedoms of speech and association, the Fifth Amendment protection against self-incrimination, and the Fourteenth Amendment guarantee of due process. The opinions in these cases include several ringing declarations on the importance of academic freedom. In *Sweezy* v. *New Hampshire,* 354 U.S. 234 (1957), for example, the Court reversed a contempt judgment against a professor who had refused to answer questions concerning a lecture delivered at the state university. The plurality opinion of four justices (with two concurring justices expressing similar thoughts) declared:

> The essentiality of freedom in the community of American universities is almost self-evident. No one should underestimate the vital role in a democracy that is played by those who guide and train our youth. To impose any straitjacket upon the intellectual leaders in our colleges and universities would imperil the future of our nation. No field of education is so thoroughly comprehended by man that new discoveries cannot yet be made. Particularly is that true in the social sciences, where few, if any, principles are accepted as absolutes. Scholarship cannot flourish in an atmosphere of suspicion and distrust. Teachers and students must always remain free to inquire, to study and to evaluate, to gain new maturity and understanding; otherwise, our civilization will stagnate and die [354 U.S. at 250].

In *Shelton* v. *Tucker,* 364 U.S. 479 (1960), where it invalidated a state statute compelling public school and college teachers to reveal all organizational affiliations or contributions for the previous five years, the Court remarked:

> The vigilant protection of constitutional freedoms is nowhere more vital than in the community of American schools. "By limiting the power of the states to interfere with freedom of speech and freedom of inquiry and freedom of association, the Fourteenth Amendment protects all persons, no matter what their calling. But, in view of the nature of the teacher's relation to the effective exercise of the rights which are safeguarded by the

---

[14]The *Perry* Court also held, in contrast, that the professor's job status, "though irrelevant to his free speech claim, is highly relevant to his procedural due process claim." The Fourteenth Amendment due process clause is the one constitutional basis for an academic freedom claim which distinguishes among faculty members on the basis of job status.

Bill of Rights and by the Fourteenth Amendment, inhibition of freedom of thought, and of action upon thought, in the case of teachers brings the safeguards of those amendments vividly into operation. Such unwarranted inhibition upon the free spirit of teachers . . . has an unmistakable tendency to chill that free play of the spirit which all teachers ought especially to cultivate and practice; it makes for caution and timidity in their associations by potential teachers" (*Wieman* v. *Updegraff,* 344 U.S. 183, 195, 73 S. Ct. 215, 221, 97 L. Ed. 216 (concurring opinion)) [364 U.S. at 487].

And in *Keyishian* v. *Board of Regents,* 385 U.S. 589 (1967), discussed below, the Court quoted both *Sweezy* and *Shelton,* and added:

Our nation is deeply committed to safeguarding academic freedom, which is of transcendent value to all of us and not merely to the teachers concerned. That freedom is therefore a special concern of the First Amendment, which does not tolerate laws that cast a pall of orthodoxy over the classroom. . . . The classroom is peculiarly the "marketplace of ideas." The nation's future depends upon leaders trained through wide exposure to that robust exchange of ideas which discovers truth "out of a multitude of tongues, [rather] than through any kind of authoritative selection" (*United States* v. *Associated Press,* 52 F. Supp. 362, 372) [385 U.S. at 603].

However, the legal principles that emerge from cases such as these are not as broad as the Court's academic freedom pronouncements might suggest. The faculty's constitutional rights evolving from the cases of the 1950s and 1960s are succinctly summarized in W. Van Alstyne, "The Constitutional Rights of Teachers and Professors, 1970 *Duke L.J.* 841, 847–48:

1. Membership per se in political organizations, not excluding the Communist Party, or economic organizations such as labor unions is not a permissible ground for terminating teachers or disqualifying applicants to the profession. Arguably, moreover, not even active and knowing membership including some degree of personal sympathy for the illegal objectives of the group may be sufficient, short of some concrete act in furtherance of an illegal objective inconsistent with one's lawful obligations as a teacher.

2. Correspondingly, disclaimer oaths requiring that one forswear activities or associations he is otherwise constitutionally privileged to pursue as a private citizen are beyond the constitutional pale. In all likelihood, the state may go no further than to require that one be willing to affirm a general commitment to uphold the Constitution and faithfully to perform the duties of the position he holds.[15]

[15](Author's footnote.) In *Cole* v. *Richardson,* 405 U.S. 676 (1972), the U.S. Supreme Court later upheld an oath that included not only a general commitment to "uphold and defend" the Constitution but also a commitment to "oppose the overthrow of the government . . . by force, violence, or by any illegal or unconstitutional method." To maintain the second commitment's constitutionality, the Court read it very narrowly as merely "a commitment not to use illegal and constitutionally unprotected force to change the constitutional system." So interpreted, the second commitment "does not expand the obligation of the first [commitment]."

3. While neither the First Amendment nor the Fifth Amendment entitles a teacher to withhold information when his employer has questioned his competence or professional integrity on the basis of reasonably specific and creditable allegations "of impropriety related to his job," information elicited under such circumstances by a public employer may not be utilized for purposes of criminal prosecution, and vague or general fishing expeditions on mere suspicion are not permissible.

The centerpiece of these constitutional developments is the Supreme Court's 1967 decision in the *Keyishian* case, quoted above. The appellants were State University of New York faculty members who refused to sign a certificate (the "Feinberg Certificate") stating that they were not and never had been Communists. This certificate was required under a set of laws and regulations designed to prevent "subversives" from obtaining employment in the state education system. The faculty members lost their jobs and sued the state on the grounds that the dismissal violated their First Amendment rights. They challenged the certificate requirements and the underlying law barring employment to members of subversive organizations, as well as other provisions authorizing dismissal for the "utterance of any treasonable or seditious word or words or the doing of any treasonable or seditious act" and for "by word of mouth or writing wilfully and deliberately advocating, advising, or teaching the doctrine of forceful overthrow of the government."

The Court held that the faculty members' First Amendment freedom of association had been violated by the existence and application of a series of laws and rules that were both vague and overbroad (see Section 3.4.1 regarding the vagueness and overbreadth doctrines). The word "seditious" was held to be unconstitutionally vague, even when defined as advocacy of criminal anarchy:

> The possible scope of "seditious utterances or acts" has virtually no limit. For under Penal Law sec. 161, one commits the felony of advocating criminal anarchy if he "publicly displays any book . . . containing or advocating, advising or teaching the doctrine that organized government should be overthrown by force, violence, or other unlawful means." Does the teacher who carries a copy of the Communist Manifesto on a public street thereby advocate criminal anarchy? . . . The teacher cannot know the extent, if any, to which a "seditious" utterance must transcend mere statement about abstract doctrine, the extent to which it must be intended to and tend to indoctrinate or incite to action in furtherance of the defined doctrine. The crucial consideration is that no teacher can know just where the line is drawn between "seditious" and nonseditious utterances and acts [385 U.S. at 598–99].

The Court also found that the state's entire system of "intricate administrative machinery" was "a highly efficient *in terrorem* mechanism. . . . It would be a bold teacher who would not stay as far as possible from utterances or acts which might jeopardize his living by enmeshing him in this intricate machinery. . . . The result may be to stifle 'that free play of the spirit which all teachers ought especially to cultivate and practice'" (385 U.S. at 601; quoting *Wieman* v. *Updegraff,* 344 U.S. 183, 195 (Frankfurter, concurring)).

The Court rejected the older case of *Adler* v. *Board of Education,* 342 U.S.

485 (1951), which permitted New York to bar employment to teachers who were members of listed subversive organizations. Noting that "the stifling effect on the academic mind from curtailing freedom of association in such a manner is manifest," the Court applied a new rule:

> Mere knowing membership without a specific intent to further the unlawful aims of an organization is not a constitutionally adequate basis for exclusion from such positions as those held by appellants. . . . Legislation which sanctions membership unaccompanied by specific intent to further the unlawful goals of the organization or which is not active membership violates constitutional limitations [385 U.S. at 606, 608].

One year after *Keyishian,* the Supreme Court stepped gingerly into a new type of academic freedom controversy. *Pickering* v. *Board of Education,* 391 U.S. 563 (1968), concerned a public high school teacher who had been dismissed for writing the local newspaper a letter in which he criticized the board of education's financial plans for the high schools. Pickering brought suit alleging that the dismissal violated his First Amendment freedom of speech. The school board argued that the dismissal was justified because the letter "damaged the professional reputations of . . . [the school board] members and of the school administrators, would be disruptive of faculty discipline, and would tend to foment 'controversy, conflict, and dissention' among teachers, administrators, the board of education, and the residents of the district."

In balancing the teacher's freedom of speech against the state's interest in maintaining an efficient educational system, the Court identified and considered the following factors: (1) Is there a close working relationship between the teacher and those he criticized? (2) Is the substance of the letter a matter of legitimate public concern? (3) Did the letter have a detrimental impact on the administration of the educational system? (4) Was the teacher's performance of his daily duties impeded? (5) Was the teacher writing in his professional capacity or as a private citizen? The Court found that Pickering had no working relationship with the board, that the letter dealt with a matter of public concern, that Pickering's letter was greeted with public apathy and therefore had no detrimental effect on the schools, that Pickering's performance as a teacher was not hindered by the letter, and that he wrote as a citizen, not a teacher. The Court concluded that under all these facts the interest of the school administration in limiting teachers' opportunities to contribute to public debate is not significantly greater than its interest in limiting a similar contribution by any member of the general public and that "in a case such as this, absent proof of false statements knowingly or recklessly made by him, a teacher's exercise of his right to speak on issues of public importance may not furnish the basis for his dismissal from public employment."

The *Pickering* balancing test was reaffirmed and further explained in two later Supreme Court cases: *Givhan* v. *Western Line Consolidated School District,* 439 U.S. 410 (1979), and *Connick* v. *Myers,* 103 S. Ct. 1684 (1983).

In *Givhan* the issue was whether *Pickering* protects public school teachers who communicate their views in private rather than in public. In a series of private meetings with her school principal, the plaintiff teacher in *Givhan* had made complaints and expressed opinions about school employment practices that she considered racially discriminatory. When the school district did not renew her contract, the teacher filed suit, claiming an infringement of her First Amendment rights. The trial court found that the school district had not renewed the teacher's contract primarily because of her criticisms of school employment practices, and it held that such action violated the First Amendment. The U.S. Court of Appeals reversed, reasoning that the teacher's expression was not protected by the First Amendment because she had expressed her views privately. The U.S. Supreme Court, in a unanimous opinion, disagreed with the appeals court and remanded the case to the trial court for further consideration. According to the Court, "neither the [First] Amendment itself nor our decisions indicate that . . . freedom [of speech] is lost to the public employee who arranges to communicate privately with his employer rather than to spread his views before the public." Rather, private expression, like public expression, is subject to the same balancing of factors that the Court utilized in *Pickering*. The Court did suggest in a footnote, however, that private expression may involve some different considerations:

> Although the First Amendment's protection of government employees extends to private as well as public expression, striking the *Pickering* balance in each context may involve different considerations. When a teacher speaks publicly, it is generally the content of his statements that must be assessed to determine whether they "in any way either impeded the teacher's proper performance of his daily duties in the classroom or . . . interfered with the regular operation of the schools generally" (*Pickering* v. *Board of Education*, 391 U.S. at 572–73). Private expression, however, may in some situations bring additional factors to the *Pickering* calculus. When a government employee personally confronts his immediate superior, the employing agency's institutional efficiency may be threatened not only by the content of the employee's message but also by the manner, time, and place in which it is delivered [439 U.S. at 415 n.4].

In *Connick* v. *Myers*, the issue was whether *Pickering* protects public employees who communicate views to office staff about office personnel matters. The plaintiff, Myers, was an assistant district attorney who had been scheduled for transfer to another division of the office. In opposing the transfer, she circulated a questionnaire on office operations to other assistant district attorneys. Later on the same day, she was discharged. In a 5-to-4 decision, the Court declined to follow *Givhan*, arguing that Givhan's statements about employment practices "involved a matter of public concern." Then, applying the *Pickering* factors, the Court majority determined that the questions posed by Myers (with one exception) "do not fall under the rubric of matters of 'public concern' "; that Myers spoke "not as a citizen upon matters of public concern, but instead as an employee upon matters only of personal interest and that circulation of the questionnaire interfered with "close working relationships" within the office. The balance of factors therefore indicated that the discharge did not violate the plaintiff's freedom of speech.

Givhan and *Myers* emphasize the need to distinguish between communications on matters of public concern and communications on matters of private or personal concern—a distinction that does not depend on whether the communication is itself made in public or in private. The dispute between the majority and dissenters in *Myers* reveals how slippery this distinction can be. Although *Myers* may appear to limit the protections originally provided by *Pickering,* the Court emphasized that its opinion was limited to the case's specific facts and that courts must remain attentive to the "enormous variety of fact situations" that other cases may present. Particularly in cases involving postsecondary faculty members, where (unlike a district attorney's office) shared governance and academic freedom may be primary values of the work place, *Myers* should not have any substantial effect on faculty members' freedom of speech.

Lower courts have often applied the *Pickering* methodology, and the principles from the *Keyishian* case and its forerunners, to determine the scope of faculty members' academic freedom. As could be expected, the court opinions have reached varying conclusions, depending on the case's specific facts and the particular court's disposition on how liberally to construe First Amendment protections, especially those in *Pickering.* Conceptually, such cases may be divided into three categories, highlighting the three arenas in which faculty members and administrators may clash over academic freedom: (1) in the classroom, (2) in institutional affairs, and (3) in private life. Sections 3.6.2 to 3.6.4 provide illustrations from each arena. Since all these cases were decided before *Givhan* and *Myers,* future courts, as well as college legal counsel, should reconsider the earlier courts' reasoning, in light of *Givhan* and *Myers,* as they apply these cases to new fact situations.

3.6.2. Academic freedom in the classroom. Courts are generally most reticent to become involved in academic freedom disputes concerning course content, teaching methods, or classroom behavior. Courts view these as matters best left to the competence of the administrators and educators who have primary responsibility over academic affairs. The following two cases illustrate this judicial attitude.

Hetrick v. *Martin,* 480 F.2d 705 (6th Cir. 1973), concerned the refusal of a state university to renew a nontenured faculty member's contract because the university disapproved of her "pedagogical attitude." Her troubles with the school administration apparently began when unnamed students and the parents of one student complained about certain of her in-class activities. Specifically, to illustrate the "irony" and "connotative qualities" of the English language, the faculty member once told her freshman students, "I am an unwed mother." At that time, she was a divorced mother of two, but she did not reveal that fact to her class. On occasion she also apparently discussed the war in Vietnam and the military draft with one of her freshman classes.

The faculty member sued the university, alleging that her First Amendment rights had been infringed. The court ruled that the nonrenewal was not based on any statements the faculty member might have made but on her "pedagogical attitude." The faculty member believed that her students should be free to organize assignments in accordance with their own interests, while the university expected her to "go by the book." Viewing the case as a dispute over teaching methods, the court refused to equate the teaching methods of professors with constitutionally protected speech:

> We do not accept plaintiff's assertion that the school administration abridged her First Amendment rights when it refused to rehire her because it considered her teaching philosophy to be incompatible with the pedagogical aims of the university. Whatever may be the ultimate scope of the amorphous

"academic freedom" guaranteed to our nation's teachers and students . . . ,
it does not encompass the right of a nontenured teacher to have her teaching
style insulated from review by her superiors when they determine whether
she has merited tenured status just because her methods and philosophy
are considered acceptable somewhere in the teaching profession [480 F.2d
at 709].

Clark v. *Holmes,* 474 F.2d 928 (7th Cir. 1972), also involved a teacher's
methods and behavior. Clark was a nontenured, temporary substitute teacher at
Northern Illinois University, a state institution. Clark had been told that he would
be rehired if he was willing to remedy certain deficiencies—namely, that he
"counseled an excessive number of students instead of referring them to NIU's
professional counselors; he overemphasized sex in his health survey course; he
counseled students with his office door closed; and he belittled other staff members
in discussions with students." After discussions with his superiors, in which he
defended his conduct, Clark was rehired; but in the middle of the year he was told
that he would not teach in the spring semester because of these same problems.
    Clark brought suit, claiming that, under *Pickering,* the university had violated
his First Amendment rights by not rehiring him because of his speech activities.
The court, disagreeing, refused to apply *Pickering* to this situation: (1) Clark's disputes
with his colleagues about course content were not matters of public concern, as
were the matters raised in Pickering's letter; and (2) Clark's disputes involved him
as a teacher, not as a private citizen, whereas Pickering's situation was just the
opposite. The court then held that the institution's interest as employer overcame
any free speech interest the teacher may have had:

> But we do not conceive academic freedom to be a license for uncon-
> trolled expression at variance with established curricular contents and inter-
> nally destructive of the proper functioning of the institution. First Amend-
> ment rights must be applied in light of the special characteristics of the
> environment in the particular case (*Tinker* v. *Des Moines Indep. Community
> School Dist.,* 393 U.S. 503, 506, 89 S. Ct. 733, 21 L. Ed. 2d 731 (1969);
> *Healy* v. *James,* 408 U.S. 169 (1972)). The plaintiff here irresponsibly made
> captious remarks to a captive audience, one, moreover, that was composed
> of students who were dependent upon him for grades and
> recommendations. . . .
>   Furthermore, *Pickering* suggests that certain legitimate interests of
> the state may limit a teacher's right to say what he pleases: for example,
> (1) the need to maintain discipline or harmony among co-workers; (2) the
> need for confidentiality; (3) the need to curtail conduct which impedes the
> teacher's proper and competent performance of his daily duties; and (4)
> the need to encourage a close and personal relationship between the employer
> and his superiors, where that relationship calls for loyalty and confidence
> [474 F.2d at 931].

3.6.3. Academic freedom in institutional affairs. Just as a faculty member's
duties extend beyond the classroom, so do the possibilities for academic freedom
disputes involving faculty members. Faculty members may claim academic freedom

protections for opinions and behavior involving other official or unofficial job responsibilities or other campus activities. In these situations the interests that both the institution and the faculty member seek to protect are different from those relating to expression or behavior in the classroom. The state may be less concerned with the effect such speech has on students. The state's main interests may be protecting the educational institution from losing public confidence and maintaining a harmonious relationship between the faculty and the institution. The faculty member is not as interested in maintaining an atmosphere of free debate within the classroom as in protecting the right to express his or her views or personality on campus without fear of reprisal.

In cases involving institutional affairs, faculty members have fared better with the courts than in the classroom cases. The following cases are illustrative.

Smith v. *Losee,* 485 F.2d 334 (10th Cir. 1973), concerned a nontenured associate professor at Dixie Junior College, a public institution in Utah, who had been denied tenure and dismissed from his position. The professor sued, claiming a denial of First Amendment rights. The trial court found, and the appellate court agreed, that college officials had dismissed the professor because he had "opposed the college administration in his capacity as president and member of the executive committee of the faculty association" and "expressed opposition to some administration policies during meetings of the . . . [association]." The appellate court also agreed that the professor's activities were exercises of First Amendment freedom of speech, for which he could not be dismissed:

> Taking the entire record and applying it to the balancing test as prescribed in [*Pickering,* above, and in the *Tinker* decision, Section 4.7.1 of this volume], it is apparent that the plaintiff's exercise of his First Amendment rights in the manner in which he did far outweighs the interest of the defendants in promoting the efficiency and harmony of Dixie College [485 F.2d at 340].

Rampey v. *Allen,* 501 F.2d 1090 (10th Cir. 1974), arose after a college president had characterized eleven professors and three staff members as "divisive" and had caused them not to be rehired. By "divisive," the court later found, the president meant that the professors refused to parrot his views or would talk to students and other faculty members about problems the school was having. The fourteen plaintiffs sued, alleging that the nonrenewal of their contracts was in retaliation for their exercise of First Amendment rights. The court agreed:

> While a college president is entitled to respect and authority within his sphere, this does not extend to the exercise of absolute control over the associations and expressions of the faculty members. Whether they demonstrate loyalty to him personally, whether they relate to him personally, and whether they have a similar philosophy is not, as we view it, a requisite and he cannot demand such attitudes at the expense of the individual rights of the faculty members, and there can be little question but that such demands infringe the rights of the faculty members to express legitimate views in the course of formulating ideas in an academic atmosphere. There is not the slightest suggestion in the evidence that the plaintiffs in exercising

their rights constituted any threat to the valid authority of President Carter in the conduct of his duties. Nor does it appear that these plaintiffs were in a relationship with Dr. Carter which required personal loyalty or devotion [501 F.2d at 1098].

In *Starsky* v. *Williams,* 353 F. Supp. 900 (D. Ariz. 1972), affirmed in pertinent part, 512 F.2d 109 (9th Cir. 1975), the plaintiff was a philosophy professor who had been dismissed on a series of eight charges, some involving on-campus activity and others involving off-campus activity. (The charges in the latter category are discussed in Section 3.6.4.) Professor Starsky was tenured and had taught at Arizona State University for six years. After several incidents, generally involving activity aimed at disseminating knowledge about socialism, the board of regents directed the president to institute proceedings against Professor Starsky. After carefully considering the evidence, the disciplinary committee found that the charges did not support a recommendation for dismissal. The board nevertheless terminated Starsky's employment, and the professor sought redress in the courts.

The district court held that the termination violated Starsky's constitutional right to free speech, and the appellate court affirmed. The district court discussed the eight charges at length, dismissing some as not being supported by the evidence. One charge found to be true was that Professor Starsky had deliberately cut a class in order to participate in a rally on campus. The court ruled that Starsky had broken no specific regulation by canceling the class and that the incident was a minor one, usually handled informally within the department. The court chastised the board for selectively enforcing its general attendance policy and dismissed the charge. Another more serious charge concerned the peaceful distribution of a leaflet to other faculty members. The leaflet was a philosophical and political discussion of activity taking place at Columbia University and quoted a Columbia student who advocated socialism. The university charged that "Professor Starsky has failed to exercise appropriate restraint or to exercise critical self-discipline and judgment in using, extending, and transmitting knowledge." The evidence stated that the university found his activity to be not in keeping with "the austere surroundings of a faculty meeting" and to have exhibited "complete disrespect for authority." The court, quoting the academic freedom declaration from the *Keyishian* case (discussed in Section 3.6.1), stated:

> There is a serious constitutional question as to whether speech can be stifled because the ideas or wording expressed upset the "austere" faculty atmosphere; certainly the board has no legitimate interest in keeping a university in some kind of intellectual austerity by an absence of shocking ideas. Insofar as the plaintiff's words upset the legislature or faculty because of the contents of his views, and particularly the depth of his social criticism, this is not the kind of detriment for which plaintiff can constitutionally be penalized [353 F. Supp. at 920].

While these cases create substantial academic freedom protections, faculty members by no means always win cases regarding institutional affairs.

Roseman v. *Indiana University of Pennsylvania,* 520 F.2d 1364 (3d Cir. 1975), is not easily reconcilable with the *Smith* v. *Losee* case above. An associate professor alleged that her contract was not renewed because she had complained to the dean, and later to the faculty at a department meeting, about the department head's alleged impropriety in the selection process for a new department chairman. The professor claimed that this complaint was First Amendment protected speech. The court, distinguishing *Pickering,* above, rejected the professor's claim because (1) her comments "were essentially private communications in which only members . . . [of the department and the dean] had any interest," whereas Pickering's letter was a public communication on a matter of public interest; and (2) her comments had a "potentially disruptive impact on the functioning of the department" because they "called into question the integrity of . . . [the department head]," whereas Pickering's letter was not directed to any person with whom he normally worked and had no disruptive impact.

The plaintiff faculty member in *Duke* v. *North Texas State University,* 469 F.2d 829 (5th Cir. 1973), had been fired after she used profane language while addressing an unauthorized meeting of students before freshman orientation. She was specifically fired on this charge: "The actions and statements of . . . [the faculty member] demonstrate a lack of academic responsibility required by Sec. II of the Statement on Academic Freedom at North Texas State University in that: (a) her actions and statements before a group of students and her participation in meetings which violate the rules and regulations of the university impair her efficiency as a teacher and her judgment as a scholar, and (b) by her actions and statements upon the occasions in question, . . . [the faculty member] failed to recognize and appreciate that the public will judge [the university] and its teaching faculty by such statements and actions, thereby demonstrating the lack of professional integrity required of the teaching faculty at North Texas State University." The court found that "the interests the university sought to protect were to maintain a competent faculty and to perpetuate public confidence in the educational institution." Weighing these interests against the faculty member's interest in free speech, the court held for the university:

> As a past and prospective instructor, Mrs. Duke owed the university a minimal duty of loyalty and civility to refrain from extremely disrespectful and grossly offensive remarks aimed at the administrators of the university. By her breach of this duty, the interests of the university outweighed her claim for protection [469 F.2d at 840].

3.6.4. Academic freedom in private life. Faculty members' activities would seem most insulated from state or institutional interference in their private lives. Indeed, the faculty member can be seen as an ordinary citizen who happens to teach in a postsecondary institution. But the faculty member's private activities are not completely immune from interference by the state or the institution, because such activities may have an impact on teaching responsibilities or other legitimate interests of the institution.

A professor's private life may involve activities not traditionally thought of as First Amendment rights. *Hander* v. *San Jacinto Junior College,* 519 F.2d 273 (5th Cir. 1975), concerned a state college's authority to enforce faculty grooming regulations. A professor was dismissed when he refused to shave his beard. In holding for the professor on due process and equal protection grounds, the court first distinguished university faculty from other government employees: "Teachers even at public institutions such as San Jacinto Junior College simply do not have the exposure or community-wide impact of policemen and other employees who deal directly with the public. Nor is the need for discipline as acute in the educational environment as in other types of public service." The court then enunciated this role for teachers:

> School authorities may regulate teachers' appearance and activities only when the regulation has some relevance to legitimate administrative or educational functions. . . .
> The mere subjective belief in a particular idea by public employers is, however, an undeniably insufficient justification for the infringement of a constitutionally guaranteed right. . . . It is illogical to conclude that a teacher's bearded appearance would jeopardize his reputation or pedagogical effectiveness with college students [519 F.2d at 277].

Another aspect of faculty freedom in private life is illustrated by *Trister* v. *University of Mississippi,* 420 F.2d 499 (5th Cir. 1969), where the court ruled that it was unconstitutional for a state law school to prohibit some part-time faculty members from working part time at outside legal jobs while allowing other faculty members to do so. Certain part-time faculty members had continued working at a legal services office of the Office of Economic Opportunity (OEO) despite a warning from the administration that they would lose their jobs at the university if they continued. There was no evidence that the OEO jobs consumed any more time than the part-time jobs of other faculty members. In upholding the plaintiffs' right to work at the OEO office, the court based its decision not on the First Amendment but on the Fourteenth Amendment equal protection clause:

> We are not willing to take the position that plaintiffs have a constitutional right to participate in the legal services program of the OEO, or in any other program. Nor do they have a constitutional right to engage in part-time employment while teaching part time at the law school. No such right exists in isolation. Plaintiffs, however, do have the constitutional right to be treated by a state agency in no significantly different manner from others who are members of the same class; that is, members of the faculty of the University of Mississippi school of law [420 F.2d at 502].

Other courts may be more willing to find a limited constitutional right to outside employment, under the First Amendment or Fourteenth Amendment due process, where such employment does not interfere with any substantial interest of the institution.

Starsky v. *Williams,* 353 F. Supp. 900 (D. Ariz. 1972), affirmed in pertinent part, 512 F.2d 109 (9th Cir. 1975), discussed in Section 3.6.3, illustrates yet another aspect of faculty freedom in private life. The plaintiff filed suit seeking reinstatement as a member of the faculty at Arizona State University. He had made a television speech criticizing the board of regents and calling them hypocrites. He had also issued a press release in which he criticized the board. The court, finding for Professor Starsky, stated:

In each of these communications, plaintiff spoke or wrote as a private citizen on a public issue, and in a place and context apart from his role as faculty member. In none of these public utterances did he appear as a spokesman for the university, or claim any kind of expertise related to his profession. He spoke as any citizen might speak, and the board was, therefore, subject to its own avowed standard that when a faculty member "speaks or writes as a citizen, he should be free from institutional censorship or discipline" [353 F. Supp. at 920].

3.6.5. Administrators' authority over faculty academic freedom. The foregoing discussions have made clear that academic freedom is an area in which the law provides no firm guidelines for administrators. This is particularly true for private institutions, since the decided cases are almost all constitutional decisions applicable only to public schools. Even the constitutional cases are sometimes incompletely reasoned or difficult to reconcile with one another. The fact that decisions often depend heavily on a vague balancing of faculty and institutional interests in light of the peculiar facts of the case makes it difficult to generalize from one case to another. Thus, it is especially crucial for institutions to develop their own guidelines on academic freedom and to have internal systems for protecting academic freedom in accordance with institutional policy. Often the AAUP guidelines (see Section 3.6.1) can be of considerable assistance in this endeavor.

The constitutional court decisions do provide some guidance, however; and they do restrict the authority of administrators to limit faculty academic freedom at public institutions. The classroom (Section 3.6.2) is clearly the arena where institutional authority is greatest and courts are most hesitant to enter. Beyond the classroom faculty members have considerable freedom to express themselves on public issues and, as private citizens, to associate with whom they please and engage in outside activities of their choice. In general, whether in the classroom or out, administrative authority over teacher behavior or activities increases as the job-relatedness of the behavior or activities increases and as the adverseness of their impact on teaching performance or other institutional functions increases.

When establishing or reviewing institutional regulations on academic freedom, administrators of public institutions should assure that such regulations avoid the constitutional dangers of "overbreadth" and "vagueness" (see Section 3.4.1). Administrators should also assure that such regulations avoid interference with the content (or substance) of faculty members' speech, particularly outside the classroom; courts permit narrow regulation of the time, place, or manner of speech but seldom of its content as such (see Section 4.7.2). In addition, administrators should assure that institutional academic freedom regulations follow procedural due process requirements in situations where their application would deprive a faculty member of a "liberty" or "property" interest (see Section 3.5.2). While these requirements bind only public institutions, they may provide useful guidance for private institutions as well.

When deciding whether to hire, renew, promote, grant tenure to, or dismiss a particular faculty member, administrators should carefully avoid decisions based on actions of that faculty member that are protected by academic freedom. Sticky problems can arise when the faculty member has engaged in possibly protected action but has also engaged in other, unprotected, action that might justify an adverse personnel decision. Suppose, for instance, that a faculty member up for renewal had made public statements critical of state policy on higher education (probably protected) and also had often failed to meet his classes (unprotected). What must an administrator do to avoid later judicial overruling of a decision not to renew?

The U.S. Supreme Court addressed this problem in *Mt. Healthy City School District Board of Education* v. *Doyle,* 429 U.S. 274 (1977). The plaintiff school teacher had made statements regarding school policy to a radio broadcaster, who promptly broadcast the information as a news item. A month later the school board informed the teacher that he would not be rehired and gave the radio broadcast as one reason. It also gave several other reasons, however, including an incident in which the teacher made an obscene gesture to two students in the school cafeteria. The Supreme Court stated that, although the radio communication was protected by the First Amendment and played a substantial part in the nonrenewal decision, the nonrenewal was valid if the school board could prove that it would not have rehired the teacher even if the radio incident had never occurred:

> Initially, in this case, the burden was properly placed upon . . . [the teacher] to show that his conduct was constitutionally protected, and that this conduct was a "substantial factor"—or, to put it in other words, that it was a "motivating factor" in the board's decision not to rehire him. [The teacher] having carried that burden, however, the district court should have gone on to determine whether the board had shown by preponderance of the evidence that it would have reached the same decision as to . . . [the teacher's] reemployment even in the absence of the protected conduct [429 U.S. at 287].

Mt. Healthy was first applied to postsecondary education in *Franklin* v. *Atkins,* 562 F.2d 1188 (10th Cir. 1977). Challenging the board of regents' refusal to appoint him to a faculty position at the University of Colorado, Bruce Franklin argued that the board had relied on constitutionally protected conduct he had engaged in while on the faculty at Stanford University. The court rejected Franklin's claim, holding that (1) he failed to prove that his conduct, described in a report from a Stanford hearing board, was constitutionally protected and (2) even if his conduct was protected, he failed to prove that it "was a 'substantial' or 'motivating factor' in the regents' decision."

After *Franklin* numerous court decisions have applied the *Mt. Healthy* test to postsecondary situations in which both proper and improper considerations are alleged to have contributed to a particular decision. In *Goss* v. *San Jacinto Junior College,* 588 F.2d 96 (5th Cir. 1979), for instance, the plaintiff was a junior college instructor whose contract had not been renewed. She claimed that the college's action was due to her political and union activities, which were protected activities under the First Amendment. The college responded that the instructor had not been rehired because of declining enrollment and poor evaluation of her work. After a jury trial, the jury agreed with the instructor and awarded her $23,400 in back pay. In affirming the jury verdict, the U.S. Court of Appeals for the Fifth Circuit issued an opinion illustrating what administrators should *not* do if they wish to avoid judicial invalidation of their personnel decisions:

> There was ample evidence to support the jury finding that Mrs. Goss had not been rehired "because of her political and/or professional activities." Dr. Spencer [the president of the college] testified that, when Mrs. Goss sought to organize a local chapter of the National Faculty Association, he distributed by campus mail a faculty newsletter expressing his concern about the organization, while denying proponents of the National Faculty Association the privilege of distributing literature by campus mail. Mrs. Goss testified that, after her husband had filed a petition to run for a seat on the board of regents, Dr. Carl Burney, chairman of the Division of Social and Behavioral Sciences, advised her to have her husband withdraw from the election. In deposition testimony, Dr. O. W. Marcom, academic dean, stated that, when Mrs. Goss presided at an organizational meeting of a local chapter of the Texas Junior College Teachers Association in the spring of 1971, he attended and voiced his objection to the group. Dr. Spencer himself testified by deposition that he had recommended the nonrenewal of Mrs. Goss's contract to discipline her for "creating or trying to create ill will or lack of cooperation . . . with the administration."
>
> There was sufficient evidence to support the jury finding that "matters other than Mrs. Goss's political and/or professional activities" were not responsible for the board of regents' action. Appellants justified the nonrenewal of Mrs. Goss's contract on the grounds that declining enrollment necessitated a staff reduction and that Mrs. Goss received a poor evaluation from Dr. Edwin Lehr, chairman of the history department, and Dr. Burney. Although Dr. Spencer had recommended a reduction of three faculty members in the history department, Mrs. Goss was one of four faculty members in the history department in 1971–72 who did not teach at San Jacinto Junior College in 1972–73.
>
> Furthermore, Dr. Lehr's evaluation of Mrs. Goss, upon which Dr. Spencer allegedly relied in making his recommendation to the board of regents, was inconsistent with the objective criteria established for the rating. The criteria by which the teachers were rated include the number of years of teaching at San Jacinto Junior College, enrollment in a doctoral program, the number of doctoral-level courses completed, the percentage of the teacher's students earning credits, and other factors. Mrs. Goss was not awarded five points to which she was entitled on the objective scale for academic courses she had taken while employed as an instructor. Thus, she was assigned eighty points, rather than eighty-five. If she had been awarded the points to which she was entitled, she would have ranked in the middle of the seventeen history instructors rather than in the bottom three [588 F.2d at 99–100].

Evidence of an intrusion into academic freedom is not always as clear to a court as it was in *Goss*. In *Allaire* v. *Rogers,* 658 F.2d 1055 (5th Cir. 1981), the court considered whether a university president had denied merit raises to a group of tenured professors because they had lobbied for increased salary appropriations at the state legislature (protected) or because of their lack of merit (unprotected). Only one of the eight original plaintiffs ultimately prevailed on appeal. In *Hillis* v. *Stephen F. Austin State University,* 665 F.2d 547 (5th Cir. 1982), the court considered whether the contract of a nontenured faculty member had not been renewed because of his private criticism of his superiors (protected) or his insubordination and uncooperativeness (unprotected). After losing at trial, the university prevailed on appeal. In *Hildebrand* v. *Board of Trustees of Michigan State University,* 607 F.2d 705 (6th Cir. 1979), appeal after remand, 662 F.2d 439 (6th Cir. 1981), the court considered whether a faculty member had been denied tenure because of his criticism of the department's curriculum (protected), his election to the departmental advisory committee (protected), or his unsuitability for the multidisciplinary emphasis of the department (unprotected). After a trial, a reversal on appeal and remand, a second trial resulting in a jury verdict for the professor, a trial judge's overturning of the jury's verdict, and a second appeal, the university eventually emerged victorious. And in *Ollman* v. *Toll,* 518 F. Supp. 1196 (D. Md. 1981), affirmed, 704 F.2d 139 (4th Cir. 1983), the court considered whether the University of Maryland's refusal to appoint the plaintiff to a department chairmanship, after his selection by a search committee, was because of his Marxist political views (protected) or because the plaintiff lacked the necessary qualifications to develop the department according to the university's plans (unprotected). The university prevailed at trial and on appeal.

By placing burdens on faculty members asserting violations of academic freedom, *Mt. Healthy* and its progeny give administrators breathing space to make personnel decisions where faculty members may have engaged in protected activity. The goal for administrators still should be a decision untainted by any consideration of protected conduct. But in the real world, this goal is not always attainable—either because under current legal standards it is difficult to determine whether particular conduct is protected or because events involving academic freedom are too widely known to completely isolate decision makers from such information. In these cases administrators can still avoid judicial invalidation if they assure that strong and dispositive grounds, independent of any grounds impinging academic freedom, exist for every adverse decision and that such independent grounds are considered in making the decision and are documented in the institution's records.

While the *Mt. Healthy* line of cases, as First Amendment precedents, bind only public institutions, they can guide private institutions in establishing review standards for their own internal hearings on personnel disputes, and they may, by analogy, assist courts in reviewing academic freedom claims based on a contract theory (see Section 3.6.1).

3.6.6. Protection of confidential academic information: "Academic freedom privilege." A line of cases from the early 1980s has created a new type of academic freedom problem for postsecondary faculty members and administrators: whether courts or administrative agencies may compel faculty members or their institutions to disclose confidential academic information if such information is relevant to issues in litigation. Faculty members may confront this problem if they are asked to provide a deposition, to answer interrogatories, or to be a witness in ongoing litigation, or if they are served with a subpoena or contempt citation or otherwise ordered by a court or administrative agency to surrender information within their control.

Administrators may become entwined in the problem if the institution seeks to assist a faculty member with such matters or, more generally, if the institution seeks to monitor institutional affairs so as to avoid litigation. Although faculty members and administrators may disagree on how best to respond to demands for confidential information, the primary clash is not between members of the academic community—as in the cases in Sections 3.6.2 to 3.6.5—but between the academic community, on the one hand, and the courts, administrative agencies, and opposing litigants on the other.

In one case, *In re Dinnan*, 661 F.2d 426 (11th Cir. 1981), a trial court had ordered a University of Georgia professor serving on a faculty committee to reveal and explain his vote on a promotion and tenure application which the committee had rejected (see this volume, Section 3.3.2.1 under "Confidentiality of Faculty Votes on Personnel Decisions"). In another case, *Dow Chemical* v. *Allen*, 672 F.2d 1262 (7th Cir. 1982), an administrative law judge had ordered two University of Wisconsin researchers to disclose their notes, reports, working papers, and raw data on a research project in progress. In legal terms the question in such cases is whether, under evidence law or under the First Amendment, the information can be said to be privileged—that is, protected from disclosure by an "academic freedom privilege" or a "researcher's privilege." *Dinnan* and *Allen* illustrate the kinds of answers courts may give to this question in particular cases.[16]

In *Dinnan* the appellate court rejected the professor's claim to an academic freedom privilege. It therefore affirmed the trial court's orders that Dinnan answer deposition questions about his committee vote and that he be fined and jailed for contempt if he continued to refuse:

> The appellant argues that the instant case is one of "academic freedom." We, however, are unable to accept this characterization and, indeed, believe that any such view of the present case requires a gross distortion of its facts.
>
> This case simply involves the law of evidence: there are no issues of constitutional dimension raised. The appellant is claiming a privilege— that is, a right to refrain from testifying, that heretofore has not been considered or recognized by any court. The issue before this court then is whether the privilege claimed by the appellant should be endorsed by this circuit.
>
> We hold that no privilege exists that would enable Professor Dinnan to withhold information regarding his vote on the promotion of the appellee. This result is required on the basis of fundamental principles of law and sound public policy. . . .
>
> Bearing in mind that there has been a notable hostility on the part of the judiciary to recognizing new privileges and that the public policy served by a new privilege must transcend the normally dominant truth-

---

[16]Although the cases in this section concern faculty members, students apparently may also raise legitimate claims of privilege in some circumstances. See *In re Grand Jury Subpoena Dated January 4, 1984*, 583 F. Supp. 991 (E.D.N.Y. 1984), where the court held that a graduate student enjoyed a qualified privilege with respect to field notes and other scholarly research generated in the course of his studies.

seeking considerations, we turn to the privilege claim brought forth in the instant case. The appellant argues that the new privilege is necessary to protect two important societal interests, "academic freedom" and the "secret ballot." We find neither argument to be even slightly persuasive; we will examine the former contention first. . . .

Academic freedom is "of transcendent value to all of us and not merely to the teachers concerned" (*Keyishian* v. *Board of Regents,* 385 U.S. 589, 603, 87 S. Ct. 675, 683, 17 L. Ed. 2d 629 (1967)). Time after time the Supreme Court has upheld academic freedom in the face of government pressure (see, for example, *Cramp* v. *Board of Public Instruction,* 368 U.S. 278, 82 S. Ct. 275, 7 L. Ed. 2d 285 (1961); *Sweezy* v. *New Hampshire,* 354 U.S. 234, 77 S. Ct. 1203, 1 L. Ed. 2d 1311 (1957; *Wieman* v. *Updegraff,* 344 U.S. 183, 73 S. Ct. 215, 97 L. Ed. 216 (1952)).

However, in all those cases there was an *attempt to suppress ideas* by the government. *Ideas may be suppressed just as effectively by denying tenure as by prohibiting the teaching of certain courses.*

Quite bluntly, this court feels that the government should stay out of academic affairs. However, these issues are not presented in the instant case. Here a *private* plaintiff is attempting to enforce her constitutional and statutory rights in an employment situation. Therefore, the reasoning behind the cited cases simply does not apply here. . . .

The appellant is frustrating the appellee's attempt to vindicate an alleged infringement of her statutory and constitutional rights. Though the case is one involving an alleged case of sex discrimination, admittedly a cause of action not especially favored by some groups at the present time, its implications are staggering. Using the appellant's logic, if a tenure committee attempted to stop the promotion of all faculty members who were not pro-abortionists, a right-to-life music professor's attempt at discovery could be barred by the concept of "academic freedom." Likewise, a physicist's application might be sabotaged because he opposed the cession of the Panama Canal where such a position was not favored by the committee. In all these cases, "academic freedom" would shield the tenure committee from having to reveal its votes, even though the decision had nothing to do with any academic grounds. In every one of these scenarios, the rights of the applicant would be infringed upon, but "academic freedom" would serve to obstruct the vindication of these rights. This possibility is a much greater threat to our liberty and academic freedom than the compulsion of discovery in the instant case [661 F.2d at 427, 430-31].

Another court in a similar case, *Gray* v. *Board of Higher Education,* 692 F.2d 901 (2d Cir. 1982), reached the same result but on much narrower grounds (see Section 3.3.2.1 under "Confidentiality of Faculty Votes on Personnel Decisions"). The *Gray* plaintiff had not been given reasons why he was denied tenure. Had he received reasons, the court suggested, the university's legitimate interests in confidentiality may have prevailed. By leaving room for recognition of an academic freedom privilege in other cases, the court in effect adopted a middle-ground position developed by the AAUP (see "A Preliminary Statement on Judicially Compelled Disclosure in the Nonrenewal of Faculty Appointments," 67 *Academe* 27 (Feb./March 1981)).

In the *Allen* case, the court recognized a claim to a researcher's privilege. It therefore refused to enforce subpoenas issued by an administrative law judge presiding over a hearing convened by the Environmental Protection Agency to consider canceling the registration of certain herbicides manufactured by Dow:

> Relevant portions of the affidavits of Dr. Allen and Mr. Van Miller [the university researchers served with the subpoenas] stated, without contradiction by Dow [the company seeking the information], that public access to the research data would make the studies an unacceptable basis for scientific papers or other research; that peer review and publication of the studies was crucial to the researchers' credibility and careers and would be precluded by whole or partial public disclosure of the information; that loss of the opportunity to publish would severely decrease the researchers' professional opportunities in the future; and that even inadvertent disclosure of the information would risk total destruction of months or years of research.
>
> The precise contours of the concept of academic freedom are difficult to define. . . . One First Amendment scholar has written: "The heart of the system consists in the right of the individual faculty member to teach, carry on research, and publish without interference from the government, the community, the university administration, or his fellow faculty members" (T. Emerson, *The System of Freedom of Expression* 594 (1970)). We think it clear that whatever constitutional protection is afforded by the First Amendment extends as readily to the scholar in the laboratory as to the teacher in the classroom (see generally Emerson at 619). Of course, academic freedom, like other constitutional rights, is not absolute and must on occasion be balanced against important competing interests. . . . Case law considering the standard to be applied where the issue is academic freedom of the university to be free of governmental interference, as opposed to academic freedom of the individual teacher to be free of restraints from the university administration, is surprisingly sparse. But what precedent there is at the Supreme Court level suggests that to prevail over academic freedom the interests of government must be strong and the extent of intrusion carefully limited. . . .
>
> In the present case, the . . . subpoenas by their terms would compel the researchers to turn over to Dow virtually every scrap of paper and every mechanical or electronic recording made during the extended period that those studies have been in progress at the university. The ALJ's [administrative law judge's] decision would have further obliged the researchers to continually update Dow on "additional useful data" which became available during the course of the proceedings. These requirements threaten substantial intrusion into the enterprise of university research, and there are several reasons to think they are capable of chilling the exercise of academic freedom. To begin with, the burden of compliance certainly would not be insubstantial. More important, enforcement of the subpoenas would leave the researchers with the knowledge throughout continuation of their studies that the fruits of their labors had been appropriated by and were being scrutinized by a not-unbiased third party whose interests were arguably antithetical to theirs. It is not difficult to imagine that that realization might

well be both unnerving and discouraging. Indeed, it is probably fair to say that the character and extent of intervention would be such that, regardless of its purpose, it would "inevitably tend to check the ardor and fearlessness of scholars, qualities at once so fragile and so indispensable for fruitful academic labor" (*Sweezy* [v. *New Hampshire,* 354 U.S. 234, 262 (1957)] (Frankfurter, J., concurring in result)). In addition, the researchers could reasonably fear that additional demands for disclosure would be made in the future. If a private corporation can subpoena the entire work product of months of study, what is to say further down the line the company will not seek other subpoenas to determine how the research is coming along? To these factors must be added the knowledge of the researchers that even inadvertent disclosure of the subpoenaed data could jeopardize both the studies and their careers. Clearly, enforcement of the subpoenas carries the potential for chilling the exercise of First Amendment rights.

We do not suggest that facts could not arise sufficient to overcome respondents' academic freedom interests in the . . . studies. Nor do we say that a waiver of the protection afforded by the First Amendment is impossible. If, for example, Dr. Allen, Mr. Van Miller, or other researchers were likely to testify about the . . . studies at the [Environmental Protection Agency] hearing, there might well be justification for granting at least partial or conditional enforcement of the subpoenas. Of course, we need not decide that question now [672 F.2d at 1273-76; footnotes omitted].

In an earlier case, *Richards of Rockford, Inc.* v. *Pacific Gas and Electric Co.,* 71 F.R.D. 388 (N.D. Cal. 1976), a federal district court judge reached a similar conclusion in an opinion that identified and balanced the various competing interests at stake. But in *Wright* v. *Jeep Corp.,* 547 F. Supp. 871 (E.D. Mich. 1982), decided seven months after *Allen,* a federal district court rejected a privilege claim and enforced a subpoena requiring a University of Michigan professor to produce research data from a study which (unlike the study in *Allen*) was apparently completed.[17]

There are few cases to date in this emerging area, and those that have been decided do not all point in the same direction. Administrators should look for further developments and work closely with counsel in anticipating and responding to problems concerning academic freedom or researchers' privileges. Close attention should be paid to the particular context in which potential issues arise. Especially important are (1) the particular procedural and evidentiary rules of the court or administrative agency that would entertain the litigation and (2) the particular impact that disclosure of the requested information would have on academic freedom.

Sec. 3.7. Staff Reduction Due to Financial Exigency and Program Discontinuance

The financial difficulties that began for postsecondary education in the late

---

[17]In a second case involving the same University of Michigan professor and the same research data, *Buchanan* v. *American Motors Corp.,* 697 F.2d 151 (6th Cir. 1983), the appellate court refused to decide the privilege issue, instead holding that to compel an "expert who has no direct connection with the litigation" to testify was "unreasonably burdensome." The court therefore quashed a subpoena seeking the professor's appearance.

1960s created a new and particularly sensitive faculty personnel issue.[18] In an era of inflation and shrinking resources, what are the legal responsibilities of an institution that must terminate an academic program or otherwise initiate a reduction in force? On this question, which should continue to stalk postsecondary education for the foreseeable future, the law is still developing. But enough judicial ink has been spilled to give administrators a fair idea of how to prepare for the unwelcome necessity of terminating faculty jobs in a financial crunch.

In 1982 debate raged on the extent to which institutions can, and should, terminate tenured faculty without a showing of bona fide institutional financial exigency. An attorney, whose position received considerable publicity, argued that institutions had been granted broad, new authority for such terminations by *Jimenez* v. *Almodovar,* a U.S. Court of Appeals case discussed in Section 3.7.1 (see R. L. Jacobson, "Colleges Advised They Need Not Declare 'Exigency' to Lay Off Tenured Professors," *Chronicle of Higher Education,* March 17, 1982, p. 1, col. 2). Reacting to this analysis, the American Association of University Professors argued that the *Jimenez* case is consistent with existing law and with AAUP policy on program discontinuance for educational reasons, and thus does not broaden institutional authority (see R. L. Jacobson, "AAUP Challenges Claim That Faculty Layoffs Need Not Be Based Mainly on 'Exigency,'" *Chronicle of Higher Education,* March 31, 1982, p. 1, col. 2; and "Faculty Tenure and University Obligations: Courts Rely on AAUP's 1940 Statement (Letter to Editor)," *Chronicle of Higher Education,* April 21, 1982, p. 19, col. 2). This debate highlighted the distinction between terminations based on institutional financial exigency and terminations based on the alternative ground of bona fide program discontinuance. Although this distinction is not developed in the earlier cases, which primarily involve financial exigency, it has now become an important distinction underlying analysis of the staff reduction problem.

3.7.1. Contractual considerations. The faculty contract (Section 3.1) is the starting point for determining both a public and a private institution's responsibilities regarding staff reductions. Administrators should consider several questions concerning the faculty contract. Does it, and should it, provide for termination due to financial exigency or program discontinuance? Does it, and should it, specify the conditions that will constitute a financial exigency or justify discontinuance of a program and stipulate how the institution will determine when such conditions exist? Does it, and should it, set forth criteria for determining which faculty members will be released? Does it, and should it, require that alternatives be explored (such as transfer to another department) before termination becomes permissible? Does it, and should it, provide a hearing or other recourse for a faculty member chosen for dismissal? Does it, and should it, provide the released faculty member with any priority right to be rehired when other openings arise or the financial situation eases?

Whenever the faculty contract has any provision on financial exigency or program discontinuance, the institution should follow it; failure to do so will likely be

---

[18]This section is limited to financial exigency and program discontinuance problems concerning faculty. But such problems also affect students, and an institution's response may occasionally give students a basis on which to sue. See *Eden* v. *Board of Trustees of State University,* 49 A.D.2d 686 (1975), discussed in Section 4.2.3; and see generally Section 4.1.3, concerning an institution's contractual obligation to students.

a breach of contract. Whether such contractual provisions exist may depend on whether the AAUP guidelines[19] have been incorporated into the faculty contract. In *Browzin* v. *Catholic University of America,* 527 F.2d 843 (D.C. Cir. 1975), for instance, the parties stipulated that the AAUP guidelines had been adopted as part of the faculty contract, and the court noted that such adoption was "entirely consistent with the statutes of the university and the university's previous responses to AAUP actions." As in *Browzin,* it is important for administrators to understand the legal status of AAUP guidelines within their institutions; any doubt should be resolved by consulting counsel.

The contract provisions for tenured and nontenured faculty members may differ, and administrators should note any differences. Nontenured faculty members generally pose far fewer legal problems, since administrators may simply not renew their contracts at the end of the contract term (see Section 3.5.2.1). If the faculty contract is silent regarding financial exigency or program discontinuance, in relation to either tenured or nontenured faculty members, the institution still may have the power to terminate. Under the common law doctrine of "impossibility," the institution may be able to extricate itself from contractual obligations if unforeseen events have made it impossible to perform those obligations. The doctrine of impossibility has been stated as follows:

> When an unforeseen event which makes impossible the performance of a contractual duty occurs subsequent to the formation of the contract, it is often held that the promisor is excused from performing. Such holdings are exceptions to the general rule that when a contractual promise is made, the promisor must perform or pay damages for his failure to perform no matter how burdensome performance has become as a result of unforeseen circumstances [J. D. Calamari and J. M. Perillo, *Contracts,* 2nd ed, sec. 13-1 at 456–77 (West, 1977); and see generally Calamari and Perillo, chap. 13].

The first major contract case on financial exigency was *AAUP* v. *Bloomfield College,* 129 N.J. Super. 249, 322 A.2d 846 (1974), affirmed, 136 N.J. Super. 442, 346 A.2d 615 (1975). On June 29, 1973, Bloomfield College, a private school, notified thirteen tenured faculty members that their services would not be needed as of June 30, 1973. The college gave financial exigency as the reason for this action. The college also notified the remaining faculty members, tenured and nontenured, that they would be put on one-year terminal contracts for 1973–74, after which they would have to negotiate new contracts with the school.

The thirteen fired faculty members brought suit based on their contracts of employment. Paragraph C(3) of the "policies" which were part of the contract provided that "a teacher will have tenure and his services may be terminated only

---

[19]See "Recommended Institutional Regulations on Academic Freedom and Tenure," Regulation 4 (62 *AAUP Bulletin* 184, 185 (1976)), and "On Institutional Problems Resulting from Financial Exigency: Some Operating Guidelines" (60 *AAUP Bulletin* 267 (1974)). The 1968 version of the AAUP guidelines, specifically the 1968 version of Regulation 4(c), was interpreted in the *Browzin* case, discussed in the text in this section. The court concluded that the defendant university had not violated the requirement that it "make every effort" to place terminated faculty members "in other suitable positions."

for adequate cause, except in case of retirement for age, or under extraordinary circumstances because of financial exigency of the institution." Paragraph C(6) provided that "termination of continuous appointment because of financial exigency of the institution must be demonstrably bona fide. A situation which makes drastic retrenchment of this sort necessary precludes expansion of the staff at other points at the same time, except in extraordinary circumstances."

The faculty members alleged that no bona fide financial exigency existed and that the hiring of twelve new staff members three months after the plaintiffs were dismissed violated the requirement that during a financial exigency new staff persons would be hired only "in extraordinary circumstances." Thus, the issues were whether there was a "demonstrably bona fide" financial exigency and whether there were such extraordinary circumstances as would justify the hiring of new faculty members.

The trial court analyzed the college's finances and determined that no bona fide financial exigency existed because the college owned a large piece of valuable property that it could have sold to meet its needs. The appellate court, however, disagreed:

> In our opinion, the mere fact that this financial strain existed for some period of time does not negate the reality that a "financial exigency" was a fact of life for the college administration within the meaning of the underlying contract. The interpretation of "exigency" as attributed by the trial court is too narrow a concept of the term in relation to the subject matter involved. A more reasonable construction might be encompassed within the phrase "state of urgency." In this context the evidence was plentiful as to the proof of the existence of the criterion of the financial exigency required by the contract.
>
> In this vein it was improper for the judge to rest his conclusion in whole or in part upon the failure of the college to sell the knoll property which had been acquired several years before in anticipation of the creation of a new campus at a different locale. . . . Whether such a plan of action to secure financial stability on a short-term basis is preferable to the long-term planning of the college administration is a policy decision for the institution. Its choice of alternative is beyond the scope of judicial oversight in the context of this litigation [346 A.2d at 617].

Though the appellate court thus held that the college was in a state of financial exigency, it was unwilling to find that the faculty members were fired because of the college's financial condition. The trial court had determined that the reason for the terminations was the college's desire to abolish tenure, and the appellate court found ample evidence to support this finding.

On the issue of whether extraordinary circumstances existed sufficient to justify the hiring of twelve new faculty members, the trial court also held in favor of the plaintiffs. The college had argued that its actions were justified because it was developing a new type of curriculum, but the court noted that the evidence put forth by the college was vague and did not suggest that any financial benefit would result from the new curriculum. The appellate court did not disturb this part of the trial court's decision, nor did it even discuss the issue.

A major overarching issue of the case concerned the burden of proof. Did the college have the burden of proving that it had fulfilled the contract conditions justifying termination? Or did the faculty members have the burden of proving that the contractual conditions had *not* been met? The issue has critical practical importance; because the evidentiary problems can be so difficult, the outcome of financial exigency litigation may often depend on who has the burden of proof. The trial court assigned the burden to the college, and the appellate court agreed:

> It is manifest that under the controlling agreement among the parties the affected members of the faculty had attained the protection of tenure after completing a seven-year probationary service. This was their vested right which could be legally divested only if the defined conditions occurred. The proof of existence of those conditions as a justifiable reason for terminating the status of the plaintiffs plainly was the burden of the defendants [346 A.2d at 616].

Since the college had not proven that it had met the contract conditions justifying termination, the courts ordered the reinstatement of the terminated faculty members.

More recently two U.S. Court of Appeals cases, one from 1978 and the other from 1981, have upheld institutional authority to terminate tenured faculty members even in the absence of any express contractual provision granting such authority. The first case, *Krotkoff* v. *Goucher College,* 585 F.2d 675 (4th Cir. 1978), concerned a termination due to bona fide financial exigency; the second case, *Jimenez* v. *Almodovar,* 650 F.2d 363 (1st Cir. 1981), concerned a termination due to discontinuance of an academic program. Both cases resort to academic custom and usage (Sections 1.3.8 and 3.1.1) to imply terms into the faculty contract. Both cases also identify implicit rights of tenured faculty members which limit the institution's termination authority.

The plaintiff in *Krotkoff* was a tenured professor at a private, liberal arts college whose appointment had been terminated during a general retrenchment prompted by financial pressures. Since her contract was silent on the question of financial exigency, the professor argued that the termination was a breach of contract. The college argued that it had implied authority to terminate in order to combat bona fide financial exigency. In a four-part opinion, the appellate court analyzed the facts regarding the overall retrenchment program and the particular termination at issue (part I); held that the faculty contract, read in light of "the national academic community's understanding of the concept of tenure," permitted termination due to financial exigency (part II); held that a bona fide financial exigency existed (part III); and held that the college had used reasonable standards in selecting which appointments to terminate and had taken reasonable measures to afford the plaintiff alternative employment (part IV). The well-reasoned and organized opinion deserves quoting at length:

I

> Krotkoff began teaching German at Goucher in 1962 and was granted "indeterminate tenure" in 1967. In June of 1975, the college notified Krotkoff that, because of financial problems, it would not renew her 1975–76 contract when it expired on June 30, 1976. The college acknowledges that

Krotkoff has at all times been a fine teacher and that the termination was not based on her performance or behavior.

Goucher is a private, liberal arts college for women in Towson, Maryland. Beginning in 1968–69, the college operated at a deficit each academic year through 1973–74. The deficit for 1973–74 was $333,561, and the total deficit from 1968–69 through 1973–74 was $1,590,965. By the end of the 1973–74 year, the college's expendable endowment, which was used to cover these deficits, amounted to less than one half of the 1973–74 deficit. In 1974–75, as a result of a substantial reduction in expenditures, the college showed a meager surplus of $1,482. This was increased to $5,051 in 1975–76, but, partially as a result of a revision of the curriculum to attract more students, the deficit in 1976–77 was anticipated to be in excess of $100,000. The college's enrollment fell every year from 1969–70 through 1976–77, reducing revenue generated by tuition and fees, a major source of income.

This financial situation convinced the trustees that action was needed to ensure the institution's future. After a review of the finances and curriculum, the board adopted a more aggressive investment policy to seek a higher rate of return on endowment and promoted rental of the auditorium and excess dormitory space. It also froze salaries, cut administrative and clerical staffs, and deferred maintenance.

As a part of its retrenchment, the college did not renew the contracts of eleven untenured and four tenured faculty members, including Krotkoff. These professors were selected largely on the bases of the dean's study of enrollment projections and necessary changes in the curriculum. In addition, the faculty elected a committee to review curricular changes suggested by the administration. Among the administration's proposals were elimination of the classics department and the German section of the modern language department, which were staffed exclusively by tenured professors. The classics department was dropped, but the faculty committee recommended that the college continue a service program in German, staffed by one teacher, for students majoring in other disciplines who needed the language as a research skill. The administration accepted this recommendation.

The German faculty consisted of Krotkoff, who taught mostly advanced literature courses, and another tenured teacher, Sybille Ehrlich, who taught chiefly introductory language courses. The dean, concurring with the chairman of the department, recommended retention of Ehrlich primarily because she had more experience teaching the elementary language courses that would be offered in a service program and because she was also qualified to teach French. The president followed this recommendation.

The faculty grievance committee, to which Krotkoff then turned, applied the criteria by which the college faculty were regularly evaluated and recommended her retention. The committee, however, did not suggest that Ehrlich's appointment be terminated, and it did not address the problem of keeping both tenured professors. The president declined to accept the committee's recommendation, and the trustees sustained her decision. The president also rejected a suggestion that both teachers be retained by assigning Krotkoff to teach the German courses, dismissing an assistant dean, and designating Ehrlich as a part-time French teacher and a part-time assistant dean.

Goucher sent Krotkoff a list of all positions available for the next year. Krotkoff insisted that any new position carry her present faculty rank, salary, and tenure. She expressed interest in a position in the economics department, but the school declined to transfer her because the department's chairman estimated that she would need two to four years of training to become qualified.

In accordance with its notice of June 1975, the college terminated her appointment on June 30, 1976.

II

The primary issue is whether as a matter of law Krotkoff's contract permitted termination of her tenure by discontinuing her teaching position because of financial exigency.

The college's 1967 letter to Krotkoff granting her "indeterminate tenure" does not define that term. The college bylaws state:

> No original appointment shall establish "tenure," i.e., the right to continued service unless good cause be shown for termination. Reappointment as professor or associate professor, after three years of service in either rank, or appointment or reappointment to any professorial rank after five years of service as instructor or in any higher rank, shall establish tenure. The term "service" as used in this section shall mean instructional service in full-time appointments.

The bylaws also specify that the college may terminate a teacher's employment at age sixty-five or because of serious disability or cause. The parties agree that Krotkoff's appointment was not terminated for any of these reasons. Financial exigency is not mentioned in the bylaws, and the college concedes that it is not considered to be a ground of dismissal for cause.

The national academic community's understanding of the concept of tenure incorporates the notion that a college may refuse to renew a tenured teacher's contract because of financial exigency so long as its action is demonstrably bona fide. Dr. Todd Furniss, director of the Office of Academic Affairs of the American Council on Education, testified on behalf of Goucher:

> The [common] understanding was that the person who held tenure would be employed for an indeterminate or indefinite period up to retirement, unless two conditions held. The first condition would be some inadequacy on that person's part, either incompetency or neglect of duty or moral turpitude. . . .
>
> The second instance under which the tenure contract might be terminated is a group that includes, of course, death, includes disability, includes resignation, obviously, but chiefly includes what has been called financial exigency.

Dr. Furniss based his opinion in part on the 1940 Statement of Principles on Academic Freedom and Tenure, which was developed by the Association of American Colleges and the American Association of University Professors. This statement was later adopted by a number of professional organizations. With respect to the security afforded by tenure, the statement explains:

> After the expiration of a probationary period, teachers or investigators should have permanent or continuous tenure, and their services should be terminated only for adequate cause, except in the case of retirement for age, or under extraordinary circumstances because of financial exigencies.
>
> In the interpretation of this principle, it is understood that the following represents acceptable academic practice:
>
> . . . . .
>
> (5) Termination of a continuous appointment because of financial exigency should be demonstrably bona fide.

Probably because it was formulated by both administrators and professors, all of the secondary authorities seem to agree that [the 1940 statement] is the "most widely accepted academic definition of tenure" (R. Brown, "Tenure Rights in Contractual and Constitutional Context," 6 *J. of Law and Education* 279, 280 (1977); see also M. Mix, *Tenure and Termination in Financial Exigency* 4 (1978); C. Byse, "Academic Freedom, Tenure, and the Law," 73 *Harvard L. Rev.* 304, 305 (1959)).

The reported cases support the conclusion that tenure is not generally understood to preclude demonstrably bona fide dismissal for financial reasons. In most of the cases, the courts have interpreted contracts which contained an explicit reference to financial exigency (see *Browzin* v. *Catholic University,* 174 U.S. App. D.C. 60, 527 F.2d 843 (1975); *Bellak* v. *Franconia College,* 386 A.2d 1266 (N.H. 1978); *American Association of University Professors* v. *Bloomfield College,* 129 N.J. Super. 249, 322 A.2d 846 (Ch. Div. 1974), affirmed, 136 N.J. Super. 442, 346 A.2d 615 (App. Div. 1975); *Scheuer* v. *Creighton University,* 199 Neb. 618, 260 N.W.2d 595 (1977)). In others, where the contracts did not mention this term, the courts construed tenure as implicitly granting colleges the right to make bona fide dismissals for financial reasons (see *Johnson* v. *Board of Regents,* 377 F. Supp. 227, 234–35 (W.D. Wis. 1974), affirmed, 510 F.2d 975 (7th Cir. 1975) (table); *Levitt* v. *Board of Trustees,* 376 F. Supp. 945 (D. Neb. 1974); cf. *Rehor* v. *Case Western Reserve University,* 43 Ohio St. 2d 224, 331 N.E.2d 416 (1975)). No case indicates that tenure creates a right to exemption from dismissal for financial reasons. . . .

A concept of tenure that permits dismissal based on financial exigency is consistent with the primary purpose of tenure. Tenure's "real concern is with arbitrary or retaliatory dismissals based on an administrator's or a trustee's distaste for the content of a professor's teaching or research, or even for positions taken completely outside the campus setting. . . . It is designed to foster our society's interest in the unfettered progress of research and learning by protecting the profession's freedom of inquiry and instruction'' (*Browzin* v. *Catholic University,* 174 U.S. App. D.C. 60, 63, 527 F.2d 843, 846 (1975); see also *Rehor* v. *Case Western Reserve University,* 43 Ohio St. 2d 224, 331 N.E.2d 416, 421 (1975); Note, ''Dismissal of Tenured Faculty for Reasons of Financial Exigency,'' 51 *Indiana L.J.* 417 n.2 (1976)). Dismissals based on financial exigency, unlike those for cause or disability, are impersonal; they are unrelated to the views of the dismissed teachers. A professor whose appointment is terminated because of financial exigency will not be replaced by another with more conventional views or better connections. Hence, bona fide dismissals based on financial exigency do not threaten the values protected by tenure.

Parties to a contract may, of course, define tenure differently in their agreement. But there is no significant evidence that Krotkoff and Goucher contracted with reference to a peculiar understanding of tenure. The Goucher bylaws and other relevant documents do not define the rights and obligations of tenured teachers during financial exigency. The only evidence of a peculiar understanding of tenure at Goucher was the testimony of Krotkoff and three other tenured professors, whose appointments had been terminated, that they understood tenure at Goucher to preclude dismissal for financial reasons. Four other tenured faculty members testified to a contrary understanding. None of these witnesses relied on any policy established by the trustees regarding the effect of financial exigency on tenure; the conclusions they expressed were largely subjective. The college introduced evidence that during the depression of the 1930s it had been forced to terminate the appointments of tenured professors because of its precarious financial condition. The former president of the college who signed Krotkoff's letter conferring ''indeterminate tenure'' testified that he used this phrase in light of the general understanding in the academic world that tenure would terminate if the position to which the professor had been appointed were eliminated either for lack of funds or lack of students.

In sum, there was no evidence of a general understanding in the Goucher community that the tenured faculty had greater protection from dismissal for financial reasons than the faculty at other colleges. The Krotkoff-Goucher contract must be interpreted consistently with the understanding of the national academic community about tenure and financial exigency. . . . By defining Krotkoff's relationship with the college in terms of tenure, the contract did not exempt her from demonstrably bona fide dismissal if the college confronted financial exigency (see Note, ''Financial Exigency as Cause for Termination of Tenured Faculty Members in Private Post Secondary Educational Institutions,'' 62 *Iowa L. Rev.* 481, 508–09 (1976)).

III

Having determined that Krotkoff's contract permitted termination of her employment because of financial exigency, we consider whether the district court erred in holding as a matter of law that the college did not breach this contract.

Krotkoff urges that the jury was entitled to assess the reasonableness of the trustees' belief that the college faced financial exigency. In support of this position, she emphasizes that the college had a large endowment and valuable land. She is entitled, she claims, to have a jury determine whether the trustees acted unreasonably in failing to secure judicial permission to invade these assets and whether the trustees should have sold the land which they were holding for a better price.

Courts have properly emphasized that dismissals of tenured professors for financial reasons must be demonstrably bona fide. Otherwise, college administrators could use financial exigency to subvert academic freedom. The leading case on this aspect of tenure is *American Association of College Professors* v. *Bloomfield College,* 129 N.J. Super. 249, 322 A.2d 846 (Ch. Div. 1974), affirmed, 136 N.J. Super. 442, 346 A.2d 615 (App. Div. 1975) [discussed above in this section]. . . .

Bloomfield, however, establishes that the trustees' decision to sell or retain a parcel of land was not a proper subject for judicial review:

> Whether . . . [the sale of land] to secure financial stability on a short-term basis is preferable to the long-term planning of the college administration is a policy decision for the institution. Its choice of alternative is beyond the scope of judicial oversight in the context of this litigation. Hence, the emphasis upon the alternative use of this capital asset by the trial judge in reaching his conclusion that a financial exigency did not exist was unwarranted and should not have been the basis of decision (346 A.2d at 617).

The same principle, we believe, should apply to the dissipation of an endowment. The reasonableness of the trustees' decision concerning the disposition of capital did not raise an issue for the jury. Stated otherwise, the existence of financial exigency should be determined by the adequacy of a college's operating funds rather than its capital assets (see Note, "Dismissal of Tenured Faculty for Reasons of Financial Exigency," 51 *Indiana L.J.* 417, 420–23 (1976); cf. *Scheuer* v. *Creighton University,* 199 Neb. 618, 260 N.W.2d 595, 599–601 (1977)).

Krotkoff has acknowledged that the trustees and other college officials did not act in bad faith. The evidence overwhelmingly demonstrates that the college was confronted by pressing financial need. As a result of the large annual deficits aggregating more than $1,500,000 over an extended period and the steady decline in enrollment, the college's financial position was precarious. Action undoubtedly was required to secure the institution's future. Because of Krotkoff's disavowal of bad faith on the part of the college and because of the unrefuted evidence concerning the college's finances and enrollment, we believe that this aspect of the case raised no question for the jury. The facts and all the inferences that properly can be drawn from them conclusively establish that the trustees reasonably believed that the college was faced with financial exigency. . . .

IV

We turn next to [the question] whether Goucher used reasonable standards in deciding not to retain Krotkoff and whether it made reasonable efforts to find her another position at the college.

The college asserts that neither of these issues is a proper subject for judicial review. It relies on a number of cases in which courts have evinced reluctance to oversee the decisions of college administrators or to intrude on the prerogatives of trustees. These cases, however, generally have involved the application of the Fourteenth Amendment to state institutions or the interpretation of statutes prohibiting racial or sexual discrimination. Since Goucher is a private college and Krotkoff does not allege the type of unlawful conduct proscribed by civil rights acts, the cases on which the college relies to forestall judicial inquiry are not dispositive.

Krotkoff's claims must be resolved by reference to her contract. This involves ascertaining, first, what contractual rights she had and, second, whether the college breached them. Viewing the evidence in the light most favorable to Krotkoff, as we must for purposes of this appeal, we believe that the district court correctly held that she was contractually entitled to insist (a) that the college use reasonable standards in selecting which faculty appointments to terminate and (b) that it take reasonable measures to afford her alternative employment.

Neither the letter granting Krotkoff tenure nor the documents setting forth Goucher's policy concerning tenure mention the procedural rights to which a faculty member is entitled when the college proposes to terminate her appointment for financial reasons. Therefore, we must examine again the academic community's understanding concerning tenure to determine the nature of this unique contractual relationship.

As we mentioned in Part II, the 1940 Statement on Academic Freedom and Tenure sanctions terminations of faculty appointments because of financial exigency. But it also stipulates: "Termination of a continuous appointment because of financial exigency should be demonstrably bona fide." The evidence discloses that the academic community commonly understands that inherent in the concept of a "demonstrably bona fide" termination is the requirement that the college use fair and reasonable standards to determine which tenured faculty members will not be reappointed. The college's obligation to deal fairly with its faculty when selecting those whose appointments will be terminated is an attribute of tenure. Consequently, it is an implicit element of the contract of appointment.

Nevertheless, the evidence questioning the reasonableness of Goucher's procedures was insufficient to submit this issue to the jury. The necessity for revising Goucher's curriculum was undisputed. A faculty committee accepted elimination of the classics department and reduction of the German section of the modern language department as reasonable responses to this need. The only substantial controversy was whether the college should have retained Krotkoff or Ehrlich, both tenured professors. Nothing in Krotkoff's contract gave her precedence, and the college did not breach it by retaining Ehrlich instead of Krotkoff. Nor was the college under any contractual obligation to retain Krotkoff by demoting Ehrlich to part-time teaching and part-time administrative work. Therefore, the district court did not err in ultimately ruling for the college on this issue.

Whether the college was contractually obliged to make reasonable

efforts to find Krotkoff alternate employment at Goucher was the subject
of conflicting evidence. It is reasonable, however, to infer from the evidence
that a demonstrably bona fide termination includes this requirement (see
Note, ''Financial Exigency as Cause for Termination of Tenured Faculty
Members in Private Post Secondary Educational Institutions,'' 62 *Iowa L.
Rev.* 481, 504–05 (1976); cf. *Browzin* v. *Catholic University,* 174 U.S. App.
D.C. 60, 64, 527 F.2d 843, 847 (1975)). On the other hand, in the absence
of an explicit contractual undertaking, the evidence discloses that tenure
does not entitle a professor to training for appointment in another discipline
(cf. *Browzin* v. *Catholic University,* 174 U.S. App. D.C. 60, 67–68, 527 F.2d
843, 850–51 (1975)).

The evidence conclusively establishes that the college did not breach
any contractual obligation concerning alternative employment. The constraints of tenure, rank, and pay that Krotkoff placed on alternative employment severely restricted the college's efforts to accommodate her. Apart
from Ehrlich's position, the only vacancy in which she expressed interest
was in the economics department. No evidence suggested that the head
of that department or the president acted unreasonably in assessing the time
and expense of retraining Krotkoff for this position or in deciding that her
transfer would not be feasible. Again, we conclude that the district court
did not err in holding that the college was entitled to judgment on these
issues.

The judgment is affirmed [585 F.2d at 677–83].

Krotkoff provides the most far-reaching analysis to date of postsecondary institutions' authority and obligations when terminating tenured faculty due to financial
exigency. The case also provides an outstanding example of judicial reliance on
academic custom and usage to resolve postsecondary education contractual disputes.

The plaintiffs in *Jimenez* v. *Almodovar,* the second case, were two professors
who had been appointed to a pilot program in physical education and recreation
at a regional college of the University of Puerto Rico. Their teaching positions were
eliminated as a result of low enrollment and poor evaluation of the program. The
court had to resolve some contractual questions in ruling on the plaintiffs' claim
of deprivation of property without procedural due process (see Section 3.5.2). The
parties stipulated that the plaintiffs had property rights established by their letters
of appointment, but the letters did not detail the extent of these rights. Therefore,
in order to determine the scope of procedures required by due process, the court
had to determine the extent of the plaintiffs' contractual rights.

According to the court:

American courts and secondary authorities uniformly recognize that,
unless otherwise provided in the agreement of the parties, or in the regulations of the institution, or in a statute, an institution of higher education
has an implied contractual right to make in good faith an *unavoidable* termination of right to the employment of a tenured member of the faculty
when his position is being eliminated as part of a change in academic program. The American court decisions are consistent with the 1940 Statement
of Principles on Academic Freedom and Tenure widely adopted by insti-

tutions of higher education and professional organizations of faculty members (60 *AAUP Bulletin* 269–72 (1974); see *Bignall* v. *North Idaho College,* 538 F.2d 245 (9th Cir. 1976); *Browzin* v. *Catholic University of America,* 527 F.2d 843 (D.C. Cir. 1975); and *Scheuer* v. *Creighton University,* 199 Neb. 618, 260 N.W.2d 595 (1977)). That the [institution's] implied right of bona fide unavoidable termination due to changes in academic program is wholly different from its right to termination for cause or on other personal grounds is plainly recognized in the following definition of tenure of the [AAUP/AAC] Commission on Academic Tenure in Higher Education [in] *Faculty Tenure: A Report and Recommendations* [Jossey-Bass, 1973]:

> An arrangement under which faculty appointments in an institu-
> tion of higher education are continued until retirement for age or dis-
> ability, subject to dismissal for adequate cause or unavoidable termina-
> tion on account of financial exigency or change of institutional program
> (emphasis in original omitted).

The foregoing authorities lead to the conclusion that, unless a Puerto Rican statute or a university regulation otherwise provides, the instant con-tracts should be interpreted as giving the University of Puerto Rico an im-plied right of bona fide unavoidable termination on the ground of change of academic program [650 F.2d at 368; footnotes omitted].

Finding no Puerto Rican statute or university regulation to the contrary, the court confirmed the university's implied contractual right to terminate tenured faculty. The court then analyzed the procedures available to the plaintiffs to challenge their terminations and concluded that they met procedural due process requirements.

The *Jimenez* decision is consistent with earlier precedents and AAUP policy in recognizing, first, a distinction between dismissals for causes personal to the indi-vidual and dismissals for impersonal institutional reasons and, second, a distinc-tion between institutional reasons of financial exigency and reasons of program discontinuance. AAUP policy on the latter distinction, however, is not found in the 1940 statement cited by the court, but in the 1976 "Recommended Institu-tional Regulations on Academic Freedom and Tenure" (62 *AAUP Bulletin* 184), which authorize program discontinuances "not mandated by financial exigency" when "based essentially upon educational considerations" and implemented accord-ing to AAUP specifications. Under this policy, if the institution adheres to it, or under the precedent now established by *Jimenez,* postsecondary institutions may, if they follow prescribed standards and procedures for doing so, terminate tenured faculty due to a bona fide academic program change. (See generally M. Clague, "*Jimenez* v. *Almodovar:* Program Discontinuance as a Cause for Termination of Tenured Faculty in Public Institutions," 9 *West's Education Law Reporter* 805 (1983).)

3.7.2. Constitutional considerations. Public institutions (see Section 1.4.2) must be concerned not only with contract considerations relating to financial exigency and program termination but also with constitutional considerations under the First and Fourteenth Amendments. Even if a termination (or other personnel decision) does not violate the faculty contract or any applicable state statutes or administrative regulations, it will be subject to invalidation by the courts if it infringes the faculty member's constitutional rights.

Under the First Amendment, a faculty member may argue that financial exigency was only a pretext for termination and that termination was actually a retaliation for the faculty member's exercise of First Amendment rights (see Note, "Economically Necessitated Faculty Dismissal as a Limit on Academic Freedom," 52 *Denver L.J.* 911 (1975); and see generally Section 3.6). The burden of proof on this issue is primarily on the faculty member (see the *Mt. Healthy* case discussed in Section 3.6.5). *Mabey* v. *Reagan,* 537 F.2d 1036 (9th Cir. 1976), is illustrative. The defendant college had not renewed the appointment of a nontenured philosophy instructor. The instructor argued that the nonrenewal was due to an argument he had had with other faculty members in an academic senate meeting and that his argument was a protected First Amendment activity. The college argued that this activity was not protected under the First Amendment and that, at any rate, the nonrenewal was also due to overstaffing in the philosophy department. In remanding the case to the trial court for further fact findings, the appellate court noted:

> We emphasize that the trier [of fact] must be alert to retaliatory termi-nations. . . . Whenever the state terminates employment to quell legitimate dissent or punishes protected expressive behavior, the termination is unlawful. . . .
> We stress that this holding does not shield those who are legitimately not reappointed. Where the complainant . . . does not meet his burden of proof that the state acted to suppress free expression, . . . the termination will stand [537 F.2d at 1045].

Under the Fourteenth Amendment, a faculty member whose job is terminated by a public institution may argue that the termination violated the due process clause. To proceed with this argument, the faculty member must show that the termina-tion infringed a "property" or "liberty" interest, as discussed in Section 3.5.2. If such a showing can be made, the questions then are (1) what procedural protec-tions is the faculty member entitled to, and (2) what kinds of arguments can the faculty member raise in his or her "defense"? A case that addresses both issues is *Johnson* v. *Board of Regents of University of Wisconsin System,* 377 F. Supp. 227 (W.D. Wis. 1974), affirmed without opinion, 510 F.2d 975 (7th Cir. 1975). The Wisconsin legislature had mandated budget reductions for the university system. To accom-modate this reduction, as well as a further reduction caused by lower enrollments on several campuses, the university officials devised a program for "laying off" tenured faculty. The chancellor of each campus determined who would be laid off, after which each affected faculty member could petition a faculty committee for "reconsideration" of the proposed layoff. The faculty committee could consider only two questions: whether the layoff decision was supported by sufficient evidence, and whether the chancellor had followed the procedures established for identifying the campus's fiscal and programmatic needs and determining who should be laid off. Thirty-eight tenured professors selected for layoff sued the university system.

The court determined that the due process clause required the following minimum procedures in a financial exigency layoff: "furnishing each plaintiff with a reasonably adequate written statement of the basis for the initial decision to lay off; furnishing each plaintiff with a reasonably adequate description of the manner in which the initial decision had been arrived at; making a reasonably adequate disclosure to each plaintiff of the information and data on which the decision makers had relied; and providing each plaintiff the opportunity to respond'' (377 F. Supp. at 240). Measuring the procedures actually used against these requirements, the court held that the university system had not violated procedural due process. The most difficult issue was the adequacy of information disclosure (the third requirement above), about which the court said:

> Plaintiffs have shown in this court that the information disclosed to them was bulky and some of it amorphous. They have shown that it was not presented to the reconsideration committees in a manner resembling the presentation of evidence in court. They have shown that in some situations . . . they encountered difficulty in obtaining a coherent explanation of the basis for the initial layoff decisions, and that, as explained in some situations, the basis included judgments about personalities. But as I have observed, the Fourteenth Amendment does not forbid judgments about personalities in this situation, nor does it require adversary proceedings. The information disclosed was reasonably adequate to provide each plaintiff the opportunity to make a showing that reduced student enrollments and fiscal exigency were not in fact the precipitating causes for the decisions to lay off tenured teachers in this department and that; and it was also reasonably adequate to provide each plaintiff the opportunity to make a showing that the ultimate decision to lay off each of them, as compared with another tenured member of their respective departments, was arbitrary and unreasonable. I emphasize the latter point. On this record, plaintiffs' allegations about the inadequacy and imprecision of the disclosure related principally to those stages of the decision making which preceded the ultimate stage at which the specific teachers, department by department, were selected.
>
> Had the disclosure as it was made not been ''reasonably adequate,'' it is possible that it could have been made adequate by permitting plaintiffs some opportunity to confront and even to cross-examine some of the decision makers. But I hold that the opportunity to confront or to cross-examine these decision makers is not constitutionally required when the disclosure is reasonably adequate, as it was here [377 F. Supp. at 242].

The court also determined that the university system could limit the issues which the faculty members could address in challenging a termination under the above procedures:

> I am not persuaded that, after the initial decisions had been made, the Fourteenth Amendment required that plaintiffs be provided an opportunity to persuade the decision makers that departments within their respective colleges, other than theirs, should have borne a heavier fiscal sacrifice; that non-credit-producing, nonacademic areas within their respective campus structures should have borne a heavier fiscal sacrifice; that campuses, other than their respective campuses, should have borne a heavier fiscal sacrifice; or that more funds should have been appropriated to the university system. However, I believe that *each plaintiff was constitutionally entitled to a fair opportunity*

*to show: (1) that the true reason for his or her layoff was a constitutionally imper-
missible reason; or (2) that, given the chain of decisions which preceded the ultimate
decision designating him or her by name for layoff, that ultimate decision was nevertheless
wholly arbitrary and unreasonable.* I believe that each plaintiff was constitutionally entitled to a fair opportunity to make such a showing in a proceeding
within the institution, in order to permit prompt reconsideration and correction in a proper case. Also, if necessary, each plaintiff was and is constitutionally entitled to a fair opportunity to make such a showing thereafter
in a court [377 F. Supp. at 239–40; emphasis added].

Although the Constitution requires that institutions avoid terminations for
a "constitutionally impermissible reason" and "wholly arbitrary" terminations,
the court made clear that the Constitution does not prescribe any particular bases
for selection of the faculty members to be terminated:

[The Constitution does not require] that the selection be made on
one specific basis or another: in inverse order of seniority within the department, for example; or in order of seniority; or in terms of record of performance or potential for performance; or in inverse order of seniority, but
with exceptions for the necessity to retain teachers in the department with
specific skills or funds of knowledge. I believe that the federal Constitution
is silent on these questions, and that the identity of the decision maker and
the choice of a basis for selection lie within the discretion of the state government [377 F. Supp. at 238].

In *Jimenez* v. *Almodovar,* 650 F.2d 363 (1st Cir. 1981) (see Section 3.7.1),
the U.S. Court of Appeals for the First Circuit rejected procedural and substantive
due process challenges to a termination of tenured faculty members due to program
discontinuance. The court's reliance on financial exigency cases such as *Johnson*
suggests that due process requirements for program discontinuance terminations
are comparable to those for financial exigency terminations.

3.7.3. Statutory considerations. A public institution's legal responsibilities
during financial exigency or program discontinuance may be defined not only by
contract and by constitutional considerations but also by state statutes or their implementing administrative regulations. The case of *Hartman* v. *Merged Area VI Community College,* 270 N.W.2d 822 (Iowa 1978), illustrates how important statutory
analysis can be.

In *Hartman* a community college had dismissed a faculty member as part
of a staff reduction occasioned by declining enrollment and a worsening financial
condition. For authority for its action, the institution relied on a state statute authorizing it to discharge faculty "for incompetency, inattention to duty, partiality, or
any good cause" (Iowa Code of 1973 sec. 279.24). The institution's position was
that the phrase *good cause* supported its action because it is a broad grant of authority
encompassing any rational reason for dismissal which the board of directors asserts
in good faith. The appellate court disagreed and invalidated the dismissal. It reasoned
that "good cause," interpreted in light of the statute's legislative history and in conjunction with other related Iowa statutes, "refer[s] only to factors personal to the
teacher"; that is, factors concerning the particular teacher which can be considered

the teacher's own "personal fault" (see Section 3.4 for a consideration of such personal factors).

While *Hartman* deals only with substantive standards for staff reduction, state statutes or administrative regulations may also establish procedures with which institutions must comply. In *Mabey* v. *Reagan,* 537 F.2d 1036 (9th Cir. 1976), for instance, a college did not renew an instructor's contract, in part because his department was overstaffed. The instructor challenged the nonrenewal, arguing that the college had followed the wrong procedures in reaching its decision. The court rejected the challenge, agreeing with the college that the applicable procedures were found in the statutes dealing with tenure and nonreappointment rather than the statutes dealing with separation for "lack of work or lack of funds."

Public institutions considering staff reductions must therefore identify not only the applicable substantive standards but also the applicable procedures specified by state law. The procedures may be contained in a legal source different from that setting out the standards (see, for example, *Council of New Jersey State College Locals* v. *State Board of Higher Education,* 91 N.J. 18, 449 A.2d 1244 (1982) (substantive criteria from state board policy on financial exigency applicable despite collective bargaining agreement, but some procedures from board policy bargainable); *Board of Trustees of Ohio State University* v. *Department of Administrative Services,* 429 N.E.2d 428 (Ohio 1981) (state administrative procedure act applicable to termination of *nonfaculty* personnel)).

3.7.4. Preparing for staff reductions. Everyone agrees that institutions, both public and private, should plan ahead to avoid the legal difficulties that can arise if financial or programmatic pressures necessitate staff reductions. Much can be done to plan ahead. Faculty contracts should be reviewed in light of the questions raised in Section 3.7.1. Where the contract does not clearly reflect the institution's desired position concerning staff reductions, its provisions should be revised to the extent possible without breaching existing contracts.

For institutional planning purposes, administrators should carefully distinguish between the two alternative approaches to faculty termination, financial exigency and program discontinuance:

1. When drafting or amending contracts for nontenured, tenure-track faculty, the institution should consider specific provisions on both alternatives. Public institutions should consult state law (Section 3.7.3 above) to determine whether it permits use of both alternatives. If the institution chooses, the AAUP's recommended regulations on either alternative (see Section 3.7.1., note 19) may be incorporated by reference into its faculty contracts. The institution may also draft provisions altogether different from the AAUP's, although it will want to give close attention to the competing policy considerations.

2. When interpreting existing tenure contracts, the institution should determine whether it has already, either expressly or by institutional custom, adopted AAUP policy for either alternative; or whether, in the face of institutional silence, courts would likely fill the gap with AAUP policy (see Section 3.7.1 above). In such circumstances the institution should consider itself bound to follow AAUP requirements and thus not free under existing contracts to strike out unilaterally on a different course.

3. When faced with circumstances mandating consideration of tenured faculty terminations, and when authorized to follow either alternative approach, the insti-

tution should carefully consider its choice. Which alternative—institution-wide financial exigency or discontinuance of specific programs—can better be substantiated by existing circumstances? Which would better serve the institution's overall mission? If the institution decides to pursue one of the alternatives, it should be careful to identify and follow the particular decision-making requirements and protections for faculty specified for that alternative.

When the institution does have authority for financial exigency staff reductions, it should have a policy and standards for determining when a financial exigency exists. It should also have a policy and standards for identifying which faculty members' positions will be terminated and procedures by which the faculty member can challenge the propriety of his or her selection for termination. If administrators make a termination decision, they should assure that (1) a financial exigency does actually exist under the institution's policy, and (2) financial exigency is in fact the reason for each termination decision that is made. In making the latter assurance, they would be wise to ascertain whether the terminations will have the effect of alleviating the exigency, as well as whether any other nonfinancial motivation for a particular termination may exist. After dismissing faculty members, administrators should be extremely careful in hiring new ones, to avoid the impression, as in the *Bloomfield* case (see Section 3.7.1), that the financial exigency was a pretext for abolishing tenure or otherwise replacing old faculty members with new. Similar considerations would apply in implementing program discontinuance authority.

Finally, administrators should remember that, in this sensitive area, some of their decisions may wind up in court despite careful planning. Administrators should thus keep complete records and documentation of their staff reduction policies, decisions, and internal review processes for possible use in court and should work closely with counsel both in planning ahead and in making the actual termination decisions.

Selected Annotated Bibliography

General

1.   AAUP/AAC Commission on Academic Tenure, *Faculty Tenure: A Report and Recommendations* (Jossey-Bass, 1973), is an evaluation by a commission cosponsored by the Association of American Colleges and the American Association of University Professors; includes special essays on "Legal Dimensions of Tenure" by V. Rosenblum and "Faculty Unionism and Tenure" by W. McHugh.
2.   American Association of University Professors, *Policy Documents and Reports* (AAUP, 1984), the "Redbook," collects the AAUP's major policy statements concerning academic freedom and tenure, collective bargaining, institutional governance, sexual harassment, part-time faculty, and other topics. Includes an appendix with selected judicial decisions referring to AAUP statements.
3.   McCarthy, J., Ladimer, I., and Sirefman, J., *Managing Faculty Disputes: A Guide to Issues, Procedures, and Practices* (Jossey-Bass, 1984), addresses the problem of faculty disputes on campus and proposes processes for resolving them. Covers both disputes that occur regularly and can be subjected to a standard dispute resolution process, and special disputes that occur irregularly and may require a resolution process tailored to the circumstances. Includes model

grievance procedures, case studies of actual disputes, and worksheets and checklists to assist administrators in implementing dispute resolution processes.

4. Chait, R. P., and Ford, A. T., *Beyond Traditional Tenure: A Guide to Sound Policies and Practices* (Jossey-Bass, 1982), includes chapters on "Tenure in Context," "Institutions Without Tenure," "Life Without Tenure," "Tenure and Nontenure Tracks," "Extended Probationary Periods and Suspension of 'Up-or-Out' Rule," "Tenure Quotas," "Sound Tenure Policy," "Evaluating Tenured Faculty," "Distributing Rewards and Applying Sanctions," and "Auditing and Improving Faculty Personnel Systems." Based on authors' survey and analysis of tenure options in existence at various institutions around the country; includes case studies of leading examples. For extended reviews of the book, see 10 *J. of College and University Law* 93–112 (1983–84).

5. Finkin, M. W., "Regulation by Agreement: The Case for Private Higher Education," 65 *Iowa L. Rev.* 1119 (1980), reprinted in 67 *AAUP Bulletin* no. 1 (1981) (Parts I and II), 67 *AAUP Bulletin* no. 2 (1981) (Part III), and 67 *AAUP Bulletin* no. 3 (1981) (Part IV), provides a multifaceted review of various problems unique to employment relations in higher education. Part I of the article serves as a general introduction; Part II discusses the nature of the contract of academic employment and various questions that arise in contract litigation; Part III discusses the continued relevance of academic organization by collective agreement, notwithstanding *NLRB* v. *Yeshiva University;* Part IV sets out a proposal for an alternative system of self-regulation of employment matters.

6. Furniss, W. T., "The Status of 'AAUP Policy,'" 59 *Educational Record* 7 (1978), reviews the role that AAUP policy statements play in the university employment scheme. The article notes the increasing use of such statements in employment litigation and urges institutions of higher education to clarify the extent to which they accept AAUP policy statements as their own institutional policy. The arguments raised in this article are challenged in a companion article: Brown, R. S., Jr., and Finkin, M. W., "The Usefulness of AAUP Policy Statements," 59 *Educational Record* 30 (1978).

7. "Tenure and Retrenchment Practices in Higher Education—A Technical Report," 31 *J. of College and University Personnel Association* nos. 3–4 (Fall–Winter 1980), is a comprehensive survey of the state of tenure in American postsecondary institutions. An introductory section surveys the development of tenure and issues related to tenure's current state. Other sections cover "Tenure Policies and Practices: A Summary," "Tenure at Doctorate-Granting Institutions," "Tenure at Comprehensive Universities and Colleges," "Tenure at Liberal Arts Colleges," "Tenure at Two-Year Colleges and Institutes," "Retrenchment Policies and Practices: A Summary," "Retrenchment at Comprehensive Universities and Colleges," "Retrenchment at Liberal Arts Colleges," and "Retrenchment at Two-Year Colleges and Institutes."

Sec. 3.1 (Contract of Employment)

1. Leslie, D., and Head, R. B., "Part-Time Faculty Rights," 60 *Educational Record* 46 (1979), is a survey of current practices concerning part-time faculty members and issues concerning part-time status.

2. McKee, P. W., "Tenure by Default: The Non-Formal Acquisition of Academic Tenure," 7 *J. of College and University Law* 31 (1980–81), analyzes the impact of *Board of Regents* v. *Roth* and *Perry* v. *Sindermann* on the concept of nonformal tenure. Distinguishes between "automatic tenure," "tenure by grant," "nonformal or de facto tenure," and "tenure by default." To resolve confusion in lower court opinions applying *Roth* and *Perry* to nonformal tenure claims, the article develops a common law analysis covering employment relationships in both private and public institutions.

3. Subcommittee on Part-Time Faculty, Committee A on Academic Freedom and Tenure, "The Status of Part-Time Faculty," 67 *Academe* no. 1 (1981), surveys problems confronting part-time instructors in postsecondary institutions and proposes a series of changes that institutions may make to accommodate part-time faculty needs; proposals include tenure policies regarding part-time faculty, part-time faculty role in academic governance, and compensation and fringe benefit policies regarding part-time employees.

Sec. 3.2. (Collective Bargaining)

1. Angell, G. W., and Kelley, E. P., Jr., *Faculty Bargaining Under Trustee Policy* (Academic Collective Bargaining Information Service, monograph 7, 1979), is a report on the status and future prospects of faculty collective bargaining at institutions not covered by state or federal collective bargaining law.

2. Angell, G. W., Kelly, E. P., Jr., and Associates, *Handbook of Faculty Bargaining* (Jossey-Bass, 1977), serves as a comprehensive guide to collective bargaining for administrators; provides information and recommendations on preparing for collective bargaining, negotiating contracts, administering contracts, and exerting institutional leadership in the bargaining context; special chapter on statewide bargaining in state postsecondary systems.

3. Bartosic, F., and Hartley, R., *Labor Relations Law in the Private Sector, 2nd ed.* (American Law Institute, in press), is a restatement and analysis of the federal law of union organization and collective bargaining. Primarily for legal counsel who are not labor law specialists; also usable by specialists as a ready-reference manual and by administrators as a readable explanatory text; can also help in dealing with public-sector labor law in states with law patterned after the federal law.

4. Finkin, M., "The NLRB in Higher Education," 5 *University of Toledo L. Rev.* 608 (1974), probes the whole gamut of NLRB authority and activity in postsecondary education. Discusses and criticizes NLRB decisions dealing with jurisdiction over private institutions; faculty status as managers, supervisors, or employees; appropriate bargaining units; and employers' unfair labor practices.

5. Head, R. B., and Leslie, D., "Bargaining Unit Status of Part-Time Faculty," 8 *J. of Law and Education* 361 (1979), discusses court cases, labor board decisions, and related problems concerning the "bargaining unit status of part-time faculty."

6. *Labor Relations in Education,* a ten-page, biweekly newsletter of Capitol Publications, provides brief, topical discussions of various developments in the area of labor relations and education, both elementary/secondary and postsecondary. Includes discussions of statutory developments, the status and impact of litigation, and newsworthy labor relations developments.

7. Lee, B. A., "Faculty Role in Academic Governance and the Managerial Ex-
    clusion: Impact of the *Yeshiva University* Decision," 7 *J. of College and University
    Law* 222 (1980–81), is an in-depth analysis of the *Yeshiva* case. Includes origins
    and definitions of the terms "supervisory," "managerial," and "professional"
    employees; treatment of the faculty's role in academic governance; and an
    examination of "the implications of the *Yeshiva* decision for both unionized
    and nonunionized colleges and universities."

8. Research Project on Students and Collective Bargaining, *Final Report* (National
    Student Education Fund, 1976), studies student participation in faculty col-
    lective bargaining; surveys current state of the law and practice regarding
    student participation; analyzes bargaining's impact on students; and discusses
    various bargaining contract provisions.

Sec. 3.3 (Nondiscrimination in Employment)

1. "The Academy in the Courts: A Symposium on Academic Freedom," 16
    University of California–Davis L. Rev. 831 (1983), is divided into two parts, the
    second of which is "Discrimination in the Academy" (see entry no. 1 for
    Section 3.6 for a description of the first part). This part contains three articles:
    C. Cooper, "Title VII in the Academy: Barriers to Equality for Faculty
    Women"; J. D. Gregory, "Secrecy in University and College Tenure
    Deliberations: Placing Appropriate Limits on Academic Freedom"; and H.
    Tepker, "Title VII, Equal Employment Opportunity, and Academic
    Autonomy: Toward a Principled Deference."

2. Baldus, D., and Cole, J., *Statistical Proof of Discrimination* (McGraw-Hill, 1980),
    is a guide to the proper uses of statistics in discrimination litigation, with
    emphasis on employment discrimination. The book will be helpful to both
    plaintiffs' and defendants' counsel in such actions. Includes useful glossary
    and bibliography.

3. Bassen, N., "Synopsis of State Laws Regulating Employment of the Han-
    dicapped," 4 *J. of College and University Law* 293 (1979), provides a state-by-
    state breakdown of statutes and regulations governing employment of the han-
    dicapped. The synopsis covers state laws that apply to state colleges and univer-
    sities and those that apply to private postsecondary institutions.

4. Bompey, S. H., and Witten, R. E., "Settlement of Title VII Disputes: Shift-
    ing Patterns in a Changing World," 6 *J. of College and University Law* 317 (1980),
    reviews the types of settlements available to plaintiffs and defendants and the
    various means of reaching such settlements. Examines the types of dispute
    resolution available to the parties from the commencement of an action by
    filing charges with the EEOC to the culmination of litigation through the
    entry of consent decrees.

5. Brooks, R. L., "Use of the Civil Rights Acts of 1886 and 1871 to Redress
    Employment Discrimination," 62 *Cornell L. Rev.* 258 (1977), analyzes the
    role that 42 U.S.C. sec. 1981 can play in employment discrimination suits;
    also discusses 42 U.S.C. secs. 1983 and 1985(3); includes consideration of
    rights and remedies available under these statutes that may not be available
    under other employment discrimination statutes, and the procedural and
    jurisdictional issues that may arise in litigation under these statutes.

6. Bureau of National Affairs, *Affirmative Action Compliance Manual* (BNA, published

and updated periodically), is a comprehensive guide for federal contractors that provides detailed and continually updated information on the federal government's affirmative action program and the compliance responsibilities and procedures of the Department of Labor, Education, Defense, and other federal agencies.

7. Carnegie Council on Policy Studies in Higher Education, *Making Affirmative Action Work in Higher Education: An Analysis of Institutional and Federal Policies with Recommendations* (Jossey-Bass, 1975), critically examines federal policies and programs of affirmative action that affect postsecondary institutions. Discusses the academic job market; salary differentials; impact of federal statutes on internal personnel decisions, goals, and timetables; and grievance and enforcement procedures; makes recommendations on the direction that federal policies should take.

8. Ford, L. C., "The Implications of the Age Discrimination in Employment Act Amendments of 1978 for Colleges and Universities," 5 *J. of College and University Law* 161 (1979), surveys the history of the 1978 amendments to the Age Discrimination in Employment Act and the exception to the amendments, which, until July 1, 1982, permitted mandatory retirement of tenured higher education faculty members at age sixty-five. Includes an overview of frequently asked questions concerning the amendments.

9. Lee, B. A., "Balancing Confidentiality and Disclosure in Faculty Peer Review: Impact of Title VII Litigation," 9 *J. of College and University Law* 279 (1982–83), analyzes recent Title VII litigation brought by faculty of higher education institutions. Includes a section on "Burdens of Proof and Persuasion," which elucidates the three stages of the Title VII case—the "prima facie case," "the institution's rebuttal," and plaintiff's proof of "pretextual behavior"—using illustrations from the higher education cases. Also reviews issues concerning "evidence admitted by courts in challenges to peer review decisions" and "standards applied by courts to the peer review process," and examines the question of whether courts should recognize an "academic freedom privilege."

10. National Association of College and University Business Officers (NACUBO), *Federal Regulations and the Employment Practices of Colleges and Universities* (1974 and periodic supp.), is a loose-leaf service that provides information and guidance on applying federal regulations affecting personnel administration in postsecondary institutions.

11. Smith, M. R., "Protecting the Confidentiality of Faculty Peer Review Records," 8 *J. of College and University Law* 20 (1981–82), emphasizes the strong interest of colleges and universities in maintaining the confidentiality of faculty personnel decisions; reviews the type of state legislation that may limit institutional confidentiality (using California statutes as a model); examines the federal legislation that permits access to personnel records; then concludes with a review of available legal arguments against federal access to and public disclosure of personnel files, and an examination of *U.S. Department of Labor v. Regents of University of California,* Case No. 78-OFCCP-7 (resolved by consent decree, Sept. 4, 1980; published in 8 *J. of College and University Law* 54 (1980–81)).

12. Sullivan, C. A., Zimmer, M. J., and Richards, R. F., *Federal Statutory Law of Employment Discrimination* (Michie/Bobbs-Merrill, 1980), is a one-volume

basic text on the federal law of employment discrimination. To be supplemented annually. Includes discussions of Title VII, the Equal Pay Act, the
Age Discrimination in Employment Act, and 42 U.S.C. sec. 1981. The authors
set out both the substantive and the procedural law developed under these
statutes and integrate this law with other areas of law, such as the National
Labor Relations Act. Extensive case citations and table of cases.

13. Symposium, "Age Discrimination," 32 *Hastings L.J.* 1093 (1981), is a collection of articles on various issues concerning age discrimination. Topics of
articles include age discrimination issues under the equal protection clause;
evidentiary standards under the ADEA; EEOC's role in enforcing age
discrimination legislation; the use of statistics in age discrimination cases;
and the relationships between federal and state pension laws. Ends with a
comprehensive bibliography of scholarly publications, government documents,
and other resources on age discrimination.

14. Yurko, R., "Judicial Recognition of Academic Collective Interests: A New
Approach to Faculty Title VII Litigation," 60 *Boston University L. Rev.* 473
(1980), proposes a new theory to govern the degree of deference to be shown
to postsecondary institutions in Title VII litigation.

Sec. 3.4 (Standards and Criteria)

1. Olswang, S. G., and Fantel, J. I., "Tenure and Periodic Performance Review:
Compatible Legal and Administrative Principles," 7 *J. of College and University Law* 1 (1980–81), examines the "separate concepts of tenure and academic
freedom and their relation to one form of accountability measure: systematic
reviews of the performance of tenured faculty." Identifies the "differences
between tenure and academic freedom" and the purposes and uses of periodic
performance reviews "in an overall system of faculty personnel management."
Includes discussion of tenure terminations for cause based on incompetence,
immorality, insubordination, and other bases.

Sec. 3.5 (Procedures for Faculty Personnel Decisions)

1. Baird, J., and McArthur, M. R., "Constitutional Due Process and the
Negotiation of Grievance Procedures in Public Employment," 5 *J. of Law
and Education* 209 (1976), compares and contrasts grievance procedures in the
public and private sectors; analyzes due process aspects of the collective
bargaining process and suggests ways that public employers can deal with
due process requirements in devising grievance procedures.

2. Olswang, S., and Lee, B., "Scientific Misconduct: Institutional Procedures
and Due Process Considerations," 11 *J. of College and University Law* 51
(1984–85), identifies the types of misconduct that qualify as "scientific misconduct," reviews appropriate and inappropriate means of investigating charges
of scientific misconduct, and examines the due process issues to be considered
before taking any action against an individual charged with scientific
misconduct.

3. See entry no. 3 in bibliography for "General" section.

4. See entry no. 2 in bibliography for Section 3.1.

Sec. 3.6 (Faculty Academic Freedom)

1. "The Academy in the Courts: A Symposium on Academic Freedom," 16
    University of California–Davis L. Rev. 831 (1983), is divided into two parts, the
    first of which is "The First Amendment in the Academy" (see entry no. 1
    for Section 3.3 for a description of the second part). This part contains three
    articles: R. O'Neil, "Scientific Research and the First Amendment: An
    Academic Privilege"; K. Katz, "The First Amendment's Protection of Ex-
    pressive Activity in the University Classroom: A Constitutional Myth"; and
    M. Malin and R. Ladenson, "University Faculty Members' Right to Dissent:
    Toward a Unified Theory of Contractual and Constitutional Protection."
    Symposium also includes a foreword by J. Poulos, which briefly recounts
    the history of institutional academic autonomy and reviews each article's
    critique of this concept.

2. Hoornstra, C. D., and Liethen, M. A., "Academic Freedom and Civil
    Discovery," 10 *J. of College and University Law* 113 (1983–84), focuses on the
    federal appeals court opinions in *Dow Chemical Co.* v. *Allen* and *Buchanan* v.
    American Motors Co. Analyzes the cases, provides a critique of "wide-open"
    approaches to pretrial discovery of the work product of academic researchers;
    and suggests limits appropriate to academic pretrial discovery. Primarily for
    counsel.

3. O'Neil, R., *Is Academic Freedom a Constitutional Right?* (Monograph 84-7, Insti-
    tute for Higher Education Law and Governance, University of Houston,
    1984), reprinted (under title "Academic Freedom and the Constitution")
    in 11 *J. of College and University Law* 275 (1984), is an argument on behalf
    of the continued vitality of constitutionally based claims of academic freedom.
    The monograph examines the current status of and conceptual difficulties
    regarding such claims and makes suggestions for faculty members and other
    academics to consider before submitting such claims to the courts for vin-
    dication. Monograph closes with a "Prospectus" of "academic freedom issues
    of the future."

4. O'Neil, R., "The Private Lives of Public Employees," 51 *Oregon L. Rev.*
    70 (1971), provides an overview of the types of problems that can arise in
    the interaction of life-style and public employment; symbolic expression, hair
    length, homosexual and heterosexual association, extracurricular writing, and
    other questions are examined. Although written primarily for the lawyer,
    the article is also instructive reading for administrators of public postsecon-
    dary institutions.

5. Zimic, L. F., "Breach of Responsibility in Extramural Utterances," 59 *Educa-
    tional Record* 45 (1978), surveys the tensions inherent in an academic setting
    in which faculty members are permitted broad freedom of speech but at the
    same time are considered bound, to a greater or lesser degree, by canons
    of academic propriety and restraint. Author examines cases in both the AAUP
    reports and court reports and finds that these cases dispel much of the am-
    biguity implicit in the standards of propriety and restraint: "[the] cases suggest
    that there is virtually no legal justification for restriction of a faculty member's
    professional or extramural expressions unless it can be shown that they are

so vituperative and disrespectful of authority as to reflect adversely on his fitness for his position.''

3.7 (Staff Reductions Due to Financial Exigency and Program Discontinuance)

1. Johnson, A., "The Problems of Contraction: Legal Considerations in University Retrenchment," 10 *J. of Law and Education* 269 (1981), examines the financial circumstances which justify retrenchment, how and by whom retrenchment decisions should be made, and the procedures to follow after the decision in order to preserve the legal rights of individuals affected by the retrenchment.
2. Mingle, J. R., and Associates, *Challenges of Retrenchment: Strategies for Consolidating Programs, Cutting Costs, and Reallocating Resources* (Jossey-Bass, 1981), describes the actual retrenchment efforts of public and private institutions through an extensive set of case studies. Analyzes the complex organizational, legal, and political issues that arise when colleges and universities lay off faculty and cut back programs and departments because of rising inflation, declining enrollments, or both.
3. Olswang, S. G., "Planning The Unthinkable: Issues in Institutional Reorganization and Faculty Reductions," 9 *J. of College and University Law* 431 (1982–83), examines the legal and policy issues inherent in institutional reorganization and faculty reduction. Analyzes the "three primary alternatives"—"financial exigency declarations, program eliminations, and program reductions"—for achieving reorganization and reduction. Also provides policy guidelines for identifying faculty for removal and discusses faculty members' rights and prerogatives when designated for removal.

✠ IV ✠

The College
and the Students

Sec. 4.1. The Legal Status of Students

4.1.1. The evolutionary process. The legal status of students in postsecondary institutions changed dramatically in the 1960s and is still evolving. For most purposes students are no longer second-class citizens under the law. They are recognized under the federal Constitution as "persons" with their own enforceable constitutional rights. They are recognized as adults, with the rights and responsibilities of adults, under many state laws. And they are accorded their own legal rights under various federal statutes. The background of this evolution is traced in Section 1.2, while the new legal status that emerges from these developments, and its impact on postsecondary administration, is explored throughout this chapter.

Perhaps the key case in forging the new student status was *Dixon* v. *Alabama State Board of Education,* discussed in Section 4.6.2. The court in this case rejected the notion that education in state schools is a "privilege" to be dispensed on whatever conditions the state in its sole discretion deems advisable; it also implicitly rejected the *in loco parentis* concept under which the law had bestowed on schools all the powers over students that parents had over minor children. The *Dixon* approach became a part of U.S. Supreme Court jurisprudence in cases such as *Tinker* v. *Des Moines School District* (see Section 4.7.1), *Healy* v. *James* (Sections 4.7.1 and 4.8.1), and *Goss* v. *Lopez* (Section 4.6.2). The impact of these public institution cases spilled over onto private institutions, as courts increasingly viewed students as contracting parties having rights under express and implied contractual relationships with the institution. Congress gave both public and private school students new rights under various civil rights acts and, in the Buckley Amendment (Section 4.12.1), gave postsecondary students certain rights which were expressly independent of and in lieu of parental rights. New state statutes lowering the age of majority also enhanced the independence of students from their parents and brought the bulk of postsecondary students, even undergraduates, into the category of adults.

The latest stage in the evolution of the legal status of students is the stage of institutional self-regulation. Increasingly, higher education associations and commentators have urged, and assisted, individual institutions to redefine and extend their own internal regulations as an alternative or supplement to government regulation. (See generally E. El-Khawas, "Solving Problems Through Self-Regulation," 59 *Educational Record* 323 (1978); C. Saunders, "How to Keep the Government from Playing the Featured Role," 59 *Educational Record* 61 (1978).)

4.1.2. The new age of majority. The age of majority is established by state law in all states. There may be a general statute prescribing an age of majority for all or most business and personal dealings in the state, or there may be specific statutes or regulations specifying varying ages of majority for specific purposes. Until the 1970s twenty-one was typically the age of majority in most states. But since the 1971 ratification of the Twenty-Sixth Amendment lowering the voting age to eighteen, most states have lowered the age of majority to eighteen or nineteen for many other purposes as well. The Michigan statute (Mich. Stat. Ann. sec. 25.244 (51), Mich. Comp. Laws Ann. sec. 722.52) illustrates the comprehensive approach adopted by some states:

> Notwithstanding any other provision of law to the contrary, a person who is eighteen years of age but less than twenty-one years of age when this Act takes effect, and a person who attains eighteen years of age thereafter, is deemed to be an adult of legal age for all purposes whatsoever and shall have the same duties, liabilities, responsibilities, rights, and legal capacity as persons heretofore acquired at twenty-one years of age.

Other states have adopted more limited or more piecemeal legislation, sometimes using different minimum ages for different purposes. Given the lack of uniformity, administrators and counsel should carefully check state law in their own states.

The new age-of-majority laws can affect many postsecondary regulations and policies. The effect of the laws may be to permit students at age eighteen to enter binding contracts without the need for a cosigner, to give consent to medical treatment, to declare financial independence, to establish a legal residence apart from the parents', and to consume alcoholic beverages. This new legal capacity enables institutions to deal with students as adults at age eighteen, but it does not necessarily require that institutions do so. Particularly in private institutions, administrators may still be able as a policy matter to require a cosigner on contracts with students, for instance, or to have higher drinking ages (or no drinking) in campus buildings. Similarly, institutions may still be able to consider the resources of parents in awarding financial aid, even though the parents have no legal obligations to support the student. An institution's legal capacity to adopt such policy positions depends on the interpretation of the applicable age-of-majority law and the possible existence of special state law provisions for postsecondary institution's. A state loan program, for instance, may have special definitions of dependency or residency, which may not conform to general age-of-majority laws; or public institutions may have special authority to set different drinking ages on campus than exist under general laws. Administrators will thus confront two questions: What do the age-of-majority laws require that I do in particular areas? And should I, where I am under no legal obligation, establish age requirements higher than the legal age in particular areas, or should I instead pattern institutional policies on the general legal standard?

4.1.3. The contractual rights of students. Both public and private institutions often have express contractual relationships with students. The most common examples are probably the housing contract or lease, the food service contract, and the loan agreement. When problems arise in these areas, the written contract, including institutional regulations incorporated by reference in the contract, is usually the first source of legal guidance.[1]

The contractual relationship between student and institution, however, extends beyond the terms of express contracts. There also exists the more amorphous contractual relationship recognized in *Carr* v. *St. John's University* (Sections 4.4.2 and 4.6.4), the modern root of the contract theory of student status. In reviewing the institution's dismissal of students for having participated in a civil marriage ceremony, the court based its reasoning on the principle that "when a student is duly admitted by a private university, secular or religious, there is an implied contract between the student and the university that, if he complies with the terms prescribed by the university, he will obtain the degree which he sought." Construing a harsh and vague regulation in the university's favor, the court upheld the dismissal because the students had failed to comply with the university's prescribed terms.

Although *Carr* dealt only with a private institution, a subsequent New York case, *Healy* v. *Larsson*, 323 N.Y.S.2d 625, affirmed, 35 N.Y.2d 653, 318 N.E.2d 608 (1971) (discussed below in this section), indicated that "there is no reason why . . . the *Carr* principle should not apply to a public university or community college."

Other courts have increasingly utilized the contract theory for both public and private institutions, as well as for both academic and disciplinary disputes. The theory, however, does not necessarily apply identically to all such situations. A public institution may have more defenses against a contract action. *Eden* v. *Board of Trustees of State University*, 49 A.D. 277, 374 N.Y.S.2d 686 (1975), for instance, recognizes both an *ultra vires* defense and the state's power to terminate a contract when necessary in the public interest. (*Ultra vires* means "beyond authority," and the defense is essentially "You can't enforce this contract against us because we didn't have authority to make it in the first place.") And courts may accord both public and private

---

[1]The contract theory is by far the primary theory for according legal status to students beyond that derived from the Constitution and state and federal statutes. Other theories have occasionally been suggested by commentators, but they are seldom reflected in court opinions (see, for example, A. L. Goldman, "The University and the Liberty of Its Students—A Fiduciary Theory," 54 *Kentucky L.J.* 643 (1966); Note, "Judicial Review of the University-Student Relationship: Expulsion and Governance," 26 *Stanford L. Rev.* 95 (1973) (common law of private associations)). For a comparison of the various theories and cites to illustrative cases, see *Tedeschi* v. *Wagner College*, 49 N.Y.2d 652, 404 N.E.2d 1302, 1304–06 (1980).

institutions more flexibility in drafting and interpreting contract terms involving academics than they do contract terms involving discipline. In holding that Georgia State University had not breached its contract with a student by withholding a master's degree, for example, the court in *Mahavongsanan* v. *Hall,* 529 F.2d 448 (5th Cir. 1976), recognized the "wide latitude and discretion afforded by the courts to educational institutions in framing their academic requirements."

In general, courts have applied the contract theory to postsecondary institutions in a deferential manner. Courts have accorded institutions considerable latitude to select and interpret their own contract terms and to change the terms to which students are subjected as they progress through the institution. In *Mahavongsanan,* for instance, the court rejected the plaintiff student's contract claim in part because an institution "clearly is entitled to modify [its regulations] so as to properly exercise its educational responsibility." Nor have institutions been subjected to the rigors of contract law as it applies in the commercial world. The plaintiff student in *Slaughter* v. *Brigham Young University* (Sections 4.4.2 and 4.6.4) had been awarded $88,283 in damages in the trial court in a suit alleging erroneous dismissal from school. The appellate court reversed:

> The trial court's rigid application of commercial contract doctrine advanced by plaintiff was in error, and the submission on that theory alone was error. . . .
>
> It is apparent that some elements of the law of contracts are used and should be used in the analysis of the relationship between plaintiff and the university to provide some framework into which to put the problem of expulsion for disciplinary reasons. This does not mean that "contract law" must be rigidly applied in all its aspects, nor is it so applied even when the contract analogy is extensively adopted. . . . The student-university relationship is unique, and it should not be and cannot be stuffed into one doctrinal category [514 F.2d at 676].

Despite the generally deferential judicial attitude, it is clear that the contract theory creates a two-way street; it has become a source of meaningful rights for students as well as institutions. In *Healy* v. *Larsson,* for instance, the plaintiff student had transferred to the Schenectady County Community College and had taken all the courses his guidance counselors specified but was denied a degree. The court held that he was contractually entitled to the degree because he had "satisfactorily completed a course of study at . . . [the] community college as prescribed to him by authorized representatives of the college." Similarly, in the *Steinberg* and *Eden* cases, discussed in Section 4.2.3, students won victories in admissions cases. Other examples include *Paynter* v. *New York University,* 319 N.Y.S.2d 893 (App. Div. 1971), and *Zumbrun* v. *University of Southern California,* 25 Cal. App. 3d 1, 101 Cal. Rptr. 499 (1972), both suits seeking tuition refunds after classes had been canceled for part of a semester during antiwar protests. Although in *Paynter* the court held in favor of the university and in *Zumbrun* it remanded the case to the trial court for further proceedings, both opinions recognized that the courses to be taken by a student and the services to be rendered in the courses are part of the student-institution contract. Moreover, the opinions indicate that the institution may make only "minor" changes in the schedule of classes and the course of study which a student has undertaken for a particular semester; more substantial deviations could constitute a breach of contract.

The contract theory is still developing. Debate continues on issues such as the means for identifying the terms and conditions of the student-institution contract, the extent to which the school catalogue constitutes part of the contract, and the extent to which the institution retains implied or inherent authority (see Section 2.1) not expressed in any written regulation or policy.

Also still debatable is the extent to which courts will rely on certain contract law concepts, such as "unconscionable" contracts and "contracts of adhesion." An unconscionable contract is one which is so harsh and unfair to one of the parties that a reasonable person would not freely and knowingly agree to it. Unconscionable contracts are not enforceable in the courts. In *Albert Merrill School* v. *Godoy,* 357 N.Y.S.2d 378 (Civ. Ct., N.Y. City, 1974), for example, the school sought to recover money due on a contract to provide data processing training. Finding that the student did not speak English well and that the bargaining power of the parties was uneven, the court held the contract unconscionable and refused to enforce it. A contract of adhesion is one offered by one party (usually the party in the stronger bargaining position) to the other party on a "take-it-or-leave-it" basis, with no opportunity to negotiate the terms. Although courts will often construe adhesion contracts in favor of the weaker party where there is ambiguity, such contracts are enforceable unless determined by the court to be unconscionable. In *K. D.* v. *Educational Testing Service,* 386 N.Y.S.2d 747 (Sup. Ct. 1976), the court viewed the plaintiff's agreement with ETS to take the Law School Admissions Test (LSAT) as a contract of adhesion, explaining:

> Where the court finds that an agreement is a contract of adhesion, effort will frequently be made to protect the weaker party from the agreement's harsher terms by a variety of pretexts, while still keeping the elementary rules of the law of contracts intact (Kessler, "Contracts of Adhesion— Some Thoughts About Freedom of Contract," 43 *Columbia L. Rev.* 629, 633 (1943)). The court may, for example, find the obnoxious clause "ambiguous," even where no ambiguity exists, and then construe it against its author; or it may find the clause to be against public policy and declare it unenforceable [386 N.Y.S.2d at 752].

Nevertheless, the court held the agreement valid because it was not "so unfair and unreasonable" that it should be disregarded by using the available "pretexts."

Since these contract principles depend on the weak position of one of the parties, and on overall determinations of "fairness," courts are unlikely to apply them against institutions that deal openly with their students—for instance, by following a good-practice code, operating grievance mechanisms for student complaints (see Sections 4.13.1 through 4.13.3), and affording students significant opportunity to participate in institutional governance.

As further developments unfold, postsecondary administrators should be sensitive to the language used in all institutional rules and policies affecting students. Language suggestive of a commitment (or promise) to students should be used only when the institution is prepared to live up to the commitment. Limitations on the institution's commitments should be clearly noted where possible. Administrators should consider the adoption of an official policy, perhaps even a "code of good practice," on fair dealing with students. (See E. H. El-Khawas, *New Expectations for Fair Practice: Suggestions for Institutional Review* (American Council on Education, 1976).)

Sec. 4.2. Admissions

4.2.1. Basic legal requirements. Postsecondary institutions have traditionally been accorded wide discretion in formulating admissions standards. The law's deference to administrators' autonomy stems from the notion that tampering with admissions criteria is tampering with the expertise of educators. In recent years, however, some doorways have been opened in the wall of deference, as dissatisfied applicants have successfully pressed the courts for relief, and legislatures and administrative agencies have sought to regulate certain aspects of the admissions process.

Administrators are subject to three general constraints in formulating admissions policies: (1) the selection process must not be arbitrary or capricious; (2) the institution may be bound, under a contract theory, to adhere to its published admissions standards and to honor its admissions decisions; and (3) the institution may not have admissions policies that unjustifiably discriminate on the basis of race, sex, age, handicap, or citizenship.

Although administrators are also constrained in the admissions process by the "Buckley" regulations on school records (Section 4.12.1), the regulations have only limited applicability to admissions records. The regulations do not apply to the records of persons who are not or have not been *students* at the institution; thus, admissions records are not covered until the applicant has been accepted and is in attendance at the institution (34 C.F.R. sec. 99.1(d), 99.3 ("student")). Admissions records may be destroyed before the applicant attends the institution if the institution so desires (34 C.F.R. sec. 99.13). The institution may also maintain the confidentiality of letters of recommendation if the student has waived the right of access; such a waiver may be sought during the application process (34 C.F.R. sec. 99.7). Moreover, when a student from one component unit of an institution applies for admission to another unit of the same institution, the student is treated as an *applicant* rather than a *student* with respect to the second unit's admissions records; those records are therefore not subject to Buckley until the student is in attendance in the second unit (34 C.F.R. sec. 99.3 ("student")).

4.2.2. Arbitrariness. The "arbitrariness" standard of review is the one most protective of the institution's prerogatives. The cases reflect a judicial hands-off attitude toward any admissions decision arguably based on academic qualifications. *Lesser* v. *Board of Education of New York,* 18 A.D.2d 388, 239 N.Y.S.2d 776 (1963), provides a classic example. Lesser sued Brooklyn College after being rejected because his grade average was below the cutoff. He argued that the college acted arbitrarily and unreasonably in not considering that he had been enrolled in a demanding high school honors program. The court declined to overturn the judgment of the college:

> Courts may not interfere with the administrative discretion exercised
> by agencies which are vested with the administration and control of educa-

tional institutions, unless the circumstances disclosed by the record leave no scope for the use of that discretion in the matter under scrutiny. . . .

More particularly, a court should refrain from interjecting its views within those delicate areas of school administration which relate to the eligibility of applicants and the determination of marking standards, unless a clear abuse of statutory authority or gross error has been shown [239 N.Y.S.2d at 779].

The court in *Arizona Board of Regents* v. *Wilson,* 24 Ariz. App. 469, 539 P.2d 943 (1975), expressed similar sentiment. In that case a woman was refused admission to the graduate school of art at the University of Arizona because the faculty did not consider her art work to be of sufficiently high quality. She challenged the admissions process on the basis that it was a rolling admissions system with no written guidelines. The court entered judgment in favor of the university:

This case represents a prime example of when a court should not interfere in the academic program of a university. It was incumbent upon appellee to show that her rejection was in bad faith, or arbitrary, capricious, or unreasonable. The court may not substitute its own opinions as to the merits of appellee's work for that of the members of the faculty committee who were selected to make a determination as to the quality of her work [539 P.2d at 946].

The review standards in these cases establish a formidable barrier for disappointed applicants to cross. But occasionally someone succeeds. *State ex rel. Bartlett* v. *Pantzer,* 158 Mont. 126, 489 P.2d 375 (1971), arose after the admissions committee of the University of Montana Law School had advised an applicant that he would be accepted if he completed a course in financial accounting. He took such a course and received a "D." The law school refused to admit him, claiming that a "D" was an "acceptable" but not a "satisfactory" grade. The student argued that it was unreasonable for the law school to inject a requirement of receiving a "satisfactory grade" after he had completed the course. The court agreed:

Thus, we look to the matter of judgment or "discretion" in the legal sense. To cause a young man, who is otherwise qualified and whose entry into law school would not interfere with the educational process in any discernible fashion, to lose a year and an opportunity for education on the technical, unpublished distinction between the words "satisfactory" and "acceptable" as applied to a credit-earning grade from a recognized institution is, in our view, an abuse of discretion [489 P.2d at 379].

All these cases involve public institutions, and whether their principles would apply to private institutions is unclear. The "arbitrary and capricious" standard apparently arises from concepts of due process and administrative law that are applicable only to public institutions. Courts may be even less receptive to arbitrariness arguments lodged against private schools, although common law may provide some relief even here. In *In re Press,* 45 U.S.L.W. 2238 (N.Y. Sup. Ct., Oct. 27, 1976), for instance, the court held that an arbitrariness claim was a valid basis on which New York University, a private institution, could be sued. And in *Levine* v. *George Washington University* and *Paulsen* v. *Golden Gate University* (Section 4.2.6), common law principles protected students at private institutions against arbitrary interpretation of institutional policy.

 4.2.3. The contract theory. The plaintiffs in *Eden* v. *Board of Trustees of State University,* 49 A.D.2d 277, 374 N.Y.S.2d 686 (1975), had been accepted for admission to a new school of podiatry being established at the State University of New York at Stony Brook. Shortly before the scheduled opening, the state suspended its plans for the school, citing fiscal pressures in state government. The students argued that they had a contract with SUNY entitling them to instruction in the podiatry school. The court agreed that SUNY's "acceptance of the petitioners' applications satisfies the classic requirements of a contract." Though the state could legally abrogate its contracts when necessary in the public interest to alleviate a fiscal crisis, and though "the judicial branch . . . must exercise restraint in questioning executive prerogative," the court nevertheless ordered the state to enroll the students for the ensuing academic year. The court found that a large federal grant as well as tuition money would be lost if the school did not open, that the school's personnel were already under contract and would have to be paid anyway, and that postponement of the opening therefore would not save money. Since the fiscal crisis would not be alleviated, the state's decision was deemed "arbitrary and capricious" and a breach of contract.

 The *Eden* case establishes that a prospective student has a contract with the school once the school accepts his or her admission application. A subsequent case takes the contract analysis one step further, applying it to applicants not yet accepted. In *Steinberg* v. *University of Health Sciences/Chicago Medical School,* 41 Ill. App. 3d 804, 354 N.E.2d 586 (1976), an intermediate appellate court held that a rejected applicant could sue for breach of contract on the theory that the medical school had deviated from the admissions criteria in its catalogue. The applicant alleged that the school had used unstated criteria, such as the existence of alumni in the applicant's family and the ability to pledge large sums of money to the school. Although conceding that it had no authority to interfere with the substance of a private school's admissions requirements, the court asserted that the school has a contractual duty to its applicants to judge their qualifications only by its published standards unless it has specifically reserved the right to reject any applicant for whatever reason it desires.

 The court reasoned that the school's catalogue was an invitation to make an offer; the applicant's application in response to that invitation was an offer; and the medical school's retention of the application fee was the acceptance of the offer.

> We believe that he [Steinberg] and the school entered into an enforceable contract; that the school's obligation under the contract was stated in the school's bulletin in a definitive manner; and that by accepting his application fee—a valuable consideration—the school bound itself to fulfill its promises. Steinberg accepted the school's promises in good faith, and he was entitled to have his application judged according to the school's stated criteria [354 N.E.2d at 591].

The court thus ordered a trial on the applicant's allegations that the school had breached a contract. The Illinois Supreme Court affirmed the order and also held that the applicant had a cause of action for fraud (69 Ill. 2d 320, 371 N.E.2d 634 (1977)).

Thus, the contract theory clearly applies to both public and private schools, although, as *Eden* suggests, public institutions may have defenses not available to private schools. While the contract theory does not require administrators to adopt or to forgo any particular admissions standard, it does require that administrators honor their acceptance decisions once made and honor their published policies in deciding whom to accept and to reject. Administrators should thus carefully review their published admissions policies and any new policies to be published. The institution may wish to omit standards and criteria from its policies in order to avoid being pinned down under the contract theory. Conversely, the institution may decide that full disclosure is the best policy. In either case administrators should make sure that published admissions policies state only what the institution is willing to abide by. If the institution needs to reserve the right to depart from or supplement its published policies, such reservation should be clearly inserted, with counsel's assistance, into all such policies.

4.2.4. The principle of nondiscrimination. Postsecondary institutions are prohibited in varying degrees and by varying legal authorities from discriminating in their admissions process on the basis of race, sex, handicap, age, residence, and alien status. The first four are discussed in this section. The other two types— discrimination against nonresidents (residents of other states) and discrimination against aliens (citizens of other countries who are residing in the United States)— are discussed in Sections 4.3.4 and 4.3.5 because the leading cases concern financial aid rather than admissions. The legal principles in these sections also apply generally to admissions. Under these principles, generally speaking, admissions preferences for state residents (see, for example, Calif. Educ. Code sec. 22522) may be permissible (see *Rosenstock* v. *Board of Governors of University of North Carolina,* 423 F. Supp. 1321, 1326–27 (M.D.N.C. 1976)), but among state residents a preference for those who are United States citizens or a bar to those who are nationals of particular foreign countries is probably impermissible (see *Tayyari* v. *New Mexico State University,* 495 F. Supp. 1365 (D.N.M. 1980)).

4.2.4.1. Race. It is clear under the Fourteenth Amendment's equal protection clause that, in the absence of a "compelling state interest" (see Section 4.2.5), no public institution may discriminate in admissions on the basis of race. The leading case, of course, is *Brown* v. *Board of Education,* 347 U.S. 483 (1954). Though *Brown* concerned elementary and secondary schools, the precedent clearly applies to postsecondary education as well, as the Supreme Court affirmed in *Florida ex rel. Hawkins* v. *Board of Control,* 350 U.S. 413 (1956). Cases involving postsecondary education have generally considered racial segregation within a state postsecondary system rather than within a single institution. One case, for instance, *Alabama State Teachers Association* v. *Alabama Public School and College Authority,* 289 F. Supp. 784 (D. Ala. 1968), affirmed without majority opinion, 393 U.S. 400 (1969), concerned the state's establishment of a branch of a predominantly white institution in a city already served by a predominantly black institution. The court rejected the plaintiff's argument that this action unconstitutionally perpetuated segregation in the state system, holding that states do not have an affirmative duty to dismantle segregated higher education (as opposed to elementary and secondary education). Similarly, *Norris* v. *State Council of Higher Education*, 327 F. Supp. 1368 (E.D. Va. 1971), affirmed without opinion, 404 U.S. 907 (1971), concerned a state plan to expand a predominantly white two-year institution into a four-year institution in an area where a predominantly black four-year institution already existed. In contrast to the Alabama case, the court overturned the action because it impeded desegregation in the state system.

Two related decisions of the U.S. Court of Appeals for the Sixth Circuit provide the leading equal protection precedents on the desegregation of higher education. In *Geier* v. *University of Tennessee*, 597 F.2d 1056 (6th Cir. 1979), the court ordered the merger of two postsecondary institutions in Tennessee, despite the state's claim that the racial imbalances at the schools were due to the students' exercise of free choice. Applying the reasoning of *Brown* and other elementary/secondary cases, the court ruled that the state's adoption of an "open-admissions" policy had not effectively dismantled the state's dual system of higher education. In a separate decision, *Richardson* v. *Blanton*, 597 F.2d 1078 (6th Cir. 1979), the same court upheld the district court's approval of the state's long-range plan for desegregating its colleges and universities.

The history of the two cases goes back to 1968, when suit was filed challenging the state's decision to expand facilities and course offerings at the traditionally all-white University of Tennessee at Nashville (UT-N). The basis of the challenge was that the proposed expansion of UT-N would impede the process of desegregation at nearby Tennessee State University (TSU), an all-black institution. The district court refused to enjoin the expansion but ordered the state to develop a long-range plan for integrating its institutions, which were formerly segregated by law. The ultimate failure of the state's plan to effectively desegregate the Nashville-area campuses led to the district court's order in *Geier* that UT-N and TSU be merged (427 F. Supp. 644 (M.D. Tenn. 1977)).

In affirming the district court's decision in *Geier*, the appellate court noted that the merger order was based on a finding that the state's failure to "dismantle a statewide dual system, the 'heart' of which was an all-black TSU," was a continuing constitutional violation. The fact that the state had not been found guilty of practicing discrimination at the schools in the recent past was irrelevant. According to the court:

> The fundamental disagreement between the district court and the appellants concerns the duty of a state to remove the vestiges of state-imposed segregation. The appellants point to the obvious differences between elementary and secondary education on the one hand and higher education on the other. One is free and compulsory, and pupils are assigned to particular schools. The other is purely elective, requires the payment of tuition and fees, and permits students to choose a particular school for a variety of reasons. Most elementary and secondary schools in a given system are roughly equal in curriculum and facilities, whereas individual colleges and universities vary greatly in their offerings and emphases. . . .

> The district court recognized these differences in the present case. Also, it agreed . . . that the "basic requirement" of the affirmative duty to dismantle a dual system of higher education was met when an open-

admissions policy was adopted and good faith was exercised in dealing with admissions, faculty, and staff. However, the district court found that something beyond this basic requirement was needed to satisfy the constitutional imperative in the present case, where segregation was once required by state law and "egregious" conditions of segregation continued to exist in public higher education in the Nashville area. What was required, the court found, was affirmative action to remove these vestiges. The district court relied principally on *Green* v. *County School Board,* 391 U.S. 430, 88 S. Ct. 1689, 20 L. Ed. 2d 716 (1968), where a "freedom-of-choice" plan was held to be an inadequate compliance by a school board with the constitutional requirement that a well-entrenched dual system be dismantled. The Court held in *Green* that in such a situation a school board is "clearly charged with the affirmative duty to take whatever steps might be necessary to convert to a unitary system in which racial discrimination would be eliminated root and branch" (391 U.S. at 437–38, 88 S. Ct. at 1694) [597 F.2d at 1065].

The court rejected the state's argument that the *Green* case did not apply to public higher education. "We agree," said the court, "that the 'state's duty is as exacting' to eliminate the vestiges of state-imposed segregation in higher education as in elementary and secondary school systems; it is only the means of eliminating segregation which differ."

The court then considered the *Geier* case in light of the facts in *Green:*

The facts of the present case are closely analogous to those in *Green.* Thirteen years after *Brown II* [*Brown* v. *Board of Education,* 349 U.S. 294 (1955), ordering that school desegregation required by the original *Brown* ruling proceed "with all deliberate speed"], the only step which the Tennessee defendants had taken toward dismantling the dual system of public higher education was inauguration of an open-admissions policy. The evidence was uncontradicted that little progress had been made. Yet the district judge did not immediately impose a plan on the state, recognizing its strong interest in making educational policy decisions. Instead, he directed the defendants to formulate a plan. Though several plans were put forward in subsequent years, none really came to grips with the Nashville situation. There the vestiges of state-imposed segregation were clear and undiminished in reality.

The Constitution may be violated by inaction as well as by deeds. Here the district court found evidence of both inaction and wrongful action in assessing conditions in public higher education in the Nashville area. During the course of this litigation, UT-N grew from a non-degree-granting "center" of the University of Tennessee to a branch of the university with a four-year degree program. During this period the student body of UT-N grew from 1,800 to 3,500, of whom 89 percent were white, while that of TSU remained virtually static. From these facts the district court concluded that the existence and expansion of the predominantly white UT-N alongside the traditionally black TSU "have impeded the dismantling of the dual system."

The appellants dispute this conclusion, pointing to the differences between TSU and UT-N. They emphasize that TSU is a "traditional university" with a broad range of offerings and a student body of traditional college age, most of whom live on campus. On the other hand, UT-N has limited offerings, primarily intended for older working students who can attend classes only in the late afternoon and at night. Granting that these distinctions exist, nevertheless the district court had abundant evidence to support its findings. More than one expert witness testified that the most likely source of white students for a traditionally black university in an urban area is older working students. Thus, the rapid development of UT-N into a degree-granting four-year branch, even though it continued to be primarily a night school, did impede the progress of desegregation of TSU [597 F.2d at 1066–67].

The court was careful to point out that the constitutional violation was not based on the mere existence of an all-black institution in the state's system. Rather, the violation was premised on the state's failure to take "meaningful actions" to facilitate desegregation of TSU while at the same time adopting a course of action with respect to UT-N which impeded the process of integration.

Next the court considered the state's argument that a merger of the two institutions was not an appropriate remedy. Noting the broad powers of a district court to fashion a desegregation remedy, the court concluded that the district court's merger order was proper:

Applying these principles, we conclude that merger was within the equitable power of the district court. The merger remedy was related to the condition found to offend the Constitution. This "condition" was failure to dismantle a dual system. The core of the problem was found to be the inability of TSU to attract a "white presence" to its campus because of the competition of UT-N for students in the Nashville area. This competition would not have been so formidable if UT-N had remained a non-degree-granting extension center. Its expansion to a four-year degree-granting institution greatly inhibited the efforts to desegregate TSU. Further, the remedy of merger effectually restores the victims of discrimination to their rightful place. The black students had a constitutional right to attend a unitary system of higher education, which was denied them by state action. The merger will permit TSU to expand as a comprehensive urban university, offering educational opportunities to students of traditional college age and older working students in a desegregated setting. The nature of the remedy does not exceed the nature and scope of the violation [597 F.2d at 1068].

Acknowledging the sensitive issues involved in modifying the state's operation of its system of postsecondary education, the court continued:

The district court stayed its hand for years in order to give the defendants an opportunity to effectuate a meaningful desegregation of TSU. The court initially approved the approach championed by the defendants of instituting joint and cooperative programs while permitting the two institutions to continue their separate existence. After nearly nine years the court found that no progress was being made with this approach and that this failure resulted largely from the inability of the governing boards to agree. The district court clearly took into account the interest of the defendants in managing higher education programs of the state on a statewide basis. However, when the authorities "fail[ed] in their affirmative obligations," the court properly invoked its equitable power. . . .

A merger of the two institutions will involve the district court in their day-to-day affairs to a much less pervasive degree than any attempt by it to divide and allocate all the various programs to one school or the other. Merger also intrudes less into the freedom of students to attend a college of their choice than any plan which might require compulsory assignments to bring about a dismantling of the dual system. The acknowledged differences between higher education and education at the primary and secondary levels appear to make such frequently used remedies as assignment and transportation of students to a particular institution unworkable as well as undesirable. . . . The appellants insist that the district court has failed to consider the vital interests of the state in being able to make educational policy decisions on a statewide basis. They contend that the court has unnecessarily interfered with decisions as to the roles and functions of the various institutions. These arguments are not persuasive. Those policy decisions of the two boards and THEC [Tennessee Higher Education Commission] which failed to take into account the state's constitutional duty to dismantle its dual system must yield to that duty. Though TSU and UT-N were given different roles in the overall scheme of public higher education, there was an abundance of expert testimony that they could be combined and that one institution could perform all the functions previously assigned to them separately [597 F.2d at 1068–69].[2]

The court found that, although the state's desegregation plan was not effective with respect to desegregation in the Nashville area, it had resulted in steady progress throughout the remainder of the state's higher education system. In its companion decision in *Richardson* v. *Blanton,* the court described the major elements of the plan:

The plan sets out separate goals of black student enrollment to be attained by 1975 and 1980 for the community colleges, the universities under control of SBR [the State Board of Regents], and the University of Tennessee. . . .

In preparing the plan, the committee did not set a single goal, applicable to all institutions. The committee recognized that many of the institutions draw large numbers of students from nearby counties and that the

---

[2]The parties subsequently reached agreement on the specifics of the merger plan and presented it to the district court for approval. The U.S. Department of Justice objected to certain provisions of the proposed settlement—for example, the use of timetables and goals for faculty and student integration—on grounds that they were beyond the court's remedial power. The court rejected these objections and approved the plan (*Geier* v. *Alexander,* 593 F. Supp. 1263 (M.D. Tenn. 1984)).

black population of Tennessee is not evenly distributed throughout the state. The distribution of the black population of Tennessee was considered along with the "drawing area" of each school. It was felt that statewide desegregation would be achieved if each institution enrolled black students in approximate proportion to the black population of its service area. . . .

In addition to setting goals for the desegregation of student bodies, faculty, and staff of the public institutions of higher learning, the long-range plan establishes a monitoring system [597 F.2d at 1080–81].

Against challenges from both the student plaintiffs and the Department of Health, Education and Welfare (now Department of Education), which established criteria for devising such plans in accord with Title VI of the 1964 Civil Rights Act (see this volume, Section 7.5.2), the appellate court affirmed the district judge's ruling that the state program was *constitutionally* adequate:

A careful weighing of many factors led the court to conclude that the long-range plan offered the most realistic promise for desegregation of public higher education within a reasonable time. Instant desegregation is not achievable and has not been required. . . . "Sequential implementation" over a period not to exceed five years is an accepted practice. . . .

We find no error in the district court's conclusion that desegregation was progressing at a steady and acceptable rate outside Nashville and that the long-range plan gave promise of continued progress. The court retained jurisdiction to implement its judgment and orders. If this progress should halt or seriously falter, the court will be in position to impose new requirements [597 F.2d at 1085–86].

Because the issue of the plan's compliance with the HEW criteria was not before the district court, the appeals court refused to address it. It did note, however, that the Tennessee plan apparently contained many of the elements of an acceptable plan as defined by the HEW criteria. Moreover, the parties were free, the court said, to return to the lower court to determine whether such was in fact the case.

As *Richardson* v. *Blanton* suggests, cases involving desegregation of state higher education systems may be decided under the Department of Education's Title VI criteria as well as under the constitutional standard. Indeed, since *Blanton* most of the controversy and activity concerning higher education desegregation has centered on the Education Department's administrative enforcement of its own desegregation criteria (see this volume, Section 7.5.2). The court's merger order in *Geier* nevertheless serves as a reminder that the Constitution is the ultimate authority on desegregation and that the states, and the Education Department as well, must measure their actions against this authority (see P. Dimond, "Constitutional Requirements," in R. Wilson (Ed.), *Race and Equity in Higher Education* (American Council on Education, 1982)).

In addition to the Constitution's equal protection clause and the desegregation criteria developed under Title VI, there are two other major legal bases for attacking racial discrimination in higher education. The first is the civil rights statute called "Section 1981" (42 U.S.C. sec. 1981) (this volume, Section 3.3.2.7). A post-Civil War statute guaranteeing the freedom to contract, Section 1981 has particular significance because (like Title VI) it applies to private as well as public institutions. In the leading case of *Fairfax-Brewster* v. *Gonzales,* 427 U.S. 160 (1976), the U.S. Supreme Court used Section 1981 to prohibit two private, white elementary schools from discriminating against blacks in their admissions policies. Since the Court has applied Section 1981 to discrimination against white persons as well as blacks (*McDonald* v. *Santa Fe Transportation Co.,* 427 U.S. 273 (1976)), this statute would also apparently prohibit predominantly minority private institutions from discriminating in admissions against white students.

The other legal source is federal income tax law. In Revenue Ruling 71-447, 1971-2 C.B. 230 (*Cumulative Bulletin,* an annual multivolume compilation of various tax documents published by the IRS), the Internal Revenue Service revised its former policy and ruled that schools practicing racial discrimination were violating public policy and should be denied tax-exempt status. Other IRS rulings enlarged on this basic rule. Revenue Procedure 72-54, 1972-2 C.B. 834, requires schools to publicize their nondiscrimination policies. Revenue Procedure 75-50, 1975-2 C.B. 587, requires that a school carry the burden of "show[ing] affirmatively . . . that it has adopted a racially nondiscriminatory policy as to students" and also establishes record-keeping and other guidelines through which a school can demonstrate its compliance. And Revenue Ruling 75-231, 1975-1 C.B. 158, furnishes a series of hypothetical cases to illustrate when a church-affiliated school would be considered to be discriminating and in danger of losing tax-exempt status. The U.S. Supreme Court upheld the basic policy of Revenue Ruling 71-447 in *Bob Jones University* v. *United States,* 103 S. Ct. 2017 (1983), discussed in Section 7.3.1 of this volume.

The combined impact of these various legal sources—the equal protection clause, Title VI, Section 1981, and IRS tax rulings—is clear: Neither public nor private postsecondary institutions may maintain admissions policies (with a possible exception for affirmative action policies, as discussed in Section 4.2.5) that discriminate against students on the basis of race, nor may states maintain plans or practices that perpetuate racial segregation in a statewide system of postsecondary education.

4.2.4.2. Sex. Title IX of the Education Amendments of 1972, 20 U.S.C. sec. 1681 *et seq.* (see this volume, Section 7.5.3), is the primary legal source governing sex discrimination in admissions policies. While Title IX and its implementing regulations, 34 C.F.R. Part 106, apply nondiscrimination principles to both public and private institutions receiving federal funds, there are special exemptions concerning admissions. For the purposes of applying these admissions exemptions, each "administratively separate unit" of an institution is considered a separate institution (34 C.F.R. sec. 106.15(b)). An "administratively separate unit" is "a school, department, or college . . . admission to which is independent of admission to any other component of such institution" (34 C.F.R. sec. 106.2(o)). *Private undergraduate institutions* are not prohibited from discriminating in admissions on the basis of sex (20 U.S.C. sec. 1681(a)(1); 34 C.F.R. sec. 106.15(d)). Nor are *public undergraduate institutions that have always been single-sex institutions* (20 U.S.C. sec. 1681(a)(5); 34 C.F.R. sec. 106.15(e); but compare the *Hogan* case, discussed later in this section). In addition, *religious institutions,* including all or any of their administratively separate units, may be exempted from nondiscrimination. The remaining institutions, which are prohibited from discriminating in admissions, are (1) graduate schools; (2) professional schools, unless part of an undergraduate institution exempted from Title IX's admissions requirements (see 34 C.F.R. sec. 106.2(m)); (3) vocational schools, unless part of an undergraduate institution exempted from Title IX's admissions requirements (see 34 C.F.R. sec. 106.2(n)); and (4) public undergraduate institutions that are not, or have not always been, single-sex schools.[3]

Institutions subject to Title IX admissions requirements are prohibited from treating persons differently on the basis of sex in any phase of admissions and recruitment (34 C.F.R. secs. 106.21–106.23). Specifically, Section 106.21(b) of the regulations provides that a covered institution, in its admissions process, shall not

(i) Give preference to one person over another on the basis of sex, by ranking applicants separately on such basis, or otherwise;
(ii) Apply numerical limitations upon the number or proportion of persons of either sex who may be admitted; or
(iii) Otherwise treat one individual differently from another on the basis of sex.

Section 106.21(c) prohibits covered institutions from treating the sexes differently in regard to "actual or potential parental, family, or marital status"; from discriminating against applicants because of pregnancy or conditions relating to childbirth; and from making preadmission inquiries concerning marital status. Sections 106.22 and 106.23(b) prohibit institutions from having admissions preference or recruitment emphases favoring single-sex or predominantly single-sex schools, if such preference or emphasis has "the effect of discriminating on the basis of sex."

Furthermore, institutions exempt from Title IX admissions requirements are not necessarily free to discriminate at will on the basis of sex. Some will be caught in the net of other statutes or of constitutional equal protection principles. A federal law prohibiting discrimination in admissions to medical, nursing, and health training schools, for instance, may catch some undergraduate programs exempted from Title IX (42 U.S.C. secs. 292(d), 298(b)(2)). A state statute such as the Massachusetts statute prohibiting sex discrimination in vocational training institutions may catch other exempted undergraduate programs (Mass. Gen. Laws Ann. ch. 151C, sec. 2A(a)). More important, the Fourteenth Amendment's equal protection clause places restrictions on public undergraduate schools even if they are single-sex schools exempt from Title IX.

After a period of uncertainty concerning the extent to which equal protection principles would restrict a public institution's admissions policies, the U.S. Supreme Court addressed the question in *Mississippi University for Women* v. *Hogan*, 102 S. Ct. 3331 (1982). In the *Hogan* case, the Court considered an admissions policy that excluded males from a professional nursing school. Ignoring the dissenting justices' protestations that Mississippi provided baccalaureate nursing programs

[3]The admissions exemption for private undergraduate institutions in the regulations may be broader than that authorized by the Title IX statute. For an argument that "administratively separate" professional and vocational components of private undergraduate institutions should not be exempt and that private undergraduate schools which are primarily professional and vocational in character should not be exempt, see W. Kaplin and M. McGillicuddy, "Scope of Exemption for Private Undergraduate Institutions from Admissions Requirements of Title IX," memorandum printed at 121 *Congressional Record* 1091 (94th Cong., 1st Sess., 1975).

at other state coeducational institutions, the majority of five struck down the institution's policy as unconstitutional sex discrimination. In the process, the Court developed an important synthesis of constitutional principles applicable to sex discrimination claims. These principles would apply not only to admissions but also to all other aspects of a public institution's operations:

> Because the challenged policy expressly discriminates among applicants on the basis of gender, it is subject to scrutiny under the equal protection clause of the Fourteenth Amendment (*Reed* v. *Reed,* 404 U.S. 71, 75 (1971)). That this statute discriminates against males rather than against females does not exempt it from scrutiny or reduce the standard of review (*Caban* v. *Mohammed,* 441 U.S. 380, 394 (1979); *Orr* v. *Orr,* 440 U.S. 268, 279 (1979)). Our decisions also establish that the party seeking to uphold a statute that classifies individuals on the basis of their gender must carry the burden of showing an "exceedingly persuasive justification" for the classification (*Kirchberg* v. *Feenstra,* 450 U.S. 455, 561 (1981); *Personnel Administrator of Massachusetts* v. *Feeney,* 442 U.S. 256, 273 (1979)). The burden is met only by showing at least that the classification serves "important governmental objectives and that the discriminatory means employed" are "substantially related to the achievement of those objectives" (*Wengler* v. *Druggists Mutual Insurance Co.,* 446 U.S. 142, 150 (1980)).
>
> Although the test for determining the validity of a gender-based classification is straightforward, it must be applied free of fixed notions concerning the roles and abilities of males and females. Care must be taken in ascertaining whether the statutory objective itself reflects archaic and stereotypic notions. Thus, if the statutory objective is to exclude or "protect" members of one gender because they are presumed to suffer from an inherent handicap or to be innately inferior, the objective itself is illegitimate (see *Frontiero* v. *Richardson,* 411 U.S. 677, 684–85 (1973) (plurality opinion)).
>
> If the state's objective is legitimate and important, we next determine whether the requisite direct, substantial relationship between objective and means is present. The purpose of requiring that close relationship is to assure that the validity of a classification is determined through reasoned analysis rather than through the mechanical application of traditional, often inaccurate, assumptions about the proper roles of men and women [102 S. Ct. at 3336–37].

Applying the principles regarding the legitimacy and importance of the state's objective, the Court reasoned:

> The state's primary justification for maintaining the single-sex admissions policy of MUW's school of nursing is that it compensates for discrimination against women and, therefore, constitutes educational affirmative action. As applied to the school of nursing, we find the state's argument unpersuasive.
>
> In limited circumstances, a gender-based classification favoring one sex can be justified if it intentionally and directly assists members of the sex that is disproportionately burdened. However, we consistently have

emphasized that "the mere recitation of a benign, compensatory purpose is not an automatic shield which protects against any inquiry into the actual purposes underlying a statutory scheme" (*Weinberger* v. *Wiesenfeld,* 420 U.S. 636, 648 (1975)). . . .

It is readily apparent that a state can evoke a compensatory purpose to justify an otherwise discriminatory classification only if members of the gender benefited by the classification actually suffer a disadvantage related to the classification. . . .

Mississippi has made no showing that women lacked opportunities to obtain training in the field of nursing or to attain positions of leadership in that field when the MUW school of nursing opened its door or that women currently are deprived of such opportunities. . . .

Rather than compensate for discriminatory barriers faced by women, MUW's policy of excluding males from admission to the school of nursing tends to perpetuate the stereotyped view of nursing as an exclusively woman's job. By assuring that Mississippi allots more openings in its state-supported nursing schools to women than it does to men, MUW's admissions policy lends credibility to the old view that women, not men, should become nurses, and makes the assumption that nursing is a field for women a self-fulfilling prophecy. Thus, we conclude that, although the state recited a "benign, compensatory purpose," it failed to establish that the alleged objective is the actual purpose underlying the discriminatory classification [102 S. Ct. at 3337–39].

Even if the state had a valid compensatory objective, its policy would still be unconstitutional, according to the Court, because it also violated other equal protection principles:

The state has made no showing that the gender-based classification is substantially and directly related to its proposed compensatory objective. To the contrary, MUW's policy of permitting men to attend classes as auditors fatally undermines its claim that women, at least those in the school of nursing, are adversely affected by the presence of men.

MUW permits men who audit to participate fully in classes. Additionally, both men and women take part in continuing education courses offered by the school of nursing, in which regular nursing students also can enroll. . . . The uncontroverted record reveals that admitting men to nursing classes does not affect teaching style, . . . and that men in coeducational nursing schools do not dominate the classroom. . . . In sum, the record in this case is flatly inconsistent with the claim that excluding men from the school of nursing is necessary to reach any of MUW's educational goals [102 S. Ct. at 3339–40].

The Court's opinion on its face invalidated single-sex admissions policies only at MUW's school of nursing and, by extension, other public postsecondary nursing schools. The majority notes: "We decline to address the question of whether MUW's admissions policy, as applied to males seeking admission to schools other than the school of nursing, violates the Fourteenth Amendment," and "We are not faced with the question of whether states can provide 'separate but equal' undergraduate institutions for males and females.'' But the majority's reasoning cannot so easily be confined, as two of the three dissenting opinions point out. It is likely that this reasoning would also serve to invalidate single-sex policies in programs other than nursing and in entire institutions. The most arguable exception to this broad reading would be a single-sex policy that serves to redress the effects of past discrimination on a professional program in which one sex is substantially underrepresented. But even such a compensatory policy would be a form of explicit sexual quota, which could be questioned by analogy to the racial affirmative action cases (this volume, Section 4.2.5).

Whatever the remaining ambiguity about the scope of the *Hogan* decision, it will not be resolved by further litigation at the Mississippi University for Women. After the Supreme Court decision, MUW's board of trustees—perhaps anticipating a broad application of the Court's reasoning—voted to admit men to all divisions of the university.

Important as *Hogan* may be to the law regarding sex discrimination in admissions, it is only part of the bigger picture, which already includes Title IX. Thus, to view the law in its current state, it is important to look both to *Hogan* and to Title IX. *Hogan* has at least limited, and apparently undermined, the Title IX exemption for public undergraduate institutions that have always had single-sex admissions policies (20 U.S.C. sec. 1681(a)(5); 34 C.F.R. sec. 106.15(e)). Thus, the only programs and institutions that are still legally free to have single-sex admissions policies are (1) private undergraduate institutions and their constituent programs and (2) religious institutions, including their graduate, professional, and vocational programs, *if* they have obtained a waiver of Title IX admission requirements on religious grounds (20 U.S.C. sec. 1681(a)(3); 34 C.F.R. sec. 106.12). A third category of institutions, the military academy, is a special case. When an academy's primary purpose is to train individuals for U.S. military service, it is exempted from Title IX entirely (not just as to admissions); although *Hogan* could limit the effect of this exemption, such a result appears doubtful because of the special deference that courts accord to government when military matters are at issue (see *Rostker* v. *Goldberg,* 101 S. Ct. 2646 (1981) (upholding male-only draft registration)).

4.2.4.3. Handicap. The country's conscience is awakening to the problem of discrimination against handicapped persons. The landmark event thus far is the passage of Section 504 of the Rehabilitation Act of 1973, 29 U.S.C. sec. 794, as amended by Section 111(a) of the Rehabilitation Act Amendments of 1974 (see Section 7.5.4). Before that Act there were a few scattered federal provisions concerning discrimination against the handicapped, such as 20 U.S.C. sec. 1684, which prohibits discrimination against blind persons by institutions receiving federal funds; and there had been a few constitutional equal protection cases on discrimination against handicapped students by public elementary and secondary schools, such as *PARC* v. *Pennsylvania,* 334 F. Supp. 1257 (E.D. Pa. 1971). But none of these developments has nearly the potential impact on postsecondary admissions that Section 504 has.

As applied to postsecondary education, Section 504 generally prohibits discrimination on the basis of handicap in federally funded programs and activities (see this volume, Section 7.5.7). Section 104.42 of the implementing regulations,

34 C.F.R. Part 105, prohibits discrimination on the basis of handicap in admissions and recruitment. This section contains several specific provisions similar to those prohibiting sex discrimination in admissions under Title IX (see this volume, Section 4.2.4.2). These provisions prohibit (1) the imposition of limitations on "the number or proportion of handicapped persons who may be admitted" (sec. 104.42(b)(1)); (2) the use of any admissions criterion or test "that has a disproportionate, adverse effect" on the handicapped, unless the criterion or test, as used, is shown to predict success validly and no alternative, nondiscriminatory criterion or test is available (sec. 104.42(b)(2)); and (3) any preadmission inquiry about whether the applicant is handicapped, unless the recipient needs the information in order to correct the effects of past discrimination or to overcome past conditions which resulted in limited participation by the handicapped (secs. 104.42(b)(4) and 104.42(c)).

These prohibitions apply to discrimination directed against "qualified handicapped" persons. A handicapped person is qualified, with respect to postsecondary and vocational services, if he or she "meets the academic and technical standards requisite to admission or participation in the recipient's education program or activity" (sec. 104.3(k)(3)). Thus, while the regulations do not prohibit an institution from denying admission to a handicapped person who does not meet the institution's "academic and technical" admissions standards, they do prohibit an institution from denying admission on the basis of the handicap as such. (After a student is admitted, however, the institution may make confidential inquiry concerning his handicaps (34 C.F.R. sec. 104.42(b)(4)). In this way the institution may obtain advance information concerning handicaps that may require accommodation.)

In addition to these prohibitions, the institution has an affirmative duty to ascertain that its admissions tests are structured to accommodate applicants with handicaps that impair sensory, manual, or speaking skills, unless the test is intended to measure these skills. Such adapted tests must be offered as often and in as timely a way as other admissions tests and must be "administered in facilities that, on the whole, are accessible" to the handicapped (sec. 104.42(b)(3)).

In *Southeastern Community College* v. *Davis,* 442 U.S. 397 (1979), the U.S. Supreme Court issued its first interpretation of Section 504. The case concerned a nursing school applicant who had been denied admission because she is deaf. The Supreme Court ruled that an "otherwise qualified handicapped individual" is one who is qualified *in spite of* (rather than except for) his handicap. Since an applicant's handicap is therefore relevant to his qualification for the program to which he seeks admission, Section 504 does not preclude a college or university from imposing "reasonable physical qualifications" on applicants for admission, where such qualifications are necessary for participation in the school's program. While the HEW (now ED) regulations implementing Section 504 provide that a handicapped applicant is "qualified" if he meets "the academic and technical standards" for admission the Supreme Court has now made clear that "technical standards" may sometimes encompass reasonable physical requirements. Under *Davis* an applicant's failure to meet such requirements can be a legitimate ground for rejection.

The Court's 9-to-0 ruling was a disappointment to many advocates on behalf of the handicapped, who feared the decision's effects on entry of handicapped persons into academic and professional pursuits and, more generally, on institutional willingness to accommodate the needs of handicapped persons. The impact of *Davis* may be substantially limited, however, by the rather narrow and specific factual context in which the case arose. As set forth by the Court, the facts are as follows:

> Respondent, who suffers from a serious hearing disability, seeks to be trained as a registered nurse. During the 1973–1974 academic year, she was enrolled in the College Parallel program of Southeastern Community College, a state institution that receives federal funds. Respondent hoped to progress to Southeastern's associate degree nursing program, completion of which would make her eligible for state certification as a registered nurse. In the course of her application to the nursing program, she was interviewed by a member of the nursing faculty. It became apparent that respondent had difficulty understanding questions asked, and on inquiry she acknowledged a history of hearing problems and dependence on a hearing aid. She was advised to consult an audiologist.
>
> On the basis of an examination at Duke University Medical Center, respondent was diagnosed as having a "bilateral, sensorineural hearing loss." A change in her hearing aid was recommended, as a result of which it was expected that she would be able to detect sounds "almost as well as a person would who has normal hearing." But this improvement would not mean that she could discriminate among sounds sufficiently to understand normal spoken speech. Her lipreading skills would remain necessary for effective communication: "While wearing the hearing aid, she is well aware of gross sounds occurring in the listening environment. However, she can only be responsible for speech spoken to her, when the talker gets her attention and allows her to look directly at the talker."
>
> Southeastern next consulted Mary McRee, executive director of the North Carolina Board of Nursing. On the basis of the audiologist's report, McRee recommended that respondent not be admitted to the nursing program. In McRee's view, respondent's hearing disability made it unsafe for her to practice as a nurse. In addition, it would be impossible for respondent to participate safely in the normal clinical training program, and those modifications that would be necessary to enable safe participation would prevent her from realizing the benefits of the program: "To adjust patient learning experiences in keeping with [respondent's] hearing limitations could, in fact, be the same as denying her full learning to meet the objectives of your nursing programs" [442 U.S. at 400–02].

The U.S. District Court had decided the case in favor of the college, concluding that the plaintiff's handicap "prevents her from safely performing in both her training program and her proposed profession" and that she therefore was not "otherwise qualified" under Section 504 (424 F. Supp. 1341 (E.D.N.C. 1976)). The U.S. Court of Appeals had reversed, concluding that the district court had erred in taking the plaintiff's handicap into account in determining whether she was "otherwise qualified" (574 F.2d 1158 (4th Cir. 1978)). Determining that the district court had the better of the argument, the Supreme Court reversed the appellate court:

Section 504 by its terms does not compel educational institutions to disregard the disabilities of handicapped individuals or to make substantial modifications in their programs to allow disabled persons to participate. Instead, it requires only that an "otherwise qualified handicapped individual" not be excluded from participation in a federally funded program "solely by reason of his handicap," indicating only that mere possession of a handicap is not a permissible ground for assuming an inability to function in a particular context.

The court [of appeals], however, believed that the "otherwise qualified" persons protected by Section 504 include those who would be able to meet the requirements of a particular program in every respect except as to limitations imposed by their handicap. Taken literally, this holding would prevent an institution from taking into account any limitation resulting from the handicap, however disabling. It assumes, in effect, that a person need not meet legitimate physical requirements in order to be "otherwise qualified." We think the understanding of the district court is closer to the plain meaning of the statutory language. An otherwise qualified person is one who is able to meet all of a program's requirements in spite of his handicap.

The regulations promulgated by the Department of Health, Education and Welfare (HEW) to interpret Section 504 reinforce, rather than contradict, this conclusion. According to these regulations, a "qualified handicapped person" is, "with respect to postsecondary and vocational education services, a handicapped person who meets the academic and technical standards requisite to admission or participation in the [school's] education program or activity" (45 C.F.R. sec. 84.3(k)(3) (1978) [now 34 C.F.R. sec. 104.3(k)(3)]). An explanatory note states: "The term 'technical standards' refers to *all* nonacademic admissions criteria that are essential to participation in the program in question" (45 C.F.R. Part 84, App. A, at p. 405 (emphasis supplied)). A further note emphasizes that legitimate physical qualifications may be essential to participation in particular programs. We think it clear, therefore, that HEW interprets the "other" qualifications which a handicapped person may be required to meet as including necessary physical qualifications [442 U.S. at 405–07].

Thus concluding that Section 504 does not preclude the use of all physical requirements for admission, the Court went on to consider their use in the circumstances of the *Davis* case. In doing so, the Court put to rest the argument that Section 504 imposes a general "affirmative action obligation" on all federal fund recipients:

It is not open to dispute that, as Southeastern's associate degree nursing program currently is constituted, the ability to understand speech without reliance on lipreading is necessary for patient safety during the clinical phase of the program. As the district court found, this ability also is indispensable for many of the functions that a registered nurse performs.

Respondent contends nevertheless that Section 504, properly interpreted, compels Southeastern to undertake affirmative action that would dispense with the need for effective oral communication. First, it is suggested that respondent can be given individual supervision by faculty members whenever she attends patients directly. Moreover, certain required courses might be dispensed with altogether for respondent. It is not necessary, she argues, that Southeastern train her to undertake all the tasks a registered nurse is licensed to perform. Rather, it is sufficient to make Section 504 applicable if respondent might be able to perform satisfactorily some of the duties of a registered nurse or to hold some of the positions available to a registered nurse.

Respondent finds support for this argument in portions of the HEW regulations discussed above. In particular, a provision applicable to postsecondary educational programs requires covered institutions to make "modifications" in their programs to accommodate handicapped persons, and to provide "auxiliary aids" such as sign-language interpreters. Respondent argues that this regulation imposes an obligation to ensure full participation in covered programs by handicapped individuals and, in particular, requires Southeastern to make the kind of adjustments that would be necessary to permit her safe participation in the nursing program.

We note first that on the present record it appears unlikely respondent could benefit from any affirmative action that the regulation reasonably could be interpreted as requiring. Section 84.44(d)(2), for example, explicitly excludes "devices or services of a personal nature" from the kinds of auxiliary aids a school must provide a handicapped individual. Yet the only evidence in the record indicates that nothing less than close, individual attention by a nursing instructor would be sufficient to ensure patient safety if respondent took part in the clinical phase of the nursing program. Furthermore, it also is reasonably clear that Section 84.44(a) does not encompass the kind of curricular changes that would be necessary to accommodate respondent in the nursing program. In light of respondent's inability to function in clinical courses without close supervision, Southeastern with prudence could allow her to take only academic classes. Whatever benefits respondent might realize from such a course of study, she would not receive even a rough equivalent of the training a nursing program normally gives. Such a fundamental alteration in the nature of a program is far more than the "modification" the regulation requires.

Moreover, an interpretation of the regulations that required the extensive modifications necessary to include respondent in the nursing program would raise grave doubts about their validity. If these regulations were to require substantial adjustments in existing programs beyond those necessary to eliminate discrimination against otherwise qualified individuals, they would do more than clarify the meaning of Section 504. Instead, they would constitute an unauthorized extension of the obligations imposed by that statute.

The language and structure of the Rehabilitation Act of 1973 reflect a recognition by Congress of the distinction between the evenhanded treatment of qualified handicapped persons and affirmative efforts to overcome the disabilities caused by handicaps. . . . Congress understood [that] accommodation of the needs of handicapped individuals may require affirmative action and knew how to provide for it in those instances where it wished to do so. . . .

Here neither the language, purpose, nor history of Section 504 reveals an intent to impose an affirmative action obligation on all recipients of federal funds. Accordingly, we hold that, even if HEW has attempted to create such an obligation itself, it lacks the authority to do so [442 U.S. at 407–11].

The Court concluded with a final word about the extent of the obligation that Section 504 imposes on postsecondary institutions:

> We do not suggest that the line between a lawful refusal to extend affir-mative action and illegal discrimination against handicapped persons always will be clear. It is possible to envision situations where an insistence on con-tinuing past requirements and practices might arbitrarily deprive genuinely qualified handicapped persons of the opportunity to participate in a covered program. Technological advances can be expected to enhance opportunities to rehabilitate the handicapped or otherwise to qualify them for some useful employment. Such advances also may enable attainment of these goals without imposing undue financial and administrative burdens upon a state. Thus, situations may arise where a refusal to modify an existing program might become unreasonable and discriminatory. Identification of those instances where a refusal to accommodate the needs of a disabled person amounts to discrimination against the handicapped continues to be an important respon-sibility of HEW.
>
> In this case, however, it is clear that Southeastern's unwillingness to make major adjustments in its nursing program does not constitute such discrimination. The uncontroverted testimony of several members of Southeastern's staff and faculty established that the purpose of its program was to train persons who could serve the nursing profession in all customary ways. This type of purpose, far from reflecting any animus against handi-capped individuals, is shared by many if not most of the institutions that train persons to render professional service. It is undisputed that respondent could not participate in Southeastern's nursing program unless the standards were substantially lowered. Section 504 imposes no requirement upon an educa-tional institution to lower or to effect substantial modifications of standards to accommodate a handicapped person. . . .
>
> Nothing in the language or history of Section 504 reflects an intention to limit the freedom of an educational institution to require reasonable physical qualifications for admission to a clinical training program. Nor has there been any showing in this case that any action short of a substantial change in Southeastern's program would render unreasonable the qualifications it im-posed [442 U.S. at 412–14].

In determining the reach of the Court's ruling, it is important to emphasize that *Davis* involved admission to a *professional, clinical* training program. The demands of such a program, designed to train students in the practice of a profession, raise far different considerations from those involved in admission to an undergraduate or a graduate academic program, or even a nonclinically oriented professional school.

While the Court approved the imposition of "reasonable physical qualifications," it did so only for requirements that the institution can justify as *necessary* to the applicant's successful participation in the particular program involved. The trial court record in *Davis* substantiated the college's determination that an applicant's ability to understand speech without reliance on lipreading is necessary to ensure patient safety and to enable the student to realize the full benefit of its nursing program. For programs without clinical components, or without professional training goals, it would be much more difficult for the institution to justify such physical requirements. Even for other professional programs, the justification may be much more difficult than in *Davis*. In a law school program, for example, the safety factor would be lacking. Moreover, in most law schools, clinical training is offered as an elective rather than a required course. By enrolling only in the nonclinical courses, a deaf student would be able to successfully complete the required program with the help of an interpreter.

Furthermore, the Court did not say that affirmative action is *never* required to accommodate the needs of handicapped applicants. Although the Court asserted that Section 504 does not require institutions "to lower or to effect substantial modifications of standards" or to make "fundamental alteration[s] in the nature of a program," the Court did suggest that less substantial and burdensome program adjustments may sometimes be required. The Court also discussed, and did not question, the regulation requiring institutions to provide certain "auxiliary aids," such as interpreters for the deaf, to qualified handicapped students (see Sections 4.3.7 and 7.5.4). Moreover, the Court said nothing that in any way precludes institutions from voluntarily making major program modifications for handicapped applicants if they choose to do so.

Several appellate court cases have applied the teachings of *Davis* to other admissions problems. The courts in these cases have added new refinements to the *Davis* analysis, especially in clarifying the burdens of proof in a discrimination suit under Section 504. In *Pushkin* v. *Regents of the University of Colorado*, 658 F.2d 1372 (10th Cir. 1981), the court affirmed the district court's decision that the plaintiff, a medical doctor suffering from multiple sclerosis, had been wrongfully denied admission to the university's psychiatric residency program. Agreeing that *Davis* permitted consideration of handicaps in determining whether an applicant is "otherwise qualified" for admission, the court outlined what the plaintiff had to prove in order to establish his case of discrimination:

> 1. The plaintiff must establish a prima facie case by showing that he was an otherwise qualified handicapped person *apart from* his handicap, and was rejected under circumstances which gave rise to the inference that his rejection was based solely on his handicap.
>
> 2. Once plaintiff establishes his prima facie case, defendants have the burden of going forward and proving that plaintiff was not an otherwise qualified handicapped person—that is, one who is able to meet all of the program's requirements *in spite of* his handicap—or that his rejection from the program was for reasons other than his handicap.
>
> 3. The plaintiff then has the burden of going forward with rebuttal evidence showing that the defendants' reasons for rejecting the plaintiff are based on misconceptions or unfounded factual conclusions, and that reasons

articulated for the rejection other than the handicap encompass unjustified consideration of the handicap itself [658 F.2d at 1387].

In another post-*Davis* case, *Doe* v. *New York University,* 666 F.2d 761 (2d Cir. 1981), the court held that the university had not violated Section 504 when it denied readmission to a woman with a long history of "borderline personality" disorders. This court also set out the elements of the case a plaintiff must make to comply with the *Davis* reading of Section 504:

> Accordingly, we hold that in a suit under Section 504 the plaintiff may make out a prima facie case by showing that he is a handicapped person under the Act and that, although he is qualified apart from his handicap, he was denied admission or employment because of his handicap. The burden then shifts to the institution or employer to rebut the inference that the handicap was improperly taken into account by going forward with evidence that the handicap is relevant to qualifications for the position sought (cf. *Dothard* v. *Rawlinson,* 433 U.S. 321, 97 S. Ct. 2720, 53 L. Ed. 2d 786 (1977)). The plaintiff must then bear the ultimate burden of showing by a preponderance of the evidence that in spite of the handicap he is qualified and, where the defendant claims and comes forward with some evidence that the plaintiff's handicap renders him less qualified than other successful applicants, that he is at least as well qualified as other applicants who were accepted [666 F.2d at 776–77].

The *Doe* summary of burdens of proof is articulated differently from the *Pushkin* summary, and the *Doe* court disavowed any reliance on *Pushkin*. In contrast to the *Pushkin* court, the *Doe* court determined that a defendant institution in a Section 504 case "does not have the burden, once it shows that the handicap is relevant to reasonable qualifications for readmission (or admission), of proving that . . . [the plaintiff] is not an otherwise qualified handicapped person" (666 F.2d at 777 n.7).

The *Doe* case is also noteworthy because, in deciding whether the plaintiff was "otherwise qualified," the court considered the fact that she had a recurring illness, even thought it was not present at the time of the readmission decision. This was an appropriate factor to consider because the illness could reappear and affect her performance after readmission:

> The crucial question to be resolved in determining whether Doe is "otherwise qualified" under the Act is the substantiality of the risk that her mental disturbances will recur, resulting in behavior harmful to herself and others. The district court adopted as its test that she must be deemed qualified if it appeared "more likely than not" that she could complete her medical training and serve as a physician without recurrence of her self-destructive and antisocial conduct. We disagree with this standard. In our view she would not be qualified for readmission if there is a significant risk of such recurrence. It would be unreasonable to infer that Congress intended to force institutions to accept or readmit persons who pose a significant risk of harm to themselves or others, even if the chances of harm were less than 50 percent. Indeed, even if she presents any appreciable risk of such

harm, this factor could properly be taken into account in deciding whether, among qualified applicants, it rendered her less qualified than others for the limited number of places available. In view of the seriousness of the harm inflicted in prior episodes, NYU is not required to give preference to her over other qualified applicants who do not pose any such appreciable risk at all [666 F.2d at 777].

Doe is thus the first major case to deal directly with the special problem of handicapping conditions that are recurring or degenerative. The question posed by such a case is this: To what extent must the university assume the risk that an applicant capable of meeting program requirements *at the time of admission* may be incapable of fulfilling these requirements *at a later date* because of changes in his handicapping conditions? *Doe* makes clear that universities may weigh such risks in making admission or readmission decisions and may consider an applicant unqualified if there is "significant risk" of recurrence (or degeneration) that would incapacitate him from fulfilling program requirements. This risk factor thus becomes a relevant consideration for both parties in carrying their respective burdens of proof in Section 504 litigation. In appropriate cases, where there is medical evidence for doing so, universities may respond to the plaintiff's prima facie case by substantiating the risk of recurrence or degeneration that would render the applicant unqualified. The plaintiff would then have to demonstrate that his condition is sufficiently stable or, if it is not, that any change during his enrollment as a student would not render him unable to complete program requirements.

Another case interpreting Section 504 in light of *Davis* is *Kling* v. *County of Los Angeles*, 633 F.2d 876 (9th Cir. 1980). The court granted a preliminary injunction admitting the plaintiff, who suffered from Crohn's disease, into the defendant's school of nursing pending the completion of litigation. The school did not argue that the plaintiff failed to meet its admissions requirements but rather that, because of her handicap, she would miss too many classes. In rejecting the school's argument, the court relied on the opinion of the plaintiff's physician that she would be able to complete the program and that hospitalization, if necessary, could be planned to minimize interruptions in her schooling.

In sum, postsecondary administrators should still proceed very sensitively in making admissions decisions concerning handicapped persons. *Davis* can be expected to have the greatest impact on professional and paraprofessional health care programs; beyond that, the circumstances in which physical requirements for admission may be used are unclear. Furthermore, while *Davis* relieves colleges and universities of any obligation to make substantial modifications in their program requirements, a refusal to make lesser modifications may in some instances constitute discrimination. Administrators and counsel should watch for further litigation involving different factual settings, as well as for possible new policy interpretations by the Department of Education.

4.2.4.4. Age. In *Massachusetts Board of Retirement* v. *Murgia*, 427 U.S. 367 (1976), the U.S. Supreme Court held that age discrimination is not subject to the high standard of justification that the Constitution requires, for instance, for race discrimination. Rather, age classifications are permissible if they "rationally further" some legitimate governmental objective. Although the Court in *Murgia* called this a "relatively relaxed standard" of review, it will not necessarily serve to uphold all public institution admissions policies that discriminate by age. In *Miller* v. *Sonoma County Junior College District*, No. C-74-0222 (N.D. Cal. 1974) (unpublished opinion decided before *Murgia*), for example, two sixteen-year-old students won the right to attend a California junior college. The court held that the college's minimum-age requirement of eighteen was an arbitrary and irrational basis for exclusion because not related to the state's interest in providing education to qualified students.

In *Purdie* v. *University of Utah*, 584 P.2d 831 (Utah 1978), a case that can usefully be compared with *Miller*, the court considered the constitutional claim of a fifty-one-year-old woman who had been denied admission to the university's department of educational psychology. Whereas the *Miller* plaintiffs were allegedly too young for admission, Purdie was allegedly too old. But in both cases the courts used the equal protection clause to limit the institution's discretion to base admissions decisions on age. In *Purdie* the plaintiff alleged, and the university did not deny, that she exceeded the normal admissions requirements and was rejected solely because of her age. The trial court held that her complaint did not state a viable legal claim and dismissed the suit. On appeal the Utah Supreme Court reversed, holding that rejection of a qualified fifty-one-year-old would violate equal protection unless the university could show that its action bore a "rational relationship to legitimate state purposes." Since the abbreviated trial record contained no evidence of the department's admissions standards or its policy regarding age, the court remanded the case to the trial court for further proceedings.

Both public and private institutions that receive federal funds are subject to the federal Age Discrimination Act of 1975, 42 U.S.C. sec. 6101 *et seq*. Section 6101 of the Act, with certain exceptions listed in Sections 6103(b) and 6103(c), originally prohibited "unreasonable discrimination on the basis of age in programs or activities receiving federal financial assistance." In 1978 Congress deleted the word "unreasonable" from the Act (see this volume, Section 7.5.5), thus lowering the statute's tolerance for discrimination and presumably making its standards more stringent than the Constitution's "rationality" standard used in *Purdie*. As amended and interpreted in the implementing regulations (45 C.F.R. Part 90), the ADA clearly applies to the admissions policies of postsecondary institutions.

The age discrimination regulations, however, do not prohibit all age distinctions. Section 90.14 of the regulations permits age distinctions that are necessary to the "normal operation" of, or to the achievement of a "statutory objective" of, a program or activity receiving federal financial assistance (see this volume, Section 7.5.5). Moreover, Section 90.15 of the regulations permits recipients to take an action based on a factor other than age—"even though that action may have a disproportionate effect on persons of different ages"—if the factor has a "direct and substantial relationship" to the program's operation or goals. The practical impact of these provisions on admissions policies is illustrated by two examples in the explanatory commentary accompanying the regulations:

> 1. A medical school receiving federal financial assistance generally does not admit anyone over 35 years of age, even though this results in turning away highly qualified applicants over 35. The school claims it has an objective, the teaching of qualified medical students who, upon graduation, will practice as long as possible. The school believes that this objective requires it to select younger applicants over older ones. The use of

such an age distinction *is not necessary* to normal operation of the recipient's program because it does not meet the requirement of Section 90.14(b). Age of the applicant may be a reasonable measure of a nonage characteristic (longevity of practice). This characteristic may be impractical to measure directly on an individual basis. Nevertheless, achieving a high average of longevity of practice cannot be considered a program objective for a medical school within the meaning of the Act. The "normal operation" exception is not intended to permit a recipient to use broad notions of efficiency or cost-benefit analysis to justify exclusion from a program on the basis of age. The basic objectives of the medical school involve training competent and qualified medical school graduates. These objectives are not impaired if the average length its graduates practice medicine is lowered by a fraction of a year (or even more) by the admission of qualified applicants over 35 years of age.

2. A federally assisted training program uses a physical fitness test as a factor for selecting participants to train for a certain job. The job involves frequent heavy lifting and other demands for physical strength and stamina. Even though older persons might fail the test more frequently than younger persons, the physical fitness test measures a characteristic that is *directly and substantially* related to the job for which persons are being trained and is, therefore, permissible under the Act [44 Fed. Reg. 33773–74 (June 12, 1979)].

State law also occasionally prohibits age discrimination against students. In its Fair Educational Practices statute, for example, Massachusetts prohibits age discrimination in admissions to graduate programs and vocational training institutions (Mass. Gen. Laws Ann. ch. 151C, secs. 2(d), 2A(a)).

Taken together, the Constitution, the federal law and regulations, and occasional state laws now appear to create a substantial legal barrier to the use of either maximum- or minimum-age policies in admissions. The federal ADA, applicable to both public and private institutions with federally funded programs or activities, is the most important of these developments; administrators should watch for further implementation of this statute via individual agency regulations.

4.2.5. Affirmative action programs. A particularly sensitive area of concern for postsecondary administrators is affirmative action programs. Designed to increase the number of minority persons admitted to educational programs, affirmative action policies pose delicate social and legal questions. Educators have agonized over the extent to which the social goal of greater minority representation justifies the admission of less or differently qualified applicants into educational programs, particularly in the professions, while courts have grappled with the complaints of qualified but rejected nonminority applicants who claim to be victims of "reverse discrimination" because minority applicants were admitted in preference to them. Though two cases have reached the U.S. Supreme Court, *DeFunis* and *Bakke* (both discussed later), neither case established comprehensive requirements regarding affirmative action. But the varied opinions of the justices in the *Bakke* decision, 438 U.S. 265 (1978), contain valuable insight and guidance concerning the legal and social issues of affirmative action. Read together with two lower court cases (discussed below) that followed it, *Bakke* forms a baseline against which all affirmative action programs should be measured.

The legal issues can be cast in both constitutional and statutory terms and apply to both public and private institutions. The constitutional issues, pertaining only to public institutions, arise under the Fourteenth Amendment's equal protection clause. The statutory issues arise under Title VI of the Civil Rights Act of 1964 and Title IX of the Education Amendments of 1972, which prohibit race and sex discrimination by public and private institutions receiving federal funds (see Sections 4.2.4.1 and 4.2.4.2) and under 42 U.S.C. sec. 1981, which has been construed to prohibit race discrimination in admissions by private schools whether or not they receive federal money (see Section 4.2.4.1). In the *Bakke* case, a majority of the justices agreed that Title VI uses constitutional standards for determining the validity of affirmative action programs (see 438 U.S. at 284–87, 328–41, 414–18). Standards comparable to the Constitution's would presumably also be used for any affirmative action question arising under 42 U.S.C. sec. 1981 or under Title IX. Thus, *Bakke* establishes the foundation for a core of uniform legal parameters for affirmative action, applicable to public and private institutions alike.

Both the Title VI and the Title IX regulations address the subject of affirmative action. These regulations preceded *Bakke* and are brief and somewhat ambiguous. After *Bakke* HEW issued a "policy interpretation" of Title VI, indicating that the department had reviewed its regulations in light of *Bakke* and "concluded that no changes in the regulation are required or desirable" (44 Fed. Reg. 58509, at 58510 (Oct. 10, 1979)). In this policy interpretation, however, HEW did set forth guidelines for applying its affirmative action regulation consistent with *Bakke*.

When an institution has discriminated in the past, the Title VI and Title IX regulations *require* it to implement affirmative action programs to overcome the effects of that discrimination (34 C.F.R. sec. 100.3(b)(6)(i) and 100.5(i); 34 C.F.R. sec. 106.3(a)).[4] When the institution has not discriminated, the regulations nevertheless *permit* affirmative action to overcome the effects of societal discrimination (34 C.F.R. secs. 100.3(b)(6)(ii) and 100.5(i); 34 C.F.R. sec. 106.3(b)). The HEW policy interpretation contains guidelines for such voluntary uses of affirmative action to increase minority student enrollments.

The first case to confront the constitutionality of affirmative action admissions programs in postsecondary education was *DeFunis* v. *Odegaard,* 507 P.2d 1169 (1973), dismissed as moot, 416 U.S. 312 (1973), on remand, 529 P.2d 438 (1974). After DeFunis, a white male, was denied admission to the University of Washington law school, he filed suit alleging that less qualified minority applicants had been accepted and that, but for the affirmative action program, he would have been admitted. He claimed that the university discriminated against him on the basis of his race, in violation of the equal protection clause.

The law school admissions committee had calculated each applicant's predicted first-year average (PFYA) through a formula that considered the applicant's Law School Admissions Test (LSAT) scores and junior-senior undergraduate

---

[4]The department, however, cannot require the institution to use admissions quotas as part of an affirmative action plan. Section 408 of the Education Amendments of 1976, 20 U.S.C. sec. 1232i(c), provides that:

> It shall be unlawful for the secretary [of education] to defer or limit any federal assistance on the basis of any failure to comply with the imposition of quotas (or any other numerical requirements which have the effect of imposing quotas) on the student admission practices of an institution of higher education or community college receiving federal financial assistance.

average. The committee had attached less importance to a minority applicant's PFYA and had considered minority applications separately from other applications. Although the committee accepted minority applicants whose PFYAs were lower than those of other applicants, in no case did it accept any person whose record indicated that he or she would not be able to complete the program successfully. The committee established no quotas; rather, its goal was the inclusion of a reasonable representation of minority groups. DeFunis's PFYA was higher than those of all but one of the minority applicants admitted in the year he was rejected.

The state trial court ordered that DeFunis be admitted, and he entered the law school. The Washington State Supreme Court reversed the lower court and upheld the law school's affirmative action program as a constitutionally acceptable admissions tool justified by several "compelling" state interests. Among them were the "interest in promoting integration in public education," the "educational interest . . . in producing a racially balanced student body at the law school," and the interest in alleviating "the shortage of minority attorneys—and, consequently, minority prosecutors, judges, and public officials."

When DeFunis sought review in the U.S. Supreme Court, he was permitted to remain in school pending the Court's final disposition of the case. Subsequently, in a *per curiam* opinion with four justices dissenting, the Court declared the case moot because, by then, DeFunis was in his final quarter of law school and the university had asserted that his registration would remain effective regardless of the case's final outcome. The Court vacated the Washington State Supreme Court's judgment and remanded the case to that court for appropriate disposition. Though the *per curiam* opinion does not discuss the merits of the case, Justice Douglas's dissent presents a thought-provoking analysis of affirmative action in admissions:

> The equal protection clause did not enact a requirement that law schools employ as the sole criterion for admissions a formula based upon the LSAT and undergraduate grades, nor does it prohibit law schools from evaluating an applicant's prior achievements in light of the barriers that he had to overcome. A black applicant who pulled himself out of the ghetto into a junior college may thereby demonstrate a level of motivation, perseverance, and ability that would lead a fair-minded admissions committee to conclude that he shows more promise for law study than the son of a rich alumnus who achieved better grades at Harvard. That applicant would be offered admission not because he is black but because as an individual he has shown he has the potential, while the Harvard man may have taken less advantage of the vastly superior opportunities offered him. Because of the weight of the prior handicaps, that black applicant may not realize his full potential in the first year of law school, or even in the full three years, but in the long pull of a legal career his achievements may far outstrip those of his classmates whose earlier records appeared superior by conventional criteria. There is currently no test available to the admissions committee that can predict such possibilities with assurance, but the committee may nevertheless seek to gauge it as best it can and weigh this factor in its decisions. Such a policy would not be limited to blacks, or Chicanos, or Filipinos, or American Indians, although undoubtedly groups such as these may in practice be the principal beneficiaries of it. But a poor

Appalachian white, or a second-generation Chinese in San Francisco, or some other American whose lineage is so diverse as to defy ethnic labels, may demonstrate similar potential and thus be accorded favorable consideration by the committee.

The difference between such a policy and the one presented by this case is that the committee would be making decisions on the basis of individual attributes, rather than according a preference solely on the basis of race. To be sure, the racial preference here was not absolute—the committee did not admit all applicants from the four favored groups. But it did accord all such applicants a preference by applying, to an extent not precisely ascertainable from the record, different standards by which to judge their applications, with the result that the committee admitted minority applicants who, in the school's own judgment, were less promising than other applicants who were rejected. Furthermore, it is apparent that because the admissions committee compared minority applicants only with one another, it was necessary to reserve some proportion of the class for them, even if at the outset a precise number of places were not set aside. That proportion, apparently 15 to 20 percent, was chosen because the school determined it to be "reasonable," although no explanation is provided as to how that number rather than some other was found appropriate. Without becoming embroiled in a semantic debate over whether this practice constitutes a "quota," it is clear that given the limitation on the total number of applicants who could be accepted, this policy did reduce the total number of places for which DeFunis could compete—solely on account of his race [416 U.S. at 331–33].

Justice Douglas did not conclude that the university's policy was therefore unconstitutional but, rather, that it would be unconstitutional unless, after a new trial, the court found that it took account of "cultural standards of a diverse rather than a homogeneous society" in a "racially neutral" way.

Five years after it avoided the issue in *DeFunis,* the Supreme Court addressed the legality of affirmative action in *Regents of the University of California* v. *Bakke,* 438 U.S. 265 (1978). The plaintiff, a white male twice rejected from the medical school of the University of California at Davis, had challenged the affirmative action program that the school used to select a portion of its entering class each year that he was rejected. The particular facts concerning this program's operation were critical to its legality and were subject to dispute in the court proceedings. They are best taken from Justice Powell's opinion in the U.S. Supreme Court, in a passage with which a majority of the justices agreed:

The faculty devised a special admissions program to increase the representation of "disadvantaged" students in each medical school class. The special program consisted of a separate admissions system operating in coordination with the regular admissions process. . . .

The special admissions program operated with a separate committee, a majority of whom were members of minority groups. On the 1973 application form, candidates were asked to indicate whether they wished to be considered as "economically and/or educationally disadvantaged" applicants;

on the 1974 form, the question was whether they wished to be considered as members of a "minority group," which the medical school apparently viewed as "blacks," "Chicanos," "Asians," and "American Indians." If these questions were answered affirmatively, the application was forwarded to the special admissions commitee. No formal definition of "disadvantaged" was ever produced, but the chairman of the special committee screened each application to see whether it reflected economic or educational deprivation. Having passed this initial hurdle, the applications then were rated by the special committee in a fashion similar to that used by the general admissions committee, except that special candidates did not have to meet the 2.5 grade point average cutoff applied to regular applicants. About one fifth of the total number of special applicants were invited for interviews in 1973 and 1974. Following each interview, the special committee assigned each special applicant a benchmark score. The special committee then presented its top choices to the general admissions committee. The latter did not rate or compare the special candidates against the general applicants but could reject recommended special candidates for failure to meet course requirements or other specific deficiencies. The special committee continued to recommend special applicants until a number prescribed by faculty vote were admitted. While the overall class size was still fifty, the prescribed number was eight; in 1973 and 1974, when the class size had doubled to 100, the prescribed number of special admissions also doubled, to sixteen.

From the year of the increase in class size—1971—through 1974, the special program resulted in the admission of twenty-one black students, thirty Mexican-Americans, and twelve Asians, for a total of sixty-three minority students. Over the same period, the regular admissions program produced one black, six Mexican-Americans, and thirty-seven Asians, for a total of forty-four minority students. Although disadvantaged whites applied to the special program in large numbers, none received an offer of admission through that process. Indeed, in 1974 at least, the special committee explicitly considered only "disadvantaged" special applicants who were members of one of the designated minority groups [438 U.S. at 272–76].

The university sought to justify its program by citing the great need for doctors to work in underserved minority communities, the need to compensate for the effects of societal discrimination against minorities, the need to reduce the historical deficit of minorities in the medical profession, and the need to diversify the student body. In analyzing these justifications, the California Supreme Court had applied a compelling state interest test, such as that used in *DeFunis*, along with a "less objectionable alternative test" (*Bakke* v. *Regents of University of California*, 18 Cal. 3d 342, 553 P.2d 1152 (1976)). Although it assumed that the university's interests were compelling, this court held the affirmative action program unconstitutional because the university had not demonstrated that the program was the least burdensome alternative available for achieving its goals. The court suggested these alternatives:

The university is entitled to consider, as it does with respect to applicants in the special program, that low grades and test scores may not accurately reflect the abilities of some disadvantaged students, and it may reasonably conclude that although their academic scores are lower, their potential for success in the school and the profession is equal to or greater than that of an applicant with higher grades who has not been similarly handicapped.

In addition, the university may properly, as it in fact does, consider other factors in evaluating an applicant, such as the personal interview, recommendations, character, and matters relating to the needs of the profession and society, such as an applicant's professional goals. . . .

In addition to flexible admission standards, the university might increase minority enrollment by instituting aggressive programs to identify, recruit, and provide remedial schooling for disadvantaged students of all races who are interested in pursuing a medical career and have an evident talent for doing so.

Another ameliorative measure which may be considered is to increase the number of places available in the medical schools, either by allowing additional students to enroll in existing schools or by expanding the schools. . . .

None of the foregoing measures can be related to race, but they will provide for consideration and assistance to individual applicants who have suffered previous disabilities, regardless of their surname or color [553 P.2d at 1166–67].

Thus concluding that the university's program did not satisfy applicable constitutional tests, the California court held that the program operated to exclude Bakke on account of his race and ordered that Bakke be admitted to medical school. It further held that the Constitution prohibited the university from giving *any* consideration to race in its admissions process and enjoined the university from doing so.

The U.S. Supreme Court affirmed this decision in part and reversed it in part (438 U.S. 265 (1978)). The justices wrote six opinions (totaling 157 pages), none of which commanded a majority of the Court. Three of these opinions deserve particular consideration: (1) Justice Powell's opinion—in some parts of which various of the other justices joined; (2) Justice Brennan's opinion—in which Justices White, Marshall, and Blackmun joined (referred to below as the "Brennan group"); and (3) Justice Stevens's opinion—in which Justices Stewart, Rehnquist, and Chief Justice Burger joined (referred to below as the "Stevens group").

A bare majority of the justices, four (the "Stevens group") relying on Title VI and one (Justice Powell) relying on the equal protection clause of the Fourteenth Amendment, agreed that the University of California at Davis program unlawfully discriminated against Bakke, thus affirming the first part of the California court's judgment (ordering Bakke's admission). A different majority of five justices—Justice Powell and the "Brennan group"—agreed that "the state has a substantial interest that legitimately may be served by a properly devised admissions program involving the competitive consideration of race and ethnic origin" (438 U.S. at 320), thus reversing the second part of the California court's judgment (prohibiting the consideration of race in admissions). The various opinions debated the issues of what equal protection tests should apply, how Title VI should be interpreted in this context, what the appropriate justifications for affirmative action programs are, and to what extent such programs can be race conscious. No majority agreed on any of these issues, however, except that Title VI embodies constitutional principles of equal protection (see previous discussion on p. 253).

Since the Supreme Court's decision in *Bakke,* two critically important state court decisions have applied the teachings of the *Bakke* opinions to uphold affirmative action programs of state professional schools in Washington and California. The first of these two cases was *McDonald* v. *Hogness,* 92 Wash. 431, 598 P.2d 707 (1979). The particular facts, like the facts in *Bakke,* were singularly important to the outcome. McDonald, a white male, sought admission to the University of Washington's medical school. After being rejected, he challenged the school's admissions policy as racially discriminatory against whites.

According to its published admissions policy then in effect, the medical school considered candidates "comparatively on the basis of academic performance, medical aptitude, motivation, maturity, and demonstrated humanitarian qualities." Unlike the admissions policy at issue in *Bakke,* the University of Washington's policy did not provide for any separate treatment or consideration of minority applicants. Nor did the policy explicitly recognize race as an admission criterion. It did, however, provide that "extenuating background circumstances are considered as they relate to [the five listed] selection factors." Similarly, the guidelines given members of the school's interviewing committee listed "special considerations, including extenuating circumstances" as one of the criteria for rating applicants. According to the Washington Supreme Court's analysis of the school's admissions practices, the race of applicants could be and was considered under this criterion.

In its opinion the Washington court further described the school's admissions policy and its application to McDonald:

> Medical school personnel believe grade point average (GPA) is the best measure of academic performance, while the Medical College Admissions Test (MCAT) score is the best measure of medical aptitude. Noncognitive criteria—motivation, maturity, and demonstrated humanitarian qualities—are assessed from the applicant's file and the interview. . . .

> The medical school's selection process was aptly summarized by the trial court:

>> The committee on admissions functions simultaneously at three levels.

>> Generally, the paper credentials of each applicant are reviewed independently by two members of the admissions committee. . . . Candidates considered potentially competitive . . . are invited to meet with an interview-conference committee. . . . Interview-conference committees evaluate the candidates' paper credentials and the candidates . . . and forward their evaluations to the executive committee [EXCOM] of the committee on admissions as a part of each . . . application. . . . [The EXCOM], which reviews applicants in the context of the total applicant pool, makes final determinations.

> The "first screen" score calculated upon receipt of an application is based on GPA and MCAT. It is the "bright-line" test for referral to the admissions committee and is considered later by admissions committee application readers and interview-conference committee members. Of the 1,703 applicants, 816 were referred to the reading committee. Interviews were granted to 546 applicants considered potentially competitive by reading committee analyses. . . .

After the twenty- to thirty-minute interview, the candidate is excused and each member [of the interview-conference committee] independently places the applicant in one of four categories: (1) Unacceptable (specific deficiencies); (2) Possible (with comparative deficiencies academically and/or with regard to noncognitive features); (3) Acceptable (no deficiencies that are not balanced by other abilities, would be an average medical student); and (4) Outstanding (no apparent deficiencies, high probability of making an excellent physician and scholar). Following each interview-conference, committee staff calculate an average of the individual committee members' ratings based on a scale of 4 for "outstanding" downward through 1 for "unacceptable." The average is entered on the interview-conference summary.

The Skeletal Consideration List (SCL) serves as a rough agenda for EXCOM selection meetings. Placement is determined by one's total score—first screen score plus interview-conference score—grouped again in categories 4, 3, 2, and 1. Placement in category 2 or 1 nearly always leads to application denial. McDonald averaged 2.17 on the interview and was placed in category 2. His SCL position was at the number 237 level. When corrected for "ties" of 546 candidates interviewed for 175 slots, more than 300 placed higher than McDonald. However, every black, Chicano, and American Indian placing higher than McDonald on the SCL had a lower "first screen" score than he did. On April 30, 1976, EXCOM voted that all candidates not otherwise acted upon, which included McDonald, be considered noncompetitive for the [1976 entering] class and his application was denied [598 P.2d at 709-10].

Noting at the outset that McDonald would not have been admitted even if the race of applicants had not been considered, the court held that this fact alone justified denying relief.[5] But because of the public importance of the case and the likelihood of its recurrence, the court proceeded to address the merits of McDonald's discrimination claim. It based its analysis on the equal protection clause and noted, as a majority of the justices in *Bakke* had held, that an admissions program which was consistent with the Fourteenth Amendment would also be consistent with Title VI of the Civil Rights Act of 1964.

In holding that the medical school's admissions program was constitutional, the court relied heavily on Justice Powell's opinion in *Bakke*. The Washington court read the Powell opinion as discouraging the separate consideration of minority applicants but permitting race to be considered as a factor in an admissions policy when its consideration "(1) is designed to promote a compelling state interest and (2) does not insulate an applicant from competition with remaining applicants." Like Justice Powell, the Washington court acknowledged that the attainment of a diverse student body is a compelling interest because it is central to the university's academic freedom:

[5]Similar problems have been encountered by plaintiffs in other affirmative action cases. In *Henson* v. *University of Arkansas*, 519 F.2d 576 (8th Cir. 1975), for example, the court affirmed the dismissal of the complaint because the petitioner had failed to show that she would have been admitted if no minority admissions program had been in effect. In the *Bakke* case, the California Supreme Court presumed that the plaintiff would have been admitted unless the defendant school could affirmatively show otherwise (18 Cal. 3d at 63-64, 553 P.2d at 1172). The U.S. Supreme Court did not pass on the issue (438 U.S. at 280 nn.13, 14).

The University of Washington argues that the denial of McDonald's application was an exercise of its constitutionally protected freedom to decide who shall be admitted to study. It quotes Mr. Justice Frankfurter's concurring opinion in *Sweezy* v. *New Hampshire,* 354 U.S. 234, 263, 77 S. Ct. 1203, 1218, 1 L. Ed. 2d 1311, 1332 (1957), also quoted by Mr. Justice Powell in *Bakke,* 438 U.S. at 312, 98 S. Ct. at 2760, 57 L. Ed. 2d at 785.

> It is the business of a university to provide that atmosphere which is most conducive to speculation, experiment, and creation. It is an atmosphere in which there prevail "the four essential freedoms" of a university—to determine for itself on academic grounds who may teach, what may be taught, how it shall be taught, and who may be admitted to study.

Like Mr. Justice Powell, we believe that the atmosphere of "speculation, experimentation, and creation" is promoted by a diverse student body. We agree that, in seeking diversity, the U.W. medical school must be viewed "as seeking to achieve a goal that is of paramount importance in the fulfillment of its mission" (438 U.S. at 313, 98 S. Ct. at 2761, 57 L. Ed. 2d at 786). But though a university must have wide discretion in making admission judgments, "constitutional limitations protecting individual rights may not be disregarded" (438 U.S. at 314, 98 S. Ct. at 2761, 57 L. Ed. 2d at 786) [598 P.2d at 712-13 n.7].

The Washington court then compared the medical school's admissions program with another program—the Harvard plan—that had been cited approvingly in *Bakke,* finding the two plans similar:

> In *dicta* Mr. Justice Powell indicates that the Harvard admission plan—which, like the plan here, employs race as an admission factor—furthers a compelling state interest in diversity of the student body (438 U.S. at 316-18, 98 S. Ct. at 2762-63, 57 L. Ed. 2d at 787-89). Justices Brennan, White, Marshall, and Blackmun also found the Harvard plan constitutional under their approach (438 U.S. at 326 n.1, 98 S. Ct. at 2767 n.1, 57 L. Ed. 2d at 793 n.1). Thus, a majority of the Court find constitutional a plan without a quota or separate consideration for minority groups but where race may be a beneficial factor. The University of Washington school of medicine's admission policies and procedures have the same redeeming characteristics [598 P.2d at 713].

For further support, the Washington court also relied on the opinion of Justice Brennan's group of four justices in *Bakke* and its own earlier opinion in *DeFunis:*

> In the second *Bakke* opinion which supports the UW medical school on this issue, Justices Brennan, White, Marshall, and Blackmun pronounce the [University of California at] Davis program constitutionally valid. In their opinion, the state need only show [that the racial criterion] (1) serves an important, articulated purpose, (2) does not stigmatize any discrete group, and (3) is reasonably used in light of the program's objectives (438 U.S.

at 361, 373–74, 98 S. Ct. at 2785, 2791, 57 L. Ed. 2d at 816, 823). The Brennan group believes Davis's goal of admitting students disadvantaged by effects of past discrimination is sufficiently important. They reasonably read Mr. Justice Powell's opinion as agreeing [that] this can constitute a compelling purpose (438 U.S. at 366 n.42, 98 S. Ct. at 2787 n.42, 57 L. Ed. 2d at 819 n.42).

In *DeFunis* v. *Odegaard,* 82 Wash. 2d 11, 507 P.2d 1169 (1973), this court rejected the argument that a state law school violated equal protection rights by denying plaintiff admission, yet accepting minority applicants with lower objective indicators than plaintiff. We stressed gross underrepresentation in law schools and the legal profession in finding an overriding interest in promoting integration in public education. We held [that] the interest in eliminating racial imbalance within public legal education is compelling (82 Wash. 2d at 33, 507 P.2d 1169).

In the instant case, the trial court determined the school had decided that, in order to serve the educational needs of the school and the medical needs of the region, the school should seek greater representation of minorities "where there has been serious underrepresentation in the school and in the medical profession." Thus, the program furthers a compelling purpose of eliminating racial imbalance within public medical education.

Furthermore, the program here meets the additional elements of the Brennan group's test. The racial classification does not stigmatize any discrete group and is reasonably used in light of its objectives [598 P.2d at 713–14].

The court in *McDonald* thus accepted the authority of both the Powell and the Brennan-group opinions in *Bakke,* holding that the University of Washington plan meets the tests established by each of these opinions. In so doing the court also accepted two separate interests—attainment of a diverse student body and elimination of racial imbalance by admitting minority students disadvantaged by past societal discrimination—as compelling interests that can justify the use of affirmative action plans.

The second affirmative action case, to be read in tandem with *McDonald,* is *DeRonde* v. *Regents of the University of California,* 28 Cal. 3d 875, 625 P.2d 220 (1981). The plaintiff was an unsuccessful applicant for admission to King Hall, the University of California at Davis law school. Following his rejection, the plaintiff was accepted at and graduated from a different law school and admitted to the state bar. The California court chose not to dismiss the case as moot, however, citing the need for "appellate resolution of important issues of substantial and continuing public interest."

The court first examined the operation of the law school's admissions policy:

The record discloses that, in selecting candidates for admission to King Hall in 1975, the university relied principally on a formula which combined an applicant's previous academic grade point average (GPA) with his or her score on the standardized Law School Admissions Test (LSAT). This formula yielded a predicted first-year average (PFYA) which, it was hoped, measured, at least roughly, the applicant's potential for law study.

Believing, however, that the foregoing formula tended to ignore other significant and relevant selection factors, the university considered several additional background elements to supplement or mitigate a lower PFYA. These factors included (1) growth, maturity, and commitment to law study (as shown by prior employment, extracurricular and community activities, advanced degrees or studies, and personal statements and recommendations); (2) factors which, while no longer present, had affected previous academic grades (such as temporary physical handicaps or disruptive changes in school or environment); (3) wide discrepancies between grades and test scores where there was indicated evidence of substantial ability and motivation; (4) rigor of undergraduate studies; (5) economic disadvantage; and (6) "ethnic minority status" contributing to diversity.

It is the consideration by the university of the final factor, "ethnic minority status," which is the principal target of DeRonde's attack. Trial testimony established that "ethnic minority status" was defined by the university as including Asians, blacks, Chicanos, Native Americans, and Filipinos. This grouping generally corresponds to the ethnic categories defined by the federal Equal Employment Opportunity Commission in its public reports. The record reflects that the university's reasons for considering minority status were primarily twofold: First, an appreciable minority representation in the student body will contribute a valuable cultural diversity for both faculty and students; and, second, a minority representation in the legal pool from which future professional and community leaders, public and private, are drawn will strengthen and preserve minority participation in the democratic process at all levels. In short, it was believed that the individual and group learning experience is enriched with broadly beneficial consequences both to the profession and to the public at large. We carefully emphasize that, although minority status was included as one of several pertinent selection factors, the university did not employ any quota system or reserve a fixed number of positions for any minority applicants in its entering class.

Just as a relatively low PFYA might be increased by utilization of any of the foregoing factors, alternatively, a relatively high PFYA could be reduced by considering (1) the applicant's prior schools attended, (2) the difficulty of his or her prior course of study, (3) variations in an applicant's multiple LSAT scores, (4) the absence of any factors indicating maturity or motivation, and (5) the applicant's advanced age.

As a consequence of this formulation, in 1975 the 406 students to whom the university offered admission included 135 minority applicants, and more than 1,800 applicants, including DeRonde, were rejected. DeRonde's 3.47 GPA and 575 LSAT score produced a 2.70 PFYA. The PFYAs of successful applicants ranged from 2.24 to 3.43. Sixty-nine minority applicants were accepted with PFYAs lower than DeRonde's. On the other hand, the more than 800 unsuccessful applicants who had higher PFYAs than DeRonde included 35 minority applicants [625 P.2d at 222–23].

Noting that the *McDonald* court had employed similar analysis, the *DeRonde* court focused on the equal protection clause and began its analysis by referring to Justice Powell's *Bakke* opinion. The court then compared the Davis program to the Harvard plan discussed by Justice Powell and similarly found it acceptable:

> In our view the admissions procedures used by the university to select its 1975 entering class at King Hall does not vary in any significant way from the Harvard program. Minority racial or ethnic origin was one of several competing factors used by the university to reach its ultimate decision whether or not to admit a particular applicant. Each application, as contemplated by the program, was individually examined and evaluated in the light of the various positive and negative admission factors. As Justice Powell pointedly observed, the primary and obvious defect in the quota system in *Bakke* was that it *precluded* individualized consideration of every applicant without regard to race (438 U.S. at 317–18 and n.52, 98 S. Ct. at 2762 and n.52). That fatal flaw does not appear in the admissions procedure before us. This is not a quota case. Thus, we conclude that the race-attentive admissions procedure used by the university in 1975 would have passed federal constitutional muster under the standards prescribed by Justice Powell in *Bakke* [625 P.2d at 225].

The *DeRonde* court then turned, as had the *McDonald* court, to Justice Brennan's opinion:

> The Brennan opinion, representing the views of four justices, would have upheld the Davis quota system invalidated by the majority in *Bakke.* It may fairly be concluded that a race-conscious law school admissions program that did not involve a quota, *a fortiori,* would be sustained by those holding the Brennan view [625 P.2d at 225].

The court noted that the Brennan group had also explicitly approved the Harvard plan but had focused on different interests than those relied on by Powell:

> Justice Brennan "agree[d] with Mr. Justice Powell that a plan like the 'Harvard' plan . . . is constitutional under our approach, at least so long as the use of race to achieve an integrated student body is necessitated by the lingering effects of past discrimination" (438 U.S. at 326, n.1, 98 S. Ct. at 2766, n.1; see also 438 U.S. at 378–79, 98 S. Ct. at 2793 (expressing the view that the Harvard plan is "no more or less constitutionally acceptable" than the Davis quota system ruled invalid by the majority)). Justice Brennan expands the foregoing requirement of a past discriminatory effect and would hold that even a racial quota system such as involved in *Bakke* was constitutional if its purpose "is to remove the disparate racial impact [the university's] actions might otherwise have and if there is reason to believe that the disparate impact is itself the product of past discrimination, whether its own or that of society at large" [625 P.2d at 225, quoting 438 U.S. at 369].

Since the *DeRonde* trial had preceded the United States Supreme Court's *Bakke* opinions, the issue whether the university's admissions program was "necessitated by the lingering effects of past discrimination'' was neither framed nor litigated by the parties. The court nevertheless studied the record and found evidence that a race-conscious admissions program was needed to prevent a disproportionate under-representation of minorities at King Hall. The primary evidence was the testimony of a former dean of the law school, who ''stressed that if admission selection was based solely upon numbers (i.e., GPA and LSAT scores), 'the greatest bulk of the minority applicants' would be excluded.'' The court then looked to the Brennan opinion to develop a nexus between past societal discrimination and present under-representation of minorities:

> Finally, the existence of a nexus between past discrimination and present disproportionate academic and professional underrepresentation was fully acknowledged in the Brennan opinion itself, wherein it was readily assumed that societal discrimination against minorities has impaired their access to equal educational opportunity. As the opinion states, ''Davis clearly could conclude that the serious and persistent underrepresentation of minorities in medicine . . . *is the result of handicaps under which minority applicants labor as a consequence of a background of deliberate, purposeful discrimination against minorities in education and in society generally,* as well as in the medical profession (438 U.S. at 370–71, 98 S. Ct. at 2788–89). . . . Judicial decrees recognizing discrimination in public education in California testify to the fact of widespread discrimination suffered by California-born minority applicants. . . . The conclusion is inescapable that applicants to medical school must be few indeed who endured the effects of *de jure* segregation, the resistance to *Brown I* [*Brown* v. *Board of Education* (1954), 347 U.S. 483, 74 S. Ct. 686, 98 L. Ed. 873], or the equally debilitating pervasive private discrimination fostered by our long history of official discrimination, and yet come to the starting line with an education equal to whites'' (438 U.S. at 372, 98 S. Ct. at 2790, italics added, footnotes omitted) [625 P. 2d at 226].

Combining its reliance on the Brennan opinion with its reliance on the Powell opinion, the court concluded:

> Accordingly, we conclude that, whether based on the Powell reasoning of assuring an academically beneficial diversity among the student body, or on the Brennan rationale of mitigating the effects of historical discrimination, it is abundantly clear that the university's 1975 admissions program would, on its face, meet federal constitutional standards as declared by a majority of the justices of the high Court [625 P.2d at 226].

Having upheld the facial validity of the Davis law school admissions policy, the court next considered DeRonde's argument that the policy had been unconstitutionally applied to his particular circumstances. In rejecting this argument, the court again relied heavily on the Powell opinion in *Bakke:*

> We readily acknowledge, of course, that a facially valid procedure may in its actual application produce a constitutionally discriminatory result.

Indeed, Justice Powell in *Bakke* fully and fairly both raised the possibility and anticipated the answer, noting:

> It has been suggested that an admissions program which considers race only as one factor is simply a subtle and more sophisticated—but no less effective—means of according racial preference than the Davis program. A facial intent to discriminate, however, is evident in petitioner's preference program and not denied in this case. *No such facial infirmity exists in an admissions program where race or ethnic background is simply one element—to be weighed fairly against other elements—in the selection process.* . . . And a court would not assume that a university, professing to employ a facially nondiscriminatory admissions policy, would operate it as a cover for the functional equivalent of a quota system. In short, *good faith would be presumed in the absence of a showing to the contrary* in the manner permitted by our cases (438 U.S. at 318-19, 98 S. Ct. at 2762-63, italics added; but see 438 U.S. at 378-79, 98 S. Ct. at 2793 (opn. of Brennan, J.)).

Again, we emphasize Justice Powell's analysis on the point because the Brennan group presumably would permit even a deliberate and systematic exclusion of white applicants if supported by the requisite showing of past discrimination.

Justice Powell further observed that "So long as the university proceeds on an individualized, case-by-case basis, there is no warrant for judicial interference in the academic process. If an applicant can establish that the institution does not adhere to a policy of individual comparisons, or can show that a systematic exclusion of certain groups results, the presumption of legality might be overcome, creating the necessity of proving legitimate educational purpose" (438 U.S. at 319, n.53, 98 S. Ct. at 2763, n. 53).

The record before us is barren of any evidence showing that the university was deliberately using the challenged admissions procedure either as a "cover" for a quota system or as a means of systematic exclusion of, or discrimination against, white male applicants such as DeRonde. The trial court made no such finding. Without proof of such an intent, the university's procedures must be upheld against a claim of unlawful racial discrimination even if accompanied by some evidence of a disproportionate impact (see *Bakke,* 438 U.S. at 289, n.27 (opn. of Powell, J.); *Arlington Heights* v. *Metropolitan Housing Corp.* (1977), 429 US. 252, 264-66, 97 S. Ct. 555, 562-63, 50 L. Ed. 2d 450).

Moreover, the evidence fails to support a finding of such disproportionate impact. The record does reflect that, between 1971 and 1977, the percentage of minorities in the entering classes at King Hall has been substantial, fluctuating from a low of 22.78 percent in 1971 to a high of 41.6 percent in 1976. From this arithmetic, DeRonde argues that "for six straight years, from 1971 to 1976, the percentage of minority students entering classes at Davis law school averaged 33 percent of those classes. This was at a time when more *highly qualified* male Caucasians were applying for admission than in the history of the school. . . . How can there be said to exist no 'disproportionate' impact when *extremely well-qualified* male Caucasian applicants outnumber *poorly qualified* minority applicants by over three to one and are admitted to the school in a lesser percentage?'' (Italics added.)

As the italicized portion of the argument reveals, the principal difficulty with DeRonde's statistical analysis is that it is based upon the faulty premise that it is only a high PFYA or GPA which truly "qualifies" an applicant for admission to law school. Yet as Justice Powell carefully explained in *Bakke,* racial or ethnic origin, as well as other "nonobjective" factors, such as personal talents, work experience, or leadership potential, properly may be considered in weighing each applicant's qualifications (438 U.S. at 317–20, 98 S. Ct. at 2762–63; for a probing analysis of the concept of "merit" within the academic context, see Fallon, "To Each According to His Ability, from None According to His Race: The Concept of Merit in the Law of Anti-discrimination," 60 *Boston University L. Rev.* 815, 871–76 (1980)).

DeRonde's statistics may indicate that the university has placed considerable weight upon racial or ethnic factors in determining the composition of its entering law classes. Yet nothing in *Bakke* prohibits such a practice, so long as individualized personal consideration is given to the varied qualifications of each applicant. Furthermore, the fact remains that male Caucasian applicants to King Hall continue to gain admission in respectable numbers. For example, according to DeRonde's own figures, in 1975, the year of DeRonde's application, 157 white males were offered admission as opposed to 133 minority applicants. We do not know the number of white females who were admitted. These statistics alone, however, would appear to contradict any assertion that the university has adopted or implemented a systematic plan or scheme to exclude male Caucasians [625 P.2d at 226–28].

Taken together, *McDonald* and *DeRonde* add considerably to the law on affirmative action. The courts adopted the same analytical approach to determining the validity of particular admissions policies. In developing this analysis, both courts affirmed the authority of the Powell and the Brennan-group opinions in *Bakke,* illustrating how these two opinions may be read together to provide a guide to the validity of affirmative action admissions plans. By accepting both opinions, the *McDonald* and *DeRonde* courts also accepted two separate justifications for implementing affirmative action: the "diverse student body" justification espoused by Powell and the "alleviation of past discrimination" justification espoused by the Brennan group.

As interpreted and applied in *McDonald* and *DeRonde,* the *Bakke* case has brought some clarity to the law of affirmative action in admissions. The legal and social issues remain sensitive, however, and administrators should involve legal counsel fully when considering any adoption or change of an affirmative action admissions policy. The following five guidelines can assist institutions in any such consideration:

1. As a threshold matter, the institution should consider whether it or the educational system of which it is a part has ever discriminated against minorities (or women) in its admissions policies. If any illegal discrimination has occurred,

the law will *require* that the institution use affirmative action to the extent necessary to overcome the present effects of the past discrimination. (See the Title VI and IX discussion above and the discussion in the *Bakke* opinions, 438 U.S. at 284, 328, and 414.) The limits that the *Bakke* decision places on the use of racial preferences do not apply to situations where "an institution has been found, by a court, legislature, or administrative agency, to have discriminated on the basis of race, color, or national origin. Race-conscious procedures that are impermissible in voluntary afirmative action programs may be required [in order] to correct specific acts of past discrimination committed by an institution or other entity to which the institution is directly related" (U.S. Dept. HEW, Policy Interpretation of Title VI, 44 Fed. Reg. 58509 at 58510 (Oct. 10, 1979)).

2. In considering whether to employ an affirmative action program, the institution should carefully determine its purposes and objectives and make its decisions in the context of these purposes and objectives. The institution may choose one or a combination of three basic approaches to affirmative action: the *uniform* system, the *differential* system, and the *preferential* system. While all three systems can be implemented lawfully, the potential for legal challenge increases as the institution proceeds down the list. The potential for substantially increasing minority enrollments also increases, however, so that an institution which is deterred by the possibility of legal action may also be forsaking part of the means to achieve its educational and societal goals.

3. A uniform system of affirmative action consists of changing the institution's general admissions standards or procedures so that they are more sensitively attuned to the qualifications and potential contributions of disadvantaged and minority individuals. These changes are then applied uniformly to all applicants. For example, all applicants might be given credit for work experience, demonstrated commitment to working in a particular geographical area, or overcoming handicaps or disadvantages. Such a system would thus allow all candidates—regardless of race, ethnicity, or sex—to demonstrate particular qualities that may not be reflected in grades or test scores. It would not preclude the use of numerical cutoffs where administrators believe that applicants with grades or test scores above or below a certain number should be automatically accepted or rejected. In *DeFunis* Justice Douglas discussed aspects of such a system (416 U.S. at 331–32), as did the California Supreme Court in *Bakke* (553 P.2d at 1165–66).

4. A differential system of affirmative action is based on the concept that equal treatment of differently situated individuals may itself create inequality; different standards for such individuals become appropriate when use of uniform standards would in effect discriminate against them. If, for instance, the institution determined that a standardized admissions test that it used was culturally biased as applied to its disadvantaged or minority applicants, it might use a different standard for assessing their performance on the test or employ some other criterion in lieu of the test.

In *Bakke* Justice Powell referred to a differential system by noting: "Racial classifications in admissions conceivably could serve a . . . purpose . . . which petitioner does not articulate: fair appraisal of each individual's academic promise in light of some bias in grading or testing procedures. To the extent that race and ethnic background were considered only to the extent of curing established inaccuracies in predicting academic performance, it might be argued that there is no 'preference' at all'' (438 U.S. at 306 n.43). Justice Douglas's *DeFunis* opinion also referred extensively to differential standards and procedures:

> Professional persons, particularly lawyers, are not selected for life in a computerized society. The Indian who walks to the beat of Chief Seattle of the Muckleshoot tribe in Washington has a different culture than examiners at law schools. . . .
>
> The admissions committee acted properly in my view in setting minority applications apart for separate processing. These minorities have cultural backgrounds that are vastly different from the dominant Caucasian. Many Eskimos, American Indians, Filipinos, Chicanos, Asian Indians, Burmese, and Africans come from such disparate backgrounds that a test sensitively tuned for most applicants would be wide of the mark for many minorities. . . .
>
> I think a separate classification of these applicants is warranted, lest race be a subtle force in eliminating minority members because of cultural differences. . . .
>
> The reason for the separate treatment of minorities as a class is to make more certain that racial factors do not militate *against an applicant or on his behalf*. . . .
>
> The key to the problem is consideration of such applications *in a racially neutral way* [416 U.S. at 334–36, 340].

To remain true to the theory of a differential system, standards or procedures can be modified only to the extent necessary to counteract the discriminatory effect of applying uniform standards, and the substituted standards or procedures must be designed to select only candidates whose qualifications and potential contributions are comparable to those of candidates selected under the general standards.

5. A preferential system of affirmative action is explicitly "race conscious" and allows some form of preference for minority applicants. The admissions programs at issue in the cases discussed above can be viewed, for the most part, as preferential systems. It is the preference available only to minorities that creates the reverse discrimination claim. Depending on the institution's objectives, some form of racial preference may indeed be necessary. In *Bakke* the Brennan group of justices agreed that:

> There are no practical means by which . . . [the university] could achieve its ends in the foreseeable future without the use of race-conscious measures. With respect to any factor (such as poverty or family educational background) that may be used as a substitute for race as an indicator of past discrimination, whites greatly outnumber racial minorities simply because whites make up a far larger percentage of the total population and therefore far outnumber minorities in absolute terms at every socioeconomic level. . . . Moreover, while race is positively correlated with differences in . . . [grades and standardized test] scores, economic disadvantage is not. Thus, it appears that economically disadvantaged whites do not score less well than economically advantaged whites while economically advantaged blacks score less well than do disadvantaged whites. These statistics graphically

illustrate that the university's purpose to integrate its classes by compensating for past discrimination could not be achieved by a general preference
for the economically disadvantaged or the children of parents of limited
education unless such groups were to make up the entire class [438 U.S.
at 376–77].

Preferential systems may fulfill objectives broader than those of differential
systems. As *McDonald* and *DeRonde* demonstrate, the leading examples are the objectives of diversifying the student body and alleviating the effects of past institutional or societal discrimination. In a preferential system, the institution must exercise special care in determining its objectives and relating its system to them.
Administrators should rely demonstrably on the institution's educational expertise
and involve policy makers at the highest levels of authority over the institution.
As emphasized by the court in an important pre-*Bakke* case, *Hupart* v. *Board of Higher
Education of City of New York,* 420 F. Supp. 1087 (S.D.N.Y. 1976):

> Every distinction made on a racial basis . . . must be justified. . . . It
> cannot be accomplished thoughtlessly or covertly, then justified after the
> fact. The defendants cannot sustain their burden of justification by coming
> to court with an array of hypothetical and *post facto* justifications for
> discrimination that has occurred either without their approval or without
> their conscious and formal choice to discriminate as a matter of official policy.
> It is not for the court to supply a rational or compelling basis (or something
> in between) to sustain the questioned state action. That task must be done
> by appropriate state officials *before* they take any action [420 F. Supp. at
> 1106].

The permissible types and scope of preference are also subject to continuing
debate. Under *Bakke* a preferential system that employs explicit racial or ethnic quotas
is, by a 5-to-4 vote, reverse discrimination and thus prohibited. But other forms
of preference are permissible. Until the U.S. Supreme Court speaks again, the best
guideline is Justice Powell's opinion in *Bakke.* The Brennan group of justices approved
of explicit, specific preferences; a fifth vote was needed to form a majority; and
of the remaining justices, only Powell acknowledged support for any form of preferential admissions system.[6] Justice Powell's opinion thus sets a boundary which administrators should stay within to reasonably assure legality.

For Powell, and thus currently for administrators, the key to a lawful
preference system is "a policy of individual comparisons" that "assures a measure
of competition among all applicants" and does not result in any "systematic exclusion of certain groups" on grounds of race or ethnicity from competition for
a portion of the places in a class (see 438 U.S. at 319 n.53). In such a system, "race

---

[6]The position of the other four justices is not entirely clear. Justice Stevens's opinion
expressing their views can be read both broadly and narrowly. He stated that, under Title VI,
"race cannot be the basis of excluding anyone from participation in a federally funded program,"
suggesting that all racial preferences may be unlawful. But he also stated that "the question whether
race can ever be used as a factor in an admissions decision is not an issue in this case,
and . . . discussion of that issue is inappropriate." If this issue is indeed left open, possibly one
or more of these four justices or their successors will in the future accept some form of racial
consideration in admissions.

or ethnic background may be deemed a 'plus' in a particular applicant's file" as long as it is only "one element—to be weighed fairly against other elements—in the selection process. . . . A court would not assume that a university, professing to employ [such] a racially nondiscriminatory admissions policy, would operate it as a cover for the functional equivalent of a quota system" (438 U.S. at 317–18). (As discussed above, Powell's model of a constitutional preference policy is the Harvard plan, a copy of which is set out in an appendix to his opinion.)

By following the five guidelines presented in this section, an institution—with the active involvement of legal counsel—can maximize the elbow room it has to make policy choices about affirmative action. By carefully considering and justifying its choice under these guidelines, the institution can reasonably assure that even an express preferential system will meet constitutional and statutory requirements.

4.2.6. Readmission. The readmission of previously excluded students can pose additional legal problems for postsecondary institutions. Although the legal principles in Section 4.2 apply generally to readmissions, the contract theory (Section 4.2.3) may assume added prominence because the student-institution contract (see Section 4.1.3) may include provisions concerning exclusion and readmission. The principles in Sections 4.4 through 4.6 may also apply generally to readmissions where the student challenges the validity of the original exclusion.

Institutions should have an explicit policy on readmission, even if that policy is simply "excluded students will never be considered for readmission." An explicit readmission policy can give students advance notice of their rights, or lack of rights, concerning readmission and, where readmission is permitted, can provide standards and procedures to promote fair and evenhanded decision making. If the institution has an explicit admissions policy, administrators should take pains to follow it, especially since its violation could be considered a breach of contract. Similarly, if administrators make an agreement with a student concerning readmission, they should firmly adhere to it. *Levine* v. *George Washington University,* C.A. (Civil Action) 8230-76 (D.C. Super. Ct. 1976), for instance, concerned a medical student who had done poorly in his first year but, by agreement with the school, was allowed to repeat the year subject to being excluded for a "repeated performance of marginal quality." On the second try, he passed all his courses but ranked low in each. The school excluded him. The court used contract principles to overturn the exclusion, finding that the school's subjective and arbitrary interpretation of "marginal quality," without prior notice to the student, breached the agreement between student and school. In contrast, the court in *Giles* v. *Howard University,* 428 F. Supp. 603 (D.D.C. 1977), held that the university's refusal to readmit a former medical student was not a breach of contract because the refusal was consistent with the "reasonable expectations" of the parties.

The California case of *Paulsen* v. *Golden Gate University* illustrates the flexibility that courts may accord institutions in devising and applying readmission standards; at the same time, however, the case illustrates the legal and practical difficulties an institution may encounter if it has no written readmission policy or does not administer its policy evenhandedly. The plaintiff in *Paulsen* had been excluded from law school at the end of his third year and petitioned the school to be allowed to attend for another year to make up his deficiencies. The school ultimately permitted him to continue on the condition that he could not receive a degree, but only a "certificate of attendance," no matter how high his grades were. After attending for a fourth year and removing his deficiencies, the student sued for a degree. The trial court ordered that the institution award the degree, and the intermediate appellate court affirmed (93 Cal. App. 3d 825, 156 Cal. Rptr. 190 (1979)). This court found that the school "apparently maintained an unwritten policy" of permitting deficient students to continue for an extra year but that no other students who had done so had been subjected to the "no-degree" condition. On this basis, the intermediate appellate court held for the student because the no-degree condition was "arbitrary, a manifest abuse of discretion, and an unreasonable discrimination between students."

On further appeal in *Paulsen,* the California Supreme Court reversed the intermediate appellate court (25 Cal. 3d 803, 159 Cal. Rptr. 858 (1979)):

> The trial court did not find that Golden Gate's decision to academically disqualify Paulsen at the end of this third year was in any way improper. It did find that the university allowed four other students to return for an additional year without a no-degree condition, and in due course awarded two of them degrees. But such students were not in fact similarly situated to Paulsen. Only he among the fourth-year students had "flunked out" at the end of the normal course of study; and the two who eventually graduated were permitted to continue in the degree program because their earlier deficiencies were due to personal factors unrelated to their academic capability (for example, serious illness).
>
> The imposition of reasonable conditions on the readmission of academically disqualified students was apparently a regular practice of Golden Gate. Although the no-degree condition may have been novel at the time, this fact in itself does not demonstrate its impermissibility. The only unacceptable conditions are those imposed for reasons extraneous to a student's qualifications for a degree (*Shuffer* v. *Board of Trustees,* 67 Cal. App. 3d 208, 220, 136 Cal. Rptr. 527). Here, there was an obvious relationship between Paulsen's special fourth-year program, even if unique, and his remarkably unsatisfactory academic record [159 Cal. Rptr. at 861–62].

Even though the institution ultimately prevailed, however, a written and consistently adhered-to readmission policy might have saved it from the uncertainties of having others guess about the bases for its decisions.

Another case, decided in 1980, illustrates the importance of carefully considering the procedures to be used in making readmission decisions. In *Evans* v. *West Virginia Board of Regents,* 271 S.E.2d 778 (W. Va. 1980), a student in good standing at a state school of osteopathic medicine had been granted a one-year leave of absence because of illness. When he sought reinstatement two months after termination of the leave, he was informed that because of his lateness he would have to reapply for admission. He did so but was rejected without explanation. The West Virginia Court of Appeals found that the student was "not in the same class as an original applicant to a professional school." Nor was he in the same position as a student who had been excluded for academic reasons, since "nothing appears of record even remotely suggesting his unfitness or inability to complete the remainder of his education.'' Rather, since he had voluntarily withdrawn after successfully completing two and a half years of his medical education, the student had a ''reasonable expectation that he would be permitted to complete his education.'' He thus had ''a sufficient property interest in the continuation and completion of his medical education to warrant the imposition of minimal due process protections.'' The court prescribed that the following procedures be accorded the student if the school again sought to deny him readmission: ''(1) a formal written notice of the reasons should he not be permitted to continue his medical education; (2) a sufficient opportunity to prepare a defense to the charges; (3) an opportunity to have retained counsel at any hearings on the charges; (4) a right to confront his accusers and present evidence on his own behalf; (5) an unbiased hearing tribunal; and (6) an adequate record of the proceedings'' (271 S.E.2d at 781).

The appellate court in *Evans* did not indicate the full terms of the school's policies regarding leave of absence and readmission or the extent to which these policies were put in writing. Perhaps, as in *Paulsen,* other schools in the defendant's position may avoid legal hot water by having a clear statement of their policies, including any procedural protections which apply and the consequences of allowing a leave of absence to expire.

Although private institutions would not be subject to the Fourteenth Amendment due process reasoning in *Evans,* they should nevertheless note the court's assertion that readmission decisions encompass different considerations and consequences than original admission decisions. Even private institutions may therefore choose to clothe readmission decisions with greater procedural safeguards than they apply to admission decisions. Moreover, private institutions, like public institutions, should clearly state their readmission policies in writing and coordinate them with their policies on exclusion and leaves of absence.

Sec. 4.3. Financial Aid

4.3.1. General principles. The legal principles affecting financial aid have a wide variety of sources. Some principles apply generally to all financial aid whether awarded as scholarships, assistantships, loans, fellowships, preferential tuition rates, or in some other form. Other principles depend on the particular source of funds being used and thus may vary with the aid program or the type of award. Sections 4.3.2 through 4.3.7 discuss the principles, and specific legal requirements resulting from them, that present the most difficult problems for financial aid administrators. This section discusses more general principles affecting financial aid.

The principles of contract law may apply to financial aid awards, since an award once made may create a contract between the institution and the aid recipient. Typically, the institution's obligation is to provide a particular type of aid at certain times and in certain amounts. The student recipient's obligation depends on the type of aid. With loans the typical obligation is to repay the principal and a prescribed rate of interest at certain times and in certain amounts. With other aid the obligation may be only to spend the funds for specified academic expenses or to achieve a specified level of academic performance in order to maintain aid eligibility. Sometimes, however, the student recipient may have more extensive obligations, such as performance of instructional or laboratory duties, participation on a varsity athletic team, or provision of particular services after graduation. The defendant student in *State of New York* v. *Coury*, 359 N.Y.S.2d 486 (Sup. Ct. 1974), for instance, had accepted a scholarship and agreed, as a condition of the award, to perform internship duties in a welfare agency for one year after graduation. When the student did not perform the duties, the state sought a refund of the scholarship money. The court held for the state because the student had "agreed to accept the terms of the contract" and had not performed as the contract required.[7]

The law regarding gifts, grants, wills, and trusts may also apply to financial aid awards. These legal principles would generally require aid administrators to adhere to any conditions that the donor, grantor, testator, or settlor placed on use of the funds. Funds provided by government agencies or private foundations, for instance, must be used in accordance with conditions in the program regulations, grant instrument, or other legal document formalizing the transaction. Section 4.3.2 illustrates such conditions in the context of federal aid programs.[8]

Similarly, funds made available to the institution under wills or trusts must be used in accordance with conditions in the will or trust instrument, unless those conditions are themselves illegal. Conditions that discriminate by race, sex, or religion have posed the greatest problems in this respect. If the government has compelled or affirmatively supported the imposition of such conditions, they will usually be considered to violate the federal Constitution's equal protection clause (see *In re Wilson*, 59 N.Y.2d 461, 465 N.Y.S.2d 900 (1983)). But if such conditions appear in a privately established and administered trust, they will usually be considered constitutional because no state action is present. In *Shapiro* v. *Columbia Union National Bank and Trust Co.* (this volume, Section 1.4.2), for instance, the Supreme Court of Missouri refused to find state action to support a claim of sex discrimination lodged against a university's involvement in a private trust established to provide scholarships exclusively for male students. Even in the absence of state action, however, a discriminatory condition in a private trust may still be declared invalid if it violates one of the federal nondiscrimination requirements applicable to federal fund recipients (see this volume, Section 4.3.3).[9]

---

[7]Illustrative cases are collected in Annot., "Construction and Application of Agreement by Medical or Social Work Student to Work in Particular Position or at Particular Location in Exchange for Financial Aid in Meeting Costs of Education," 83 A.L.R.3d 1273 (1978 plus periodic supp.). State age-of-majority laws (regarding a parent's obligation to support a child) are an important supplement to general contract law principles. These laws help the institution determine whether it should contract with the parent or the child in awarding aid and whether it should take parental resources into account in computing the amount of aid. Administrative and policy problems in determining dependency and possible constitutional challenges to the dependency determinations of public institutions are discussed in D. J. Hanson, *The Lowered Age of Majority: Its Impact on Higher Education*, pp. 11–17, 36–37 (Association of American Colleges, 1975).

[8]As to trusts generally, see G. C. Bogert and G. T. Bogert, *Handbook of the Law of Trusts*, 5th ed. (West, 1973). As to wills, see T. E. Atkinson, *Handbook of the Law of Wills*, 2nd ed. (West, 1953). As to grants, see R. Cappalli, *Rights and Remedies Under Federal Grants* (Bureau of National Affairs, 1979).

[9]The relevant cases are collected in Annot., "Validity and Effect of Gift for Charitable

Conditions in testamentary or *inter vivos* trusts can sometimes be modified by a court under the *cy pres* doctrine. In *Howard Savings Institution* v. *Peep,* 34 N.J. 494, 170 A.2d 39 (1961), Amherst College had been unable to accept a trust establishing a scholarship loan fund because one of its provisions violated the college's charter. The provision, stipulating that recipients of the funds had to be "Protestant" and "Gentile," was deleted by the court. Similarly, in *Wilbur* v. *University of Vermont,* 129 Vt. 33, 270 A.2d 889 (1970), the court deleted a provision in a financial aid trust that had placed numerical restrictions on the size of the student body at the university's college of arts and sciences. In each case the court found that the dominant purpose of the person establishing the trust could still be achieved with the restriction removed. As the court in the *Peep* case explained, "The doctrine of *cy pres* is a judicial mechanism for the preservation of a charitable trust when accomplishment of the particular purpose of the trust becomes impossible, impracticable, or illegal. In such a situation, if the settlor manifested an intent to devote the trust to a charitable purpose more general than the frustrated purpose, a court, instead of allowing the trust to fail, will apply the trust funds to a charitable purpose as nearly as possible to the particular purpose of the settlor" (170 A.2d at 42).

A third relevant body of legal principles is that of constitutional due process. These principles apply generally to public institutions and apply to private institutions when they make awards from public funds (see Section 1.4.2). Since termination of aid may affect both "property" and "liberty" interests (see Section 3.5.2) of the student recipients, courts may sometimes require that termination be accompanied by some form of procedural safeguards. *Corr* v. *Mattheis,* 407 F. Supp. 847 (D.R.I. 1976), for instance, involved students who had had their federal aid terminated in midyear under a federal student unrest statute, after they had participated in a campus protest against the Vietnam War. The court found that the students had been denied a property interest in continued receipt of funds awarded to them, as well as a liberty interest in being free from stigmas foreclosing further educational or employment opportunities. Termination thus had to be preceded by notice and a meaningful opportunity to contest the decision. In other cases, if the harm or stigma to students is less, the required procedural safeguards may be less stringent. Moreover, if aid is terminated for academic rather than disciplinary reasons, procedural safeguards may be almost nonexistent, as courts follow the distinction between academic deficiency problems and misconduct problems drawn in Section 4.6.3.

Federal and state laws regulating lending and extensions of credit provide a fourth body of applicable legal constraints. At the federal level, for example, the Truth-in-Lending Act, 15 U.S.C. sec. 1601 *et seq.,* establishes various requirements regarding disclosure terms of loans and credit sales (see R. Rohner, *The Law of Truth in Lending* (Warren, Gorham, and Lamont, 1984)). Such provisions are of concern not only to institutions with typical loan programs but also to institutions with credit plans allowing students or parents to defer payment of tuition for extended periods of time. The federal Truth-in-Lending Act, however, exempts National Direct Student Loans, Guaranteed Student Loans, and Auxiliary Loans to Assist Students (see Section 4.3.2) from its coverage (15 U.S.C. sec. 1603(6)).

Purposes Which Excludes Otherwise Qualified Beneficiaries Because of Their Race or Religion," 25 A.L.R.3d 736 (1969 plus periodic supp.).

4.3.2. Federal programs. The federal government provides or guarantees many millions of dollars per year in student aid for postsecondary education. To protect its investment and assure the fulfillment of national priorities and goals, the federal government imposes many requirements on the way institutions manage and spend funds under federal programs. Some are general requirements applicable to student aid and all other federal assistance programs. Others are specific programmatic requirements applicable to one student aid program or to a related group of such programs. These requirements constitute the most prominent—and, critics would add, most prolific and burdensome—source of specific restrictions on an institution's administration of financial aid.

The most prominent general requirements are the nondiscrimination requirements discussed in Section 4.3.3, which apply to all financial aid, whether or not it is provided under federal programs. In addition, the federal Buckley Amendment (discussed in Section 4.12.1) imposes various requirements on the institution's record-keeping practices regarding all financial aid. The Buckley regulations, however, do partially exempt financial aid records from nondisclosure requirements. They provide that an institution may disclose personally identifiable information from a student's records, without the student's consent, to the extent "necessary for such purposes as" determining the student's eligibility for financial aid, determining the amount of aid and the conditions that will be imposed regarding it, or enforcing the terms or conditions of the aid (34 C.F.R. sec. 99.31(a)(4)).

The specific programmatic restrictions on federal student aid depend on the particular program. Under some programs the federal government provides funds to institutions to establish revolving loan funds, as in the National Direct Student Loan (NDSL) program, 20 U.S.C. sec. 1087aa *et seq.,* 34 C.F.R. Part 674, and the Health Professions Student Loan program, 42 U.S.C. sec. 294m *et seq.,* 42 C.F.R. Part 57, subpart C. Under other programs the government grants funds to institutions, which in turn grant them to students, as in the Supplemental Educational Opportunity Grant (SEOG) program, 20 U.S.C. sec. 1070b *et seq.,* 34 C.F.R. Part 676, and the College Work-Study (CWS) program, 42 U.S.C. sec. 2751, 34 C.F.R. Part 675. Sometimes the institution merely participates in government-sponsored programs by performing certain functions for students who receive funds from the federal government, as in the GI Bill program, 38 U.S.C. sec. 1651, 38 C.F.R. 21.1020, and the Pell Grant program (formerly Basic Educational Opportunity Grant program), 20 U.S.C. sec. 1070a, 34 C.F.R. Part 690; from the federal government through the states, as in the State Student Incentive Grant (SSIG) program, 20 U.S.C. sec. 1070c *et seq.,* 34 C.F.R. Part 692; or from third-party lenders, as in the Guaranteed Student Loan (GSL) program, 20 U.S.C. sec. 1071 *et seq.,* 34 C.F.R. Part 682. There is also a new loan program, auspiciously called ALAS (Auxiliary Loans to Assist Students), whose regulations are to be published at 34 C.F.R. Part 638. This program originated in the Education Amendments of 1980 as the Parent Loan (PLUS) program but was renamed ALAS, modified in its borrowing terms, and extended to graduate students and independent undergraduate students (in addition to parents) by the Omnibus Reconciliation Act of 1981. Each of these programs has its own regulations placing various requirements on the institution.

A further controversy was interjected into the student aid arena in 1982, when Congress amended the Military Selective Service Act to require that students subject to the draft registration law must register as a condition to receiving federal student financial aid (Defense Department Authorization Act of 1983, 96 Stat. 718 sec. 1113; 50 U.S.C. App. sec. 462(f)). In order to receive aid, students required to register with Selective Service must file statements with the institutions they attend, certifying that they have complied with the Selective Service law and regulations. The validity of this requirement was upheld by the U.S. Supreme Court in *Selective Service System* v. *Minnesota Public Interest Research Group,* 104 S. Ct. 3348 (1984). Regulations implementing the certification requirement are published in 34 C.F.R. Part 668 (the Student Assistance General Provisions), secs. 668.24–28.

4.3.3. Nondiscrimination. The legal principles of nondiscrimination apply to the financial aid process in much the same way they apply to the admissions process (see Sections 4.2.4 and 4.2.5). The same constitutional principles of equal protection apply to financial aid. The relevant statutes and regulations on nondiscrimination—Title VI, Title IX, Section 504, and the ADA—all apply to financial aid, although Title IX's and Section 504's coverage and specific requirements for financial aid are different from those for admissions. And the affirmative action problem poses difficulties for financial aid programs similar to those it poses for admissions programs.

Of the federal statutes, Title IX has the most substantial impact on the financial aid programs and policies of postsecondary institutions. The regulations (34 C.F.R. sec. 106.37), with four important exceptions, prohibit the use of sex-restricted scholarships and virtually every other sex-based distinction in the financial aid program. Section 106.37(a)(1) prohibits the institution from providing "different amounts or types" of aid, "limiting eligibility" for "any particular type or source" of aid, "applying different criteria," or otherwise discriminating "on the basis of sex" in awarding financial aid. Section 106.37(a)(2) prohibits giving any assistance, "through solicitation, listing, approval, provision of facilities, or other services," to any "foundation, trust, agency, organization, or person" that discriminates on the basis of sex in providing financial aid to the institution's students. Section 106.37(a)(3) also prohibits aid eligibility rules that treat the sexes differently "with regard to marital or parental status."

The four exceptions to this broad nondiscrimination policy permit sex-restricted financial aid under certain circumstances. Section 106.37(b) permits an institution to "administer or assist in the administration of" sex-restricted financial assistance which is "established pursuant to domestic or foreign wills, trusts, bequests, or similar legal instruments or by acts of a foreign government." Institutions must administer such awards, however, so that their "overall effect" is "nondiscriminatory" according to standards set out in Section 106.37(b)(2). Section 106.31(c) creates the same kind of exception for sex-restricted foreign study scholarships awarded to the institution's students or graduates. Such awards must be established through the same legal channels specified for the first exception, and the institution must make available "reasonable opportunities for similar [foreign] studies for members of the other sex." The third exception, for athletic scholarships, is discussed in Section 4.11.2. A fourth exception was added by an amendment to Title IX included in the Education Amendments of 1976. Section 412(a)(4) of the amendments (20 U.S.C. sec. 1681(a)(9)) permits institutions to award financial assistance to winners of pageants based on "personal appearance, poise, and talent," even though the pageant is restricted to members of one sex.

Section 504 of the Rehabilitation Act of 1973 (see Section 7.5.4), as implemented by the ED regulations, restricts postsecondary institutions' financial aid processes as they relate to handicapped persons. Section 104.46(a) of the regulations (34 C.F.R. Part 104) prohibits the institution from providing "less assistance" to qualified handicapped students, from placing a "limit [on] eligibility for assistance," and from otherwise discriminating or assisting any other entity to discriminate on the basis of handicap in providing financial aid. The major exception to this nondiscrimination requirement is that the institution may still administer financial assistance provided under a particular discriminatory will or trust as long as "the overall effect of the award of scholarships, fellowships, and other forms of financial assistance is not discriminatory on the basis of handicap" (34 C.F.R. sec. 104.46(a)(2)).

Regulations were issued in June 1979 under the Age Discrimination Act of 1975, 42 U.S.C. sec. 6101 *et seq.* (see Section 7.5.5 of this volume). Being general regulations applicable to all government agencies dispensing federal aid, they have no specific provisions on financial aid as do the Title IX and Section 504 regulations. But the individual agency regulations, particularly those of the Department of Education, will likely have specific financial aid provisions. It is clear from the general regulations that the ADA will apply to the financial aid programs of postsecondary institutions receiving federal funds and that age distinctions will be prohibited under Section 90.12 unless they fit within one of the narrow exceptions in Sections 90.3, 90.14, and 90.15 or constitute affirmative action under Section 90.49. (See generally Sections 4.2.4.4, 7.5.5, and 7.5.6 of this volume.)

While the ADA regulations generally do not cover "employment practice[s]" (sec. 90.3), aid administrators should note that they "do cover any program or activity [such as the College Work-Study program] which is both a program of federal financial assistance and provides employment" (44 Fed. Reg. 33769, June 12, 1979).

The affirmative action/reverse discrimination dilemma hit the financial aid area in *Flanagan* v. *President and Directors of Georgetown College,* 417 F. Supp. 377 (D.D.C. 1976). The law school at Georgetown had allocated 60 percent of its financial aid for the first-year class to minority students, who constituted 11 percent of the class. The remaining 40 percent of the aid was reserved for nonminorities, the other 89 percent of the class. Within each category, funds were allocated on the basis of need; but, because of Georgetown's allocation policy, the plaintiff, a white law student, received less financial aid than some minority students even though his financial need was greater. The school's threshold argument was that this program *did not discriminate by race* because disadvantaged white students were also included within the definition of minority. The court quickly rejected this argument:

> Certain ethnic and racial groups are automatically accorded "minority" status, while whites or Caucasians must make a particular showing in order to qualify. . . . Access to the "favored" category is made more difficult for one racial group than another. This in itself is discrimination as prohibited by Title VI as well as the Constitution [417 F. Supp. at 382].

The school then defended its policy as part of an affirmative action program to increase minority enrollment. The student argued that the policy discriminated against nonminorities in violation of Title VI of the Civil Rights Act (see Section 7.5.2). The court sided with the student:

Where an administrative procedure is permeated with social and cultural factors (as in a law school's admission process), separate treatment for "minorities" may be justified in order to insure that all persons are judged in a racially neutral fashion.

But in the instant case, we are concerned with the question of financial need, which, in the final analysis, cuts across racial, cultural, and social lines. There is no justification for saying that a "minority" student with a demonstrated financial need of $2,000 requires more scholarship aid than a "nonminority" student with a demonstrated financial need of $3,000. To take such a position, which the defendants have, is reverse discrimination on the basis of race, which cannot be justified by a claim of affirmative action [417 F. Supp. at 384].

Although *Flanagan* broadly concludes that allotment of financial aid on an explicit racial basis is impermissible, the subsequent *Bakke* decision and cases following it (see Section 4.2.5) do preserve some room for racial considerations in financial aid programs. To fit within *Bakke*, however, the institution would have to demonstrate that its use of race was necessary to diversify the student body, rectify past discrimination, or achieve some comparably important goal. Moreover, to fit within Justice Powell's requirements in *Bakke*, the institution would apparently have to award aid on an individual competitive basis, using race as one of a mix of evaluative criteria, and not systematically exclude any group from competition for any portion of the aid.

4.3.4. Discrimination against nonresidents. State institutions have often imposed significantly higher tuition fees on out-of-state students. Courts have generally permitted such discrimination in favor of the state's own residents. The U.S. Supreme Court, in the context of a related issue, said, "We fully recognize that a state has a legitimate interest in protecting and preserving the quality of its colleges and universities and the right of its own bona fide residents to attend such institutions on a preferential tuition basis (*Vlandis* v. *Kline*, 412 U.S. 441, 452–53 (1973)). Not all preferential tuition systems, however, are beyond constitutional challenge.

In a variety of cases, students have questioned the constitutionality of the particular criteria used by states to determine who is a resident for purposes of the lower tuition rate.[10] In *Starns* v. *Malkerson*, 326 F. Supp. 234 (D. Minn. 1970), students challenged a regulation that stipulated: "No student is eligible for resident classification in the university, in any college thereof, unless he has been a bona fide domiciliary of the state for at least a year immediately prior thereto." The students argued, as have the plaintiffs in similar cases, that discrimination against nonresidents affects "fundamental" rights to travel interstate and to obtain an education and that such discrimination is permissible under the equal protection clause only if necessary to the accomplishment of some "compelling state interest." The court dismissed the students' arguments, concluding that "the one-year waiting

---

[10]Citations to state statutes and regulations on residency determinations, and an analysis of the governance structure by which each state implements its requirements, are contained in M. Olivas and others, "State Residency Requirements: Postsecondary Authorization and Regulations," 13 *College Law Digest* 157, printed in *West's Education Law Reporter* (NACUA Special Pamphlet, Feb. 1983). Further studies and compilations of state residency requirements are being prepared by this article's author at the Institute for Higher Education Law and Governance, University of Houston.

period does not deter any appreciable number of persons from moving into the state. There is no basis in the record to conclude, therefore, that the one-year waiting period has an unconstitutional 'chilling effect' on the assertion of the constitutional right to travel.'' The U.S. Supreme Court affirmed the decision without opinion (401 U.S. 985 (1971)).

Other cases are consistent with *Starns* in upholding durational residency requirements of up to one year for public institutions. Courts have agreed that equal protection law requires a high standard of justification when discrimination infringes fundamental rights. But, as in *Starns,* courts have not agreed that the fundamental right to travel is infringed by durational residency requirements. Since they have also rejected the notion that access to postsecondary education is a fundamental right (see *San Antonio Independent School District* v. *Rodriguez,* 411 U.S. 1 (1973)), courts have not applied the compelling interest test to durational residency requirements of a year or less. In *Sturgis* v. *Washington,* 414 U.S. 1057 (1973), affirming 368 F. Supp. 38 (W.D. Wash. 1973), the Supreme Court again recognized these precedents by affirming, without opinion, the lower court's approval of Washington's one-year durational residency statute.

However, in *Vlandis* v. *Kline* (discussed earlier in this section), the Supreme Court held another kind of residency requirement to be unconstitutional. A Connecticut statute provided that a student's residency at the time of application for admission would remain her residency for the entire time she was a student. The Supreme Court noted that, under such a statute, a person who had been a lifelong state resident, except for a brief period in another state just prior to admission, could not reestablish Connecticut residency as long as she remained a student. But a lifelong out-of-state resident who moved to Connecticut before applying could receive in-state tuition benefits even if she had lived in the state for only one day. Because such unreasonable results could flow from Connecticut's ''permanent irrebuttable presumption'' of residency, the Court held that the statute violated due process. At the same time, the Court reaffirmed the state's broad discretion to use more flexible and individualized criteria for determining residency, such as ''year-round residence, voter registration, place of filing tax returns, property ownership, driver's license, car registration, marital status, vacation employment,'' and so on. In subsequent cases the Court has explained *Vlandis* as applying only to ''those situations in which a state 'purports to be concerned with [domicile but] at the same time den[ies] to one seeking to meet its test of [domicile] the opportunity to show factors clearly bearing on that issue' '' (*Elkins* v. *Moreno,* 435 U.S. 647 (1978); quoting *Weinberger* v. *Salfi,* 422 U.S. 749, 771 (1975)).

Other rulings on different residency criteria include *Kelm* v. *Carlson,* 473 F.2d 1267 (6th Cir. 1973), where a U.S. Court of Appeals invalidated a University of Toledo requirement that a law student show proof of employment in Ohio before being granted resident status. In a later decision, the same court rejected a student's claim that voter registration alone showed state residency for lower state tuition purposes (*Hayes* v. *Board of Regents of Kentucky State University,* 495 F.2d 1326 (6th Cir. 1974)). And in *Samuel* v. *University of Pittsburgh,* 375 F. Supp. 1119 (W.D. Pa. 1974), a class action brought by female married students, the court invalidated a residency determination rule that made a wife's residency status dependent on her husband's residency. While the state defended the rule by arguing the factual validity of the common law presumption that a woman has the domicile of her husband, the court held that the rule discriminated on the basis of sex and thus violated equal protection principles.

In addition to issues concerning criteria, issues may also arise concerning the procedures that institutions must utilize in making residency determinations. State statutes or administrative regulations may establish procedures that institutions must follow. The federal due process clause could also have some impact. In *Lister* v. *Hoover,* 706 F.2d 796 (7th Cir. 1983), however, the court held that the due process clause did not obligate the University of Wisconsin to provide students denied resident status with a written statement of reasons for the denial; see also *Michaelson* v. *Cox,* 476 F. Supp. 1315 (S.D. Iowa, 1979).

4.3.5. Discrimination against aliens. In *Nyquist* v. *Jean-Marie Mauclet,* 432 U.S. 1 (1977), the U.S. Supreme Court set forth constitutional principles applicable to discrimination against aliens in student financial aid programs. The case involved a New York state statute that barred resident aliens from eligibility for regents' college scholarships, tuition assistance awards, and state-guaranteed student loans. Resident aliens denied financial aid argued that the New York law unconstitutionally discriminated against them in violation of the equal protection clause of the Fourteenth Amendment. The Supreme Court agreed.

The Supreme Court's opinion makes clear that alienage, somewhat like race, is a "suspect classification." Discrimination against aliens in awarding financial aid can thus be justified only if the discrimination is necessary in order to achieve some legitimate and substantial governmental interest. The *Nyquist* opinion indicates that offering an incentive for aliens to become naturalized, or enhancing the educational level of the electorate, is not a state governmental interest sufficient to justify discrimination against resident aliens with regard to financial aid. (For a different analysis of alienage classifications, which may apply when government uses citizenship as an employment criterion, see Section 3.3.3.)

Since the case was brought against the state rather than against individual postsecondary institutions, *Nyquist*'s most direct effect is to prohibit states from discriminating against resident aliens in state financial aid programs. It does not matter whether the state programs are for students in public institutions, in private institutions, or both, since in any case the state has created the discrimination. In addition, the case clearly would prohibit public institutions from discriminating against resident aliens in operating their own separate financial aid programs. Private institutions are affected by these constitutional principles only to the extent that they are participating in government-sponsored financial aid programs or are otherwise engaging in "state action" (see Section 1.4.2) in their aid programs.

Administrators whose institutions are subject to the *Nyquist* principles can comply by assuring that United States citizenship, applying for such citizenship, or filing a statement of intent to do so is not used as an eligibility requirement for financial aid administered by the institution. This does not mean that *all* aliens must be eligible for aid. While *Nyquist* indicates that resident aliens as a class do not differ sufficiently from United States citizens to permit different treatment, courts may not reach the same conclusion regarding temporary nonresident aliens. Institutions may deem temporary nonresident aliens ineligible, at least if the aliens have no demonstrable present intention to become permanent residents. (See the similar eligibility standard for the federal Guaranteed Student Loan program, 34 C.F.R. sec. 682.201.)

Moreover, since *Nyquist* does not affect state residency requirements, aliens who are not state residents may still be deemed ineligible when the principles discussed in Section 4.3.3 permit it—not because they are aliens but because they are nonresidents of the state. Although state residency for aliens may be determined in part by their particular status under federal immigration law (see especially 8 U.S.C. sec. 1101(a)(15)), it is well to be cautious in relying on federal law. In *Elkins* v. *Moreno,* 435 U.S. 647 (1978), the University of Maryland had denied "in-state" status, for purposes of tuition and fees, to aliens holding G-4 nonimmigrant visas (for employees of international treaty organizations and their immediate families) under federal law. The university argued that their federal status precluded such aliens from demonstrating an intent to become permanent Maryland residents. The U.S. Supreme Court rejected this argument, holding that G-4 aliens (unlike some other categories of nonimmigrant aliens) are not incapable under federal law of becoming permanent residents and thus are not precluded from forming an intent to reside permanently in Maryland. The Court then certified to the Maryland Court of Appeals the question whether G-4 aliens or their dependents are incapable of establishing Maryland residency under the state's common law.

In "act 2" of this litigation drama, *Toll* v. *Moreno,* 284 Md. 425, 397 A.2d 1009 (1979), judgment vacated, 441 U.S. 458 (1979), the Maryland court answered no to the Supreme Court's question. In the interim, however, the university had adopted a new in-state policy, which no longer used state residency as the paramount factor in determining in-state status for tuition and fees. Because the changed policy raised new constitutional issues, the Supreme Court ended act 2 by vacating the Maryland court's judgment and remanding the case to the district court where the *Elkins* case had begun.

After the district court invalidated Maryland's new policy and the U.S. Court of Appeals affirmed, the case returned to the U.S. Supreme Court (*Toll* v. *Moreno,* 102 S. Ct. 2977 (1982)) for act 3. The Court held that the university's new policy, insofar as it bars G-4 aliens and their dependents from acquiring in-state status, violates the supremacy clause (Art. VI, clause 2) of the United States Constitution. The supremacy clause recognizes the primacy of federal regulatory authority over subjects within the scope of federal constitutional power and prevents state law from interfering with federal law regarding such subjects. Since the federal government's broad constitutional authority over immigration has long been recognized, federal law on immigration is supreme, and states may not interfere with it. Applying these principles in *Toll,* the Supreme Court reasoned:

> [Our cases] stand for the broad principle that "state regulation not congressionally sanctioned that discriminates against aliens lawfully admitted to the country is impermissible if it imposes additional burdens not contemplated by Congress" (*De Canas* v. *Bica,* 424 U.S. 351, 358 n.6 (1976)). . . .
>
> The Immigration and Nationality Act of 1952, 66 Stat. 163, as amended, 8 U.S.C. sec. 1101 *et seq.,* . . . recognizes two basic classes of aliens, immigrant and nonimmigrant. With respect to the nonimmigrant class, the Act establishes various categories, the G-4 category among them. For many of these nonimmigrant categories, Congress has precluded the covered alien from establishing domicile in the United States. But signifi-

cantly, Congress has allowed G-4 aliens—employees of various international organizations and their immediate families—to enter the country on
terms permitting the establishment of domicile in the United States. In light
of Congress's explicit decision not to bar G-4 aliens from acquiring domicile,
the state's decision to deny "in-state" status to G-4 aliens, *solely* on account
of the G-4 alien's federal immigration status, surely amounts to an ancillary
"burden not contemplated by Congress" in admitting these aliens to the
United States. We need not rely, however, simply on Congress's decision
to permit the G-4 alien to establish domicile in this country; the federal
government has also taken the additional affirmative step of conferring
special tax privileges on G-4 aliens.

As a result of an array of treaties, international agreements, and
federal statutes, G-4 visa holders employed by the international organizations described in 8 U.S.C. sec. 1101(a)(15)(G)(iv) are relieved of federal
and, in many instances, state and local taxes on the salaries paid by the
organizations. . . .

The tax benefits serve as an inducement for these organizations to
locate significant operations in the United States. By imposing on those
G-4 aliens who are domiciled in Maryland higher tuition and fees than
are imposed on other domiciliaries of the state, the university's policy
frustrates these federal policies. Petitioners' very argument in this Court
only buttresses this conclusion. One of the grounds on which petitioners
have sought to *justify* the discriminatory burden imposed on the named
respondents is that the salaries their parents receive from the international
banks for which they work are exempt from Maryland income tax. Indeed,
petitioners suggest that the "dollar differential . . . at stake here [is] an
amount roughly equivalent to the amount of state income tax an international bank parent is spared by treaty each year" (Brief for Petitioners 23).
But to the extent this is indeed a justification for the university's policy
with respect to the named respondents, it is an impermissible one: the state
may not recoup indirectly from respondents' parents the taxes that the federal
government has expressly barred the state from collecting [102 S. Ct. at
2983–85].

As a result of the *Elkins/Toll* litigation, it is now clear that postsecondary
institutions may not use G-4 aliens' immigration status as a basis for denying them
in-state status for tuition and fees purposes. It does not follow, however, that institutions are similarly limited with respect to other categories of nonimmigrant aliens.
Most nonimmigrant categories, other than G-4, are comprised of aliens who enter
the United States temporarily for a specific purpose and must maintain residence
in a foreign country (see, for example, 8 U.S.C. sec. 1101(a)(15)(B) (temporary
visitors for pleasure or business); sec. 1101(a)(15)(C) (aliens in transit); sec.
1101(a)(15)(F) (foreign students); sec. 1101(a)(15)(H) (temporary workers); see
generally this volume, Section 7.2.6). Such restrictions, not applicable to G-4s,
preclude these other classes of nonimmigrant aliens from forming an intent to
establish permanent residency (or domicile), which is required under the residency
laws of most states. Thus, federal and state law would apparently still support public
institutions that deny in-state status to nonimmigrant aliens other than G-4s.

It also remains important, after *Elkins/Toll,* to distinguish between nonimmigrant (nonresident) and immigrant (resident) aliens. Because immigrant aliens, like G-4 aliens, are permitted under federal law to establish United States and state residency, denial of in-state status because of their alienage would apparently violate the federal supremacy principles relied on in *Toll* (act 3). Such discrimination against immigrant aliens is also prohibited by the equal protection clause of the Fourteenth Amendment, as established in *Nyquist* v. *Jean-Marie Mauclet* (discussed earlier in this section).[11]

4.3.6. Collection of student debts. When a postsecondary institution extends financial aid to its students in the form of loans, it has the additional problem of assuring that students repay their loans according to the schedule and conditions in the loan agreement. Enforcing payment of loans can involve the institution in a legal quagmire, several aspects of which are discussed in this section.

4.3.6.1. Federal bankruptcy law. Student borrowers have often sought to extinguish their loan obligations to their institutions by filing for bankruptcy under the federal Bankruptcy Code contained in Title 11 of the *United States Code.* The Bankruptcy Code supersedes all state law inconsistent with its provisions or with its purpose of allowing the honest bankrupt a "fresh start," free from the burden of indebtedness. A debtor may institute bankruptcy proceedings by petitioning the appropriate federal court for discharge of all his provable debts. Following receipt of the bankruptcy petition, the court issues an order fixing times for the filing and hearing of objections to the petition before a bankruptcy judge. Notice of this order is given to all potential creditors, usually by mail.

Debtors may petition for bankruptcy under either Chapter 7 or Chapter 13 of the Bankruptcy Code. Under a Chapter 7 "straight" bankruptcy, debts are routinely and completely discharged unless the creditors can show reasons why no discharge should be ordered (11 U.S.C. sec. 727) or unless a creditor can demonstrate why its particular claim should be "excepted" from the discharge order as a "nondischargeable debt" (11 U.S.C. sec. 523). Chapter 13, on the other hand, provides for the adjustment of debts for debtors with regular income. After the debtor has filed a Chapter 13 petition, he must submit a plan providing for full or partial repayment of his debts (11 U.S.C. secs. 1321-23), and the bankruptcy court must hold a hearing and decide whether to confirm the plan (11 U.S.C. secs. 1324-25, 1327). Prior to the hearing, the bankruptcy court must notify all creditors whom the debtor has included in the plan; these creditors may then object to the plan's confirmation (11 U.S.C. sec. 1324). If the plan is confirmed and the debtor makes the payments according to the plan's terms, the bankruptcy court will issue a discharge of those debts included in the plan (11 U.S.C. sec. 1328(a)).

In 1976, responding to an escalation in defaults on student loans and in the number of students seeking discharge of their loans in bankruptcy, Congress amended the Higher Education Act to prohibit the discharge, under certain circumstances, of loans guaranteed or insured under the federal Guaranteed Student Loan program

---

[11]There are some circumstances where the equal protection clause will also protect nonimmigrant and illegal (undocumented) aliens from state discrimination in the delivery of educational services (see *Plyler* v. *Doe,* 102 S. Ct. 2382 (1982); M. Olivas, C. Ramirez, and S. Vera, *Postsecondary Implications of Plyler* v. *Doe and Toll* v. *Moreno: Adults and "Endured Disability"* (Monograph 84-4, Institute for Higher Education Law and Governance, University of Houston, 1985), to be reprinted in 15 *J. of Law and Educ.* (in press).

(20 U.S.C. sec. 1087-3). Subsequently, Congress replaced this provision with a broader provision, included in the Bankruptcy Reform Act of 1978. In 1979 Congress amended this new provision in order to clarify its language and correct some inequities that it had inadvertently created. As amended, the new student bankruptcy provision took effect, along with the rest of the revised Bankruptcy Code, on October 1, 1979. The provision is contained in 11 U.S.C. sec. 523(a)(8):

> *Section 523. Exceptions to discharge:*
> (a) A discharge under Section 727, 1141, or 1328(b) of this title does not discharge an individual debtor from any debt—
> . . .
> (8) for an educational loan made, insured, or guaranteed by a governmental unit, or made under any program funded in whole or in part by a governmental unit or a nonprofit institution of higher education, unless—
> (A) such loan first became due before five years (exclusive of any applicable suspension of the repayment period) before the date of the filing of the petition; or
> (B) excepting such debt from discharge under this paragraph will impose an undue hardship on the debtor and the debtor's dependents.

Section 523(a)(8) covers loans made under any Department of Education student loan program as well as student loans made, insured, guaranteed, or funded by other "governmental units," such as state and local governments, and by nonprofit higher education institutions. Loans made by profit-making postsecondary institutions or privately owned banks (and not guaranteed or insured under a government program) are not covered by the provision and thus continue to be dischargeable. Moreover, Section 523(a)(8) is written to apply primarily to Chapter 7 bankruptcies, as explained below, so that for most purposes the provision will not prevent discharge of student loans under Chapter 13.

In re Shore, 707 F.2d 1337 (11th Cir. 1983), illustrates the broad scope of the "governmental unit" language of Section 523(a)(8). A student at Columbus College, part of the University of Georgia System, had borrowed money from the Greentree-Sevier Trust, a trust to benefit Columbus College and its students. The student sought to discharge the loan in bankruptcy, arguing that the loan was made by a trust fund rather than a governmental unit and therefore did not fall within the reach of Section 523. The Eleventh Circuit disagreed:

> Columbus College is the beneficiary of the Greentree-Sevier Trust. Columbus College made the educational loan to Shore using funds from this trust. Appellant agreed "to pay to Columbus College" the sum of the amount signed for in the space provided on the Loan Agreement. An educational loan "made by" a governmental unit within the meaning of Section 523(a)(8) is one in which a governmental unit is the lender and the holder of the loan obligation. The particular fund on which the governmental unit draws to fund the loan does not alter the definition [707 F.2d at 1339].

The new student-loan bankruptcy provision defuses what previously had been a major issue in Chapter 7 student bankruptcies: the issue of "provability." The role of this issue under the old code is illustrated by *State* v. *Wilkes,* 41 N.Y.2d 655, 303 N.E.2d 555 (1977). The college in that case had initiated collection procedures against a student who claimed that his prior bankruptcy had discharged his student loans (a point not made clear in the bankruptcy proceeding). The New York Court of Appeals rejected the student's claim. It held that contingencies such as a repayment plan extending over ten years, provision for termination of the debt if the student died or became disabled, and provision for reduction of the debt if the student taught in certain schools made the "ultimate amount of liability impossible to ascertain or even approximate." The debt was therefore not "provable," and because not provable it was nondischargeable.

Section 523(a)(8) obviates the need for an institution to raise lack of prova-bility in order to prevent the discharge of student loans that have been due for less than five years. During that period the student loan is ordinarily nondischargeable, regardless of provability. Thus, the institution no longer has the burden of filing a proof of claim and asserting lack of provability as a bar to discharge unless the debt has been due for five years or more. Instead, Section 523(a)(8) "is intended to be self-executing and the lender or institution is not required to file a complaint to deter-mine the nondischargeability of any student loan" (S. Rpt. No. 95–989, 95th Cong., 2d Sess., reprinted in 1978 *U.S. Code Congressional and Administrative News,* p. 5865).[12]

Even if a student loan is nondischargeable under Chapter 7, the filing of a bankruptcy petition may nevertheless affect the institution's efforts to collect the debt. Under the Bankruptcy Code, creditors are automatically prohibited during the pendency of the bankruptcy proceedings from continuing with collection efforts (11 U.S.C. sec. 362). The bankruptcy judge may modify or cancel this prohibition during the proceedings, however, if the institution can show cause why such action should be taken (11 U.S.C. sec. 362(d)(1)).

There has been considerable litigation on the scope of the "undue hardship" exception to nondischargeability in Section 523(a)(8)(B). In general, bankruptcy courts have interpreted this exception narrowly, looking to the particular facts of each case (see J. Kasel, "Running the Gauntlet of 'Undue Hardship'—The Discharge of Student Loans in Bankruptcy," 11 *Golden Gate University L. Rev.* 457 (1981)). Primary importance has been attached to whether the student debtor's economic straits were foreseeable and within his control. In *In re Perkins,* 11 Bankr. Rptr. (*Bankruptcy Reporter*) 160 (D. Vt. 1980), the court held that the undue hard-ship exception "is not intended to shelter the debtor from self-imposed hardship resulting from a reluctance to live within his means." *In re Price,* 1 Bankr. Rptr. 768 (D. Hawaii 1980), held that the bankrupt's sending three children to private schools constituted a failure to live within means; and *In re Brock,* 4 Bankr. Rptr. 491 (S.D.N.Y. 1980), held that "the necessity of careful budgeting is not evidence of undue hardship." Even unemployment or underemployment will not suffice for a hardship discharge when future prospects are bright (see, for example, *In re Hemmen,* 7 Bankr. Rptr. 63 (N.D. Ala. 1980); *In re Tobin,* 18 Bank. Rptr. 560 (W.D. Wisc. 1982)). On the other hand, courts will consider such factors as insufficient

---

[12]There may nevertheless be practical difficulties for college counsel in determining how and when to respond to a notice of the student's filing of a bankruptcy petition (see T. Ayres and D. Sagner, "The Bankruptcy Reform Act and Student Loans: Unraveling New Knots," 9 *J. of College and University Law* 361, 385–88 (1982–83)).

income to maintain a minimum standard of living, excessive unavoidable debts and expenses, and the failure of education to increase the debtor's earning power. In *In re Diaz,* 5 Bankr. Rptr. 253 (W.D.N.Y. 1980), for instance, the bankruptcy judge discharged the student loans of a debtor with personal and family medical problems and poor employment prospects; and in *In re Birden,* 17 Bankr. Rptr. 891 (E.D. Pa. 1982), the bankruptcy judge, in deciding to discharge the student loans, considered the presence of large nondischargeable obligations for taxes and child support payments.

As mentioned, Section 523(a)(8) applies to all Chapter 7 bankruptcies but does not apply to most repayment plans adopted under Chapter 13. Chapter 13 thus provides a large escape hatch for many student debtors who would not be able to discharge their loans under Chapter 7. In *In re Eichelberger,* 6 Bankr. Rptr. 705 (S.D. Miss. 1980), the court held that "Congress intended a broader discharge under Chapter 13 than available under Chapter 7." Echoing the arguments of numerous other courts, the court in *Eichelberger* determined that long-term debts and family support obligations are the only exceptions to dischargeability authorized for Chapter 13 proceedings under Section 1328(a).

There is one circumstance, however, in which Section 523(a)(8) could apply to Chapter 13 bankruptcies and could result in a determination of nondischargeability of student loans. If, after the bankruptcy judge has confirmed the repayment plan, the bankrupt is unable to complete the plan, he may ask for a discharge of his debts due to "circumstances for which the debtor should not justly be held accountable" (11 U.S.C. sec. 1328(b)(1)). Whether a student loan may be included in such a discharge is determined under the standards of Section 523(a)(8). Thus, if the loan has been due less than five years, it will not be dischargeable unless the Chapter 13 debtor can meet the same undue hardship standards as apply to Chapter 7 bankruptcies.

The primary means by which an institution may contest a Chapter 13 bankruptcy is to show that the debtor has not offered his repayment plan "in good faith" (11 U.S.C. sec. 1325(a)(3)) (see C. K. Cyr, "The Chapter 13 'Good Faith' Tempest: An Analysis and a Proposal for Change," 55 *American Bankruptcy L.J.* 271 (1981)). The Bankruptcy Code does not fix any minimum repayment required to sustain a showing of good faith, and bankruptcy courts have split over what constitutes a good-faith effort. The majority have required a substantial and meaningful payment (see, for example, *In re Yee,* 7 Bankr. Rptr. 747 (E.D.N.Y. 1980)). Other courts have required the best efforts of the debtor regardless of the amount of repayment, and have thus accepted zero payment or nominal payment plans when the debtor could do no better (see *In re Scher,* 12 Bankr. Rptr. 258 (D. Kan. 1981); *In re Barnes,* 13 Bankr. Rptr. 997 (D.D.C., 1981), modified on unrelated points and affirmed, 689 F.2d 193 (D.C. Cir. 1982)). Courts apparently agree, however, that good faith does not exist when the sole purpose of the Chapter 13 filing is to avoid the nondischargeability of student loans under Chapter 7. In *In re Johnson,* 17 Bankr. Rptr. 78 (S.D. Ind. 1981), for instance, the debtor's only debts were student loans. The court held the Chapter 13 petition to be in bad faith and an abuse of the Bankruptcy Code because the debtor was attempting to circumvent nondischargeability under Section 523(a)(8).[13]

[13]In *Northern Pipeline Construction Co.* v. *Marathon Pipeline Co.,* 102 S. Ct. 2858 (1982), the

4.3.6.2. Withholding certified transcripts. Like its predecessor, the revised (1978) Bankruptcy Code generally forbids creditors from resorting to the courts or other legal process to collect debts discharged in bankruptcy (11 U.S.C. sec. 524(a)(2)). Under the old Bankruptcy Act, however, there was considerable debate on whether informal means of collection, such as withholding certified grade transcripts from a student bankrupt, were permissible. In *Girardier* v. *Webster College,* 563 F.2d 1267 (8th Cir. 1977), decided under the old Act, the court held that the Act did not prohibit private institutions from withholding certified transcripts. Besides reducing the scope of this problem by limiting the dischargeability of student loans, the 1978 Bankruptcy Act appears to have legislatively overruled the result in the *Girardier* case.

The provision of the old Act that was applied in *Girardier* prohibited formal attempts, by "action" or "process," to collect discharged debts. The 1978 Act rewrote this provision to read (with further amendments in 1984):

A discharge in a case under this title . . . operates as an injunction against the commencement or continuation of an action, the employment of process, or an act, to collect, recover or offset any such debt as a personal liability of the debtor, whether or not discharge of such debt is waived [11 U.S.C. sec. 524(a)(2)].

The new language, especially the phrase "or an act," serves to extend the provision's coverage to informal, nonjudicial means of collection, thus "insur[ing] that once a debt is discharged, the debtor will not be pressured in any way to repay it" (S. Rpt. No. 95–989, 95th cong., 2nd Sess., reprinted in 1978 *U.S. Code Congressional and Administrative News,* p. 5866).

The 1978 Act also added the words "any act" to a related provision, Section 362(a)(6), which prohibits creditors from attempting to collect debts during the pendency of a bankruptcy proceeding. Bankruptcy courts have construed this new language to apply to attempts to withhold certified transcripts (see *In re Lanford,* 10 Bank. Reptr. 132 (D. Minn. 1981)). This legislative change, together with the change in Section 524(a)(2), apparently prevents postsecondary institutions from withholding transcripts both during the pendency of a bankruptcy proceeding and after the discharge of debts, under either Chapter 7 or Chapter 13.[14]

The situation is different if, as in the majority of situations, the student has not filed a bankruptcy petition. Nothing in the Bankruptcy Code would prohibit

---

U.S. Supreme Court held that the Bankruptcy Reform Act conferred judicial powers on bankruptcy judges that, under the U.S. Constitution, could be exercised only by judges with life tenure. Because the Act provided only fourteen-year terms for judges, the Court declared that the bankruptcy court system established in the Act was prospectively unconstitutional and called on Congress to remedy the problem. In late 1984 Congress finally enacted the Bankruptcy Amendments and Federal Judgeship Act, 98 Stat. 333, which restructured the bankruptcy courts to comply with the *Northern Pipeline* ruling.

[14]Public institutions may also be restrained by Section 525 of the Code, which forbids "governmental units" from discriminating against bankrupts in various ways—apparently including denial of transcripts (see *In re Howren,* 10 Bankr. Rptr. 303 (D. Kans. 1980)).

postsecondary institutions from withholding transcripts from such student debtors. Moreover, the Code does not prevent institutions from withholding transcripts if the bankruptcy court has refused to discharge the student-loan debts. In *Johnson* v. *Edinboro State College*, 728 F.2d 163 (3d Cir. 1984), for example, the bankruptcy court had declared a former student to be bankrupt but did not discharge his student loans because he had failed to prove that a hardship existed. Nevertheless, the bankruptcy court had held that the college was obligated to issue the student a transcript because of the Bankruptcy Code's policy to guarantee debtors "fresh starts." When the college appealed, the Court of Appeals overruled the bankruptcy court, holding that when a bankrupt's student loans are nondischargeable under Section 523(a)(8), the policy of that section overrides the Code's general fresh-start policy. The college therefore remained free to withhold transcripts from the student.

Similarly, nothing in the federal Buckley Amendment on student records (Section 4.12.1) prohibits institutions from withholding certified transcripts from student debtors. If an institution enters grades in a student's records, the Buckley Amendment would give the student a right to see and copy the grade records. But the Buckley Amendment would not give the student any right to a *certified* transcript of grades, nor would it obligate the institution to issue a certified transcript or other record of grades to third parties (see *Girardier* v. *Webster College*, 421 F. Supp. 45, 48 (D. Mo. 1976)).

The most likely legal difficulty would arise under the federal Constitution's due process clause, whose requirements limit only public institutions (see Section 1.4.2). The basic issue is whether withholding a certified transcript deprives the student of a "liberty" or "property" interest protected by the due process clause (see generally Section 3.5.2). If so, the student would have the right to be notified of the withholding and the reason for it, and to be afforded some kind of hearing on the sufficiency of the grounds for withholding. Courts have not yet defined liberty or property interests in this context. But under precedents in other areas, if the institution has regulations or policies entitling students to certified transcripts, these regulations or policies could create a property interest that would be infringed by withholding without notice or hearing. And withholding certified transcripts from a student applying to professional or graduate school, or for professional employment, may so foreclose the student's freedom to pursue education or employment opportunities as to be a deprivation of liberty. Thus, despite the lack of cases in point, administrators at public institutions should consult counsel before implementing a policy of withholding transcripts for failure to pay loans, or for any other reason.

4.3.6.3. Debt collection requirements in federal student loan programs.[15] The National Direct Student Loan (NDSL) program statute and regulations contain several provisions affecting the institution's debt collection practices. The statute provides, in 20 U.S.C. sec. 1087cc(5), that where a note or written agreement evidencing

[15]Besides these student loan requirements, there is a growing body of state and federal statutes and court decisions on debt collection practices. See generally Uniform Consumer Credit Code, sec. 5.108(5) (Commissioners on Uniform State Laws, 1974); R. Geltzer and L. Woocher, "Debt Collection Regulation: Its Development and Direction for the 1980's," 37 *Business Lawyer* 1401 (1982); S. Rester, "Regulating Debt Collection Practices: The Social and Economic Needs and a Congressional Response," 11 *Clearing-House Review* 547 (1977); M. Greenfield, "Coercive Collection Tactics—An Analysis of the Interests and the Remedies," 1972 *Washington University L.Q.* 117 (1972).

such a loan has been in default for at least two years despite the institution's due diligence in attempting to collect the debt, the institution may assign its rights under the note or agreement to the United States without recompense. If the debt is thereafter collected by the United States, the sums are deposited in the general Treasury fund. The NDSL regulations, 34 C.F.R. sec. 674.42 *et seq.,* provide that each institution maintaining an NDSL fund must accept responsibility for, and use due diligence in effecting, collection of all amounts due and payable to the fund. Due diligence includes the following elements: (1) providing borrowers with full disclosure of their rights and obligations when or before they sign promissory notes (34 C.F.R. sec. 674.42(a)); (2) conducting exit interviews with borrowers when they leave the institution and providing them with copies of repayment schedules that indicate the total amount of the loans and the dates and amounts of installments as they come due (34 C.F.R. sec. 674.42(b)-(c)); (3) keeping a written record of interviews and retaining signed copies of borrowers' repayment schedules (34 C.F.R. sec. 674.42(d)); and (4) staying in contact with borrowers both before and during the repayment period in order to facilitate billing and keep the borrowers informed of changes in the program that may affect rights and obligations (34 C.F.R. sec. 674.43). The institution must also use specified "billing procedures" (set forth at 34 C.F.R. sec. 674.44), including statements of notice and account and demands for payment on accounts that are more than fifteen days overdue. If an institution is unable to locate a borrower, it must do an address search (34 C.F.R. sec. 674.45). If the billing procedures are unsuccessful, the institution must either obtain the services of a collection agency or utilize its own resources to compel repayment (34 C.F.R. sec. 674.46(a)). (See J. Hunter, "Collecting Defaulted Student Loans: How Much Diligence is Due?" 9 *J. of College and University Law* 149 (1982–83).)

The Guaranteed Student Loan (GSL) program includes fewer provisions related to debt collection, since postsecondary institutions are not usually the lenders under the program (see T. Naegele, "The Guaranteed Student Loan Program: Do Lenders' Risks Exceed Their Rewards?" 34 *Hastings L.J.* 599 (1983)). The regulations require, at 34 C.F.R. sec. 682.62(a), that participating institutions establish and maintain such administrative and fiscal procedures and records as may be necessary to protect the United States from unreasonable risk of loss due to defaults. Another approach to debt collection, with more specifics than GSL but fewer than NDSL, is illustrated by the Health Professions Student Loan program, 42 C.F.R. Part 57, subpart C. Participating institutions must exercise "due diligence" in collecting loan payments (42 C.F.R. sec. 57.210(b)) and must maintain complete repayment records for each student borrower, including the "date, nature, and result of each contact with the borrower or proper endorser in the collection of an overdue loan" (42 C.F.R. sec. 57.215(c)). The regulations also establish a quantitative performance standard, requiring institutions to maintain a "borrower delinquency rate" or a "dollar delinquency rate" of not more than 5 percent (42 C.F.R. sec. 57.216(a)).

4.3.7. Related support services. Recent litigation has raised provocative questions on the extent of a postsecondary institution's obligation to provide support other than financial aid to students in order to remove other practical impediments to their full participation in the institution's educational program. Courts have addressed these questions in two contexts: auxiliary aids for handicapped students (see this volume, Section 7.5.4), in particular interpreter services for hearing-impaired students; and child care facilities for women students with young children.

The most publicized case on interpreter services is *University of Texas* v. *Camenisch,* 101 S. Ct. 1830 (1981). In that case a deaf graduate student at the University of Texas alleged that the university had violated Section 504 of the Rehabilitation Act of 1973 by refusing to provide him with sign language interpreter services, which he claimed were necessary to the completion of his master's degree. The university had denied the plaintiff's request for interpreter services on the grounds that he did not meet the university's established criteria for financial assistance to graduate students and should therefore pay for his own interpreter. The district court had issued a preliminary injunction (an injunction providing temporary relief pending the results of the trial) ordering the university to provide the interpreter services, irrespective of the student's ability to pay for them. The U.S. Court of Appeals affirmed the district court (616 F.2d 127 (5th Cir. 1980)). The U.S. Supreme Court, however, held that the issue concerning the propriety of the preliminary injunction had become moot because the plaintiff had graduated. Refusing to address the merits of the plaintiff's claim for interpreter services, the Supreme Court vacated the appellate court's decision and returned the case to the district court for trial.

The result of this technical dueling is that the *Camenisch* case did not furnish answers to questions concerning universities' responsibilities to provide interpreter services and other auxiliary aids to handicapped students. A regulation promulgated under Section 504 of the Rehabilitation Act of 1973 does obligate institutions to provide such services, and this obligation apparently is not negated by the student's ability to pay. But the courts have not ruled definitively on whether this regulation (sec. 84.44(d), now sec. 104.44(d)), so interpreted, is consistent with the Section 504 statute. That is the issue raised but not answered in *Camenisch.*

A related issue concerns the obligations of federally funded state vocational rehabilitation (VR) agencies to provide auxiliary services for eligible college students. The plaintiff in *Camenisch* argued that Section 84.44(d) does not place undue financial burdens on the universities because "a variety of outside funding sources," including the VR agencies, "are available to aid universities" in fulfilling their obligation. This line of argument suggests two further questions: whether the state VR agencies are legally obligated to provide auxiliary services to handicapped college students and, if so, whether their obligation serves to diminish the obligation of universities to pay the costs (see J. Orleans and M. A. Smith, "Who Should Provide Interpreters Under Section 504 of the Rehabilitation Act?" 9 *J. of College and University Law* 177 (1982–83)).

Two cases decided since *Camenisch* provide answers to these questions. In *Schornstein* v. *New Jersey Division of Vocational Rehabilitation Services,* 519 F. Supp. 773 (D.N.J. 1981), affirmed, 688 F.2d 824 (3d Cir. 1982), the court held that Title I of the Rehabilitation Act of 1973 (29 U.S.C. sec. 100 *et seq.*) requires state VR agencies to provide eligible college students with interpreter services they require to meet their vocational goals. In *Jones* v. *Illinois Department of Rehabilitation Services,* 504 F. Supp. 1244 (N.D. Ill. 1981), affirmed, 689 F.2d 724 (7th Cir. 1982), the court agreed that state VR agencies have this legal obligation. But it also held that colleges have a similar obligation under Section 104.44(d) and asked whose responsibility is primary. The court concluded that the state VR agencies have primary financial responsibility, thus diminishing universities' responsibility in situations where the student is eligible for state VR services.

There is a catch, however, in the application of these cases to the *Camenisch* problem. As the district court in *Schornstein* noted, state VR agencies may consider the financial need of handicapped individuals in determining the extent to which the agency will pay the costs of rehabilitation services (see 34 C.F.R. sec. 361.47). Thus, in a situation where the VR agency employs a financial need test and finds that a particular handicapped student does not meet it, the primary obligation would again fall on the university and the issue raised in *Camenisch* would again predominate.

The second context in which a court has addressed support services—child care—was the focus of *De La Cruz* v. *Tormey,* 582 F.2d 45 (9th Cir. 1978). Suit was brought in the U.S. District Court for the Northern District of California by several low-income women challenging the lack of child care facilities on the campuses of the San Mateo Community College District. The plaintiffs alleged that the impact of the district's decision not to provide child care facilities fell overwhelmingly on women, effectively barring them from the benefits of higher education and thus denying them equal educational opportunity. The women claimed that the policy constituted sex discrimination in violation of the equal protection clause and Title IX of the Education Amendments of 1972. The district court dismissed the case for failure to state any claim on which relief could be granted, and the plaintiffs appealed.

The U.S. Court of Appeals for the Ninth Circuit reversed the district court, ruling that the complaint could not be summarily dismissed on the pleadings and remanded the case to the lower court for a trial on the plaintiffs' allegations. Although the district's policy did not rest on an explicit classification by sex, the appellate court acknowledged that such a facially neutral policy could still violate equal protection if it affected women disproportionately and was adopted or enforced with discriminatory intent. And while Title IX would similarly require proof of disproportionate impact, "a standard less stringent than intentional discrimination" may be appropriate in considering a plaintiff's claim under the statute. (For other developments regarding discriminatory intent, see Sections 3.3.3 and 7.5.7.2.)

Regarding disproportionate impact, the court explained:

> There can be little doubt that a discriminatory effect, as that term is properly understood and has been used by the Supreme Court, has been adequately alleged. The concrete human consequences flowing from the lack of sufficient child care facilities, very practical impediments to beneficial participation in the district's educational programs, are asserted to fall over-whelmingly upon women students and would-be students. . . . The essence of the plaintiffs' grievance is that the absence of child care facilities renders the *included* benefits less valuable and less available to women; in other words, that the effect of the district's child care policy is to render the entire "package" of its programs of lesser worth to women than to men. . . . Were the object of the challenge simply a refusal to initiate or support a program or course of particular interest and value to women—women's studies, for instance—the case might be a much easier one [582 F.2d at 53, 56].

After remand the parties in *De La Cruz* agreed to an out-of-court settlement, which provided for the establishment of child care centers on the defendant's campuses. A trial was never held. It is therefore not yet known whether the novel claim raised in *De La Cruz,* or similar claims regarding other support services or other forms of discrimination, will be recognized by the courts.

An additional problem may arise if the support service is funded by a student activities fee or other mandatory fee. If the institution is public, state statutes, agency regulations, or board of trustees rules may limit the uses to be made of mandatory fees. Moreover, students who do not use the support service or who oppose it on grounds of conscience may object to the reliance on mandatory fees levied on all students. The sparse law on this point suggests, however, that such challenges will not often succeed. In *Erzinger* v. *Regents of University of California,* 137 Cal. App. 3d 389, 187 Cal. Rptr. 164 (1982), for instance, students objected to the defendants' use of mandatory fees to provide abortion and pregnancy counseling as part of campus student health services. The court rejected the students' claim that such use infringed their free exercise of religion. (See also the cases in Section 4.8.2.)

Sec. 4.4. Disciplinary Rules and Regulations

Postsecondary institutions customarily have rules of conduct or behavior, which students are expected to follow. It has become increasingly common to commit these rules to writing and embody them in codes of conduct binding on all students. Although the trend toward written codes is a sound one, legally speaking, because it gives students fairer notice of what is expected from them and often results in a better-conceived and administered system, written rules also provide a specific target to aim at in a lawsuit. Thus, in many cases students subjected to disciplinary action have contested the validity of the rule under which they were reprimanded.

4.4.1. Public institutions. In public institutions students frequently contend that the rule violates some specific guarantee of the Bill of Rights as made applicable to state institutions by the Fourteenth Amendment (see Section 1.4.2). These situations, the most numerous of which implicate the free speech and press clauses of the First Amendment, are discussed in various sections of this chapter. In other situations the contention is a more general one—that the rule is so vague that its enforcement violates due process; that is, the rule is unconstitutionally "vague" or "void for vagueness."

Soglin v. *Kauffman,* 418 F.2d 163 (7th Cir. 1969), is illustrative. The University of Wisconsin had expelled students for engaging in protest activity attempting to block access to an off-campus recruiter. The university had charged the students under a rule prohibiting "misconduct" and argued in court that it had inherent power to discipline, which need not be exercised through specific rules. Both the U.S. District Court and the U.S. Court of Appeals held that the misconduct policy was unconstitutionally vague. The appellate court reasoned:

> No one disputes the power of the university to protect itself by means of disciplinary action against disruptive students. Power to punish and the rules defining the exercise of that power are not, however, identical. Power alone does not supply the standards needed to determine its application to types of behavior or specific instances of "misconduct." As Professor Fuller has observed: "The first desideratum of a system for subjecting human conduct to the governance of rules is an obvious one: there must be rules" (L. Fuller, *The Morality of Law,* p. 46 ([Yale University Press,] rev. ed. 1969)). The proposition that government officers, including school administrators, must act in accord with rules in meting out discipline is so fundamental

that its validity tends to be assumed by courts engaged in assessing the propriety of specific regulations. . . . The [doctrine] of vagueness . . . , already applied in academic contexts, [presupposes] the existence of rules whose coherence and boundaries may be questioned. . . . These same considerations also dictate that the rules embodying standards of discipline be contained in properly promulgated regulations. University administrators are not immune from these requirements of due process in imposing sanctions. Consequently, in the present case, the disciplinary proceedings must fail to the extent that the defendant officials of the University of Wisconsin did not base those proceedings on the students' disregard of university standards of conduct expressed in reasonably clear and narrow rules.

. . . The use of "misconduct" as a standard in imposing the penalties threatened here must therefore fall for vagueness. The inadequacy of the rule is apparent on its face. It contains no clues which could assist a student, an administrator, or a reviewing judge in determining whether conduct not transgressing statutes is susceptible to punishment by the university as "misconduct."

Pursuant to appropriate rule or regulation, the university has the power to maintain order by suspension or expulsion of disruptive students. Requiring that such sanctions be administered in accord with preexisting rules does not place an unwarranted burden upon university administration. We do not require university codes of conduct to satisfy the same rigorous standards as criminal statutes. We only hold that expulsion and prolonged suspension may not be imposed on students by a university simply on the basis of allegations of "misconduct" without reference to any preexisting rule which supplies an adequate guide [418 F.2d at 167–68].

While similar language about vagueness is often found in other court opinions, the actual result in *Soglin* (the invalidation of the rule) is unusual. Most university rules subjected to judicial tests of vagueness have survived, sometimes because the rule at issue is less egregious than the "misconduct" rule in *Soglin,* sometimes because a court accepts the "inherent power to discipline" argument raised by the *Soglin* defendants and declines to undertake any real vagueness analysis, and sometimes because the student conduct at issue was so contrary to the judges' own standards of decency that they tended to ignore the defects in the rules in light of the obvious "defect" in behavior. The case most often cited in opposition to *Soglin, Esteban* v. *Central Missouri State College,* 415 F.2d 1077 (8th Cir. 1969), reveals all three of these distinctions. In this case students contested their suspension under a regulation prohibiting "participation in mass gatherings which might be considered as unruly or unlawful." In upholding the suspension, the court emphasized the need for "flexibility and reasonable breadth, rather than meticulous specificity, in college regulations relating to conduct" and recognized the institution's "latitude and discretion in its formulation of rules and regulations." The approach has often been followed in later cases—for instance, in *Jenkins* v. *Louisiana State Board of Education,* 506 F.2d 992 (5th Cir. 1975), where the court upheld a series of regulations dealing with disorderly assembly and disturbing the peace on campus.

Although the judicial trend suggests that most rules and regulations will be upheld, administrators should not thus assume that they have a free hand in promulgating codes of conduct. *Soglin* signals the institution's vulnerability where it has no written rules at all or where the rule provides no standard to guide conduct. And even the *Esteban* court warned: "We do not hold that any college regulation, however loosely framed, is necessarily valid." To avoid such pitfalls, disciplinary rules should provide standards sufficient to guide both the students in their conduct and the disciplinarians in their decision making. A rule will likely pass judicial scrutiny if the standard "conveys sufficiently definite warning as to the proscribed conduct when measured by common understanding and practices" (*Sword* v. *Fox*, 446 F.2d 1091 (4th Cir. 1971), upholding a regulation that "demonstrations are forbidden in any areas of the health center, inside any buildings, and congregating in the locations of fire hydrants"). Regulations need not be drafted by a lawyer— in fact, heavy student involvement in drafting may be valuable to ensure an expression of their "common understanding"—but it would usually be wise to have a lawyer play a general advisory role in the process.

   4.4.2. Private institutions. Private institutions, not being subject to federal constitutional constraints (see Section 1.4.2), have even more latitude than public institutions do in promulgating disciplinary rules. Courts are likely to recognize a broad right to discipline that is inherent in the private student-institution relationship or to find such a right implied in some contractual relationship between student and school. Under this broad construction, private institutional rules will not be held to specificity standards such as those in *Soglin* above. Thus, in *Dehaan* v. *Brandeis University*, 150 F. Supp. 626 (D. Mass. 1957), the court upheld the plaintiff's suspension for misconduct under a policy where the school "reserves the right to sever the connection of any student with the university for appropriate reason"; and in *Carr* v. *St. John's University, New York*, 17 A.D.2d 632, 231 N.Y.S.2d 410, affirmed, 12 N.Y.2d 802, 187 N.E.2d 18 (1962), the court upheld the dismissal of four students for off-campus conduct under a regulation providing that "in conformity with the ideals of Christian education and conduct, the university reserves the right to dismiss a student at any time on whatever grounds the university judges advisable."

   Despite the breadth of such cases, the private school administrator, like his or her public counterpart, should not assume a legally free hand in promulgating disciplinary rules. Under one developing theory or another (see Section 1.4.3), courts can now be expected to protect private school students from clearly arbitrary disciplinary actions. When a school has disciplinary rules, courts may overturn administrators' actions taken in derogation of the rules. And when there is no rule or the applicable rule provides no standard of behavior, courts may overturn suspensions for conduct which the student could not reasonably have known was wrong. Thus, in *Slaughter* v. *Brigham Young University*, 514 F.2d 622 (10th Cir. 1975), though the court upheld the expulsion of a graduate student for dishonesty under the student code of conduct, it first asked "whether the . . . [expulsion] was arbitrary" and indicated that the university's findings would be accorded a presumption of correctness only "if the regulations concerned are reasonable [and] if they are known to the student or should have been." To avoid such situations, it is wise for private institutions to adhere to much the same guidelines for promulgating rules as are suggested above for public institutions.

Sec. 4.5. Grades, Credits, and Degrees

   Fewer legal restrictions pertain to both public and private institutions' application of academic standards to students than to their application of behavioral standards.[16] Courts are more deferential to academia when evaluation of academic work is the issue, believing that such evaluation resides in the expertise of the faculty rather than the court.

In one leading case, *Connelly* v. *University of Vermont*, 244 F. Supp. 156 (D. Vt. 1965), a medical student challenged his dismissal from medical school. He had failed the pediatrics-obstetrics course and was excluded, under a College of Medicine rule, for having failed 25 percent or more of his major third-year courses. The court described its role, and the institution's legal obligation, in such cases as follows:

> Where a medical student has been dismissed for a failure to attain a proper standard of scholarship, two questions may be involved; the first is, was the student in fact delinquent in his studies or unfit for the practice of medicine? The second question is, were the school authorities motivated by malice or bad faith in dismissing the student, or did they act arbitrarily or capriciously? In general, the first question is not a matter for judicial review. However, a student dismissal motivated by bad faith, arbitrariness, or capriciousness may be actionable. . . .
>
> This rule has been stated in a variety of ways by a number of courts. It has been said that courts do not interfere with the management of a school's internal affairs unless "there has been a manifest abuse of discretion or where [the school officials'] action has been arbitrary or unlawful" (*State ex rel. Sherman* v. *Hyman*, 180 Tenn. 99, 171 S.W.2d 822, certiorari denied, 319 U.S. 748, 63 S. Ct. 1158, 87 L. Ed. 1703 (1942)), or unless the school authorities have acted "arbitrarily or capriciously" (*Frank* v. *Marquette University*, 209 Wis. 372, 245 N.W. 125 (1932)), or unless they have abused their discretion (*Coffelt* v. *Nicholson*, 224 Ark. 176, 272 S.W.2d 309 (1954); *People ex rel. Bluett* v. *Board of Trustees of University of Illinois*, 10 Ill. App. 2d 207, 134 N.E.2d 635, 58 A.L.R.2d 899 (1956)), or acted in "bad faith" (*Barnard* v. *Inhabitants of Shelburne* . . . [216 Mass. 19, 102 N.E. 1095 (1913)] and see 222 Mass. 76, 109 N.E. 818 (same case)).
>
> The effect of these decisions is to give the school authorities absolute discretion in determining whether a student has been delinquent in his studies, and to place the burden on the student of showing that his dismissal was motivated by arbitrariness, capriciousness, or bad faith. The reason for this rule is that, in matters of scholarship, the school authorities are uniquely qualified by training and experience to judge the qualifications of a student, and efficiency of instruction depends in no small degree upon

---

[16]The cases in this section concern institutional *refusals* to enter specific grades or award credits and degrees; they do not directly consider institutional *revocation* of grades, credits, or degrees already awarded. The principles developed here, however, would also apply to the revocation situation. Generally, both public and private institutions have authority to revoke improperly awarded degrees when good cause for doing so (for instance, discovery of fraud or misrepresentation) is shown (see S. Steinbach, E. Gulland, and J. P. Byrne, "Amicus Curiae Brief Filed in *Waliga* v. *Kent State University*," 14 *College Law Digest* 255, printed in *West's Education Law Reporter* (NACUA Special Pamphlet, May 3, 1984)). The institution must, however (at least if it is public), afford the degree recipient notice and an opportunity for a hearing before making a decision on whether to revoke the degree (see *Crook* v. *Baker*, 584 F. Supp. 1531 (E.D. Mich. 1984); and see generally Section 4.6 of this volume).

the school's faculty's freedom from interference from other noneducational tribunals. It is only when the school authorities abuse this discretion that a court may interfere with their decision to dismiss a student [244 F. Supp. at 159–60].

The plaintiff had alleged that his instructor decided before completion of the course to fail him regardless of the quality of his work. The court held that these allegations met its requirements for suits. They therefore stated a cause of action, which if proven at trial would justify the entry of judgment against the college.

In 1975 the U.S. Court of Appeals for the Tenth Circuit issued an important reaffirmation of the principles underlying the *Connelly* case. *Gaspar* v. *Bruton*, 513 F.2d 843 (10th Cir. 1975), concerned a practical nurse student who had been dismissed for deficient performance in clinical training. In rejecting the student's suit against the school, the court held that:

> Courts have historically refrained from interfering with the authority vested in school officials to drop a student from the rolls for failure to attain or maintain prescribed scholastic rating (whether judged by objective and/or subjective standards), absent a clear showing that the officials have acted arbitrarily or have abused the discretionary authority vested in them. . . .
>
> The courts are not equipped to review academic records based upon academic standards within the particular knowledge, experience, and expertise of academicians. Thus, when presented with a challenge that the school authorities suspended or dismissed a student for failure re academic standards, the court may grant relief, as a practical matter, only in those cases where the student presents positive evidence of ill will or bad motive [513 F.2d at 850–51].

Although the U.S. Supreme Court has not expressly adopted the judicial review standards of cases such as *Connelly* and *Gaspar*, it did address the issue briefly in *Board of Curators of the University of Missouri* v. *Horowitz*, 435 U.S. 78 (1978) (discussed in Section 4.6.3). A dismissed medical student claimed that the school applied stricter standards to her because of her sex, religion, and physical appearance. Referring particularly to *Gaspar* v. *Bruton*, the Court rejected the claim in language inhospitable to substantive judicial review of academic decisions:

> A number of lower courts have implied in dictum that academic dismissals from state institutions can be enjoined if "shown to be clearly arbitrary or capricious." . . . Even assuming that the courts can review under such a standard an academic decision of a public educational institution, we agree with the district court that no showing of arbitrariness or capriciousness has been made in this case. Courts are particularly ill equipped to evaluate academic performance. The factors discussed . . . with respect to procedural due process [see Section 4.6.3] speak *a fortiori* here and warn against any such judicial intrusion into academic decision making [435 U.S. at 91–92].

Courts may resolve legal questions concerning the award of grades, credits, or degrees not only by applying standards of arbitrariness or bad faith but also by applying the terms of the student-institutional contract (Section 4.1.3). A 1979 Kentucky case, *Lexington Theological Seminary* v. *Vance,* 596 S.W.2d 11 (Ky. App. 1979), illustrates the deference that may be accorded postsecondary institutions— especially church-related institutions—in identifying and construing the contract. The case also illustrates the problems that may arise when institutions attempt to withhold academic recognition from students because of their homosexuality.

The Lexington Theological Seminary, a seminary training ministers for the Disciples of Christ and other denominations, had denied Vance, a student who had successfully completed all his academic requirements, a Master of Divinity degree because of his admitted homosexuality. The student had enrolled in the seminary in 1972. In September 1975 he advised the dean of the school and the president of the seminary of his homosexuality. In January 1976 the student was informed that his degree candidacy would be deferred until completion of one additional course. In May 1976, after he had successfully completed the course, the faculty voted to grant the Master of Divinity degree. The seminary's executive committee, however, voted not to approve the faculty recommendation, and the board of trustees subsequently ratified the committee's decision. The student brought suit, seeking conferral of the degree.[17]

The trial court dealt with the suit as a contract case and held that the seminary had breached its contract with the plaintiff student. The Kentucky Court of Appeals, although overruling the trial court, also agreed to apply contract principles to the case: "The terms and conditions for graduation from a private college or university are those offered by the publications of the college at the time of enrollment and, as such, have some of the characteristics of a contract."

The appellate court relied on various phrases from the seminary's catalogue, such as "Christian ministry," "gospel transmitted through the Bible," "servants of the Gospel," "fundamental character," and "display traits of character and personality which indicate probable effectiveness in the Christian ministry," which it determined to be contract terms. It held that these terms created "reasonably clear standards" and interpreted them to permit the seminary to bar a homosexual student from receiving a degree. The court found that the seminary, being a religious institution preparing ministers to preach the gospel, had "a most compelling interest" in allowing only "persons possessing character of the highest Christian ideals" to graduate and that it had exercised sound discretion in denying the degree.

The court's reasoning sparked a strong dissenting opinion, which examined not only the language in the seminary catalogue but also the conduct of the seminary's dean, president, and faculty. To the dissenting judge, "Since neither the dean, the president, nor the faculty understood the catalogue to clearly exclude homosexuals, their view certainly cloud[ed] any contrary meaning." The dissent also argued that the language used in the catalogue was not sufficiently clear: "In the future, the board should consider revising the catalogue to be more explicit on what is meant by 'fundamental character.' The board might also make it clear that applications for degree candidacy will not only be 'evaluated by the faculty' but will also be reviewed by the board."

---

[17]See generally Annot., "Certificates and Certification: Student's Right to Compel School Officials to Issue Degree, Diploma, or the Like," 11 A.L.R.4th 1182 (1982 plus periodic supp.).

The *Lexington Theological Seminary* case illustrates that courts may resolve questions of academic credits or degrees by viewing the school catalogue as a contract binding on both student and institution. The majority opinion also illustrates the flexibility that courts may accord postsecondary institutions in drafting and interpreting this contract, and the special deference that may be accorded church-related institutions in enforcing terms dealing with morality. The dissent in this case, however, deserves as much attention as the majority opinion. It emphasizes that administrative conduct may have an effect on the construction of ambiguous contract terms (see Section 1.3.8) and illustrates the potential for ambiguity that resides in general terms such as "fundamental character." Postsecondary administrators should heed these warnings. Other courts may not be as deferential to the institution as the Kentucky Court of Appeals was, especially in cases that involve life-style or off-campus behavior rather than the quality of academic works as such. Even if administrators could confidently expect broad deference from the courts, the dissent's cautions are still valuable as suggestions for how institutions can do better, of their own accord rather than through judicial compulsion, in ordering their own internal affairs.

A 1980 New York case, *Olsson* v. *Board of Higher Education of the City of New York,* 4 N.Y.2d 408, 402 N.E.2d 1150 (1980), illustrates a third type of analysis of grading issues. A student had not passed a comprehensive examination and therefore had not been awarded the M.A. degree for which he had been working. He claimed that his professor had misled him concerning the required passing grade on the examination. The professor had meant to say that a student must score three out of a possible five points on four of the five questions; instead, the professor said that a student must pass three of five questions. The student relied on the estoppel doctrine—the doctrine that justifiable reliance on a statement or promise estops the other from contradicting it if the reliance led directly to a detriment or injustice to the promisee. He argued that (1) he had justifiably relied on the professor's statement in budgeting both his study and test time, (2) he had achieved the grade the professor had stated was necessary, and (3) injustice would result if the university was not estopped from denying the degree.

The trial court and intermediate appellate court both accepted the student's argument. The state's highest appellate court, however, did not. Deferring to the academic judgment of the institution, and emphasizing that the institution had offered the student an opportunity to retake the exam, the court refused to grant a "degree by estoppel":

> In reversing the determinations below, we are mindful that this case involves more than a simple balancing of equities among various competing commercial interests. While it is true that in the ordinary case, a principal must answer for the misstatements of his agent when the latter is clothed with a mantle of apparent authority (see, for example, *Phillips* v. *West Rockaway Land Co.,* 226 N.Y. 507, 124 N.E. 87), such hornbook rules cannot be applied mechanically where the "principal" is an educational institution and the result would be to override a determination concerning a student's academic qualifications. Because such determinations rest in most cases upon the subjective professional judgment of trained educators, the courts have quite properly exercised the utmost restraint in applying

traditional legal rules to disputes within the academic community (see, for example, *Board of Curators, University of Missouri* v. *Horowitz,* 435 U.S. 78, 98 S. Ct. 948, 55 L. Ed. 2d 124 . . .).

This judicial reluctance to intervene in controversies involving academic standards is founded upon sound considerations of public policy. When an educational institution issues a diploma to one of its students, it is, in effect, certifying to society that the student possesses all of the knowledge and skills that are required by his chosen discipline. In order for society to be able to have complete confidence in the credentials dispensed by academic institutions, however, it is essential that the decisions surrounding the issuance of these credentials be left to the sound judgment of the professional educators who monitor the progress of their students on a regular basis. Indeed, the value of these credentials from the point of view of society would be seriously undermined if the courts were to abandon their longstanding practice of restraint in this area and instead began to utilize traditional equitable estoppel principles as a basis for requiring institutions to confer diplomas upon those who have been deemed to be unqualified.

Certainly [in this case John Jay College] was not obliged to confer a diploma upon Olsson before he demonstrated his competence in accordance with the institution's academic standards. The mere circumstance that Olsson may have been misled by Professor Kim's unfortunate remark cannot serve to enhance the student's position in this regard. Despite Olsson's speculative contention that he might have passed the examination had he not been misinformed about the grading criteria, the fact remains that neither the courts nor the college authorities have any way of knowing whether the outcome of the testing would have been different if Olsson had not "relied" upon Professor Kim's misstatement. Indeed, the fact that 23 of the 35 students enrolled in Professor Kim's review course managed to pass the examination despite the faculty member's "slip-of-the-tongue" serves to demonstrate that there was no necessary connection between Olsson's exposure to the "three out of five" comment and his failure to achieve a passing score. Under these circumstances, requiring the college to award Olsson a diploma on equitable estoppel grounds would be a disservice to society, since the credential would not represent the college's considered judgment that Olsson possessed the requisite qualifications [402 N.E.2d at 1152–53].

Although the court refused to apply the estoppel doctrine to the particular facts of this case, it indicated that in other, more extreme, circumstances estoppel could apply to problems concerning grading and other academic judgments:

To be distinguished from the present case are those situations in which a student has fulfilled all of the academic requirements for graduation, but has neglected some technical prerequisite in reliance upon the assurances of a faculty member. The facts in *Matter of Blank* v. *Board of Higher Education,* 51 Misc. 2d 724, 273 N.Y.S.2d 796 [see this volume, Section 2.2.2], are illustrative in this regard. There, the student had elected to pursue the college's "professional option plan" after consulting with his prelaw adviser at the college. Under the plan, a student who had completed at least three quarters of his studies at the college could become entitled to a baccalaureate degree if he completed one year's full-time work in an approved law school. The only proviso was that the student's course of study had to "constitute, in the opinion of the dean of faculty, an acceptable program for the A.B. degree." Since he lacked four required courses at the time he was preparing to enter law school, the student approached the guidance officer of the college and the chairperson of the applicable academic department in an effort to work out an acceptable program. The student, who was planning to attend an out-of-town law school, was unequivocally advised that he would have to enroll in the required courses at the college, but was told that he could obtain the necessary credits without actually attending classes if the individual instructors agreed. Pursuant to this advice, the student in *Blank* took two of the required courses over the summer "in residence" and then made arrangements with college instructors to take the two remaining courses on a "correspondence" basis. Although he passed the final examinations in each of the last two courses with a grade of "B" and received full course credit from the individual instructors, the student in *Blank* was denied his diploma after the dean determined that he had failed to comply with the college's "in residence" requirement. Under these circumstances, [the court] correctly held that the dean of the college should be estopped from asserting the "in residence" requirement as a ground for withholding the student's diploma, since the requirement had, in effect, been waived by several faculty members, all of whom could be regarded agents of the dean.

The outstanding feature which differentiates *Blank* from the instant case is the unavoidable fact that in *Blank* the student unquestionably had fulfilled the academic requirements for the credential he sought. Unlike the student here, the student in *Blank* had demonstrated his competence in the subject matter to the satisfaction of his professors. Thus, there could be no public policy objection to [the court's] decision to award a "diploma by estoppel" (accord *Matter of Healy* v. *Larsson,* 67 Misc. 2d 374, 323 N.Y.S.2d 625, affirmed, 42 A.D.2d 1051, 348 N.Y.S.2d 971, affirmed, 35 N.Y.2d 653, 360 N.Y.S.2d 419, 318 N.E.2d 608). Moreover, although the distinction is not dispositive, it cannot be overlooked that the student in *Blank* had relied upon a continuous series of deliberate and considered assurances from several faculty members, while Olsson, the student in this case, premised his estoppel claim upon a single inadvertent "slip-of-the-tongue" made by one professor during the course of a single presentation [402 N.E.2d at 1153–54].[18]

The *Olsson* case thus provides both an extensive justification of "aca-

---

[18]Another case in which the court ordered the award of a degree is *Kantor* v. *Schmidt,* 73 A.D.2d 670, 423 N.Y.S.2d 208 (1979), a mandamus proceeding under New York law. The State University of New York at Stony Brook had withheld the degree because the student had not made sufficient progress, within established time limits, toward completion of the degree. The court ordered the defendant to award a B.A. degree to the student because the university had not complied with the state commissioner of education's regulations on student progress and informing students of progress. The student had completed the 120 credits required for the degree.

demic deference''—that is, judicial deference to an educational institution's academic judgments—and an extensive analysis of when courts, rather than deferring, should invoke estoppel principles to protect students challenging academic decisions. Synthesizing its analysis, the court concluded:

> It must be stressed that the judicial awarding of an academic diploma is an extreme remedy which should be reserved for the most egregious of circumstances. In light of the serious policy considerations which militate against judicial intervention in academic disputes, the courts should shun the ''diploma by estoppel'' doctrine whenever there is some question as to whether the student seeking relief has actually demonstrated his competence in accordance with the standards devised by the appropriate school authorities. Additionally, the courts should be particularly cautious in applying the doctrine in cases such as this, where a less drastic remedy, such as retesting, may be employed without seriously disrupting the student's academic or professional career [402 N.E.2d at 1154].

A second case from 1980, *Alexander* v. *Yale University,* 631 F.2d 178 (2d Cir. 1980), illustrates yet another, and newly emerging, way in which the law may apply to disputes over academic evaluations and awards. *Alexander* was a case brought by five female students who alleged that Yale's practices and procedures for dealing with sexual harassment of students violated Title IX of the Education Amendments of 1972 (this volume, Section 7.5.3). One of the plaintiffs alleged that a faculty member had ''offered to give her a grade of 'A' in the course in exchange for her compliance with his sexual demands'' and that, when she refused, he gave her a ''C,'' which ''was not the result of a fair evaluation of her academic work but the result of her failure to accede to [the professor's] sexual demands.'' The remaining plaintiffs made other allegations concerning acts of harassment and the inadequacies of campus procedures to deal with them.

The district court entered judgment for Yale, and the U.S. Court of Appeals affirmed. With the exception of the lowered grade claim of one plaintiff, all the various claims and plaintiffs were dismissed for technical reasons: the plaintiffs had graduated and their claims were therefore ''moot''; Yale had already adopted procedures for dealing with sexual harassment and thus, in effect, had already granted the primary remedy requested in the suit; other claims of harm were too ''speculative'' or ''uncertain.'' The lowered grade claim was dismissed because the plaintiff, at trial, did not prove the allegations.

Although rejecting all claims, the *Alexander* court by no means shut the door on Title IX actions alleging that the integrity of grading or other academic processes has been compromised by faculty's sexual harassment of students. Both trial and appellate courts made clear that the grade claim was a ''justifiable claim for relief under Title IX.'' A denial or threatened denial of earned academic awards would be a deprivation of an educational benefit protected by Title IX; and when imposed for sexual reasons, that deprivation becomes sex discrimination prohibited by Title IX. As the district court held, and the appellate court quoted with apparent approval, ''Academic advancement conditioned upon submission to sexual demands constitutes sex discrimination in education'' (459 F. Supp. 1, 4 (D. Conn. 1977), 631 F.2d at 182). In this respect, the sensitive problem of sexual harassment, finally a visible academic problem attracting serious attention (see National Advisory Council on Women's Educational Programs, *Sexual Harassment: A Report on the Sexual Harassment of Students* (U.S. Department of Education, 1980)), is also a matter of law. Title IX thus provides a new legal perspective, in one specific area of concern, on the award of grades, credits, and degrees.

Sec. 4.6. Procedures for Suspension, Dismissal, and Other Sanctions

4.6.1. General principles. As Sections 4.4 and 4.5 indicate, both public and private postsecondary institutions have the clear right to dismiss, suspend, or impose lesser sanctions on students for behavioral misconduct or academic deficiency. But just as that right is limited by the principles set out in those sections, so it is also circumscribed by a body of procedural requirements which institutions must follow in effecting disciplinary or academic sanctions. These procedural requirements tend to be more specific and substantial than the requirements set out above, although they do vary depending on whether behavior or academics is involved and whether the institution is public or private (see Section 1.4.2).

At the threshold level, whenever an institution has established procedures that apply to the imposition of sanctions, the law will usually require that they be followed. In *Woody* v. *Burns,* 188 So. 2d 56 (Fla. 1966), for example, the court invalidated an expulsion from a public institution because a faculty committee had "circumvented . . . [the] duly authorized [disciplinary] committee and arrogated unto itself the authority of imposing its own penalty for appellant's misconduct." And in *Tedeschi* v. *Wagner College,* 49 N.Y.2d 652, 404 N.E.2d 1302 (1980), New York's highest court invalidated a suspension from a private institution, holding that "when a university has adopted a rule or guideline establishing the procedure to be followed in relation to suspension or expulsion, that procedure must be substantially observed."

There are two exceptions, however, to this "follow-the-rules" principle. An institution may be excused from following its own procedures if the student knowingly and freely waives his or her right to them, as in *Yench* v. *Stockmar,* 483 F.2d 820 (10th Cir. 1973), where the student neither requested that the published procedures be followed nor objected when they were not. Second, deviations from established procedures may be excused when they do not disadvantage the student, as in *Winnick* v. *Manning,* 460 F.2d 545 (2d Cir. 1972), where the student contested the school's use of a panel other than that required by the rules, but the court held that the "deviations were minor ones and did not affect the fundamental fairness of the hearing."

4.6.2. Public institutions: Disciplinary sanctions. State institutions may be subject to state administrative procedure acts, state board of higher education rules, or other state statutes or administrative regulations specifying particular procedures for suspensions or expulsions. In *Moresco* v. *Clark,* 100 A.D.2d 41, 473 N.Y.S.2d 843 (1984), the court refused to apply New York State's Administrative Procedure Act to a suspension proceeding at SUNY-Cortland; but in *Mull* v. *Oregon Institute of Technology,* 538 P.2d 87 (Or. 1975), the court applied that state's administrative procedure statutes to a suspension for misconduct and remanded the case to the college with instructions to enter findings of fact and conclusions of law as required by one of the statutory provisions. The primary external source of procedural requirements for public institutions, however, is the due process clause of the federal Constitution. Since the early 1960s, the concept of procedural due process has been one of the primary legal forces shaping the administration of postsecondary education.

A landmark 1961 case on suspension procedures, *Dixon* v. *Alabama State Board of Education,* 294 F.2d 150 (5th Cir. 1961), is still very instructive. Several black students at Alabama State College had been expelled during a period of intense civil rights activity in Montgomery, Alabama. The students, supported by the NAACP, sued the state board, and the court faced the question "whether [the] due process [clause of the Fourteenth Amendment] requires notice and some opportunity for hearing before students at a tax-supported college are expelled for misconduct." On appeal this question was answered in the affirmative, with the court establishing standards by which to measure the adequacy of a public institution's expulsion procedures:

> The notice should contain a statement of the specific charges and grounds which, if proven, would justify expulsion under the regulations of the board of education. The nature of the hearing should vary depending upon the circumstances of the particular case. The case before us requires something more than an informal interview with an administrative authority of the college. By its nature, a charge of misconduct, as opposed to a failure to meet the scholastic standards of the college, depends upon a collection of the facts concerning the charged misconduct, easily colored by the point of view of the witnesses. In such circumstances, a hearing which gives the board or the administrative authorities of the college an opportunity to hear both sides in considerable detail is best suited to protect the rights of all involved. This is not to imply that a full-dress judicial hearing, with the right to cross-examine witnesses, is required. Such a hearing, with the attending publicity and disturbance of college activities, might be detrimental to the college's educational atmosphere and impractical to carry out. Nevertheless, the rudiments of an adversary proceeding may be preserved without encroaching upon the interests of the college. In the instant case, the student should be given the names of the witnesses against him and an oral or written report on the facts to which each witness testifies. He should also be given the opportunity to present to the board, or at least to an administrative official of the college, his own defense against the charges and to produce either oral testimony or written affidavits of witnesses in his behalf. If the hearing is not before the board directly, the results and findings of the hearing should be presented in a report open to the student's inspection. If these rudimentary elements of fair play are followed in a case of misconduct of this particular type, we feel that the requirements of due process of law will have been fulfilled [294 F.2d at 158–59].

Since the *Dixon* case, courts at all levels have continued to recognize and extend the due process safeguards available to students charged by college officials with misconduct. Such safeguards must now be provided for all students in publicly supported schools not only before expulsion, as in *Dixon,* but before suspension and other serious disciplinary action as well. In 1975 the U.S. Supreme Court itself recognized the vitality and clear national applicability of such developments when it held that even a secondary school student faced with a suspension of less than ten days is entitled to "oral or written notice of the charges against him and, if he denies them, an explanation of the evidence the authorities have and an opportunity to present his side of the story" (*Goss* v. *Lopez,* 419 U.S. 565 (1975)).

Probably the case that has set forth due process requirements in greatest detail is *Esteban* v. *Central Missouri State College,* 277 F. Supp. 649 (W.D. Mo. 1967) (see also later litigation in this case, discussed in Section 4.4.1 above). The plaintiffs had been suspended for two semesters for engaging in protest demonstrations. The lower court held that the students had not been accorded procedural due process and ordered the school to provide the following protections for them: (1) a written statement of the charges, for each student, made available at least ten days before the hearing; (2) a hearing before the person(s) having power to expel or suspend; (3) the opportunity for advance inspection of any affidavits or exhibits the college intends to submit at the hearing; (4) the right to bring counsel to the hearing to advise them (but not to question witnesses); (5) the opportunity to present their own version of the facts, by personal statements as well as affidavits and witnesses; (6) the right to hear evidence against them and question (personally, not through counsel) adverse witnesses; (7) a determination of the facts of each case by the hearing officer solely on the basis of the evidence presented at the hearing; (8) a written statement of the hearing officer's findings of fact; and (9) the right, at their own expense, to make a record of the hearing.

The judicial imposition of specific due process requirements rankles many administrators. By and large, courts have been sufficiently sensitive to avoid such detail in favor of administrative flexibility (see, for example, *Moresco* v. *Clark,* 100 A.D.2d 41, 473 N.Y.S.2d 843 (1984); *Henson* v. *Honor Committee of the University of Virginia,* 719 F.2d 69 (4th Cir. 1983), discussed in Section 4.6.2.2). Yet for the internal guidance of an administrator responsible for disciplinary procedures, the *Esteban* requirements provide a very useful checklist. The listed items not only suggest the outer limits of what a court might require but also identify those procedures most often considered valuable for ascertaining facts where they are in dispute. Within this framework of concerns, the constitutional focus remains on the notice-and-opportunity-for-hearing concept of *Dixon.*

4.6.2.1. Notice. Notice should be given of both the conduct with which the student is charged and the rule or policy which allegedly proscribes that conduct. The charges need not be drawn with the specificity of a criminal indictment, but they should be "in sufficient detail to fairly enable . . . [the student] to present a defense" at the hearing (*Jenkins* v. *Louisiana State Board of Education,* 506 F.2d 992 (5th Cir. 1975), holding notice in a suspension case to be adequate, particularly in light of information provided by the defendant subsequent to the original notice). Factual allegations not enumerated in the notice may be developed at the hearing if the student could reasonably have expected them to be included.

There is no clear constitutional requirement concerning how much advance notice the student must have of the charges. As little as two days before the hearing has been held adequate (*Jones* v. *Tennessee State Board of Education,* 279 F. Supp. 190 (M.D. Tenn. 1968), affirmed, 407 F.2d 834 (6th Cir. 1969)). *Esteban* required ten days, however, and in most other cases the time has been longer than two days. In general, courts handle this issue case by case, asking whether the amount of time was fair under all the circumstances.

4.6.2.2. Hearing. The minimum requirement is that the hearing provide students with an opportunity to speak in their own defense and explain their side of the story. Since due process apparently does not require an open or public hearing, the institution has the discretion to close or partially close the hearing or to leave the choice to the accused student. But courts usually will accord students the right to hear the evidence against them and to present oral testimony or, at minimum, written statements from witnesses. Formal rules of evidence need not be followed. Cross-examination, the right to counsel, the right to a transcript, and an appellate procedure have generally not been constitutional essentials, but where institutions have voluntarily provided these procedures, courts have often cited them approvingly as enhancers of the hearing's fairness. In upholding the validity of the University of Virginia's student-operated honor system, for example, the court in *Henson* v. *Honor Committee of the University of Virginia,* 719 F.2d 69 (4th Cir. 1983), reasoned that:

> The university's honor system provides the accused student with an impressive array of procedural protections. The student, for example, receives what is essentially an indictment, specifying both the charges and the factual allegations supporting them (Virginia Honor Code, Art. III sec. C(1)). He has a right to a hearing before a committee of his peers. He is entitled, at no personal cost, to have a student lawyer represent his interests at all critical stages in the proceedings. He may also retain a practicing attorney to assist in his defense, although the attorney can assume no active role in the honor trial itself (Art. III sec. C(1)). The individuals who brought the charges must face the student at the hearing and state the basis of their allegations (Art. III sec. D(2)). They, in turn, must submit to cross-examination by the student, or his designated student counsel, and by the members of the hearing committee. The student then has the right to present evidence in opposition to the charges and to offer witnesses for the sole purpose of bolstering his character (Art. III sec. D(5)(a)). He may, if he chooses, demand that the hearing be conducted in public, where impartial observers can make an independent assessment of the proceeding's fairness (Art. VIII sec. E). If, after hearing the evidence, four fifths (4/5) of the committee members find the student guilty beyond a reasonable doubt, he has the right to appeal the decision to a five-member board comprised of members of the student government (Art. V). This board is empowered to review the record of the honor trial and to grant new trials when, in its judgment, the correct procedures were not followed or the evidentiary findings of the trial committee were deficient.
>
> In some respects, these procedures concededly fall short of the stringent protections afforded the criminal defendant; that is not, however, a defect of constitutional dimension. . . . The Supreme Court has made it plain that "the judicial model of an evidentiary hearing is neither a required, nor even the most effective, method of decision making in all circumstances." . . .
>
> It is true that Henson [the student plaintiff] was not permitted to have a practicing attorney conduct his defense, but this is not a right generally available to students facing disciplinary charges (*Gabrilowitz* v. *Newman,* 582 F.2d 100, 104 (1st Cir. 1978)). Henson was provided with two student

lawyers, who consulted extensively with his personally retained attorney at all critical stages of the proceedings. The due process clause would impose no greater obligations on the university than it placed on itself in conducting its disciplinary proceedings [719 F.2d at 73–74].

When the conduct with which the student is charged in the disciplinary proceeding is also the subject of a criminal court proceeding, the due process obligations of the institution will likely increase. Since the student then faces additional risks and strategic problems, some of the procedures usually left to the institution's discretion may become constitutional essentials. In *Gabrilowitz* v. *Newman*, 582 F.2d 100 (1st Cir. 1978) (discussed in Section 4.13.3), for example, the court required that the institution allow the student to have a professional lawyer present to advise him during the disciplinary hearing.

The person(s) presiding over the disciplinary proceedings and the person(s) with authority to make the final decision must decide the case on the basis of the evidence presented and must, of course, weigh the evidence impartially. Generally the student must show malice, bias, or conflict of interest on the part of the hearing officer or panel member before a court will make a finding of partiality. In *Blanton* v. *State University of New York*, 489 F.2d 377 (2d Cir. 1973), the court held that—at least where students had a right of appeal—due process was not violated when a dean who had witnessed the incident at issue also sat on the hearing committee. And in *Jones* v. *Tennessee State Board of Education*, 279 F. Supp. 190 (M.D. Tenn. 1968), affirmed, 407 F.2d 834 (6th Cir. 1969), the court even permitted a member of the hearing committee to give evidence against the accused student, in the absence of proof of malice or personal interest. But other courts may be less hospitable to such practices, and it would be wise to avoid them whenever possible.

The hearing must normally take place before the suspension or expulsion goes into effect. The leading case on this point has been *Stricklin* v. *Regents of University of Wisconsin*, 297 F. Supp. 416 (W.D. Wis. 1969), where the court limited the use of interim suspensions, pending a final decision, to situations where "the appropriate university authority has reasonable cause to believe that danger will be present if a student is permitted to remain on campus pending a decision following a full hearing." The court also noted that "an interim suspension may not be imposed without a prior preliminary hearing, unless it can be shown that it is impossible or unreasonably difficult to accord it prior to an interim suspension," in which case "procedural due process requires that . . . [the student] be provided such a preliminary hearing at the earliest practical time." These requirements would protect a student from being "suspended in ex parte proceedings . . . without any opportunity, however brief and however limited, to persuade the suspending authority that there is a case of mistaken identity or that there was extreme provocation or that there is some other compelling justification for withholding or terminating the interim suspension." While case law on these points has been sparse, the U.S. Supreme Court's 1975 ruling in *Goss* v. *Lopez* (Section 4.6.2) affirms that at least part of *Stricklin* applies nationwide:

> As a general rule notice and hearing should precede removal of the student from school. We agree . . . , however, that there are recurring situations in which prior notice and hearing cannot be insisted upon. Students

whose presence poses a continuing danger to persons or property or an ongoing threat of disrupting the academic process may be immediately removed from school . . . [and notice and hearing] should follow as soon as practicable [419 U.S. at 583 (1975)].

The extent to which the notice and hearing procedures set forth above apply to disciplinary sanctions less severe than suspension or expulsion is unclear. On the one hand, a pre-*Goss* case, *Yench* v. *Stockmar* (Section 4.6.1), held the due process clause inapplicable to disciplinary probation cases. On the other hand, any penalty that deprives the student of substantial educational benefits or seriously affects his reputation and employment prospects is, under *Goss,* arguably subject to at least the "rudimentary" protections of due process. In general, an institution should provide increasingly more formal and comprehensive due process procedures as the severity of the potential penalty increases and should gear its procedures to the *maximum* penalty that can be meted out in each type of proceeding it authorizes.

4.6.3. Public institutions: Academic sanctions. The Fourteenth Amendment's due process clause also applies to students facing suspension or dismissal from publicly supported schools for deficient academic performance. But even though academic dismissals may be even more damaging to students than disciplinary dismissals, due process affords substantially less protection to students in the former situation. Courts grant less protection because they recognize that they are less competent to review academic evaluative judgments than factually based determinations of misconduct and that hearings and the attendant formalities of witnesses and evidence are less meaningful in reviewing grading than in determining misconduct.

Gaspar v. *Bruton,* 513 F.2d 843 (10th Cir. 1975), was apparently the first case to provide any procedural due process rights to a student facing an academic suspension or dismissal. The plaintiff was a forty-four-year-old high school graduate pursuing practical nurse training in a vocational-technical school. After completing more than two thirds of the program, she was dismissed for deficient performance in clinical training. She had been on probation for two months owing to such deficiencies and had been informed that she would be dismissed if they were not corrected. When they were not, she was notified of dismissal in a conference with the superintendent and some of her instructors and was subsequently offered a second conference and an opportunity to question other staff-faculty members who had participated in the dismissal decision.

The trial and appellate courts upheld the dismissal, rejecting the student's contention that before dismissal she should have been confronted with and allowed to challenge the evidence supporting the dismissal and allowed to present evidence in her defense. Although the appellate court recognized a "property interest" in continued attendance, it held that school officials had only minimal due process obligations in this context:

> Gaspar was provided much more due process than that which we hold must be accorded in cases involving academic termination or suspension. We hold that school authorities, in order to satisfy due process prior to termination or suspension of a student for deficiencies in meeting minimum academic performance, need only advise that student with respect to such deficiencies in any form. All that is required is that the student

be made aware prior to termination of his failure or impending failure to meet those standards [513 F.2d at 850–51].

More significant protection was afforded in *Greenhill* v. *Bailey,* 519 F.2d 5 (8th Cir. 1975), where another U.S. Court of Appeals invalidated a medical student's dismissal because he had not been accorded procedural due process. The school had dismissed the student for "lack of intellectual ability or insufficient preparation" and had conveyed that information to the liaison committee of the Association of American Medical Colleges, where it was available to all other medical schools. The court ruled that "the action by the school in denigrating Greenhill's intellectual ability, as distinguished from his performance, deprived him of a significant interest in liberty, for it admittedly 'imposed on him a stigma or other disability that foreclose[s] his freedom to take advantage of other . . . opportunities' (*Board of Regents* v. *Roth,* 408 U.S. at 573, 92 S. Ct. at 2707)." In such circumstances, due process required more than the school had provided:

> At the very least, Greenhill should have been notified in writing of the alleged deficiency in his intellectual ability, since this reason for his dismissal would potentially stigmatize his future as a medical student elsewhere, and should have been accorded an opportunity to appear personally to contest such allegation.
> We stop short, however, of requiring full trial-type procedures. . . . But an "informal give-and-take" between the student and the administrative body dismissing him—and foreclosing his opportunity to gain admission at all comparable institutions—would not unduly burden the educational process and would, at least, give the student "the opportunity to characterize his conduct and put it in what he deems proper context" (*Goss* v. *Lopez,* 419 U.S. at 584, 95 S. Ct. at 741) [519 F.2d at 9].

The next year the same U.S. Court of Appeals extended its *Greenhill* ruling in another medical school case, *Horowitz* v. *Board of Curators of University of Missouri,* 538 F.2d 1317 (8th Cir. 1976). But on appeal the U.S. Supreme Court clipped this court's wings and put an apparent halt to the development of procedural due process in academic disputes (*Board of Curators of the University of Missouri* v. *Horowitz,* 435 U.S. 78 (1978)). The university had dismissed the student, who had received excellent grades on written exams, for deficiencies in clinical performance, peer and patient relations, and personal hygiene. After several faculty members repeatedly expressed dissatisfaction with her clinical work, the school's council on evaluation recommended that Horowitz not be allowed to graduate on time and that, "absent radical improvement" in the remainder of the year, she be dropped from the program. She was then allowed to take a special set of oral and practical exams, administered by practicing physicians in the area, as a means of appealing the council's determination. After receiving the results of these exams, the council reaffirmed its recommendation. At the end of the year, after receiving further clinical reports on Horowitz, the council recommended that she be dropped from school. The school's coordinating committee, then the dean, and finally the provost for health sciences affirmed the decision.

Though there was no evidence that the reasons for the dismissal were conveyed to the liaison committee, as in *Greenhill,* the appellate court held that "Horowitz's dismissal from medical school will make it difficult or impossible for her to obtain employment in a medically related field or to enter another medical school." The court concluded that dismissal would so stigmatize the student as to deprive her of liberty under the Fourteenth Amendment and that, under the circumstances, the university could not dismiss the student without providing "a hearing before the decision-making body or bodies, at which she shall have an opportunity to rebut the evidence being relied upon for her dismissal and accorded all other procedural due process rights."

The Supreme Court found it unnecessary to decide whether Horowitz had been deprived of a liberty or property interest. Even assuming she had, Horowitz had no right to a hearing:

> Respondent has been awarded at least as much due process as the Fourteenth Amendment requires. The school fully informed respondent of the faculty's dissatisfaction with her clinical progress and the danger that this posed to timely graduation and continued enrollment. The ultimate decision to dismiss respondent was careful and deliberate. These procedures were sufficient under the due process clause of the Fourteenth Amendment. We agree with the district court that respondent
>
>> was afforded full procedural due process by the [school]. In fact, the court is of the opinion, and so finds, that the school went beyond [constitutionally required] procedural due process by affording [respondent] the opportunity to be examined by seven independent physicians in order to be absolutely certain that their grading of the [respondent] in her medical skills was correct [435 U.S. at 85].

The Court relied on the distinction between academic and disciplinary cases that lower courts had developed in cases prior to *Horowitz,* finding that distinction to be consistent with its own due process pronouncements, especially *Goss* v. *Lopez* (Section 4.6.2):

> The Court of Appeals apparently read *Goss* as requiring some type of formal hearing at which respondent could defend her academic ability and performance. . . . But we have frequently emphasized that "the very nature of due process negates any concept of inflexible procedures universally applicable to every imaginable situation" (*Cafeteria Workers* v. *McElroy,* 367 U.S. 886, 895 (1961)). The need for flexibility is well illustrated by the significant difference between the failure of a student to meet academic standards and the violation by a student of valid rules of conduct. This difference calls for far less stringent procedural requirements in the case of an academic dismissal. . . .
>
> A school is an academic institution, not a courtroom or administrative hearing room. In *Goss,* this Court felt that suspensions of students for disciplinary reasons have a sufficient resemblance to traditional judicial and administrative fact finding to call for a "hearing" before the relevant school authority. . . .

Academic evaluations of a student, in contrast to disciplinary determinations, bear little resemblance to the judicial and administrative fact-
finding proceedings to which we have traditionally attached a full hearing requirement. In *Goss,* the school's decision to suspend the students
rested on factual conclusions that the individual students had participated
in demonstrations that had disrupted classes, attacked a police officer,
or caused physical damage to school property. The requirement of a hearing, where the student could present his side of the factual issue, could
under such circumstances "provide a meaningful hedge against erroneous action." The decision to dismiss respondent, by comparison, rested
on the academic judgment of school officials that she did not have the
necessary clinical ability to perform adequately as a medical doctor and
was making insufficient progress toward that goal. Such a judgment is
by its nature more subjective and evaluative than the typical factual questions presented in the average disciplinary decision. Like the decision of
an individual professor as to the proper grade for a student in his course,
the determination whether to dismiss a student for academic reasons requires an expert evaluation of cumulative information and is not readily
adapted to the procedural tools of judicial or administrative decision making
[435 U.S. at 85–90].

Horowitz signals the Court's lack of receptivity to procedural requirements
for academic dismissals. Clearly, an adversary hearing is not required. Nor are
all the procedures used by the university in *Horowitz* required, since the Court suggested that Horowitz received *more* due process than she was entitled to. But the
Court's opinion does not say that *no* due process is required. Institutions apparently
must afford some minimal protections, the exact character of which is not yet clear.
Due process probably requires the institution to inform the student of the inadequacies in performance and their consequences on academic standing. Apparently,
due process also generally requires that the institution's decision making be "careful
and deliberate." For the former requirements, courts are likely to be lenient on
how much information or explanation the student must be given and also on how
far in advance of formal dismissal the student must be notified. For the latter requirement, courts are likely to be very flexible, not demanding any particular procedure
but rather accepting any decision-making process that, overall, supports reasoned
judgments concerning academic quality. Even these minimal requirements would
be imposed on institutions only when their academic judgments infringe on a student's "liberty" or "property" interests, and it is not yet clear what constitutes
such infringements in the postsecondary context.

Since courts attach markedly different due process requirements to academic
sanctions than to disciplinary sanctions, it is crucial to be able to place particular
cases in one category or the other. The characterization required is not always easy.
The *Horowitz* case is a good example. The student's dismissal was not a typical case
of inadequate scholarship, such as poor grades on written exams; rather, she was
dismissed at least partly for inadequate peer and patient relations and personal hygiene.
It is arguable that such a decision involves "fact finding," as in a disciplinary case,
more than an "evaluative," "academic judgment." Indeed, the Court split on this
issue: five judges applied the "academic" label to the case, two judges applied the

"disciplinary" label or argued that no labeling was appropriate, and two judges refused to determine either which label to apply or "whether such a distinction is relevant."

Another illustration of the categorization difficulty is provided by a pre-*Horowitz* case, *Brookins* v. *Bonnell,* 362 F. Supp. 379 (E.D. Pa. 1973). A nursing student was dismissed from a community college for (1) failing to submit a state-required physical examination report, (2) failing to inform the college that he had previously attended another nursing school, and (3) failing to attend class regularly. The student disputed these charges and argued that he should have been afforded a hearing before his dismissal. The court indicated that the right to a hearing depended on whether the student had been dismissed "because of disciplinary misconduct" or "solely because of an academic failure." After noting that the situation "does not fit neatly" into either category, the court decided the issue as follows:

> This case is not the traditional disciplinary situation where a student violates the law or a school regulation by actively engaging in prohibited activities. Plaintiff has allegedly failed to act and comply with school regulations for admission and class attendance by passively ignoring these regulations. These alleged failures do not constitute misconduct in the sense that plaintiff is subject to disciplinary procedures. They do constitute misconduct in the sense that plaintiff was required to do something. Plaintiff contends that he did comply with the requirements. Like the traditional disciplinary case, the determination of whether plaintiff did or did not comply with the school regulations is a question of fact. Most importantly, in determining this factual question, reference is not made to a standard of achievement in an esoteric academic field. Scholastic standards are not involved, but rather disputed facts concerning whether plaintiff did or did not comply with certain school regulations. These issues adapt themselves readily to determination by a fair and impartial "due process" hearing [362 F. Supp. at 383].

The distinction made by the court is sound and is generally supported in the various justices' opinions in *Horowitz.* When dismissal or other serious sanctions depend more on disputed factual issues concerning conduct than on expert evaluation of academic work, the student should be accorcded procedural rights akin to those for disciplinary cases (Section 4.6.2) rather than the lesser rights for academic deficiency cases. Of course, even when the academic label is clearly appropriate, administrators may choose to provide more procedural safeguards than the Constitution requires. Indeed, there may be good reason to provide some form of hearing prior to academic dismissal whenever the student has some basis for claiming that the academic judgment was arbitrary, in bad faith, or discriminatory (see Section 4.5). The question for the administrator, therefore, is not merely what procedures are constitutionally required but also what procedures would make the best policy for the particular institution.

There have been few reported opinions applying *Horowitz* to other academic dismissal problems in public institutions. Typical of those cases that have been reported is *Sofair* v. *SUNY Upstate Medical Center College of Medicine,* 44 N.Y.2d 475, 377 N.E.2d 730 (1978), in which the New York Court of Appeals relied on *Horowitz* to reject a medical student's claim that his academic dismissal violated constitutional due process requirements:

In this instance, as in *Horowitz*, the student had previously been informed of the school's dissatisfaction with his progress, and the dismissal was for academic (as opposed to disciplinary) cause—failure to demonstrate sufficient clinical aptitude for the practice of medicine. . . .

No contention is advanced on behalf of this student that the dismissal was made in bad faith or that the assignment of academic cause was a calculated pretext—arguments which if substantiated might present factual issues appropriate to be resolved in a judicial evidentiary hearing [377 N.E.2d at 731].

(See also *Delaney* v. *Heimstra*, 288 N.W.2d 769 (S.D. 1980); *Gamble* v. *University of Minnesota*, 639 F.2d 452 (8th Cir. 1981).)

More frequently, courts have relied on *Horowitz* for guidance in contexts other than student academic dismissals from public institutions—challenges to academic decisions other than dismissals, challenges to academic dismissals from *private* institutions, challenges to judgments concerning faculty rather than students. In *Olsson* v. *Board of Higher Education of the City of New York*, 4 N.Y.2d 408, 402 N.E.2d 1150 (1980) (this volume, Section 4.5), for example, the court cited *Horowitz* in rejecting a public college student's challenge to an examination grade. In *Maas* v. *Corporation of Gonzaga University*, 618 P.2d 106 (Wash. App. 1980), and *Miller* v. *Hamline University School of Law*, 601 F.2d 970 (8th Cir. 1979), the courts used *Horowitz* to reject student challenges to academic decisions of private institutions. And in *Clark* v. *Whiting*, 607 F.2d 634 (4th Cir. 1979), another court relied on *Horowitz* to reject an associate professor's challenge to a denial of promotion to full professor.

Overall, two trends are emerging from the reported decisions in the wake of *Horowitz*. First, extensive appellate litigation challenging academic dismissals is not occurring, and the cases that have been reported have been decided in favor of the institutions. Apparently *Horowitz*, with its strong support for institutional discretion in devising academic dismissal procedures, has depressed the market for such litigation. Second, courts have read *Horowitz* as a case whose message has meaning well beyond the context of constitutional due process and academic dismissal. Thus, *Horowitz* also supports the broader concept of "academic deference," or judicial deference to the full range of an academic institution's academic decisions. Both trends help insulate postsecondary institutions from judicial intrusion into their dealings with students and other members of the academic community. But just as surely, these trends serve to emphasize the institution's own responsibilities to deal fairly with students and others and to provide appropriate internal means of accountability regarding institutional academic decision making.

4.6.4. Private institutions. Federal constitutional guarantees of due process do not bind private institutions unless their imposition of sanctions falls under the state action doctrine explained in Section 1.4.2. But the inapplicability of constitutional protections, as Sections 4.4 and 4.5 suggest, does not necessarily mean that the student stands procedurally naked before the authority of the school.

The old view of a private institution's authority is illustrated by *Anthony* v. *Syracuse University*, 224 A.D. 487, 231 N.Y.S. 435 (1928), where a student's dismissal was upheld even though "no adequate reason [for it] was assigned by the university authorities." The court held that "no reason for dismissing need be given," though the institution "must . . . have a reason" which falls within its dismissal regulation. "Of course, the university authorities have wide discretion in determining what situation does and what does not fall within . . . [its regulation], and the courts would be slow indeed in disturbing any decision of the university authorities in this respect."

In more recent times, however, many courts have become faster on the draw with private schools. In *Carr* v. *St. John's University, New York* (see Section 4.4.2)— a case limiting the impact of *Anthony* within New York State—the court indicated that a private institution dismissing a student must act "not arbitrarily but in the exercise of an honest discretion based on facts within its knowledge that justify the exercise of discretion." In subsequently applying this standard to a discipline case, another New York court ruled that "the college or university's decision to discipline that student [must] be predicated on procedures which are fair and reasonable and which lend themselves to a reliable determination" (*Kwiatkowski* v. *Ithaca College,* 368 N.Y.S.2d 973 (Sup. Ct. 1975)).

A U.S. Court of Appeals has taken a similar approach. *Slaughter* v. *Brigham Young University,* 514 F.2d 622 (10th Cir. 1975), concerned a student who was dismissed for violating the honesty provision of the student code, having made unauthorized use of a professor's name as coauthor of an article. After the lower court had awarded $88,283 in damages to the student, the appellate court set aside the judgment and upheld the dismissal. But in doing so, it tested "whether the action was arbitrary" by investigating both the "adequacy of the procedure" and the substantiality of the evidence supporting the institution's determination. In judging the procedures, the court used *constitutional* due process as a guide, holding that the "proceedings met the requirements of the constitutional procedural due process doctrine as it is presently applied to public universities," and it is therefore unnecessary "to draw any distinction, *if there be any,* between the requirements in this regard for private and for public institutions" (emphasis added).

Cases such as these indicate a judicial trend toward increased protections for private school students. As is true of public institutions, this trend is much more evident in the misconduct area than in the academic sphere. In *Militana* v. *University of Miami,* 236 So. 2d 162 (Fla. App. 1970), for example, the court upheld the dismissal of a medical student, stating flatly that notice and opportunity to be heard, though required in discipline cases, are "not required when the dismissal is for academic failure." Yet even here, the contract theory (see Section 4.1.3) may provide some lesser procedural protections for students in academic jeopardy at private institutions.

Also as true for public institutions, the line between academic and disciplinary cases may be difficult to draw. In *Napolitano* v. *Trustees of Princeton University,* 453 A.2d 263 (N.J. Super. Ct., App. Div. 1982), the court reviewed the university's withholding of a degree, for one year, from a student whom a campus committee had found guilty of plagiarizing a term paper. In upholding the university's action, the court determined that the problem was one "involving academic standards and not a case of violation of rules of conduct." In so doing, the court distinguished "academic disciplinary actions" from disciplinary actions involving other types of "misconduct," according greater deference to the institution's decisions in the former context and suggesting that lesser "due process" protection was required. The resulting dichotomy differs from the "academic/disciplinary" dichotomy delineated in Section 4.6.3 and suggests the potential relevance of a third, middle category for "academic disciplinary" cases. Because such cases involve academic standards, courts should be sufficiently deferential to avoid interference with the institution's expert judgments on such matters; however, because such cases may also involve disputed factual issues concerning student conduct, courts should afford greater due process rights than they would in academic cases involving only the evaluation of student performance.

While the doctrinal bases for procedural rights in the public and private sectors are different, and while the law accords private institutions greater flexibility, a rough similarity of treatment nevertheless appears to be developing in the courts. The *Slaughter* case above provides a good illustration. So does *Miller* v. *Hamline University School of Law*, 601 F.2d 970 (8th Cir. 1979), which applies the *Horowitz* due process analysis (Section 4.6.3) to a private school's dismissal of a student for academic deficiency. It may thus be prudent for private school administrators to use constitutional due process principles (Sections 4.6.2 and 4.6.3) as general guides in implementing their own procedural systems. And if a private school makes a conscious policy choice not to use certain procedures which due process would require for public schools, that choice should be clearly reflected in its rules and regulations, so as to inhibit a court from finding such procedures implicit in the rules or in the student-institution relationship.

Sec. 4.7. Student Protest and Demonstrations

4.7.1. General principles. In a line of cases arising mainly from the campus unrest of the late 1960s and early 1970s, courts have affirmed that students have a right to peacefully protest and demonstrate—a right that public institutions may not infringe. This right stems from the free speech clause of the First Amendment as reinforced by that amendment's freedom of assembly and freedom to petition for redress of grievances. The keystone case is *Tinker* v. *Des Moines School District*, 393 U.S. 503 (1969). Several high school students had been suspended for wearing black armbands to school to protest the United States' Vietnam War policy. The U.S. Supreme Court ruled that the protest was a nondisruptive exercise of free speech and could not be punished by suspension from school. The Court made clear that "First Amendment rights, applied in light of the special characteristics of the school environment, are available to teachers and students" and that students "are possessed of fundamental rights which the state must respect, just as they themselves must respect their obligations to the state." The Court also made clear that the First Amendment protects more than just words; it also protects certain "symbolic acts" which are done "for the purpose of expressing certain views."

Though *Tinker* involved secondary school students, the Supreme Court soon applied its principles to postsecondary education in *Healy* v. *James*, 408 U.S. 169 (1972), discussed further in Section 4.8.1. The *Healy* opinion carefully notes the First Amendment's important place on campus:

> State colleges and universities are not enclaves immune from the sweep of the First Amendment. . . . Of course, as Mr. Justice Fortas made clear in *Tinker*, First Amendment rights must always be applied "in light of the special characteristics of the . . . environment" in the particular case. And, where state-operated educational institutions are involved, this Court has long recognized "the need for affirming the comprehensive authority

of the states and of school officials, consistent with fundamental constitutional safeguards, to prescribe and control conduct in the schools'' [*Tinker*
at 507]. Yet, the precedents of this Court leave no room for the view that,
because of the acknowledged need for order, First Amendment protections
should apply with less force on college campuses than in the community
at large. Quite to the contrary, ''The vigilant protection of constitutional
freedoms is nowhere more vital than in the community of American schools''
(*Shelton* v. *Tucker*, 364 U.S. 479, 487 (1960)). The college classroom with
its surrounding environs is peculiarly the '''marketplace of ideas,''' and
we break no new constitutional ground in reaffirming this nation's dedica-
tion to safeguarding academic freedom [408 U.S. at 180].

Despite occasional rhetoric to the contrary, *Tinker* and *Healy* clearly do not
create the total permissive society on campus. The *Tinker* opinion repeats many
times that freedom to protest does not constitute freedom to disrupt: ''conduct by
the student, in class or out of it, which for any reason—whether it stems from time,
place, or type of behavior—materially disrupts classwork or involves substantial
disorder or invasion of the rights of others is . . . not immunized by the constitutional guarantee of freedom of speech.'' *Healy* makes the same point.

4.7.2. Regulation of student protest. Postsecondary institutions may promulgate student conduct rules that prohibit group demonstrations or other forms
of group or individual protest falling within the *Tinker/Healy* guidelines above.
Students may be suspended if they violate such rules by actively participating in
a disruptive demonstration—for example, entering the stands during a college football
game and ''by abusive and disorderly acts and conduct'' depriving the spectators
''of the right to see and enjoy the game in peace and with safety to themselves''
(*Barker* v. *Hardway*, 283 F. Supp. 228 (S.D. W. Va.), affirmed, 399 F.2d 638 (4th
Cir. 1968)) or physically blocking entrances to campus buildings and preventing
personnel or other students from using the buildings (*Buttney* v. *Smiley*, 281 F. Supp.
280 (D. Colo. 1968)).

The critical problem in enforcing rules prohibiting disruptive protest activity
is determining when the activity has become sufficiently disruptive to lose its protection under *Tinker* and *Healy*. It is clearly not sufficient that administrators suspect
or fear that there will be disruption:

Undifferentiated fear or apprehension of disturbance is not enough
to overcome the right to freedom of expression. Any departure from absolute
regimentation may cause trouble. Any variation from the majority's opinion
may inspire fear. Any word spoken, in class, in the lunchroom, or on the
campus, that deviates from the views of another person may start an argument or cause disturbance. But our Constitution says we must take this
risk (*Terminiello* v. *Chicago*, 337 U.S. 1 (1949)); and our history says that
it is this sort of hazardous freedom—this kind of openness—that is the basis
of our national strength and of the independence and vigor of Americans
who grow up and live in this relatively permissive, often disputatious, society
[*Tinker* at 508–09].

Yet substantial disruption need not be a fait accompli before administrators can take action. It is sufficient that administrators have actual evidence on which they can "reasonably . . . forecast" (*Tinker* at 514) that substantial disruption is imminent.

The administrator should also determine whether the disruption is created by the protesters themselves or by the onlookers' reaction to their presence. In striking down a regulation limiting off-campus speakers at Mississippi state colleges, the court in *Stacy* v. *Williams,* 306 F. Supp. 963 (N.D. Miss. 1969), emphasized that "one simply cannot be restrained from speaking, and his audience cannot be prevented from hearing him, unless the feared result is likely to be engendered by what the speaker himself says or does." Either the protesters' own conduct must be disruptive, as in *Barker* and *Buttney* above, or their words and acts must be "directed to inciting or producing imminent" disruption by others and "likely to produce" such disruption (*Brandenburg* v. *Ohio,* 395 U.S. 444 (1969)) before an administrator may stop the protest or discipline the protesters. Where the onlookers rather than the protesters have created the disruption, the administrator's proper recourse is against the onlookers.

Besides adopting regulations prohibiting disruptive protest, public institutions may also promulgate "reasonable regulations with respect to the time, the place, and the manner in which student groups conduct their speech-related activities" (*Healy* at 192–93). Students who violate such regulations may be disciplined even if their violation did not create substantial disruption. To be valid, however, such regulations must cover only times, places, or manners of expression that are "basically incompatible with the normal activity of a particular place at a particular time" (*Grayned* v. *Rockford,* 408 U.S. 104, 116 (1972)). Incompatibility must be determined by the physical impact of the speech-related activity on its surroundings and not by the content of the speech: "Above all else, the First Amendment means that government has no power to restrict expression because of its message, its ideas, its subject matter, or its content" (*Police Department* v. *Mosley,* 408 U.S. 92, 95 (1972)). Time, place, and manner regulations must also be drafted "with narrow specificity," so that students are clearly informed about what the institution requires or prohibits (see *Hynes* v. *Mayor and Council of Oradell,* 425 U.S. 610 (1976)).

These requirements concerning time, place, and manner regulations are derived from the doctrines of "overbreadth" and "vagueness," also discussed in Sections 3.4 and 4.4.1. The overbreadth doctrine provides that regulation of speech-related activities must be "necessary to further significant governmental interests" and "narrowly tailored" to further those interests in a way which has the least restrictive impact on free expression (*Grayned* v. *Rockford,* 408 U.S. 104, 115 (1972)). The vagueness doctrine provides that regulations of conduct must be sufficiently clear to be understandable by persons of common intelligence. Vagueness principles apply more stringently when the regulations deal with speech-related activity: " 'Stricter standards of permissible statutory vagueness may be applied to a statute having a potentially inhibiting effect on speech; a man may the less be required to act at his peril here, because the dissemination of ideas may be the loser' " (*Hynes* at 620, quoting *Smith* v. *California,* 361 U.S. 147, 151 (1959)). Both doctrines have a general application to all the regulations governing student protest discussed in Sections 4.7.2, 4.7.3, and 4.7.4. The *Grayned* case contains an excellent discussion, in the school context, of the relationship between the two doctrines.

Shamloo v. *Mississippi State Board of Trustees,* 620 F.2d 516 (5th Cir. 1980), comprehensively illustrates the legal limits on an institution's authority to regulate student protests. The plaintiffs, Iranian nationals, were students at Jackson State University. In the fall of 1979, they had participated in two on-campus demonstrations in support of the regime of Ayatollah Khomeini in Iran. The university disciplined the students for having violated campus regulations which required scheduling, at least three days in advance, of any "student parade, serenade, demonstration, rally, and/or other meeting or gathering for any purpose." The students filed suit claiming that the regulations and the disciplinary action violated their First Amendment rights.

The appellate court first addressed the defendant's argument that the protests were sufficiently disruptive to lose any protection under the First Amendment. The court asked whether the demonstration had "materially and substantially interfered with the requirements of appropriate discipline in the operation of the school"—the standard developed in an earlier Fifth Circuit case and adopted by the U.S. Supreme Court in *Tinker*. Applying this standard to the facts of the case, the court rejected the defendant's claim:

> There was no testimony by the students or teachers complaining that the demonstration was disrupting and distracting. Shamloo testified that he did not think any of the classes were disrupted. Dr. Johnson testified that the demonstration was quite noisy. Dr. Smith testified that he could hear the chanting from his office and that, in his opinion, classes were being disrupted. The only justification for his conclusion is that there are several buildings within a close proximity of the plaza that students may have been using for purposes of study or for classes. There is no evidence that he received complaints from the occupants of these buildings.
>
> The district court concluded that "the demonstration had a disruptive effect with respect to other students' rights." But this is not enough to conclude that the demonstration was not protected by the First Amendment. The court must also conclude (1) that the disruption was a *material* disruption of classwork or (2) that it involved *substantial* disorder or invasion of the rights of others. It must constitute a *material* and *substantial* interference with discipline. The district court did not make such a conclusion and we certainly cannot, especially in light of the conflicting evidence found in the record. We cannot say that the demonstration did not constitute activity protected under the First Amendment [620 F.2d at 522].

Having determined that the plaintiffs' demonstration activities were protected by the First Amendment, the court then considered whether the regulations which the university had applied to the protest were valid under the First Amendment. The court focused its attention on a portion of the regulations which required that "all events sponsored by student organizations, groups, or individual students must be registered with the director of student activities, who, in cooperation with the vice-president for student affairs, approves activities of a wholesome nature." In concluding that this requirement was unconstitutional, the court reasoned:

> While the idea of a regulation being unconstitutionally vague and overbroad has previously been applied to regulations of an educational institution, it is important to realize that school disciplinary regulations need

not be drawn with the same precision of a criminal code. . . . But the regulations must be reasonable as limitations on the time, place, and manner of the protected speech and its dissemination (*Papish* v. *Board of Curators of the University of Missouri*, 410 U.S. 667, 93 S. Ct. 1197, 35 L. Ed. 2d 618 (1973); *Healy* v. *James*, 408 U.S. 169, 92 S. Ct. 2338, 33 L. Ed. 2d 266 (1972)). Disciplinary action may not be based on the disapproved *content* of the protected speech (*Papish*, 410 U.S. at 670, 93 S. Ct. at 1199)).

The reasonableness of a similar university regulation was previously addressed by this court in *Bayless* v. *Martine*, 430 F.2d 872, 873 (5th Cir. 1970). In *Bayless* ten students sought injunctive relief from their suspension for violating a university regulation. The regulation in *Bayless* created a Student Expression Area that could be reserved forty-eight hours in advance for any nonviolent purpose. All demonstrations similar to the one held by the Iranian students were regulated to the extent that they could only be held at the Student Expression Area "between the hours of 12:00 noon to 1:00 P.M. and from 5:00 to 7:00 P.M." but there was no limitation on the *content* of the speech. This court noted that the requirement of forty-eight hours advance notice was a reasonable method to avoid the problem of simultaneous and competing demonstrations and it also provided advance warning of the possible need for police protection. This court upheld the validity of the regulation as a valid exercise of the right to adopt and enforce reasonable nondiscriminatory regulations as to the time, place, and manner of a demonstration.

There is one critical distinction between the regulation examined in *Bayless* and the Jackson State regulation. The former made no reference to the *content* of the speech that would be allowed in the Student Expression Area. As long as there was no interference with the flow of traffic, no interruption of the orderly conduct of university affairs, and no obscene material, the students were not limited in what they could say. Apparently, the same cannot be said with respect to the Jackson State regulations, which provide that only "activities of a *wholesome* nature" will be approved. And if a demonstration is not approved, the students participating may be subjected to disciplinary action, including the possibility of dismissal.

Limiting approval of activities only to those of a "wholesome" nature is a regulation of *content* as opposed to a regulation of time, place, and manner. Dr. Johnson testified that he would disapprove a student activity if, in his opinion, the activity was unwholesome. The presence of this language converts what might have otherwise been a reasonable regulation of time, place, and manner into a restriction on the content of speech. Therefore, the regulation appears to be unreasonable on its face.

The restriction on activities other than those of a "wholesome" nature raises the additional issue that the Jackson State regulation may be void for vagueness. . . . An individual is entitled to fair notice or a warning of what constitutes prohibited activity by specifically enumerating the elements of the offense (*Smith* v. *Goguen*, 415 U.S. 566, 94 S. Ct. 1242, 39 L. Ed. 2d 605 (1974)). The regulation must not be designed so that different officials could attach different meaning to the words in an arbitrary and discriminatory manner (*Smith* v. *Goguen, supra*). But, of course, we cannot expect "mathematical certainty" from our language (*Grayned* v. *City of Rockford*, 408 U.S. 104, 92 S. Ct. 2294, 33 L. Ed. 2d 222 (1972) . . .). The approach adopted by this court with respect to university regulations is to examine whether the college students would have any "difficulty in understanding what conduct the regulations allow and what conduct they prohibit."

The requirement that an activity be "wholesome" before it is subject to approval is unconstitutionally vague. The testimony revealed that the regulations are enforced or not enforced depending on the purpose of the gathering or demonstration. Dr. Johnson admitted that whether or not something was wholesome was subject to interpretation and that he, as the vice-president of student affairs, and Dr. Jackson, director of student activities, could come to different conclusions as to its meaning. . . . The regulation's reference to wholesome activities is not specific enough to give fair notice and warning. A college student would have great difficulty determining whether or not his activities constitute prohibited unwholesome conduct. The regulation is void for vagueness [620 F.2d at 522–24].

The court's opinion in *Shamloo* follows, seriatim, three major issues in First Amendment analysis. First, it considers whether the demonstrating students were disruptive and could be punished for that reason consistent with the First Amendment. Second, it considers whether the regulations the university applied to the protest are unconstitutionally overbroad because they regulate the content, rather than the time, place, or manner, of speech. Third, it considers whether the university's regulations comply with the constitutional requirement prohibiting vagueness. A fourth issue, raised by the students but not addressed by the court, was whether the regulations constitute an unconstitutional prior restraint on speech. Under applicable legal principle (see Section 4.7.3), this issue would also probably have been decided in the plaintiffs' favor. The court's analysis of the first three issues and its likely negative answer to the fourth illuminate pitfalls that administrators will wish to avoid in devising and enforcing their own campus's demonstration regulations.

4.7.3. Prior approval of protest activities. Sometimes institutions have attempted to avoid disruption and disorder on campus by requiring that protest activity be approved in advance and by approving only those activities that will not pose problems. Under this strategy a protest would be halted, or its participants disciplined, not because the protest was in fact disruptive or violated reasonable time, place, and manner requirements but merely because it had not been approved in advance. Administrators at public institutions should be extremely leery of such a strategy. A prior approval system constitutes a "prior restraint" on free expression—that is, a temporary or permanent prohibition of expression imposed before the expression has occurred rather than a punishment imposed afterward. Prior restraints "are the most serious and the least tolerable infringement of First Amendment rights" (*Nebraska Press Association* v. *Stuart*, 427 U.S. 539, 559 (1976)).

Hammond v. *South Carolina State College*, 272 F. Supp. 947 (D.S.C. 1967), provides a classic example of prior restraint. The defendant college had a rule providing that "the student body is not to celebrate, parade, or demonstrate on the campus at any time without the approval of the office of the president." Several students were expelled for violating this rule after they held a demonstration for which they had not obtained prior approval. The court found the rule to be "on its face a prior restraint on the right to freedom of speech and the right to assemble" and held the rule and the expulsions under it to be invalid.

The courts have not asserted, however, that all prior restraints on expression are invalid. *Healy* v. *James* (Sections 4.7.1 and 4.8.1) summarizes the current judicial attitude: "While a college has a legitimate interest in preventing disruption on campus, which under circumstances requiring the safeguarding of that interest may justify . . . [a prior] restraint, a 'heavy burden' rests on the college to demonstrate the appropriateness of that action." It is extremely difficult to determine what prior restraints would be valid under *Healy*. Prior approval requirements probably could be imposed on student protest activities to assure that such activities will not violate time, place, or manner regulations meeting the guidelines in Section 4.7.2. They probably could also be imposed for the limited purpose of determining that, under those guidelines, protest activities will not cause substantial disruption. In either case, however, it is questionable whether prior approval requirements would be appropriate if applied to small-scale protests that have no reasonable potential for disruption. Also in either case, prior approval regulations would have to contain a clear definition of the protest activity to which they apply, precise standards to limit the administrator's discretion in making approval decisions, and procedures for assuring an expeditious and fair decision-making process. The administrator must always assume the burden of proving that the protest activity would violate a reasonable time, place, or manner regulation or would cause substantial disruption.[19]

Given these complexities, prior approval requirements may invite substantial legal challenges. Administrators should carefully consider whether and when the prior approval strategy is worth the risk. There are always alternatives: disciplining students who violate regulations prohibiting disruptive protest; establishing time, place, or manner requirements, as set out in Section 4.7.2; or using injunctive or criminal processes, as set out in Section 4.7.4.

4.7.4. Court injunctions and criminal prosecutions. When administrators are faced with a mass disruption which they cannot end by discussion, negotiation, or threat of disciplinary action, they may want to seek judicial assistance. A court injunction terminating the demonstration is one option. Arrest and criminal prosecution is the other. Although both options involve critical tactical considerations and risks, commentators favor the injunction for most situations, primarily because it provides a more immediate judicial forum for resolving disputes and because it shifts the responsibility for using law enforcement officials from administrators to the court. Injunctions may also be used in some instances to enjoin future disruptive conduct, whereas criminal prosecutions are limited to punishing past conduct. The use of the injunctive process does not legally foreclose the possibility of later criminal prosecutions; and injunctive orders or criminal prosecutions do not legally prevent the institution from initiating student disciplinary proceedings. Under U.S. Supreme

---

[19]These prior restraint requirements have been established in bits and pieces in various court cases. *Healy* is a leading case on burden of proof. *Kunz* v. *New York,* 340 U.S. 290 (1951), and *Shuttlesworth* v. *Birmingham,* 394 U.S. 147 (1969), are leading cases on standards to guide administrative discretion. *Southeastern Promotions* v. *Conrad,* 420 U.S. 546 (1975), is a leading case on procedural requirements.

Court precedents, none of these combinations would constitute double jeopardy. (For other problems regarding the relationship between criminal prosecutions and disciplinary proceedings, see Section 4.13.3.)

The legality of injunctions or criminal prosecutions depends on two factors. First, the conduct at issue must be unlawful under state law. In the case of an injunction, the conduct must be an imminent or continuing violation of property or civil rights protected by state law; in the case of a criminal arrest and prosecution, the conduct must violate the state criminal code. Second, the conduct at issue must not constitute expression protected by the First Amendment. Both injunctive orders and criminal convictions are restraints on speech-related activity and would be tested by the principles discussed in Section 4.7.2, concerning the regulation of student protest. Since injunctions act to restrain future demonstrations, they may operate as prior restraints on expression and would also be subject to the First Amendment principles described in Section 4.7.3.

When the assistance of the court is requested, public and private institutions are on the same footing. Since the court, rather than the institution, will ultimately impose the restraint, and since the court is clearly a public entity subject to the Constitution, both public and private institutions' use of judicial assistance must comply with First Amendment requirements. Also, for both public and private institutions, judicial assistance depends on the same technical requirements regarding the availability and enforcement of injunctions and the procedural validity of arrests and prosecutions.

Sec. 4.8. Student Organizations

4.8.1. Right to organize. Students in public postsecondary institutions have a general right to organize; to be officially recognized whenever the school has a policy of recognizing student groups; and to use meeting rooms, bulletin boards, and similar facilities open to campus groups. Occasionally a state statute will accord students specific organizational rights (see *Student Association of the University of Wisconsin–Milwaukee* v. *Baum*, 74 Wis. 2d 283, 246 N.W.2d 622 (1976), discussed in Section 2.2.3). More generally, organizational rights are protected by the freedom of association and freedom of expression concepts of the First Amendment. It is also clear, however, that public institutions retain authority to withhold or revoke recognition in certain instances and to evenhandedly regulate the organizational use of campus facilities. The balance between the organization's rights and the institution's authority was struck in *Healy* v. *James*, 408 U.S. 169 (1972), the leading case in the field.[20]

Healy arose after a student request at Central Connecticut State College for recognition as a local Students for a Democratic Society (SDS) organization had been approved by the college's student affairs committee. But the college's president denied recognition, asserting that the organization's philosophy was antithetical

---

[20]The later case of *Widmar* v. *Vincent*, discussed in Section 4.8.4, affirms many of the principles of *Healy* and adds important new guidance on the particular question of when a student group may have access to meeting rooms and other campus facilities. See also *Gay Student Services* v. *Texas A&M University*, 737 F.2d 1317, 1331–33 (5th Cir. 1984), in which the court used *Widmar*'s "public forum" analysis in invalidating the defendant's refusal to recognize the plaintiff groups.

to the college's commitment to academic freedom and that the organization would be a disruptive influence on campus. The denial of recognition had the effect of prohibiting the student group from using campus meeting rooms and campus bulletin boards and placing announcements in the student newspaper. The U.S. Supreme Court found the president's reasons insufficient under the facts to justify the extreme effects of nonrecognition on the organization's ability to "remain a viable entity" on campus and "participate in the intellectual give and take of campus debate." The Court therefore overruled the president's decision and remanded the case to the lower court, ruling that the college had to recognize the student group if the lower court determined that the group was willing to abide by all reasonable campus rules.

The associational rights recognized in *Healy* are not limited to situations where recognition is the issue. In *Gay Students Organization of the University of New Hampshire* v. *Bonner,* 509 F.2d 652 (1st Cir. 1974), for instance, the plaintiff (GSO) was an officially recognized campus organization. After it sponsored a dance on campus, the state governor criticized the university's policy regarding GSO; in reaction, the university announced that GSO could no longer hold social functions on campus. GSO filed suit, and the U.S. Court of Appeals for the First Circuit found that the university's new policy violated the students' freedom of association and expression. *Healy* was the controlling precedent even though GSO had not been denied recognition:

> The Court's analysis in *Healy* focused not on the technical point of recognition or nonrecognition, but on the practicalities of human interaction. While the Court concluded that the SDS members' right to further their personal beliefs had been impermissibly burdened by nonrecognition, this conclusion stemmed from a finding that the "primary" impediment to free association flowing from nonrecognition is the denial of use of campus facilities for meetings and other appropriate purposes." The ultimate issue at which inquiry must be directed is the effect which a regulation has on organizational and associational activity, not the isolated and for the most part irrelevant issue of recognition per se [509 F.2d at 658–59].

Healy and related cases reveal three broad bases on which administrators may regulate the recognition of student organizations without violating associational rights. First,

> a college administrator may impose a requirement . . . that a group seeking official recognition affirm in advance its willingness to adhere to reasonable campus law. Such a requirement does not impose an impermissible condition on the students' associational rights. Their freedom to speak out, to assemble, or to petition for changes in school rules is in no sense infringed. It merely constitutes an agreement to conform to reasonable standards respecting conduct. This is a minimal requirement, in the interest of the entire academic community, of any group seeking the privilege of official recognition [*Healy* at 193].

Such standards of conduct, of course, must not themselves violate the First Amendment or other constitutional safeguards. Recognition, for instance, could not be conditional on the organization's willingness to abide by a rule prohibiting all peaceful protest demonstrations on campus (see Section 4.7.2) or requiring all campus newspaper announcements to be approved in advance by the administration (see Section 4.9.1). But as long as campus rules avoid such pitfalls, student organizations must comply with them, just as individual students must. If the organization refuses to agree in advance to obey campus law, recognition may be denied until such time as the organization does agree. If a recognized organization violates campus law, its recognition may be suspended or withdrawn for a reasonable period of time.

Second, "associational activities need not be tolerated where they . . . interrupt classes . . . or substantially interfere with the opportunity of other students to obtain an education" (*Healy* at 189). Thus, administrators may also deny recognition to a group that would create substantial disruption on campus, and they may revoke the recognition of a group that has created such disruption. In either case the institution has the burden of demonstrating with reasonable certainty that substantial disruption will or did in fact result from the organization's actions—a burden that the college failed to meet in *Healy*. This burden is a heavy one because "denial of recognition . . . [is] a form of prior restraint" of First Amendment rights (*Healy* at 184).

Third, the institution may act to prevent organizational activity that is itself illegal under local, state, or federal laws, as well as activity "directed to inciting or producing imminent lawless action and . . . likely to incite or produce such action" (*Brandenburg* v. *Ohio*, 395 U.S. 444, 447 (1969), quoted in *Healy* at 188). While the *GSO* case specifically supported this basis for regulation, the court found that the institution had not met its burden of demonstrating that the group's activities were illegal or inciting. A similar conclusion was reached in *Gay Lib* v. *University of Missouri*, 558 F.2d 848 (8th Cir. 1977), reversing 416 F. Supp. 1350 (W.D. Mo. 1976). The trial court found, on the basis of the university's expert evidence, that recognition of the student group "would predictably lead to increased homosexual activities, which include sodomy [a felony under state law] as one of the most prevalent forms of sexual expression in homosexuality." Relying on this finding and on the fact that sodomy is an illegal activity that can be prohibited, the trial court upheld the university's refusal to recognize the group. Overruling the trial court, the appellate court held that the university's proof was insufficient to demonstrate that the student organization intended to breach university regulations or advocate or incite imminent lawless acts. At most, the group intended peaceably to advocate the repeal of certain criminal laws—expression that constitutionally could not be prohibited. Thus, the appellate court concluded that the university's denial of recognition impermissibly penalized the group's members because of their status rather than their conduct. (To the same effect, see *Gay Activists Alliance* v. *Board of Regents*, 638 P.2d 1116 (Okla. 1981); and see generally Note, "The Rights of Gay Student Organizations," 10 *J. of College and University Law* 397 (1983–84).)

All rules and decisions regarding student organizations should be supportable on one or more of these three regulatory bases. Rules should be applied evenhandedly, carefully avoiding selective applications to particular groups whose philosophy or activities are repugnant to the institution. Decisions under the rules should be based on a sound factual assessment of the impact of the group's activity rather than on speculation or on what the Supreme Court calls "undifferentiated fear or apprehension." Decisions denying organizational privileges should be preceded by "some reasonable opportunity for the organization to meet the university's contentions" or "to eliminate the basis of the denial" (*Wood* v. *Davison,* 351 F. Supp. 543, 548 (N.D. Ga. 1972)). Keeping these points in mind, administrators can retain substantial yet sensitive authority over the recognition of student groups.

4.8.2. Right not to organize. The right-to-organize concept has a flip side. Students often are organized into a large campus-wide or college-wide association recognized by the institution as a student government or similar representational organization. Mandatory student activities fees sometimes are collected by the institution and channeled to the student association. Where such circumstances pertain at a public institution, may students argue that their constitutional rights are violated—either by a requirement that they be members of the association or by a requirement that their activity fees be used to support the association? Or, where nonrepresentational, special-purpose student organizations are concerned, may a public institution channel funds from a mandatory student activities fee to such an organization when other students object to supporting the organization's beliefs or statements?

Although the law on these questions is still fairly sparse, the case of *Good* v. *Associated Students of the University of Washington,* 86 Wash. 2d 94, 542 P.2d 762 (1975), provides substantial guidance in developing answers. In *Good* some students challenged the university's support of the ASUW, a nonprofit corporation purporting to represent all students at the university but with whose political viewpoints the plaintiff students disagreed. All university students were required to be members of the ASUW, and the ASUW was the recipient of part of a mandatory student activities fee that the university collected from all students. After finding that the university had authority under state law to support such a corporation as long as it is "in essence an agency of the university and subject to ultimate control by the board [of regents]," the court asked whether compulsory membership and financial support violated the students' "freedom to associate, [which] carries with it a corresponding right to not associate."

The court first held that mandatory *membership* is unconstitutional:

> Notwithstanding the convolutions of the . . . opinions of the United States Supreme Court, we have no hesitancy in holding that the state, through the university, may not compel membership in an association, such as the ASUW, which purports to represent *all* the students at the university, including these plaintiffs. That association expends funds for political and economic causes to which the dissenters object and promotes and espouses political, social, and economic philosophies which the dissenters find repugnant to their own views. There is no room in the First Amendment for such absolute compulsory support, advocation, and representation [542 P.2d at 768].

The court was not willing, however, to place an absolute ban on the mandatory *fee.* This issue called for a delicate balance:

> We must balance the plaintiffs' First Amendment rights against the traditional need and desirability of the university to provide an atmosphere of learning, debate, dissent, and controversy. Neither is absolute. If we allow mandatory financial support to be unchecked, the plaintiffs' rights

may be meaningless. On the other hand, if we allow dissenters to withhold the nominal financial contributions required, we would permit a possible minority view to destroy or cripple a valuable learning adjunct of university life. . . .

When a student enrolls at a university, he or she enters an academic community—a world which allows the teaching, advocacy, and dissemination of an infinite range of ideas, theories, and beliefs. They may be controversial or traditional, radical or conformist. But the university is the arena in which accepted, discounted—even repugnant—beliefs, opinions, and ideas challenge each other [542 P.2d at 768–69].

Considering these factors, the court concluded that "dissenting students should not have the right to veto every event, speech, or program with which they disagree." Accordingly, student associations like the ASUW may use mandatory fees as long as (1) such use does not "exceed the statutory purposes" for which fees may be spent and (2) the group does not "become the vehicle for the promotion of one particular viewpoint, political, social, economic, or religious" (542 P.2d at 769).[21]

A similar approach can be taken toward the validity of mandatory fee allocations to special-purpose organizations (such as minority or foreign student groups, social action groups, and academic or honorary societies). If students have no "right to veto every event, speech, or program" they disagree with, then neither should students be able to veto university support for every organization with which they disagree. Thus, unlike broad representational groups such as the ASUW, special-purpose groups can promote a "particular viewpoint." In *Larson* v. *Board of Regents of the University of Nebraska,* 204 N.W.2d 568 (Neb. 1973), for instance, the court rejected student challenges to mandatory fee allocations for the student newspaper and the visiting-speakers program, whose views the plaintiffs opposed. The limit appears to be that the institution's fee allocations, as a whole, must provide a forum for a broad spectrum of viewpoints rather than selectively supporting particular ones with which the institution feels comfortable. Each special-purpose organization, of course, must use the funds only for purposes permitted under any state statutes or regulations governing the use of student activity fees.

Thus, in overseeing student organizations, administrators should avoid imposing compulsory membership requirements. In allocating mandatory student fees, they should develop evenhanded processes devoid of artificial limits on the number or type of viewpoints that may be supported. If the process does include limits on the

---

[21]Although the U.S. Supreme Court has not addressed the problem of student activity fees, lawyers will want to consult *Abood* v. *Detroit Board of Education,* 431 U.S. 209 (1977), a case involving similar issues respecting mandatory service fees charged teachers by the collective bargaining representative for teachers. The Court permits such fees but allows individual teachers to get rebates for fees used for ideological activities unrelated to collective bargaining. Apparently, the *Abood* reasoning can be applied to support mandatory student fees in the university setting. When students could get rebates is less apparent, since it is unclear when a fee expenditure would be unrelated to the university's purpose in establishing the fee system. Overall, the *Good* approach appears consistent with *Abood.* See also *Galda* v. *Bloustein,* 686 F.2d 159 (3d Cir. 1982), which analyzes *Abood* and the refund issue in a special context: when the university agrees to collect a mandatory but refundable fee for an independent student organization (here, PIRG) not officially recognized by the institution.

purposes or groups that may be supported, these limits should be demonstrably consistent with the three bases for regulation set out in Section 4.8.1 above or some other substantial and evenly applied educational priority of the institution, and with the special rules regarding discrimination (Section 4.8.3) and religious activities (Section 4.8.4).

4.8.3. Principle of nondiscrimination. While the law prohibits administrators from imposing certain kinds of restrictions on student organizations, as Sections 4.8.1 and 4.8.2 indicate, there are other kinds of restrictions which administrators may be *required* to impose. The primary example concerns discrimination, particularly on the basis of race or sex. Just as the institution usually cannot discriminate on grounds of race or sex, neither can the student organization discriminate—either as the agent of (see generally Section 2.1) or with the substantial support of the institution. The institution has an obligation either to prohibit discrimination by student organizations in these circumstances or to withhold institutional support from those that do discriminate.

In public institutions student organizations may be subject to constitutional equal protection principles under the state action doctrine (Section 1.4.2) if they act as agents of the institution or make substantial use of institutional facilities, resources, or funds. Thus, in *Joyner* v. *Whiting,* 477 F.2d 456 (4th Cir. 1973) (also discussed in Section 4.9.2), a black-oriented student newspaper allegedly had a segregationist editorial policy and had discriminated by race in staffing and in accepting advertising. Although prohibiting the university president from permanently cutting off the paper's funds because of the restraining effect of such a cutoff on free press, the court did hold that the president could and must prohibit the discrimination in staffing and advertising: "The equal protection clause forbids racial discrimination in extracurricular activities of a state-supported institution . . . and freedom of the press furnishes no shield for discrimination."

Uzzell v. *Friday,* 547 F.2d 801 (4th Cir. 1977), concerned certain rules of student organizations at the University of North Carolina. The Campus Governing Council, legislative branch of the student government, was required under its constitution to have at least two minority students, two males, and two females among its eighteen members. The student Honor Court, under its rules, permitted defendants to demand that a majority of the judges hearing the case be of the same race or the same sex as the defendant. Eschewing the need for any extended analysis, the court invalidated each of the provisions as race discrimination: "Without either reasonable basis or compelling interest, the composition of the council is formulated on the basis of race. This form of constituency blatantly fouls the letter and the spirit of both the Civil Rights Act [42 U.S.C. sec. 2000d] and the Fourteenth Amendment." (The sex discrimination aspects of the provisions were not challenged by the plaintiff students or addressed by the court.) In *Friday* v. *Uzzell,* 438 U.S. 912 (1978), the U.S. Supreme Court, seeing possible affirmative action issues underlying this use of racial considerations, vacated the appellate court's judgment and remanded the case for further consideration in light of the *Bakke* decision (see Section 4.2.5).

In 1979 the appeals court reconsidered its earlier decision and, by a vote of 4 to 3, again invalidated the rules (*Uzzell* v. *Friday,* 591 F.2d 997 (4th Cir. 1979) (*en banc*)). The majority held that the rules were contrary to the teaching of *Bakke:*

> The permeating defect in the organization of . . . the governing council
> is the imposition of an artificial racial structure upon this elective body that
> bars nonminority students from eligibility for appointment to the council.
> This resort to race affronts *Bakke*. Although the regulation seeks to provide
> "protective representation," its effect is to establish a racial classification,
> as it relies exclusively on race to preclude nonminority students from enjoying
> opportunities and benefits available to others [591 F.2d at 998].

The minority, reading *Bakke* more liberally, argued that more facts were necessary
before the court could ascertain whether the student government rules were invalid
race discrimination, on the one hand, or valid affirmative action, on the other.
They therefore asserted that the case should be returned to the district court for
a full trial:

> The present record simply does not permit a firm conclusion as to
> the extent of discrimination at the University of North Carolina and the
> need for and efficacy of the present regulations. The majority's condem-
> nation of the regulations because they impinge upon the rights of others
> is simplistic. *Bakke* teaches that as a necessary remedial measure a victimized
> group may be preferred at the expense of other innocent persons. What
> cries out for determination in the instant case is whether such preferment
> is justified under the principles of *Bakke* [591 F.2d at 1001].

In June 1980 the Fourth Circuit recalled its 1979 decision because the *en
banc* court which had heard the appeal was improperly constituted: a senior judge
sat as a member of the panel—a violation of a federal statute (28 U.S.C. sec. 46)
requiring that an *en banc* panel consist only of active circuit court judges. The new
rehearing *en banc* placed the matter before the appeals court for the third time (*Uzzell
v. Friday*, 625 F.2d 1117 (4th Cir. 1980) (*en banc*)). On this occasion the court ruled
5 to 3 to remand the case to the district court for a full development of the record
and reconsideration in light of *Bakke*. In so ruling, the court expressly adopted the
dissenting view of the 1979 decision. The majority indicated that racially conscious
actions which impinge on one class of persons in order to ameliorate past discrimination against another class are not unlawful per se, and that "the university should
have the opportunity to justify its regulations so that the district court can apply
the *Bakke* test: is the classification necessary to the accomplishment of a constitutionally permissible purpose?"

In private institutions as well as public, federal civil rights laws (see Section
7.5) may require institutions to assure, as a condition to receiving federal funds,
that student organizations do not discriminate. The Title VI regulations (Section
7.5.2) contain several provisions broad enough to cover student organizations; in
particular, 34 C.F.R. sec. 100.3(b)(1) prohibits institutions from discriminating
by race, either "directly or through contractual or other arrangements," and 34
C.F.R. sec. 100.3(b)(4) prohibits discrimination respecting any service or benefit
provided "in or through a facility" constructed or operated in whole or part with
federal funds. And the Title IX regulations (Section 7.5.3) prohibit institutions from
"providing significant assistance" to any organization "which discriminates on

the basis of sex in providing any aid, benefit, or service to students'' (34 C.F.R. sec. 106.31(b)(7); see also sec. 106.6(c)). Title IX does not apply, however, to the membership practices of tax-exempt social fraternities and sororities (20 U.S.C. sec. 1681(a)6(A)). (For a discussion of the civil rights statutes' application to student organizations and other activities that do not receive federal funds, see this volume, Section 7.5.7.)

In light of such constitutional and regulatory requirements, it is clear that administrators cannot ignore alleged discrimination by student organizations. In some areas of concern, discrimination being the primary example, administrators must deal affirmatively with the rules and practices of campus student organizations in order to fulfill their institution's obligations under the law.

4.8.4. Religious activities. In *Widmar* v. *Vincent*, 102 S. Ct. 269 (1981), a case involving the University of Missouri–Kansas City (UMKC), the United States Supreme Court established important rights for student religious groups at public postsecondary institutions who seek to use the institution's facilities. In 1972 the board of curators of UMKC promulgated a regulation prohibiting the use of university buildings or grounds ''for purposes of religious worship or religious teaching.'' In 1977 UMKC applied this regulation to a student religious group called Cornerstone and denied it permission to continue meeting in university facilities. According to the Court:

> Cornerstone is an organization of evangelical Christian students from various denominational backgrounds. . . . Cornerstone held its on-campus meetings in classrooms and in the student center. These meetings were open to the public and attracted up to 125 students. A typical Cornerstone meeting included prayer, hymns, Bible commentary, and discussion of religious views and experiences [102 S. Ct. at 272 n.2].

Following this denial, eleven members of Cornerstone sued the university, alleging that it had abridged their rights to free exercise of religion and freedom of speech under the First Amendment. The district court rejected the students' arguments, holding that UMKC's regulation was necessary to fulfill the university's obligation, under the establishment clause of the First Amendment, to refrain from supporting religion (*Chess* v. *Widmar*, 480 F. Supp. 907 (W.D. Mo. 1979)). The U.S. Court of Appeals for the Eighth Circuit reversed the district court (635 F.2d 1310 (8th Cir. 1980)). It determined that the group's activities were protected by the free speech clause of the First Amendment. Applying a classic free speech analysis, the appellate court held that the university had violated the students' rights by placing content-based restrictions on their speech. The Supreme Court agreed with the appellate court.

For the Supreme Court, as for the lower courts, the threshold question was whether the case would be treated as a free speech case. In considering this question, Justice Powell's opinion for the Court (with Justice White dissenting) characterized the students' activities as ''religious speech,'' which, like other speech, is protected by the free speech clause. The university, by making its facilities generally available to student organizations, had created a ''forum'' open to speech activities, which the Court described both as a ''limited public forum'' and an ''open forum.'' The free speech clause therefore applied to the situation. This clause did not require

UMKC to establish a forum; once UMKC had done so, however, the clause required it to justify any exclusion of a student group from this forum because of the content of its activities:

> In order to justify discriminatory exclusion from a public forum based on the religious content of a group's intended speech, the university must satisfy the standard of review appropriate to content-based exclusions. It must show that its regulation is necessary to serve a compelling state interest and that it is narrowly drawn to achieve that end [102 S. Ct. at 274].

In attempting to justify its regulation under this standard, UMKC relied on both the First Amendment's establishment clause and the establishment clause in the Missouri state constitution. Its argument was that maintaining separation of church and state, as mandated by these clauses, was a "compelling state interest" which justified its no-religious-worship regulation under the free speech clause. Resorting to establishment clause jurisprudence, the Court rejected this argument:

> The university first argues that it cannot offer its facilities to religious groups and speakers on the terms available to other groups without violating the establishment clause of the Constitution of the United States. We agree that the interest of the university in complying with its constitutional obligations may be characterized as compelling. It does not follow, however, that an "equal access" policy would be incompatible with this Court's establishment clause cases. Those cases hold that a policy will not offend the establishment clause if it can pass a three-pronged test: "First, the [governmental policy] must have a secular legislative purpose; second, its principal or primary effect must be one that neither advances nor inhibits religion . . . ; finally, the [policy] must not foster 'an excessive government entanglement with religion'" (*Lemon* v. *Kurtzman*, 403 U.S. 602, 612–13, 91 S. Ct. 2105, 2111, 29 L. Ed. 2d 745 (1971)). (See *Committee for Public Education* v. *Regan*, 444 U.S. 646, 653, 100 S. Ct. 840, 846, 63 L. Ed. 2d 94 (1980); *Roemer* v. *Maryland Public Works Board*, 426 U.S. 736, 748, 96 S. Ct. 2337, 2345, 49 L. Ed. 2d 179 (1976).)
>
> In this case two prongs of the test are clearly met. Both the district court and the court of appeals held that an open-forum policy, including nondiscrimination against religious speech, would have a secular purpose and would avoid entanglement with religion. But the district court concluded, and the university argues here, that allowing religious groups to share the limited public forum would have the "primary effect" of advancing religion.
>
> The university's argument misconceives the nature of this case. The question is not whether the creation of a religious forum would violate the establishment clause. The university has opened its facilities for use by student groups, and the question is whether it can now exclude groups because of the content of their speech (see *Healy* v. *James*, 408 U.S. 169, 92 S. Ct. 2338, 33 L. Ed. 2d 266 (1972)). In this context we are unpersuaded that the primary effect of the public forum, open to all forms of discourse, would be to advance religion.

We are not oblivious to the range of an open forum's likely effects. It is possible—perhaps even foreseeable—that religious groups will benefit from access to university facilities. But this Court has explained that a religious organization's enjoyment of merely ''incidental'' benefits does not violate the prohibition against the ''primary advancement'' of religion (*Committee for Public Education* v. *Nyquist,* 413 U.S. 756, 771, 93 S. Ct. 2955, 2964, 37 L. Ed. 2d 948 (1973); see, for example, *Roemer* v. *Maryland Public Works Board,* 426 U.S. 736, 96 S. Ct. 2337, 49 L. Ed. 2d 179 (1976); *Hunt* v. *McNair,* 413 U.S. 734, 93 S. Ct. 2868, 37 L. Ed. 2d 923 (1972); *McGowan* v. *Maryland,* 366 U.S. 420, 422, 81 S. Ct. 1101, 1103, 6 L. Ed. 2d 393 (1961)).

We are satisfied that any religious benefits of an open forum at UMKC would be ''incidental'' within the meaning of our cases. Two factors are especially relevant.

First, an open forum in a public university does not confer any imprimatur of state approval on religious sects or practices. As the court of appeals quite aptly stated, such a policy ''would no more commit the university . . . to religious goals'' than it is ''now committed to the goals of the Students for a Democratic Society, the Young Socialist Alliance,'' or any other group eligible to use its facilities (*Chess* v. *Widmar,* 635 F.2d at 1317).

Second, the forum is available to a broad class of nonreligious as well as religious speakers; there are over 100 recognized student groups at UMKC. The provision of benefits to so broad a spectrum of groups is an important index of secular effect (see, for example, *Wolman* v. *Walter,* 433 U.S. 229, 240-41, 97 S. Ct. 2593, 2601, 53 L. Ed. 2d 714 (1977); *Committee for Public Education* v. *Nyquist,* 413 U.S. at 756, 781-82, and n.38, 93 S. Ct. at 2955, 2969-70 (1973)). If the establishment clause barred the extension of general benefits to religious groups, ''a church could not be protected by the police and fire departments, or have its public sidewalk kept in repair'' (*Roemer* v. *Maryland Public Works Board,* 426 U.S. 736, 747, 96 S. Ct. 2337, 2345, 49 L. Ed. 2d 179 (1976) (plurality opinion); quoted in *Committee for Public Education* v. *Regan,* 444 U.S. 646, 658 n.6, 100 S. Ct. 840, 849, 63 L. Ed. 2d 94 (1980)). At least in the absence of empirical evidence that religious groups will dominate UMKC's open forum, we agree with the court of appeals that the advancement of religion would not be the forum's ''primary effect.''

Arguing that the state of Missouri has gone further than the federal Constitution in proscribing indirect state support for religion, the university claims a compelling interest in complying with the applicable provisions of the Missouri constitution.

The Missouri courts have not ruled whether a general policy of accommodating student groups, applied equally to those wishing to gather to engage in religious and nonreligious speech, would offend the state constitution. We need not, however, determine how the Missouri courts would decide this issue. It is also unnecessary for us to decide whether, under the supremacy clause, a state interest, derived from its own constitution, could ever outweigh free speech interests protected by the First Amendment. We limit our holding to the case before us.

On one hand, respondents' First Amendment rights are entitled to special constitutional solicitude. Our cases have required the most exacting scrutiny in cases in which a state undertakes to regulate speech on the basis of its content (see, for example, *Carey* v. *Brown,* 447 U.S. 455, 100 S. Ct. 2286, 65 L. Ed. 2d 263 (1980); *Police Dept.* v. *Mosley,* 408 U.S. 92, 92 S. Ct. 2286, 33 L. Ed. 2d 212 (1972)). On the other hand, the state interest asserted here—in achieving greater separation of church and state than is already ensured under the establishment clause of the federal Constitution—is limited by the free exercise clause and in this case by the free speech clause as well. In this constitutional context, we are unable to recognize the state's interest as sufficiently "compelling" to justify content-based discrimination against respondents' religious speech [102 S. Ct. at 274–77].

Since UMKC could not justify its content-based restriction on access to the forum it had created, the Court declared the university's regulation unconstitutional. The plaintiff students thereby obtained the right to have their religious group hold its meetings in campus facilities generally open to student groups. It follows that other student religious groups at other public postsecondary institutions have the same right to use campus facilities; institutions may not exclude them, whether by written policy or otherwise, on the basis of the religious content of their activities.[22]

Widmar thus may have substantial impact on public institutions, most of which have created forums like that existing at UMKC. The opinion falls far short, however, of requiring institutions to relinquish all authority over student religious groups. There are substantial limits to the opinion's reach:

1. *Widmar* does not require (nor does it permit) institutions to create forums especially for religious groups, or to give them any other preferential treatment. As the Court noted, "Because this case involves a forum already made generally available to student groups, it differs from those cases in which this Court has invalidated statutes permitting school facilities to be used for instruction by religious groups but not by others" (102 S. Ct. at 275 n.10; see also 102 S. Ct. at 276 n.13).

2. Nor does *Widmar* require institutions to create a forum for student groups generally, or continue to maintain one, if they choose not to do so. The case applies only to situations where the institution has created and voluntarily continues to maintain a forum for student groups.

3. *Widmar* requires access only to facilities that are part of a forum created by the institution, not to any other facilities. Similarly, *Widmar* requires access only for students: "We have not held . . . that a campus must make all of its facilities equally available to students and nonstudents alike, or that a university must grant free access to all of its grounds or buildings" (102 S. Ct. at 273 n.5).

4. *Widmar* does not prohibit all regulation of student organizations' use of forum facilities; it prohibits only content-based restrictions on access. Thus, the

---

[22]In 1984 Congress passed and the President signed the Equal Access Act, 98 Stat. 377, giving limited statutory recognition to the principles underlying *Widmar.* By its terms, however, the Act extends these principles to, and applies *only* to, "public secondary school[s] . . . receiv[ing] federal financial assistance."

Court noted that "a university's mission is education, and decisions of this Court have never denied its authority to impose reasonable regulations compatible with that mission upon the use of its campus and facilities" (102 S. Ct. at 273 n.5). In particular, according to the Court, the *Widmar* opinion "in no way undermines the capacity of the university to establish reasonable time, place, and manner regulations" (102 S. Ct. at 278) for use of the forum. Such regulations must be imposed on all student groups, however, not just student religious organizations, and must be imposed without regard to the content of the group's speech activities (see *Heffron* v. *International Society for Krishna Consciousness,* 101 S. Ct. 2559 (1981)). If a student religious group or other student group "violate[s] [such] reasonable campus rules or substantially interfere[s] with the opportunity of other students to obtain an education" (102 S. Ct. at 278), the institution may deny the group use of campus facilities for its activities.

5. *Widmar* does not rule out every possible content-based restriction on access to a forum. The Court's analysis quoted above makes clear that a content-based regulation would be constitutional under the First Amendment if it were "necessary to serve a compelling state interest and . . . narrowly drawn to achieve that end." As *Widmar* and other First Amendment cases demonstrate, this standard is exceedingly difficult to meet. But the *Widmar* opinion suggests at least two possibilities, the contours of which are left for further development should the occasion arise. First, the Court hints that, if there is "empirical evidence that religious groups will dominate . . . [the institution's] open forum" (102 S. Ct. at 277, also quoted above), the institution apparently may regulate access by these groups to the extent necessary to prevent domination. Second, if the student demand for use of forum facilities exceeds the supply, the institution may "make academic judgments as to how best to allocate scarce resources" (102 S. Ct. at 278). In making such academic judgments, the institution may apparently prefer the educational content of some group activities over others and allocate its facilities in accord with these academic preferences. Justice Stevens' opinion concurring in the Court's judgment contains an example for consideration:

> If two groups of twenty-five students requested the use of a room at a particular time—one to view Mickey Mouse cartoons and the other to rehearse an amateur performance of *Hamlet*—the First Amendment would not require that the room be reserved for the group that submitted its application first. . . . A university should be allowed to decide for itself whether a program that illuminates the genius of Walt Disney should be given precedence over one that may duplicate material adequately covered in the classroom. . . . A university legitimately may regard some subjects as more relevant to its educational mission than others. But the university, like the police officer, may not allow its agreement or disagreement with the viewpoint of a particular speaker to determine whether access to a forum will be granted [102 S. Ct. at 279].

For another example of a content-based restriction—approved by a federal appellate court subsequent to *Widmar*—see *Chapman* v. *Thomas,* 743 F.2d 1056 (4th Cir. 1984). In this case the court ruled that North Carolina State University could prohibit a student from door-to-door canvassing in dormitories to publicize campus Bible study meetings, even though it permitted candidates for top student government offices to campaign door to door.

Sec. 4.9. Student Press

4.9.1. General perspectives. A public institution's relationships with student newspapers, magazines, and other publications should be viewed in the first instance under the same principles that are set out in the preceding section on student organizations. Often student publications are under the auspices of some student organization (such as the newspaper staff), which may be recognized by the school or funded from mandatory student activity fees. Such organizations can claim the same freedom of association as the organizations discussed in the preceding section, and a public institution's regulation of such organizations is limited by the principles set out in that section. Objecting students, moreover, have no more right to challenge the allocation of mandatory student fees to student newspapers that express a particular viewpoint than they have to challenge such allocations to other student organizations expressing particular viewpoints. In *Arrington* v. *Taylor,* 380 F. Supp. 1348 (M.D.N.C. 1974), affirmed, 526 F.2d 587 (4th Cir. 1975), for example, the court rejected a challenge to the University of North Carolina's use of mandatory fees to subsidize its campus newspaper, the *Daily Tar Heel.* Since the paper did not purport to speak for the entire student body nor did its existence inhibit students from expressing or supporting opposing viewpoints, the subsidy did not infringe First Amendment rights.

However, student publications must also be viewed from an additional perspective, not directly involved in the section on student organizations: the perspective of freedom of the press. As perhaps the most staunchly guarded of all First Amendment rights, the right to a free press protects student publications from virtually all encroachments on their editorial prerogatives by public institutions. In a series of forceful cases, courts have implemented this student press freedom, using First Amendment principles akin to those that would apply to a big-city daily published by a private corporation.

The chief concern of the First Amendment's free press guarantee is censorship. Thus, whenever a public institution seeks to control or coercively influence the *content* of a student publication, it will have a legal problem on its hands. The problem will be exacerbated if the institution imposes a prior restraint on publication; that is, a prohibition imposed in advance of publication rather than a sanction imposed subsequently (see Section 4.7.3). Conversely, the institution's legal problems will be alleviated if the institution's regulations (concerning, for example, the allocation of office space or limitations on the time, place, or manner of distribution) do not affect the message, ideas, or subject matter of the publication and do not permit prior restraints on publication.

4.9.2. Permissible scope of regulation. *Joyner* v. *Whiting,* 477 F.2d 456 (4th Cir. 1973), arose after the president of North Carolina Central University permanently terminated university financial support for the campus newspaper. The president asserted that the newspaper had printed articles urging segregation and had advocated the maintenance of an all-black university. The court held that the president's action violated the student staff's First Amendment rights:

It may well be that a college need not establish a campus newspaper, or, if a paper has been established, the college may permanently discontinue publication for reasons wholly unrelated to the First Amendment. But if a college has a student newspaper, its publication cannot be suppressed because college officials dislike its editorial comment. . . .

The principles reaffirmed in *Healy* [v. *James,* Section 4.7.1] have been extensively applied to strike down every form of censorship of student publications at state-supported institutions. Censorship of constitutionally protected expression cannot be imposed by suspending the editors, suppressing circulation, requiring imprimatur of controversial articles, excising repugnant materials, withdrawing financial support, or asserting any other form of censorial oversight based on the institution's power of the purse [477 F.2d at 460].

The president had also asserted, as grounds for terminating the paper's support, that the newspaper would employ only blacks and would not accept advertising from white-owned businesses. While such practices were not protected by the First Amendment and could be enjoined, the court held that the permanent cutoff of funds was an inappropriate remedy for such problems because of its broad effect on all future ability to publish.

Bazaar v. *Fortune,* 476 F.2d 570, rehearing, 489 F.2d 225 (5th Cir. 1973), is also illustrative. The University of Mississippi had halted publication of an issue of *Images,* a student literary magazine written and edited with the advice of a professor from the English department, because a university committee had found two stories objectionable on grounds of "taste." While the stories concerned interracial marriage and black pride, the university disclaimed objection on this basis and relied solely on the stories' inclusion of "earthy" language. The university argued that the stories would stir an adverse public reaction, and, since the magazine had a faculty adviser, their publication would reflect badly on the university. The court held that the involvement of a faculty adviser did not enlarge the university's authority over the magazine's content. The university's action violated the First Amendment because "speech cannot be stifled by the state merely because it would perhaps draw an adverse reaction from the majority of people, be they politicians or ordinary citizens, and newspapers. To come forth with such a rule would be to virtually read the First Amendment out of the Constitution and, thus, cost this nation one of its strongest tenets."

Schiff v. *Williams,* 519 F.2d 257 (5th Cir. 1975), concerned the firing of the editors of the *Atlantic Sun,* the student newspaper of Florida Atlantic University. The university's president based his action on the poor quality of the newspaper and on the editors' failure to respect university guidelines regarding the publication of the paper. The court characterized the president's action as a form of direct control over the paper's content and held that such action violated the First Amendment. Poor quality, even though it "could embarrass, and perhaps bring some element of disrepute to the school," was not a permissible basis on which to limit free speech. The university president in *Schiff* attempted to bolster his case by arguing that the student editors were employees of the state. The court did not give the point the attention it deserved. Presumably, if a public institution chose to operate its own publication (such as an alumni magazine) and hired a student editor, the institution could fire that student if the technical quality of his or her work was inadequate. The situation in *Schiff* did not fit this model, however, because the newspaper was not set up as the university's own publication. Rather, it was recognized by the university as a publication primarily by and for the student body, and the student editors were paid from a special student activities fee fund under the general control of the student government association. While such arrangements may insulate the student newspaper from university control, might the newspaper's use of mandatory student fees and university facilities constitute state action (see Section 1.4.2), subjecting the student editors themselves to First Amendment restraints when dealing with other students and with outsiders? (See *Mississippi Gay Alliance* v. *Goudelock*, 536 F.2d 1073 (5th Cir. 1976) (state action argument rejected over strong dissent).)

Joyner, Bazaar, and *Schiff* clearly illustrate the very substantial limits on an administrator's authority to control the student press in public institutions. Though each case involves a different regulatory technique and a different rationale for regulation, the administrators lost each time. Yet even these cases suggest grounds on which student publications can be subjected to some regulation. The *Joyner* case indicates that the student press can be prohibited from racial discrimination in its staffing and advertising policies. *Bazaar* indicates that institutions may dissociate themselves from student publications to the extent of requiring or placing a disclaimer on the cover or format of the publication. (The court specifically approved the following disclaimer after it reheard the case: "This is not an official publication of the university.") *Schiff* suggests enigmatically that there may be "special circumstances" where administrators may regulate the press to prevent "significant disruption on the university campus or within its educational processes."

In these and other student press cases, the clear lesson is not "don't regulate" but rather "don't censor." As long as administrators avoid direct or indirect control of content, they may regulate publications by student organizations or individual students in much the same way they may regulate organizations (Section 4.8) or students generally (Section 4.7). Even content need not be totally beyond an administrator's concern. A disclaimer requirement can be imposed to avoid confusion concerning the publication's status within the institution. And, as the next two sections discuss, content that is illegal under state law because it is obscene or libelous may be regulated. Advertising in a publication also can be controlled to some extent. *Pittsburgh Press Co.* v. *Pittsburgh Commission on Human Relations,* 413 U.S. 376 (1973), upheld a regulation prohibiting newspapers from publishing "help-wanted" advertisements in sex-designated columns. And *Virginia State Board of Pharmacy* v. *Virginia Citizens Consumer Council,* 425 U.S. 748 (1976), while invalidating a statutory ban on advertising prescription drug prices, did affirm the state's authority to regulate false or misleading advertising and advertising that proposes illegal transactions.

4.9.3. Obscenity. It is clear that public institutions may discipline students or student organizations for having published obscene material. Public institutions may even halt the publication of such material *if* they do so under carefully constructed and conscientiously followed procedural safeguards. A leading case is *Antonelli* v. *Hammond,* 308 F. Supp. 1329 (D. Mass. 1970), which invalidated a system of prior review and approval by a faculty advisory board. The system's major defects were the failure to place the burden of proving obscenity on the board, the failure to provide for a prompt review and internal appeal of the board's decisions, and the failure to provide for a prompt final judicial determination. *Baughman* v. *Freimuth,*

478 F.2d 1345 (4th Cir. 1973), which sets out prior review requirements in the secondary school context, is also illustrative. Clearly, the constitutional requirements for prior review are stringent, and the creation of a constitutionally acceptable system is a very difficult and delicate task. (For U.S. Supreme Court teaching on prior review, see *Southeastern Promotions, Ltd.* v. *Conrad,* 420 U.S. 546 (1975).)

Moreover, institutional authority extends only to material that is actually obscene, and the definition or identification of obscenity is, at best, an exceedingly difficult proposition. In a leading Supreme Court case, *Papish* v. *Board of Curators of the University of Missouri,* 410 U.S. 667 (1973), the plaintiff was a graduate student who had been expelled for violating a board of curators bylaw prohibiting distribution of newspapers "containing forms of indecent speech." The newspaper at issue had a political cartoon on its cover which "depicted policemen raping the Statue of Liberty and the Goddess of Justice. The caption under the cartoon read: 'With Liberty and Justice for All.'" The newspaper also "contained an article entitled 'M---- F---- Acquitted,' which discussed the trial and acquittal on an assault charge of a New York City youth who was a member of an organization known as 'Up Against the Wall, M---- F----.'" After being expelled, the student sued the university, alleging a violation of her First Amendment rights.

The Supreme Court ruled unanimously in favor of the student:

> We think *Healy* [v. *James,* Section 4.7.1] makes it clear that the mere dissemination of ideas—no matter how offensive to good taste—on a state university campus may not be shut off in the name alone of "conventions of decency." Other recent precedents of this Court make it equally clear that neither the political cartoon nor the headline story involved in this case can be labeled as constitutionally obscene or otherwise unprotected [410 U.S. at 670].

Obscenity, then, is not definable in terms of an institution's or an administrator's own personal conceptions of taste, decency, or propriety. Obscenity can be defined only in terms of the guidelines that courts have constructed to prevent the concept from being used to choke off controversial social or political dialogue:

> We now confine the permissible scope of . . . regulation [of obscenity] to works which depict or describe sexual conduct. That conduct must be specifically defined by the applicable state law, as written or authoritatively construed. A state offense must also be limited to works which, taken as a whole, appeal to the prurient interest in sex, which portray sexual conduct in a patently offensive way, and which, taken as a whole, do not have serious literary, artistic, political, or scientific value [*Miller* v. *California,* 413 U.S. 15, 24 (1973)].

Although these guidelines were devised for the general community, the Supreme Court made clear in *Papish* that "the First Amendment leaves no room for the operation of a dual standard in the academic community with respect to the content of speech." Administrators devising campus rules for public institutions are thus bound by the same obscenity guidelines that bind the legislators promulgating obscenity laws. Under these guidelines the permissible scope of regulation is very narrow, and the drafting or application of rules is a technical exercise that administrators should undertake with the assistance of counsel, if at all.

4.9.4. Libel. As they may for obscenity, institutions may discipline students or organizations that publish libelous matter. Here again, however, the authority of public institutions extends only to matter that is libelous according to technical legal definitions. It is not sufficient that a particular statement be false or misleading. Common law and constitutional doctrines require that (1) the statement be false; (2) the publication cause at least nominal injury to the person libeled, usually including but not limited to injury to reputation; and (3) the falsehood be attributable to some fault on the part of the person or organization publishing it. The degree of fault depends on the subject of the alleged libel. If the subject is a public official or what the courts call a "public figure," the statement must have been made with "actual malice"; that is, with knowledge of its falsity or with reckless disregard for its truth or falsity. In all other situations governed by the First Amendment, the statement need only have been made negligently. Courts make this distinction in order to give publishers extra breathing space when reporting on certain matters of high public interest.[23]

Given the complexity of the libel concept, administrators should approach it most cautiously. Because of the need to assess both injury and fault, as well as identify the defamatory falsehood, libel may be even more difficult to combat than obscenity. Suppression in advance of publication is particularly perilous, since injury can only be speculated about at that point, and reliable facts concerning fault may not be attainable. Much of the material in campus publications, moreover, may involve public officials or public figures and thus be protected by the higher fault standard of actual malice.

Though these factors might reasonably lead administrators to forgo any regulation of libel, there is a countervailing consideration: Institutions or administrators may occasionally be held liable in court for libelous statements in student publications. (See Sections 2.3.1 and 2.4.1 for a general discussion of tort liability.) Such liability could exist where the institution sponsors a publication (such as a paper operated by the journalism department as a training ground for its students), employs the editors of the publication, establishes a formal committee to review material in advance of publication, or otherwise exercises some control (constitutionally or unconstitutionally) over the publication's content. In any case, liability would exist only for statements deemed libelous under the criteria set out above.

Such potential liability, however, need not necessarily prompt increased surveillance of student publications. Increased surveillance would demand regulations that stay within constitutional limits yet are strong enough to weed out all libel— an unlikely combination. And since institutional control of the publication is the predicate to the institution's liability, increased regulation increases the likelihood of liability should a libel be published. Thus, administrators may choose to handle liability problems by lessening rather than enlarging control. The privately

---

[23]The U.S. Supreme Court has developed the constitutional boundaries of libel law in a progression of decisions beginning with *New York Times* v. *Sullivan*, 376 U.S. 254 (1964). See also *Curtis Publishing Co.* v. *Butts*, 388 U.S. 130 (1967); *Associated Press* v. *Walker*, 388 U.S. 162 (1967); *Gertz* v. *Robert Welch, Inc.*, 418 U.S. 323 (1974); and *Time, Inc.* v. *Firestone*, 424 U.S. 448 (1976).

incorporated student newspaper operating independently of the institution would
be the clearest example of a no-control/no-liability situation.

A 1981 decision by the New York State Court of Claims provides a leading
example of libel law's application to student newspapers at public institutions. The
court's opinion in the case, *Mazart* v. *State,* 441 N.Y.S.2d 600 (Ct. Cl. 1981), illustrates the basic steps in establishing libel and affirms that institutional control over
the newspaper, or lack thereof, is a key to establishing or avoiding institutional
liability. The opinion also discusses the question whether an institution can ever
restrain in advance the planned publication of libelous material.

The plaintiffs (claimants) in *Mazart* were two students at SUNY-Binghamton
who were the targets of an allegedly libelous letter to the editor published in the
student newspaper, the *Pipe Dream.* The letter described a prank that had occurred
in a male dormitory and characterized it as an act of prejudice against homosexuals.
The plaintiffs' names appeared at the end of the letter, although they had not in
fact written it, and the body of the letter identified them as "members of
the gay community." Applying accepted principles of libel law to the educational
context in which the incident occurred, the court determined that this letter was libelous:

> Did the letter in the *Pipe Dream* expose claimants to hatred, contempt,
> or aversion, or induce an evil or unsavory opinion of them in the minds
> of a substantial number of the community? The answer to the question
> is far from simple. In general, the community we are concerned with here
> was the university community located on a campus outside of the City of
> Binghamton, Broome County, New York. According to the chairman of
> the English Department at the university, homosexuals were able to function
> in the university community with less of a problem than say Anita Bryant
> might have. This witness was of the view that sexual orientation had no
> more bearing in the classroom than religious affiliation. The assistant vice-
> president for finance, management, and control of the university opined
> that the published letter had a "very low, very little effect" on the campus
> community.
>
> No doubt the impact of the published letter on the collective mind
> of the university was considerably less than it might have been had the letter
> been published in a conservative rural American village. Nonetheless, the
> court finds that an unsavory opinion of the claimants did settle in the minds
> of a substantial number of persons in the university community. . . . The
> question of homosexuality was a significant one on the university campus. . . .
> Both claimants testified that they were accosted by numerous fellow students
> after the event and queried about their sexual orientation, and the court
> finds their testimony, in this respect, credible. Deviant sexual intercourse
> and sodomy were crimes in the state of New York at the time the letter
> was published (Penal Law, secs. 130 and 130.38). Certainly those members
> of the university community who did not personally know the claimants
> would logically conclude that claimants were homosexual, since the letter
> identified them as being members of the "gay community." The court finds
> that a substantial number of the university community would naturally
> assume that the claimants engaged in homosexual acts from such identifica-
> tion [441 N.Y.S.2d at 603–04].

The court then rejected the state's argument that, even if the letter was libelous, its publication was protected by a qualified privilege because the subject matter was of public concern. Again using commonly accepted libel principles, the court concluded that a privilege did not apply because

> the editors of the *Pipe Dream* acted in a grossly irresponsible manner by failing to give due consideration to the standards of information gathering and dissemination. It is obvious that authorship of a letter wherein the purported author appears to be libeled should be verified. Not only was the authorship of the letter herein not verified but it appears that the *Pipe Dream,* at least in November of 1977, had no procedures or guidelines with regard to the verification of the authorship of any letters to the editor [441 N.Y.S.2d at 604].

Third, the court held that, although the letter was libelous and not privileged, the university (and thus the state) was not liable for the unlawful acts of the student newspaper. In its analysis the court considered and rejected two theories of liability: "(1) [that] the state, through the university, may be vicariously liable for the torts of the *Pipe Dream* and its editors on the theory of *respondeat superior* (that is, the university, as principal, might be liable for the torts of its agents, the student paper and editors); and (2) [that] the state, through the university, may have been negligent in failing to provide guidelines to the *Pipe Dream* staff regarding libel generally and, specifically, regarding the need to review and verify letters to the editor."

In rejecting the first theory, the court relied heavily on First Amendment principles:

> The state could be held vicariously liable if the university and the *Pipe Dream* staff operated in some form of agency relationship. However, it is characteristic of the relationship of principal and agent that the principal has a right to control the conduct of the agent with respect to matters entrusted to him. While this control need not apply to every detail of an agent's conduct and can be found where there is merely a right held by the principal to make management and policy decisions affecting the agent, there can be no agency relationship where the alleged principal has no right of control over the alleged agent.
>
> There are severe constitutional limitations on the exercise of any form of control by a state university over a student newspaper . . . (*Panarella* v. *Birenbaum,* 37 A.D.2d 987, 327 N.Y.S.2d 755, affirmed, 32 N.Y.2d 108, 343 N.Y.S.2d 333, 296 N.E.2d 238). . . . Censorship or prior restraint of constitutionally protected expression in student publications at state-supported institutions has been uniformly proscribed by the courts. Such censorship or prior restraint cannot be imposed by suspending editors (*Scoville* v. *Board of Education of Joliet Township High School District 204,* 425 F.2d 10), by suppressing circulation (*Channing Club* v. *Board of Regents of Texas Tech. University,* 317 F. Supp. 688), by requiring prior approval of controversial articles (*Quarterman* v. *Byrd,* 453 F.2d 54 (4th Cir.); *Trujillo* v. *Love,* 322 F. Supp. 1266; *Antonelli* v. *Hammond,* 308 F. Supp. 1329), by excising or

suppressing distasteful material (*Trujillo* v. *Love, supra; Korn* v. *Elkins,* 317 F. Supp. 138; *Zucker* v. *Panitz,* 299 F. Supp. 102), or by withdrawing financial support (*Joyner* v. *Whiting,* 477 F.2d 456 (4th Cir.); *Antonelli* v. *Hammond, supra).*

Claimants' counsel argues that "the issue of prior restraint has never been extended to libel . . . cases." . . . In fact, in the absence of special circumstances, the publication of libelous material will not be restrained by the courts:

> A court of equity will not, except in special circumstances, issue an injunctive order restraining libel or slander or otherwise restricting free speech.
>
> To enjoin any publication, no matter how libelous, would be repugnant to the First Amendment to the Constitution (. . . *Parker* v. *Columbia Broadcasting System, Inc.,* 320 F.2d 937 (2d Cir. 1963); cf. *Near* v. *State of Minnesota, ex rel. Olson,* 283 U.S. 697, 51 S. Ct. 625, 75 L. Ed. 1357 (1931)), and to historic principles of equity [*Konigsberg* v. *Time, Inc.,* 288 F. Supp. 989 (S.D.N.Y. 1968)].

Thus, it appears that a policy of prior approval of items to be published in a student newspaper, even if directed only to restraining the publication of potentially libelous material (cf. *Trujillo* v. *Love, supra*), would run afoul of *Near* v. *State of Minnesota, supra,* wherein the Court stated that "liberty of the press, historically considered and taken up by the federal Constitution, has meant, principally although not exclusively, immunity from previous restraints or censorship" (283 U.S. at 716, 51 S. Ct. at 631). . . . The court, therefore, finds that the university was powerless to prevent the publication of the letter.

Although claimants' counsel suggests in his argument that the university's involvement with the funding of the *Pipe Dream* might afford it some measure of control, this involvement affords little, if any, actual control over the funding and expenditures of the newspaper . . . and, in any event, it is settled that no form of editorial control over constitutionally protected expression in student publications can be based on the university's power of the purse.

No doubt the university benefits, and did benefit at the time of the publication of the letter, from the existence of the *Pipe Dream.* That the university recognized participation on the newspaper as a form of independent study indicates that it received educational benefits. Furthermore, the *Pipe Dream* served as a means of disseminating information to the university community and as a forum for debate and discussion for members of the university community. However, these factors, which might suggest an agency relationship, are insufficient to overcome the university's lack of control over the newspaper.

The fact that the university created a climate wherein the student newspaper flourished by furnishing office space and janitorial services hardly creates an agency relationship which would permit recovery against the state. Such accoutrements are nothing more than a form of financial aid to the newspaper which cannot be traded off in return for editorial control (see *Joyner* v. *Whiting, supra; Antonelli* v. *Hammond, supra).*

The court recognizes that the *Pipe Dream* and its staff may be incapable of compensating claimants for any damages flowing from the libel. But, in light of the university's eschewing control, editorial or otherwise, over the paper and the constitutionally imposed barriers to the exercise by the university of any editorial control over the newspaper, the court must reluctantly conclude that the relationship of the university and the *Pipe Dream* is not such as would warrant the imposition of vicarious liability on the state for defamatory material appearing in the student newspaper (see "Tort Liability of a University for Libelous Material in Student Publications," 71 *Michigan L. Rev.* 1061) [441 N.Y.S.2d at 604–06; some citations omitted].

Focusing on the tort law concept of "duty," the court then rejected the claimant's second liability theory:

The second theory . . . involves the question of whether the state university, and therefore the state, can be cast in damages in simple negligence for failing to provide to the student editors guidelines and procedures designed to avoid the publication of libelous material. As discussed above, there are constitutional limitations on the actual exercise of editorial control by the university, but this does not necessarily preclude the existence of a duty on the part of the university to furnish guidance.

In view of the absolute hands-off policy adopted by the university administration, it is clear that no such guidelines were furnished, and from the evidence adduced at trial, it does not appear that student editors verified the authorship of controversial letters to the editor prior to the subject publication. The issue then is whether there was a duty on the part of the university administration. The court concludes that there was not. It is clear from a reading of the published cases dealing with the rights of college students that the courts uniformly regard them as young adults and not children. . . .

Furthermore, the establishment by statute of the minimum voting age (Election Law, sec. 5-102), drinking age (Alcoholic Beverage Control Law, sec. 65), and the age of consent for marriage (Domestic Relations Law, sec. 7) at 18 years, is indicative of a recognition, at least on the part of the legislature, of a substantial degree of maturity in college-aged persons.

In view of this societal recognition of adulthood, can the court conclude that the university had a duty to supply guidelines to the *Pipe Dream* editors in order to better enable the editors to avoid libeling an innocent party, even though such guidelines are generally considered within the common knowledge of mature laypersons? In rejecting the need for expert affidavits on a motion for summary judgment in a libel action, the court in *Greenberg* v. *CBS, Inc.,* 69 A.D.2d 693, 419 N.Y.S.2d 988, stated: "The elementary standards of basic news reporting are common knowledge. News articles and broadcasts must contain the answers to the essential inquiries of who, what, where, when, why, and how" (419 N.Y.S.2d 988). Certainly the need to verify the authorship of a letter wherein the purported author appears to be libeled is rudimentary. A conclusion that the university had a duty to furnish guidance to the *Pipe Dream* concerning libel would in effect be a finding that the *Pipe Dream* editors lacked that degree of maturity and common sense necessary to comprehend the normal procedures for information gathering and dissemination. But surely such a finding would be anomalous since those editors' contemporaries might well be selected to sit on a jury (Judiciary Law, sec. 510(2)), assigned the task of determining, without the aid and guidance of expert testimony, whether a newspaper (the *Pipe Dream* or any other) had failed to adhere to generally followed standards, resulting in the publication of libel. . . .

The court must, therefore, find that the university had no duty to supply news gathering and dissemination guidelines to the *Pipe Dream* editors since they were presumed to already know those guidelines. Admittedly, it appears that the student editors of the *Pipe Dream* in 1977 either did not know or simply ignored common-sense verification guidelines with regard to the publication of the instant letter. But that was not the fault of the university. In either event, there was no duty on the part of the university. The editors' lack of knowledge of or failure to adhere to standards which are common knowledge (*Greenberg* v. *CBS, Inc., supra*) and ordinarily followed by reasonable persons . . . was not reasonably foreseeable [441 N.Y.S.2d at 606–07].

Mazart v. *State* is an extensively reasoned precedent in an area where there has been a dearth of precedent. The court's opinion provides much useful guidance for administrators of public institutions. The opinion's reasoning depends, however, on particular circumstances concerning the campus setting in which the libel occurred, the irresponsibility of the student editors, the degree of control the institution exercised over the newspaper, and the foreseeability of the student editors' irresponsible acts. Administrators will therefore want to consult with counsel before attempting to apply the principles in *Mazart* to occurrences on their own campuses.

4.9.5. Obscenity and libel in private institutions. Since the First Amendment does not apply to private institutions that are not engaged in state action (Section 1.4.2), such institutions have a freer hand in regulating obscenity and libel. Yet private institutions should devise their regulatory role cautiously. Regulations broadly construing libel and obscenity based on lay concepts of those terms could stifle the flow of dialogue within the institution, while attempts to avoid this problem with narrow regulations may lead the institution into the same definitional complexities that public institutions face when seeking to comply with the First Amendment. Moreover, in devising their policies on obscenity and libel, private institutions will want to consider the potential impact of state law. Violation of state obscenity or libel law by student publications could subject the responsible students to injunctions, damage actions, and even criminal prosecutions, causing unwanted publicity for the institution. But if the institution regulates the student publications to prevent such problems, it could be held liable along with the students if it exercises sufficient control over the publication. (See Sections 2.1 and 4.9.4.)

Sec. 4.10. Student Housing

4.10.1. Housing regulations. Postsecondary institutions with residential campuses usually have policies specifying which students may, and which students must, live in campus housing. Institutions also typically have policies regulating living conditions in campus housing. Several such housing policies have been challenged in court cases brought by students in public institutions.[24]

Where institutional regulations require students to live on campus, such regulations sometimes apply only to certain groups of students. The classifications may be based on the student's age, sex, class, or marital status. In *Prostrollo* v. *University of South Dakota,* 507 F.2d 775 (8th Cir. 1974), students claimed that the university's regulation requiring all single freshmen and sophomores to live in university housing was unconstitutional because it denied them equal protection under the Fourteenth Amendment and infringed their constitutional rights of privacy and freedom of association. The university admitted that one purpose of the regulation was to maintain a certain level of dormitory occupancy to secure revenue to repay dormitory construction costs. But the university also offered testimony that the regulation was instituted to ensure that younger students would educationally benefit from the experience in self-government, community living, and group discipline, and the opportunities for relationships with staff members that dormitory life provides. In addition, university officials contended that the dormitories provided easy access to study facilities and to films and discussion groups.

After evaluating these justifications, the lower court determined that the primary purpose of the housing regulation was financial and that the regulation's differentiation of freshmen and sophomores from upper-division students had no rational relationship to the purpose of ensuring housing income. The lower court therefore held the regulation unconstitutional under the equal protection clause. The U.S. Court of Appeals for the Eighth Circuit reversed the lower court's decision. It reasoned that, even if the regulation's primary purpose was financial, there was no denial of equal protection because there was another rational basis for differentiating freshmen and sophomores from upper-division students: the university officials' belief that the regulation contributed to the younger students' adjustment to college life. The appellate court also rejected the students' right-to-privacy and freedom-of-association challenges. The court gave deference to school authorities' traditionally broad powers in formulating educational policy.

A similar housing regulation that used an age classification to prohibit certain students from living off campus was at issue in *Cooper* v. *Nix,* 496 F.2d 1285 (5th Cir. 1974). The regulation required all unmarried full-time undergraduate students, regardless of age and whether or not emancipated, to live on campus. The regulation contained an exemption for certain older students, which in practice the school enforced by simply exempting all undergraduates twenty-three years old and over. Neither the lower court nor the appeals court found any justification in the record for a distinction between twenty-one-year-old students and twenty-three-year-old students. Though the lower court had enjoined the school from requiring students twenty-one and older to live on campus, the appeals court narrowed the remedy to require only that the school not automatically exempt all twenty-three-year-olds. Thus, the school could continue to enforce the regulation if it exempted students over twenty-three only on a case-by-case basis.

---

[24]The cases are collected in Annot., "Validity, Under Federal Constitution, of Policy or Regulation of College or University Requiring Students to Live in Dormitories or Residence Halls," 31 A.L.R. Fed. 813 (1977 plus periodic supp.).

A regulation that allowed male students but not female students to live off campus has also been challenged. In *Texas Woman's University* v. *Chayklintaste,* 521 S.W.2d 949 (Tex. Civ. App. 1975), the court found such a regulation to be unconstitutional. Though the university convinced the court that it did not have the space or the money to provide on-campus male housing, the court held that mere financial reasons could not justify the discrimination. The court held that the university was unconstitutionally discriminating against its male students by not providing them any housing facilities and also unconstitutionally discriminating against its female students by not permitting them to live off campus.

The university subsequently made housing available to males and changed its regulations to require both male and female undergraduates under twenty-three to live on campus. Although the regulation was now like the one found unconstitutional in *Cooper,* above, the Texas Supreme Court upheld its constitutionality in a later appeal of *Texas Woman's University* v. *Chayklintaste,* 530 S.W.2d 927 (1975). In this case the university justified the age classification with reasons similar to those used in *Prostrollo,* above, which upheld the freshman and sophomore classification. The university argued that on-campus dormitory life added to the intellectual and emotional development of its students and supported this argument with evidence from two professional educational journals and the testimony of a vice-president of student affairs, a professor of education, and an instructor of social work.

In *Bynes* v. *Toll,* 512 F.2d 252 (2d Cir. 1975), another challenge was brought against a university concerning a housing regulation that permitted married students to live on campus but barred their children from living on campus. The court found that there was no denial of equal protection, since the university had several very sound safety reasons for not allowing children to reside in the dorms. The court also found that the regulation did not interfere with the marital privacy of the students or their natural right to bring up their children.

Housing regulations limiting dormitory visitation privileges have also been challenged. In *Futrell* v. *Ahrens,* 88 N.M. 284, 540 P.2d 214 (1975), students claimed that a regulation prohibiting visitation by members of the opposite sex in dormitory bedrooms violated their rights of privacy and free association. The regulation did not apply to the lounges or lobbies of the dorms. The court held for the institution, reasoning that even if the regulation affected rights of privacy and association, it was a reasonable time and place restriction on exercise of those rights, since it served legitimate educational interests and conformed with accepted standards of conduct.

Taken together, these cases indicate that the Constitution affords public universities broad leeway in regulating on-campus student housing. An institution may require some students to live on campus; may regulate living conditions to fulfill legitimate health, safety, or educational goals; and may apply its housing policies differently to different student groups. If students are treated differently, however, the Constitution requires that the basis for classifying them be reasonable. The cases above suggest that classification based solely on financial considerations may not meet that test. Administrators should thus be prepared to offer sound non-financial justifications for classifications in their residence rules—such as the promotion of educational goals, the protection of the health and safety of students, or the protection of other students' privacy interests. Differing treatment of students based on sex may require a relatively stronger showing of justification, and differing treatment based on race would require a justification so compelling that perhaps none exists.

Besides these limits on administrators' authority over student housing, the Constitution also limits public administrators' authority with regard to the entry of student rooms (see Section 4.10.2) and regulation of solicitation, canvassing, and voter registration in student residences (see Sections 5.4.3 and 5.6.4).

For private institutions as well as public, federal civil rights regulations also limit administrators' authority to treat students differently on grounds of race, sex, or age, or because they are handicapped. The Title VI regulations (see Section 7.5.2) apparently prohibit any and all different treatment of students by race (34 C.F.R. secs. 100.3(b)(1)-(b)(5) and 100.4(d)). The Title IX regulations (see Section 7.5.3) have specific provisions requiring that the institution provide amounts of housing for female and male students proportionate to the number of housing applicants of each sex, that such housing be comparable in quality and in cost to the student, and that the institution not have different housing policies for each sex (34 C.F.R. secs. 106.32 and 106.33). The Section 504 regulations on discrimination against the handicapped (see Section 7.5.4) require institutions to provide "comparable, convenient, and accessible" housing for handicapped students at the same cost as for nonhandicapped students (34 C.F.R. sec. 104.45). And the Age Discrimination Act regulations (see Section 7.5.5) apparently apply to discrimination by age in campus housing. Being general regulations applicable to all federal agencies dispensing federal aid, they have no specific provisions on student housing as do the Title IX and Section 504 regulations. But the Department of Education's own regulations, yet to be issued, may have such specific provisions.

As implemented in the general regulations, the ADA apparently limits administrators' authority to use explicit age distinctions (such as those used in *Cooper* v. *Nix* and *Texas Woman's University* v. *Chayklintaste*) in formulating housing policies. Policies that distinguish among students according to their class (such as those used in *Prostrollo* v. *University of South Dakota*) may also be affected by the ADA, since they may have the *effect* of distinguishing by age. Such age distinctions will be prohibited under Section 90.12 of the general regulations unless they fit within one of the narrow exceptions in Sections 90.13, 90.14, and 90.15, or constitute affirmative action under Section 90.49 (see generally Sections 7.5.5 and 7.5.6 of this volume). The best bet for fitting within an exception may be Section 90.14, which permits age distinctions that are "necessary to the normal operation . . . of a program or activity." But administrators should note that the four-part test set out in the regulation carefully circumscribes this exception. For policies based on the class of students, administrators may also be helped by Section 90.15, which would permit the use of a nonage factor with an age-discriminatory effect "if the factor bears a direct and substantial relationship to the normal operation of the program or activity."

4.10.2. Searches and seizures. The Fourth Amendment secures an individual's expectation of privacy against government encroachment by providing that "the right of the people to be secure in their persons, houses, papers, and effects, against unreasonable searches and seizures, shall not be violated, and no warrants shall issue, but upon probable cause, supported by oath or affirmation, and particularly describing the place to be searched, and the persons or things to be seized." Searches or seizures conducted pursuant to a warrant meeting the requirements of this provision are deemed reasonable. Warrantless searches may also be found reasonable if they are conducted with the consent of the individual involved, if they are incidental to a lawful arrest, or if they come within a few narrow judicial exceptions, such as an emergency situation.

The applicability of these Fourth Amendment mandates to postsecondary institutions has not always been clear. In the past, when administrators' efforts to provide a "proper" educational atmosphere resulted in noncompliance with the Fourth Amendment, the deviations were defended by administrators and often upheld by courts under a variety of theories. While the previously common justification of *in loco parentis* is no longer appropriate (see Section 4.1.1), several remaining theories retain vitality. The leading case of *Piazzola* v. *Watkins*, 442 F.2d 284 (5th Cir. 1971), provides a good overview of these theories and their validity.

Piazzola involved the dean of men at a state university, who was informed by the police that they had evidence that marijuana was in the dormitory rooms of certain students. In response to a police request, the dean pledged the cooperation of university officials in searching the rooms. At the time of the search, the university had the following regulation in effect: "The college reserves the right to enter rooms for inspection purposes. If the administration deems it necessary, the room may be searched and the occupant required to open his personal baggage and any other personal material which is sealed." Both defendants' rooms were searched without their consent and without a warrant by police officers and university officials. When police found marijuana in each room, the defendants were arrested, tried, convicted, and sentenced to five years in prison. The U.S. Court of Appeals for the Fifth Circuit reversed the convictions, holding that "a student who occupies a college dormitory room enjoys the protection of the Fourth Amendment" and that the warrantless searches were unreasonable and therefore unconstitutional under that amendment.

Piazzola and similar cases establish that administrators of public institutions cannot avoid the Fourth Amendment simply by asserting that a student has no reasonable expectation of privacy in institution-sponsored housing. Similarly, administrators can no longer be confident of avoiding the Fourth Amendment by asserting the *in loco parentis* concept or by arguing that the institution's landlord status, standing alone, authorizes it to search to protect its property interests. Nor does the landlord status, by itself, permit the institution to consent to a search by police, since it has been held that a landlord has no authority to consent to a police search of a tenant's premises (see, for example, *Chapman* v. *United States*, 365 U.S. 610 (1961)).

However, two limited bases remain on which administrators of public institutions or their delegates can enter a student's premises uninvited and without the authority of a warrant.[25] Under the first approach, the institution can obtain the student's consent to entry by including such consent in a written housing agreement

---

[25]In *New Jersey* v. *T.L.O.*, 105 S. Ct. 733 (1985), the U.S. Supreme Court created a judicial exception to the warrant requirement for certain searches of public school students. However, the Court's opinion directly applies only to public elementary and secondary schools. Moreover, the opinion applies (1) only to searches of the person or property (such as a purse) carried on the person, as opposed to searches of dormitory rooms, lockers, desks, or other such locations (105 S. Ct. at 741 n.5); and (2) only to "searches carried out by school authorities acting alone and on their own authority," as opposed to "searches conducted by school officials in conjunction with or at the behest of law enforcement agencies" (105 S. Ct. at 744 n.7).

or in housing regulations incorporated in the housing agreement. *Piazzola* explains the substantial limits on this approach. Citing the regulation quoted above, the court explained that

> The university retains broad supervisory powers which permit it to adopt . . . [this regulation], provided that regulation is reasonably construed and is limited in its application to further the university's function as an educational institution. The regulation cannot be construed or applied so as to give consent to a search for evidence for the primary purpose of a criminal prosecution. Otherwise, the regulation itself would constitute an unconstitutional attempt to require a student to waive his protection from unreasonable searches and seizures as a condition to his occupancy of a college dormitory room [442 F.2d at 289].

Thus, housing agreements or regulations must be narrowly construed to permit only such entry and search as is expressly provided, and in any case to permit only entries undertaken in pursuit of an educational purpose rather than a criminal enforcement function.

Under the second approach to securing entry to a student's premises, the public institution can sometimes conduct searches (often called "administrative searches") whose purpose is the protection of health and safety. Unconsented administrative searches to enforce health regulations or fire and safety codes usually require a warrant, under this second approach, but it may be obtained under less stringent standards than those for obtaining a criminal search warrant. The leading case is *Camara* v. *Municipal Court*, 387 U.S. 523 (1967), where the U.S. Supreme Court held that a person cannot be prosecuted for refusing to permit city officials to conduct a warrantless code-enforcement inspection of his residence. The Court held that such a search required a warrant, which could be obtained "if reasonable legislative or administrative standards for conducting an area inspection are satisfied"; such standards need "not necessarily depend upon specific knowledge of the condition of the particular dwelling."

In emergency situations where there is insufficient time to obtain a warrant, health and safety searches may be conducted without one. The U.S. Supreme Court emphasized in the *Camara* case (387 U.S. at 539) that "nothing we say today is intended to foreclose prompt inspections, even without a warrant, that the law has traditionally upheld in emergency situations." In other cases courts have recognized firefighters' authority to enter "a burning structure to put out the blaze" and remain there to investigate its cause (*Michigan* v. *Tyler*, 436 U.S. 499 (1978)), and police officers' authority to "enter a dwelling without a warrant to render emergency aid and assistance to a person whom they reasonably believe to be in distress and in need of that assistance" (*Root* v. *Gauper*, 438 F.2d 361 (8th Cir. 1971)).

For genuine health and safety searches, it may often be possible to obtain the specific consent of the student(s) whose premises will be entered. Administrators should obtain such consent whenever feasible for reasons of courtesy as well as because it reinforces the validity of the entry. (The same might be said for searches provided for in the housing agreement, even though the student has already consented generally by entering the agreement.) As *Camara* suggests, administrators may not take

disciplinary action against a student for refusing to consent where such consent
was not previously required in the housing agreement or regulations.

In addition to these two limited approaches (housing agreements and administrative searches) to securing entry, other even narrower exceptions to Fourth
Amendment warrant requirements may be available to security officers of public
institutions who have arrest powers. Such exceptions involve the intricacies of Fourth
Amendment law on arrests and searches (see generally *Welsh* v. *Wisconsin,* 104 S.
Ct. 2091 (1984)). The case of *State of Washington* v. *Chrisman,* 102 S. Ct. 812 (1982),
is illustrative. A campus security guard at Washington State University had arrested
a student, Overdahl, for illegally possessing alcoholic beverages. The officer accompanied Overdahl to his dormitory room when Overdahl offered to retrieve his identification. Overdahl's roommate, Chrisman, was in the room. While waiting at
the doorway for Overdahl to find his identification, the officer observed marijuana
seeds and a pipe lying on a desk in the room. The officer then entered, confirmed
the identity of the seeds, and seized them. Chrisman was later convicted of possession of marijuana and of LSD, which security officers also found in the room.

By a 6-to-3 vote, the U.S. Supreme Court applied the "plain view" exception to the Fourth Amendment and upheld the conviction. The plain view doctrine
allows a law enforcement officer to seize property which is clearly incriminating
evidence or contraband when that property is in "plain view" in a place where
the officer has a right to be. The Court determined that, since an arresting officer
has a right to maintain custody of a subject under arrest, this officer lawfully could
have entered the room with Overdahl and remained at Overdahl's side for the entire
time Overdahl was in the room. Thus, the officer not only had the right to be where
he could observe the drugs; he also had the right to be where he could seize the
drugs. According to the Court, "It is of no legal significance whether the officer
was in the room, on the threshold, or in the hallway, since he had a right to be
in any of these places as an incident of a valid arrest. . . . This is a classic instance
of incriminating evidence found in plain view when a police officer, for unrelated
but entirely legitimate reasons, obtains lawful access to an individual's area of
privacy."

Chrisman thus recognizes that a security officer may enter a student's room
"as an incident of a valid arrest" of either that student or his roommate. The case
also indicates that an important exception to search warrant requirements—the plain
view doctrine—retains its full vitality in the college dormitory setting. The Court
accorded no greater or lesser constitutional protection from search and seizure to
student dormitory residents than to the population at large. Clearly, under *Chrisman*
students do enjoy Fourth Amendment protections on campus; but, just as clearly,
the Fourth Amendment does not accord dormitory students special status or subject
campus security officials to additional restrictions that are not applicable to the
nonacademic world.

Administrators at private institutions are generally not subject to Fourth
Amendment restraints, since their actions are usually not "state action" (Section
1.4.2). But if local, state, or federal law enforcement officials are in any way involved in a search at a private institution, such involvement may be sufficient to
make the search state action and therefore subject to the Fourth Amendment. In
People v. *Boettner,* 362 N.Y.S.2d 365 (Sup. Ct. 1974), affirmed, 50 A.D.2d 1074,
376 N.Y.S.2d 59 (1975), for instance, the question was whether a dormitory room

search by officials at the Rochester Institute of Technology, a private institution, was state action. The court answered in the negative only after establishing that the police had not expressly or implicitly requested the search; that the police were not aware of the search; and that there was no evidence of any implied participation of the police by virtue of a continuing cooperative relationship between university officials and the police. And in a leading case involving a security officer of a private business firm, another court judged the validity of the search by determining whether the officer had "acted at the behest or suggestion, with the aid, advice, or encouragement, or under the direction or influence of" government law enforcement officials (*United States* v. *Clegg,* 509 F.2d 605 (5th Cir. 1975)). Thus, a private institution's authority to conduct searches unshackled by the Fourth Amendment depends on the absence of direct or indirect involvement of such officials in such searches. In addition, if security officers at a private institution have been given public arrest or search powers, they and their institution will be subject to Fourth Amendment strictures in exercising these state-delegated powers (see *People* v. *Zelinski,* 24 Cal. 3d 357, 594 P.2d 1000(1979), discussed in this volume, Section 4.14.1).

Sec. 4.11. Athletics

4.11.1. General principles. Athletics, as a subsystem of the postsecondary institution, is governed by the general principles set forth elsewhere in this chapter and this book. These principles, however, must be applied in light of the particular characteristics and problems of curricular, extracurricular, and intercollegiate athletics programs. A student athlete's eligibility for financial aid, for instance, would be viewed under the general principles in Section 4.3, but aid conditions related to the student's eligibility for or performance in intercollegiate athletics may create a special focus for the problem. In *Taylor* v. *Wake Forest,* 191 S.E.2d 379 (N.C. App. 1972), for instance, the court held that a student athlete's refusal to participate in practice was a breach of his contractual obligations under his athletic scholarship. Similarly, the due process principles in Section 4.6 above may apply when a student athlete is disciplined, and the First Amendment principles in Section 4.7 may apply when student athletes engage in protest activities. But in each case the problem may have a special focus.

In a discipline situation, the penalty may be suspension from the team, thus raising the issue whether the procedural protections accompanying suspension from school are also applicable to suspension from a team. For institutions engaging in state action (see Sections 1.4.2 and 4.11.4), the constitutional issue is whether the student athlete has a "property interest" or "liberty interest" in continued intercollegiate competition sufficient to make suspension of that interest a deprivation of "liberty or property" within the meaning of the due process clause. (The same general issue arises with respect to due process's applicability to faculty dismissals (see Section 3.5.2) as well as to suspension of students from school (Section 4.6.2).) Several federal court cases have addressed this question.

In *Behagen* v. *Intercollegiate Conference of Faculty Representatives,* 346 F. Supp. 602 (D. Minn. 1972), a suit brought by University of Minnesota basketball players suspended from the team for participating in an altercation during a game, the court reasoned that participation in intercollegiate athletics has "the potential to bring [student athletes] great economic rewards" and is thus as important as con-

tinuing in school. The court therefore held that the students' interest in intercollegiate participation were protected by procedural due process and granted the suspended athletes the protections established in the *Dixon* case (Section 4.6.2). In
Regents of University of Minnesota v. *NCAA,* 422 F. Supp. 1158 (D. Minn. 1976), the
same district court reaffirmed and further explained its analysis of student athletes'
due process rights. The court reasoned that the opportunity to participate in intercollegiate competition is a property interest entitled to due process protection, not
only because of the possible remunerative careers that result but also because such
participation is an important part of the student athlete's educational experience.
(Although the appellate court reversed this decision, 560 F.2d 352 (8th Cir. 1977),
it did so on other grounds and did not question the district court's due process
analysis.) (To the same effect, see *Hall* v. *University of Minnesota,* 530 F. Supp. 104
(D. Minn. 1982).)

In contrast, the court in *Colorado Seminary* v. *NCAA,* 417 F. Supp. 885 (D.
Colo. 1976), relying on an appellate court's opinion involving high school athletes
(*Albach* v. *Odle,* 531 F.2d 983 (10th Cir. 1976)), held that college athletes have no
property or liberty interests in participating in intercollegiate sports, participating
in postseason competition, or appearing on television. The court did suggest,
however, that revocation of an athletic scholarship would infringe property or liberty
interests of the student and require due process safeguards (see Section 4.3.1). The
appellate court affirmed (570 F.2d 320 (10th Cir. 1978)). Given this disagreement
among the courts, the extent of student athletes' procedural due process protections remains an open question, and administrators should tread cautiously in this
area.

In a protest situation, the First Amendment rights of protesting athletes must
be viewed in light of the institution's particular interest in maintaining order and
discipline in its athletic programs. An athlete's protest that disrupts an athletics
program would no more be protected by the First Amendment than any other student
protest that disrupts institutional functions. While the case law regarding athletes'
First Amendment rights is even more sparse than that regarding their due process
rights, *Williams* v. *Eaton,* 468 F.2d 1079 (10th Cir. 1972), does specifically apply
the *Tinker* case (Section 4.7.1) to a protest by intercollegiate football players. Black
football players had been suspended from the team for insisting on wearing black
armbands during a game to protest the alleged racial discrimination of the opposing
church-related school. The court held that the athletes' protest was unprotected
by the First Amendment because it would interfere with the religious freedom rights
of the opposing players and their church-related institution. The *Williams* opinion
is unusual in that it mixes considerations of free speech and freedom of religion.
The court's analysis would have little relevance to situations where religious freedom
is not involved. Since the court did not find that the athletes' protest was disruptive,
it relied solely on the seldom-used "interference with the rights of others" branch
of the *Tinker* case.

More recently, in *Marcum* v. *Dahl,* 658 F.2d 731 (10th Cir. 1981), the court
considered a First Amendment challenge to an institution's nonrenewal of the scholarships of several student athletes. The plaintiffs, basketball players on the University
of Oklahoma's women's team, had been involved during the season in a dispute
with other players over who should be the team's head coach. At the end of the
season, they had announced to the press that they would not play the next year

if the current coach was retained. The plaintiffs argued that the institution had refused to renew their scholarships because of this statement to the press and that the statement was constitutionally protected. The trial court and then the appellate court disagreed. Analogizing the scholarship athletes to public employees for First Amendment purposes (see Section 3.6.1), the appellate court held that (1) the dispute about the coach was not a matter of "general public concern" and the plaintiffs' press statement on this subject was therefore not protected by the First Amendment and (2) the plaintiffs' participation in the dispute *prior* to the press statement, and the resultant disharmony, provided an independent basis for the scholarship nonrenewal.

Tort law is another area where athletics programs present special problems. Because of the physical nature of athletics and because athletics programs often require travel to other locations, the danger of injury to students and the possibilities for institutional liability are greater than those resulting from other institutional functions. These problems are subject to the tort liability principles set out in Sections 2.3.1 and 2.4.1, applied in light of the special characteristics of athletics programs. In *Scott* v. *State,* 158 N.Y.S.2d 617 (Ct. Cl. 1956), for instance, a student collided with a flagpole while chasing a fly ball during an intercollegiate baseball game; the student was awarded $12,000 damages because the school had negligently maintained the playing field in a dangerous condition and the student had not assumed the risk of such danger. But in *Rubtchinsky* v. *State University of New York at Albany,* 260 N.Y.S.2d 256 (Ct. Cl. 1965), discussed in Section 2.3.1.1, a student injured in an extracurricular pushball game did not collect damages; the student was injured when clipped by another player, and the court held that he had assumed the risk of such injury. When the alleged negligence is that of a public institution (as in the two cases above), the general principles of tort immunity may also apply to athletic injury cases. In *Lowe* v. *Texas Tech University,* 530 S.W.2d 337 (Tex. Civ. App. 1975), for instance, a varsity football player with a knee injury had his damages suit dismissed by the intermediate appellate court because the university had sovereign immunity; but on further appeal, the suit was reinstituted because it fell within a specific statutory waiver of immunity (540 S.W.2d 297 (1976)).

More generally, major new legal and policy issues have surfaced in the national debate on the status of "big-time" intercollegiate athletics within the higher education world. The debate has focused on academic entrance requirements for student athletes (see L. Greene, "The New NCAA Rules of the Game: Academic Integrity or Racism?" 28 *St. Louis University L.J.* 101 (1984)), postsecondary institutions' recruiting practices, alleged doctoring of high school and college transcripts to obtain or maintain athletic eligibility, drug use among athletes and mandatory drug testing to curb such use, low graduation rates of college athletes, alleged exploitation of black athletes, National Collegiate Athletic Association (NCAA) authority over individual schools, NCAA regulation of women's sports and the relationship between NCAA and the Association for Intercollegiate Athletics for Women (AIAW), and control of television rights to broadcast or cablecast intercollegiate athletic contests (see Section 7.2.10). The overall issue being framed by this debate is one of integrity: the integrity of individual institutions' athletic programs, the integrity of academic standards at institutions emphasizing major intercollegiate competition, the integrity of higher education's mission in an era when athletics has assumed such a substantial role in the operation of the system.

4.11.2. Sex discrimination. Sex discrimination has become a major issue in athletics programs. Before the passage of Title IX, 20 U.S.C. sec. 1681 *et seq.* (see Section 7.5.3), the legal aspects of this controversy centered on the Fourteenth Amendment's equal protection clause. As in the case of admissions (Section 4.2.4.2), courts searched for an appropriate standard by which to ascertain the constitutionality of sex-based classifications in athletics. Most of the cases concerned female high school athletes seeking the opportunity to try out for male teams. Although the decisions were not all in agreement, a rough consensus apparently developed on one point: When the sport is a "noncontact sport"—that is, a sport involving little bodily contact among participants—the female athlete must be afforded an equal opportunity to compete for the traditionally male team *if* there is no comparable athletic activity provided for females.[26]

Since the implementation in 1975 of the Title IX regulations (34 C.F.R. Part 106), the equal protection aspects of sex discrimination in high school and college athletics have been playing second fiddle to Title IX. Since Title IX applies to both public and private institutions receiving federal aid, it has a broader reach than equal protection, which applies only to public institutions (see this volume, Section 1.4.2). Moreover, Title IX has several provisions on athletics which establish requirements more extensive than anything yet devised under the banner of equal protection.

Section 106.41 of the Title IX regulations is the primary provision on athletics; it establishes various equal opportunity requirements applicable to "interscholastic, intercollegiate, club, or intramural athletics." Section 106.37(c) establishes equal opportunity requirements regarding the availability of athletic scholarships. Physical education classes are covered by Section 106.34, and extracurricular activities related to athletics, such as cheerleading and booster clubs, are covered generally under Section 106.31. The regulations apparently impose nondiscrimination requirements on these activities whether or not they are directly subsidized by federal funds. The validity of this expansive interpretation of Title IX's scope is discussed in Section 7.5.7.4 of this volume.

One of the greatest controversies stirred by Title IX concerns the issue of sex-segregated versus unitary (integrated) athletic teams. The regulations develop a compromise approach to this issue, which roughly parallels the equal protection principles that have emerged from the court cases.[27] Under Section 106.41(b):

---

[26]The cases are collected in Annot., "Validity, Under Federal Law, of Sex Discrimination in Athletics," 23 A.L.R. Fed. 664 (1975 and periodic supp.).

[27]It is still an open question whether Title IX's athletic regulations fully comply with constitutional equal protection and due process requirements. There is some basis for arguing that the Title IX regulations do not fully meet the equal protection requirements that courts have constructed or will construct in this area. (See W. Kaplin and S. Marmur, "Validity of the 'Separate but Equal' Policy of the Title IX Regulations on Athletics," a memorandum reprinted in 121 *Congressional Record* 1090, 94th Cong., 1st Sess. (1975).) One court has ruled on the question, holding Title IX regulation 86.41(b) (now 106.41(b)) unconstitutional as applied to exclude physically qualified girls from competing with boys in contact sports (*Yellow Springs Exempted Village School District* v. *Ohio High School Athletic Association,* 443 F. Supp. 753 (S.D. Ohio 1978)). On appeal (647 F.2d 651 (6th Cir. 1981)), however, a U.S. Court of Appeals reversed the district court's ruling. The appellate court held that, because of the posture of the case and the absence of evidence in the record, "we believe it inappropriate for this court to make any ruling on the matter at this time." The majority opinion and a concurring/dissenting opinion include extensive analysis of sex segregation in athletic teams.

[An institution] may operate or sponsor separate teams for members of each sex where selection for such teams is based upon competitive skill or the activity involved is a contact sport. However, where a recipient operates or sponsors a team in a particular sport for members of one sex but operates or sponsors no such team for members of the other sex, and athletic opportunities for members of that sex have previously been limited, members of the excluded sex must be allowed to try out for the team offered unless the sport involved is a contact sport. For the purposes of this part, contact sports include boxing, wrestling, rugby, ice hockey, football, basketball, and other sports the purpose or major activity of which involves bodily contact.

This regulation requires institutions to operate unitary teams only for noncontact sports where selection is not competitive. Otherwise, the institution may operate either unitary or separate teams and may even operate a team for one sex without having any team in the sport for the opposite sex, as long as the institution's overall athletics program "effectively accommodate[s] the interests and abilities of members of both sexes" (34 C.F.R. sec. 106.41(c)(1)). In a noncontact sport, however, if an institution operates only one competitively selected team, it must be open to both sexes whenever the "athletic opportunities" of the traditionally excluded sex "have previously been limited" (34 C.F.R. sec. 106.41(b)).

Regardless of whether its teams are separate or unitary, the institution must "provide equal athletic opportunity for members of both sexes" (34 C.F.R. sec. 106.41(c)). While equality of opportunity does not require either equality of "aggregate expenditures for members of each sex" or equality of "expenditures for male and female teams," an institution's "failure to provide necessary funds for teams for one sex" is a relevant factor in determining compliance (34 C.F.R. sec. 106.41(c)). Postsecondary administrators grappling with this slippery equal opportunity concept will be helped by Section 106.41(c)'s list of ten nonexclusive factors by which to measure overall equality:

1. Whether the selection of sports and levels of competition effectively accommodate the interests and abilities of members of both sexes.
2. The provision of equipment and supplies.
3. Scheduling of games and practice time.
4. Travel and per diem allowance.
5. Opportunity to receive coaching and academic tutoring.
6. Assignment and compensation of coaches and tutors.
7. Provision of locker rooms, practice and competitive facilities.
8. Provision of medical and training facilities and services.
9. Provision of housing and dining facilities and services.
10. Publicity.

The equal opportunity focus of the regulations also applies to athletic scholarships. Institutions must "provide reasonable opportunities for such awards for members of each sex in proportion to the number of each sex participating in . . . intercollegiate athletics" (34 C.F.R. sec. 106.37(c)(1)). If the institution operates separate teams for each sex, as permitted in Section 106.41, it may allocate athletic scholarships on the basis of sex to implement its separate team philosophy, as long as the overall allocation achieves equal opportunity.

In December 1979, after a period of substantial controversy, HEW (now ED) issued a lengthy "policy interpretation" of its Title IX regulations as they apply to intercollegiate athletics (44 Fed. Reg. 71413 (Dec. 11, 1979)). In this sensitive area, the ED policy interpretation provides important guidance to institutions seeking to comply with the Title IX statute and regulations.

4.11.3. Discrimination on the basis of handicap. Under Section 504 of the Rehabilitation Act of 1973 (this volume, Section 7.5.4), institutions must afford handicapped students an equal opportunity to participate in physical education and athletics programs. The ED regulations set forth the basic requirement:

(1) In providing physical education courses and athletics and similar programs and activities to any of its students, a recipient to which this subpart applies may not discriminate on the basis of handicap. A recipient that offers physical education courses or that operates or sponsors intercollegiate, club, or intramural athletics shall provide to qualified handicapped students an equal opportunity for participation in these activities.

(2) A recipient may offer to handicapped students physical education and athletic activities that are separate or different only if separation or differentiation is consistent with the requirements . . . [that the programs and activities be operated in "the most integrated setting appropriate"] and only if no qualified handicapped student is denied the opportunity to compete for teams or to participate in courses that are not separate or different [34 C.F.R. sec. 104.47(a)].

Like the Title IX regulations, this Section 504 regulation apparently applies to athletics activities even if they are not directly subsidized by federal funds (see Section 7.5.7.4 of this volume for discussion of the validity of this broad application).

In *Wright* v. *Columbia University,* 520 F. Supp. 789 (S.D.N.Y. 1981), the court relied on Section 504 to protect a handicapped student's right to participate in intercollegiate football. The student had been blind in one eye since infancy; because of the potential danger to his "good" eye, the institution had denied him permission to participate. In issuing a temporary restraining order against the university, the court accepted (pending trial) the student's argument that the institution's decision was discriminatory within the meaning of Section 504 because the student was qualified to play football despite his handicap and capable of making his own decisions about "his health and well-being."

4.11.4. Athletic associations and conferences. Legal issues regarding athletics often arise as a result of the activity of the various athletic associations and conferences that regulate intercollegiate athletics. Individual institutions have become involved in such legal issues in two ways. Student athletes penalized for violating conference or association rules have sued both the conference or association and the institution over the enforcement of these rules. And institutions themselves have sued conferences or associations over their rules, policies, or decisions. Either situation presents the difficult threshold problem of determining what legal principles apply to the dispute.

The bulk of such disputes have involved the National Collegiate Athletic

Association (NCAA), the primary regulator of intercollegiate athletics in the United States. In a series of cases, courts have considered whether the NCAA, an institutional membership association for both public and private collegiate institutions, is engaged in "state action" (see Section 1.4.2) and thus is subject to the constraints of the U.S. Constitution, such as due process and equal protection. An early leading case, *Parish* v. *NCAA,* 506 F.2d 1028 (5th Cir. 1975), concerned sanctions applied against Centenary College for granting athletic eligibility to several basketball players who did not meet the NCAA academic requirement. The players, later joined by the college, challenged the constitutionality of the academic requirement (then known as the "1.600 rule"). The court rejected the NCAA's argument that it is a private association not subject to the Constitution:

> We see no reason to enumerate again the contacts and the degree of participation of the various states, through their colleges and universities, with the NCAA. Suffice it to say that state-supported educational institutions and their members and officers play a substantial, although admittedly not pervasive, role in the NCAA's program. State participation in or support of nominally private activity is a well-recognized basis for a finding of state action. . . . Moreover, we cannot ignore the states'—as well as the federal government's—traditional interest in all aspects of this country's educational system. Organized athletics play a large role in higher education, and improved means of transportation have made it possible for any college, no matter what its location, to compete athletically with other colleges throughout the country. Hence, meaningful regulation of this aspect of education is now beyond the effective reach of any one state. In a real sense, then, the NCAA by taking upon itself the role of coordinator and overseer of college athletics—in the interest both of the individual student and of the institution he attends—is performing a traditional governmental function [506 F.2d at 1032–33].

Thus, the court, using first the "government contacts" theory and then the "public function" theory (both of which are explained in Section 1.4.2), held the NCAA to be engaged in state action. (Most other cases reaching this result—for example, *Howard University* v. *NCAA,* 510 F.2d 213 (D.C. Cir. 1975)—rely only on the government contacts theory.) Having found the NCAA to be engaged in state action, the court proceeded to examine the NCAA's rule under due process and equal protection principles, finding the rule valid in both respects.

Subsequent to the decisions in *Parish* and other similar NCAA cases, the U.S. Supreme Court issued several opinions that narrow the circumstances under which courts will find state action, the most important of which is *Rendell-Baker* v. *Kohn,* discussed in Section 1.4.2. In *Arlosoroff* v. *NCAA,* 746 F.2d 1019 (4th Cir. 1984), the U.S. Court of Appeals for the Fourth Circuit relied on these Supreme Court opinions to reach a result contrary to the *Parish* line of cases. The plaintiff had played varsity tennis in his freshman year at Duke University (a private institution). Thereafter the NCAA declared him ineligible for further competition because he had participated in amateur competition for several years before enrolling at Duke. The plaintiff claimed that the bylaw under which the NCAA had acted was invalid under the due process and equal protection clauses. The court held that the NCAA's promulgation and enforcement of the bylaw was not state action and therefore declined to reach the merits of the plaintiff's challenge. First, the court considered the applicability of the public function theory:

> In a sense, the NCAA may be said to perform a public function as the overseer of the nation's intercollegiate athletics. It introduces some order into the conduct of its programs and enforces uniform rules of eligibility. The regulation of intercollegiate athletics, however, is not a function "traditionally exclusively reserved to the state" (*Jackson* v. *Metropolitan Edison Co.*, 419 U.S. 345, 352, 95 S. Ct. 449, 454, 42 L. Ed. 2d 477 (1975)). . . . The operation of a school (*Rendell-Baker* v. *Kohn*, 457 U.S. 830, 842, 102 S. Ct. 2764, 2772, 73 L. Ed. 2d 418 (1982)) is [not] traditionally an exclusive prerogative of the state.
>
> The fact that NCAA's regulatory function may be of some public service [therefore] lends no support to the finding of state action, for the function is not one traditionally reserved to the state [746 F.2d at 1021].

Then the court considered the government contacts theory:

> Formally, the NCAA is a private entity. Approximately one half of its members are public institutions, and those institutions provide more than one half of the NCAA's revenues. Those facts, however, do not alter the basic character of the NCAA as a voluntary association of public and private institutions. Nor do they begin to suggest that the public institutions, in contrast to the private institutional members, caused or procured the adoption of the bylaw.
>
> It is not enough that an institution is highly regulated and subsidized by a state. If the state in its regulatory or subsidizing function does not order or cause the action complained of, and the function is not one traditionally reserved to the state, there is no state action. A private school's discharge of employees was not state action in spite of the fact that the school was extensively regulated and highly subsidized by the state. The state's regulatory and funding activities had not compelled the discharge of those employees (*Rendell-Baker* v. *Kohn*, 457 U.S. 830, 102 S. Ct. 2764, 73 L. Ed. 2d 418 (1982); see also *Blum* v. *Yaretsky*, 457 U.S. 991, 102 S. Ct. 2777, 73 L. Ed. 2d 534 (1982)), just as they had not compelled a private nursing home's involuntary transfer and discharge of a group of Medicaid patients. (See also *Polk County* v. *Dodson*, 454 U.S. 312, 102 S. Ct. 445, 70 L. Ed. 2d 509 (1982) (autonomous decisions of public defender not under color of law).)
>
> *Rendell-Baker* . . . control[s] here. There is no suggestion in this case that the representatives of the state institutions joined together to vote as a block to effect adoption of the bylaw over the objection of private institutions. There is simply no showing that the state institutions controlled or directed the result.
>
> The NCAA serves the common need of member institutions for regulation of athletics while correlating their diverse interests. Through the representatives of all of the members, Bylaw 5-1-(d)-(3) was adopted, not

as a result of governmental compulsion, but in the service of the common interests of the members. The adoption of the bylaw was private conduct, not state action [746 F.2d at 1021-22].

Arlosoroff casts doubt on the continuing validity of the earlier case law and its proposition that NCAA activities are state action. It is thus questionable, after this case, whether the NCAA will continue to be subject to federal constitutional constraints. Administrators and counsel should watch for further cases testing whether *Arlosoroff* will ultimately prevail over the earlier case law.

Even if the courts refrain from applying the Constitution to most activities of the NCAA and other athletic associations, these associations will still be limited by another relevant body of legal principles: the common law of "voluntary, private associations."[28] Primarily, these principles would require the NCAA and other conferences and associations to adhere to their own rules and procedures, fairly and in good faith, in their relations with their member institutions. *California State University, Hayward* v. *NCAA*, 47 Cal. App. 3d 533, 121 Cal. Rptr. 85 (1975), for instance, arose after the NCAA had declared the university's athletic teams indefinitely ineligible for postseason play. The university argued that the NCAA's decision was contrary to the NCAA's own constitution and bylaws. The court affirmed the trial court's issuance of a preliminary injunction against the NCAA, holding the following principle applicable to the NCAA:

> Courts will intervene in the internal affairs of associations where the action by the association is in violation of its own bylaws or constitution. "It is true that courts will not interfere with the disciplining or expelling of members of such associations where the action is taken in good faith and in accordance with its adopted laws and rules. But if the decision of the tribunal is contrary to its laws or rules, or it is not authorized by the bylaws of the association, a court may review the ruling of the board and direct the reinstatement of the member" [quoting another case] [47 Cal. App. 3d at 539, 121 Cal. Rptr. at 88, 89].

The case then went back to the lower court for a trial on the merits. The lower court again held in favor of the university and made its injunction against the NCAA permanent. In a second appeal, under the name *Trustees of State Colleges and Universities* v. *NCAA*, 82 Cal. App. 3d 461, 147 Cal. Rptr. 187 (1978), the appellate court again affirmed the lower court, holding that the NCAA had not complied with its constitution and bylaws in imposing a penalty on the institution. The appellate court also held that, even if the institution had violated NCAA rules, under the facts of the case the NCAA was estopped from imposing a penalty on the institution. (The *Hayward* case is extensively discussed in J. D. Dickerson and M. Chapman, "Contract Law, Due Process, and the NCAA," 5 *J. of College and University Law* 197 (1978-79).)

---

[28]This same body of common law also applies to private accrediting associations, as discussed in Sections 8.1 and 8.2. Regarding the application of voluntary private association law to the NCAA, see Note, "Judicial Review of Disputes Between Athletes and the National Collegiate Athletic Association," 24 *Stanford L. Rev.* 903, 909-16 (1972).

As these legal developments indicate, postsecondary institutions do have legal weapons to use in disputes with the NCAA and other athletic associations. The common law clearly applies to such disputes; the U.S. Constitution may or may not apply, depending on the particular circumstances at issue and on the trend of future case law. Antitrust law also has some applicability (see Section 7.2.10; and see J. Weistart, "Antitrust Issues in the Regulation of College Sports," 5 *J. of College and University Law* 77 (1977-78)). Administrators should be aware, however, that these weapons are two-edged: student athletes may also use them against the institution when the institution and the athletic association are jointly engaged in enforcing athletic rules against the student. In such circumstances the institution may be so aligned with the athletic association that it is subject to the same legal principles that bind the association. Moreover, if the institution is public, the U.S. Constitution may apply to the situation even if the courts do not consider the association itself to be engaged in state action.

Sec. 4.12. Student Files and Records

4.12.1. The Buckley Amendment. The Family Educational Rights and Privacy Act of 1974, 20 U.S.C. sec. 1232g, popularly known as the Buckley Amendment, has created a substantial role for the federal government with respect to student records. The Act and its implementing regulations, 34 C.F.R. Part 99, apply to all public and private educational agencies or institutions that receive federal funds from the U.S. Department of Education or whose students receive such funds (under the Guaranteed Student Loan program, for example) and pay them to the agency or institution (34 C.F.R. sec. 99.1). While the Buckley Amendment does not invalidate common law or state statutory law applicable to student records (see this volume, Section 4.12.2), the regulations are so extensive that they are the predominant legal consideration in dealing with student records.[29]

The Buckley Amendment and regulations establish requirements pertaining to (1) students' right of access to their education records (34 C.F.R. secs. 99.11-99.13); (2) students' right to challenge the content of their records (34 C.F.R. secs. 99.20-99.22); (3) disclosure of "personally identifiable" information from these records to personnel of the institution or to outsiders (34 C.F.R. secs. 99.30-99.37); (4) the institution's obligation to notify students of their rights under the Act and regulations (34 C.F.R. secs. 99.5-99.6); and (5) recourse for students and the federal government when an institution may have violated the Act or regulations (34 C.F.R. secs. 99.60-99.67). Recourse includes a formal system for receipt, investigation, and adjudication of complaints by the Family Educational Rights and Privacy Act Office of the Department of Education and by a review board (34 C.F.R. sec.

---

[29]The Buckley regulations provide that "an educational agency or institution which determines that it cannot comply with the requirements . . . [of the Act or regulations] because a state or local law conflicts with . . . [their] provisions . . . shall so advise the . . . [Family Educational Rights and Privacy Act Office] within forty-five days of any such determination, giving the text and legal citation of the conflicting law" (34 C.F.R. sec. 99.61). Where such conflict exists, the federal law will take precedence unless the institution is willing to relinquish federal funding (see generally *Rosado* v. *Wyman,* 397 U.S. 397, 420-23 (1970)). The federal government would, however, allow a period of negotiation and encourage the institution to seek an official interpretation of the state law compatible with Buckley or an amendment of the state law.

99.60.[30] All students enrolled or formerly enrolled in postsecondary institutions have rights under the Act and regulations regardless of whether they are eighteen and regardless of whether they are dependent on their parents (34 C.F.R. secs. 99.1(d) and 99.4). (If students are dependents for federal income tax purposes, however, they cannot prevent their parents from seeing their education records (sec. 99.31(a)(8)).)

Students have rights with respect to all "those records which (1) are directly related to a student, and (2) are maintained by an educational agency or institution or by a party acting for the agency or institution" (20 U.S.C. 1232g(a)(4)(A); 34 C.F.R. sec. 99.3). This section of the regulations contains five exceptions to this definition, which exclude from coverage certain personal and private records of institutional personnel, certain campus law enforcement records, certain student employment records, certain records regarding health care, and "records . . . [such as alumni records] which contain only information relating to a person after that person was no longer a student at the . . . institution." There is also a partial exception for "directory information," which is exempt from the regulations' nondisclosure requirements under certain conditions (34 C.F.R. sec. 99.37).

The key to success in dealing with the Buckley Amendment is a thorough understanding of the implementing regulations. Administrators should keep copies of the regulations at their fingertips and should not rely on secondary sources to resolve particular problems. Counsel should review the institution's record-keeping policies and practices, and every substantial change in them, to assure compliance with the regulations. Administrators and counsel should work together to maintain appropriate legal forms to use in implementing the regulations, such as forms for a student's waiver of his rights under the Act or regulations (34 C.F.R. sec. 99.7), forms for securing a student's consent to release personally identifiable information from his records (34 C.F.R. sec. 99.30), and forms for notifying parties to whom information is disclosed of the limits on the use of that information (34 C.F.R. sec. 99.33). Questions concerning the interpretation or application of the regulations may be directed to the Family Educational Rights and Privacy Act Office at the U.S. Department of Education.

4.12.2. State law. In a majority of states, courts now recognize a common law tort of invasion of privacy, which, in some circumstances, protects individuals against the public disclosure of damaging private information about them and against intrusions into their private affairs. A few states have similarly protected privacy with a statute or constitutional provision. Although this body of law has seldom been applied to educational record-keeping practices, the basic legal principles appear applicable to record-keeping abuses by postsecondary institutions. This body of right-to-privacy law could protect students against abusive collection and retention practices where clearly intrusive methods are used to collect information concerning private affairs. In *White* v. *Davis,* 13 Cal. 3d 757, 533 P.2d 222 (1975) (see

---

[30]It is not yet clear whether courts will permit students injured by an institution's violation of the Buckley Amendment to sue the institution in court. Nor is it clear, if such a "private cause of action" (see Section 7.5.9) is recognized, whether the complainant must first pursue the complaint process within ED. One court, however, has refused (after brief analysis) to recognize a private cause of action (*Girardier* v. *Webster College,* 563 F.2d 1267, 1277 (8th Cir. 1977); see also K. Cudlipp, "The Buckley Amendment Two Years Later," a memo printed at 122 *Congressional Record* 16447 (94th Cong., 2d Sess., 1976)).

Section 5.5), for example, the court held that undercover police surveillance of university classes and meetings violated the right to privacy because "no professor or student can be confident that whatever he may express in class will not find its way into a police file." Similarly, right-to-privacy law could protect students against abusive dissemination practices that result in unwarranted public disclosure of damaging personal information.

In addition to this developing right-to-privacy law, many states also have statutes or administrative regulations dealing specifically with record keeping. These include subject access laws, open or public record laws, and confidentiality laws. Such laws usually apply only to state agencies, and a state's postsecondary institutions may or may not be considered state agencies subject to record-keeping laws. Occasionally a state statute deals specifically with postsecondary education records. Massachusetts, for instance, has a statute making it an "unfair educational practice" for any "educational institution," including public and private postsecondary institutions, to request information or make or keep records concerning certain arrests or misdemeanor convictions of students or applicants (Mass. Gen. Laws Ann. ch. 151C, sec. 2(f)).

Since state laws on privacy and records vary greatly from state to state, administrators should check with counsel to determine the law in their particular state. Since state record requirements may occasionally conflict with the Buckley Amendment regulations, it is especially important for counsel to determine whether any such conflict exists (see this volume, Section 4.12.1, note 29). Regarding right-to-privacy concepts, an institution in compliance with the Buckley Amendment regulations is not likely to be violating any state right to privacy. The two exceptions concern information collection practices and the particular types of records kept, which are not treated in the Buckley regulations (except that Buckley (sec. 99.32) requires that a "record of disclosures" of information be kept). In these situations, developing state laws may carve out requirements, as in the *White* case and the Massachusetts statute above, independent of and supplementary to Buckley.

4.12.3. The federal Privacy Act. The Privacy Act of 1974, 88 Stat. 1896, partly codified in 5 U.S.C. sec. 552a, applies directly to federal government agencies and, with two exceptions discussed below, does not restrict postsecondary educational institutions. The Act accords all persons—including students, faculty members, and staff members—certain rights enforceable against the federal government regarding information about them in federal agency files, whether collected from a postsecondary institution or from any other source. The Act grants the right to inspect, copy, and correct such information and limits its dissemination by the agency.

The first situation where the Act applies to postsecondary institutions concerns Social Security account numbers. Section 7 of the Act prohibits federal, state, and local government agencies from requiring persons to disclose their Social Security numbers. This provision applies to public but not to private postsecondary institutions and thus prevents public institutions from requiring either students or employees to disclose their Social Security numbers. The two exceptions to this nondisclosure requirement permit an institution to require disclosure (1) where it is required by some other federal statute and (2) where the institution maintains "a system of records in existence and operating before January 1, 1975, if such disclosure was required under statute or regulation adopted prior to such date to verify the identity of an individual" (88 Stat. 1896 at 1903).

The second provision of the Act potentially relevant to some postsecondary institutions is Section 3(m) (5 U.S.C. sec. 552a(m)), which applies the Act's requirements to government contractors who operate record-keeping systems on behalf of a federal agency pursuant to the contract.

Sec. 4.13. Disciplinary and Grievance Systems

4.13.1. Establishment of systems. It is clear from much of the material in this chapter that postsecondary institutions have extensive authority to regulate both the academic and the nonacademic activities and behavior of students. This power is summarized in an often-cited judicial statement:

> In the field of discipline, scholastic and behavioral, an institution may establish any standards reasonably relevant to the lawful missions, processes, and functions of the institution. It is not a lawful mission, process, or function of . . . [a public] institution to prohibit the exercise of a right guaranteed by the Constitution or a law of the United States to a member of the academic community in the circumstances. Therefore, such prohibitions are not reasonably relevant to any lawful mission, process, or function of . . . [a public] institution.
>
> Standards so established may apply to student behavior on and off the campus when relevant to any lawful mission, process, or function of the institution. By such standards of student conduct the institution may prohibit any action or omission which impairs, interferes with, or obstructs the missions, processes, and functions of the institution.
>
> Standards so established may require scholastic attainments higher than the average of the population and may require superior ethical and moral behavior. In establishing standards of behavior, the institution is not limited to the standards or the forms of criminal laws ["General Order on Judicial Standards of Procedure and Substance in Review of Student Discipline in Tax-Supported Institutions of Higher Education," 45 F.R.D. 133, 145 (W.D. Mo. 1968)].

It is not enough, however, for an administrator to understand the extent and limits of institutional authority. The administrator must also skillfully implement this authority through various systems for the resolution of disputes concerning students. Such systems should include procedures for processing and resolving disputes; substantive standards or rules to guide the judgment of the persons responsible for dispute resolution; and mechanisms and penalties with which decisions are enforced. The procedures, standards, and enforcement provisions should be written and made available to all students. Dispute-resolution systems, in their totality, should create a two-way street; that is, they should provide for complaints *by* students *against* other members of the academic community as well as complaints *against* students *by* other members of the academic community.

The choice of structures for resolving disputes depends on policy decisions made by administrators, preferably in consultation with representatives of various interests within the institution. Should a single system cover both academic and nonacademic disputes, or should there be separate systems for separate kinds of disputes? Should there be a separate disciplinary system for students, or should there be a broader system covering other members of the academic community as well? Will the systems use specific and detailed standards of student conduct, or will they operate on the basis of more general rules and policies? To what extent will students participate in establishing the rules governing their conduct? To what extent will students, rather than administrators or faculty members, be expected to assume responsibility for reporting or investigating violations of student conduct codes or honor codes? To what extent will students take part in adjudicating complaints by or against students? What kinds of sanctions can be levied against students found to have been engaged in misconduct? Can they be fined, made to do volunteer work on campus, expelled from the institution, given a failing grade in a course or denied a degree, or required to make restitution? To what extent will the president, provost, or board of trustees retain final authority to review decisions concerning student misconduct?

Devices for creating dispute-resolution systems may include honor codes or codes of academic ethics; codes of student conduct; bills of rights, or rights and responsibilities, for students or for the entire academic community; the use of various legislative bodies, such as a student or university senate; a formal judiciary system for resolving disputes concerning students; and the establishment of grievance mechanisms for students, such as an ombudsman system or a grievance committee. On most campuses security guards or some other campus law enforcement system will also be involved in the resolution of disputes and regulation of student behavior.

Occasionally, specific procedures or mechanisms will be required by law. Constitutional due process, for instance, requires the use of certain procedures before a student is suspended or dismissed from a public institution (see this volume, Section 4.6). The Title IX regulations (Section 7.5.3) and the Buckley Amendment regulations (Section 4.12.1) require both public and private institutions to establish certain procedures for resolving disputes under those particular statutes. Even when specific mechanisms or procedures are not required by law, the procedures or standards adopted by an institution will sometimes be affected by existing law. A public institution's rules regarding student protest, for instance, must comply with First Amendment strictures protecting freedom of speech (Section 4.7). And its rules regarding administrative access to or search of student rooms, and the investigatory techniques of its campus police, must comply with Fourth Amendment strictures regarding search and seizure (Section 4.10.2). Though an understanding of the law is thus crucial to the establishment of disciplinary and grievance systems, the law by no means rigidly controls their form and operation. To a large extent, the kind of system adopted will depend on the institution's notions of good administrative practice.

Fair and accessible dispute-resolution systems, besides being useful administrative tools in their own right, can also serve to insulate institutions from lawsuits. Students who feel that their arguments or grievances will be fairly considered within the institution may forgo resort to the courts. If students ignore internal mechanisms in favor of immediate judicial action, the courts may refer the students to the institution. Under the "exhaustion of remedies" doctrine (see Section 3.5.3), courts may require plaintiffs to exhaust available remedies within the institution before bringing the complaint to court. In *Pfaff* v. *Columbia-Greene Community College,* 472 N.Y.S.2d 480 (App. Div. 1984), for example, the New York courts dismissed the complaint of a student who had sued her college, contesting a "C" grade entered in a course, because the college had an internal appeal process and the student "failed to show that pursuit of the available administrative appeal would have been fruitless."

4.13.2. Codes of student conduct. If a code of conduct defines the offenses for which a student may be penalized by a public institution, that code must comply with constitutional due process requirements concerning vagueness. The requirement is a minimal one, generally requiring the code to be sufficiently clear that students can understand the standards with which their conduct must comply and that the code is not susceptible to arbitrary enforcement (see this volume, Section 4.4). A public institution's code of conduct must also comply with the constitutional doctrine of overbreadth in any area where the code could affect First Amendment rights. Basically, this doctrine requires that the code not be drawn so broadly and vaguely as to include protected First Amendment activity along with behavior subject to legitimate regulation (see Section 4.7.2). And finally, a public institution's student conduct code must comply with a general requirement of evenhandedness. This means that the code cannot arbitrarily discriminate in the range and type of penalties, or in the procedural safeguards, afforded various classes of offenders. *Paine* v. *Board of Regents of the University of Texas System,* 355 F. Supp. 199 (W.D. Tex. 1972), affirmed *per curiam,* 474 F.2d 1397 (5th Cir. 1973), concerned such discriminatory practices. The institution had treated students convicted of drug offenses differently from all other code offenders, including those charged with equally serious offenses, giving them a harsher penalty and fewer procedural safeguards. The court found this differential treatment to violate the equal protection and due process clauses.

As noted in the judicial statement quoted in Section 4.13.1, codes of conduct can apply to the off-campus actions as well as the on-campus activity of students. But the extension of a code to off-campus activity can pose significant legal and policy questions. In the *Paine* case above, the institution automatically suspended students who had been put on probation by the criminal courts for possession of marijuana. The court invalidated the suspensions partly because they were based on an off-campus occurrence—court probation—which did not automatically establish a threat to the institution. And in *Thomas* v. *Granville Board of Education,* 607 F.2d 1043 (2d Cir. 1979), a high school case with pertinent ramifications for postsecondary education, several students had been suspended for their off-campus activities in publishing a newspaper of sexual satire. The court also invalidated these suspensions, according the students the same First Amendment rights as citizens generally and emphasizing that "our willingness to grant school officials substantial autonomy within their academic domain rests in part on the confinement of that power within the metes and bounds of the school itself." To avoid such problems, administrators should ascertain that an off-campus act has a direct detrimental impact on the institution's educational functions before using that act as a basis for disciplining students.

Private institutions not subject to the state action doctrine (see Section 1.4.2) are not constitutionally required to follow these principles regarding student codes. Yet these principles reflect basic notions of fairness, which can be critical components of good administrative practice; thus, administrators of private institutions may wish to use them as policy guides in formulating their codes.

4.13.3. Judicial systems. Judicial systems that adjudicate complaints of student misconduct must be very sensitive to procedural safeguards. The membership of judicial bodies, the procedures they use, the extent to which their proceedings are open to the academic community, the sanctions they may impose, the methods by which they may initiate proceedings against students, and provisions for appealing their decisions should be set out in writing and made generally available within the institution.

Whenever the charge could result in a punishment as serious as suspension, a public institution's judicial system must provide the procedures required by the due process clause (see Section 4.6.2). The focal point of these procedures is the hearing at which the accused student may present evidence and argument concerning the charge. The institution, however, may wish to include preliminary stages in its judicial process for more informal disposition of complaints against students. The system may provide for negotiations between the student and the complaining party, for instance, or for preliminary conferences before designated representatives of the judicial system. Full due process safeguards need not be provided at every such preliminary stage. *Andrews* v. *Knowlton,* 509 F.2d 898 (2d Cir. 1975), dealt with the procedures required at a stage preceding an honor code hearing. The court held that due process procedures were not required at that time because it was not a "critical stage" which could have a "prejudicial impact" on the final honor code determination. Thus, administrators have broad authority to construct informal preliminary proceedings so long as a student's participation in such stages does not adversely affect his or her ability to defend the case in the final stage.

Occasionally, a campus judicial proceeding may involve an incident that is also the subject of criminal court proceedings. The same student may thus be charged in both forums at the same time. In such circumstances the postsecondary institution is not legally required to defer to the criminal courts by canceling or postponing its proceedings. As held in *Paine* (Section 4.13.2) and other cases, even if the institution is public, such dual prosecution is not double jeopardy because the two proceedings impose different kinds of punishment to protect different kinds of state interests. The Constitution's double jeopardy clause applies only to successive *criminal* prosecutions for the same offense. Nor will the existence of two separate proceedings necessarily violate the student's privilege against self-incrimination. Several courts have rejected student requests to stay campus proceedings on this ground pending the outcome of criminal trials, such as in *Grossner* v. *Trustees of Columbia University,* 287 F. Supp. 535 (S.D.N.Y. 1968). One court emphasized, however, that if students in campus proceedings "are forced to incriminate themselves . . . and if that testimony is offered against them in subsequent criminal proceedings, they can then invoke . . . [Supreme Court precedents] in opposition to the offer" (*Furutani* v. *Ewigleben,* 297 F. Supp. 1163 (N.D. Cal. 1969)). A student's claim that being identified in campus disciplinary proceedings would increase the possibility of misidentification by witnesses at his criminal trial was rejected as speculative in *Nzuve* v. *Castleton State College,* 335 A.2d 321 (Vt. 1975).

While neither double jeopardy nor self-incrimination need tie the administrator's hands, administrators may nevertheless choose, for policy reasons, to delay or dismiss particular campus proceedings when the same incident is in the criminal courts. It is possible that the criminal proceedings will adequately protect the institution's interests. Or, as *Furutani* and *Nzuve* suggest, student testimony at a campus proceeding could create evidentiary problems for the criminal court.

If a public institution proceeds with its campus action while the student is subject to charges still pending in criminal court, the institution may have to permit the student to have a lawyer with him during the campus proceedings. In *Gabrilowitz v. Newman*, 582 F.2d 100 (1st Cir. 1978), a student challenged a University of Rhode Island rule that prohibited the presence of legal counsel at campus disciplinary hearings. The student obtained an injunction prohibiting the university from conducting the hearing without permitting the student the advice of counsel. The appellate court, affirming the lower court's injunction order, held that when a criminal case based on the same conduct giving rise to the disciplinary proceeding is pending in the courts, "the denial to [the student] of the right to have a lawyer of his own choice to consult with and advise him during the disciplinary proceeding would deprive [him] of due process of law."

The court emphasized that the student was requesting the assistance of counsel to consult with and advise him during the hearing, not to conduct the hearing on the student's behalf. Such assistance was critical to the student because of the delicacy of the legal situation he faced:

> Were the appellee to testify in the disciplinary proceeding, his statement could be used as evidence in the criminal case, either to impeach or as an admission if he did not choose to testify. Appellee contends that he is, therefore, impaled on the horns of a legal dilemma: if he mounts a full defense at the disciplinary hearing without the assistance of counsel and testifies on his own behalf, he might jeopardize his defense in the criminal case; if he fails to fully defend himself or chooses not to testify at all, he risks loss of the college degree he is within weeks of receiving, and his reputation will be seriously blemished [582 F.2d at 103].

If a public institution delays campus proceedings, and then uses a conviction in the criminal proceedings as the basis for its campus action, the institution must take care to protect the student's due process rights. In the *Paine* case, a university rule required the automatic two-year suspension of any student convicted of a narcotics offense. The court held that the students must be given an opportunity to show that, despite their conviction and probation, they posed "no substantial threat of influencing other students to use, possess, or sell drugs or narcotics." Thus, a criminal conviction does not automatically provide the basis for suspension; administrators should still ascertain that the conviction has a detrimental impact on the campus, and the affected student should have the opportunity to make a contrary showing.

Sec. 4.14. Campus Security

4.14.1. Security officers. The powers and responsibilities of campus security officers should be carefully delineated. Administrators must determine whether such officers should be permitted to carry weapons and under what conditions. They must determine the security officers' authority to investigate crime on campus or to investigate violations of student codes of conduct. Record-keeping practices must be devised.[31] The relationship that security officers will have with local and state

---

[31]For a general discussion of the legal restrictions on record keeping, see Section 4.12. The Buckley Amendment, discussed there, has a specific provision relating to campus law enforcement

police must be cooperatively worked out with local and state police forces. Because campus security officers may play dual roles, partly enforcing public criminal laws and partly enforcing the institution's codes of conduct, administrators should carefully delineate the officers' relative responsibilities in each role.

Administrators must also determine whether their campus security guards do, or should, have arrest powers under state or local law. For public institutions, state law may grant full arrest powers to certain campus security guards. In *People* v. *Wesley*, 365 N.Y.S.2d 593 (City Ct., Buffalo, 1975), for instance, the court determined that security officers at a particular state campus were "peace officers" under the terms of Section 355(2)(m) of the New York Education Law. For public institutions not subject to such statutes, and for private institutions, deputization under city or county law or the use of "citizen's arrest" powers may be options.

Although security guards may have authority to make arrests off campus as well as on campus, their off-campus authority may be more limited. In *State* v. *Lyon*, 584 P.2d 844 (Utah 1978), for instance, the Supreme Court of Utah vacated the conviction of a motorcyclist (Lyon) who had been arrested by a college security officer four blocks from the campus. The state argued that, under Utah law, the officer had "all of the powers possessed by a policeman" and was "required" to make the arrest to protect the interests of the college. The court rejected this argument, noting that the officer's "suspicion" that Lyon had committed vandalism or theft did not justify the off-campus arrest. Rather, the court stated, for the arrest to be valid, a "present danger" to the college, its students, or its employees must have been evident. (See D. Berman, "Law and Order on Campus: An Analysis of the Role and Problems of the Security Police," 49 *J. of Urban Law* 513 (1971–72).)

Police work is subject to a variety of constitutional restraints concerning such matters as investigations, arrests, and searches and seizures of persons or private property. Security officers for public institutions are subject to all these restraints. In private institutions security officers who are operating in conjunction with local or state police forces (see Section 4.10.2) or who have arrest powers (see *Zelinski* case below) may also be subject to constitutional restraints under the state action doctrine (see Section 1.4.2). In devising the responsibilities of such officers, therefore, administrators should be sensitive to the constitutional requirements regarding police work.

In *People* v. *Zelinski*, 24 Cal. 3d 357, 594 P.2d 1000 (1979), the California Supreme Court issued a major opinion concerning the applicability of constitutional restraints to private security personnel. Although it concerned security guards at a department store rather than a college campus, and applied the state constitution rather than the United States Constitution, the case nevertheless speaks meaningfully to the question of when a private college's security officers would be subject to state or federal constitutional restraints on their activities. In reversing the conviction

---

records. Section 99.3 of the regulations exempts from the amendment all the records of a law enforcement unit of an educational agency or institution that are (1) maintained apart from student education records, (2) maintained solely for law enforcement purposes, and (3) not disclosed to individuals other than law enforcement officials of the same jurisdiction, provided that the education records maintained by the agency or institution are not disclosed to the personnel of the law enforcement unit (34 C.F.R. sec. 99.3, definition of "education records," paragraph (b)(2)).

of a person who had been arrested and searched by private store detectives, the *Zelinski* court reasoned:

> Here the store security forces did not act in a purely private capacity but rather were fulfilling a public function in bringing violators of the law to public justice. For reasons hereinafter expressed, we conclude that under such circumstances—that is, *when private security personnel conduct an illegal search or seizure while engaged in a statutorily authorized citizen's arrest and detention of a person in aid of law enforcement authorities*—the constitutional proscriptions of Article I, Section 13 [whose words parallel the Fourth Amendment to the U.S. Constitution] are applicable. . . .
>
> The store employees arrested defendant pursuant to the authorization contained in Penal Code Section 837 [citizen's arrest], and the search which yielded the narcotics was conducted incident to that arrest. Their acts, engaged in pursuant to the statute, were not those of a private citizen acting in a purely private capacity. Although the search exceeded lawful authority, it was nevertheless an integral part of the exercise of sovereignty allowed by the state to private citizens. In arresting the offender, the store employees were utilizing the coercive power of the state to further a state interest. Had the security guards sought only the vindication of the merchant's private interests, they would have simply exercised self-help and demanded the return of the stolen merchandise. Upon satisfaction of the merchant's interests, the offender would have been released. By holding defendant for criminal process and searching her, they went beyond their employer's private interests.
>
> Persons so acting should be subject to the constitutional proscriptions that secure an individual's right to privacy, for their actions are taken pursuant to statutory authority to promote a state interest in bringing offenders to public accounting. Unrestrained, such action would subvert state authority in defiance of its established limits. It would destroy the protection those carefully defined limits were intended to afford to everyone, the guilty and innocent alike. It would afford de facto authorizations for searches and seizures incident to arrests or detentions made by private individuals that even peace officers are not authorized to make. Accordingly, we hold that in any case *where private security personnel assert the power of the state to make an arrest or to detain another person for transfer to custody of the state*, the state involvement is sufficient for the court to enforce the proper exercise of that power (cf. *People* v. *Haydel* (1974) 12 Cal. 3d 190, 194 [115 Cal. Rptr. 394, 534 P.2d 866]) by excluding the fruits of illegal abuse thereof [594 P.2d at 1006; emphasis added].

Administrators should also be sensitive to the tort law principles applicable to security work (see generally Sections 2.3.1, 2.4.1, and 2.5). Like athletic activities (Section 4.11), campus security actions are likely to expose the institution to a substantial risk of tort liability. Using physical force or weapons, detaining or arresting persons, entering or searching private property can all occasion tort liability if they are undertaken without justification or accomplished carelessly. *Jones* v. *Wittenberg University*, 534 F.2d 1203 (6th Cir. 1976), for example, dealt with a university security guard who had fired a warning shot at a fleeing student. The shot pierced the student's chest and killed him. The guard and the university were held liable for the student's death, even though the guard did not intend to hit the student and may have had justification for firing a shot to frighten a fleeing suspect. The appellate court reasoned that the shooting could nevertheless constitute negligence "if it was done so carelessly as to result in foreseeable injury."

4.14.2. Protection against violent crime on campus. The extent of the institution's obligation to protect students from crime on campus—particularly, violent crimes committed by outsiders from the surrounding community—has become a sensitive issue for higher education. The number of such crimes reported, especially sexual attacks on women, has increased in recent years (see L. Middleton, "Many Campuses Losing Ground in War Against Crime," *Chronicle of Higher Education,* Oct. 7, 1981, p. 5, col. 1). As a result, postsecondary institutions now face substantial tactical and legal problems concerning the planning and operation of their campus security systems. In a 1976 case, *P. D.* v. *Catholic University,* Civ. No. 75-2198 (D.D.C. 1976), a jury found the defendant liable for injuries incurred by a student who was raped in the locker room of the campus gym. While the case supports the general proposition that institutions have some legal duty to protect their students against outside criminal assailants, the court did not issue any opinion explaining the source or extent of this duty. Now several other courts have provided some answers to the questions raised in the *P. D.* case.

Duarte v. *State of California,* 151 Cal. Rptr. 727 (1979), was a suit brought by the mother of a student who had been raped and murdered in her dormitory room at California State University, San Diego. In her complaint the plaintiff alleged that repeated incidents of rape and other violence had been occurring on the campus for some time, and she set forth various legal theories that could be used to establish the state's liability. In its answer to the complaint, the state did not challenge the facts that plaintiff had alleged but denied that these facts established any legal liability. The trial court dismissed the case, and Duarte appealed. The appeals court reversed the trial court, holding that the facts if proven would create liability under the legal theories set out by the plaintiff.

The appeals court determined that three of Duarte's legal theories could be applied to the campus security problem. The first theory is based on principles of tort law (see Section 2.3.1). Traditionally, the court said, a person has no duty under tort law to control the conduct of another or to warn those endangered by another's conduct. But exceptions to this general rule have evolved "where the defendant stands in a special relationship to the person whose conduct needs controlling, or to the victim." Relationships that have been recognized by law to fit this classification include carrier-passenger, innkeeper-guest, and landlord-tenant. Concluding that the relationship between a university and a resident student is analogous to that of a landlord-tenant, the court examined cases that have held landlords of urban apartment buildings liable for injuries to tenants resulting from criminal assault, where the attack was foreseeable and the landlord failed to take reasonable steps to protect the tenants (see, for example, *Kline* v. *1500 Massachusetts Avenue Apartment Corp.,* 439 F.2d 477 (D.C. Cir. 1970)). Applying these cases, the court reasoned:

> [The decedent] was not a victim of a sudden outburst. She had a landlord-tenant relationship-plus with the university. [She] had in many substantial respects surrendered the control of her person, control of her own security to the university. . . . No security devices were instituted, let

alone minimal safety precautions such as warning of the degree of danger. The university allegedly had superior knowledge and also the means of instituting some reasonable protective measures. The university not only had control over the campus area and the residential facilities but also many aspects of personal activities. [The student] herself could not purchase and install security devices or hire a private police force. She could not possess a dog or a firearm [151 Cal. Rptr. at 735].

Thus, under this theory, insofar as a university knows that there is a high incidence of crime on campus, it is obligated as a landlord to take reasonable protective measures to prevent outside assailants from intentionally causing harm to students residing in its dormitories.

The *Duarte* plaintiff's second theory also focuses on the university's responsibilities as a landlord, but, unlike the first theory, it relies on principles of contract law. According to this theory, a duty to protect can be implied from the lease agreement between the university-landlord and the student-tenant. The lease entitled the student, according to the court, "not only to a safe roof and adequate walls, but essentially to a safe place of residence." Failure to provide a dormitory reasonably safe from intruders would, under this theory, breach a "covenant of habitability" implicit in the lease and thus constitute a breach of contract on the part of the university.

The third theory approved by the appellate court is a theory of negligent misrepresentation. Under this theory, the university could be liable if persons in authority falsely represented that the campus was reasonably safe for female students and had no reasonable grounds for believing their representation to be true. When the listener believes the statement and relies on it to her detriment, the speaker is responsible for the injury inflicted by the reliance. Thus, if the university falsely and knowingly represented its campus to be safe, and in reliance on that representation the victim failed to take precautions, the university would be liable in tort for the student's death.[32]

In a second case, *Mullins* v. *Pine Manor College*, 389 Mass. 47, 449 N.E.2d 331 (1983), the court approved two additional legal theories for establishing institutional liability in campus security cases. As in *Duarte*, the court applied these theories specifically to the problem of security in campus housing; the theories themselves, however, appear to have broader potential applications to security breaches which affect resident students when they are on other parts of the campus. The student in *Mullins* had been abducted from her dormitory room and raped on the campus

[32]Having determined that the plaintiff's complaint raised legal issues meriting further consideration, the appellate court remanded the case to the lower court for trial. Subsequently, the California Supreme Court declined to review the appellate court's decision but ordered that the appellate court's opinion not be published in the official California case reporter (Cal. App.) (see 151 Cal. Rptr. at 727). Although the California Supreme Court's action may diminish *Duarte*'s precedential value in California (see *Baldwin* v. *Zoradi*, 123 Cal. App. 3d 275, 294, 176 Cal. Rptr. 809, 821 (1981)), the opinion remains an instructive discussion of the theoretical foundations of liability in security cases involving campus housing. The principles underlying the first *Duarte* theory were later applied in *Miller* v. *State of New York*, 62 N.Y.2d 506, 467 N.E.2d 493 (1984), a case in which the state was held liable after a student was abducted from an unlocked basement laundry room in her dormitory and raped.

of Pine Manor College, a women's college located in a suburban area. Although the court found that the college was located in a low-crime area and that there was relatively little crime on campus, it nevertheless held the college liable.

Developing its first theory, the *Mullins* court determined that residential colleges have a general legal duty to exercise due care in providing campus security:

> We think it can be said with confidence that colleges of ordinary prudence customarily exercise care to protect the well-being of their resident students, including seeking to protect them against the criminal acts of third parties. An expert witness hired by the defendant testified that he had visited eighteen area colleges, and, not surprisingly, all took steps to provide an adequate level of security on their campus. He testified also that standards had been established for determining what precautions should be taken. Thus, the college community itself has recognized its obligation to protect resident students from the criminal acts of third parties. This recognition indicates that the imposition of a duty of care is firmly embedded in a community consensus.
>
> This consensus stems from the nature of the situation. The concentration of young people, especially young women, on a college campus, creates favorable opportunities for criminal behavior. The threat of criminal acts of third parties to resident students is self-evident, and the college is the party which is in the position to take those steps which are necessary to ensure the safety of its students. No student has the ability to design and implement a security system, hire and supervise security guards, provide security at the entrance of dormitories, install proper locks, and establish a system of announcement for authorized visitors. Resident students typically live in a particular room for a mere nine months and, as a consequence, lack the incentive and capacity to take corrective measures. College regulations may also bar the installation of additional locks or chains. Some students may not have been exposed previously to living in a residence hall or in a metropolitan area and may not be fully conscious of the dangers that are present. Thus, the college must take the responsibility on itself if anything is to be done at all [449 N.E.2d at 335].

Developing its second theory, the court determined "that a duty voluntarily assumed must be performed with due care." Quoting from Section 323 of the *Restatement of Torts Second,* a scholarly work of the American Law Institute, the court held that when a college has taken responsibility for security, it is "subject to liability . . . for physical harm resulting from [the] failure to exercise reasonable care to perform [the] undertaking." An institution may be held liable under this theory, however, only if the plaintiff can establish that its "failure to exercise due care increased the risk of harm, or . . . the harm is suffered because of the student's reliance on the undertaking."

Analyzing the facts of the case under these two broad theories, the appellate court affirmed the trial court's judgment in favor of the student. The facts relevant to establishing the college's liability included the ease of scaling or opening the gates that led to the dormitories, the small number of security guards on night shift, the lack of a system for supervising the guards' performance of their duties, and the lack of deadbolts or chains for dormitory room doors.

Another case, *Jesik* v. *Maricopa County Community College District*, 611 P.2d 547 (Ariz. 1980), did not involve campus dormitory security as did *Duarte* and *Mullins*. Moreover, unlike these other two cases, *Jesik* concerned a specific threat of harm to a particular student rather than a general threat of crime on campus:

> On August 22, 1973, the decedent Peter Jesik, II, was registering as a student for the fall semester at Phoenix College. In the late morning, Charles Doss after having "words" with the decedent told decedent that he was going home to get a gun and coming back to the college campus to kill him. The decedent reported this threat to Scott Hilton, a security guard employed by Phoenix College, and received assurances of help and protection. The decedent then continued with his registration. Hilton, the complaint alleges, failed to arm himself or take any other precautionary measures. Approximately an hour later Doss returned to campus carrying a briefcase. He proceeded to the gymnasium where the decedent was continuing his registration. The decedent again contacted Hilton and pointed out Doss and the briefcase. Again the decedent was assured of help and protection, and he remained in the gymnasium in reliance on these assurances. Hilton approached Doss, questioned him, and, apparently satisfied, turned his back on Doss and walked away. Doss immediately pulled a gun from his briefcase and shot and killed the decedent. Doss was subsequently convicted of murder (see *State* v. *Doss*, 116 Ariz. 156, 568 P.2d 1054 (1977)) [611 P.2d at 548].

The plaintiff, the father of the murdered student, sued the president and the individual members of the governing board of the Community College District, the executive dean and dean of students at Phoenix College, the security guard (Hilton), and the Community College District. The trial court summarily dismissed the case as to all defendants except the security guard. The plaintiff appealed this dismissal to the Arizona Supreme Court.

The appellate court first considered the potential liability of the officials and administrators. The plaintiff argued that "[the individual] defendants controlled an inadequate and incompetent security force [and thus should be] liable for any breach of duty by that security force." To establish the "duty" that had been breached, the plaintiff relied on a series of Arizona statutes which required the Community College District's governing board, where necessary, to appoint security officers (Ariz. Rev. Stat. Ann. sec. 15-679(A)(3) and (9)), "to adopt rules and regulations for the maintenance of public order" (Ariz. Rev. Stat. Ann. sec. 13-1093), and to prevent "trespass upon the property of educational institutions [or] interference with its lawful use" (Ariz. Rev. Stat. Ann. sec. 13-1982). The court rejected this argument, finding that the statutes in question did not establish any specific standard of care but "only set forth a general duty to provide security to members of the public on school property."

Having discovered no specific legal duty chargeable to the individual defendants (excluding the security officer, whose potential liability the trial court had not rejected), the Arizona court next considered the liability of the Community College District itself. Rejecting the plaintiff's request to adopt two liability principles from the *Restatement of Torts Second*,[33] the court found this principle controlling in Arizona:

> A public school district in Arizona is liable for negligence when it fails to exercise ordinary care under the circumstances. [Arizona cases have] established that students are invitees and that schools have a duty to make the premises reasonably safe for their use. If a dangerous condition exists, the invitee must show that the employees of the school knew of or created the condition at issue [611 P.2d at 550].

The court then determined that the *respondeat superior* doctrine applies to governmental defendants under Arizona law, so that the Community College District could be held liable for the negligence of its employees. Therefore, if the plaintiff could show at trial that the district's security guard had breached the duty set out above, while acting within the scope of employment, the district would be liable (along with the employee) for the death of the plaintiff's son.

The *Jesik* court also discussed an Arizona statute (Ariz. Rev. Stat. Ann. sec. 15-442(A)(16)) that imposes a standard of care on public school districts and community college districts (see 611 P.2d at 550 (original opinion) and 551 (supplemental opinion)). The court did not base its decision on this statute because it was not yet in effect at the time the crime was committed. But the court's discussions provide a useful illustration of how state statutes may affect liability questions about campus security. In a later case, *Peterson* v. *San Francisco Community College District*, 36 Cal. 3d 799, 205 Cal. Rptr. 842, 685 P.2d 1193 (1984), the court did rely on a statutory provision to impose liability on the defendant. The plaintiff was a student who had been assaulted while leaving the campus parking lot. Her assailant had concealed himself behind "unreasonably thick and untrimmed foliage and trees." Several other assaults had occurred at the same location and in the same manner. Community college officials had known of these assaults but did not publicize them. The court held that the plaintiff could recover damages under Section 835 of the California Tort Claims Act (Cal. Code, Government, sec. 810 *et seq.*), which provides that "a public entity is liable for injury caused by a dangerous condition of its property" if the dangerous condition was caused by a public employee acting in the scope of his employment or if the entity "had actual or constructive notice of the dangerous condition" and failed to correct it. The court concluded that the failure to trim the foliage or to warn students of the earlier assaults constituted the creation of such a dangerous condition.

Another case, *Relyea* v. *State of Florida*, 385 So. 2d 1378 (Fla. 1980), like *Jesik*, deals with campus security in a context other than dormitories; unlike *Jesik*, it does not deal with a specific threat. The plaintiffs were the parents of two Florida

---

[33]Section 318 of the *Restatement* deals with the duty of a possessor of land to control the conduct of persons permitted to use the land. Section 344 deals with the duty of a possessor of land held open to the public for business purposes to protect members of the public from physical harm caused by third persons.

Atlantic University (FAU) students who were abducted from the FAU campus and murdered. The abduction occurred in the early evening near a classroom building some distance from the main group of campus buildings. The two students had attended class in the building. The plaintiffs sued, among others, the state, the board of regents, and the board of regents' insurance company. The court held that sovereign immunity (see this volume, Section 2.3.1) protected the state and the board of regents from suit. This immunity, however, did not extend to the insurance company. Since the insurance company could therefore be held liable for negligent acts of the board, the court proceeded to determine the liability of the board under Florida law.

In delineating the applicable duty of care, the court relied on legal principles applicable to landowners generally (rather than crafting a principle specifically for postsecondary institutions, as in *Mullins*):

> As a basic principle of law, a property owner has no duty to protect one on his premises from criminal attack by a third person (62 Am. Jur. 2d, Premises Liability, sec. 200 (1972)). Even though one's negligence may be a cause in fact of another's loss, he will not be liable if an independent, intervening, and unforeseeable criminal act also causes the loss (see *Nicholas v. Miami Burglar Alarm Co.*, 339 So. 2d 175, 177 (Fla. 1979)). If, however, the criminal attack is reasonably foreseeable, a duty may arise between a landowner and his invitee. But it must be borne in mind that a landowner is not an insurer of the safety of his invitees and is not required to take precautions against a sudden attack from a third person which he has no reason to anticipate (see *Totten* v. *More Oakland Residential House, Inc.*, 63 Cal. App. 3d 538, 134 Cal. Rptr. 29 (1976)).
>
> In order to impose a duty upon a landowner to protect an invitee from criminal acts of a third person, a plaintiff invitee must allege and prove that the landowner had actual or constructive knowledge of prior, *similar* criminal acts committed upon invitees. The landowner is not bound to anticipate criminal activities of third persons where, as here, the wrongdoers were complete strangers to the landowner and to the victims, and where the incident occurred precipitously. . . . Appellants simply failed to allege or prove that any prior assaults upon persons had been committed in the area of the abduction and murder or, for that matter, anywhere on the campus. In fact, the proof showed there had not been one serious crime against a person since the school was founded in 1963. The reported incidents involved minor larcenies from automobiles and school buildings, hit-and-run complaints for minor automobile damage, and miscellaneous incidents such as malicious mischief. These facts do not give rise to the foreseeability of violent assaults, which, in turn, may give rise to a duty to protect [385 So. 2d at 1382–83].

Based on this lack of foreseeability, the court held that the trial court had correctly determined that the board of regents' insurer was not liable for damages. (See also, for a similar case with the same result, *Hall* v. *Board of Supervisors, Southern University*, 405 So. 2d 1125 (La. 1981).)

The cases in this section illustrate a variety of campus security problems and a variety of legal theories for analyzing them. Each court's choice of theories depended on the common and statutory law of the particular jurisdiction and the specific factual setting of the case. The theories used in *Duarte,* where the security problem occurred in campus housing and the institution's role was comparable to a landlord's, differ from the theories used in *Jesik* and *Relyea,* where the security problems occurred elsewhere and the student was considered the institution's "invitee." Similarly, the first theory used in *Mullins,* establishing a standard of care specifically for postsecondary institutions, differs from theories in the other cases, which borrow and apply standards of care for landlords or landowners generally. Despite the differences, however, a common denominator can be extracted from these cases that can serve as a guideline for postsecondary administrators: When an institution has foreseen or ought to have foreseen that criminal activity will likely occur on campus, it must take reasonable, appropriate steps to safeguard its students and other persons whom it has expressly or implicitly invited onto its premises. In determining whether this duty has been met in a specific case, the key issues are the foreseeability of violent criminal activity on the particular campus and the reasonableness and appropriateness of the institution's response to that particular threat.

Selected Annotated Bibliography

General

1. Carnegie Council on Policy Studies in Higher Education, *Fair Practices in Higher Education: Rights and Responsibilities of Students and Their Colleges in a Period of Intensified Competition for Enrollments* (Jossey-Bass, 1979), focuses on the ethical conduct of institutions and their students. Concluding that serious ethical decay has occurred, the council directs numerous recommendations to institutions, students, accrediting associations, the states, and the federal government. The council specifically recommends that institutions provide more and better information on institutional practices and develop codes of rights and responsibilities covering such matters as admissions, financial aid, tuition, record keeping, academic requirements, support services, student conduct penalties for infractions, and grievance procedures.

2. "Joint Statement on Rights and Freedoms for Students," 52 *AAUP Bulletin* 365 (1967), provides a set of model guidelines for implementing students' rights on campus, drafted by the Association of American Colleges, the American Association of University Professors, the National Student Association, the National Association of Student Personnel Administrators, and the National Association of Women Deans and Counsellors, and endorsed by a number of other professional organizations. This document should be read in conjunction with W. Van Alstyne's discussion of the Joint Statement in G. W. Holmes (Ed.), *Student Protest and the Law,* pp. 181–186 (Institute of Continuing Legal Education, Ann Arbor, 1969).

3. Laudicina, R., and Tramutola, J., Jr., *A Legal Overview of the New Student as Educational Consumer, Citizen, and Bargainer* (Thomas, 1976), is a survey of legal developments concerning students and their impact on postsecondary administration; suggests legal and administrative models for dealing with legal

and policy developments. Written by an administrator and a lawyer, with commentary by many other contributors.

4. Tice, T. N., *Student Rights, Decisionmaking, and the Law* (ERIC/Higher Education Research Report no. 10, American Association for Higher Education, 1976), includes an essay on the impact of laws and morals on campus administration, a set of guidelines for administrative decisions concerning students, and an extensive annotated bibliography on student rights and responsibilities.

5. Young, D. P., and Gehring, D., *The College Student and the Courts* (College Administration Publications, 1973 and periodic supp.), provides briefs and supporting comments on court cases concerning students, with the addition of new cases by quarterly supplements.

Sec. 4.1 (The Legal Status of Students)

1. Comment, "Consumer Protection and Higher Education—Student Suits Against Schools," 37 *Ohio State L.J.* 608 (1976), surveys the types of problems being addressed as part of the student consumerism movement, the legal theories used by courts in student consumerism cases, and the steps that institutions might take to alleviate the problems and attendant lawsuits.

2. Hanson, D. J., *The Lowered Age of Majority: Its Impact on Higher Education* (Association of American Colleges, 1975), provides a very helpful overview of how the lowered age of majority affects a range of legal issues regarding student status, such as determining dependency for financial aid purposes, determining residency for tuition purposes, and devising residence hall regulations; written by a lawyer but primarily for nonlawyers.

3. Jennings, E. K., "Breach of Contract Suits Against Postsecondary Institutions: Can They Succeed?" 7 *J. of College and University Law* 191 (1980–81), is a detailed study of suits brought by students alleging breach of contract. Cases are divided into the categories of "Tuition and Fees," "Scholarships," "Student Discipline," "Miscellaneous," and "The Academic Relationship." In the last category, cases are subdivided into "Program Termination," "Quality of Academic Program," "Refusal to Grant Degree," "Change of Requirements During Student's Tenure," and "Academic Dismissal Procedures."

4. Nordin, V. D., "The Contract to Educate: Toward a More Workable Theory of the Student-University Relationship," 8 *J. of College and University Law* 141 (1981–82), is a historical and theoretical overview of the development and current interpretation of the "contract to educate." Includes discussion of the academic abstention doctrine, the application of implied contract and quasi-contract theories to education, the reasonable expectations of the parties, and the legal significance of the college bulletin.

5. Olswang, S. G., Cole, E. K., and Wilson, J. B., "Program Elimination, Financial Emergency, and Student Rights," 9 *J. of College and University Law* 163 (1982–83), analyzes one particular aspect of the contract relationship between institution and student: the obligations the institution may have to the student when the institution has slated an academic program for elimination. A useful supplement to the articles in items no. 3 and 4 above.

Sec. 4.2 (Admissions)

1. Baxter, F. V., "The Affirmative Duty to Desegregate Institutions of Higher Education—Defining the Role of the Traditionally Black College," 11 *J. of Law and Education* 1 (1982), provides "an analytical framework to assess, in a consistent fashion, the role which [black] institutions should play in a unitary system." Reviews various legal strategies to deflect the "very real threat to black colleges that is posed by administrative and judicial efforts to desegregate state systems of higher education."

2. Bell, D. A., Jr., "Black Colleges and the Desegregation Dilemma," 28 *Emory L.J.* 949 (1979), reviews the development of desegregation law and its impact on black colleges. The author argues that black colleges continue to provide a special service to black Americans and that litigation and legislation should be tailored to accommodate and promote this service.

3. Gellhorn, E., and Hornby, D. B., "Constitutional Limitations on Admissions Procedures and Standards—Beyond Affirmative Action," 60 *Virginia L. Rev.* 975 (1974), discusses legal issues concerning law school admissions procedures and, more generally, analyzes due process and equal protection limitations on postsecondary admissions; includes a general analysis of courts' treatment of educational administration questions and gives specific recommendations for law school admissions procedures.

4. Hornby, D. B., *Higher Education Admission Law Service* (Educational Testing Services, 1973, with subsequent additions), is a looseleaf service revised and updated annually. Particularly useful for admissions officers in both public and private institutions.

5. McCormack, W. (Ed.), *The Bakke Decision: Implications for Higher Education Admissions* (American Council on Education, 1978), is a report of the American Council on Education/Association of American Law Schools committee convened to study *Bakke*. The report reviews the various opinions in *Bakke* and discusses their implications for admissions and financial aid. It also "analyzes the various objectives to be served by race and ethnic group–conscious admission programs and examines several models of admission procedures and criteria that might be used to serve these objectives."

6. O'Neil, R. M., *Discriminating Against Discrimination: Preferential Admissions and the DeFunis Case* (Indiana University Press, 1975), provides a detailed examination of the *DeFunis* case and the continuing issues emerging from it. The author, a lawyer and university administrator, argues in favor of special admissions programs for minorities, considering and rejecting various nonracial alternatives in the process.

7. Orleans, J. H., "Memorandum: First Thoughts on *Southeastern Community College* v. *Davis*," 6 *J. of College and University Law* 263 (1979–80), analyzes the U.S. Supreme Court's *Davis* opinion and explores the case's impact on the postsecondary institution's obligations to handicapped students. It also explores the potential impact of the case on other issues under the federal Section 504 regulations, such as "Academic Treatment, Adjustments, and Assistance" and "Preadmission Inquiries."

8. Preer, J., "Lawyers v. Educators: Changing Perceptions of Desegregation in Public Higher Education," 11 *North Carolina Central L.J.* 74 (1979), reprinted

in 53 *J. of Higher Education* 119 (1982), examines lawyers' and educators' perceptions of public higher education desegregation, and the tension between these perceptions. Discusses three historical examples: The Morrill Act of 1890, "the reactions of civil rights lawyers and educators to the regional educational compact of the 1940s," and the "legal and educational paradoxes" of *Adams* v. *Richardson* (see this volume, Sections 7.5.2 and 7.5.8). The author concludes that "both lawyers and educators need to expand their vision." For an extended version of these themes, see the author's book *Lawyers* v. *Educators: Black Colleges and Desegregation in Public Higher Education* (Greenwood Press, 1982); especially rich in historical materials.

9. Sindler, A. P., *Bakke, DeFunis, and Minority Admissions: The Quest for Equal Opportunity* (Longman, 1979), is a thought-provoking analysis of the various issues raised by affirmative admissions policies. Traces the issues and their implications through the U.S. Supreme Court's pronouncement in *Bakke*.

10. "Symposium: *Regents of the University of California* v. *Bakke,*" 67 *California L. Rev.* 1 (1979), contains articles, comments, and a book review on issues relating to *Bakke*. Lead articles, all by noted legal scholars, are D. A. Bell, Jr., "*Bakke*, Minority Admissions, and the Usual Price of Racial Remedies"; V. Blasi, "*Bakke* as Precedent: Does Mr. Justice Powell Have a Theory?"; R. G. Dixon, Jr., "*Bakke:* A Constitutional Analysis"; K. Greenawalt, "The Unresolved Problems of Reverse Discrimination"; L. Henkin, "What of a Right to Practice a Profession?"; R. M. O'Neil, "*Bakke* in Balance: Some Preliminary Thoughts"; and R. A. Posner, "The *Bakke* Case and the Future of Affirmative Action."

11. Tribe, L., "Perspectives on *Bakke:* Equal Protection, Procedural Fairness, or Structured Justice," 92 *Harvard L. Rev.* 864 (1978), is a theoretical discussion of *Bakke*'s ramifications. Draws on broad themes of constitutional law of particular interest to lawyers.

12. Wilson, R. (Ed.), *Race and Equity in Higher Education* (Macmillan, 1983), contains five essays produced by the American Council on Education–Aspen Institute Seminar on the Desegregation of Higher Education. Essays examine the history and politics of higher education desegregation, provide data on demographic changes in recent decades, analyze constitutional standards and remedies, evaluate desegregation plans of states involved in *Adams* v. *Richardson* (see Sections 7.5.2 and 7.5.8) litigation, and propose new policies and agendas. Essays by J. Egerton, J. E. Blackwell, J. L. Prestage, P. R. Dimond, and A. L. Berrian.

Sec. 4.3 (Financial Aid)

1. Ayres, T. D., and Sagner, D. R., "The Bankruptcy Reform Act and Student Loans: Unraveling New Knots," 9 *J. of College and University Law* 361 (1982–83), reviews legal issues presented by the Bankruptcy Reform Act of 1978 and other efforts to curtail discharge of student loans in bankruptcy. Examines discharge of debts under both Chapter 7 and Chapter 13 of the Bankruptcy Code and reviews the case law explicating bankruptcy law concepts such as the "undue hardship" exception and the "good faith and related tests." Includes, in appendices, a listing of the "documents composing the

legislative history of the Bankruptcy Reform Act of 1978," a standard inter-rogatory form used by university counsel, "selected resources on bankruptcy law," and a discussion of bankruptcy procedures under the 1978 act.

2. Carnegie Council on Policy Studies, *Next Steps for the 1980s in Student Financial Aid: A Fourth Alternative* (Jossey-Bass, 1979), is divided into three parts: "Making Better Use of Existing Resources," "The Current System [as of 1979] in Operation," and "Opportunities for Improvement." Although numerous changes have been made in federal student aid programs since publication of this report, its overview of the federal/state/private financial aid system, identification and analysis of policy issues, and specific recommendations are of clear continuing importance.

3. Cohen, A. B., *Bankruptcy, Secured Transactions, and Other Debtor-Creditor Matters* (Michie, 1981), is a comprehensive volume providing an overview of this area of the law, including the new bankruptcy code; case citations; and an analysis of important issues that arise. A general resource rather than one focusing specifically on problems of student aid.

4. Fenske, R. H., Huff, R. P., and Associates, *Handbook of Student Financial Aid: Programs, Procedures, and Policies* (Jossey-Bass, 1983), is an overview of the issues involved in financial aid programs and planning. Divided into four parts: "Development, Scope, and Purposes of Student Aid," "Delivering Aid to Students on Campus," "Ensuring Effectiveness in Administering Aid Pro-grams," and "Importance of Aid in Meeting Student Needs and Institutional Goals." Includes discussion of federal student aid programs and their require-ments, and problems of student borrower bankruptcies.

5. Jenkins, H., "Regulation of Colleges and Universities Under the Guaranteed Student Loan Program," 4 *J. of College and University Law* 13 (1977), explains and defends the federal regulations of a major student loan program and com-pares them with provisions in the Education Amendments of 1976, which impose similar regulatory requirements on the other major federal student aid programs.

6. Lines, P. M., "Tuition Discrimination: Valid and Invalid Uses of Tuition Differentials," 9 *J. of College and University Law* 241 (1982–83), addresses the constitutional validity of tuition differentials between state residents, on one hand, and nonresidents, aliens, or new residents, on the other. Reviews issues arising under equal protection clauses of federal and state constitutions, the federal privileges and immunities clause, the irrebuttable presumption doctrine of federal due process, and the federal supremacy clause.

7. Orleans, J. H., and Johnson, E. D., "Nondiscrimination Doesn't Have to Not Work: Restricted Scholarships, H.E.W., and I.R.S.," 7 *J. of Law and Education* 493 (1978), discusses the interplay of constitutional, statutory, and administrative policy regarding race- and sex-restricted scholarships.

8. Sagner, D., "Consumer Credit and Higher Education," 6 *J. of College and University Law* 3 (1979), discusses the truth-in-lending provisions of the Con-sumer Credit Protection Act of 1968, 15 U.S.C. sec. 160 *et seq.,* and the univer-sity's obligations of disclosure regarding the terms of student loans and credit sales.

9. Verville, R. E., and Leyton, P. S., "Department of Education Student Financial Assistance Audit and Regulatory Proceedings: Limitations, Suspen-sions, and Terminations," 36 *Administrative L. Rev.* 1 (1984), is a practical

article reviewing the enforcement proceedings used in the Pell Grant, College Work-Study, NDSL, and GSL programs. Topics include who may conduct an audit; the objectives to be achieved by an audit; procedures for the suspension, freezing, and termination of federal assistance; the statutory and regulatory authorization for these procedures; and the procedural safeguards afforded institutions facing regulatory proceedings.

Sec. 4.4 (Disciplinary Rules and Regulations)

See the bibliography for Section 4.13 below.

Sec. 4.5 (Grades, Credits, and Degrees)

1. Crocker, P. L., and Simon, A. E., "Sexual Harassment in Education," 10 *Capital University L. Rev.* 541 (1981), is an overview of sexual harassment problems, especially those affecting students in higher education, and the law relevant to their resolution. The article analyzes the range of injuries that sexual harassment encompasses and the range of legal remedies available to sexual harassment victims under the federal Title IX statute, state tort law, state contract law, and state criminal law. Includes a section on "litigation issues."
2. LaMorte, M., and Meadows, R., "Educationally Sound Due Process in Academic Affairs," 8 *J. of Law and Education* 197 (1979), analyzes cases up to and including *Board of Curators of the University of Missouri* v. *Horowitz*, 435 U.S. 78 (1978), and provides extended discussion of educationally and legally sound practices in student evaluation, academic dismissals, and awarding of degrees.
3. See Jennings article in bibliography for Section 4.1 (item 3), especially pp. 204–215.

Sec. 4.6 (Procedures for Suspension, Dismissal, and Other Sanctions)

1. Dessem, R. L., "*Board of Curators of the University of Missouri* v. *Horowitz:* Academic Versus Judicial Expertise," 39 *Ohio State L.J.* 476 (1978), thoroughly canvasses the ramifications and limitations of the *Horowitz* decision.
2. Golden, E. J., "Procedural Due Process for Students at Public Colleges and Universities," 11 *J. of Law and Education* 337 (1982), reviews postsecondary education's response to *Goss* v. *Lopez*, 419 U.S. 565 (1975), the leading Supreme Court case on disciplinary procedures, and the later *Horowitz* case on academic procedures. After reviewing *Goss*'s and *Horowitz*'s application to dismissals and long-term suspensions, the author reports results of his survey of procedural protections extended by public colleges and universities to students faced with disciplinary or academic dismissal. Includes data on notice, hearing, evidentiary standards, and other procedural issues.

Sec. 4.7 (Student Protest and Demonstrations)

1. Blasi, V., "Prior Restraints on Demonstrations," 68 *Michigan L. Rev.* 1482 (1970), is a comprehensive discussion of First Amendment theory and case

law and the specific manner in which the law bears on the various components of a student demonstration.

2.   Herman, J., "Injunctive Control of Disruptive Student Demonstrations," 56
      Virginia L. Rev. 215 (1970), analyzes strategic, constitutional, and procedural
      issues concerning the use of injunctions to control disruptive student protest.

3.   Holmes, G. W., *Student Protest and the Law* (Institute of Continuing Legal Educa-
      tion, Ann Arbor, 1969), is a collection of papers, panel discussions, and sup-
      porting documents (such as pleadings and injunctive orders) presented at a
      national conference; covers a broad range of topics relevant to student protest
      and to student affairs generally. Though somewhat outdated, still a useful,
      practical resource for both lawyers and administrators.

Sec. 4.8 (Student Organizations)

1.   Meabon, D. L., Alexander, R. E., and Hunter, K. E., *Student Activity Fees:
      A Legal and National Perspective* (National Entertainment and Campus Activities
      Association, 1979), provides information on student activities fees and on
      various issues regarding their use. Chapters include "Student Activity Fees:
      A Backward Glance"; "Legal Issues Involved in the Collection, Control and
      Allocation of Student Activity Fees"; "Student Activity Fees: A National
      Study"; and "Recommendations for Local Student Activity Fee Guidelines."
      Also includes a set of appendices providing, among other things, texts of
      guidelines already in use at several postsecondary institutions.

2.   Comment, " 'Fee Speech': First Amendment Limitations on Student Fee Ex-
      penditures," 20 *Cal. Western L. Rev.* 279 (1984), focuses on the particular
      problem of "using mandatory student fees to finance political or ideological
      activities." The comment analyzes the constitutional issues raised by this prac-
      tice, from the perspectives of both the university and the students who object
      to such uses of mandatory fees; reviews prior cases on student fees as well
      as on mandatory labor union dues; and proposes a new analytical scheme
      for determining the constitutionality of particular mandatory student fees.

Sec. 4.9 (Student Press)

1.   Comment, "Student Editorial Discretion, the First Amendment, and Public
      Access to the Campus Press," 16 *U. Cal.-Davis L. Rev.* 1089 (1983), reviews
      the constitutional status of student newspapers under the First Amendment,
      analyzes the applicability of the state action doctrine to student newspapers
      on public campuses, and discusses the issue of whether noncampus groups
      have any right to have material published in campus newspapers on public
      campuses.

2.   Duscha, J., and Fischer, T., *The Campus Press: Freedom and Responsibility*
      (American Association of State Colleges and Universities, 1973), is a hand-
      book that provides historical, philosophical, and legal information on college
      newspapers. Not only discusses case law that affects the campus press but also
      illustrates the variety of ways the press may be organized on campus and the
      responsibilities the institution may have for its student publications.

3.   Nichols, J. E., "Vulgarity and Obscenity in the Student Press," 10 *J. of Law
      and Education* 207 (1981), examines the legal definitions of vulgarity and obscenity

as they apply to both higher education and secondary education and reviews the questions these concepts pose for the student press.

4. Note, "Tort Liability of a University for Libelous Material in Student Publications," 71 *Michigan L. Rev.* 1061 (1973), provides the reader with a general understanding of libel law and discusses the various theories under which a university may be held liable for the torts of its student press. The author also recommends preventive measures to minimize university liability.

Sec. 4.10 (Student Housing)

1. Delgado, R., "College Searches and Seizures: Students, Privacy and the Fourth Amendment," 26 *Hastings L.J.* 57 (1975), provides a broad view of the legal issues involved in dormitory searches and analyzes the validity of the various legal theories used to justify such searches.

2. Gehring, D. D. (Ed.), *Administering College and University Housing: A Legal Perspective* (College Administration Publications, 1983), is an overview of legal issues that can arise in the administration of campus housing. Written in layperson's language and directed to all staff involved with campus housing. Chapters include "Legal Information: A Part of the Decision Making Process," by D. Gehring; "Constitutional Issues in the Residence Halls," by G. Pavela; "Statutes and Regulations Affecting Residence Hall Operations and Staff," by D. Gehring; "Contracts and Their Use in Housing," by S. Miller; "Torts: Your Legal Duties and Responsibilities," by D. Moore and L. Murray; and "Managing the Risk," by S. Miller. Includes an appendix with a "Checklist of Housing Legal Issues" for use in doing legal audits of housing programs.

3. Note, "Admissibility of Evidence Seized by Private University Officials in Violation of Fourth Amendment Standards," 56 *Cornell L. Rev.* 507 (1971), discusses the applicability of Fourth Amendment standards to actions by private universities; addresses the degree of involvement by school and police authorities that may render private university actions subject to the state action doctrine.

Sec. 4.11 (Athletics)

1. Appenzeller, H., and Appenzeller, T., *Sports and the Courts* (Michie, 1980), is an overview of various legal issues regarding sports, particularly at the amateur level, and suggestions for dealing with them. Emphasizes the practical rather than the theoretical. Primarily for athletic directors and coaches.

2. Cross, H. M., "The College Athlete and the Institution," 38 *Law and Contemporary Problems* 151 (1973), provides a legal analysis of the student athlete's status within the institution; discusses admissions, recruitment, athletic eligibility, and the athlete's status as a member of the student body. Written by a law professor and former NCAA president.

3. Gaal, J., DiLorenzo, L. P., and Evans, T. S., "HEW's Final Policy Interpretation on Title IX and Intercollegiate Athletics," 6 *J. of College and University Law* 345 (1980), is a critical analysis of HEW's (now Department of Education's) final guidelines on how Title IX applies to postsecondary athletic programs. The article should be read together with J. Gaal and L. P. DiLorenzo, "The Legality and Requirements of HEW's Proposed Policy Interpretation

of Title IX and Intercollegiate Athletics,'' 6 *J. of College and University Law*
161 (1979–80), an earlier article on the proposed guidelines and the underlying
Title IX regulations.

4. Langerman, S., and Fidel, N., "Sports Injury—Negligence," 15 *Proof of Facts*
    2d 1 (American Jurisprudence, 1978, with supplementation), is a thorough
    examination of the issues involved in this increasingly litigated area of the
    law. Covers "Duty of Administrator of Sports Program," "Unsafe Facilities
    or Equipment," "Inadequate Coaching or Supervision," "Effect of Age and
    Experience of Plaintiff," "Contributory Negligence," "Assumption of Risk,"
    and other topics. Includes "Practice Comments" of the authors and model
    question-and-answer dialogues with expert witnesses. Primarily for lawyers.

5. "On Collegiate Athletics," 60 *Educational Record* no. 4 (Fall 1979), is a sym-
    posium with articles and other material, including E. H. El-Khawas, "Self-
    Regulation and Collegiate Athletics"; C. H. Lowell, "The Law and Collegiate
    Athletics in Public Institutions"; and "Responsibilities in the Conduct of Col-
    legiate Athletic Programs: American Council on Education Policy Statements"
    (three policy statements, directed respectively to institutional trustees,
    presidents, and athletic directors, developed by ACE and its Commission on
    Collegiate Athletics).

6. "Symposium on Athletics in Higher Education," 8 *J. of College and University
    Law* 291 (1981–82), contains the following lead articles: A. V. Thomas, and
    J. S. Wildgen, "Women in Athletics: Winning the Game but Losing the Sup-
    port"; L. R. Thompson and J. T. Young, "Taxing the Sale of Broadcast
    Rights to College Athletics—An Unrelated Trade or Business?"; R. H. Ruxin,
    "Unsportsmanlike Conduct: The Student Athlete, the NCAA, and Agents";
    and E. Branchfield and M. Grier, "*Aiken* v. *Lieuallen* and *Peterson* v. *Oregon
    State University:* Defining Equity in Athletics" (includes a conciliation agree-
    ment settling the *Peterson* case).

7. "Symposium on Postsecondary Athletics and the Law," 5 *J. of College and
    University Law* nos. 1 and 2 (1978–79), provides extended discussion and
    research on a variety of issues. Contains these articles: (1) J. D. Dickerson
    and M. Chapman, "Contract Law, Due Process, and the NCAA"; (2) E.
    P. Edmonds, "Postsecondary Athletics and the Law: A Selected
    Bibliography"; (3) A. M. C. Hermann, "Sports and the Handicapped: Section
    504 of the Rehabilitation Act of 1973 and Curricular, Intramural, Club, and
    Intercollegiate Athletic Programs in Postsecondary Educational Institutions";
    (4) P. R. Hochberg, "The Four Horsemen Ride Again: Cable Communica-
    tions and Collegiate Athletics"; (5) S. Horn, "Intercollegiate Athletics: Waning
    Amateurism and Rising Professionalism"; (6) M. A. Kadzielski, "Postsecon-
    dary Athletics in an Era of Equality: An Appraisal of the Effects of Title IX";
    (7) W. A. Kaplin, "An Overview of Legal Principles and Issues Affecting
    Postsecondary Athletics"; (8) C. H. Lowell, "Judicial Review of Rule-Making
    in Amateur Athletics"; (9) J. C. Weistart, "Antitrust Issues in the Regulation
    of College Sports"; (10) H. L. Zuckman, "Throw 'em to the Lions (or
    Bengals): The Decline and Fall of Sports Civilization as Seen Through the
    Eyes of a United States District Court."

8. Weistart, J. C., "Legal Accountability and the NCAA," 10 *J. of College and
    University Law* 167 (1983–84), is an essay exploring the unique status and role
    of the NCAA in intercollegiate athletics. Reviews structural deficiencies, such

as NCAA's alleged failure to provide any accommodation to the interests of student athletes in its governance structure; and suggests that the NCAA should be considered to have a fiduciary relationship to its member institutions. Also considers the role of judicial supervision of NCAA activities and its effect on NCAA's regulatory objectives (that is, preservation of academic integrity and regulation of the commercial aspects of collegiate athletics).

9. Weistart, J. C., and Lowell, C. H., *The Law of Sports* (Michie, 1979), is a reference work, with comprehensive citations to authorities, treating the legal issues concerning sports. Of particular relevance to postsecondary institutions are the chapters on "Regulation of Amateur Athletics," "Public Regulation of Sports Activities," and "Liability for Injuries in Sports Activities."

Sec. 4.12 (Student Files and Records)

1. American Association of Collegiate Registrars and Admissions Officers, Task Force on Buckley Amendment, *A Guide to Postsecondary Institutions for Implementation of the Family Educational Rights and Privacy Act of 1974 as Amended* (AACRAO, 1975), explains the Act and its regulations, as well as the procedures and strategies for compliance, and provides sample forms for use in complying and a copy of the Act and its regulations.

2. Michigan Law Review Editorial Board, "Government Information and the Rights of Citizens, 73 *Michigan L. Rev.* 971 (1975), provides an exhaustive review of federal and state constitutional, statutory, and common law protections of the right to privacy; includes lengthy discussions of the Privacy Act of 1974 and state law applicable to education records, as well as a brief discussion of the Buckley Amendment; focuses primarily on the limitations applicable to public agencies and institutions.

3. Schatken, S., "Student Records at Institutions of Postsecondary Education: Selected Issues Under the Family Educational Rights and Privacy Act of 1974," 4 *J. of College and University Law* 147 (1977), identifies the major Buckley issues, explains why they are issues, suggests resolutions, and gives practical advice for administrators and counsel dealing with student records.

4. Trubow, G. B., *Law Enforcement Information and the Family Educational Rights and Privacy Act* (American Bar Association, 1982), a report of the ABA's Section on Individual Rights and Responsibilities, explores the Buckley Amendment's "effect on the flow of information between institutions of higher education and law enforcement agencies." Summarizes Buckley Amendment requirements; reviews kinds of records kept by postsecondary institutions; examines the problem of third-party access to student records, especially law enforcement records; and presents the results of a survey on how postsecondary institutions are complying with Buckley.

Sec. 4.13 (Disciplinary and Grievance Systems)

1. Beaney, W. M., and Cox, J. C. S., "Fairness in University Disciplinary Proceedings," 22 *Case Western L. Rev.* 390 (1971), provides legal and policy analyses, and suggested guidelines, concerning the development of fair disciplinary proceedings on campus.

2. Pavela, G., "Limiting the Pursuit of Perfect Justice on Campus: A Proposed

Code of Student Conduct," 6 *J. of College and University Law* 137 (1980), provides a well-drafted code, including both standards of conduct and hearing
procedures, with comprehensive annotations explaining particular provisions
and cites to relevant authorities. The code represents an alternative to the
procedural complexities of the criminal justice model.

3.   Pavela, G., "Therapeutic Paternalism and the Misuse of Mandatory
     Psychiatric Withdrawals on Campus," 9 *J. of College and University Law* 101
     (1982–83), analyzes the pitfalls associated with postsecondary institutions' use
     of "psychiatric withdrawals" of students. Pitfalls include violations of Sec-
     tion 504 (on handicap discrimination) and of students' substantive and pro-
     cedural due process rights. The article concludes with "Policy Considera-
     tions," which review the limits of psychiatric diagnosis, the danger of
     substituting a "therapeutic" approach as a solution for disciplinary problems,
     and the "appropriate uses for a psychiatric withdrawal policy." For a later
     monograph adapted from this article, with model standards and procedures,
     hypothetical case studies, and a bibliography, see G. Pavela, *The Dismissal
     of Students with Mental Disorders: Legal Issues, Policy Considerations, and Alternative
     Responses* (College Administration Publications, 1985).

4.   U.S. District Court, Western District of Missouri (*en banc*), "General Order
     on Judicial Standards of Procedure and Substance in Review of Student
     Discipline in Tax-Supported Institutions of Higher Education," 45 *Federal
     Rules Decisions* 133 (1968), provides a set of guidelines promulgated for the
     guidance of that court in deciding students' rights cases. The guidelines are
     similarly useful to administrators and counsel seeking to comply with federal
     legal requirements.

Sec. 4.14 (Campus Security)

1.   Blumer, D. H., and Witsil, J. L., "Security on the Campus," in D. H. Blumer
     (Ed.), *Legal Issues for Postsecondary Education: Briefing Papers,* vol. 2, pp. 35–44
     (American Association of Community and Junior Colleges, 1976), reviews
     the legal and policy problems regarding campus security and provides possible
     solutions.

2.   Hauserman, N., and Lansing, P., "Rape on Campus: Postsecondary Insti-
     tutions as Third Party Defendants," 8 *J. of College and University Law* 182
     (1981–82), traces the evolution of tort actions by rape and assault victims
     against third-party institutional defendants. Other sections of the article review
     the procedural issues that may be raised by such suits, the availability and
     scope of sovereign and charitable immunity defenses, the elements a plaintiff
     must prove in order to establish the case, and the potential availability of
     Title IX as an additional ground for litigation.

3.   Sims, D. S., Jr. (Ed.), *New Directions in Campus Law Enforcement: A Handbook
     for Administrators* (University of Georgia Center for Continuing Education,
     1971), is a series of papers setting forth case studies, proposals, and advice
     concerning law enforcement on campus.

V

The College
and the Community

Sec. 5.1. General Principles

Postsecondary institutions are typically subject to the regulatory authority of one or more local government entities, such as a city, village, town, or county government. Local regulations sometimes are relatively noncontroversial, as in the case of some fire and safety codes. In other situations regulations may be highly controversial. In 1976–77, for instance, Cambridge, Massachusetts, attempted to regulate genetic experimentation on the Harvard and MIT campuses. Prohibition of nuclear weapons research within the city was an issue in Cambridge in 1983 and in Ann Arbor, Michigan (home of the University of Michigan), in 1984. Also, in 1984 Normal, Illinois (home of Illinois State University), passed an ordinance requiring permits for large-group gatherings at which alcohol will be served. And various other cities in the early 1980s passed ordinances restricting smoking in the work place. When dealing with issues such as these, postsecondary administrators should be aware of the extent of, and limits on, each local government's regulatory authority.

A local government has only that authority which the state has delegated to it by state law. When a local government has been delegated "home rule" powers, its authority will usually be broadly interpreted; otherwise, its authority will usually be narrowly construed. Even where a local body has general authority, it cannot exercise that authority in a way that conflicts with state law, which generally prevails over local law in case of conflict.[1] Nor can a local government regulate matters that the state otherwise has "preempted" by its own extensive regulation of the field or matters that are considered protected by the state's sovereign immunity. Nor, of course, can local governments regulate in a way that violates the federal Constitution.

Both public and private institutions will be bound by local government regulations that are interpreted to apply to them and that satisfy the foregoing principles concerning authority. Public institutions, however, are more likely than private institutions to escape the local regulatory net. Although the preemption doctrine applies to both public and private institutions, public institutions are more heavily regulated by the states (see Section 6.2) and thus more likely in particular cases to have preemption defenses. Public institutions may also defend against local regulation by asserting sovereign immunity, a defense not available to private institutions.

The preemption doctrine governs situations in which state and local regulatory activities overlap. If a local government ordinance regulates the same kind of activity as a state law, the institution may be bound only by the state law. Courts will resolve any apparent overlapping of state law and local ordinances by a case-by-case determination whether state law has preempted the field and precluded local regulation. In *Hall* v. *City of Taft,* 47 Cal. 2d 177, 302 P.2d 574 (1956), the court held that detailed state regulation of public school construction preempted the field, so that public schools built in the municipality did not have to conform with local building codes. But in *Port Arthur Independent School District* v. *City of Groves,* 376 S.W.2d 330 (Tex. 1974), the court held that local public school buildings were subject to municipal building codes, in the absence of explicit state regulation of construction standards, because "to hold otherwise would be to leave a hiatus in regulation necessary to the health and safety of the community."

A rather unusual case concerning colleges and universities illustrates the application of these principles. *Board of Trustees* v. *City of Los Angeles,* 49 Cal. App. 3d 45, 122 Cal. Rptr. 361 (1975), arose after a state university leased one of its facilities to a circus and claimed that the municipal ordinance regulating circus operations was preempted by a state statute authorizing the board of regents to promulgate rules for the governance of state colleges. In upholding the ordinance, the court found as follows:

> The general statutory grant of authority ([Cal. Educ.] Code secs. 23604, 23604.1, 23751) to promulgate regulations for the governing of the state colleges and the general regulations promulgated pursuant to that authority (Cal. Admin. Code Title 5, sec. 4000 *et seq.*) contain no comprehensive state scheme for regulating the conduct of circuses or similar exhibitions with specific references to the safety, health, and sanitary problems attendant on such activities. Nor can the board point to any attempt by it to control the activities of its lessees for the purpose of protecting the public, the animals, or the neighboring community.

[1]Occasionally, state laws may be held invalid because they regulate matters of "purely local concern" which the state constitution reserves to local "home rule" governments or because they constitute "local" or "special" legislation prohibited by the state constitution. In such a case, there is no conflict, and local law may prevail.

In the absence of the enforcement of the city's ordinance, there would be a void in regulating circuses and similar exhibitions when those activities were conducted on university property, thereby creating a status for tenants of the university which would be preferential to tenants of other landowners. This preferential status, under the circumstances, serves no governmental purpose. The subject matter of Los Angeles Municipal Code section 53.50 has not been preempted by the state [122 Cal. Rptr. at 365].

The sovereign immunity doctrine holds that state institutions, as arms of state government, cannot be regulated by a lesser governmental authority which has only those powers delegated to it by the state. In order to claim sovereign immunity, the public institution must be performing state "governmental" functions, not acting in a merely "proprietary" capacity. In *Board of Trustees* v. *City of Los Angeles,* above, the court rejected the board's sovereign immunity defense by using this distinction:

In the case at bar, the board leases . . . [its facilities] as a revenue-producing activity. The activities which are conducted thereon by private operators have no relation to the governmental function of the university. "The state is acting in a proprietary capacity when it enters into activities . . . to amuse and entertain the public. The activities of [the board] do not differ from those of private enterprise in the entertainment industry" (*Guidi* v. *California,* 41 Cal. 2d 623, 627, 262 P.2d 3, 6). The doctrine of sovereign immunity cannot shield the university from local regulation in this case. Even less defensible is the university's attempt here to extend its immunity to private entrepreneurs who are involved in the local commercial market where their competitors are subject to local regulation. By the terms of the lease, the university specifically disavowed any governmental status for its lessee [122 Cal. Rptr. at 364].

In contrast, a sovereign immunity defense was successful in *Board of Regents of Universities* v. *City of Tempe,* 88 Ariz. 299, 356 P.2d 399 (1960). The board sought an injunction to prohibit the city from applying its local construction codes to the board. In granting the board's request, the court reasoned:

The essential point is that the powers, duties, and responsibilities assigned and delegated to a state agency performing a governmental function must be exercised free of control and supervision by a municipality within whose corporate limits the state agency must act. The ultimate responsibility for higher education is reposed by our constitution in the state. The legislature has empowered the board of regents to fulfill that responsibility subject only to the supervision of the legislature and the governor. It is inconsistent with this manifest constitutional and legislative purpose to permit a municipality to exercise its own control over the board's performance of these functions. A central, unified agency, responsible to state officials rather than to the officials of each municipality in which a university or college is located, is essential to the efficient and orderly administration of a system of higher education responsive to the needs of all the people of the state [356 P.2d at 406–07].

Sec. 5.2 Zoning and Land Use Regulation

5.2.1. Overview. The zoning and other land use regulations of local governments can influence the operation of postsecondary institutions in many ways.[2] Where the institution is located, the size of its campus, the institution's ability to expand its facilities, the density and character of its building, the traffic and parking patterns of its campus—all can be affected by zoning laws. Zoning problems are not the typical daily fare of administrators; but when problems do arise, they can be critical to the institution's future development. Building programs, the expansion of the campus area, the use of unneeded land for commercial real estate ventures, the development of branch campuses or additional facilities in other locations (see especially the *New York Institute of Technology* case in Section 5.2.4), program changes that affect the size and character of the student body or the times during which the campus is heavily used (see especially the *Marjorie Webster Junior College* case in Section 5.2.4)—all can be limited, even prevented, by local land use laws. Thus, administrators should be careful not to underestimate the formidable challenge that zoning and other land use laws can present in such circumstances. Since successful maneuvering through such laws necessitates many legal strategy choices and technical considerations, administrators should involve counsel at the beginning of any land use problem.

Local governments that have the authority to zone typically do so by enacting zoning ordinances, which are administered by a local zoning board. Ordinances may altogether exclude educational uses of property from certain zones (called exclusionary zoning). Where educational uses are permitted, the ordinances may impose general regulations—such as architectural and aesthetic standards, set-back requirements, and height and bulk controls—which limit the way that educational property may be used (called regulatory zoning). Public postsecondary institutions are more protected from zoning, just as they are from other types of local regulation, than are private institutions, because public institutions often have sovereign immunity.

5.2.2. Sovereign immunity of public institutions. The courts have employed three tests to determine whether a unit of government, such as a state university, is subject to another government's local zoning law. As summarized in *City of Temple Terrace* v. *Hillsborough Association,* 322 So. 2d 571 (Fla. App. 1975), affirmed without opinion, 332 So. 2d 610 (1976), these tests are (1) the superior sovereign test, (2) the governmental/proprietary distinction, and (3) the balancing test. The court's opinion summarizes the case law on the first two tests:

> One approach utilized by a number of courts is to rule in favor of the superior sovereign. Thus, where immunity from a local zoning ordinance is claimed by an agency occupying a superior position in the governmental hierarchy, it is presumed that immunity was intended in the absence of express statutory language to the contrary. . . . A second test frequently employed is to determine whether the institutional use proposed for the

[2]The relevant cases and authorities are collected in Annot., "Zoning Regulations as Applied to Colleges, Universities, or Similar Institutions for Higher Education," 64 A.L.R.3d 1138 (1975 and periodic supp.).

land is "governmental" or "proprietary" in nature. If the political unit is found to be performing a governmental function, it is immune from the conflicting zoning ordinance. . . . On the other hand, when the use is considered proprietary, the zoning ordinance prevails. . . . Where the power of eminent domain has been granted to the governmental unit seeking immunity from local zoning, some courts have concluded that this conclusively demonstrates the unit's superiority where its proposed use conflicts with zoning regulations. . . . Other cases are controlled by explicit statutory provisions dealing with the question of whether the operation of a particular governmental unit is subject to local zoning. . . .

When the governmental unit which seeks to circumvent a zoning ordinance is an arm of the state, the application of any of the foregoing tests has generally resulted in a judgment permitting the proposed use. This has accounted for statements of horn-book law to the effect that a state agency authorized to carry out a function of the state is not bound by local zoning regulations [322 So. 2d at 576; citations omitted].

In applying these tests to postsecondary education, the court in *City of Newark* v. *University of Delaware,* 304 A.2d 347 (Del. Ch. 1973), used a traditional sovereign immunity analysis combining tests 1 and 2: "It has generally been held that a state agency is immune from local zoning ordinances. . . . The University of Delaware is an agency of the state of Delaware. . . . Its function is governmental. . . . It has the power of eminent domain. . . . Traditionally these characteristics and/or power have been cited as establishing immunity" (304 A.2d at 348).

Rutgers, State University v. *Piluso,* 60 N.J. 142, 286 A.2d 697 (1972), is the leading case on the third and newest test—the balancing test. A balancing approach weighs the state's interest in providing immunity for the institution against the local interest in land use regulation. In determining the strength of the state's interest, the *Rutgers* court analyzed the implied legislative intent to confer immunity on the university:

The rationale which runs through our cases and which we are convinced should furnish the true test of immunity in the first instance, albeit a somewhat nebulous one, is the legislative intent in this regard with respect to the particular agency or function involved. That intent, rarely specifically expressed, is to be divined from a consideration of many factors, with a value judgment reached on an overall evaluation. All possible factors cannot be abstractly catalogued. The most obvious and common ones include the nature and scope of the instrumentality seeking immunity, the kind of function or land use involved, the extent of the public interest to be served thereby, the effect local land use regulation would have upon the enterprise concerned, and the impact upon legitimate local interests. . . . In some instances one factor will be more influential than another or may be so significant as to completely overshadow all others. No one, such as the granting or withholding of the power of eminent domain, is to be thought of as ritualistically required or controlling. And there will undoubtedly be cases, as there have been in the past, where the broader public interest is so important that immunity must be granted even though the local interests may be great. The point is that there is no precise formula or set of criteria which will determine every case mechanically and automatically [286 A.2d at 702–03].

On the facts of the *Rutgers* case, the court decided that the legislative intent was to immunize the university from local zoning laws:

> With regard to a state university . . . there can be little doubt that, as an instrumentality of the state performing an essential governmental function for the benefit of all the people of the state, the legislature would not intend that its growth and development should be subject to restriction or control by local land use regulation. Indeed, such will generally be true in the case of all state functions and agencies [286 A.2d at 703].

The court emphasized, however, that immunity is not absolute and may be conditioned by local needs:

> Even where . . . [immunity] is found to exist, it must not . . . be exercised in an unreasonable fashion so as to arbitrarily override all important legitimate local interests. This rule must apply to the state and its instrumentalities as well as to lesser governmental entities entitled to immunity. For example, it would be arbitrary, if the state proposed to erect an office building in the crowded business district of a city where provision for off-street parking was required, for the state not to make some reasonable provision in that respect. And, at the very least, even if the proposed action of the immune governmental instrumentality does not reach the unreasonable stage for any sufficient reason, the instrumentality ought to consult with the local authorities and sympathetically listen and give every consideration to local objections, problems, and suggestions in order to minimize the conflict as much as possible [286 A.2d at 703].

The court then held that, under the facts of the case, the local interests did not outweigh the university's claim of immunity:

> As far as Rutgers' proposal here, to erect the student family housing on the Kilmer tract, is concerned, we fail to see the slightest vestige of unreasonableness as far as Piscataway's local interests are concerned or in any other respect. (The university did present the proposal to the local authorities by its variance application.) The possible additional local cost of educating children living in the housing is clearly not a legitimate local interest from any proper land use impact point of view [286 A.2d at 703].

State institutions may be in a stronger position to successfully assert sovereign immunity than are community colleges sponsored by local governments. In confrontations with a local zoning board, a state institution is clearly the superior sovereign, whereas an institution of another local government may not be. Moreover, the legislature's intent regarding immunity may be clearer for state institutions than for local ones. (For an example of a case where a community college was subjected to local zoning laws, see *Appeal of Community College of Delaware County*, 435 Pa. 264, 254 A.2d 641 (1969).) Constitutionally autonomous state universities (see Section 6.2.2) would usually have the strongest claim to immunity. In *Regents of the University of California* v. *City of Santa Monica*, 77 Cal. App. 3d 130, 143 Cal. Rptr. 276 (1978), for example, the city had attempted to apply various requirements in its zoning and building codes to a construction project undertaken within the city by the university. Relying on various provisions of the California constitution and statutes, and applying a variation of the superior sovereign test; the court held the university to be immune from such regulation:

> In view of the virtually plenary power of the regents in the regulation of affairs relating to the university and the use of property owned or leased by it for educational purposes, it is not subject to municipal regulation. . . . Thus, the regents in constructing improvements solely for educational purposes are exempt from local building codes and zoning regulations [case citations omitted] and also specifically exempt from payment of local permit and inspection fees [143 Cal. Rptr. at 279–80; statutory provisions omitted].

    5.2.3. Private institutions and zoning regulations. In seeking redress against a local government's zoning regulations, private postsecondary institutions may challenge the zoning board's interpretation and application of the zoning ordinance or may argue that the ordinance conflicts with the federal Constitution or some state law limitation on the local government's zoning authority. Where those arguments are unavailing, the institution may seek an exception (Section 5.2.4), a variance (Section 5.2.5), or an amendment to the zoning ordinance (Section 5.2.6).
    A leading case dealing with the constitutional argument is *Nectow* v. *Cambridge*, 277 U.S. 183 (1928), where the Court stated that "the governmental power to interfere . . . with the general rights of the landowner by [establishing zoning regulations that restrict] the character of his use is not unlimited, and, other questions aside, such restriction cannot be imposed if it does not bear a substantial relation to the public health, safety, morals, or general welfare" (277 U.S. at 188). Despite this precedent, however, constitutional challenges of zoning laws seldom succeed. One major success is *Prentiss* v. *American University*, 214 F.2d 282 (D.C. Cir. 1954), where a U.S. Court of Appeals overturned a rezoning action of the local zoning board because it did not bear a substantial relation to the public welfare and therefore constituted an unconstitutional taking of property without due process. A second, more recent, success is *Northwestern College* v. *City of Arden Hills*, 281 N.W.2d 865 (Minn. 1979), in which the court ruled that, in the particular circumstances, the city's denial of a zoning variance to the college was arbitrary and discriminatory, thus violating constitutional equal protection principles.
    In several cases educational institutions have challenged zoning ordinances that exclude educational uses of land in residential zones. In *Yanow* v. *Seven Oaks Park*, 11 N.J. 341, 94 A.2d 482 (1953), a postsecondary religious training school challenged the reasonableness of an ordinance that excluded schools of higher or special education from residential zones where elementary and secondary schools were permitted. The court, determining that the former schools could be "reasonably placed in a separate classification" from the latter, upheld the exclusion. But in

Long Island University v. *Tappan,* 202 Misc. 956, 113 N.Y.S.2d 795, affirmed, 305 N.Y. 893, 114 N.E.2d 432 (1952), the institution won its battle against an exclusionary ordinance. After the university had obtained a certificate of occupancy from the local township, a nearby village annexed the tract of land where the university was located. The village then passed a zoning ordinance that would have prohibited the operation of the university. The court concluded: "Insofar as the zoning ordinance seeks to prohibit entirely the use of plaintiff's lands in the village for the purposes for which it is chartered, the zoning ordinance is void and ineffectual, as beyond the power of the village board to enact and as bearing no reasonable relation to the promotion of the health, safety, morals, or general welfare of the community" (113 N.Y.S.2d at 799).

Even when the zoning ordinance permits all or particular kinds of educational institutions to operate in a residential or other zone, the zoning board may not consider all the institution's uses of its land and buildings to be educational use.[3] The distinction is much the same as that drawn in local taxation law (see Section 5.3), where the tax status of an educational institution's property depends not only on the character of the institution but also on whether the particular property is being used for educational purposes. When there are no specific definitions or restrictions in the ordinance itself, courts tend to interpret phrases such as "educational use" broadly, to permit a wide range of uses. In *Scheuller* v. *Board of Adjustment,* 95 N.W.2d 731 (Iowa 1959), the court held that a seminary's dormitory building was an educational use under an ordinance that permitted educational uses but did not permit apartment houses or multiple dwellings. And in *Property Owners Association* v. *Board of Zoning Appeals,* 123 N.Y.S.2d 716 (Sup. Ct. 1953), the court held that seating to be constructed adjacent to a college's athletic field was an educational use.

Where a zoning ordinance prohibits or narrowly restricts educational uses in a particular zone, an educational institution may be able to argue that its proposed use is a permissible noneducational use under some other part of the ordinance. In *Application of LaPorte,* 2 A.D.2d 710, 152 N.Y.S.2d 916, affirmed, 2 N.Y.2d 921, 161 N.Y.S.2d 886, 141 N.E.2d 917 (1956), a college was allowed to construct a residence to accommodate more than sixty students because the residence came within the ordinance's authorization of single-family dwelling units:

> The city's legislative body has the right to define the term "family." It has done so, placing no limitation on the number of persons constituting a family, nor does it require that the members thereof be related by blood or marriage. We may not impose any restrictions not contained in the ordinance. The petition does not allege, nor does the record disclose, facts from which it can be determined that the proposed building does not constitute a single dwelling unit, or that the members of the order will occupy the dwelling unit other than as a "single, nonprofit housekeeping unit," within the purview of the ordinance [152 N.Y.S.2d at 918].

---

[3]The relevant cases and authorities are collected in Annot., "What Constitutes 'School,' 'Educational Use,' or the Like Within Zoning Ordinance," 64 A.L.R.3d 1087 (1975 and periodic supp.); and in Annot., "Zoning Regulations as Applied to Colleges, Universities, or Similar Institutions for Higher Education," 64 A.L.R.3d 1138, secs. 9–11 (1975 and periodic supp.).

Fraternity houses may be excluded from residential districts or may be a permissible educational or noneducational use, depending on the terms of the ordinance and the facts of the case.[4] In *City of Baltimore* v. *Poe,* 224 Md. 428, 168 A.2d 193 (1961), a fraternity was permitted in a zone that excluded any "club, the chief activity of which is a service customarily carried on as a business." The court found that "the chief activities carried on at this fraternity house . . . have clearly been established to be social and educational functions for the benefit of the whole membership." But in *Theta Kappa, Inc.* v. *City of Terre Haute,* 226 N.E.2d 903 (Ind. 1967), the court found that a fraternity did not come within the term "dwelling" as defined by the zoning ordinance and was therefore not a permissible use in the residential district in which it was located.

Other problems concerning zoning ordinances arise not because the ordinances exclude a particular use of property but because they regulate the way in which the land holder implements the permitted use. The validity of such "regulatory zoning" also often depends on the interpretation and application of the ordinance and its consistency with state law. In *Franklin and Marshall College* v. *Zoning Hearing Board of the City of Lancaster,* 29 Pa. Commw. Ct. 478, 371 A.2d 557 (1977), for example, the college sought to convert a single-family home it owned into a fraternity house. The fraternity house was a permissible use under the ordinance. The town opposed the conversion, however, arguing that it would violate other provisions of the zoning ordinance dealing with the adequacy of parking and the width of side yards. Applying these provisions, the court held that the proposed number of parking spaces was adequate but that the width of the side yard would have to be increased before the conversion would be allowed.

In *Sisters of Holy Cross* v. *Brookline,* 347 Mass. 486, 198 N.E.2d 624 (1964), a state statute was the focus of the dispute about regulatory zoning. A local zoning authority had attempted to apply construction requirements for single-family homes to the facilities of a private college. A state statute provided that "no ordinance or bylaw which prohibits or limits the use of land for any church or other religious purpose or for any educational purpose . . . shall be valid." The court rejected the town's claim that the statute did not cover ordinances regulating the dimensions of buildings: "We think that this bylaw, as applied to Holy Cross, 'limits the use' of its land and, therefore, we think such application valid." In contrast, the court in *Radcliffe College* v. *City of Cambridge,* 350 Mass. 613, 215 N.E.2d 892 (1966), held that the same state statute did not conflict with a Cambridge zoning ordinance requiring the college to provide off-street parking for newly constructed facilities:

> Providing for the parking or housing of the automobiles of students, instructors, and employees of an educational institution is within the broad scope of the educational powers of the institution, just as is providing for the feeding and housing of such personnel. These are secondary functions incidental to the main educational purpose. Hence, a regulation that requires that some of the college land be used for parking does not lessen the availability of all or any of the institution's land for some appropriate educational purpose. We think the statute does not bar such regulation. Plainly the

[4]The relevant cases and authorities are collected in Annot., "Application of Zoning Regulations to College Fraternities and Sororities," 25 A.L.R.3d 921 (1969 and periodic supp.).

statute does not do so in express terms. At most the Cambridge ordinance requires choices among the proper educational purposes of the institution. In so doing, it does not impede the reasonable use of the college's land for its educational purposes. We rule, therefore, that it does not limit "the use of [its] land for any . . . educational purpose" within the meaning of . . . [the statute] [215 N.E.2d at 895–96].

5.2.4. Special exceptions. Particular educational or noneducational uses may be permitted as "conditional uses" in an otherwise restricted zone. In this situation the institution must apply for a special exception, "a special use which is considered by the local legislative body to be essential or desirable for the welfare of the community and its citizenry and not essentially incompatible with basic uses in the zone involved, but not at every or any location therein or without restrictions or conditions being imposed on such use" (*Piscatelli* v. *Township of Scotch Plains,* 103 N.J. Super. 589, 248 A.2d 274, 277 (1968)). An educational institution may seek a special exception by demonstrating that it satisfies the conditions imposed by the zoning board. If it cannot do so, it may challenge the conditions as being unreasonable or beyond the zoning board's authority under the ordinance or state law.

The plaintiff in *Marjorie Webster Junior College* v. *District of Columbia Board of Zoning Adjustment,* 309 A.2d 314 (D.C. 1973), had operated a girls' finishing school in a residential zone under a special exception granted by the zoning board. The discretion of the zoning board was limited by a regulation specifying that exceptions would be granted only where "in the judgment of the board such special exceptions will be in harmony with the general purpose and intent of the zoning regulations and maps and will not tend to affect adversely the use of neighboring property in accordance with said zoning regulations and maps." Another regulation specifically authorized exceptions for colleges and universities, but only if "such use is so located that it is not likely to become objectionable to neighboring property because of noise, traffic, number of students, or other objectionable conditions." The college was sold to new owners, who instituted new programs (mostly short-term continuing education programs) that altered the curriculum of the school and attracted a new clientele to the campus. After a citizens' group complained that this new use was outside the scope of the college's special exception, the college filed an amendment to the campus plan which constituted the basis for its special exception. The zoning board rejected the amendment after extensive hearings, concluding that, under the applicable regulations, the new use of the college property would not be in harmony with the general purpose and intent of the zone and would adversely affect neighboring property by attracting large numbers of transient men and women to the campus and increasing vehicular traffic in the neighborhood. On appeal by the college, the court held that the zoning regulations contained adequate standards to control the board's discretion and that the board's decision was supported by sufficient evidence.

New York Institute of Technology v. *LeBoutillier,* 33 N.Y.2d 125, 350 N.Y.S.2d 263, 305 N.E.2d 754 (1973), took up a similar issue. A private college had entered an agreement with the local government regarding the use of the college's existing property. Subsequent to the agreement, the college acquired property not contiguous with the main campus, in a residential zone that permitted educational use by special exception. The college's application for a special exception was denied by the zoning board, and the court upheld the board's decision in an interesting opinion combining fact, policy, and law:

> Several factors persuade us that there should be an affirmance in this case. To begin with, the institute seeks to expand an existing educational use without a demonstrable need to expand. Need, of course, is not a criterion for granting a special exception permit. But a reading of the cases dealing with the expansion of existing educational or religious uses clearly indicates that need was apparent. . . .
>
> The institute already owns in excess of four hundred acres in Old Westbury. To date it has built on only about 1 percent of its land, whereas, pursuant to the 1965 agreement, it is permitted to build on up to 10 percent. Moreover, its master plan contemplates buildings on only about 8 percent of its acreage, again less than the allowable percentage. Then, too, student enrollment is only about three thousand, whereas the permissible enrollment under the agreement is seventy-five hundred. Need to expand, it seems, is highly questionable.
>
> The institute contends, however, that it is more feasible economically to purchase the Holloway estate and to renovate the existing structures for its teacher education program than to undertake new construction at its main campus. It also contends that certain aspects of the planned teacher education program make separation from the main campus desirable. There is force to the argument that these judgments should be made by college administrators, not zoning boards of appeal or courts. But at some point, probably not definable with precision, a college's desire to expand, here by the path of least economic resistance, should yield to the legitimate interests of village residents. The village has, in the past, acceded to the incorporation of after-acquired properties into the site plan for the campus. But the right to expand is not absolute. . . .
>
> Here, the 1965 agreement becomes relevant. That agreement, although not expressly applicable to after-acquired property, governs the relationship between the institute and the village. By its adoption it became part of the village's comprehensive plan. Approval of this application would constitute a substantial departure from that agreement. The property is not contiguous with the existing campus. It is located in the center of the village in a single-family residential district with two-acre minimum building lots, one-half mile straight-line distance from the main campus, and about four miles over interior village roads. Approval of the institute's application would negate village planning objectives of keeping college uses on the perimeter of the village in an area buffered by golf courses, thereby minimizing the impact on area residents. Approval would also negate the planning objective of routing traffic to and from the colleges over perimeter county roads, rather than interior village routes. There is ample evidence that a traffic problem already exists on Wheatley Road, which the planning board found would be aggravated by students commuting between the main campus and the proposed one at the Holloway estate.
>
> Finally, it should be quite evident that Old Westbury, containing

parts of four college campuses occupying substantial acreage in the village, is not pursuing a policy of exclusion or insularism. On the contrary, it has attempted to accommodate these uses to the essentially residential character of the community by placing reasonable restrictions upon them. Moreover, it has, in the past, approved incorporations of contiguous properties into the institute's campus. However, having approved expansion of the institute on previous applications does not require the board to grant the institute's present request to expand its existing educational use irrespective of the effect it may have on the overall character of the community [305 N.E.2d at 758–59].

5.2.5. *Variances.* If a proposed use by an educational institution does not conform to the general standards of the zone or to the terms of a special exception, the institution may seek a variance. "A variance is an exercise of the power of the governmental authority to grant relief, in a proper case, from the liberal application of the terms of an ordinance. It is to be used where strict application of the ordinance would cause unnecessary and substantial hardship to the property holder peculiar to the property in question, without serving a warranted and corresponding benefit to the public interest" (*Arcadia Development Corp.* v. *Bloomington,* 267 Minn. 211, 125 N.W.2d 846, 851 (1964)).

Zoning boards may grant variances only in these narrow circumstances and only on the basis of standards created by state or local law. Variances that constitute substantial changes in the zoning plan or alter the boundaries of established zones may be considered in excess of the zoning board's authority. The college in *Ranney* v. *Institute Pontificio Delle Maestre Filippini,* 20 N.J. 189, 119 A.2d 142 (1955), had applied for a variance to expand its existing facilities, located in a restrictive residential zone. The zoning board granted the variance. The New Jersey Supreme Court reversed the board's decision, however, relying on a statutory provision that authorized variances only where there would be no "substantial detriment to the public good" and "the intent and purpose of the zone plan and zoning ordinance" would not be "substantially impair[ed]" (N.J. Stat. Ann. sec. 40:55-39(d)):

> The existing use and structure cannot justify an enlargement in the face of a zoning plan which has prescribed and fostered the overwhelmingly residential character of the area in which Villa Walsh is located. . . . A variance here would be directly antagonistic to the design and purpose of the ordinance and sound zoning. The "disintegrating process would be set in motion" (*Beirn* v. *Morris* . . . [14 N.J. 529, 103 A.2d 365]). "The zoning act does not contemplate variations which would frustrate the general regulations and impair the overall scheme which is set up for the general welfare of the several districts and the entire community" (*Dolan* v. *DeCapua,* 16 N.J. 599, 611, 109 A.2d 615, 621 (1954)) [119 A.2d at 147].

5.2.6. *Amendment of zoning ordinances.* If an educational institution's proposed use is prohibited within a zone, and the institution cannot obtain an exception or a variance, it may petition the local government to amend the zoning ordinance. Unlike an exception or a variance, an amendment is designed to correct an intrinsic flaw in the zoning ordinance, rather than to relieve individual hardship imposed by zoning requirements. An institution seeking an amendment should be prepared to demonstrate that the proposed change is in the public interest rather than just for its own private advantage.

Jurisdictions vary in the presumptions and standards applied to zoning amendments. Some jurisdictions give amendments a presumption of reasonableness. Others presume that the original ordinance was reasonable and require that any amendment be justified. Many jurisdictions require that an amendment conform to the comprehensive zoning plan. ''Spot zoning,'' which reclassifies a small segment of land, is frequently overturned for nonconformance with a comprehensive plan.

Bidwell v. *Zoning Board of Adjustment,* 4 Pa. Commw. Ct. 327, 286 A.2d 471 (1972), illustrates many of the important legal considerations regarding zoning amendments. An amendment reclassified a tract of land from single-family to multi-family residential and granted an exception to a college to allow the construction of a library, a lecture hall, and off-street parking. The court upheld the amendment:

> From the very nature of the proposed use as a library and lecture hall, it is not unreasonable to conclude that commercial activity will not intensify. Nor is there evidence that danger to residents will be significantly increased. Excessive congestion is also not a factor since off-street parking is to be provided. The ordinance in question here merely extended a preexisting zone in accordance with the legislative judgment. . . .
>
> Appellants have not borne their burden of proving that the amendments in question were not in accordance with a comprehensive plan. . . . Public hearings regarding the proposed changes were held and the well-contemplated decision of the legislative body was to amend the zoning ordinance. Considering the presumption afforded this judgment, and taking into account the tenor of the general area, we are of the opinion that this legislation reflects and implements the ''totality of a municipality's program of land utilization, considering both the land resources available and the needs and desires of the community'' (*Donohue* v. *Zoning Board of Adjustment,* 412 Pa. 332, 335, 194 A.2d 610, 612 (1963)) [286 A.2d at 473, 474].

5.2.7. Rights of other property owners. In considering various approaches to zoning problems, administrators should be aware that other property owners may challenge zoning decisions favorable to the institution or may intervene in disputes between the institution and the zoning board. The procedures of the zoning board may require notice to local property owners and an opportunity for a hearing before certain zoning decisions are made. Thus, zoning problems may require administrators to ''do battle'' with the local community in a very real and direct way.

Landowners usually can challenge a zoning decision if they have suffered a special loss different from that suffered by the public generally. Adjacent landowners almost always are considered to have suffered such loss and thus to have ''standing'' (that is, a legal capacity) to challenge zoning decisions regarding the adjacent land. Property owners' associations may or may not have standing based on their special loss or that of their members, depending on the jurisdiction. In *Peirce Junior College* v. *Schumaker,* 17 Pa. Commw. Ct. 604, 333 A.2d 510 (1975), neighboring landowners were denied permission to intervene in a local college's appeal of a zoning decision because they were not the owners or tenants of the property directly involved. But in *Citizens Association of Georgetown* v. *District of Columbia Board of Zoning Adjustment*, 365 A.2d 372 (D.C. 1976), a citizens' association from the neighboring area was successful in challenging and overturning, on procedural grounds, a special exception granted to Georgetown University.

Sec. 5.3. Local Government Taxation

5.3.1. General tax concepts. Local government taxation is one of the most traditional problems in postsecondary education law. Although the basic concepts are more settled here than they are in many areas, these concepts often prove difficult to apply in particular cases. Moreover, in an era of tight budgets, where local governments seek new revenue sources and postsecondary institutions attempt to minimize expenditures, the sensitivity of local tax questions has increased.

The real property tax is the most common tax imposed by local governments on educational institutions. Sales taxes and admissions taxes are also imposed in a number of jurisdictions. A local government's authority to tax is usually grounded in state enabling legislation, which delegates various types of taxing power to various types of local governments. Most local tax questions involving postsecondary institutions concern the interpretation of this state legislation, particularly its exemption provisions. A local government must implement its taxing power by local ordinance, and questions may also arise concerning the interpretation of these ordinances.

A public institution's defenses against local taxation may differ from those of a private institution. Public institutions may be shielded from local taxation by tax exemptions for state government contained in state constitutional provisions or statutes. Public institutions may also make sovereign immunity claims (see Section 5.1) against attempts by a local government to impose taxes or tax collection responsibilities on them. Private institutions, on the other hand, depend on state constitutional or statutory exemptions that limit the local government's authority to tax. Although the provisions vary, most tax codes contain some form of tax exemption for religious, charitable, and educational organizations. These exemptions are usually "strictly construed to the end that such concessions will be neither enlarged nor extended beyond the plain meaning of the language employed" (*Cedars of Lebanon Hospital* v. *Los Angeles County*, 35 Cal. 2d 729, 221 P.2d 31, 34 (1950)). The party requesting the exemption has the burden of proving that the particular activity for which it seeks exemption is covered by the exemption provision. The strictness with which exemptions are construed depends on the state and the type of exemption involved.

5.3.2. Property taxes. Public institutions are often exempt from local real property taxation under state law exemptions for state property. In applying these exemptions, questions sometimes arise concerning whether the particular property at issue is actually that of the institution or state. In *Southern Illinois University* v. *Booker,* 98 Ill. App. 3d 1062, 425 N.E.2d 465 (1981), for instance, the county in which Southern Illinois University is located attempted to assess a property tax on low-cost housing that the university maintained for its married students. The housing consisted of apartments financed by the Federal Housing Administration and the Southern Illinois University Foundation. The foundation was the legal owner of the property. It is a nonprofit corporation whose purpose, under its bylaws, is "to buy, sell, lease, own, manage, convey, and mortgage real estate" and "in a manner specified by the board of trustees of Southern Illinois University, to act as the business agent of the said board in respect to . . . acquisition, management, and leasing of real property and buildings."

The university claimed that the married student apartments were state property and thus exempt from local government taxation. The county argued, however, that legal ownership vested in the foundation, not the university, thus making the exemption for state property inapplicable. In rejecting the county's argument, the court relied on the time-honored distinction between "legal title" and "equitable title":

> With respect to control and enjoyment of the benefits of the property, the stipulated facts show that the university, not the foundation, in fact controls the property and has the right to enjoy the benefits of it in the manner of an owner in fee simple absolute. The foundation acquired title to the property from the university solely as a convenience to the university with regard to long-term financing. The property is used to house students of the university. The facilities are controlled, operated, and maintained by the university. From funds derived from the operation of the property, the university pays annually as rent the amount of the foundation's mortgage payment and, as agent of the foundation, transmits that sum to the Federal National Mortgage Association. Furthermore, when the mortgage is eventually retired, the university will receive title to the improved property with no further payment whatsoever required as consideration for the transfer. The foundation holds but naked legal title to property plainly controlled and enjoyed by the university and, hence, the state. . . .
>
> Although the foundation is a corporate entity legally distinct from that of the university, the function of the one is expressly "to promote the interests and welfare" of the other, and some of the highest officers of the university are required, under the bylaws of the foundation, to serve in some of the highest positions of the foundation. Thus, a further reality of the ownership of this property is the identification to a certain extent between the holder of bare legal title and the state as holder of the entire equitable interest. In this case, then, not only does the foundation hold but naked legal title to property controlled and enjoyed by the state, but a certain identity exists as well between the holder of naked legal title and the state. For these reasons we hold the property exempt from taxation as property belonging to the state [425 N.E.2d at 471].

Private nonprofit institutions are also often exempt from local real property taxation. Generally, the applicable state law provisions will exempt property of institutions organized for an educational purpose if the property at issue is used for that purpose. Sometimes such exemptions will extend to public institutions as well as private. In the *Southern Illinois University* case above, for example, the court held the married student housing to be exempt not only as state property but also as property of an educational institution devoted to an educational use. (The latter feature of this case is discussed later in this section.)

The states vary in the tests they apply to implement the educational use exemption. Some require that the property be used "exclusively" for educational purposes to qualify for an exemption. Others require only that the property be used "primarily" for educational purposes. The cases below illustrate the variety of decisions reached under different standards of "use" and differing factual circumstances.

Appeal of University of Pittsburgh, 407 Pa. 416, 180 A.2d 760 (1962), is a leading case concerning the exemption of houses provided by postsecondary institutions for their presidents. The court allowed an exemption under a lenient standard of use:

> The head of such an institution, whether he be called president or chancellor, represents to the public eye the "image" of the institution. Both an educator and an administrator of the tremendous "business" which any university or college now is, he must also be the official representative to host those who, for one reason or the other, find the university or college a place of interest and, if he is to assume the full scope and responsibility of his duties to the university or college, he must be universal in his contacts. Many years ago the Supreme Court of Massachusetts in *Amherst College v. Assessors,* 193 Mass. 168, 169, 170, 79 N.E. 248, stated: "At the same time the usage and customs of the college impose upon the president certain social obligations. . . . The scope, observations, and usage of the character mentioned are not matters of express requirement or exaction. They are, however, required of a president in the use of the house, and noncompliance with them unquestionably would subject him to unfavorable comment from the trustees and others, or, at least, be regarded as a failure on his part to discharge the obligations and hospitality associated with his official position." . . . The residence of the head of a university or college necessarily renders a real function, tangibly and intangibly, in the life of the institution. While its utility to the purposes and objectives of the institution is incapable of *exact* measurement and evaluation, it is nonetheless real and valuable [180 A.2d at 763].

Another court, citing the *Pittsburgh* case and using the same lenient test, denied an exemption for the house of a president emeritus. The court made a finding of fact that the house was not actually used for institutional purposes:

> [The court in the *Pittsburgh* case] held that a president's or chancellor's residence could enjoy tax exemption where the record showed that the majority of the events for which the residence was utilized bore a direct relationship to the proper functioning of the University of Pittsburgh and served its aims and objectives. In this appeal the record does not support the test laid down in [that case]. This record reflects that the president emeritus is retained on a consultative basis in development and public relations. The residence provided the president emeritus by the trustees appears to properly afford him an appropriate dwelling house commensurate with his past worthy service to Albright College. The record does not support, as in the case of the chancellor's residence of the University of Pittsburgh, that the residence in fact was used for the general purposes of Albright College [*In re Albright College,* 213 Pa. Super. Ct. 479, 249 A.2d at 835 (1968)].

In *Cook County Collector* v. *National College of Education,* 41 Ill. App. 633, 354 N.E.2d 507 (1976), the institution introduced extensive evidence of the institutional use of the president's house. The vice-president for business affairs testified that the house, "although used as the residence of the president, . . . is used as well for a number of educational, fund-raising, business, alumni, and social activities of the college," citing many examples. The exemption was denied, however, because the evidence did not satisfy the more stringent use test applied in that jurisdiction:

> On cross-examination . . . [the vice-president] stated that classes are not held in the home; that access to the home is by invitation only; and that the primary use of the premises is to house the president and his family.
> The trial court found that the property was not exempt, stating that it is used primarily for residential purposes as an accommodation for the president and only incidentally for college-related purposes [354 N.E.2d at 508].

Cases dealing with faculty and staff housing illustrate a similar split of opinions, depending on the facts of the case and the tests applied. In *MacMurray College* v. *Wright,* 38 Ill. 2d 272, 230 N.E.2d 846 (1967), for example, the court, applying a primary use test, denied a tax exemption:

> The colleges have failed to demonstrate clearly that the faculty and staff housing was primarily used for purposes which were reasonably necessary for the carrying out of the schools' educational purposes. The record does not show that any of the faculty or staff members of either college were required, because of their educational duties, to live in these residences or that they were required to or did perform any of their professional duties there. Also, though both records before us contain general statements that there were associations between the concerned faculty and students outside the classroom, there was no specific proof presented, aside from one isolated example, to show that student, academic, faculty, administrative, or any other type of college-connected activities were ever actually conducted at home by any member of the faculty or staff of either of the colleges [230 N.E.2d at 850].

Student dormitories are usually exempt from property taxation, even if the institution charges students rent. Other types of student housing, however, may present additional complexities. In *Southern Illinois University* v. *Booker,* 98 Ill. App. 3d 1062, 425 N.E.2d 465 (1981) (discussed above in this section), the court considered whether apartments for married students were exempt from taxation. The question was whether this housing was more like dormitory housing for single students, which is generally considered an exempt educational use in Illinois, or like faculty and staff housing, which is generally not considered an exempt educational use in Illinois. Making ample use of the facts, the court chose the former:

> Without belaboring the point, we think that married students, for purposes of the comparison with faculty members, are first and foremost

students. They are, therefore, more nearly analogous to single students, whose dormitory housing, as we have said, has long enjoyed tax-exempt status in Illinois. Married students seeking an education seem analogous to faculty members, for purposes of this comparison, only insofar as faculty members are often married and raising families. Faculty members, however, have usually completed their educations and are obviously employed, whereas students, by their very nature, have not completed their educations and are, if not unemployed, generally living on quite limited incomes. If a student cannot both attend school and afford to support his or her family in private housing, family obligations being what they are, the student cannot attend school, at least in the absence of low-cost family housing of the kind in issue here. Similarly, if a student cannot find available private housing for his or her family in a community crowded by students seeking housing not provided by the educational institution itself, the student cannot attend school. Therefore, we consider married student housing as necessary to the education of a married student as single-student housing is to a single student. Since the use of dormitory housing, serving essentially single students, is deemed primarily educational rather than residential, the use of family housing for married students should likewise be deemed primarily educational, and such property should enjoy tax-exempt status [425 N.E.2d at 474].

Similarly, courts may or may not accord sorority and fraternity houses the same tax treatment as student dormitories. If the institution itself owns the property, it must prove that the property is used for the educational purposes of the institution. In *Alford* v. *Emory University,* 216 Ga. 391, 116 S.E.2d 596 (1960), the court held that fraternity houses operated by the university as part of its residential program were entitled to a tax exemption:

Under the evidence in this case, these fraternity buildings were built by the university; they are regulated and supervised by the university; they are located in the heart of the campus, upon property owned by the university, required to be so located and to be occupied only by students of the university; adopted as a part of the dormitory and feeding system of the college, and an integral part of the operation of the college. In our opinion these fraternity houses are buildings erected for and used as a college, and not used for the purpose of making either private or corporate income or profit for the university, and our law says that they shall be exempt from taxes [116 S.E.2d at 601].

More recently *Alford* was followed in *Johnson* v. *Southern Greek Housing Corporation,* 307 S.E.2d 491 (Ga. 1983). Georgia Southern College, part of the University of Georgia System, organized the Southern Greek Housing Corporation in order to provide the college's fraternities and sororities with housing close to campus. The corporation, not the college, held title to the property on which the fraternity houses were to be built. The Georgia Supreme Court concluded that the fraternity and sorority houses would be " 'buildings erected for and used as a college' [quoting *Alford*] and that such buildings [would be] used for the operation of an educational

institution.'' The court held that, even though the property was owned by a corporation and not the college, the fact that the corporation ''performs an educational
function with and under the auspices of'' the college sufficed to bring the case within
Alford.

In contrast, the court in *Cornell University* v. *Board of Assessors,* 24 A.D. 526,
260 N.Y.S.2d 197 (1965), focused on the social uses of university-owned fraternity
houses to deny an exemption under an ''exclusive use'' test:

> It is true, of course, that the fraternities perform the essential func-
> tions of housing and feeding students, but it is clear that, in each case, the
> use of the premises is also devoted, in substantial part, to the social and
> other personal objectives of a privately organized, self-perpetuating club,
> controlled by graduate as well as student members. The burden of
> demonstrating these objectives to be educational purposes was not sustained
> and thus . . . [the lower court] properly found that the premises were not
> used ''exclusively'' for educational purposes, within the intendment of the
> exemption statute [260 N.Y.S.2d at 199].

But in a later case, *University of Rochester* v. *Wagner,* 63 A.D.2d 341, 408
N.Y.S.2d 157 (1978), affirmed, 47 N.Y.2d 833, 418 N.Y.S.2d (1979), the New
York courts qualified the *Cornell University* holding. The University of Rochester
owned nine fraternity houses for which it sought tax-exempt status. Unlike the *Cornell*
case, where the houses served ''social and other personal objectives'' (but somewhat
like the *Alford* case), the University of Rochester houses had become integrated into
the university's housing program: the university controlled the houses' ''exterior
grounds, walkways, and access points''; the houses' dining programs were part
of the university dining program; the university periodically ''review[ed] the health
and viability'' of the houses; and the university occasionally assigned nonfraternity
members to live in the houses. Applying the ''exclusive use'' test, and analogizing
these fraternity houses to dormitories, the courts granted the university's application for tax exemption:

> Like dormitories, the fraternity houses here serve the primary func-
> tion of housing and feeding students while they attend the university and
> complete the required curriculum. This use has been held to be in further-
> ance of the university's educational purposes. Moreover, the social inter-
> course and recreational activities that take place in the fraternity houses
> are similar both in quantity and quality to that which occurs in the dor-
> mitories. This social activity, although incidental to the primary use of the
> facilities, is essential to the personal, social, and moral development of the
> student and should not be found to change the character of the property
> from one whose use is reasonably incident to and in furtherance of the univer-
> sity's exempt purposes to a use which is not. For the same reason that dor-
> mitories have traditionally been held tax exempt, we see no reason why
> under the facts of this case the fraternity houses should not be accorded
> similar treatment [408 N.Y.S.2d at 164–65].

If an independently incorporated fraternity or sorority seeks its own property tax exemption, it must demonstrate an educational, religious, or charitable purpose independent of the university and prove that the property is used for that purpose. Greek letter and other social fraternities usually do not qualify for exemptions. In *Kappa Alpha Educational Foundation* v. *Holliday,* 226 A.2d 825 (Del. 1967), the court found that a fraternity house was being held as an investment by the corporation that owned it and therefore did not qualify for exemption. Professional fraternities may be somewhat more successful in establishing the educational purpose and use of their property in order to qualify for exemption. In *City of Memphis* v. *Alpha Beta Welfare Association,* 174 Tenn. 440, 126 S.W.2d 323 (1939), the appellate court upheld a district court's finding of fact that a medical fraternity's house was used exclusively for educational purposes:

> It is shown in proof that the student members of the fraternity by reason of being housed together receive medical, ethical, and cultural instruction that they otherwise would not get. The acquisition of the property in order that the students might be housed together was but the means to the end that the purpose of the Phi Chi Medical Fraternity to promote the welfare of medical students morally and scientifically might be more effectively carried out [126 S.W.2d at 326].

Even if a campus sorority or fraternity does not qualify for an educational exemption, it may qualify under a general statutory exemption for social organizations. In *Gamma Phi Chapter of Sigma Chi Building Fund Corp.* v. *Dade County,* 199 So. 2d 717 (Fla. 1967), the court held that the property of a national college fraternity was eligible for a statutory exemption designed for fraternal lodges. The exemption was denied on a technicality, however, because the fraternity missed the filing date.[5]

Athletic and recreational facilities owned by an educational institution may be exempt if the institution can prove that the facilities are used for educational purposes. Facilities far in excess of the institution's potential use may be subject to judicial scrutiny. In *Trustees of Rutgers University* v. *Piscataway Township,* 134 N.J.L. 85, 46 A.2d 56 (1946), the court held that a stadium with a seating capacity of twenty thousand owned by an institution with a student body of seventeen hundred was not entitled to a property tax exemption.

Dining facilities that are located on the property of an educational institution and whose purpose is to serve the college community rather than to generate a profit have long been recognized as part of the educational program and therefore entitled to a property tax exemption.[6] *Goodman* v. *University of Illinois Foundation,* 388 Ill. 363, 58 N.E.2d 33 (1944), upheld an exemption for dining halls (as well as dormitory and recreational facilities) even though the university derived incidental income by charging for the services. Dining facilities may be tax exempt even if the institution contracts with a private caterer to provide food services. In *Blair Academy* v. *Blairstown,* 95 N.J. Super. 583, 232 A.2d 178 (1967), the court held:

---

[5]The relevant cases on sorority and fraternity houses are collected in Annot., "Exemption from Taxation of College Fraternity or Sorority House," 66 A.L.R.2d 904 (1959 and periodic supp.).

[6]Cases on dining facilities are collected in Annot., "Property Used as Dining Rooms or Restaurants as Within Tax Exemptions Extended to Property of Religious, Educational, Charitable, or Hospital Organizations," 60 A.L.R.2d 521 (1960 and periodic supp.).

The use of a catering system to feed the students and faculty of this boarding school cannot be regarded as a commercial activity or business venture of the school. Blair pays for this catering service an annual charge of $376 per person. It has been found expedient by the management of the school to have such a private caterer, in lieu of providing its own personnel to furnish this necessary service. The practice has been carried on for at least ten years. Nor do we find material as affecting Blair's nonprofit status that the catering system uses Blair's kitchen equipment and facilities in its performance or that some of the caterer's employees were permitted by the school to occupy quarters at the school, rent-free [232 A.2d at 181–82].

Exemptions of various other kinds of institutional property also depend on the particular use of the property and the particular test applied in the jurisdiction. In *Princeton University Press* v. *Borough of Princeton*, 35 N.J. 209, 172 A.2d 420 (1961), a university press was denied exemption under an "exclusive use" test.

There is no question that the petitioner has been organized exclusively for the mental and moral improvements of men, women, and children. The press's publication of outstanding scholarly works, which the trade houses would not be apt to publish because of insufficient financial returns, carries out not only the purposes for which it was organized but also performs a valuable public service. It cannot be likewise concluded, however, that the property is *exclusively used* for the mental and moral improvement of men, women, and children as required by the statute. A substantial portion of the press's activity consists of printing work taken in for the purpose of offsetting the losses incurred in the publication of scholarly books. Such printing, which includes work done for educational and nonprofit organizations other than Princeton University, is undertaken for the purpose of making a profit. Hence, in this sense the printing takes on the nature of a commercial enterprise and, therefore, it cannot be said that the property is *exclusively used* for the statutory purpose [172 A.2d at 424].

But in *District of Columbia* v. *Catholic Education Press*, 199 F.2d 176 (D.C. Cir. 1952), a university press was granted an exemption:

The Catholic Education Press does not stand alone. It is a publishing arm of the [Catholic University of America]. It is an integral part of it. It has no separate life except bare technical corporate existence. It is not a private independent corporation, but to all intents and purposes it is a facility of the university. . . .

If the Catholic University of America, in its own name, should engage in activities identical with those of its subsidiary, the Catholic Education Press, we suppose its right to exemption from taxation on the personal property used in such activities would not be questioned. We see no reason for denying the exemption to the university merely because it chooses to do the work through a separate nonprofit corporation [199 F.2d at 178–79].

In *City of Ann Arbor* v. *University Cellar*, 401 Mich. 270, 258 N.W.2d 1 (1977), the issue was the application of a local personal property tax to the inventory of a campus bookstore at the University of Michigan. The statute provided an exemption for property "belonging to" the state or to an incorporated educational institution. The bookstore, the University Cellar, was a nonprofit corporation whose creation had been authorized by the university's board of regents. The majority of the corporation's board of directors, however, were appointed by the student government. The court determined that the directors did not represent the board of regents or the university administration and that the regents did not control the operation of the bookstore. Distinguishing the *Catholic Education Press* case, where the separately incorporated entity was essentially the alter ego of the university, the court denied the exemption because the property could not be said to "belong to" the university.

As a number of the above cases demonstrate, if an otherwise eligible postsecondary institution establishes or affiliates with a separately incorporated entity, the entity's property may or may not be eligible for tax exemption. Similarly, if a postsecondary institution leases some of its property to another entity, the property may or may not retain its exempt status. In such cases, exemption again depends on the use of the property and the exemption tests applied in the jurisdiction,[7] and particular consideration may be given to the extent to which the institution controls the property in the hands of the separate entity.

If institutional property is denied an exemption and subjected to property taxation, the institution's administrators must then deal with the problem of valuation. After a property tax assessor makes the initial assessment, the institution may challenge the assessment through procedures established by the local government. The assessment of institutional property may be difficult because of the absence of comparable market values. In *Dartmouth Corp. of Alpha Delta* v. *Town of Hanover*, 332 A.2d 390 (N.H. 1975), an independent fraternity challenged the assessment of its property. To arrive at an evaluation, the town had compared the fraternity property to dormitory facilities. The court upheld the assessor's estimate, reasoning that "in view of the functional similarity between fraternities and dormitories and considering that the college regulates the rents of both types of facilities, it was not unlawful for the board to consider the income and costs of the fraternity buildings if used as dormitories in ascertaining their assessed value."

5.3.3. Sales and admission taxes. A local government may have authority to impose a sales tax on the sales or purchases of an educational institution. The institution may claim a specific exemption based on a particular provision of the sales tax ordinance or a general exemption provided by a state statute or the state constitution. The language of the provision may limit the exemption only to the sales or to the purchases of an educational institution or may cover both. The institution's eligibility for exemption from these taxes, as from property taxes, depends on the language of the provision creating the exemption, as interpreted by the courts, and the particular factual circumstances.[8]

---

[7]Cases dealing with leased property are collected in Annot., "Tax Exemption—Leased Property," 55 A.L.R.3d 430 (1974 and periodic supp.).

[8]The relevant cases on sales taxes, as well as "use" taxes sometimes levied in place of sales taxes, are collected in Annot., "Exemption of Charitable or Educational Organization from Sales or Use Tax," 53 A.L.R.3d 748 (1973 and periodic supp.).

New York University v. *Taylor,* 251 A.D. 444, 296 N.Y.S. 848 (1937), arose after the comptroller of the city of New York tried to impose a sales tax on both the sales and the purchases of a nonprofit educational institution. The law in effect at that time provided that "receipts from sales or services . . . by or to semipublic institutions . . . shall not be subject to tax hereunder." Semipublic institutions were defined as "those charitable and religious institutions which are supported wholly or in part by public subscriptions or endowment and are not organized or operated for profit." The court made a finding of fact that the university was a "semipublic institution" within the meaning of the statute and therefore was not subject to taxation on its sales or purchases.

Sales by an educational institution may be exempt even if some of the institution's activities generate a profit. The exemption will depend on the use of the profits and the language of the exemption. In *YMCA* v. *City of Philadelphia,* 139 Pa. Super. Ct. 332, 11 A.2d 529 (1940), the court held that the sale was not subject to taxation under an ordinance that exempted sales by or to semipublic institutions:

> Certainly, the ordinance contemplated a departure by such institutions from the activities of a public charity, which, in its narrowest sense, sells nothing and is supported wholly by public subscriptions and contributions or endowment; and may be said to recognize that many institutions organized for charitable purposes and supported in part by public subscriptions or endowment do engage in certain incidental activities, of a commercial nature, the proceeds of which, and any profits derived therefrom, are devoted to the general charitable work of the institution and applied to no alien or selfish purpose [11 A.2d at 531].

City of Boulder v. *Regents of the University of Colorado,* 501 P.2d 123 (Colo. 1972), concerned the attempt of the local government to impose an admission tax on various events, including intercollegiate football games, held on the University of Colorado campus. The court held that the city could not impose tax collection responsibilities on the university because the university as a branch of the state government could claim sovereign immunity. The Supreme Court of Colorado quoted the trial court's opinion with approval:

> "In the instant case the city is attempting to impose duties on the board of regents which would necessarily interfere with the regents' control of the university. The constitution establishes a statewide university and vests control in the board of regents. The board of regents has *exclusive* control and direction of all funds of, and appropriations to, the university. . . . Thus, the city of Boulder cannot force the regents to apply any funds toward the collection of the tax in question. Even if the city claims that sufficient funds would be generated by the tax to compensate the regents for collection expense and, arguably, such funds could be paid to the regents by the city, the regents are still vested with the 'general supervision' of the university. The university would necessarily be required to expend both money and manpower for the collection, identification, and payment of such funds to the city. This interferes with the financial conduct of the university and the allocation of its manpower for its statewide educational duties. . . .

"Thus, since the constitution has established a statewide university at Boulder and vested general supervisory control in a statewide board of regents and management in control of the state, a city, even though a home rule city, has no power to interfere with the management or supervision of the activities of the University of Colorado. If the city of Boulder was allowed to impose duties on the university, such duties would necessarily interfere with the functions of the state institution. There is no authority to permit the city of Boulder to force a state institution to collect such a local tax. Consequently, the city of Boulder cannot require the board of regents of the University of Colorado, to become involuntary collectors of the city of Boulder's admission tax" [501 P.2d at 125].

The court also held, over two dissents, that the admission tax was itself invalid as applied to various university functions.

When academic departments of the university, or others acting under the auspices of the university, sponsor lectures, dissertations, art exhibitions, concerts, and dramatic performances, whether or not an admission fee is charged, these functions become a part of the educational process. This educational process is not merely for the enrolled students of the university, but it is a part of the educational process for those members of the public attending the events. In our view the home rule authority of a city does not permit it to tax a person's acquisition of education furnished by the state. We hold that the tax is invalid when applied to university lectures, dissertations, art exhibitions, concerts, and dramatic performances [501 P.2d at 126].

With respect to football games, however, the tax's validity was affirmed because the university had not made "a showing that football is so related to the educational process that its devotees may not be taxed by a home rule city." This latter ruling is "probably academic," as the court acknowledged, since under sovereign immunity the university cannot be required to collect the tax, even if it is valid.[9]

Sec. 5.4. Student Voting in the Community

The passage of the Twenty-Sixth Amendment to the U.S. Constitution, lowering the voting age to eighteen, created several new problems for postsecondary administrators. On some voting issues, administrators may at most play an intermediary or advocate role in disputes between students and the community. Other issues require positive action by administrators to establish guidelines for voting activities on campus.

5.4.1. Registering to vote. The extension of the franchise did not automatically give every citizen over eighteen the right to vote. All potential voters must register with the board of elections of their legal residence in order to exercise their right.

---

[9]Relevant cases on admission taxes are collected in Annot., "Validity of Municipal Admission Tax for College Football Games or Other College Sponsored Events, " 60 A.L.R.3d 1027 (1974 and periodic supp.).

Determining the legal residence of students attending residential institutions has created major controversies. Some small communities near colleges and universities, fearful of the impact of the student vote, have tried to limit student registration, while students eager to participate in local affairs and to avoid the inconveniences of absentee voting have pushed for local registration.

The trend of the cases has been to overturn statutes or practices that impede student registration. At issue in *Jolicoeur* v. *Mihaly*, 5 Cal. 3d 565, 488 P.2d 1 (1971), was a statute which created an almost conclusive presumption that an unmarried minor's residence was her parents' home. The court held that this statute violated the equal protection clause and the Twenty-Sixth Amendment:

> Sophisticated legal arguments regarding a minor's presumed residence cannot blind us to the real burden placed on the right to vote and associated rights of political expression by requiring minor voters residing apart from their parents to vote in their parents' district. . . .
>
> An unmarried minor must be subject to the same requirements in proving the location of his domicile as is any other voter. Fears of the way minors may vote or of their impermanency in the community may not be used to justify special presumptions—conclusive or otherwise—that they are not bona fide residents of the community in which they live.
>
> It is clear that respondents have abridged petitioners' right to vote in precisely one of the ways that Congress sought to avoid—by singling minor voters out for special treatment and effectively making many of them vote by absentee ballot. . . .
>
> Respondents' policy would clearly frustrate youthful willingness to accomplish change at the local level through the political system. Whether a youth lives in Quincy, Berkeley, or Orange County, he will not be brought into the bosom of the political system by being told that he may not have a voice in the community in which he lives, but must instead vote wherever his parents live or may move to. Surely as well, such a system would give any group of voters less incentive "in devising responsible programs" in the town in which they live [488 P.2d at 4, 7].

Another court has invalidated a Michigan statute that created a rebuttable presumption that students are not voting residents of the district where their institution is located. The statute was implemented through elaborate procedures applicable only to students. The court held that the statute infringed the right to vote, in violation of the equal protection clause (*Williams* v. *Bentley*, 385 Mich. 670, 189 N.Y.2d 423 (1971)). And in *United States* v. *State of Texas*, 445 F. Supp. 1245 (S.D. Tex. 1978), a three-judge federal court enjoined the voting registrar of Waller County from applying a burdensome presumption of nonresidency to unmarried dormitory students at Prairie View A&M University. The U.S. Supreme Court summarily affirmed the lower court's decision without issuing any written opinion (*Symm* v. *United States*, 439 U.S. 1105 (1979)).

In contrast, courts have upheld statutory provisions making attendance at a local college or university irrelevant as a factor in determining a student's residence. In *Whittingham* v. *Board of Elections*, 320 F. Supp. 889 (N.D.N.Y. 1970), a special three-judge court upheld a "gain or loss provision" of the New York constitution.

This provision, found in many state constitutions and statutes, requires a student to prove residency by indicia other than student status. The *Whittingham* case was followed by *Gorenberg* v. *Onondaga County Board of Elections,* 38 A.D.2d 145, 328 N.Y.S.2d 198 (1972), modified, 31 N.Y.2d 36, 286 N.E.2d 247 (1972), upholding a New York State statute specifying criteria for determining student residence, including dependency, employment, marital status, age, and location of property.

A few general rules for determining student residency emerge. Mere presence as a student is not sufficient to establish residency. A student must manifest intent to establish residency in the community. Present intent to establish residency is probably sufficient. Students who intend to leave the community after graduation do not have such intent. Students who are uncertain about their postgraduate plans, but consider the home community their home for the time, probably do have such intent. A statute that required proof of intent to remain *indefinitely* in the community after graduation was held a denial of equal protection in *Whatley* v. *Clark,* 482 F.2d 1230 (5th Cir. 1973).

Uncertainties concerning future plans and the difficulties of proving intent complicate the application of these general rules. The indicia used by boards of election to determine whether a student intends to establish residency include vacation activity, the type of home established, the location of property, the choice of banks and other services, membership in community groups, and the declaration of residence for other purposes such as tax payment and auto registration.

5.4.2. Scheduling elections. The only reported case that deals with the timing of an election in a district with a substantial student population is *Walgren* v. *Board of Selectmen of Town of Amherst,* 519 F.2d 1364 (1st Cir. 1975). The appellate court's opinion lays out the special facts of the case:

> The controversy arises from events which took place over a ten-day period in December 1972, during which the town selectment, at plaintiff Walgren's urging, endeavored to change the scheduled date for the town caucus, the primary election in which nominees for the positions of town officer and town meeting member are selected. On December 10, 1972, Walgren protested the then recently published schedule for the 1973 elections on the ground that the caucus date of January 19 would be during the winter recess of the University of Massachusetts, when some ten thousand dormitory students would be out of town. On December 11, the board voted to reconsider the schedule at its December 18 meeting. After a week of public reaction, both pro and con, a long and animated meeting was held on December 18, at the end of which the board voted to establish a new calendar. But the dates for the caucus and the final election proposed by Walgren, January 29 and March 1, raised the possibility of a conflict with a state requirement that thirty-one days separate the two dates. The board, being of the opinion that statutory notice for the proposed new dates would have to be published by the following day, provisionally adopted them, subject to advice of counsel. When, on December 19, the advice was received that the dates would be illegal, the board, at a special meeting in the evening, turned down its counsel's proposal that the town meeting itself be moved ahead by a week, and reinstated the original calendar [519 F.2d at 1365].

The lower court refused to set aside the election. Although disagreeing with the lower court's finding that the burden on students' and faculty members' right to vote was insignificant, the appellate court relied on the good-faith efforts of the selectmen to schedule an appropriate date:

> In short, we would be disturbed if, given time to explore alternatives and given alternatives which would satisfy all reasonable town objectives, a town continued to insist on elections during vacations or recess, secure in the conviction that returning to town and absentee voting would be considered insignificant burdens.
>
> The critical element which in our view serves to sustain the 1973 election is the foreshortened time frame within which the selectment were forced to face up to and resolve a problem which was then novel. . . .
>
> We would add that, under the circumstances of this case, even if we had found the burden impermissible, we would have looked upon the novelty and complexity of the issue, the shortness of time, and the good-faith efforts of the defendants as sufficient justification for refusing to order a new election at this late date [519 F.2d at 1368].

The special facts of the case and the narrowness of the court's holding limit *Walgren*'s authority as precedent. But *Walgren* does suggest that purposefully scheduling an election so as to disenfranchise an identifiable segment of the student electorate can be successfully challenged under some circumstances.

5.4.3. Canvassing and registration on campus. The regulation of voter canvassing and registration on campus is the voting issue most likely to require the direct involvement of college and university administrators. Any regulation must accommodate the First Amendment rights of the canvassers, the First Amendment rights of the students who may be potential listeners, the privacy interests of those students who may not wish to be canvassed, the requirements of local election law, and the institution's interests in order and safety. Not all of these considerations have been explored in litigation.

In *James v. Nelson,* 349 F. Supp. 1061 (N.D. Ill. 1972), Northern Illinois University had for some time prohibited all canvassing in student living areas. After receiving requests to modify this prohibition, the university proposed a new regulation, which would have permitted canvassing under specified conditions. Before the new regulation could go into effect, however, it had to be adopted in a referendum by two thirds of the students in each dormitory, after which individual floors could implement it by a two-thirds vote. The court held that this referendum requirement unconstitutionally infringed the freedom of association and expression rights of the students who wished to canvas or be canvassed. The basis for the *James* decision is difficult to discern. The court emphasized that the proposed canvassing regulation was not "in any way unreasonable or beyond the powers of the university administration to impose in the interests of good order and the safety and comfort of the student body." If the proposed regulation was constitutional, a referendum adopting it would not infringe anyone's constitutional rights. The court's implicit ruling must be that the university's blanket prohibition on canvassing was an infringement of First Amendment rights, and a requirement that this prohibition could be removed only by a two-thirds vote of the students in each dormitory and each floor was also an infringement on the rights of those students who would desire a liberalized canvassing policy.

National Movement for the Student Vote v. *Regents of the University of California,* 50 Cal. App. 3d 131, 123 Cal. Rptr. 141 (1975), was decided on statutory grounds. A local statute permitted registrars to register voters at their residence. University policy, uniformly enforced, did not allow canvassing in student living areas. Registrars were permitted to canvass in public areas of the campus and in the lobbies of the dormitories. The court held that the privacy interest of the students limited the registrars' right to canvass to reasonable times and places and that the limitations imposed by the university were reasonable and in compliance with the law. In determining reasonableness, the court emphasized the following facts:

> There was evidence and findings to the effect that dining and other facilities of the dormitories are on the main floor; the private rooms of the students are on the upper floors; the rooms do not contain kitchen, washing, or toilet facilities; each student must walk from his or her room to restroom facilities in the halls of the upper floors in order to bathe or use the toilet facilities; defendants, in order to "recognize and enhance the privacy" of the students and to minimize assaults upon them and thefts of their property, have maintained a policy and regulations prohibiting solicitation, distribution of materials, and recruitment of students in the upper-floor rooms; students in the upper rooms complained to university officials about persons coming to their rooms and canvassing them and seeking their registrations; defendants permitted signs regarding the election to be posted throughout the dormitories and permitted deputy registrars to maintain tables and stands in the main lobby of each dormitory for registration of students; students in each dormitory had to pass through the main lobby thereof in order to go to and from their rooms; a sign encouraging registration to vote was at each table, and students registered to vote at the tables [123 Cal. Rptr. at 146].

Though the *National Movement* v. *Regents* decision is based on a statute, the court's language suggests that similar principles and factors would be used in considering the constitutionality of a public institution's canvassing regulations under the First Amendment. In a later case, *Harrell* v. *Southern Illinois University,* 120 Ill. App. 3d 161, 457 N.E.2d 971 (1983), the court did use similar reasoning in upholding, against a First Amendment challenge, a university policy that prohibited political candidates from canvassing dormitory rooms except during designated hours in the weeks preceding elections. The court also indicated that the First Amendment (as well as that state's election law) would permit similar restrictions on canvassing by voter registrars. Thus, although public institutions may not completely prohibit voter canvassing on campus, they may impose reasonable restrictions on the "time, place, and manner" of canvassing in dormitories and other locations on campus. (See also Section 5.6.4.2.)

5.4.4. Reapportionment. A series of U.S. Supreme Court decisions in the early 1960s established that "the fundamental principle of representative government in this country is one of equal representation for equal numbers of people,

without regard to race, sex, economic status, or place of residence within a state"
(*Reynolds* v. *Sims,* 377 U.S. 533, 560–61 (1964)). This "one person, one vote" stan-
dard was extended to local government elections in *Avery* v. *Midland County,* 390
U.S. 474 (1968) and *Hadley* v. *Junior College District,* 397 U.S. 50 (1970):

> Whenever a state or local government decides to select persons by
> popular election to perform governmental functions, the equal protection
> clause of the Fourteenth Amendment requires that each qualified voter must
> be given an equal opportunity to participate in that election, and when
> members of an elective body are chosen from separate districts, each district
> must be established on a basis that will insure, as far as is practicable, that
> equal numbers of voters can vote for proportionately equal numbers of of-
> ficials [397 U.S. at 56].

Consistent with this basic constitutional requirement, local and state governments must periodically "reapportion" the populations of election districts and
redraw their boundaries accordingly. If the election districts containing the largest
percentages of student voters were to include more voters per elected official than
other districts, thus diluting the voting strength of district voters (malapportion-
ment), students or other voters could claim a violation of "one person, one vote"
principles. Even if the districts with concentration of student voters have populations
substantially equal to those of other districts, students could still raise an equal protection challenge if the district lines were drawn in a way that minimized their voting
strength (gerrymandering). Case law indicates, however, that both types of claims
would be very difficult to sustain. Beginning with *Abate* v. *Mundt,* 403 U.S. 182
(1971) (local elections) and *Mahan* v. *Howell,* 410 U.S. 315 (1973) (state elections),
the U.S. Supreme Court has accepted various justifications for departing from strict
population equality among districts, thus making it harder to prevail on malap-
portionment claims. And in *Gaffney* v. *Cummings,* 412 U.S. 735 (1973), and later
cases, the Court has flagged its reluctance to scrutinize gerrymandering that is undertaken to balance or maintain the voting strengths of political groups within the
jurisdiction.

In re House Bill 2620, 225 Kan. 827, 595 P.2d 334 (1979)—apparently the
only reported case dealing with student challenges to reapportionment—also illustrates the difficulty of prevailing on such claims. The student senate of the University
of Kansas (and others) filed suit objecting to the reapportionment of two state
legislative districts covering the city of Lawrence. Prior to reapportionment, the
three voting precincts with the most concentrated student vote ("L," "K," and
"O") were located in one legislative district. The reapportionment plan placed two
of these precincts in one district and the third in a separate district. The students
contended that this redistricting was done in order to split the student vote, thus
diluting student voting power. The Kansas Supreme Court disagreed, holding that
the redistricting did not invidiously discriminate against students:

> There are presently 22,228 students enrolled in the University of
> Kansas. It is stated [that] a large portion of the students hold similar political
> beliefs, and those living in precincts identified as "L," "K," and "O"
> form a cohesive homogenous unit that cannot be separated without discri-

mination. . . In 1978 there were 5,138 "census persons" residing in these three precincts, and 3,156 voters were registered on October 27, 1978. Even assuming that all registered voters in these three precincts were students, which is highly questionable, the three precincts involved would represent no more than 14.2 percent of the students in the university.

Other factors militate against a solid cohesive student body. The students come from different family and political backgrounds and from different localities. Many students vote in their home districts. It is extremely doubtful that all would be of one party. Considering modern trends in higher education, each student is trained for independent thinking. Unanimity among a student body seems unlikely. Keeping all these factors in mind, we cannot say that removing precincts K and O from District 44 and placing them in the newly constituted District 46 was done for the purpose of canceling the voting strength of the 22,228 students attending the University of Kansas. We are not convinced that invidious discrimination resulted [595 P.2d at 343–44].

Sec. 5.5. Relations with Local Police

Since the academic community is part of the surrounding community, it will generally be within the geographical jurisdiction of one or more local (town, village, city, county) police forces. The circumstances under which local police may and will come onto the campus, and their authority once on campus, are thus of concern to every administrator. Their role on campus depends on a mixture of considerations: the state and local law of the jurisdiction, federal constitutional limitations on police powers, the adequacy of the institution's own security services, and the terms of any explicit or implicit understanding between local police and campus authorities.

If the institution has its own uniformed security officers, administrators must decide what working relationships these officers will have with local police. This decision will depend partly on the extent of the security officers' authority, especially regarding arrests, searches, and seizures—authority that should also be carefully delineated (see generally Section 4.14.1). Similarly, administrators must understand the relationship between arrest and prosecution in local courts, on the one hand, and campus disciplinary proceedings on the other (see Section 4.13.3). Although administrators cannot make crime an internal affair by hiding evidence of crime from local police, they may be able to assist local law enforcement officials in determining prosecution priorities. Campus and local officials may also be able to cooperate in determining whether a campus proceeding should be stayed pending the outcome of a court proceeding, or vice versa.

The powers of local police are circumscribed by various federal constitutional provisions, particularly the Fourth Amendment strictures on arrests, searches, and seizures. These provisions limit local police authority on both public and private campuses. Under the Fourth Amendment, local police must often obtain a warrant before arresting or searching a member of the academic community or searching or seizing any private property on the campus (see Section 4.10.2). On a private institution's campus, nearly all the property may be private, and local police may need a warrant or the consent of whoever effectively controls the property before entering most areas of the campus. On a public institution's campus, it is more difficult to determine which property would be considered public and which private, and thus more difficult to determine when local police must have a warrant or consent prior to entry. In general, for both public and private institutions, police will need a warrant or consent before entering any area in which members of the academic community have a "reasonable expectation of privacy" (see generally *Katz* v. *United States,* 389 U.S. 347 (1967)). The constitutional rules and concepts are especially complex in this area, however; and administrators should consult counsel whenever questions arise concerning the authority of local police on campus.

In *People* v. *Dickson,* 91 Cal. App. 3d 409, 154 Cal. Rptr. 116 (1979), a California appellate court considered the validity of a warrantless search of a chemistry laboratory conducted by local police and campus security officers at the Bakersfield campus of California State University. The search uncovered samples of an illegal drug and materials used in its manufacture—evidence that led to the arrest and conviction of the defendant, a chemistry professor who used the laboratory. The court upheld the search and the conviction because, under the facts of the case (particularly facts indicating ready access to the laboratory by many persons, including campus police), the professor had no "objectively reasonable expectation of privacy" in his laboratory. That this particular search was upheld even though the officers did not procure a warrant, however, does not mean that the practice of obtaining warrants can be routinely dispensed with. When there is time to do so, procuring a warrant or the consent of the person whose expectation of privacy may be invaded is still the surest policy.

In 1980 Congress enacted legislation that limits police search-and-seizure activities on college campuses. The legislation, the Privacy Protection Act of 1980, 42 U.S.C. sec. 2000aa *et seq.,* was passed in part to counter the U.S. Supreme Court's decision in *Zurcher* v. *Stanford Daily,* 436 U.S. 547 (1978). In *Zurcher* the Palo Alto, California, Police Department had obtained a warrant to search the files of the *Stanford Daily,* a student newspaper, for photographs of participants in a demonstration during which several police officers had been assaulted. The lower court found probable cause to believe that the *Stanford Daily*'s files did contain such photographs, but no probable cause to believe that the newspaper itself was engaged in any wrongdoing. The U.S. Supreme Court held that the *Stanford Daily,* even though an innocent third party and even though engaged in publication activities, had no First or Fourth Amendment rights to assert against the search warrant.

The Privacy Protection Act's coverage is not confined to newspapers, the subject of the *Zurcher* case. As its legislative history makes clear, the Act also protects scholars and other persons engaged in "public communication"—that is, the "flow of information to the public" (see S. Rep. No. 874, 96th Congress, 2d Sess., in 4 *United States Code Congressional and Administrative News* 3950, 3956 (1980)).

Section 101(a) of the Act pertains to the "work product materials" of individuals intending "to disseminate to the public a newspaper, book, broadcast, or other similar form of public communication." The section prohibits the searching for or seizure of the work product of such individuals by any "government officer or employee [acting] in connection with the investigation or prosecution of a criminal offense." There are several exceptions, however, to the general prohibition in Section 101(a). First, search and seizure of work product material is permitted where "there is probable cause to believe that the person possessing such materials has committed or is committing the criminal offense to which the materials relate'' and this offense does not consist of ''the receipt, possession, communication, or withholding of such materials.'' Second, search and seizure is permitted where there is probable cause to believe that the possessor has committed or is committing an offense consisting ''of the receipt, possession, or communication of information relating to the national defense, classified information, or restricted data'' prohibited under specified provisions of national security laws. Third, search and seizure of work product is permitted when ''there is reason to believe that the immediate seizure of such materials is necessary to prevent the death of, or serious bodily injury to, a human being.''

Section 101(b) of the Act covers ''documentary materials, other than work product materials.'' The section prohibits search and seizure of such materials in the same way that Section 101(a) prohibits search and seizures of work product. The same exceptions to the general prohibition also apply. There are also two additional exceptions unique to 101(b), under which search and seizure of documentary materials is permitted if:

> (3) there is reason to believe that the giving of notice pursuant to a subpoena duces tecum would result in the destruction, alteration, or concealment of such materials; or
> (4) such materials have not been produced in response to a court order directing compliance with a subpoena duces tecum, and—
>> (A) all appellate remedies have been exhausted; or
>> (B) there is reason to believe that the delay in an investigation or trial occasioned by further proceedings relating to the subpoena would threaten the interests of justice.

Section 106 of the Act authorizes a civil suit for damages for any person subjected to a search or seizure that is illegal under Section 101(a) or 101(b).

The Act's language and legislative history clearly indicate that the Act applies to local and state, as well as federal, government officers and employees. It thus limits the authority of city, town, and county police officers both on campus and in off-campus investigations of campus scholars or journalists. The Act limits police officers and other government officials, however, only when they are investigating criminal, as opposed to civil, offenses. Scholars and journalists thus are not protected, for example, from the seizure of property to satisfy outstanding tax debts or from the regulatory inspections or compliance reviews conducted by government agencies administering civil laws. Moreover, the Act's legislative history makes clear that traditional subpoena powers and limitations are untouched by the Act (see S. Rep. No. 874, 96th Congress, 2d Sess., in 4 *United States Code Congressional and Administrative News* 3950, 3956–60 (1980)). (Subpoenas of scholarly information are discussed in this volume, Section 3.6.5.)

Different problems arise when local police enter a campus not to make an arrest or conduct a search but to engage in surveillance of members of the institutional community. In *White* v. *Davis,* 13 Cal. 3d 757, 120 Cal. Rptr. 94, 533 P.2d 222 (1975), a history professor at UCLA sued the Los Angeles police chief to enjoin the use of undercover police agents for generalized surveillance in the university. Unidentified police agents had registered at the university and compiled dossiers on students and professors based on information obtained during classes and public meetings. The California Supreme Court held that such action was a prima facie violation of students' and faculty members' First Amendment freedoms of speech, assembly, and association, as well as the "right-to-privacy" provision of the California constitution. The case was returned to the trial court to determine whether the police were acting on any compelling state interest that would justify the infringement of constitutional rights.

The court's opinion differentiates the First Amendment surveillance problem from the more traditional Fourth Amendment search-and-seizure problem:

> The most familiar limitations on police investigatory and surveillance activities, of course, find embodiment in the Fourth Amendment of the federal Constitution and article I, section 13 (formerly art. I, sec. 19) of the California constitution. On numerous occasions in the past, these provisions have been applied to preclude specific ongoing police investigatory practices. Thus, for example, the court in *Wirin* v. *Parker*, 48 Cal. 2d 890, 313 P.2d 844, prohibited the police practice of conducting warrantless surveillance of private residences by means of concealed microphones. . . .
>
> Unlike these past cases involving the limits on police surveillance prescribed by the constitutional "search-and-seizure" provisions, the instant case presents the more unusual question of the limits placed upon police investigatory activities by the guarantees of freedom of speech (U.S. Const. 1st and 14th Amends.; Cal. Const., art. I, sec. 2). As discussed below, this issue is not entirely novel; to our knowledge, however, the present case represents the first instance in which a court has confronted the issue in relation to ongoing police surveillance of a university community.
>
> Our analysis of the limits imposed by the First Amendment upon police surveillance activities must begin with the recognition that with respect to First Amendment freedoms "the Constitution's protection is not limited to direct interference with fundamental rights" (*Healy* v. *James* (1972) 408 U.S. 169, 183, 92 S. Ct. 2338, 2347, 33 L. Ed. 2d 266). Thus, although police surveillance of university classrooms and organizations' meetings may not constitute a direct prohibition of speech or association, such surveillance may still run afoul of the constitutional guarantee if the effect of such activity is to chill constitutionally protected activity. . . .
>
> As a practical matter, the presence in a university classroom of undercover officers taking notes to be preserved in police dossiers must inevitably inhibit the exercise of free speech both by professors and students [533 P.2d at 228–29].

The court also emphasized the special danger that police surveillance poses for academic freedom:

> The threat to First Amendment freedoms posed by any covert intelligence gathering network is considerably exacerbated when, as in the instant case, the police surveillance activities focus upon university classrooms and their environs. As the United States Supreme Court has recognized time and again: "The vigilant protection of constitutional freedoms is nowhere more

vital than in the community of American schools" (*Shelton* v. *Tucker,* 364 U.S. 479, 487, 81 S. Ct. 247, 251, 5 L. Ed. 2d 231 (1960)).

The police investigatory conduct at issue unquestionably poses . . . [a] debilitating . . . threat to academic freedom. . . . According to the allegations of the complaint, which for purposes of this appeal must be accepted as true, the Los Angeles Police Department has established a network of undercover agents which keeps regular check on discussions occurring in various university classes. Because the identity of such police officers is unknown, no professor or student can be confident that whatever opinion he may express in class will not find its way into a police file. . . . The crucible of new thought is the university classroom; the campus is the sacred ground of free discussion. Once we expose the teacher or the student to possible future prosecution for the ideas he may express, we forfeit the security that nourishes change and advancement. The censorship of totalitarian regimes that so often condemns developments in art, science, and politics is but a step removed from the inchoate surveillance of free discussion in the university; such intrusion stifles creativity and to a large degree shackles democracy [533 P.2d at 229–31].

The principles of *White* v. *Davis* would apply equally to local police surveillance at a private institution. As an agency of government, the police are prohibited from violating any person's freedom of expression or right to privacy, whether on a public campus or a private one.[10]

Sec. 5.6. Community Access to Institutional Property

5.6.1. Public versus private institutions. Postsecondary institutions have often been the location for many types of events that attract people from the surrounding community and sometimes from other parts of the state, country, or world. Because of their capacity for large audiences and the sheer numbers of students and faculty and staff members on campus every day, postsecondary institutions provide an excellent forum for speakers, conferences, exhibits, pamphleteering, and other kinds of information exchanges. In addition, cultural, entertainment, and sporting events attract large numbers of outside persons. Whether public or private, postsecondary institutions have considerable authority to determine how and when their property will be used for such events and to regulate access to such events by outside persons. Although a public institution's authority is more limited than that of a private institution, the case of *State* v. *Schmid,* 84 N.J. 535, 423 A.2d 615 (1980), diminishes the distinction between public and private institutions' authority to deny access to outsiders who want to engage in expressional activities. (For discussion see this volume, Section 5.6.3.)

[10]The right-to-privacy reasoning used in *White* v. *Davis* would apply only to states that recognize an individual right to privacy similar to that created under the California constitution. The applicability of the case's First Amendment reasoning may be limited to states whose courts would grant professors or students standing to raise illegal surveillance claims. The *White* plaintiffs obtained standing under a California "taxpayer standing" statute. They apparently would not have succeeded in the federal court, since the U.S. Supreme Court has held, in *Laird* v. *Tatum,* 408 U.S. 1 (1972), that government surveillance does not cause the type of specific harm necessary to establish federal court standing.

Both private and public institutions customarily have ownership or leasehold interests in their campuses and buildings—interests protected by the property law of the state. Subject to this statutory and common law, both types of institution have authority to regulate how and by whom their property is used. Typically, an institution's authority to regulate use by its students and faculty members is limited by the contractual commitments it has made to these groups (see Sections 3.1 and 4.1.3). Thus, for instance, students may have contractual rights to the reasonable use of dormitory rooms and the public areas of residence halls or of campus libraries and study rooms; and faculty members may have contractual rights to the reasonable use of office space or classrooms. With respect to the outside community, however, such contractual rights usually do not exist.

A public institution's authority to regulate the use of its property is further limited by the federal Constitution, in particular the First Amendment, and may also be affected by state statutes or regulations applicable to state property in general or specifically to the property of state educational institutions. Unlike contract law limitations, these limitations on institutional authority may provide rights of access and use not only to faculty members and students (see, for example, Sections 4.7.1, 4.7.2, and 4.8.1 on the First Amendment usage rights of students) but also to the outside community.

The following subsections explore various statutes, regulations, and constitutional considerations that affect outsiders' access to the property of postsecondary institutions.

5.6.2. Speaker bans. Administrators who seek to avoid disruption by banning particular speakers or events have inevitably clashed not only with the participants but with those on campus who demand the right to hear the speaker or attend the event. These clashes have sometimes resulted in litigation. Most of the cases on access to campus facilities have involved regulations on off-campus speakers, commonly referred to as "speaker bans."

Since rules regulating off-campus speakers provide a convenient target for a First Amendment attack, such rules should be drafted with extreme care. Much of the law that has developed concerning faculty members' and students' free speech rights on campus also applies to the issue of off-campus speakers (see Sections 3.6 and 4.7).

Under the First Amendment, administrators of public institutions may reasonably regulate the time, place, and manner of speeches and other communicative activities, whether engaged in by on- or off-campus persons. Problems arise when these basic rules of order are expanded to include regulations under which a speaker can be banned because of the content of his speech or his political affiliation or persuasion. Such regulations are particularly susceptible to judicial invalidation because they are prior restraints on speech (Section 4.7.3). *Stacy* v. *Williams,* 306 F. Supp. 963 (N.D. Miss. 1969), is a leading example. The board of trustees of the Institutions of Higher Learning of the State of Mississippi promulgated rules providing, in part, that "all speakers invited to the campus of any of the state institutions of higher learning must first be investigated and approved by the head of the institution involved and when invited the names of such speakers must be filed with the executive secretary of the board of trustees." The regulations were amended several times to prohibit "speakers who will do violence to the academic atmosphere," "persons in disrepute from whence they come," persons "charged with crime or other moral wrongs," any person "who advocates a philosophy of the overthrow of the

United States,'' and any person ''who has been announced as a political candidate or any person who wishes to speak on behalf of a political candidate.'' In addition, political or sectarian meetings sponsored by any outside organization were prohibited.

Under the authority of these regulations, the board prevented political activists Aaron Henry and Charles Evers from speaking on any Mississippi state campus. Students at several schools joined faculty members and other persons as plaintiffs in an action to invalidate the regulations. The court struck down the regulations because they created a prior restraint on the students' and faculties' First Amendment right to hear speakers. Not all speaker bans, however, are unconstitutional under the court's opinion. When the speech ''presents a 'clear and present danger' of resulting in serious substantive evil,'' a ban would not violate the First Amendment:

> For purpose of illustration, we have no doubt that the college or university authority may deny an invitation to a guest speaker requested by a campus group if it reasonably appears that such person would, in the course of his speech, advocate (1) violent overthrow of the government of the United States, the state of Mississippi, or any political subdivision thereof; (2) willful destruction or seizure of the institution's buildings or other property; (3) disruption or impairment, by force, of the institution's regularly scheduled classes or other educational functions; (4) physical harm, coercion, or intimidation or other invasion of lawful rights of the institution's officials, faculty members, or students; or (5) other campus disorder of violent nature. In drafting a regulation so providing, it must be made clear that the ''advocacy'' prohibited must be of the kind which prepares the group addressed for imminent action and steels it to such action, as opposed to the abstract espousal of the moral propriety of a course of action by resort to force; and there must be not only advocacy to action but also a reasonable apprehension of imminent danger to the essential functions and purposes of the institution, including the safety of its property and the protection of its officials, faculty members, and students [306 F. Supp. at 973–74].

The court also promulgated a set of ''Uniform Regulations for Off-Campus Speakers,'' which it determined to comply with the First Amendment (306 F. Supp. at 979–80). These regulations provide that all speaker requests come from a recognized student or faculty group, thus precluding any outsider's insistence on using the campus as a forum. This approach accords with the court's basis for invalidating the regulations: the rights of students or faculty members to hear a speaker.

Besides meeting a ''clear and present danger'' or comparable test, speaker ban regulations must use language that is sufficiently clear and precise to be understood by the average reader. Ambiguous or vague regulations run the risk of being struck down, under the First and Fourteenth Amendments, as ''void for vagueness'' (see Sections 4.4.1 and 4.7.2). In *Dickson* v. *Sitterson,* 280 F. Supp. 486 (M.D.N.C. 1968), the court relied on this ground to invalidate a state statute and regulations prohibiting a person from speaking at state colleges or universities if he was a ''known member of the Communist party,'' was ''known to advocate the overthrow of the Constitution of the United States or the state of North Carolina,'' or had ''pleaded the Fifth Amendment'' in response to questions relating to the Communist party or other subversive organizations.

The absence of rules can be just as risky as poorly drafted ones, since either situation leaves administrators and affected persons with insufficient guidance. *Brooks* v. *Auburn University,* 412 F.2d 1171 (5th Cir. 1969), is illustrative. A student organization, the Human Rights Forum, had requested that the Reverend William Sloan Coffin speak on campus. After the request was approved by the Public Affairs Seminar Board, the president of Auburn overruled the decision because the Reverend Coffin was "a convicted felon and because he might advocate breaking the law." Students and faculty members filed suit contesting the president's action, and the U.S. Court of Appeals upheld their First Amendment claim:

> Attributing the highest good faith to Dr. Philpott in his action, it nevertheless is clear under the prior restraint doctrine that the right of the faculty and students to hear a speaker, selected as was the speaker here, cannot be left to the discretion of the university president on a pick and choose basis. As stated, Auburn had no rules or regulations as to who might or might not speak and thus no question of a compliance with or a departure from such rules or regulations is presented. This left the matter as a pure First Amendment question; hence the basis for prior restraint. Such a situation of no rules or regulations may be equated with a licensing system to speak or hear and this has been long prohibited.
>
> It is strenuously urged on behalf of Auburn that the president was authorized in any event to bar a convicted felon or one advocating lawlessness from the campus. This again depends upon the right of the faculty and students to hear. We do not hold that Dr. Philpott could not bar a speaker under any circumstances. Here there was no claim that the Reverend Coffin's appearance would lead to violence or disorder or that the university would be otherwise disrupted. There is no claim that Dr. Philpott could not regulate the time or place of the speech or the manner in which it was to be delivered. The most recent statement of the applicable rule by the Supreme Court, perhaps its outer limits, is contained in the case of *Brandenburg* v. *Ohio,* decided June 9, 1969, 395 U.S. 444, 89 S. Ct. 1927, 23 L. Ed. 2d 430: " . . . These later decisions have fashioned the principle that the constitutional guarantees of free speech and free press do not permit a state to forbid or proscribe advocacy of the use of force or of law violation except where such advocacy is directed to inciting or producing imminent lawless action and is likely to incite or produce such action." . . . There was no claim that the Coffin speech would fall into the category of this exception [412 F.2d at 1172–73].

Under these cases regulations concerning off-campus speakers present sensitive legal issues for public institutions. If such regulations are determined to be necessary, they should be drafted with the aid of counsel. The cases clearly permit reasonable regulation of "the time or place of the speech or the manner in which it . . . [is] delivered," as the *Brooks* opinion notes. But regulating a speech because of its content is permissible only in the narrowest of circumstances, such as those set out in *Stacy* and in *Brooks.* The regulations promulgated by the court in *Stacy* provide useful guidance in drafting legally sound regulations.

5.6.3. Trespass statutes and ordinances. States and local governments often have trespass or unlawful entry laws that limit the use of a postsecondary institution's facilities by outsiders. Such statutes or ordinances typically provide that offenders are subject to ejection from the campus and that violation of an order to leave, made by an authorized person, is punishable as a misdemeanor. These laws, and the court decisions interpreting them, should be carefully examined to determine each law's particular coverage. Some laws may cover all types of property; others may cover only educational institutions. Some laws may cover all postsecondary institutions, public or private; others may apply only to public or only to private institutions. Some laws may be broad enough to restrict members of the campus community under some circumstances; others may be applicable only to outsiders. There may also be technical differences in the standards for determining what acts will be considered a trespass or when an institution's actions will constitute implied consent to entry. (For an illustrative case, see *People* v. *Leonard*, 62 N.Y.2d 404, 405 N.E.2d 831 (1984), in which the court reviewed the applicability of state trespass law to the exclusion of a sometime student from the SUNY-Binghamton campus.)

A number of reported cases have dealt with the federal and state constitutional limitations on a state or local government's authority to apply trespass laws to the campus setting. *Braxton* v. *Municipal Court*, 10 Cal. 3d 138, 514 P.2d 697 (1973), is a leading example. Several individuals had demonstrated on the San Francisco State campus against the publication of campus newspaper articles that they considered "racist and chauvinistic." A college employee notified the protestors that they were temporarily barred from campus. When they disobeyed this order, they were arrested and charged under Section 626.4 of the California Penal Code. This statute authorized "the chief administrative officer of a campus or other facility of a community college, state college, or state university or his designate" to temporarily bar a person from the campus if there was "reasonable cause to believe that such person has wilfully disrupted the orderly operation of such campus or facility." The protestors argued that the state trespass statute was unconstitutional for reasons of overbreadth and vagueness (see Sections 3.4.1, 4.4.1, and 4.7.2).

The California Supreme court rejected the protestors' argument. Regarding overbreadth, the court concluded:

> Without a narrowing construction, Section 626.4 would suffer First Amendment overbreadth. For example, reasoned appeals for a student strike to protest the escalation of a war, or the firing of the football coach, might "disrupt" the "orderly operation" of a campus; so, too, might calls for the dismissal of the college president or for a cafeteria boycott to protest employment policies or the use of nonunion products. Yet neither the "content" of speech nor freedom of association can be restricted merely because such expression or association disrupts the tranquillity of a campus or offends the tastes of school administrators or the public. Protest may disrupt the placidity of the vacant mind just as a stone dropped in a still pool may disturb the tranquillity of the surface waters, but the courts have never held that such "disruption" falls outside the boundaries of the First Amendment. . . .

> Without a narrowing construction, Section 626.4 would also suffer overbreadth by unnecessarily restricting conduct enmeshed with First Amendment activities. Although conduct entwined with speech may be regulated if it is completely incompatible with the peaceful functioning of the campus, Section 626.4 on its face fails to distinguish between protected

activity such as peaceful picketing or assembly and unprotected conduct that is violent, physically obstructive, or otherwise coercive. . . .

In order to avoid the constitutional overbreadth that a literal construction of Section 626.4 would entail, we interpret the statute to prohibit only incitement to violence or conduct physically incompatible with the peaceful functioning of the campus. We agree with the attorney general in his statement: "The word 'disrupt' is commonly understood to mean a *physical* or *forcible* interference, interruption, or obstruction. In the campus context, disrupt means a physical or forcible interference with normal college activities."

The disruption must also constitute "a substantial and material threat" to the orderly operation of the campus or facility (*Tinker* v. *Des Moines School District* (1969) 393 U.S. 503, 514, 89 S. Ct. 733, 21 L. Ed. 2d 731). The words "substantial and material" appear in the portion of the statute which authorizes reinstatement of permission to come onto the campus (Penal Code sec. 626.4(c)). Accordingly, we read those words as expressing the legislature's intent as to the whole function of the statute; we thus construe Section 626.4 to permit exclusion from the campus only of one whose conduct or words are such as to constitute, or incite to, a substantial and material physical disruption incompatible with the peaceful functioning of the academic institution and of those upon its campus. Such a substantial and material disruption creates an emergency situation justifying the statute's provision for summary, but temporary, exclusion [514 P.2d at 701–05].

The court then also rejected the vagueness claim:

Petitioners point out that even though the test of substantial and material physical disruption by acts of incitement of violence constitutes an acceptable constitutional standard for preventing overbroad applications of the statute in specific cases, the enactment still fails to provide the precision normally required in criminal legislation. Thus, for example, persons subject to summary banishment must guess at *what* must be disrupted (classes or the attendance lines for athletic events), and *how* the disruption must take place (by picketing or by a single zealous shout in a classroom or by a sustained sit-in barring use of a classroom for several days).

Our examination of the legislative history and purposes of Section 626.4 reveals, however, that the legislature intended to authorize the extraordinary remedy of summary banishment only when the person excluded has committed acts illegal under other statutes; since these statutes provide ascertainable standards for persons seeking to avoid the embrace of Section 626.4, the instant enactment is not void for vagueness [514 P.2d at 705].

In *Kirstel* v. *State*, 13 Md. App. 482, 284 A.2d 12 (1971), another court upheld a similar state statute against constitutional attack. This Maryland statute (since recodified as Md. Ann. Code, Education, sec. 26-102) authorized the "highest official or governing body" of each public college or university to deny campus access to individuals "who have no lawful business to pursue at the institution, or who are

acting in a manner disruptive or disturbing to the normal educational functions
of the institution." Like the litigants in *Braxton,* Kirstel argued that the statute was
vague and overbroad, asserting in particular the vagueness of the "no lawful
business" language in the statute. Also like *Braxton,* the court had to work hard
to clarify and thus justify a statute that would not win any awards for precision.
By equating the phrase "lawful business" with the similarly vague and technical
phrase "constitutionally protected" activity, however, the *Kirstel* opinion adds little
to an understanding of the Maryland statute.

One case that does strike down a trespass statute is *Grady* v. *State,* 278 N.E.2d
280 (Ind. 1972), where the law at issue provided:

> It shall be a misdemeanor for any person to refuse to leave the
> premises of any institution established for the purpose of the education of
> students enrolled therein when so requested, regardless of the reason, by
> the duly constituted officials of any such institution [Ind. Code Ann. sec.
> 10-4533].

The court held that the law was void on its face owing to vagueness and overbreadth
in violation of the First and Fourteenth Amendments:

> This statute attempts to grant to some undefined school "official"
> the power to order cessation of *any* kind of activity whatsoever, by *any* person
> whatsoever, and the official does not need to have any special reason for
> the order. The official's power extends to teachers, employees, students,
> and visitors and is in no way confined to suppressing activities that are
> interfering with the orderly use of the premises. This statute empowers the
> official to order any person off the premises because he does not approve
> of his looks, his opinions, his behavior, no matter how peaceful, or *for no
> reason at all.* Since there are *no* limitations on the reason for such an order,
> the official can request a person to leave the premises solely because the
> person is engaging in expressive conduct even though that conduct may
> be clearly protected by the First Amendment. If the person chooses to con-
> tinue the First Amendment activity, he can be prosecuted for a crime under
> sec. 10-4533. This statute is clearly overbroad [278 N.E.2d at 282-83].

Even if a regulation or statute is neither vague nor overbroad, it may be
vulnerable to a procedural due process attack. There is authority for the proposition that notice and a hearing are required before a noncampus person can be
expelled from a public campus. The court in the *Braxton* case, for example, having
narrowly construed the California statute to avoid vagueness and overbreadth, then
declared:

> We recognize, likewise, that the statute must be construed so as not
> to violate the precepts of procedural due process; hence, we interpret Section
> 626.4 to require notice and a hearing on alleged misconduct before the issu-
> ance of any exclusion order unless the campus administrator reasonably
> finds that the situation is such an exigent one that the continued presence
> on the campus of the person from whom consent to remain is withdrawn
> constitutes a substantial and material threat of significant injury to persons

or property (sec. 626.4(c)). Even when an exclusion order issues without a hearing, a postexclusion hearing must be held as soon as reasonably possible not later than seven days following a request by the person excluded [514 P.2d at 700].

Similarly, in *Dunkel* v. *Elkins,* 325 F. Supp. 1235 (D. Md. 1971), the court construed the Maryland statute upheld in *Kirstel* to require that the institution provide notice and an opportunity for a hearing before excluding an outsider from campus. If a prior hearing is not feasible because of emergency conditions, then a prompt hearing must be held after the expulsion. The burden of proof is on the institution to establish that the person to be excluded fell within the terms of the statute.

A notice and a hearing were also required in *Watson* v. *Board of Regents of the University of Colorado,* 182 Colo. 307, 512 P.2d 1162 (1973). The plaintiff, a consultant to the University of Colorado Black Student Alliance with substantial ties to the campus, was rejected for admission to the university. Believing that a particular admissions committee member had made the decision to reject him, the plaintiff threatened his safety. The university president then notified the plaintiff in writing that he would no longer be allowed on campus. Nevertheless, the plaintiff returned to campus and was arrested for trespass. Relying on *Dunkel* v. *Elkins,* the court agreed that the exclusion violated procedural due process:

> Where students have been subjected to disciplinary action by university officials, courts have recognized that procedural due process requires— prior to imposition of the disciplinary action—adequate notice of the charges, reasonable opportunity to prepare to meet the charges, an orderly administrative hearing adapted to the nature of the case, and a fair and impartial decision. . . . The same protection must be afforded nonstudents who may be permanently denied access to university functions and facilities.
>
> As part of a valid regent's regulation of this type, in addition to providing for a hearing, there should be a provision for the person or persons who will act as adjudicator(s).
>
> In the present posture of this matter we should not attempt to "spell out" all proper elements of such a regulation. This task should be undertaken first by the regents. We should say, however, that when a genuine emergency appears to exist and it is impractical for university officials to grant a prior hearing, the right of nonstudents to access to the university may be suspended without a prior hearing, so long as a hearing is thereafter provided with reasonable promptness [512 P.2d at 1165].

Most trespass litigation concerning postsecondary education, such as the cases above, has probed federal constitutional and state statutory limits on public institutions' authority. The debate has been extended to private institutions, however, by the litigation in *State* v. *Schmid,* 84 N.J. 535, 423 A.2d 615 (1980), known as the *Princeton University* case.

Chris Schmid, a nonstudent and a member of the United States Labor Party, was arrested for trespass when he attempted to distribute political materials on the campus of Princeton University and was subsequently convicted. Princeton's regulations required nonstudents and non-university-affiliated organizations to obtain permission to distribute materials on campus. No such requirement applied to students or campus organizations. The regulations did not include any standards for when permission would be granted or for what times, manners, or places of expression were appropriate. Schmid claimed that the regulations violated his rights to freedom of expression under both the federal Constitution and the New Jersey state constitution.

First addressing the federal constitutional claim under the First Amendment, the court acknowledged that "in particular settings, private entities, including educational institutions, may so impact upon the public or share enough of the essential features of governmental bodies as to be engaged functionally in 'state action' for First Amendment purposes." The court also emphasized, however, that this "state action" requirement, a predicate to the application of the First Amendment, "is not readily met in the case of a private educational institution." Reviewing the various theories on which state action has been grounded, the court extensively analyzed their applicability to the case but declined to hold that Princeton's exclusion of Schmid constituted state action under any of the theories. (See this volume, Section 1.4.2.)

Although, in the absence of a state action finding, the federal First Amendment could not apply to Schmid's claim, the court did not find itself similarly constrained in applying the state constitution. Addressing Schmid's state constitutional claim, the court determined that the state constitutional provisions protecting freedom of expression (even though similar to the First Amendment provision) could be construed more expansively than the First Amendment so as to reach Princeton's actions. The court reaffirmed that state constitutions are independent sources of individual rights; that state constitutional protections may surpass the protections of the federal constitution; and that this greater expansiveness could exist even if the state provision is identical to the federal provision because state constitutional rights are not intended to be simply mirror images of federal rights. (See this volume, Section 1.4.3.)

Whether the more expansive state constitutional protections did protect Schmid against the trespass claim depended on balancing the "legitimate interests in private property with individual freedoms of speech and assembly." According to the court:

> The state constitutional equipoise between expressional rights and property rights must be . . . gauged on a scale measuring the nature and extent of the public's use of such property. Thus, even as against the exercise of important rights of speech, assembly, petition, and the like, private property itself remains protected under due process standards from untoward interferences with or confiscatory restrictions upon its reasonable use. . . .
>
> On the other hand, it is also clear that private property may be subjected by the state, within constitutional bounds, to reasonable restrictions upon its use in order to serve the public welfare. . . .
>
> We are thus constrained to achieve the optimal balance between the protections to be accorded private property and those to be given to expressional freedoms exercised upon such property [423 A.2d at 629].

To strike the required balance, the court announced a "test" encompassing several "elements" and other "considerations":

> We now hold that, under the state constitution, the test to be applied to ascertain the parameters of the rights of speech and assembly upon privately

owned property and the extent to which such property reasonably can be restricted to accommodate these rights involves several elements. This standard must take into account (1) the nature, purposes, and primary use of such private property, generally, its "normal" use, (2) the extent and nature of the public's invitation to use that property, and (3) the purpose of the expressional activity undertaken upon such property in relation to both the private and public use of the property . . . subject to suitable restrictions, the reasonable exercise by individuals of the constitutional freedoms of speech and assembly.

Even when an owner of private property is constitutionally obligated under such a standard to honor speech and assembly rights of others, private property rights themselves must nonetheless be protected. The owner of such private property, therefore, is entitled to fashion reasonable rules to control the mode, opportunity, and site for the individual exercise of expressional rights upon his property. It is at this level of analysis—assessing the reasonableness of such restrictions—that weight may be given to whether there exist convenient and feasible alternative means to individuals to engage in substantially the same expressional activity. While the presence of such alternatives will not eliminate the constitutional duty, it may lighten the obligations upon the private property owner to accommodate the expressional rights of others and may also serve to condition the content of any regulations governing the time, place, and manner for the exercise of such expressional rights [423 A.2d at 630].

Applying each of the three elements in its test to the particular facts concerning Princeton's campus and Schmid's activity on it, the court concluded that Schmid did have state constitutional speech and assembly rights, which Princeton was obligated to honor:

The application of the appropriate standard in this case must commence with an examination of the primary use of the private property, namely, the campus and facilities of Princeton University. Princeton University itself has furnished the answer to this inquiry [in its university regulations] in expansively expressing its overriding educational goals, viz:

The central purposes of a university are the pursuit of truth, the discovery of new knowledge through scholarship and research, the teaching and general development of students, and the transmission of knowledge and learning to society at large. Free inquiry and free expression within the academic community are indispensable to the achievement of these goals. The freedom to teach and to learn depends upon the creation of appropriate conditions and opportunities on the campus as a whole as well as in classrooms and lecture halls. All members of the academic community share the responsibility for securing and sustaining the general conditions conducive to this freedom. . . .

Free speech and peaceable assembly are basic requirements of the university as a center for free inquiry and the search for knowledge and insight.

No one questions that Princeton University has honored this grand ideal and has in fact dedicated its facilities and property to achieve the educational goals expounded in this compelling statement.

In examining next the extent and nature of a public invitation to use its property, we note that a public presence within Princeton University is entirely consonant with the university's expressed educational mission. Princeton University, as a private institution of higher education, clearly seeks to encourage both a wide and continuous exchange of opinions and ideas and to foster a policy of openness and freedom with respect to the use of its facilities. The commitment of its property, facilities, and resources to educational purposes contemplates substantial public involvement and participation in the academic life of the university. The university itself has endorsed the educational value of an open campus and the full exposure of the college community to the "outside world"—that is, the public at large. Princeton University has indeed invited such public uses of its resources in fulfillment of its broader educational ideas and objectives.

The further question is whether the expressional activities undertaken by the defendant in this case are discordant in any sense with both the private and public uses of the campus and facilities of the university. There is nothing in the record to suggest that Schmid was evicted because the purpose of his activities, distributing political literature, offended the university's educational policies. The reasonable and normal inference thus to be extracted from the record in the instant case is that defendant's attempt to disseminate political material was not incompatible with either Princeton University's professed educational goals or the university's overall use of its property for educational purposes. Further, there is no indication that, even under the terms of the university's own regulations, Schmid's activities . . . directly or demonstrably "disrupt[ed] the regular and essential operations of the university" or that, in either the time, the place, or the manner of Schmid's distribution of the political materials, he "significantly infringed on the rights of others" or caused any interference or inconvenience with respect to the normal use of university property and the normal routine and activities of the college community [423 A.2d at 630–31].

Princeton, however, invoked the other considerations included in the court's test. It argued that, to protect its private property rights as an owner and its academic freedom as a higher education institution, it had to require that outsiders have permission to enter its campus and that its regulations reasonably implemented this necessary requirement. The court did not disagree with the first premise of Princeton's argument, but it did disagree that Princeton's regulations were a reasonable means of protecting its interests:

In addressing this argument, we must give substantial deference to the importance of institutional integrity and independence. Private educational institutions perform an essential social function and have a fundamental responsibility to assure the academic and general well-being of their communities of students, teachers, and related personnel. At a minimum, these needs, implicating academic freedom and development, justify an educational institution in controlling those who seek to enter its domain. The singular need to achieve essential educational goals and regulate activities that impact upon these efforts has been acknowledged even with respect to public educational institutions (see, for example, *Healy* v. *James,* 408 U.S. at 180, 92 S. Ct. at 2345, 33 L. Ed. 2d at 279; *Tinker* v. *Des Moines Indep. Community School Dist.,* 393 U.S. 503, 513-14, 89 S. Ct. 733, 740-41, 21 L. Ed. 2d 731, 741-42 (1969). Hence, private colleges and universities must be accorded a generous measure of autonomy and self-governance if they are to fulfill their paramount role as vehicles of education and enlightenment.

In this case, however, the university regulations that were applied to Schmid . . . contained no standards, aside from the requirement for invitation and permission, for governing the actual exercise of expressional freedom. Indeed, there were no standards extant regulating the granting or withholding of such authorization, nor did the regulations deal adequately with the time, place, or manner for individuals to exercise their rights of speech and assembly. Regulations thus devoid of reasonable standards designed to protect both the legitimate interests of the university as an institution of higher education and the individual exercise of expressional freedom cannot constitutionally be invoked to prohibit the otherwise noninjurious and reasonable exercise of such freedoms. . . .

In these circumstances, given the absence of adequate reasonable regulations, the required accommodation of Schmid's expressional and associational rights, otherwise reasonably exercised, would not constitute an unconstitutional abridgment of Princeton University's property rights. . . . It follows that, in the absence of a reasonable regulatory scheme, Princeton University did in fact violate defendant's state constitutional rights of expression in evicting him and securing his arrest for distributing political literature upon its campus [423 A.2d at 632-33].

Since Schmid did have free expression rights on the Princeton campus, and since Princeton did not have in place a reasonable regulatory scheme for limiting Schmid's access, Schmid could not constitutionally be convicted for trespass. The court reversed his conviction.

Princeton sought U.S. Supreme Court review of the New Jersey court's decision. The university argued that the court's interpretation of *state* constitutional law violated its rights under *federal* law. Specifically, it claimed a First Amendment academic freedom right (a claim to *institutional,* rather than individual faculty or student, academic freedom)[11] and a Fifth Amendment right to protect its property from infringement by government (here the New Jersey court). In a *per curiam* opinion, the Supreme Court declined to address the merits of Princeton's arguments (*Princeton University and State of New Jersey* v. *Schmid,* 455 U.S. 100 (1982)). Instead, it declared the appeal moot because Princeton had changed its regulations since the time of Schmid's con-

---

[11]The arguments for and against the existence of an institutional academic freedom right are well developed in the briefs of the parties and the *amici curiae.* Lawyers facing this important issue will want to consult these briefs and the resources they cite. See particularly the *Brief Amicus Curiae of the American Association of University Professors,* filed August 20, 1981, in *Princeton University and State of New Jersey* v. *Chris Schmid,* No. 80-1576, U.S. Supreme Court, Oct. Term 1980.

viction. Since the prior regulations, which had been at issue before the New Jersey court, were no longer in effect, there was no longer a live controversy between the parties. Although the Supreme Court therefore dismissed the appeal, the dismissal had no negative effect on the New Jersey court's opinion, which stands as authoritative law for that state.

The New Jersey court's reasoning was subsequently approved and followed by the Pennsylvania Supreme Court in *Pennsylvania* v. *Tate*, 432 A.2d 1382 (1981). The defendants had been arrested for trespassing at Muhlenberg College, a private institution, when they distributed leaflets on campus announcing a community-sponsored lecture by the then FBI director. The Pennsylvania court developed an analysis similar to the New Jersey court's and invoked the free expression guarantees of the Pennsylvania state constitution. The standardless nature of the college's regulations was again a crucial factor rendering the trespass conviction a violation of state constitutional rights.

State v. *Schmid* is a landmark case and the first case to impose constitutional limitations on the authority of private institutions to exclude outsiders from their campuses. *Schmid* does not, however, create a new nationwide rule. The applicability of its analysis to private campuses in states other than New Jersey and Pennsylvania will vary, depending on the particular individual rights clauses in a state's constitution, the existing precedents construing their application to private entities, and the receptivity of a state's judges to the New Jersey court's view of the nature and use of private campuses. Even in New Jersey and Pennsylvania, the *Schmid* and *Tate* precedents do not create the same access rights to all private campuses; as *Schmid* emphasizes, the degree of access required depends on the primary use for which the institution dedicates its campus property and the scope of the public invitation to use that particular property. Administrators dealing with access of outsiders should consult counsel concerning their own state's law and their institution's status under it.

Nor does *Schmid* prohibit private institutions from regulating the activity of outsiders to whom they must permit entry. Institutions may still adopt regulatory standards that impose reasonable time, place, and manner restrictions on access. Indeed, the new regulations adopted by Princeton after Schmid's arrest were cited favorably by the New Jersey court. Although they were not at issue in the case, since they were not the basis of the trespass charge, the court noted that "these current amended regulations exemplify the approaches open to private educational entities seeking to protect their institutional integrity while at the same time recognizing individual rights of speech and assembly and accommodating the public whose presence nurtures academic inquiry and growth." The new Princeton regulations, which are set out in full in the court's opinion (423 A.2d at 617–18 n.2), thus provide substantial guidance for institutions that are subject to state law such as New Jersey's or that as a matter of educational policy desire to change their access regulations.

5.6.4. Soliciting and canvassing. Not only for speakers, pamphleteers, and canvassers conveying a social, political, or religious message, but also for companies selling merchandise to college students, the university campus may be an attractive marketplace. Whether the enterprising outsider wishes to develop a market for ideas or for commodities, the public institution's authority to restrict contact with its students is limited by the First Amendment. As in other circumstances, because of the First Amendment's applicability, a public institution's authority to regulate soliciting and canvassing is more limited than that of a private institution.

Historically, litigation and discussion of free speech have focused on rights attending the communication of political or social thought. The U.S. Supreme Court's opinion in *Virginia State Board of Pharmacy* v. *Virginia Citizens Consumer Council*, 425 U.S. 748 (1976), however, made clear that the protection of the First Amendment likewise extends to purely "commercial speech." According to the Court, even where the communication is simply "I will sell you X at Y price," it falls within the ambit of protected speech. Nonetheless, the degree of protection afforded commercial speech may be less than that afforded noncommercial speech.

The Supreme Court has consistently approved time, place, and manner restrictions on speech where they (1) are not based on the speech's "content or subject matter," (2) "serve a significant governmental interest," and (3) "leave open ample alternative channels for communication of the information" (*Heffron* v. *International Society for Krishna Consciousness*, 452 U.S. 640 (1981)). Within these guidelines public institutions may subject both commercial and noncommercial speech to reasonable regulation of the time, place, and manner of delivery. In addition, however, public institutions may regulate the content of commercial advertising in ways that would not be permissible for other types of speech.

5.6.4.1. Commercial solicitation. Two cases involving American Future Systems, Inc., a corporation specializing in the sale of china and crystal, are the first to address the regulation of commercial speech by a public university. In *American Future Systems* v. *Pennsylvania State University,* 618 F.2d 252 (3d Cir. 1980) (*American Future Systems I*), the plaintiff corporation challenged the defendant university's regulations on commercial activities in campus residence halls. The regulations in question barred "the conducting of any business enterprise for profit" in student residence halls except where an individual student invites the salesperson to his or her room for the purpose of conducting business only with that student. No rules prevented businesses from placing advertisements in student newspapers or on student radio, or from making sales attempts by telephone or mail.

American Future Systems (AFS) scheduled a number of sales demonstrations in Penn State residence halls in the fall of 1977. When Penn State officials attempted to stop the sales demonstrations, AFS argued that such action violated its First Amendment "commercial speech" rights. At this point Penn State informed AFS "that it would be permitted to conduct the demonstration portion of its show if no attempts were made to sell merchandise to the students during the presentation" (618 F.2d at 254). Claiming that the sales transactions were essential to its presentation, AFS ceased its activity and commenced its lawsuit. AFS based its argument on the *Virginia State Board of Pharmacy* case:

> Plaintiff AFS is correct that in *Virginia Pharmacy Board* the Supreme Court ruled that commercial speech is entitled to some level of protection by the First Amendment (425 U.S. at 770, 96 S. Ct. at 1829). This holding, by itself, does not resolve the issue presented by this case, however. The statutory scheme discussed in *Virginia Pharmacy Board* effectively suppressed all dissemination of price information throughout the state. The case at hand presents a dramatically different fact situation, implicating many different concerns.
>
> Penn State argues that it can restrict the use of its residence halls to purposes which further the educational function of the institution. It urges that transacting sales with groups of students in the dormitories does not

further the educational goals of the university and, therefore, can be lawfully prohibited. It emphasizes that AFS seeks a ruling that its sales and demonstrations be permitted in the residence halls, areas which are not open to the general public. In light of all the facts of this case, we believe Penn State is correct [618 F.2d at 255].

To reach its conclusion, the *American Future Systems I* court began by inquiring whether Penn State had established a "public forum" for free speech activity (see *Widmar* v. *Vincent,* this volume, Section 4.8.4) in the residence halls:

> When the state restricts speech in some way, the court must look to the special interests of the government in regulating speech in the particular location. The focus of the court's inquiry must be whether there is a basic incompatibility between the communication and the primary activity of an area (*Grayned* v. *City of Rockford,* 408 U.S. 104, 116, 92 S. Ct. 2294, 2303, 33 L. Ed. 2d 222 (1972)).
>
> Pennsylvania State University was established for educational purposes by statute in 1855. . . . From its beginnings to this day, it has maintained its identity as an institution dedicated to education.
>
> As discussed above, members of the general public do not have unrestricted access to Penn State residence halls. "No Trespassing" signs are posted near the entrances to all the residence halls. Although nonresidents of the halls may enter the lobbies, they may not proceed freely to the private living areas. We believe that these facts demonstrate that the arena at issue here, the residence halls at Penn State, does not constitute a "public forum" under the First Amendment [618 F.2d at 256].

The court then inquired whether, despite the absence of a public forum, AFS could still claim First Amendment protection for solicitation and sales activities occurring in the residence halls. According to the court, such a claim depends on whether the activity impinges on the primary business for which the area in question is used:

> We recognize that the absence of a "public forum" from this case does not end our inquiry, however. There are some "non-public-forum" areas where the communication does not significantly impinge upon the primary business carried on there. Penn State asserts that the AFS group sales do impinge significantly on the primary activities of a college dormitory. Penn State argues that its residence halls are "exclusively dedicated to providing a living environment which is conducive to activities associated with being a student and succeeding academically." It contends that group sales activities within the residence halls would disrupt the proper study atmosphere and the privacy of the students. It reiterates that there is no history of allowing group commercial transactions to take place in the dormitories. We conclude that Penn State has articulated legitimate interests which support its ban on group sales activity in the dormitories. We also conclude that these interests are furthered by the proscription against commercial transactions [618 F.2d at 256-57].

To complete its analysis, the court addressed, and rejected, a final argument made by AFS: that Penn State cannot distinguish between commercial and noncommercial speech in making rules for its residence halls and that, since Penn State permits political and other noncommercial group activities, it must permit commercial activities as well. The court replied:

> In a case decided two years after *Virginia Pharmacy Board,* the Supreme Court explicitly rejected plaintiff's view that commercial and noncommercial speech must be treated exactly alike.
>
>> We have not discarded the "commonsense" distinction between speech proposing a commercial transaction, which occurs in an area traditionally subject to government regulation, and other varieties of speech. . . . To require a parity of constitutional protection for commercial and noncommercial speech alike could invite dilution, simply by a leveling process, of the force of the amendment's guarantee with respect to the latter kind of speech. Rather than subject the First Amendment to such a devitalization, we instead have afforded commercial speech a limited measure of protection, commensurate with its subordinate position in the scale of First Amendment values, while allowing models of regulation that might be impermissible in the realm of noncommercial expression (*Ohralick* v. *Ohio State Bar Association,* 436 U.S. 447, 455–56, 98 S. Ct. 1912, 1918, 56 L. Ed. 2d 444 (1978)). . . .

Here Penn State has not totally suppressed the speech of plaintiff. It has restricted that speech somewhat, however. Although AFS sales representatives are allowed into the residence halls to present demonstrations to groups of students, they cannot consummate sales at these gatherings. Even that restriction is removed if the sales representative is invited to the hall by an individual student who decides to purchase the merchandise marketed by AFS.

As noted above, Penn State has advanced reasonable objectives to support its ban on group commercial activity in the residence halls. Further, it has emphasized that traditionally there has been an absence of such activity in the halls. This places commercial speech in a quite different category from activities historically associated with college life, such as political meetings or football rallies. We cannot say that the record in this case reveals any arbitrary, capricious, or invidious distinction between commercial and noncommercial speech. We therefore conclude that AFS is incorrect in its assertion that the Penn State policy violates the First Amendment because it treats noncommercial speech differently from commercial speech [618 F.2d at 257–59].

Having determined that AFS's activities were commercial speech entitled to First Amendment protection, but that Penn State's regulations complied with First Amendment requirements applicable to such speech, the court in *American Future Systems I* upheld the regulations and affirmed the lower court's judgment for Penn State.

It was not long, however, before a second generation of litigation was born.

After the first lawsuit, and in accordance with its understanding of the appellate court's opinion, AFS requested Penn State to allow group demonstrations that would not include consummation of sales and would take place only in residence hall common areas. AFS provided the university with a copy of its "script" for these demonstrations, a series of seventy-six cue cards. Penn State responded that AFS could use certain cue cards with information the university considered to have "educational value," but not cue cards with "price guarantee and payment plan information," which the university considered "an outright group commercial solicitation."

AFS sued again, along with several Penn State students, arguing that Penn State's censorship of its cue cards violated its right to commercial speech and contradicted the court's opinion in *American Future Systems I*. After losing again in the trial court, AFS finally gained a victory when the appellate court ruled in its favor (*American Future Systems* v. *Pennsylvania State University*, 688 F.2d 907 (1982) (*American Future Systems II*)). The appellate court carefully distinguished this litigation from the prior litigation in *American Future Systems I* and identified the new issue presented to it:

> It is important at the outset to clarify which issues are not before us. Although AFS construes our decision in *American Future Systems I* as having established its constitutional free speech right to conduct demonstrations of a commercial product in common areas within the university's residence halls, we do not read that opinion so broadly. Penn State has not sought to bar all commercial activity from its residence halls. It has limited what ostensibly appears to be such a ban through its definition of "commercial," which excludes student contact with a peddler "if the contact was invited by the individual student involved." Therefore, we need not decide whether a state university may properly ban all commercial activity in its residence halls. Similarly, AFS does not challenge the distinction which the earlier opinion made between an actual consummation or completion of the "commercial transaction" and a group demonstration of AFS's products (618 F.2d at 258–59). Instead, it seeks only to conduct the demonstration in the common areas without censorship of the contents of that demonstration.
>
> Finally, although the university has conceded that portions of the demonstration may have some educational value, and it and the district court sought to draw the line between those portions of the demonstration which they deem educational and those portions which they deem commercial, it is unmistakable that the demonstration is geared to the sales of the products and represents commercial speech. Thus, the only issue is whether Penn State may censor the content of AFS's commercial speech conducted in the dormitory common rooms, where AFS has been permitted by the university to conduct its sales demonstration [688 F.2d at 912].

In resolving this issue, the court first reviewed U.S. Supreme Court precedents. These precedents confirmed that "commercial speech is protected from unwarranted governmental interference" and that the "protection extends to price information as well as advertising"; but they also indicated that "commercial speech . . . allows greater regulation than noncommercial speech." The most recent precedent, *Central Hudson Gas & Electric Corp.* v. *Public Service Commission*, 447 U.S. 557 (1980), also establishes a test for ascertaining the validity of regulations of commercial speech:

> For commercial speech to come within [the First Amendment], it at least must concern lawful activity and not be misleading. Next, we ask whether the asserted governmental interest is substantial. If both inquiries yield positive answers, we must determine whether the regulation directly advances the government interest asserted and whether it is not more extensive than is necessary to serve that interest [688 F.2d at 913, quoting *Central Hudson* at 566].

Applying this test, the court determined that Penn State's prohibition of AFS's demonstration violated AFS's First Amendment rights:

> In the instant situation, there has been no allegation that AFS's commercial speech activities are fraudulent, misleading, or otherwise unlawful. . . .
>
> We, therefore, must first determine whether the university has advanced a substantial government interest to be achieved by the restrictions at issue. The only interest advanced by Penn State for precluding information on the price of the company's products and the nature of the contract it enters into with purchasers is that asserted in the prior action before this court—that is, its interest in maintaining the proper study atmosphere in its dormitories and in protecting the privacy of the students residing in those facilities. Restrictions on the *contents* of the demonstration as distinguished from the conduct of the demonstration cannot further these interests. The Supreme Court cases provide ample precedent for the proposition that price information has value (see *Virginia State Board of Pharmacy* v. *Virginia Citizens Consumer Council, Inc.*, 425 U.S. at 754, 96 S. Ct. at 1821; *Bates* v. *State Bar of Arizona*, 433 U.S. at 364, 97 S. Ct. at 2699). The university does not contend that the mere act of convening a group in the common areas of the residence halls is inimical to the study atmosphere, since its policy permits such group activity. We conclude that Penn State has failed to show a substantial state interest, much less a plausible explanation, for its policy differentiating between the nature of the information contained in the AFS demonstration [688 F.2d at 913].

The court therefore reversed the lower court's entry of summary judgment for Penn State and remanded the case for trial.

Several students were also plaintiffs in *American Future Systems II*. They claimed that the university had violated their First Amendment rights to make purchases in group settings in the residence hall common areas and to host and participate in sales demonstrations in the private rooms of residence halls. The students argued that these rights are not aspects of commercial speech, as AFS's rights are, but noncommercial speech, freedom of association, and due process rights, which deserve higher protection. The appellate court determined that the lower court's record

was not sufficiently developed on these points and remanded the students' claims
to the lower court for further consideration—thus leaving these arguments unresolved.[12]

The two appellate court opinions in the complex *American Future Systems* litigation
yield considerable guidance for administrators concerned with commercial activity
in public institutions. A public institution clearly has considerable authority to place
restrictions on outsiders' access to its campus for such purposes. The institution
may reasonably restrict the "time, place, and manner" of commercial activity—
as by limiting the places where group demonstrations may be held in residence halls,
prohibiting the consummation of sales during group demonstrations, or prohibiting
commercial solicitations in libraries or classrooms. The institution may also regulate
the content of commercial activity to ensure that it is not fraudulent or misleading
or does not propose illegal transactions. Other content restrictions—namely, restrictions that directly advance a substantial institutional interest and are no more extensive than necessary to serve that interest—are also permissible. Administrators
cannot comfortably assume, however, that this authority is broad enough to validate
every regulation of commercial activity. Regulations that censor or sharply curtail
the mere dissemination of commercial information may infringe the First Amendment. *American Future Systems II* is a leading example. Similarly, a regulation prohibiting all in-person contacts with students, even when the representative does
not attempt to close a deal or when the student has initiated the contact, may be
invalid. In some locations, moreover, the institution's interest in regulating may
be sufficiently weak to be incapable of justifying particular restrictions. Possible
examples include orderly solicitations in the common areas of student unions or
other less private or studious places on campus; solicitations of individual students
conducted in the student's own room by prior arrangement; and solicitations at the
request of student organizations in locations customarily used by such organizations,
when such solicitations involve no deceptive practices and propose no illegal activity.

It is also clear from U.S. Supreme Court precedents (see, for example, *Consolidated Edison Co.* v. *Public Service Commission,* 447 U.S. 530 (1980)) that not all
speech activity of commercial entrepreneurs is "commercial" speech. Activity whose
purpose is not to propose or close a commercial transaction—for example, an educational seminar or a statement on political, economic, or other issues of public
interest—may fall within First Amendment protections higher than those accorded
commercial speech. Administrators should also be guided by this distinction when
regulating, since their authority to limit access to campus and their authority to
restrict the content of what is said will be narrower when entrepreneurs wish to
engage in "public interest" rather than "commercial" speech.

5.6.4.2. Noncommercial canvassing. As discussed in Sections 5.6.4 and 5.6.4.1,
noncommercial speech is afforded greater protection under the First Amendment
than commercial speech. Consequently, a public institution's authority to regulate
political canvassing, charitable solicitations, public opinion polling, and other types

---

[12]In further proceedings, after remand to the trial court, the plaintiff students obtained
a preliminary injunction against Penn State's ban on group sales demonstrations in individual
students' rooms (*American Future Systems* v. *Pennsylvania State University,* 553 F. Supp. 1268 (M.D.
Pa. 1982) (*American Future Systems III*). Subsequently, the court entered a permanent injunction
against this policy (*American Future Systems* v. *Pennsylvania State University,* 568 F. Supp. 666 (M.D.
Pa. 1983)).

of noncommercial speech is more limited than its authority to regulate commercial sales and solicitations.

In *Brush* v. *Pennsylvania State University,* 414 A.2d 48 (Pa. 1980), students at Penn State challenged university restrictions on canvassing in residence halls. The regulations permitted canvassing (defined as "any attempt to influence student opinion, gain support, or promote a particular cause or interest") by registered individuals in the living areas of a dormitory if the residents of that building had voted in favor of open canvassing. A majority vote to ban canvassing precluded access to living areas by canvassers unless they were specifically invited in advance by a resident. All canvassers remained free, however, to reach students by mail or telephone and to contact residents in the dining halls, lobbies, and conference rooms of each dormitory.

The Supreme Court of Pennsylvania upheld these regulations. It determined that the university had substantial interests in protecting the privacy of its students, preventing breaches of security, and promoting quiet study conditions. The regulations reasonably restricted the time, place, and manner of speech in furtherance of these government interests. Additionally, insofar as the regulations did not eliminate effective alternatives to canvassing inside the living areas, the university had afforded canvassers ample opportunity to reach hall residents.

On the basis of *Brush,* public institutions can confidently exclude canvassers from the actual living quarters of student residence facilities when a majority of the residents have voted to preclude such access. Similar restrictions applied to dining halls, student unions, sidewalks, or other less private areas, however, may violate the First Amendment rights of the speakers and of the potential listeners who are not in favor of the restriction. No-canvassing rules imposed on student living areas with separate living units, such as married student garden apartments or townhouses, may also be unconstitutional; in such circumstances the institution's interests in security and study conditions may be weaker, and the students' (or student family's) interest in controlling their individual living space is greater.

Whether rules such as Penn State's would be valid if imposed directly by the administration and not decided by the student vote is not addressed in *Brush.* But given the strong institutional interests in security and in preserving conditions appropriate for study, it is likely that narrowly drawn no-canvassing rules limited to living areas of dorms would be constitutional even without approval by student vote. In *Chapman* v. *Thomas,* 743 F.2d 1056 (4th Cir. 1984), the court upheld such a restriction, calling the dorm living area a "nonpublic forum" (see *Perry Education Association* v. *Perry Local Educators' Association,* 103 S. Ct. 948, 954–55 (1983)) to which the institution may prohibit or selectively regulate access. For the same reason, no-canvassing rules would probably be constitutional, even without student vote, as applied to study halls, library stacks and reading rooms, laboratories, and similar restricted areas.

For discussion of the related topic of voter canvassing and registration, see Section 5.4.3.

Sec. 5.7. Community Activities of Faculty Members and Students

Besides being part of the academic community, faculty members and students are also private citizens, whose private lives may involve them in the broader local community. Thus, a postsecondary institution may be concerned not only with its authority over matters arising when the community comes onto the campus, as in Section 5.6, but also with its authority over matters arising when the campus goes out into the community.

Generally, an institution has much less authority over a student's or faculty member's activities in the community than on the campus. The faculty-institution contract (Section 3.1) and the student-institution contract (Section 4.1.3) may have little or no application to the off-campus activities that faculty or students engage in as private citizens, or the contract may affirmatively protect faculty members or students from institutional interference in their private lives. In public institutions, faculty members (Section 3.6.4) and students (Section 4.13.2) have constitutional rights that protect them from undue institutional interference in their private lives.

In relation to First Amendment rights, a landmark teacher case, *Pickering* v. *Board of Education,* 391 U.S. 563 (1968) (see Section 3.6.1), created substantial protection for teachers against being disciplined for expressing themselves in the community on issues of public concern. A U.S. Court of Appeals case, *Pickings* v. *Bruce,* 430 F.2d 595 (8th Cir. 1970), establishes similar protections for students. The issue in *Pickings* was that Southern State College had placed SURE (Students United for Rights and Equality), an officially recognized campus group, on probation for writing a letter to a local church criticizing its racial policies. SURE members claimed that the college's action deprived them of their First Amendment rights. In holding for the students, the court made this general statement concerning campus involvement in the community:

> Students and teachers retain their rights to freedom of speech, expression, and association while attending or teaching at a college or university. They have a right to express their views individually or collectively with respect to matters of concern to a college or to a larger community. They are [not] required to limit their expression of views to the campus or to confine their opinions to matters that affect the academic community only. It follows that here the administrators had no right to prohibit SURE from expressing its views on integration to the College View Baptist Church or to impose sanctions on its members or advisors for expressing these views. Such statements may well increase the tensions within the college and between the college and the community, but this fact cannot serve to restrict freedom of expression (*Tinker* v. *Des Moines Community School Dist.,* 393 U.S. at 508–09, 89 S. Ct. 733) [430 F.2d at 598].

For another case protecting the activities of students in the community, see *Thomas* v. *Granville Board of Education,* 607 F.2d 1043 (2d Cir. 1979), discussed in this volume, Section 4.13.2.

Selected Annotated Bibliography

Sec. 5.1 (General Principles)

Reynolds, O. M., *Local Government Law* (West, 1982), is a comprehensive, well-documented review of local government law. Divided into twenty-two chapters, including "Limits on State Control of Municipalities," "Relationship of

Municipalities to Federal Government," "Powers of Municipalities," "Finances of Local Government," "Local Control of the Use of Property," and "Local Regulation of Trade, Business, and Other Enterprises."

Sec. 5.2 (Zoning and Land Use Regulation)

1. Hagman, D., *Urban Planning and Land Development Control Law* (West, 1975), is a thorough survey of land use law. Includes chapters on "Land-Use Planning," 'Types of Zones and Uses," "Zoning Procedures," "Eminent Domain," "Urban Renewal," and other topics.
2. Johnston, R., "Recent Cases in the Law on Intergovernmental Zoning Immunity: New Standards Designed to Maximize the Public Interests," 8 *Urban Lawyer* 327 (1976), provides a concise analysis of traditional zoning immunity concepts and trends in the case law.
3. "Special Project: The Private Use of Public Power: The Private University and the Power of Eminent Domain," 27 *Vanderbilt L. Rev.* 681 (1974), is a lengthy study of eminent domain as a land use planning technique to benefit private universities. Emphasis is on the use of eminent domain in conjunction with federal urban renewal programs. A case study involving Nashville, Tennessee, is included.

Sec. 5.3 (Local Government Taxation)

Ginsberg, W. R., "The Real Property Tax Exemption of Nonprofit Organizations: A Perspective," 53 *Temple L.Q.* 291 (1980), is an overview of the issues involved in granting tax exempt status to nonprofit organizations. Author discusses the judicial and statutory tests used to determine exempt status, the theoretical foundations for property tax exemption, and the problems unique to educational and religious uses of property. Numerous citations to state constitutional and statutory provisions on property tax exemption are included.

Sec. 5.4 (Student Voting in the Community)

Reiff, J. D., "Ohio Residence Law for Student Voters—Its Implications and a Proposal for More Effective Implementation of Residency Statutes," 28 *Cleveland State L. Rev.* 449 (1979), is an article written in the wake of an Ohio Supreme Court decision invalidating an Ohio statute that applied different voter eligibility standards to students and nonstudents. Author argues that this decision has created its own type of unfairness, allowing many temporary residents to influence local elections. Includes discussion of the concept of domicile, critique of arguments favoring student enfranchisement at the place of college residence, and review of the "judicial treatment of student voters" by courts across the nation.

Sec. 5.5 (Relations with Local Police)

1. Bickel, R., "The Relationship Between the University and Local Law Enforcement Agencies in Their Response to the Problem of Drug Abuse on the Campus," in D. P. Young (Ed.), *Higher Education: The Law and Campus Issues,*

pp. 17–27 (Institute of Higher Education, University of Georgia, 1973), provides a practical discussion of the general principles of search and seizure,
double jeopardy, and confidentiality in the campus drug abuse context; also
discusses the necessity of administrators' having the advice of counsel.

2.   Cowen, L., "The Campus and the Community: Problems of Dual Jurisdiction," in D. P. Young (Ed.), *Proceedings of a Conference on Higher Education:
The Law and Student Protest,* pp. 28–32 (Institute of Higher Education, University
of Georgia, 1970), is a brief discussion of the policy considerations governing the division of authority between the institution and local law enforcement agencies.

3.   Ferdico, J., *Criminal Procedure for the Law Enforcement Officer,* 2nd ed. (West,
1979), is an introductory text on police and criminal court procedure, including arrest, search, admissions, investigation, and evidence.

4.   Kalaidjian, E., "Problems of Dual Jurisdiction of Campus and Community,"
in G. Holmes (Ed.), *Student Protest and the Law,* pp. 131–148 (Institute of Continuing Legal Education, University of Michigan, 1969), addresses issues arising out of concurrent criminal and disciplinary proceedings and police entry
onto campus.

5.   Note, "Privacy Protection Act of 1980: Curbing Unrestricted Third-Party
Searches in the Wake of *Zurcher* v. *Stanford Daily,*" *14 University of Michigan
J. of Law Reform* 519 (1981), reviews the constitutional law implications of
the *Zurcher* case and analyzes the various provisions of the Act passed by Congress in response to *Zurcher.*

Sec. 5.6 (Community Access to Institutional Property)

1.   "Comment: The University and the Public: The Right of Access by
Nonstudents to University Property," 54 *California L. Rev.* 132 (1966), discusses
the appropriateness and constitutionality of using state trespass laws to limit
the public's access to state university and college campuses; California's
criminal trespass law designed for state colleges and universities (Cal. Penal
Code sec. 602-7, 1965), since amended and recodified as Cal. Penal Code
sec. 626.6 (West, supplement, 1977), is highlighted.

2.   Finkin, M., "On 'Institutional' Academic Freedom," 61 *Texas L. Rev.* 817
(1983), analyzes the historical and theoretical underpinnings for the claim
of "institutional academic freedom." Taking as his starting point the distinction between institutional autonomy and academic freedom, the author reviews
the nineteenth-century development of academic freedom in the United States
and the adaptations of the European ideal that American conditions necessitated; considers the constitutional recognition accorded concepts of academic
freedom and the collapsing, in recent cases, of the distinction between institutional autonomy and academic freedom; and applies this discussion to *State*
v. *Schmid,* the *Princeton University* case.

Sec. 5.7 (Community Activities of Faculty Members and Students)

McKay, R., "The Student as Private Citizen," 45 *Denver L.J.* 558 (1968), with
three responding commentaries by other authors, provides a legal and policy
overview of students' status as private citizens of the larger community.

VI

The College
and the State
Government

Sec. 6.1. General Background

Unlike the federal government (see Section 7.1) and local governments (Section 5.1), state governments have general rather than limited powers and can claim all power not denied them by the federal Constitution or their own state constitution. Thus, the states have the greatest reservoir of legal authority over postsecondary education, although the extent to which this source is tapped varies greatly from state to state. In states that do assert substantial authority over postsecondary education, questions may arise concerning whether particular functions are lodged in the legislative or in the executive branch (or, sometimes, in a board or official constitutionally autonomous from either branch). Questions may also arise concerning the state's legal authority, in relation to the federal government's, under federal spending or regulatory programs. In *Shapp* v. *Sloan,* 480 Pa. 449, 391 A.2d 595 (1978), for instance, the specific problems were (1) whether, under Pennsylvania state law, the state legislature or the governor was legally entrusted with control over federal funds made available to the state; and (2) whether, under federal law, state legislative control of federal funds was consistent with the supremacy clause of the Constitution and the provisions of the funding statutes. In a lengthy opinion addressing an array of legal complexities, the Pennsylvania Supreme Court held that the legislature had control of the federal funds under state law and that such control had not been exercised inconsistently with federal law.

The states' functions in matters concerning postsecondary education include planning, coordinating, regulating, and funding. These functions are performed through myriad agencies, including boards of regents; statewide planning or coordinating boards; departments of education or higher education; institutional licensure boards or commissions; State Approval Agencies (SAAs), which operate under contract to the federal Veterans Administration to approve courses for which veterans' benefits may be expended; and various professional and occupational licensure boards, which indirectly regulate postsecondary education by evaluating programs of study and establishing educational prerequisites for taking licensure exams.

Other state agencies whose primary function is not education (such as workers' compensation boards and labor boards) may also regulate postsecondary education as part of a broader class of covered institutions, corporations, or government agencies. States also have broad authority to tax postsecondary education. All private institutions, or their property, within the state are presumed subject to taxation under the existing tax statutes unless a specific statutory or constitutional provision grants an exemption. *In re Middlebury College Sales and Use Tax,* 137 Vt. 28, 400 A.2d 965 (1979), is illustrative. Although the Vermont statute granted general tax-exempt status to private institutions meeting federal standards for tax exemption under the Internal Revenue Code (see this volume, Section 7.3.1), the statute contained an exception for institutional "activities which are mainly commercial enterprises." Middlebury College operated a golf course and a skiing complex, the facilities of which were used for its physical education program and other college purposes. The facilities were also open to the public upon payment of rates comparable to those charged by commercial establishments. When the state sought to tax the college's purchases of equipment and supplies for the facilities, the college claimed that its purchases were tax exempt under the Vermont statute. The court rejected Middlebury's claim, holding that the college had failed to meet its burden of proving that the golfing and skiing activities were not "mainly commercial enterprises."

In addition to performing the above functions through its agencies and boards, the state, through its court system, is the source of the "common law" (see Section 1.3.5) that provides general legal context for most of the transactions and disputes in which institutions may become involved. Agency law is a critical component of this common law (see Sections 2.1 and 2.2). Contract law (Sections 2.3.2 and 2.4.2) and tort law (Sections 2.3.1 and 2.4.1) are comparably important. For example, common law contract and tort principles constrain an institution's freedom to terminate the employment of its personnel. Under the traditional formulation of contract principles, called the "employment at will" doctrine, if the parties do not "fix the period of service and prescribe the conditions on which the contract may be terminated," then the "right of the employee to quit the service of the employer, for whatever reason, is the same as the right of the employer, for whatever reason, to dispense with the services of such employee" (*Adair* v. *United States,* 208 U.S. 161, 174-75 (1908)). These principles have often provided institutions wide latitude in dealing with their administrators and support staffs. Courts in recent cases, however, have modified contract and tort law principles to create exceptions to the "employment at will" doctrine. In a leading example, *Monge* v. *Beebe Rubber Company,* 114 N.H. 130, 316 A.2d 549 (1974), the court held that an employee discharge made in bad faith is a breach of the employment contract; it then invalidated the discharge of an employee for refusing to date her foreman. And in *Fortune* v. *National Cash Register,* 373 Mass. 96, 364 N.E.2d 1251 (1977), the court held that the employer's discharge of an employee to avoid paying him employee bonuses constituted a breach. Other courts have used tort law principles to limit the "employment at will" doctrine. In *Tameny* v. *Atlantic Richfield Co.*, 27 Cal. 3d 167, 164 Cal. Rptr. 839, 610 P.2d 1330 (1980), for instance, the court recognized a "tort of wrongful discharge" applicable to situations where the reasons for the discharge violate state public policy.

Given the considerable, and growing, state involvement suggested by the above discussion, postsecondary administrators can expect increasingly to bump against state agencies and legal requirements in the course of their daily institutional duties. Administrators should therefore stay abreast of state requirements and approval processes and integrate these considerations into their institutional planning. Administrators should also encourage their legal counsel or their government relations office to monitor the growing body of state law and keep key institutional personnel apprised of developments.

Sec. 6.2. State Provision of Public Postsecondary Education

Public postsecondary education systems vary in type and organization from state to state. Such systems may be established by the state constitution, by legislative acts, or by a combination of the two, and may encompass a variety of institutions—from the large state university to smaller state colleges or teachers colleges, to community colleges, technical schools, and vocational schools.

Every state has at least one designated body that bears statewide responsibility for at least some aspects of its public postsecondary system.[1] These bodies are known by such titles as Board of Higher Education, Commission on Higher Education, Board of Regents, Regents, Board of Educational Finance, or Board of Governors. Most such boards are involved in some phase of planning, program review and approval, and budget development for the institutions under their control or within their sphere of influence. Other responsibilities—such as the development of data bases and management information systems or the establishment of new degree-granting institutions—might also be imposed. Depending on their functions, boards are classifiable into two groups: governing and coordinating. Governing boards are legally responsible for the management and operation of the institutions under their control. Coordinating boards have the lesser responsibilities that their name implies. Most governing boards work directly with the institutions for which they are responsible. Coordinating boards may or may not do so. Although community colleges are closely tied to their locales, most come within the jurisdiction of some state board or agency.

The legal status of the institutions within the public postsecondary system varies from state to state and may vary as well from institution to institution within the same state. Typically, institutions established directly by a state constitution have more authority than institutions established by statute and, correspondingly, have more autonomy from the state governing board and the state legislature. In dealing with problems of legal authority, therefore, one must distinguish between "statutory" and "constitutional" institutions and, within these basic categories,

[1]The information in this paragraph is drawn heavily from R. M. Millard, *State Boards of Higher Education* (American Association for Higher Education, ERIC Higher Education Research Rpt. No. 4, 1976).

carefully examine the terms of the provisions granting authority to each particular institution.

State constitutional and statutory provisions may also grant certain authority over institutions to the state governing board or some other state agency or official. It is thus also important to examine the terms of any such provisions that are part of the law of the particular state. The relevant statutes and constitutional clauses do not always project clear answers, however, to the questions that may arise concerning the division of authority among the individual institution, the statewide governing or coordinating body, the legislature, the governor, and other state agencies (such as a civil service commission or a budget office) or officials (such as a commissioner of education). Because of the uncertainties, there has been litigation in a number of states in which the courts have had to determine who holds the ultimate authority to make various critical decisions regarding public postsecondary education.

The litigated issues include the registration of doctoral programs (*Moore* v. *Board of Regents of University of the State of New York,* 390 N.Y.S.2d 582 (Sup. Ct. 1977), affirmed, 59 A.D. 44, 397 N.Y.S.2d 449 (1977), affirmed, 44 N.Y.2d 593, 407 N.Y.S.2d 452, 378 N.E.2d 1022 (1978)); the establishment of tuition rates (*Kowalski* v. *Board of Trustees of Macomb County Community College,* 67 Mich. App. 74, 240 N.W.2d 272 (1976)); the ability to make binding agreements with faculties (*Busboom* v. *Southeast Nebraska Technical Community College,* 194 Neb. 488, 232 N.W.2d 24 (1975)); the authority to authorize expenditures by a constitutionally established university (*Regents of University of Michigan* v. *State of Michigan,* 395 Mich. 52, 235 N.W.2d 1 (1975); *Board of Regents of University of Nebraska* v. *Exon,* 199 Neb. 146, 256 N.W.2d 330 (1977); *State of New Mexico* v. *Kirkpatrick,* 86 N.M. 359, 524 P.2d 975 (1974)); the approval of budget amendments and the appropriation of funds for the university system (*Board of Regents of Higher Education* v. *Judge,* 543 P.2d 1323 (Mont. 1975)); the power to determine the residency requirements for in-state tuition rates (*Schmidt* v. *Regents of University of Michigan,* 63 Mich. App. 54, 233 N.W.2d 855 (1975)); the establishment of salary scales (*San Francisco Labor Council* v. *Regents of University of California,* 26 Cal. 3d 785, 608 P.2d 277 (1980)); control of building design and construction (*State of Mississippi* v. *Board of Trustees of Institutions of Higher Learning,* 387 So. 2d 89 (Miss. 1980)); and control over the expenditure of "self-generated funds"—that is, funds raised directly by the institution through contracts with private entities and other measures that the institution undertakes by its own initiative (*State of Mississippi* case above).

6.2.1. Statutorily based institutions. A public institution established by state statute is usually characterized, for legal purposes, by terms such as "state agency," "public corporation," or state "political subdivision." Such institutions—particularly institutions considered "state agencies"—are subject to substantial state legislative control. A state agency, for example, is usually subject to the state's administrative procedure act and other requirements of state administrative law. State agencies, and sometimes other statutory institutions, may also be able to assert the legal defenses available to the state, such as sovereign immunity. In *Board of Trustees of Howard Community College* v. *John K. Ruff, Inc.,* 278 Md. 580, 366 A.2d 360 (1976), for instance, the court's holding that the board of a regional community college was a state agency enabled the board to assert sovereign immunity as a defense against a suit for breach of contract.

The case of *Moore* v. *Board of Regents of University of the State of New York,* 390
N.Y.S.2d 582 (Sup. Ct. 1977), affirmed, 59 A.D. 44, 397 N.Y.S.2d 449 (1977),
affirmed, 44 N.Y.2d 593, 407 N.Y.S.2d 452, 378 N.E.2d 1022 (1978), illustrates
the problem of dividing authority between a statutory institution and other entities
claiming some authority over it. The trustees and chancellor of the State University
of New York, together with several professors and doctoral students in the affected
departments, sought a declaratory judgment that the university trustees were responsible under the law for providing the standards and regulations for the organization and operation of university programs, courses, and curricula in accordance
with the state's master plan. The defendants were the state board of regents and
the state commissioner of education. The case concerned the commissioner's
deregistration of the doctoral programs in history and English at the State University of New York at Albany. In statements for the news media, each of the opposing
litigants foresaw an ominous impact from a decision for the other side: if the commissioner and the state board won, the institution would continue to be subjected
to "unprecedented intervention"; if the trustees won, the university would be placed
beyond public accountability (*Chronicle of Higher Education,* March 8, 1976, p. 3,
cols. 1–2).

On the basis of its analysis of the state's constitution, Education Law, and
administrative regulations, the court concluded that the commissioner, acting for
the board of regents, which was established by the state constitution, had the authority
to make the decision:

> In support of this conclusion, the court points out that the board
> of regents is a constitutional body which was created in 1784 under the
> name of the Regents of the University of the State of New York (N.Y. Const.
> art. XI, sec. 2). The University of the State of New York (not to be con-
> fused with the State University of New York) is the name given to the entire
> educational community under the jurisdiction of the board of regents. It
> includes "all institutions of higher education which are now or may hereafter
> be incorporated in this state" (Laws of 1892, ch. 378; see Education Law,
> sec. 214).
>
> As of 1784, the regents were vested with full power and authority
> to make ordinances for the government of the colleges which should compose
> the university. In 1892, prior to the adoption of the 1894 constitution, the
> legislature granted broad powers to the regents; these powers included the
> power to charter institutions and colleges, and the legislation prohibited
> institutions not holding university or college degree-conferring powers from
> assuming the appellation of college or university or conferring degrees. These
> and other powers were, in effect, confirmed by the constitution of 1894
> [references omitted].
>
> In its *amicus curiae* brief, the Commission on Independent Colleges
> and Universities notes that since 1787 the regents have registered programs
> and since 1910 they have conducted such registration through the com-
> missioner. In construing the statute to allow the regents, through the com-
> missioner, to register programs, the court relies not only on the historical
> grants of extensive power to the regents, but also on the rule that a long
> continued course of action by those administering a statute is entitled to

great weight (see McKinney's *Cons. Laws of N.Y.,* Book 1, Statutes, sec. 129). Moreover, it would appear that the legislature has recognized the existence and exercise of this authority (Education Law, sec. 224, subd. 4). . . .

   The court also rejects plaintiffs' contention that, notwithstanding the existence of any power the regents and the commissioner may have to register programs in other institutions, they have no power to approve programs in the State University of New York. The State University of New York was created by the legislature on July 1, 1948 (Laws of 1948, ch. 695 [Education Law, sec. 352]), as a corporation within the State Education Department and the University of the State of New York. In 1961, chapter 388 of the Laws of 1961 gave the Board of Trustees of the State University of New York the authority to administer the internal affairs of the State University. Nothing contained in that statute, or in the legislative history leading to its passage, indicates that the State University was to become *sui generis* and not subject to the same requirements imposed by the regents and commissioner on private institutions of higher education in this state [390 N.Y.S.2d at 585–86].

This decision was affirmed by the appellate division of the New York Supreme Court (an intermediate appellate court) and subsequently by the New York Court of Appeals. In affirming, however, the New York Court of Appeals cautioned that the broad "policy-making" and "rule-making" power of the regents "is not unbridled and is not an all-encompassing power permitting the regents' intervention in the day-to-day operations of the institutions of higher education in New York."

   6.2.2. Constitutionally based institutions. A public institution established by the state's constitution is usually characterized, for legal purposes, as a "public trust," an "autonomous university," a "constitutional university," or a "constitutional body corporate." Such institutions enjoy considerable freedom from state legislative control and generally are not subject to state administrative law. Such institutions also may not be able to assert all the defenses to suit that the state may assert. If the institution is considered a public trust, its trustees must fulfill the special fiduciary duties of public trustees and administer the trust for the educational benefit of the public.

   The case of *Regents of University of Michigan* v. *State of Michigan,* 395 Mich. 52, 235 N.W.2d 1 (1975), illustrates both the greater autonomy of constitutional (as opposed to statutory) institutions and the differing divisions of authority that are likely between the institution and other entities claiming authority over it. The University of Michigan, Michigan State University, and Wayne State University, all "constitutional" universities, challenged the constitutionality of various provisions in legislative appropriation acts that allegedly infringed on their autonomy. The court affirmed that, although the legislature could impose conditions on its appropriations to the institutions, it could not do so in a way which would "interfere with the management and control of those institutions." Thus, when one is addressing the constitutionality of any particular condition in an appropriation act, the question is whether that condition constitutes an interference with institutional autonomy. The court refused to answer this question for most of the provisions challenged because they were no longer in effect and the controversy was therefore moot. But the court did address the challenge to a provision prohibiting the institutions from contracting for the construction of any "self-liquidating project" (a project that would ultimately pay for itself) without first submitting to the legislature schedules for liquidation of the debt incurred for construction and operation of the project. The court upheld this provision because it "is a mere reporting measure, without corollary of supervision or control on the part of the [legislative] committees receiving the information. . . . Universities may still enter into construction contracts for self-liquidating projects without prior legislative approval."

The institutions also challenged the State Board of Education's authority over higher education. The State Board of Education argued that it had the authority to approve program changes or new construction at the universities. Relying on the express terms of a constitutional provision setting out the board's powers and their relationship to powers of individual institutions, the court held that the State Board of Education's authority over the institutions was advisory only. The institutions were required only to inform the board of program changes, so that it could "knowledgeably carry out its advisory duties." Thus, although constitutionally created institutions may have exclusive authority over their own operations, some requirements may be imposed on them to accommodate the authority given other state agencies or branches of government. (See also *Regents of University of Michigan* v. *Michigan Employment Relations Commission,* 389 Mich. 96, 204 N.W.2d 218 (1973), where the court held that the University of Michigan is a public employer and subject to the Public Employees Relations Act.)

Similarly, in *San Francisco Labor Council* v. *Regents of University of California,* 26 Cal. 3d 785, 163 Cal. Rptr. 460, 608 P.2d 277 (1980), the court gave substantial protection to a constitutionally based institution's autonomy. The plaintiff labor council argued that the regents had failed to comply with a requirement set forth in the State Education Code—namely, that the board of regents, in setting salaries, must take account of prevailing minimum and maximum salaries in various localities. The board asserted that the state constitution exempted it from the Education Code's mandate. The California Supreme Court agreed with the board.

The state constitutional provision at issue (as quoted by the court) reads:

> The University of California shall constitute a public trust, to be administered by the existing corporation known as "The Regents of the University of California," *with full powers of organization and government, subject only to such legislative control* as may be necessary to insure the security of its funds and compliance with the terms of the endowments of the university and such competitive bidding procedures as may be made applicable to the university by statute for the letting of construction contracts, sales of real property, and purchasing of materials, goods, and services [Cal. Const. art. IX, sec. 9].

The court (608 P.2d at 278) discussed the autonomy that the board enjoyed under this constitutional provision:

> Article IX, section 9, grants the regents broad powers to organize and govern the university and limits the legislature's power to regulate either the university or the regents. This contrasts with the comprehensive power of regulation the legislature possesses over other state agencies.

The courts have also recognized the broad powers conferred upon the regents as well as the university's general immunity from legislative regulation. "The regents have the general rule-making power in regard to the university . . . and are . . . fully empowered with respect to the organization and government of the university. . . . The power of the regents to operate, control, and administer the university is virtually exclusive" (*Regents of University of California* v. *Superior Court* (1970), 3 Cal. 3d 529, 540 [91 Cal. Rptr. 57, 476 P.2d 457]; *California State Employees' Association* v. *Flournoy* (1973), 32 Cal. App. 3d 219, 233 [108 Cal. Rptr. 251]; *California State Employees' Association* v. *State of California* (1973), 32 Cal. App. 3d 103, 109 [108 Cal. Rptr. 60]; *Ishimatsu* v. *Regents of University of California* (1968), 266 Cal. App. 2d 854, 859–60 [72 Cal. Rptr. 756]; *California State Employees' Association* v. *Regents of University of California* (1968), 267 Cal. App. 2d 667, 671 [73 Cal. Rptr. 449].

We recently pointed out "the university is intended to operate as independently of the state as possible (see Cal. Const. art. IX, sec. 9)" (*Regents of University of California* v. *Superior Court* (1976), 17 Cal. 3d 533, 537 [131 Cal. Rptr. 228, 551 P.2d 844]). In that case we concluded the university is so autonomous that, unlike other state agencies, it is subject to the usury laws then applicable to private persons and private universities (17 Cal. 3d at 536–37).

Nevertheless, the board of regents is not totally independent of state legislative control. The court (608 P.2d at 278, 279) outlined three areas where the legislature may regulate the board:

It is true the university is not completely free from legislative regulation. In addition to the specific provisions set forth in article IX, section 9, there are three areas of legislative regulation. First, the legislature is vested with the power of appropriation, preventing the regents from compelling appropriations for salaries (*California State Employees Association* v. *Flournoy, supra; California State Employees' Association* v. *State of California, supra,* at 109–10).

Second, it is well settled that general police power regulations governing private persons and corporations may be applied to the university (*Regents of University of California* v. *Superior Court, supra,* at 536–37; *City Street Imp. Co.* v. *Regents* (1908), 153 Cal. 776, 778 *et seq.* [96 P. 801]; *Estate of Royer* (1899), 123 Cal. 614, 624 [56 P. 461]. For example, workers' compensation laws applicable to the private sector may be made applicable to the university.

Third, legislation regulating public agency activity not generally applicable to the public may be made applicable to the university when the legislation regulates matters of statewide concern not involving internal university affairs (*Tolman* v. *Underhill* (1952), 39 Cal. 2d 708, 712 [249 P.2d 280]).

The court then held that the Education Code provision relied on by the plaintiff did not fit any of the three areas where the legislature could intervene and thus did not bind the board of regents.

Another case, *Board of Regents of University of Oklahoma* v. *Baker,* 638 P.2d 464 (Okla. 1981), is similar to the *San Francisco Labor Council* case in both facts and outcome. The Oklahoma legislature had directed all state agencies, including the board of regents, to increase employee salaries by 6 percent. The board withheld the increase from certain university employees. The employees sued, arguing that the board had no authority to deny them raises authorized by the legislature. The Oklahoma Supreme Court rejected this argument, finding that "the determination of faculty salaries is clearly an integral part of the power to govern the university and a function essential in preserving the independence of the board." In reaching its conclusion, the court relied in part on the *San Francisco Labor Council* case.

Sec. 6.3. State Chartering and Licensure of Private Postsecondary Institutions

6.3.1. Scope of state authority. The authority of states to regulate private postsecondary education is not as broad as their authority over their own public institutions (see Section 1.4.1). Nevertheless, under their police powers, states do have extensive regulatory authority. In a leading case, *Shelton College* v. *State Board of Education,* 48 N.J. 501, 226 A.2d 612 (1967), the court reviewed the authority of New Jersey to license degree-granting institutions and approve the basis and conditions on which they grant degrees. The State Board of Education had refused to approve the granting of degrees by the plaintiff college, and the college challenged the board's authority on a variety of grounds. In an informative opinion, the New Jersey Supreme Court rejected all the challenges and broadly upheld the board's decision and the validity of the statute under which the board had acted.

Similarly, in *Warder* v. *Board of Regents of University of the State of New York,* 53 N.Y.2d 186, 423 N.E.2d 352 (1981), the court rejected state administrative law and constitutional due process challenges to New York's authority to charter postsecondary institutions. The Unification Theological Seminary, a subdivision of the Unification Church (the church of Reverend Moon), sought to incorporate in New York and offer a master's degree in religious education. It applied for a provisional charter. In reviewing the application, the state education department subjected the seminary to an unprecedented lengthy and intensive investigation. The department had been concerned about charges of brainwashing and deceptive practices directed against the Unification Church. The department's investigation did not substantiate these charges but did uncover evidence suggesting other deficiencies. Ultimately, the department determined that the seminary had misrepresented itself as having degree-granting status, had refused to provide financial statements, and had not enforced its admissions policies.

The New York Court of Appeals held that, despite the singular treatment the seminary had received, the education department had a rational basis for its decision to deny the charter:

> Petitioners do not and cannot dispute that the board validly could deny a provisional charter to an institution that engaged in "brainwashing" and deception. That the broad investigation revealed no evidence of such practices does not mean that it was improperly undertaken in the first instance. The board cannot now be faulted because it discharged its responsibility for ensuring ethical educational programs of quality and in the process discovered serious deficiencies in the conduct of the academic program [423 N.E.2d at 357].

The seminary also charged that the legislature's grant of authority to the education department was vague and overbroad, and that the department had reviewed the seminary in a discriminatory and biased manner. Dispensing with the latter argument, the court found that the record did not contain evidence of discrimination or bias. Also rejecting the former argument, the court held that the New York statutes constituted a lawful delegation of authority to the state's board of regents:

> The board of regents is charged with broad policy-making responsibility for the state's educational system (Education Law sec. 207) and is specifically empowered to charter institutions of higher education (Education Law secs. 216, 217). In the meaningful discharge of those functions and to "encourage and promote education" (Education Law sec. 201), the regents ensure that acceptable academic standards are maintained in the programs offered (see *Moore* v. *Board of Regents of University of the State of New York,* 44 N.Y.2d 593, 407 N.Y.S.2d 452, 378 N.E.2d 1022). Thus, before an institution may be admitted to the academic community with degree-granting status, it must meet established standards (see 8 NYCRR [New York Code, Rules and Regulations] 3.21, 3.22, 52.1, 52.2); its purposes must be, "in whole or in part, of educational or cultural value deemed worthy of recognition and encouragement" (Education Law sec. 216). Given the broad responsibility of the board of regents for the quality of education provided in this state, it must be given wide latitude to investigate and evaluate institutions seeking to operate within the system [423 N.E.2d at 357].

Authority over private postsecondary institutions is exercised, in varying degrees depending on the state, in two basic ways. The first is incorporation or chartering, a function performed by all states. In some states postsecondary institutions are subject to the nonprofit corporation laws applicable to all nonprofit corporations; in others postsecondary institutions come under corporation statutes designed particularly for charitable institutions; and in a few states there are special statutes for incorporating educational institutions. Proprietary (profit-making) schools often fall under general business corporation laws. The states also have laws applicable to "foreign" corporations (that is, those chartered in another state), under which states may "register" or "qualify" out-of-state institutions that seek to do business in their jurisdiction.

The second method for regulating private postsecondary institutions is licensure. Imposed as a condition to offering education in the state or to granting degrees or using a collegiate name, licensure is a more substantial form of regulation than chartering. An overview of the kinds of provisions that are or can be included in state licensing systems, as well as some of the policy choices involved, can be found in *Model State Legislation: Report of the Task Force on Model State Legislation for Approval of Postsecondary Educational Institutions and Authorization to Grant Degrees* (Education Commission of the States, Rpt. No. 39, June 1973).

There are three different approaches to licensure:

> First, a state can license on the basis of *minimum standards*. The state may choose to specify, for example, that all degree-granting institutions

have a board, administration, and faculty of certain characteristics, an organized curriculum with stipulated features, a library of given size, and facilities defined as adequate to the instruction offered. Among states pursuing this approach, the debate centers on what and in what detail the state should prescribe—some want higher levels of prescription to assure "quality," others want to allow room for "innovation."

A second approach follows models developed in contemporary regional accreditation and stresses *realization of objectives.* Here the focus is less on a set of standards applicable to all than on encouragement for institutions to set their own goals and realize them as fully as possible. The role of the visiting team is not to inspect on the basis of predetermined criteria but to analyze the institution on its own terms and suggest new paths to improvement. This help-oriented model is especially strong in the eastern states with large numbers of well-established institutions; in some cases, a combined state-regional team will be formed to make a single visit and joint recommendation.

A third model would take an *honest practice* approach. The essence of it is that one inspects to verify that an institution is run with integrity and fulfills basic claims made to the public. The honesty and probity of institutional officers, integrity of the faculty, solvency of the balance sheet, accuracy of the catalogue, adequacy of student records, equity of refund policies—these related matters would be the subject of investigation. If an institution had an occupation-related program, employment records of graduates would be examined. It is unclear whether any state follows this model in its pure form, though it is increasingly advocated, and aspects of it do appear in state criteria. A claimed advantage is that, since it does not specify curricular components or assess their strengths and weaknesses (as the other two models might), an "honest practice" approach avoids undue state "control" of education [*Approaches to State Licensing of Private Degree-Granting Institutions,* pp. 17–19 (Postsecondary Education Convening Authority, George Washington University, 1975)].

Although almost all states have some form of licensing laws applicable to proprietary institutions, not all of these states have licensing laws for nonprofit degree-granting institutions. Among the states that do have such laws, their strength and the effectiveness of their enforcement vary considerably. Often, by statutory mandate or the administrative practice of the licensing agency, regionally accredited institutions (see Section 8.1) are exempted from all or most licensing requirements.

State corporation laws ordinarily do not pose significant problems for postsecondary institutions, since their requirements can usually be met easily and routinely. Although licensing laws contain more substantial requirements, even in the more rigorous states these laws present few problems for established institutions, either because they are exempted by accreditation or because their established character makes compliance easy. For these institutions problems with licensing laws are most likely to arise if they establish new programs in other states and must therefore comply with the various licensing laws of those other states (see Section 6.4). The story is quite different for new institutions, especially if they have innovative (nontraditional) structures, programs, or delivery systems, or if they operate across state lines (Section 6.4). For these institutions licensing laws can be quite burdensome, because such laws may not be adapted to the particular characteristics of nontraditional education or receptive to out-of-state institutions.

When an institution does encounter problems with state licensing laws, administrators may have several possible legal arguments to raise, which generally stem from state administrative law or the due process clauses of state constitutions or the federal Constitution. Administrators should insist that the licensing agency proceed according to written standards and procedures, that it make them available to the institution, and that it scrupulously follow its own standards and procedures. If any standard or procedure appears to be outside the authority delegated to the licensing agency by state statute, it may be questioned before the licensing agency and challenged in court. Occasionally, even if standards and procedures are within the agency's delegated authority, the authorizing statute itself may be challenged as an unlawful delegation of legislative power. In *Packer Collegiate Institute* v. *University of the State of New York,* 298 N.Y. 184, 81 N.E.2d 80 (1948), the court invalidated New York's licensing legislation because "the legislature has not only failed to set out standards or tests by which the qualifications of the schools might be measured, but has not specified, even in most general terms, what the subject matter of the regulations is to be." *State* v. *Williams,* 253 N.C. 337, 117 S.E.2d 444 (1960), used similar reasoning to invalidate a North Carolina law. However, a much more hospitable approach to legislative delegations of authority is found in more recent cases, such as *Shelton College* and *Warder,* both discussed earlier in this section, where the courts upheld state laws against charges that they were unlawful delegations of authority.

Perhaps the soundest legal argument for an institution involved with a state licensing agency is that the agency must follow the procedures in the state's administrative procedure act (where applicable) or the constitutional requirements of procedural due process. *Blackwell College of Business* v. *Attorney General,* 454 F.2d 928 (D.C. Cir. 1971), a case involving a federal agency function analogous to licensing, provides a good illustration. The case involved the withdrawal by the Immigration and Naturalization Service (INS) of Blackwell College's status as a school approved for attendance by nonimmigrant alien students under Section 1101(a)(15)(F) of the Immigration and Nationality Act. The INS had not afforded the college a hearing on the withdrawal of its approved status, but only an interview with agency officials and an opportunity to examine agency records concerning the withdrawal. The appellate court found that "the proceedings . . . were formless and uncharted" and did not meet the requirements of either the federal Administrative Procedure Act or constitutional due process. Invalidating the INS withdrawal of approval because of this lack of procedural due process, the court established guidelines for future government proceedings concerning the withdrawal of a school's license or approved status:

> The notice of intention to withdraw approval . . . should specify in reasonable detail the particular instances of failure to . . . [comply with agency requirements]. The documentary evidence the school is permitted to submit . . . can then be directed to the specific grounds alleged. In addition, if requested, the school should be granted a hearing before an official other than the one upon whose investigation the [agency] has relied for initiating its withdrawal proceedings. If the evidence against the school

is based upon authentic records, findings may be based thereon, unless the purport of the evidence is denied, in which event the school may be required to support its denial by authentic records or live testimony. If, however, the data presented in support of noncompliance [are] hearsay evidence, the college, if it denies the truth of the evidence, shall have opportunity, if it so desires, to confront and cross-examine the person or persons who supplied the evidence, unless the particular hearsay evidence is appropriate for consideration under some accepted exception to the hearsay rule. In all the proceedings the school, of course, shall be entitled to representation and participation by counsel. The factual decision of the [agency] shall be based on a record thus compiled; and the record shall be preserved in a manner to enable review of the decision. . . . We should add that we do not mean that each and every procedural item discussed constitutes by itself a prerequisite of procedural due process. Rather our conclusion of unfairness relates to the totality of the procedure. . . . The ultimate requirement is a procedure that permits a meaningful opportunity to test and offer facts, present perspective, and invoke official discretion [454 F.2d at 936].

Although state incorporation and licensing laws are often sleeping dogs, they can sometimes bite hard. Institutional administrators—especially in new, expanding, or innovating institutions—should remain aware of the potential impact of these laws and the legal arguments available should problems arise.

6.3.2. Chartering and licensure of church-related institutions. In some respects, church-related institutions stand on the same footing as private secular institutions with respect to state chartering and licensure. The *Warder* case (Section 6.3.1), for example, involved a religious seminary that encountered the same kinds of problems as a secular institution might have encountered and raised the same kinds of legal issues as a secular institution might have raised. In other respects, however, the problems encountered and issues raised by church-related institutions may be unique to their religious mission and status. The predominant consideration in such situations is likely to be whether the church-related institution may invoke the freedom of religion guarantees in the federal Constitution or the state constitution—thus obtaining a shield against state regulation not available to secular institutions. The following two cases are illustrative.

In the first case, *New Jersey Board of Higher Education* v. *Shelton College,* 90 N.J. 470, 448 A.2d 988 (1982), the New Jersey Supreme Court held that a state law requiring a license to grant degrees applied to religious as well as nonreligious private colleges. The court also held that application of the law to Shelton, a small fundamentalist Presbyterian college, did not violate either the free exercise clause or the establishment clause of the First Amendment (see Section 1.5).[2] The college had begun offering instruction leading to the baccalaureate degree without first obtaining a state license. The state sought to enjoin Shelton from engaging in this activity within the state, and the New Jersey court granted the state's request.

While acknowledging that the state's licensing scheme imposed some burdens on Shelton's free exercise rights, the court found that the state had an overriding

---

[2]The court refers to this litigation as *Shelton II* to distinguish it from *Shelton I* (*Shelton College* v. *State Board of Education,* discussed in Section 6.3.1).

interest in regulating education and maintaining minimum academic standards.
Given the strength of the state's interest in regulating and the absence of less restrictive means for fulfilling this interest, the state interest outweighed the college's
religious interests:

> Legislation that impedes the exercise of religion may be constitu-
> tional if there exists no less restrictive means of achieving some overriding
> state interest. . . .
>
> The legislation at issue here advances the state's interest in ensuring
> educational standards and maintaining the integrity of the baccalaureate
> degree. . . .
>
> That maintenance of minimum educational standards in all schools
> constitutes a substantial state interest is now beyond question. . . .
>
> [Moreover,] the First Amendment does not require the provision
> of religious exemptions where accommodation would significantly interfere
> with the attainment of an overriding state interest. . . .
>
> Here, accommodation of defendants' religious beliefs would entail
> a complete exemption from state regulation. . . . Such accommodation
> would cut to the heart of the legislation and severely impede the achieve-
> ment of important state goals. Furthermore, if an exemption were created
> here, Shelton College would receive an advantage at the expense of those
> educational institutions that have submitted to state regulation. Such a
> development would undermine the integrity of the baccalaureate degree,
> erode respect for the state higher education scheme, and encourage others
> to seek exemptions. Thus, the uniform application of these licensing require-
> ments is essential to the achievement of the state's interests. . . .
>
> In sum, although defendants' freedom of religion may suffer some
> indirect burden from this legislation, the constitutional balance nonetheless
> favors the state interest in uniform application of these higher education
> laws [448 A.2d at 995–97].

Nor did the state regulations result in any "excessive entanglement" with
religion or otherwise infringe the establishment clause. Instead, the New Jersey
law on its face created a religiously neutral regulatory scheme:

> The allegation of excessive entanglement rests on speculation about
> the manner in which these statutes and regulations might be applied.
> Although one could imagine an unconstitutional application of this
> regulatory scheme, we are confident that the board of higher education will
> pursue the least restrictive means to achieve the state's overriding concerns.
> Of course, should the board exercise its discretion in a manner that un-
> necessarily intrudes into Shelton's religious affairs, the college would then
> be free to challenge the constitutionality of such action [448 A.2d at 998].

In a similar case decided the same month as *Shelton College,* the Supreme Court
of Tennessee upheld that state's authority to regulate degree granting by religious
colleges. In *State ex rel. McLemore* v. *Clarksville School of Theology,* 636 S.W.2d 706
(Tenn. 1982), the school had also been offering instruction leading to a degree without

obtaining a state license. When the state sought to enjoin it from offering degrees, the school argued that application of the state law would infringe its freedom of religion under the First Amendment.

The court agreed with the state's contention that the award of degrees is a purely secular activity and that the state's licensing requirement therefore did not interfere with the school's religious freedoms:

> The school is inhibited in no way by the Act as far as religion is concerned, the Act only proscribing the issuance of educational credentials by those institutions failing to meet the minimum requirements. The court holds, therefore, that applying the Act to defendant school does not violate the free exercise of religion clause of the Constitution, state or federal. . . .
>
> If the Act placed a burden upon the free exercise of religion by the defendants or posed a threat of entanglement between the affairs of the church and the state, the state would be required to show that "some compelling state interest" justified the burden and that there exists no less restrictive or entangling alternative (*Sherbert* v. *Verner,* 374 U.S. 398, 83 S. Ct. 1790, 10 L. Ed. 2d 965 (1963); *Wisconsin* v. *Yoder,* 406 U.S. 205, 92 S. Ct. 1526, 32 L. Ed. 2d 15 (1972)).
>
> We conclude, however, that this Act places neither a direct nor [an] indirect burden upon the free exercise of religion by the defendants nor threatens an entanglement between the affairs of church and state. . . .
>
> The Act does not regulate the beliefs, practices, or teachings of any institution; it merely sets forth minimum standards which must be met in order for an institution to be authorized to issue degrees. Moreover, the evidence shows that the granting of degrees is a purely secular activity. It is only this activity that brings the school under the regulation of the Act [636 S.W.2d at 708–09].

The court emphasized that the licensing statute did not interfere with the content of the school's teaching or with the act of teaching itself. But when the school sought to provide educational credentials as an end product of that teaching, it was properly subject to the state's authority to regulate a secular activity intimately related to the public welfare:

> The fact remains that the state is merely regulating the awarding of educational degrees. The supposed predicament of the school is not a result of the state's regulation of its religious function of *training ministers* but of its preeminent role of *awarding degrees* which is, as conceded by its president and founder, a purely secular activity [636 S.W.2d at 711].

The Tennessee court thus rejected the school's First Amendment claims because the state regulation did not burden any religious activity of the school. In contrast, the New Jersey court recognized that the state regulation burdened Shelton College's religious activities but rejected the school's First Amendment claims because the state's educational interests were sufficiently strong to justify the burden. By these varying paths, both cases broadly uphold state licensing authority over religiously affiliated degree-granting institutions. (For a dissenting view on the issues involved, see R. Kirk, "*Shelton College* and State Licensing of Religious Schools: An Educator's View of the Interface Between the Establishment and Free Exercise Clauses," 44 *Law and Contemporary Problems* 169 (1981).)

Sec. 6.4. State Regulation of Out-of-State Institutions

Postsecondary institutions are increasingly departing from the traditional mold of a campus-based organization existing at a fixed location within a single state.[3] Nowadays both established and new institutions, public as well as private, are establishing branch campuses, off-campus programs, colleges without walls, learning "clusters" or centers, TV and other media-based programs, and other innovative systems for delivering education to a wider audience (see K. P. Cross, J. R. Valley, and Associates, *Planning Non-Traditional Programs: An Analysis of the Issues for Postsecondary Education* (Jossey-Bass, 1974)). This nontraditional education (NTE) movement often takes institutions into states other than their home states, where they were incorporated, and subjects institutions to the regulatory jurisdiction of those other states.

For these multistate institutions, whether public or private, legal problems increase both in number and in complexity. Not only must they meet the widely differing and possibly conflicting legal requirements of the various states, but they must also be prepared to contend with laws or administrative practices that are not suited to or hospitable to either out-of-state or nontraditional programs. Institutional administrators contemplating the development of any program that will cross state lines should be sensitive to this added legal burden and to the legal arguments that may be used to lighten it.

A multistate institution may seek to apply the legal arguments in Section 6.3 to states that prohibit or limit the operation of the institution's programs within their boundaries; these legal arguments apply to all state regulations, whether it concerns out-of-state institutions or not. Out-of-state institutions may also raise particular questions concerning the state's authority over out-of-state, as opposed to in-state, institutions. Is the state licensing agency authorized under state law to license out-of-state schools that award degrees under the authority of their home states? Is the licensing agency authorized to apply standards to an out-of-state school which are higher than or different from the standards it applies to in-state schools? And, most intriguing, may the agency's authority be challenged under provisions of the federal or state constitution—in particular, the commerce clause or the First Amendment of the federal Constitution?

The commerce clause, for example, in addition to being a rich lode of power for the federal government (see Section 7.1), also limits the authority of states to use their regulatory powers in ways that interfere with the free movement of goods and people across state lines. As the U.S. Supreme Court has emphasized, "the very purpose of the commerce clause was to create an area of free trade among the

[3]Some of the material in this section is drawn from prior work of the author included in Chapter Nine of *Nova University's Three National Doctoral Degree Programs* (Nova/N.Y.I.T. Press, 1977) and in Section 4.3 of *Legal and Other Constraints to the Development of External Degree Programs* (report done under Grant NE-G-00-3-0208, National Institute of Education, Jan. 1975).

several states. . . . By its own force [the clause] created an area of trade free from interference by the states'' (*Great A&P Tea Co.* v. *Cottrell,* 424 U.S. 366 (1976)). The term *commerce* has been very broadly construed by the courts. It includes both business and nonbusiness, profit and nonprofit activities. It encompasses the movement of goods or people, the communication of information or ideas, the provision of services that cross state lines, and all component parts of such transactions. Interstate educational activities were specifically found to fall within the category of commerce as far back as 1910 in *International Textbook Co.* v. *Pigg,* 217 U.S. 91, where the Supreme Court held that an out-of-state correspondence school could not constitutionally be subjected to Kansas's foreign corporation requirements.[4]

What protection, then, might the commerce clause yield for multistate institutions? The zone of protection has been clearly identified in one circumstance: when the state subjects an out-of-state program to requirements that are different from and harsher than those applied to in-state (domestic) programs. Such differentiation is clearly unconstitutional. For one hundred years, it has been settled that states may not discriminate against interstate commerce, or goods or services from other states, in favor of their own intrastate commerce, goods, and services.

Beyond this principle of nondiscrimination or evenhandedness, the commerce clause's umbrella of protection against state regulation becomes more uncertain and more dependent on the facts of each particular case. Although a state may evenhandedly regulate the in-state or "localized" activities of out-of-state institutions, a potential commerce clause problem arises when the state regulation burdens the institution's ability to participate in interstate commerce. To resolve such problems, the courts engage in a delicate balancing process, attempting to preserve the right of states to protect their governmental interests while protecting the principle of free trade and intercourse among the states. After a long period of feeling its way, the Supreme Court in 1970 finally agreed unanimously on this general approach:

> Where the statute regulates evenhandedly to effectuate a legitimate local public interest, and its effects on interstate commerce are only incidental, it will be upheld unless the burden imposed on such commerce is clearly excessive in relation to the putative local benefits. If a legitimate local purpose is found, then the question becomes one of degree. And the extent of the burden that will be tolerated will, of course, depend on the nature of the local interest involved, and on whether it could be promoted as well with a lesser impact on interstate activities [*Pike* v. *Bruce Church,* 397 U.S. 137, 142 (1970)].

Under this test the state's interest must be "legitimate"—a label that courts have sometimes refused to apply to parochial, internal economic interests prompted

---

[4]Lawyers will want to compare the *Pigg* case with *Eli Lilly and Co.* v. *Sav-On Drugs,* 366 U.S. 276 (1961), where the Supreme Court distinguished between the *intrastate* and *interstate* activities of a foreign corporation engaged in interstate commerce and permitted the state to regulate the corporation's intrastate activities. See generally Annot., "Regulation and Licensing of Correspondence Schools and Their Canvassers or Solicitors," 92 A.L.R.2d 522 (1963 plus periodic supp.).

by a state's desire to protect its own economy from out-of-state competition. In one famous case, which arose after a state had refused to license an out-of-state business because the in-state market was already adequately served, the Court said that the state's decision was ''imposed for the avowed purpose and with the practical effect of curtailing the volume of interstate commerce to aid local economic interests'' and held that ''the state may not promote its own economic advantages by curtailment or burdening of interstate commerce'' (*H. P. Hood & Sons* v. *DuMond*, 336 U.S. 525 (1949)). While an economically based state regulation is not invariably invalid, it is usually suspect, and the underlying interest may be accorded little or no weight. On the other hand, under the *Pike* test, state interests in safety, fair dealing, accountability, or institutional competence would be legitimate interests to be accorded considerable weight. States clearly may regulate the localized activities of out-of-state institutions (along with in-state institutions) in order to promote such legitimate interests. In doing so, however, states must regulate sensitivity, minimizing the impact on the institutions' interstate activities and assuring that each regulation actually does further the interest asserted.

Commerce clause issues, or other constitutional or statutory issues concerning state authority, are most likely to arise in situations where a state denies entry to an out-of-state program or places such burdensome restrictions on its entry that it is excluded in effect. A state might, for instance, deny entry to an out-of-state program by using academic standards higher than those applied to in-state programs. A state might impose a ''need requirement'' to which in-state programs are not subjected. Or a state might institute a need requirement applicable to both out-of-state and in-state programs but which serves to freeze and preserve a market dominated by in-state schools. A state might also deny entry for lack of approval by a regional or statewide coordinating council dominated by in-state institutions. The relevant legal principles point to the possible vulnerability of state authority in each instance.

In *Nova University* v. *Board of Governors of the University of North Carolina*, 47 N.C. App. 638, 267 S.E.2d 596 (1980), affirmed, 305 N.C. 156, 287 S.E.2d 872 (1982), the North Carolina courts issued the first published court opinions exploring the legal questions raised in this section. By a 4-to-2 vote, the state's Supreme Court held that the state did not have the authority to regulate out-of-state institutions that operate educational programs in North Carolina but award degrees under the auspices of their home states. The plaintiff, Nova University, was licensed to award degrees under Florida law but organized small-group ''cluster'' programs in other states, including North Carolina. Successful participants received graduate degrees awarded in Florida. The board of governors of the University of North Carolina (pursuant to North Carolina General Statute 116-15, which authorized it to license degree-conferring institutions) claimed that Nova's curriculum was deficient and sought to deny the institution authority to operate its cluster programs in the state. The board claimed that the statute which authorized it to license degree conferrals included, by implication, the power to license teaching as well.

In rejecting the board's argument, the court acknowledged the important constitutional questions that the board's position would raise:

> Were we . . . to interpret G.S. 116-15 as the Board suggests, serious constitutional questions arising under the First Amendment and the interstate commerce and Fourteenth Amendment due process clauses of the

United States Constitution and the law of the land clause of the North Carolina constitution would arise [287 S.E.2d at 879].

Looking to the language of G.S. 116-15, the court determined that it could reasonably be interpreted, and should be interpreted, to avoid these constitutional issues:

> All that Nova does in North Carolina is teach. Teaching and academic freedom are "special concern[s]" of the First Amendment to the United States Constitution (*Keyishian* v. *Board of Regents of New York*, 385 U.S. 589, 603, 87 S. Ct. 675, 683, 17 L. Ed. 2d 629 (1967)); and the freedom to engage in teaching by individuals and private institutions comes within those liberties protected by the Fourteenth Amendment to the United States Constitution. . . .
>
> To say that it is conducting a "degree program" which is somehow different from or more than mere teaching, as the board would have it, is nothing more than the board's euphemization. Teaching is teaching and learning is learning, notwithstanding what reward might follow either process. The board's argument that the power to license teaching is necessarily implied from the power to license degree conferrals simply fails to appreciate the large difference, in terms of the state's power to regulate, between the two kinds of activities. The board accuses Nova of trying to accomplish an "end run" around the statute. In truth, the board, if we adopted its position, would be guilty of an "end run" around the statutory limits on its licensing authority. . . .
>
> Here the legislature has clearly authorized the board to license only degree conferrals, not teaching. Because of the statute's clear language limiting the board's authority to license only degree conferrals and not separately to license the teaching which may lead to the conferral, the statute is simply not reasonably susceptible to a construction which would give the board the power to license such teaching [287 S.E.2d at 878, 881–82].

Thus, the court in *Nova University* not only analyzed the state statutory issues but also outlined the sensitive constitutional issues that loom on the horizon if state authority is construed broadly. In contrast to other recent cases, which broadly construe state licensing authority over in-state institutions (see Section 6.3), the *Nova* case narrowly construes state authority over out-of-state schools. Although a more broadly and explicitly worded statute could serve to expand such authority in North Carolina or other states, this broader authority would still have to be tested against the federal and state constitutional limitations suggested by the *Nova* court. The *Nova* litigation therefore affirms that the legal principles in this section do provide substantial ammunition to out-of-state institutions, making it likely that they can hit the mark in cases where state regulation stifles the development of legitimate interstate postsecondary programs.

Sec. 6.5. Other State Regulatory Laws Affecting Postsecondary Education Programs

Aside from the body of state law specifically designed for postsecondary education, discussed in Sections 6.2 and 6.3, public and private postsecondary institutions are subject to a variety of state statutes and regulations that are not specifically tailored to educational operations. Most of this law concerns the institution's role either as employer or, in the case of public schools, as a government agency.

In some regulatory areas, especially with regard to private institutions, federal legislation has "preempted the field," leaving little or no room for state law. Private-sector collective bargaining is a major example (see Section 7.2.2). The federal government has the power to preempt and thereby to exclude state law in any field of concern encompassed by its constitutional powers (see Section 7.1). In other areas, where there is little or no federal legislation, state legislation is primary. Major examples include collective bargaining laws covering public sector employment; workers' compensation laws; deceptive practices laws (for nonprofit entities); and open-meeting laws, administrative procedure acts, ethics codes, civil service laws, and contract and competitive bidding procedures for public agencies. In yet other areas, federal and state governments may share regulatory responsibilities, with some overlap and coordination of federal and state laws. Fair employment laws, occupational health and safety laws, environmental protection laws, unfair trade laws, unemployment compensation laws, and laws on solicitation of funds by charitable organizations are major examples. In this latter area, federal law will prevail over state law in case of conflict if the subject being regulated is within the federal government's constitutional powers.

As these examples suggest, state regulatory law may intrude upon campus operations in many important respects. The cases in the sections below illustrate the kinds of legal disputes that may arise under the laws listed above. But many other state laws—ranging from state liquor-licensing laws (applicable to the campus union) to landlord-tenant laws (sometimes applicable to residence halls)—are also part of the campus's daily legal life. Administrators and counsel should stay attuned to the various state regulations existing in their own jurisdiction, and to their particular applications to the campus.

   6.5.1. Open meetings and public disclosure. Open-meeting laws provide a particularly good illustration of the controversy and litigation that can be occasioned by applying general state law to the particular circumstances of postsecondary education. In an era of skepticism about public officials and institutions, public postsecondary administrators must be especially sensitive to laws whose purpose is to promote openness and accountability in government. As state entities, public postsecondary institutions are often subject to open-meeting laws and similar legislation, and the growing body of legal actions under such laws indicates that the public intends to make sure that public institutions comply.

   Litigation to enforce or to clarify the effect of open-meeting laws on public institutions has been initiated by the media, faculty members, students, education associations, and members of the general public. In *Arkansas Gazette Co.* v. *Pickens,* 522 S.W.2d 350 (Ark. 1975), for instance, a newspaper and one of its reporters argued that committees of the University of Arkansas board of trustees, and not just the full board itself, were subject to the Arkansas Freedom of Information Act. The reporter had been excluded from a committee meeting on a proposed rule change that would have allowed students of legal age to possess and consume intoxicating beverages in university-controlled facilities at the Fayetteville campus. The Arkansas Freedom of Information Act provided in part: "It is vital in a democratic society that public business be performed in an open and public manner so that the electors shall be advised of the performance of public officials and of the decisions that are reached in public activity and in making public policy. Toward this end this Act is adopted, making it possible for them or their representatives to learn and to report fully the activities of the public officials" (Ark. Stat. Ann. sec. 12-2802). The board of trustees contended, and the lower court agreed, that meetings of the board's committees were not "public meetings" within the meaning of the act. The Arkansas Supreme Court reversed, reasoning that the "intent of the legislature, as so emphatically set forth in its statement of policy, [was] that *public business* be performed in an open and public manner" (522 S.W.2d at 353). The court could find no distinction between the board's business and that of its committees and thus applied the open-meeting requirement to both.

A more recent case, *Wood* v. *Marston*, 442 So. 2d 934 (Fla. 1983), concerned the application of Florida's open-meeting law to a University of Florida search-and-screen committee formed to recommend candidates for dean of the law school. The Florida statute stated that (with certain specified exceptions) "all meetings of any board or commission of any state agency . . . at which official acts are to be taken are declared to be public meetings open to the public at all times" (Fla. Stat. Ann. sec. 286.011). The plaintiffs, members of the local news media, sought to enjoin the search-and-screen committee from meeting in private session. Under existing Florida case law, committees that performed only advisory or "fact-gathering" functions, as distinguished from "decision-making" functions, did not perform "official acts" within the statute's meaning and thus were not covered by the statute. The defendants argued that, because the search-and-screen committee's decisions were subject to further review, the committee should be considered an advisory body exempted from the statute. The court rejected this claim:

> The search-and-screen committee had an admitted "fact-gathering" role in the solicitation and compilation of applications. It had an equally undisputed decision-making function in screening the applicants. In deciding which of the applicants to reject from further consideration, the committee performed a policy-based, decision-making function delegated to it by the president of the university through the faculty as a whole. Nor does the fact that the results were submitted to the faculty as a whole, which had the authority to review the work of the screening committee, render the committee's function any less policy based or decision making [442 So. 2d at 938–39].

Similarly, in *University of Alaska* v. *Geistauts*, 666 P.2d 424 (Alaska 1983), the Alaska Supreme Court applied the state's open-meeting law to the meetings of a university tenure committee. The statute provided in part that "all meetings of . . . subordinate units . . . of the state or of any of its political subdivisions are open to the public" (Alaska Stat. sec. 44.62.310(a)). The plaintiff, a disappointed tenure applicant, argued that the statute applied to the committee's deliberations on his tenure application. The university argued that the committee's deliberations fit into a statutory exception permitting closed sessions when the "subjects [to be discussed] tend to prejudice the reputation or character of any person," unless the affected individual requested that the session be open (Alaska Stat. sec. 44.62.310(c)(2)). The court held that the statutory exception applied. It then further held, however, that the tenure committee had failed to notify the plaintiff of the committee's meetings and that this failure deprived him of his statutory right to request that the meetings be open. The court therefore concluded that the committee's decision denying tenure was void and ordered that the plaintiff be reinstated for an additional year with the option to reapply for tenure and be considered by the then-current tenure committee. Left undiscussed by the Alaska court is the impact of the statute and decision on third parties whose opinions of the applicant may be sought, perhaps with a tacit or express understanding of confidentiality, in the course of the tenure review.

Not all cases, however, have been resolved in favor of openness. In *Associated Students of University of Colorado* v. *Regents of University of Colorado,* 543 P.2d 59 (Colo. 1975), the plaintiffs sought to enjoin the regents from holding executive sessions barred to the public. After the trial court applied the state's open-meeting law to the board of regents and enjoined it from holding executive sessions except when matters covered by the attorney-client privilege would be discussed, the Colorado Supreme Court reversed. It held that the board was not subject to the open-meeting law because it was a constitutional body corporate (see Section 6.2.2) with broad powers under the state constitution and statutes to supervise its own affairs. And in *The Missoulian* v. *Board of Regents of Higher Education,* 675 P.2d 962 (Mont. 1984), the court rejected a Montana newspaper's claim that the state's open-meeting law applied to the board of regents' periodic review of Montana state college presidents. Adopting a balancing test that weighed the individual's right to privacy against the public's right to know, the court held that the right to privacy prevailed under the particular facts of the case.

As cousins of open-meeting laws, state public document acts and freedom of information acts also have had important impact on postsecondary education. In *Redding* v. *Brady,* 606 P.2d 1193 (Utah 1980), the plaintiff was the editor of the student newspaper at Weber State College. He sued under the Utah Information Practices Act and the State Public and Private Writings Act to compel the release of salary figures for all Weber State employees. When the court decided in Redding's favor,[5] the legislature responded by enacting the Publication of Higher Education Salary Data Act, which authorized limited disclosure of salaries of groups of employees but generally forbade the disclosure of "personally identifiable salary data." Redding then sued a second time, arguing that both the Utah state constitution and the federal constitution's First Amendment created a public right of access to documents like those he sought and that accordingly the legislation was unconstitutional.

In the second suit, *Redding* v. *Jacobsen,* 638 P.2d 503 (Utah 1981), the Utah Supreme Court agreed that there was an emerging right of access to government documents under recent First Amendment decisions of the U.S. Supreme Court. This emerging right, however, had to be balanced against employees' rights of privacy, which the state legislation sought to protect. Determining that the right to

[5]For other examples of cases in which plaintiffs have succeeded in obtaining information, see *Carter* v. *Alaska Public Employees Association,* 663 P.2d 916 (Alaska 1983) (use of public records disclosure act to obtain a list of university employees and their job titles and locations); *Arkansas Gazette Co.* v. *Southern State College,* 620 S.W.2d 258 (Ark. 1981) (use of state freedom of information act to obtain disclosure of the amounts of money that member schools of an athletic conference dispensed to student athletes).

gather news should not prevail, in this particular instance, over a right to privacy which the legislature had deemed paramount, the court upheld the legislation's constitutionality.

As these cases demonstrate, the general problem created by open-meeting statutes and similar laws is how to balance the public's right to know with an individual's right to privacy or an institution's need for confidentiality. Administrators must consider the complex interplay of all these interests. Sometimes the legislation provides guidelines or rules for striking this balance. Even in the absence of such provisions, some courts, like the *Missoulian* court, have narrowly construed open-meeting laws to avoid intrusion on compelling interests of privacy or confidentiality.

6.5.2. State administrative procedure laws. State administrative law is another area of state law that has had an impact on the campus. Like the federal government, many states have statutes requiring that state agencies follow prescribed procedures when formulating binding rules. State boards and institutions of higher education may be considered state agencies subject to these rule-making statutes. In *Florida State University* v. *Dann,* 400 So. 2d 1304 (Dist. Ct. App. 1980), for instance, several faculty members challenged university procedures used to determine merit raises and other salary increases. The faculty members argued that the university had not conformed to the state rule-making statute when it created the salary increase procedures. The court agreed and invalidated the procedures.

Similarly, in *Board of Trustees* v. *Department of Administrative Services,* 429 N.E.2d 428 (Ohio 1981), laid-off employees of Ohio State University argued that they were entitled to reinstatement and other relief because their layoffs were executed under improperly issued rules. The court agreed. It considered the university's rules to be state agency rules subject to the state's Administrative Procedure Act. This Act required public notice of rule making, filing of rules with the executive and legislative branches of government, a public hearing on proposed rules, and notification of persons who would be especially affected by the rules. The university had failed to follow these procedures. Moreover, it had erroneously issued the rules under the aegis of its board of trustees. The applicable statutory provision grants such rule-making authority to the personnel departments of state universities, not the boards of trustees.

6.5.3. Unemployment compensation laws. Another active area of general law affecting the college campus is unemployment compensation. As developed in Section 7.3.3 of this volume, federal law requires most postsecondary institutions, public or private, to make contributions to a state unemployment insurance program. Participating institutions are treated the same as other employers within the state. As for all employers, an unemployment compensation scheme will cover only persons who have an "employment" relationship with the institution. *Vermont Institute of Community Development* v. *Department of Employment Security,* 436 A.2d 765 (Vt. 1981), for instance, concerned a loosely structured postsecondary institution which employed a small administrative staff, for whom it made unemployment contributions, and a faculty, primarily adjuncts, for whom it did not. Faculty members had written contracts with the school, under which they were paid according to the numbers of students enrolled in their classes. The institute approved the courses taught, but the faculty members selected the time and provided the place for the instruction.

The institute argued that this relationship with faculty members did not constitute "employment" under the Vermont unemployment compensation statute and that the institute therefore was not required to make unemployment contributions on behalf of its faculty members. The statute provided, however, that all services for wages are considered as employment except when:

> (i) Such individual has been and will continue to be free from control or direction over the performance of such services, both under his contract of service and in fact; and
> (ii) Such service is either outside the usual course of the business for which such service is performed, or . . . such service is performed outside of all the places of business of the enterprise for which such service is performed; and
> (iii) Such individual is customarily engaged in an independently established trade, occupation, profession, or business [21 Vt. Stat. Ann. sec. 1301(6)(B)].

The court held that the institute's relationship with its employees did not fall within this exception. Such factors as the institute's setting a minimum number of hours of instruction and requiring end-of-course evaluations negated the institute's argument that it had satisfied condition (i). The institute also failed in its argument that it satisfied condition (iii) because its faculty members were all engaged primarily in nonteaching fields; the court held "that in order to satisfy the provision, the employees must be independently established, providing the same or similar services as they provide for the employer."

6.5.4. Workers' compensation laws. Workers' compensation law provides yet another illustration of general state law with substantial impact on the campus. Like unemployment compensation laws, workers' compensation laws cover postsecondary institutions much as they would any other employer. They provide compensation to the employee or the employee's family in cases where the employee has been injured or killed in the course of employment. The concept of "employment" is again the key coverage issue (see A. Larson, The Law of Workmen's Compensation, vol. 1C, secs. 43–48 (Matthew Bender, 1982)). Several recent cases, for instance, have raised the question whether a varsity scholarship athlete has an employment relationship with his institution and is therefore covered by workers' compensation when he loses the scholarship because he is injured and unable to play. In Rensing v. Indiana State University Board of Trustees, 444 N.E.2d 1170 (1983), the Supreme Court of Indiana upheld the Industrial Board of Indiana's denial of workers' compensation to a scholarship athlete who was permanently disabled by an injury received in football practice. Indiana's intermediate appellate court had overruled the board's decision (437 N.E.2d 78 (Ind. App. 1982)). In reversing the appeals court and reinstating the board's decision, the supreme court held that "there was no intent to enter into an employer-employee relationship" when the student and the university entered into the scholarship agreement. Since the plaintiff athlete was therefore not considered an "employee" under the Indiana Workmen's Compensation Act (Ind. Code sec. 22-3-6-1(b)), he was not eligible for benefits under the Act. (For critical commentary see A. Larson, The Law of Workmen's Compensation, vol. 1A, sec. 22.21 (Matthew Bender, Dec. 1983 Supp.); Note, "Workers' Compensation and College Athletes: Should Universities Be Responsible for Athletes Who Incur Serious Injuries?" 10 J. of College and University Law 197 (1983–84).)

In another case illustrating the operation of workers' compensation statutes, *California State Polytechnic University–Pomona* v. *Workers' Compensation Appeals Board,* 127 Cal. App. 2d 514, 179 Cal. Rptr. 605 (1982), a claim had been filed on behalf of a former stenographer at the university who had been shot to death while working at her desk. A great deal of circumstantial evidence implicated a former boyfriend of the deceased as the likely suspect. The boyfriend was never prosecuted for the shooting because of what the court termed "evidentiary problems." The deceased's family argued that the deceased was killed in the course of employment. The university argued that the deceased was killed out of "personal motives," a defense that would shield it from the workers' compensation claim. The court decided the case in favor of the university.

Selected Annotated Bibliography

Sec. 6.1 (General Background)

1. Hustoles, T., "Faculty and Staff Dismissals: Developing Contract and Tort Theories," 10 *J. of College and University Law* 479 (1983–84), reviews the "employment at will" doctrine and its decline, with special reference to higher education. Examines the contract and tort theories, recently devised by the courts, that have made it more difficult to dismiss employees serving under indefinite or "terminable at will" contracts. Article has greater application to administrative and staff positions than to regular faculty positions, which often are for a stated contract term or have the protection of tenure.

2. Schwartz, B., *Administrative Law,* 2nd ed. (Little, Brown, 1984), is a comprehensive overview of the principles of administrative law. Although the book does not focus on education, its analyses can be applied to state postsecondary systems (to the extent that they are considered state agencies), to state agencies that charter or license private institutions, and to other state agencies whose regulatory authority extends to postsecondary institutions.

Sec. 6.2 (State Provision of Public Postsecondary Education)

1. Beckham, J., "Reasonable Independence for Public Higher Education: Legal Implications of Constitutionally Autonomous Status," 7 *J. of Law and Education* 177 (1978), is a call "for a suitable mechanism to insure reasonable autonomy on selected issues of college and university governance." Author's thesis is that this mechanism should be a constitutional grant of "limited autonomy" to "the state's higher education system." Article also discusses related issues, such as the constitutionality of legislative attempts to transfer power from an autonomous system, the effect "legislation relating to statewide concerns" has on an autonomous system, and the distinction between "appropriations and expenditures."

2. Crockett, R. B., "Constitutional Autonomy and the North Dakota State Board of Higher Education," 54 *North Dakota L. Rev.* 529 (1978), is a study of the autonomy granted to North Dakota public postsecondary education by amendment to the state constitution. Article examines judicial decisions both in North Dakota and in neighboring jurisdictions. Author concludes that "a grant of

autonomy is significant and the constitutional authority of a governing board to control, manage, administer, or supervise the institutions under its jurisdiction may not be invoked or interfered with by a state legislature.''

3. Horowitz, H. W., "The Autonomy of the University of California Under the State Constitution," 25 *UCLA L. Rev.* 23 (1977), is a discussion of the state constitutional provisions that grant the University of California "constitutional" rather than "statutory" legal status. Article analyzes judicial decisions interpreting the relative position of the board of regents under the state constitution vis à vis other branches of state government, and proposes a theory that would limit legislative interference with the governance of the university.

4. Millard, R. M., *State Boards of Higher Education* (American Association for Higher Education, ERIC/Higher Education Research Rpt. No. 4, 1976), discusses the history, structure, functions, and future directions of state governing and coordinating boards for higher education; includes state-by-state tables and a bibliography.

5. Schaefer, H., "The Legal Status of the Montana University System Under the New Montana Constitution," 35 *Montana L. Rev.* 189 (1974), compares and analyzes the new and old Montana constitutional provisions and discusses comparable provisions in other state constitutions; considers the impact of such provisions on the state institution's relationships with other branches of state government.

Sec. 6.3 (State Chartering and Licensure of Private Postsecondary Institutions)

1. Dutile, F., and Gaffney, E., *State and Campus: State Regulation of Religiously Affiliated Higher Education* (Notre Dame Press, 1983), explores the relationship between state governments and church-related colleges and universities, and reviews the various types of state regulations and their validity under federal and state constitutions.

2. Jung, S., and others, *The Final Technical Report—A Study of State Oversight in Postsecondary Education* (American Institutes for Research, Palo Alto, 1977), is an extensive report done by AIR under contract with the U.S. Office of Education. Compiles and assesses statutes and administrative regulations under which state agencies regulate postsecondary institutions. Includes studies of consumer protection incidents reported by state officials. Office (now Dept.) of Education reference: HEW, USOE, Contract No. 300-76-0377. AIR reference: AIR-59400-1277-FR.

3. Millard, R. M., "Postsecondary Education and 'The Best Interests of the People of the States,'" 50 *J. of Higher Education* 121 (1979), discusses the status of licensing in the fifty states and other developments with respect to licensing.

4. *The Nonprofit Counsel* (Charitable Productions Co.) is a monthly newsletter covering a range of legal matters pertinent to nonprofit corporations. Presents information and analysis on new legislation, administrative regulations, and current developments at both state and federal levels. Legal topics include taxation, tax exemption, regulation of fund raising, charitable giving, and rules regarding private foundations.

5. O'Neill, J. P., and Barnett, S., *Colleges and Corporate Change: Merger, Bankruptcy and Closure* (Conference of Small Colleges, Princeton, N.J., 1981), is a hand-

book primarily for trustees and administrators but also useful to attorneys. Chapters include "Indicators of Institutional Health," "Options for Collegiate Corporate Change," "Merger," and "Dissolution of the College Corporation." Discusses procedures for amending the college charter, disposition of assets, placement of faculty, and reorganization under federal bankruptcy law. Also includes state-by-state summary of laws and regulations governing collegiate corporate changes and state-by-state summary of regulations regarding institutional responsibility for student records.

6. Postsecondary Education Convening Authority, *Approaches to State Licensing of Private Degree-Granting Institutions* (George Washington University, Institute for Educational Leadership Rpt. No. 8, 1975), is the conference report on the first conference of state officials who license private degree-granting institutions; explores the concepts of chartering and licensing, the current status of licensing in the fifty states, and the policy and legal problems facing licensing officials; makes recommendations for the future.

Sec. 6.4 (State Regulation of Out-of-State Institutions)

Hughes, E., and others, *Nova University's Three National Doctoral Degree Programs* Nova University, 1977), is a Ford Foundation–funded case study on the development of multistate education programs. Chap. 9 (by F. Nelson and W. Kaplin) provides a discussion of "Legal and Political Constraints on Nova University's External Degree Programs."

Sec. 6.5 (Other State Regulatory Laws Affecting Postsecondary Education Programs)

1. See entry no. 1 for Section 6.3.
2. Bakaly, C., and Grossman, J., *Modern Law of Employment Contracts: Formation, Operation and Remedies for Breach* (Harcourt Brace Jovanovich, 1983 and periodic supp.), is a practical handbook on the legal relationship between employer and nonunionized employee. Topics include application of state contract law principles to employment contracts, issues regarding employee handbooks and employment manuals, wrongful discharge and the "employment at will" doctrine, and internal dispute resolution mechanisms for employment disputes. Also includes appendices with state-by-state review of wrongful discharge law, sample provisions for employee handbooks, and sample employment contract provisions.
3. Cleveland, H., *The Costs and Benefits of Openness: Sunshine Laws and Higher Education* (Association of Governing Boards of Universities and Colleges, 1985), is a research report that reviews state "open meeting" laws and the court decisions and state attorney general opinions construing these laws. Compares the various state laws using a list of twenty-three characteristics relating to openness. Author analyzes the costs and benefits of openness under these laws, concluding that the costs generally outweigh the benefits. Report includes an appendix of attorney general opinions and a bibliography.
4. Hopkins, B., *Charity Under Siege: Government Regulation of Fund Raising* (Wiley, 1980), describes and analyzes the governmental scheme for regulating fund raising by nonprofit organizations. Presents state-by-state summary of laws

on charitable solicitations; analyzes constitutional questions raised by government regulation of fund raising; explores federal IRS oversight of tax-exempt organizations and the activities of private agencies as part of the overall regulatory scheme; and offers advice on how to comply with existing rules.

5. Madden, M., *Employer's Complete Guide to Unemployment Compensation* (Central Commercial Publishing Corp., 1979), is a practical guide to this important area of responsibility shared by state and federal governments. Handbook includes tables summarizing the details of unemployment compensation laws in each of the states, practice forms, and discussion of the particular problems of education institutions.

6. Madsen, H. H., "New State Legislation on Informing Workers About Hazardous Substances in the Workplace: Will It Impact on University Teaching and Research?" 9 *J. of College and University Law* 325 (1982–83), reviews the legal situation in states that have enacted "laws giving employees the right to obtain basic information about hazardous substances with which they work." Author provides an overview of some major issues involved in this area of regulation, contrasting different states' responses (or lack of response) to these issues. Author also discusses factors that could improve state regulation of hazardous substances in the higher education context.

7. Simon, A. M., "The Application of State Sunshine Laws to Institutions of Higher Education," 4 *J. of College and University Law* 83 (1977), explores the state open-meeting and disclosure laws from every angle of concern to postsecondary administrators and their counsel. Includes extensive citations to cases and statutes, three appendices collecting and categorizing state laws, and a bibliography.

8. See entry no. 2 in bibliography for Chapter 7, Section 7.2.

❖ VII ❖

The College
and the Federal
Government

Sec. 7.1. Federal Constitutional Powers over Education

The federal government is a government of limited powers; it has only those powers that are expressly conferred by the U.S. Constitution or can reasonably be implied from those conferred. The remaining powers are, under the Tenth Amendment, "reserved to the states respectively, or to the people." Although the Constitution does not mention education, let alone delegate power over it to the federal government, it does not follow that the Tenth Amendment reserves the handling of education to the states or the people. Many federal constitutional powers—particularly the spending power, the taxing power, the commerce power, and the civil rights enforcement power—are broad enough to extend to many matters concerning education. Whenever an activity falls within the scope of these federal powers (such as making conditional grants to, or contracting with, postsecondary institutions; regulating unfair labor practices or unfair trade practices that affect interstate commerce; taxing graduate assistantships; prohibiting sex discrimination in postsecondary employment practices), the federal government may regulate it. (See, for example, *Case v. Bowles,* 327 U.S. 92 (1946), where the Court rejected a Tenth Amendment challenge to federal emergency price controls on sales of property owned by the states and used for school purposes.)

    7.1.1. Spending power. The current federal involvement in education stems primarily from the "spending power"—that is, Congress's power under Article I, section 8, clause 1, to spend its funds for the "general welfare of the United States."

The spending power is the basis of the federal aid to education programs discussed in Section 7.4 and the civil rights requirements discussed in Section 7.5. It is also the basis of the student records (Buckley Amendment) requirements analyzed in Section 4.12.1. The practice of placing conditions on grants to postsecondary education was approved as long ago as 1907, when in *Wyoming ex rel. Wyoming Agricultural College* v. *Irvin,* 206 U.S. 278 (1907), the U.S. Supreme Court upheld a condition attached to grants under the Land-Grant College Acts. Since then, especially after the Supreme Court's validation of innovative spending legislation passed during Roosevelt's New Deal, the spending power has been broadly construed to permit virtually any spending program that Congress believes will further the general welfare (see, for example, *Helvering* v. *Davis,* 301 U.S. 619 (1937)) and any condition on spending, whether imposed on governmental or private entities, which is "reasonable" and "relevant to federal interest in the project and the overall objective thereof" (*Ivanhoe Irrigation District* v. *McCracken,* 357 U.S. 275, 295 (1958)). The spending power, however, does not give the federal government a roving commission to regulate postsecondary education. What leverage the federal government exerts through the spending power arises from its establishment of the purposes and conditions for its expenditure of funds. Though fund recipients are subject to federal requirements, they can avoid the requirements by not accepting the funds.

In a 1981 case, *Pennhurst State School and Hospital* v. *Halderman,* 101 S. Ct. 1531 (1981), the U.S. Supreme Court made its most important pronouncement on the spending power since the New Deal cases of the 1930s. The plaintiff, a mentally retarded resident of a special school and hospital operated by the state of Pennsylvania, claimed that she had a right to "appropriate treatment"—a right derived in part from conditions that the federal government had attached to certain grants received by the school. The Court rejected the plaintiff's claim, asserting that Congress had not conditioned the grants on the state's willingness to guarantee appropriate treatment and that the language about treatment in the grant statute "represent[s] general statements of federal policy, not newly created legal duties."

To reach its decision, the Court adopted an interpretation of the spending power which emphasizes Congress's responsibility to speak clearly if it seeks to create "entitlements" or "rights" that states (and, apparently, other grantees) must recognize as a condition to receiving federal money:

> Our cases have long recognized that Congress may fix the terms on which it shall disburse federal money to the states. . . . However, legislation enacted pursuant to the spending power is much in the nature of a contract: in return for federal funds, the states agree to comply with federally imposed conditions. The legitimacy of Congress's power to legislate under the spending power thus rests on whether the state voluntarily and knowingly accepts the terms of the "contract" (see *Steward Machine Co.* v. *Davis,* 301 U.S. 548, 585-98, 57 S. Ct. 883, 890-96, 81 L. Ed. 2d 1279 (1937)). There can, of course, be no knowing acceptance if a state is unaware of the conditions or is unable to ascertain what is expected of it. Accordingly, if Congress intends to impose a condition on the grant of federal moneys, it must do so unambiguously. . . . By insisting that Congress speak with a clear voice, we enable to states to exercise their choice knowingly, cognizant of the consequences of their participation [101 S. Ct. at 1539-40].

Although this interpretation clearly benefits states in their dealings with the federal government, it does not create new substantive limits on the number or type of conditions that Congress may impose under the spending power. Instead, *Pennhurst* limits the circumstances in which courts may rcognize, and federal agencies may enforce, grant conditions upon grantees. If Congress and the federal agencies fit within these circumstances by defining their conditions clearly before they award grants, they may impose such conditions to the same extent after *Pennhurst* as they could before.

   7.1.2. Taxing power. The federal taxing power also comes from Article I, section 8, clause 1, which authorizes Congress "to lay and collect taxes" in order to raise the money it spends for the general welfare. The tax power is the basis for the laws discussed in Section 7.3. Though the purpose of the tax power is to raise revenue rather than to regulate, as such, the power has been broadly construed to permit tax measures with substantial regulatory effects. The application of the tax power to postsecondary education was upheld in *Allen* v. *Regents of the University System of Georgia,* 304 U.S. 439 (1938), which concerned an admissions tax that the federal government had levied on state college football games. The tax power may be somewhat greater over private than over public institutions, since public institutions may enjoy a constitutional immunity from federal taxation of their sovereign functions (see Section 7.3.1), and the federal tax laws often treat public and private institutions differently.

   7.1.3. Commerce power. The federal commerce power stems from Article 1, section 8, clause 3 of the Constitution, which authorizes Congress "to regulate commerce with foreign nations, and among the several states." This is the major regulatory power that has been applied to postsecondary education and is the basis for most of the laws discussed in Section 7.2. The commerce power has been broadly construed to permit the regulation of activities which either are *in* interstate or foreign commerce or *affect* it. As the U.S. Supreme Court has often acknowledged, "Congress's power under the commerce clause is very broad. Even activity that is purely intrastate in character may be regulated by Congress, where the activity, combined with like conduct by others similarly situated, affects commerce among the states or with foreign nations" (*Fry* v. *United States,* 421 U.S. 542, 547 (1975)).

   In a series of opinions in the late 1970s and early 1980s, the U.S. Supreme Court did attempt to limit Congress's use of the commerce power as a basis for regulating state and local governments. The key case was *National League of Cities* v. *Usery,* 426 U.S. 833 (1976). By a 5-to-4 vote, the Court relied on the Tenth Amendment to invalidate federal wage and hours laws as applied to state and local government employees, reasoning that "their application will significantly alter or displace the states' abilities to structure employer-employee relationships . . . in areas of traditional governmental functions." The Court premised this decision on a general principle that "Congress may not exercise . . . [the commerce] power so as to force directly upon the states its choices as to how essential decisions regarding the conduct of integral governmental functions are to be made." In subsequent years, however, lower courts and the Supreme Court itself struggled to understand and apply *National League's* enigmatic distinctions between "traditional" and "nontraditional," and "integral" and "nonintegral," government functions. Finally, in *Garcia* v. *San Antonio Metropolitan Transit Authority,* 105 S.Ct. 1005 (1985), by a 5-to-4 vote, the court overruled *National League:*

We therefore now reject, as unsound in principle and unworkable in practice, a rule of state immunity from federal regulation that turns on a judicial appraisal of whether a particular governmental function is "integral" or "traditional." . . .

The principal and basic limit on the federal commerce power is that inherent in all congressional action—the built-in restraints that our system provides through state participation in federal governmental action. The political process ensures that laws that unduly burden the states will not be promulgated. . . .

The model of democratic decision making [that] the court [identified in *National League*] underestimated, in our view, the solicitude of the national political process for the continued vitality of the states. Attempts by other courts since then to draw guidance from this model have proved it both impracticable and doctrinally barren. In sum, in *National League of Cities* the court tried to repair what did not need repair [105 S. Ct. at 1016, 1020-2].

7.1.4. Civil rights enforcement power. The civil rights enforcement power is the fourth major federal power applicable to education. Its source is the enforcement clauses of various constitutional amendments, particularly the Fourteenth Amendment (due process and equal protection), whose fifth section provides that "the Congress shall have power to enforce, by appropriate legislation, the provisions of this article." In *Katzenbach* v. *Morgan*, 384 U.S. 641 (1966), the U.S. Supreme Court held that section 5 of the Fourteenth Amendment empowers Congress to "exercise its discretion in determining whether and what legislation is needed to secure the [amendment's] guarantees," as long as the legislation is "adapted to carry out the objects the . . . [amendment has] in view" and is not otherwise prohibited by the Constitution.

The civil rights enforcement powers are the basis for some of the federal employment discrimination laws (see Section 3.3.2). In *Fitzpatrick* v. *Bitzer*, 427 U.S. 445 (1976), for instance, the Court upheld the 1972 extension of Title VII to state and local governments as an appropriate exercise of the Fourteenth Amendment enforcement power. These powers are also the basis for various civil rights regulatory statutes that have some application to postsecondary education (statutes such as 42 U.S.C. sec. 1981, discussed in Sections 3.3.2.7 and 4.2.4.1; and 42 U.S.C. sec. 1983, discussed in Section 2.3.3). Although the enforcement powers clearly apply to public institutions, some uncertainty remains concerning the scope of these powers as applied to the public sector (see *Oregon* v. *Mitchell*, 400 U.S. 112 (1970)). There is also some uncertainty concerning the application of Congress's enforcement powers to the private sector, although Section 1981 (passed pursuant to the Thirteenth Amendment enforcement power to eradicate "badges" and "incidents" of slavery) does clearly extend to private institutions (see *Fairfax-Brewster* v. *Gonzales*, 427 U.S. 160 (1976), discussed in Section 4.2.4.1). The issues regarding the scope of the enforcement powers are complex and vary with the civil rights statute being addressed and the constitutional amendment (Thirteenth, Fourteenth, or Fifteenth) under which the statute was passed.[1]

---

[1]For a theoretical examination of Congress's enforcement powers, see J. Choper, "Congressional Power to Expand Judicial Definitions of the Substantive Terms of the Civil War Amend-

Sec. 7.2. Federal Regulation of Postsecondary Education

Institutions and their national associations are increasingly seeking to develop arguments for limiting the impact of federal regulations and federal funding conditions on postsecondary education. The 1979 *Davis* case (discussed in Section 7.5.4) is a major example of the use of legislative history and statutory construction to narrow the reach of administrative agency regulations. Another prominent strategy is to strengthen self-regulation by institutions and associations and to utilize self-regulation as a justification for decreasing federal regulation.

The subsections below examine developments in federal regulatory areas of particular concern to postsecondary education. Other federal statutes, not listed in these subsections, may also become important in particular circumstances. The federal bankruptcy law (11 U.S.C. sec. 101 *et seq.*), for instance, is important when a student loan recipient declares bankruptcy (see Section 4.3.6.1) and when an institution encounters severe financial distress. The Export Administration Act, 50 U.S.C. sec. 2401 *et seq.*, can become important when the federal government seeks to restrict the flow of technical data to other countries (see R. Sullivan and N. Bader, "The Application of Export Control Laws to Scientific Research at Universities," 9 *J. of College and University Law* 451 (1982–83)). The Military Selective Service Act, 50 U.S.C. sec. 451 *et seq.*, is important when the federal government seeks to prohibit nonregistrants from receiving federal student aid (see Section 4.3.2). The Communications Act of 1934, as amended, 47 U.S.C. sec. 151 *et seq.*, is important when a postsecondary institution seeks or holds a Federal Communications Commission license to operate an instructional television channel or other broadcasting license. The Lanham Act, 15 U.S.C. sec. 1051 *et seq.*, providing for registration and protection of trademarks and other "marks," becomes important whenever an institution needs to protect its logos and other symbols of identity (see entries 2 and 7 in the bibliography for Section 7.2). The Resource Conservation and Recovery Act, 90 Stat. 2795 (1976) (adding various sections to Title 42, U.S.C.) and the Comprehensive Environmental Response, Compensation, and Liability Act ("Superfund"), 94 Stat. 2767 (1980) (adding various sections to Titles 26, 33, 42, and 49, U.S.C.), both of which deal with management and disposal of hazardous waste, are important if the institution has laboratories or other installations that generate such waste. And the Medicare (42 U.S.C. sec. 1395 *et seq.*) and Medicaid (42 U.S.C. sec. 1396 *et seq.*) statutes are important for institutions with teaching hospitals or other health programs delivering services for which the institution or staff members seek Medicare or Medicaid reimbursements (see C. Hitchner, "Medicare and Medicaid Reimbursement of Teaching Hospitals and Faculty Physicians," 10 *J. of College and University Law* 79 (1983–84)).

---

ments," 67 *Minnesota L. Rev.* 299 (1982). For an extended analysis of congressional power to combat private discrimination, see Note, "Federal Power to Regulate Private Discrimination: The Revival of the Enforcement Clauses of the Reconstruction Era Amendments," 74 *Columbia L. Rev.* 449 (1974). For an analysis of congressional power under the Thirteenth Amendment and an argument that this power extends to enforcing affirmative action, see C. A. Baldwin, "The Thirteenth Amendment as an Effective Source of Constitutional Authority for Affirmative Action Legislation," 18 *Columbia J. of Law and Social Problems* 77 (1983). For a review of enforcement issues under Section 1981 and the Thirteenth Amendment, see "Developments in the Law—Section 1981," 15 *Harvard Civil Rights–Civil Liberties L. Rev.* 29 (1981).

7.2.1. Occupational Safety and Health Act. Private postsecondary institutions must conform to the federal Occupational Safety and Health Act of 1970 (OSHA), 29 U.S.C. sec. 651 *et seq.* Under this Act a private institution must "furnish to each of [its] employees employment and a place of employment which are free from recognized hazards that are causing or are likely to-cause death or serious physical harm" (29 U.S.C. sec. 654). Violations may result in fines or imprisonment (sec. 666). The Act does not preempt any rights employees may have to pursue civil actions or other remedies under state laws (sec. 653(b)(4)).

Though public postsecondary institutions are not subject to OSHA, they may be required to conform to state occupational safety and health laws or equivalent state legislation or administrative regulations.

7.2.2. Labor-Management Relations Act. The Labor-Management Relations Act, 29 U.S.C. sec. 141 *et seq.*, protects the employees of covered employers in "the exercise . . . of full freedom of association, self-organization, and designation of representatives of their own choosing, for the purpose of negotiating the terms and conditions of their employment or other mutual aid or protection" (29 U.S.C. sec. 151). The LMRA's application to faculty members is discussed in Section 3.2.

The Act defines "employee" to exclude "any individual employed as a supervisor" (29 U.S.C. sec. 152(3)); a "supervisor" is defined as "any individual having authority, in the interest of the employer, to hire, transfer, suspend, lay off, recall, promote, discharge, assign, reward, or discipline other employees, or responsibly to direct them, or to adjust their grievances, or effectively to recommend such action, if in connection with the foregoing the exercise of such authority is not of a merely routine or clerical nature, but requires the use of independent judgment" (sec. 152(11)). The Act defines "employer" to exclude "any state or political subdivision thereof," thereby removing public employers, including public postsecondary institutions, from the Act's coverage (29 U.S.C. sec. 152(2)). The LMRA thus applies only to private postsecondary institutions and, under current National Labor Relations Board rules, only to those with gross annual revenues of at least one million dollars (29 C.F.R. sec. 103.1).

Public institutions, though not subject to the LMRA, are often subject to similar legislation at the state level (see Section 3.2.1).

7.2.3. Fair Labor Standards Act. The Fair Labor Standards Act (FLSA), 29 U.S.C. sec. 201 *et seq.*, establishes the minimum hourly wage and the piecework rates as well as the maximum hours allowed for certain nonsupervisory employees. The FLSA has always applied to private postsecondary institutions (except for some religious schools, as discussed below). But the Act's application to public postsecondary institutions has been the subject of historical turmoil. In 1966 Congress extended the Act's coverage to public hospitals and schools, including public postsecondary schools. Two years later the U.S. Supreme Court upheld this extension in *Maryland* v. *Wirtz*, 392 U.S. 183 (1968). But the Court expressly overruled its *Wirtz* opinion in *National League of Cities* v. *Usery*, 426 U.S. 833 (1976), thus prohibiting the federal government from enforcing the FLSA against public postsecondary institutions and other state and local government employers that Congress had brought under the Act's coverage in 1974. Then, completing the circle, the court overruled its *National League of Cities* opinion in *Garcia* v. *San Antonio Metropolitan Transit Authority*, 105 S. Ct. 1005 (1985) (see Section 7.1.3). The *Garcia* opinion apparently opens the way for Congress and the Department of Labor to again regulate public postsecondary institutions under the FLSA; administrators and counsel should watch for further developments.

In situations where an applicable state law establishes a minimum wage rate that conflicts with the federal standard, the higher rate must prevail (29 U.S.C. sec. 218).

The FLSA specifically exempts "any employee employed in a bona fide executive, administrative, or professional capacity" from the minimum wage and maximum hour requirements (29 U.S.C. sec. 213(a)(1)). The Department of Labor has promulgated regulations implementing this provision (29 C.F.R. Part 541). The regulations establish the conditions of employment that must exist before an employer may consider an employee to be an "executive," or an "administrative," or a "professional" employee. Of particular interest to higher education, the term *administrative* includes persons who perform "functions in the administration of [an] . . . educational establishment or institution, or of a department or subdivision thereof" (29 C.F.R. sec. 541.2(a)(2)) and meet the other conditions set by the regulations. Similarly, the term *professional* includes persons whose primary duty is "teaching, tutoring, instructing, or lecturing . . . and who are employed and engaged in this activity as a teacher in the . . . educational establishment or institution by which he is employed (29 C.F.R. sec. 541.3(a)(3)), if they also meet the regulations' other conditions.

The DOL regulations were applied in *Prakash* v. *American University,* 727 F.2d 1174 (D.C. Cir. 1984), a case brought by a former physics professor seeking payment at the minimum wage rate for regular and overtime work previously performed. The university claimed that the professor was a professional exempted from the FLSA's coverage and thus not entitled to the statutory minimum wage. The appellate court remanded the case to the trial court for a determination of whether the university could prove that the professor's position had met all the conditions of professional capacity established in the DOL regulations.

Even more basic than whether one is a professional, executive, or administrative employee is the question whether one can be classified at all as an employee. In *Marshall* v. *Regis Educational Corp.,* 666 F.2d 1324 (10th Cir. 1981), the secretary of labor contended that the college's student resident-hall assistants (RAs) were "employees" within the meaning of the Act and therefore must be paid the prescribed minimum wage. The college argued that its RAs were not employees and that, even if they were, application of the Act to these RAs would violate the college's academic freedom protected by the First Amendment. Affirming the district court, the appellate court accepted the college's first argument and declined to consider the second. The court's opinion focuses on the unique circumstances of academic life:

> During the years [at issue], the college was aided in its resident-hall program by some 47 students who served as RAs. RAs resided in the dormitories where they assisted the residence directors and actively participated in the development and implementation of programs designed to enhance the quality of resident-hall living. Students seeking appointment as RAs were required to submit applications for the position, and candidates were screened by a committee of administrators and students. Successful applicants participated in a training workshop prior to the beginning of the fall semester.

The duties of an RA . . . were specified in a written contract called an "employment agreement." . . . Regis entered into a Resident Assistant Grant-in-Aid agreement with each RA. The terms of this agreement, which avoided the words "employment" and "employee," were substantially the same as the "employment agreement." RAs were required to participate in training programs and were responsible for miscellaneous administrative tasks, such as telephone coverage, mail distribution, unlocking doors, and the like. RAs, moreover, had broader responsibilities in maintaining discipline and order within the halls and in encouraging participation in campus activities. Although RAs did not work a specified number of hours per day, they were generally available in the halls for an estimated twenty hours a week. In order to keep their status as RAs they were required to maintain a specified grade point average. In exchange for the performance of these duties, RAs received a reduced rate on their rooms, the use of a free telephone, and a $1,000 tuition credit. . . .

The government contends that RAs were "employees" because they received compensation and the college enjoyed an immediate economic benefit from their services. The government emphasizes that RAs displaced employees whom Regis would otherwise have been required to hire. Regis counters that the primary purpose of the RA program was educational, that RAs at Regis were not "employees," but student recipients of financial aid. The college rejects the argument that RAs displace other employees, stressing that the peer counseling and educational aspects of the resident assistant program would be lost if it were operated without students. . . .

[Section 203 of 29 U.S.C.] defines an "employee" as "any individual employed by an employer," and defines "employ" as "to suffer to permit to work." . . . In *Rutherford Food Corp.* v. *McComb,* 331 U.S. 722 (1947), . . . the Supreme Court declared that the determination of employment under the FLSA ought not depend on isolated factors but upon the "circumstances of the whole activity" (331 U.S. at 730). This test is controlling in the case at bar.

The government urges that RAs were employees because their services had an immediate economic impact on the "business" of operating a college. In so asserting, the government views the college as being in the "business" of providing educational and support services and concludes that when the college enlists students to help in promoting safe and secure accommodations, it is, in fact, *employing* students. The college is deemed by the government as being in the "business" of providing security for the learning environment.

We believe the government's perspective to be so limited as to ignore not only the broad educational purpose of this private liberal arts college, but also the expressed educational objectives of the student resident assistant program. . . .

Our holding that RAs are not employees does not require the conclusion that no student working at the college would be within the scope of the FLSA. No such inference should be drawn. There are undoubtedly campus positions which can be filled by students and which require compliance with the FLSA. Students working in the bookstore selling books, working with maintenance, painting walls, etc., could arguably be "employees." . . .

The record shows that student athletes who receive tuition grants are required to maintain a specified academic average and to fulfill certain duties with respect to training programs and to participate in sports events on campus; student leaders in the student government associations are similarly situated. Selected student leaders have specified duties and responsibilities and receive tuition credits. . . .

We agree with the district court (considering the totality of the circumstances) in finding that RAs at Regis were legally indistinguishable from athletes and leaders in student government who received financial aid. We therefore hold that the RAs at Regis College were not "employees" within the meaning of the Act, but student recipients of financial aid [666 F.2d at 1326–28].

7.2.4. Employee Retirement Income Security Act. The Employee Retirement Income Security Act of 1974 (known as the Pension Reform Act or ERISA) establishes "standards of conduct, responsibility, and obligation for fiduciaries of employee benefit plans" (29 U.S.C. sec. 1001(b)). The terms *employee benefit plan* and *employee pension plan* are defined to encompass various health benefits, death benefits, disability benefits, unemployment benefits, retirement plans, and income deferral programs (29 U.S.C. sec. 1002(1) and (2)). The ERISA requirements for the creation and management of these plans are codified partly in the federal tax law (26 U.S.C. sec. 401 *et seq.*) and partly in the federal labor law (29 U.S.C. sec. 1001 *et seq.*). These requirements apply only to private postsecondary institutions. The plans of public institutions are excluded from coverage as "governmental plan(s)" under 29 U.S.C. sec. 1002(32) and 26 U.S.C. sec. 414(d).

The ERISA standards have been construed as *minimum* federal standards designed to curb the funding and disclosure abuses of employee pension and benefit plans (*Wadsworth* v. *Whaland,* 562 F.2d 70 (1st Cir. 1977)). Rules and regulations have been issued covering reporting and disclosure requirements, minimum standards of conduct, and fiduciary responsibilities (see 29 C.F.R. Parts 2510, 2520, 2530, and 2550). Interpretive bulletins explaining the Act have also been issued and reprinted at 29 C.F.R. Part 2509.

Some special rules apply to benefit plans for teachers and other employees of tax-exempt educational institutions. Under certain circumstances, for instance, such employees may delay their participation in a benefit plan until they reach the age of twenty-six (26 U.S.C. sec. 410(a)(1)(B)(ii); 29 U.S.C. sec. 1052(a)(1)(B)(ii)).

ERISA was amended by the Retirement Equity Act of 1984, 98 Stat. 1426 *et seq.* The new Act's purpose, as stated in its preamble, is to "provide for greater equity under private pension plans for workers and their spouses and dependents by taking into account changes in work patterns, the status of marriage as an economic partnership, and the substantial contribution to that partnership of spouses who work both in and outside the home." Section 102(e) of the Act contains provisions that protect employees' pension benefits during periods of maternity or paternity leave; Section 103 establishes requirements regarding the provision, by pension plans, of joint and survivor annuities and preretirement survivor annuities for surviving spouses of employees; and Section 104 establishes rules for the assignment of rights to pension benefits in divorce proceedings.

With various listed exceptions, ERISA supersedes any and all state laws "insofar as they may now or hereinafter relate to any employee benefit plan" subject to the ERISA statute (29 U.S.C. sec. 1144(a)). The exceptions are for state laws regulating insurance, banking, or securities, and state criminal laws, none of which are superseded by ERISA (29 U.S.C. sec. 1144(b)). These provisions, and their relation to other provisions in the statute, have been the subject of varying interpretations by the courts, and it has often proved difficult in particular cases to determine when ERISA preempts state law. (See generally P. Turza and L. Halloway, "Preemption of State Laws Under the Employee Retirement Income Security Act of 1974," 28 *Catholic University L. Rev.* 163 (1979).)

Two U.S. Supreme Court cases address the ERISA preemption issue from different, but not contradictory, perspectives. In *Alessi* v. *Raybestos-Manhattan*, 451 U.S. 504 (1981), the Court considered whether a state law prohibiting workers' compensation benefits from being used to offset pension benefits was preempted by ERISA. The Court held that the state statute was preempted: "ERISA makes clear that even indirect state action bearing on private pension plans may encroach upon the area of exclusive federal concern. . . . ERISA's authors clearly meant to preclude the states from avoiding through form the substance of the preemption provision." In *Shaw* v. *Delta Airlines*, 103 S. Ct. 2890 (1983), an airline and other employers sought to have two New York State statutes preempted by ERISA insofar as they applied to employee benefit plans: the New York Human Rights Law, a comprehensive antidiscrimination statute prohibiting, among other actions, discrimination on the basis of pregnancy; and the New York Disability Benefits Law, which required employers (among other things) to pay sick leave benefits to employees unable to work because of pregnancy. The Court determined that the ERISA preemption provision (sec. 1144(a)) should be broadly construed and that both New York statutes "relate to" employee benefit plans within the meaning of that provision. The Court then proceeded, in painstakingly intricate analysis, to save both statutes from preemption (with some qualifications) by resorting to other ERISA provisions which limit the reach of the preemption clause.

After these Supreme Court rulings, the relationship between ERISA and state laws remains complex and should be a focal point of the postsecondary institution's legal planning with respect to its fringe benefit programs.

7.2.5. Employment discrimination laws. Aside from the nondiscrimination requirements that it imposes as conditions on federal spending (see Section 7.5), the federal government also directly regulates employment discrimination under several other statutes. Primary among them is Title VII of the Civil Rights Act of 1964, 42 U.S.C. sec. 2000e *et seq.* These statutes are set out and discussed in Section 3.3.2, which examines their particular applications to faculty members.

7.2.5.1. Application to administrators and staff. Courts have often been deferential to higher education institutions when considering employment discrimination claims brought against them. Usually, however, courts have displayed this deference in cases where the institution's refusal to hire, renew, or tenure *a faculty member* is alleged to be discriminatory. In such cases the reluctance of courts to intervene may stem from a recognition of the limits of their competence to second-guess decisions resulting from a peer review process that emphasizes subjective evaluation of scholarly work. Such considerations are usually absent in cases brought by administrators or staff personnel in positions without faculty status. Since the justifications for according deference to higher education institutions do not apply with the same force to these nonfaculty cases, courts may be more activist in applying federal nondiscrimination laws to them.

In addition to the differing degrees of deference, employment decisions regarding administrators and staff may raise different types of issues under federal nondiscrimination laws than do employment decisions regarding faculty. Two cases, both decided under the Age Discrimination in Employment Act (Section 3.3.2.5), illustrate two such issues. In *EEOC* v. *University of Texas Health Science Center*, 710 F.2d 1091 (5th Cir. 1983), the court considered the ADEA's application to a campus security force. The plaintiff had been refused employment because he exceeded the force's maximum hiring age of forty-five. The center argued that age was a bona fide occupational qualification (BFOQ) for the position of security officer, not subject to the Act's prohibition, because the job demanded an exceptional level of physical fitness. The court held in favor of the center—but only because it was able to present "consistent testimony at trial that physical strength, agility, and stamina are important to the training and performance of campus policemen." In *EEOC* v. *Board of Trustees of Wayne County Community College*, 723 F.2d 509 (6th Cir. 1983), the court considered the applicability, to a community college president, of an ADEA provision excluding high-level public appointees in policy-making positions from the Act's protections. The EEOC argued that, because the college's board of trustees exercised broad policy-making powers, the president did not fall within the exclusion and was therefore protected by the Act. The court rejected this argument, reasoning that "shared, overlapping, and complementary authority [is] no less capable of being denominated policy making than is exclusive authority."

7.2.5.2. Applicability to religious institutions. A major coverage issue under federal employment discrimination statutes is their applicability to religious institutions. The issue parallels those that recently arose under federal collective bargaining law (see the *Catholic Bishop* case in Section 3.2.1), unemployment compensation law (see the *St. Martin's* case in Section 7.3.3), and federal tax law (see the *Bob Jones* case in Section 7.3.1). In two cases decided in 1980 and 1981, the U.S. Court of Appeals for the Fifth Circuit thoroughly analyzed the extent to which religious schools are subject to Title VII of the Civil Rights Act of 1964, 42 U.S.C. sec. 2000e *et seq.* The cases also include useful analysis of how a religious college may respond to investigatory subpoenas and other information requests served on it by the Equal Employment Opportunity Commission (EEOC).

The first case, *Equal Employment Opportunity Commission* v. *Mississippi College*, 626 F.2d 477 (5th Cir. 1980), concerned a four-year coeducational school owned by the Mississippi Baptist Convention, an organization of Southern Baptist churches in Mississippi. According to the court:

> The Convention conceives of education as an integral part of its Christian mission. It acquired the college in 1850 and has operated it to the present day to fulfill that mission by providing educational enrichment in a Christian atmosphere. . . . The college has a written policy of preferring active members of Baptist churches in hiring. The evidence the college presented to the district court indicates that approximately 95 percent of the college's full-time faculty members are Baptists. The evidence also shows that 88 percent of the college's students are Baptists. . . . Because no woman has been ordained as a minister in a Southern Baptist church in Mississippi, the college hires only males to teach courses concerning the Bible [626 F.2d at 479].

A part-time member of the college's faculty, Dr. Summers, had filed a charge with the EEOC after the college denied her application for a vacancy on the full-time faculty. Dr. Summers alleged that the college's choice of a male for the position was an act of sex discrimination. She also alleged that the college discriminated against women as a class and against minorities in hiring. When the EEOC attempted to investigate these allegations, the college refused to cooperate, and the EEOC sought court enforcement of a subpoena directed to the college.

As to Dr. Summers' individual claim, the college asserted that it had chosen the male applicant partly because he was a Baptist and Summers was not. Thus, argued the college, its decision was based on religion and was clearly within the exemption for religious educational institutions in Section 702 of Title VII:

> This title [Title VII, 42 U.S.C. sec. 2000e *et seq.*] shall not apply to . . . a religious corporation, association, educational institution, or society with respect to the employment of individuals of a particular religion to perform work connected with the carrying on by such corporation, association, educational institution, or society of its activities [42 U.S.C. sec. 2000e-1].

The court agreed in principle with the college but indicated the need for additional evidence on whether the college had accurately characterized its failure to hire Summers:

> If a religious institution of the kind described in Section 702 presents convincing evidence that the challenged employment practice resulted from discrimination on the basis of religion, Section 702 deprives the EEOC of jurisdiction to investigate further to determine whether the religious discrimination was a pretext for some other form of discrimination. This interpretation of Section 702 is required to avoid the conflicts that would result between the rights guaranteed by the religion clauses of the First Amendment and the EEOC's exercise of jurisdiction over religious educational institutions. . . . If the district court determines on remand that the college applied its policy of preferring Baptists over non-Baptists in granting the faculty position to Bailey rather than Summers, then Section 702 exempts that decision from the application of Title VII and would preclude any investigation by the EEOC to determine whether the college used the preference policy as a guise to hide some other form of discrimination. On the other hand, should the evidence disclose only that the college's preference policy could have been applied, but in fact it was not considered by the college in determining which applicant to hire, Section 702 does not bar the EEOC's investigation of Summers' individual sex discrimination claim [626 F.2d at 485–86].

The college also argued, as to Summers' individual claim and her allegation of class discrimination against women and blacks, (1) that the employment relationship between a church-related school and its faculty is not within the purview of Title VII; and (2) that, if this relationship is within Title VII, its inclusion violates both the establishment clause and the free exercise clause of the First Amendment.

The court easily rejected the first argument, reasoning that the relationship between a church-related school and its faculty is not comparable to the church-minister relationship, which is outside Title VII. The court spent more time on the second argument but rejected it as well.

Addressing the establishment clause issue first, the court relied on the *Lemon* v. *Kurtzman* (403 U.S. 602 (1971)) line of cases to determine whether application of Title VII to the college would foster "excessive government entanglement with religion" (see Section 1.5). The court reasoned:

> The nature of the burden that might be imposed upon the college by the application of Title VII to it is largely hypothetical at this stage of the proceedings. The information requested by the EEOC's subpoena does not clearly implicate any religious practices of the college. The college's primary concern is that the EEOC's investigation will not cease should it comply with the subpoena, but instead will intrude further into its operations. The college worries that the EEOC will seek to require it to alter the employment practices by which it seeks to ensure that its faculty members are suitable examples of the Christian ideal advocated by the Southern Baptist faith. These hypothetical concerns are of limited validity. As noted previously, the exemption granted to religious institutions by Section 702 of Title VII must be construed broadly to exclude from the scope of the Act any employment decision made by a religious institution on the basis of religious discrimination. This construction of Section 702 largely allays the college's primary concern that it will be unable to continue its policy of preferring Baptists in hiring. The only practice brought to the attention of the district court that is clearly predicated upon religious beliefs that might not be protected by the exemption of Section 702 is the college's policy of hiring only men to teach courses in religion. The bare potential that Title VII would affect this practice does not warrant precluding the application of Title VII to the college. Before the EEOC could require the college to alter that practice, the college would have an opportunity to litigate in a federal forum whether Section 702 exempts or the First Amendment protects that particular practice. We thus determine that, in the factual context before us, the application of Title VII to the college could have only a minimal impact upon the college's religion-based practices.
>
> The relationship between the federal government and the college that results from the application of Title VII does have limits both in scope and effect. It is true that the subpoena issued to the college by the EEOC presages a wide-ranging investigation into many aspects of the college's hiring practices. Furthermore, should the EEOC conclude that cause exists to believe that the college discriminates on the basis of sex or race, the college in all likelihood would be subjected to a court action if it did not voluntarily agree to alter its actions. The college would, however, be entitled to a de novo determination of whether its practices violate Title VII. In that action the college could reassert the protection of the First Amendment prior to being ordered to amend its practices. If the challenged employment practices survived the scrutiny of the district court, the EEOC could not attack again those particular practices absent some change in circumstances.

Although the college is a pervasively sectarian institution, the minimal burden imposed upon its religious practices by the application of Title VII and the limited nature of the resulting relationship between the federal government and the college cause us to find that application of the statute would not foster excessive government entanglement with religion. . . . We conclude that imposing the requirements of Title VII upon the college does not violate the establishment clause of the First Amendment [626 F.2d at 487–88].

The court then considered whether application of Title VII to the college would violate the free exercise clause:

In determining whether a statutory enactment violates the free exercise of a sincerely held religious belief, the Supreme Court has examined (1) the magnitude of the statute's impact upon the exercise of the religious belief, (2) the existence of a compelling state interest justifying the burden imposed upon the exercise of the religious belief, and (3) the extent to which recognition of an exemption from the statute would impede the objectives sought to be advanced by the state. . . .

As discussed previously, the impact of Title VII upon the exercise of the religious belief is limited in scope and degree. Section 702 excludes from the scope of Title VII those employment practices of the college that discriminate on the basis of religion. We acknowledge that, except for those practices that fall outside of Title VII, the impact of Title VII on the college could be profound. To the extent that the college's practices foster sexual or racial discrimination, the EEOC, if unable to persuade the college to alter them voluntarily, could seek a court order compelling their modification, imposing injunctive restraints upon the college's freedom to make employment decisions, and awarding monetary relief to those persons aggrieved by the prohibited acts. However, the relevant inquiry is not the impact of the statute upon the institution, but the impact of the statute upon the institution's exercise of its sincerely held religious beliefs. The fact that those of the college's employment practices subject to Title VII do not embody religious beliefs or practices protects the college from any real threat of undermining its religious purpose of fulfilling the evangelical role of the Mississippi Baptist Convention, and allows us to conclude that the impact of Title VII on the free exercise of religious beliefs is minimal.

Second, the government has a compelling interest in eradicating discrimination in all forms. . . . Congress manifested that interest in the enactment of Title VII and the other sections of the Civil Rights Act of 1964. The proscription upon racial discrimination in particular is mandated not only by congressional enactments but also by the Thirteenth Amendment. We conclude that the government's compelling interest in eradicating discrimination is sufficient to justify the minimal burden imposed upon the college's free exercise of religious beliefs that results from the application of Title VII.

Moreover, we conclude that creating an exemption from the statutory enactment greater than that provided by Section 702 would seriously undermine the means chosen by Congress to combat discrimination and is not constitutionally required. Although the number of religious educational institutions is minute in comparison to the number of employers subject to Title VII, their effect upon society at large is great because of the role they play in educating society's young. If the environment in which such institutions seek to achieve their religious and educational goals reflects unlawful discrimination, those discriminatory attitudes will be perpetuated with an influential segment of society, the detrimental effect of which cannot be estimated. Because the burden placed upon the free exercise of religion by the application of Title VII to religious educational institutions is slight, because society's interest in eradicating discrimination is compelling, and because the creation of an exemption greater than that provided by Section 702 would seriously undermine Congress's attempts to eliminate discrimination, we conclude [that] the application of Title VII to educational institutions such as Mississippi College does not violate the free exercise clause of the First Amendment [626 F.2d at 488–89].

In *Equal Employment Opportunity Commission* v. *Southwestern Baptist Theological Seminary,* 651 F.2d 277 (5th Cir. 1981), the same court refined its *Mississippi College* analysis in the special context of religious seminaries. The defendant seminary was a nonprofit corporation owned, operated, supported, and controlled by the Southern Baptist Convention. This seminary offers degrees only in theology, religious education, and church music, and its purposes and character were described by the court as "wholly sectarian." The EEOC had asked the seminary to complete form EEO-6, a routine information report. When the seminary refused, the EEOC sued to compel compliance under 42 U.S.C. sec. 2000e-8(c), Title VII's record-keeping and reporting provision.

The court determined that the general principles set out in *Mississippi College* applied to this case but that the differing factual setting of this case required a result partly different from that in *Mississippi College.* In particular, the court held that "Title VII does not apply to the employment relationship between this seminary and its faculty." Reasoning that the Southwestern Baptist Seminary, unlike Mississippi College, was "entitled to the status of 'church'" and that its faculty "fit the definition of 'ministers,'" the court determined that Congress did not intend to include within Title VII this ecclesiastical relationship, which is the special concern of the First Amendment. Using the same reasoning, the court also excluded from Title VII administrative positions that are "traditionally ecclesiastical or ministerial," citing as likely examples the "president and executive vice-president of the seminary, the chaplain, the dean of men and women, the academic deans, and those other personnel who equate to or supervise faculty." But the court refused to exclude other administrative and support staff from Title VII, even if the employees filling those positions are ordained ministers.

Having held "nonministerial" staff to be within Title VII, the court then considered whether the First Amendment would prohibit the EEOC from applying its reporting requirement to those employees. Again using the principles of *Mississippi College,* the court concluded that the First Amendment was not a bar and that the EEOC could require the seminary to provide the information requested in the EEO-6 form for its nonministerial employees. The court left open the question whether the First Amendment would prohibit the EEOC from obtaining further information on the seminary's nonministerial employees by use of the more intrusive investigatory subpoena, as was done in *Mississippi College.*

By attending at length to both statutory and constitutional issues, the opinions in the *Mississippi College* and *Southwestern Baptist Theological Seminary* cases clarify and validate Title VII's application to church-related colleges. The cases develop a balanced interpretation of the Section 702 exemption against the backdrop of First Amendment law. The exemption protects only employment decisions based on the *religion* of the applicant or employee. Once the college has shown that religion was the basis for its decision, the complainant may not attempt to rebut this proof with evidence that religion was a pretext for some other form of discrimination. Thus, in the narrow range covered by Section 702, the college is treated more favorably than in other Title VII contexts, where the complainant may show pretext (see this volume, Section 3.3.2.1).

The First Amendment, in most circumstances, does not provide additional special treatment for the church-related college; Section 702 itself provides the full extent of protection the First Amendment requires. There is one exception recognized by the *Southwestern Baptist Theological Seminary* case: If the college is a seminary, the First Amendment may prohibit application of Title VII to "ministerial" employees and may limit the scope of the EEOC's investigation and enforcement activities regarding "nonministerial" employees. A second possible exception, not urged in either *Mississippi College* or *Southwestern Baptist Theological Seminary,* may be urged in other contexts: If an institution practices some form of discrimination prohibited by Title VII, but can prove that its discrimination is based on religious belief, it may argue that the First Amendment protects such discrimination. The developing case law does not yet provide a definitive response to this argument. But the U.S. Supreme Court's opinion in the *Bob Jones* case (Section 7.3.1)—although addressing a tax benefit rather than a regulatory program such as Title VII—does suggest a general approach that courts may use in responding to the argument.

7.2.6. Immigration laws. Many citizens of foreign countries come to the United States to study, teach, lecture, or do research at American higher education institutions. The conditions under which such foreign nationals may enter and remain in the United States are governed by a complex set of federal statutes codified in Title 8 of the *United States Code* and by regulations promulgated and administered primarily by the U.S. Department of State and the Immigration and Naturalization Service (INS) of the U.S. Department of Justice. The statutes and regulations establish numerous categories and subcategories for aliens entering the United States, with differing eligibility requirements and conditions of stay attaching to each.

Under Title 8 aliens may enter the United States either as immigrants or as nonimmigrants. Immigrants are admitted for permanent residence in the country. Nonimmigrants are admitted only for limited time periods to engage in narrowly defined types of activities. Eligibility for the immigrant class is subject to various numerical limitations and various priorities or preferences for certain categories of aliens (8 U.S.C. secs. 1151–1159). The nonimmigrant class is not limited numerically, but it is subdivided into thirteen specific categories (A through M), which define, and thus serve to limit, eligibility for nonimmigrant status. Of the two classes, immigrant and nonimmigrant, the latter is the greater source of problems for postsecondary institutions and is the focus for the remainder of this section.

In 1979–80, when the federal government responded to the Iranian crisis by imposing new restrictions on foreign students from Iran, higher education institutions were sensitized anew to immigration law's potential impact on campuses. Aside from such political crises, higher education institutions have a general interest in knowing the immigration status of each foreign national whom they enroll as a student, hire for a faculty or other position, or invite to the campus as a temporary guest, and in helping these foreign nationals maintain their legal status for the term of their stay. In these situations administrators and counsel will need to be conversant with the federal laws and regulations governing immigration.

The immigration status of foreign students will be of particular concern to higher education in future years, since the proportion of applicants and students from foreign countries is expected to grow dramatically. In 1980–81 there were approximately 312,000 foreign students on American campuses, accounting for 2.7 percent of the student population. By the early 1990s, those figures could increase to over one million, or 10 percent (see Committee on Foreign Students and Institutional Policy, *Foreign Students and Institutional Policy: Toward an Agenda for Action* (American Council on Education, 1982)).

Nonimmigrant students usually qualify for admission to the United States under one of three categories: "academic" student (8 U.S.C. sec. 1101(a)(15)(F)), "vocational" or "nonacademic" student (8 U.S.C. sec. 1101(a)(15)(M)), or "exchange visitor" (8 U.S.C. sec. 1101(a)(15)(J)).[2] In each category the statute provides that the "alien spouse and minor children" of the student may also qualify for admission "if accompanying him or following to join him."

The first of these three categories is for aliens in the United States "temporarily and solely . . . to pursue a full course of study . . . at an established college, university, seminary, conservatory, . . . or other academic institution or in a language training program" (8 U.S.C. sec. 1101(a)(15)(F)(i)). The second category is for aliens in the United States "temporarily and solely . . . to pursue a full course of study . . . at an established vocational or other recognized nonacademic institution (other than a language training program)" (8 U.S.C. sec. 1101(a)(15)(M)(i)). The former category is called "F-1," and included students are "F-1s;" the latter category is called "M-1" and the students "M-1s." The spouses and children of these students are called "F-2s" and "M-2s."

The third category, exchange visitor, is known as the "J" category. It includes any alien (and the family of any alien) "who is a bona fide student, scholar, trainee, teacher, professor, research assistant, specialist, or leader in a field of specialized knowledge or skill, or other person of similar description, who is coming temporarily to the United States as a participant in a program designated by the secretary of state, for the purpose of teaching, instructing or lecturing, studying, observing, conducting research, consulting, demonstrating special skills, or receiving training" (8 U.S.C. sec. 1101(a)(15)(J)). Exchange visitors who will attend medical

---

[2]A fourth relevant category, for "trainees," is established by 8 U.S.C. sec. 1101(a)(15) (H)(iii). Regulations for this "H-3" category are at 8 C.F.R. sec. 214.2(h)(4) and 22 C.F.R. sec. 41.55(c). A fifth category into which some foreign students fall, the "G-4" category, was at issue in the *Elkins* v. *Moreno* litigation discussed in Section 4.3.5. This category, for employees of international treaty organizations and their immediate families, is established by 8 U.S.C. sec. 1101(a)(15)(G). Pertinent regulations are in 8 C.F.R. sec. 214.2(g) and 22 C.F.R. sec. 41.50.

school, and the institutions they will attend, are subject to additional requirements under this section and 8 U.S.C. sec. 1182(j). Another provision of the statute, 8 U.S.C. sec. 1182(e), establishes the conditions under which an alien who has been an exchange visitor may remain in or return to the United States for purposes of employment.[3]

The Department of State's role in regulating foreign students is shaped by its power to grant or deny visas to persons applying to enter the United States. Consular officials verify whether an applicant alien has met the requirements under one of the pertinent statutory categories and the corresponding requirements established by State Department regulations. The State Department's regulations for academic student visas are in 22 C.F.R. sec. 41.45 and those for vocational or nonacademic students are in 22 C.F.R. sec. 41.68. Requirements for exchange visitor status are in 22 C.F.R. sec. 41.65.

The Immigration and Naturalization Service has authority to approve the schools which foreign students may attend and for which they may obtain F-1 or M-1 visas from the State Department (8 C.F.R. sec. 214.3). The INS is also responsible for assuring that foreign students do not violate the conditions of their visas once they enter the United States. In particular, the INS must determine that holders of F-1 and M-1 student visas are making satisfactory progress toward the degree or other academic objective which they are pursuing. The regulations under which INS fulfills this responsibility are in 8 C.F.R. sec. 214.2(f) for academic students and 8 C.F.R. sec. 214.2(m) for vocational students. These regulations specify the periods of time for which foreign students may be admitted into the country and the circumstances that will constitute a "full course of study." In addition, the regulations establish the ground rules for on-campus employment of foreign students, off-campus employment (much more restricted than on-campus employment), transfers to another school, temporary absences from the country, and extensions of stay beyond the period of initial admission. Another regulation, 8 C.F.R. sec. 248, establishes the ground rules for changing nonimmigrant status from a student category to a nonstudent category and vice versa. There are substantial differences in the regulatory provisions applicable to F-1 students and those applicable to M-1s.

A third federal government agency, the International Communication Agency, also has responsibilities regarding foreign students. It operates the exchange visitor program. This agency's regulations implementing the program are codified in 22 C.F.R. Part 514. Section 514.2(a) defines the status of the "student" for purposes of these regulations. Sections 514.11 to 514.17 outline the role of postsecondary institutions and other organizations that sponsor exchange visitor programs.

In addition to its impact on enrollment of foreign students, immigration law also circumscribes the postsecondary institution's decisions on employing aliens in

[3]The statute defines various categories of exchange visitors who must have returned to their homeland or last foreign residence, and been physically present there for at least two years after departing the United States, to be eligible for a visa or permanent residence (see Annot., "Foreign Residence Requirement for Educational (Exchange) Visitors under sec. 212(e) of Immigration and Nationality Act [8 U.S.C. sec. 1182(e)]," 48 A.L.R. Fed. 509 (1980), plus periodic supp.). Proposed legislation stalled in a House-Senate conference committee in 1984 (House bill H.R. 1510; Senate bill S. 529: the "Simpson-Mazzoli bill") would revise this "two-year" rule and extend it to categories of students other than exchange visitors. Administrators and counsel should check for further developments regarding these controversial proposals.

faculty or staff positions and inviting aliens to campus to lecture or otherwise participate in campus life. Again, three nonimmigrant categories are particularly important: "exchange visitor" (8 U.S.C. sec. 1101(a)(15)(J)), "temporary visitor" (8
U.S.C. sec. 1101(a)(15)(B)), and "temporary worker" (8 U.S.C. sec.
1101(a)(15)(H)). For the first and third, but not the second, of these categories,
the statute also provides that the "alien spouse and minor children" of the alien
may qualify for admission "if accompanying him or following to join him."

The first category, exchange visitor, is the "J" category already discussed
with reference to students. The statutory definition, quoted above, is broad enough
to include some types of employees as well. The second, or "B" category, is for
aliens "visiting the United States temporarily for business or temporarily for
pleasure," except those "coming for the purpose of study or of performing skilled
or unskilled labor or as a representative of foreign press, radio, film, or other foreign
information media coming to engage in such vocation" (8 U.S.C. sec.
1101(a)(15)(B)). Visitors for business are B-1s, and visitors for pleasure are B-2s.
The third, or "H," category includes three subcategories of temporary alien workers:
those "of distinguished merit and ability" who will "perform services of an exceptional nature requiring such merit and ability" (H-1s); those who will "perform
temporary services or labor" when "unemployed persons capable of performing
such service or labor cannot be found in this country" (H-2s); and those who will
act as trainees (H-3s) (8 U.S.C. sec. 1101(a)(15)(H)(i)–(iii)). For each subcategory
the statute prescribes more limited rules for alien medical school graduates.

It is sometimes difficult to distinguish the temporary "business" visitor
belonging in category B from the temporary worker belonging in category H. INS
regulations provide this clarification:

> The term "business" as used in Section 1101(a)(15)(B) of the Act
> [8 U.S.C. sec. 1101(a)(15)(B)] refers to legitimate activities of a commercial
> or professional character. It does not include purely local employment or
> labor for hire. An alien seeking to enter as a nonimmigrant for employ-
> ment or labor pursuant to a contract or other prearrangement shall be re-
> quired to qualify under the provisions of [22 C.F.R.] sec. 41.55 [the regula-
> tion dealing with the admission of "temporary workers"]. An alien of
> distinguished merit and ability seeking to enter the United States temporarily
> with the idea of performing temporary services of an exceptional nature,
> requiring such merit and ability, but having no contract or other prear-
> ranged employment, may be classified as a nonimmigrant temporary visitor
> for business [22 C.F.R. sec. 41.25(b)].

The State Department and the INS play roles with respect to these categories
comparable to their roles respecting foreign students. The U.S. Department of Labor
also has an important role in issuing "labor certifications" for H-2 aliens indicating
that their employment will not displace or adversely affect American workers (8
C.F.R. sec. 214(h)(3)(i)). Pertinent State Department regulations are in 22 C.F.R.
sec. 41.25 (temporary visitors) and 22 C.F.R. sec. 41.55 (temporary workers). Pertinent INS regulations are in 8 C.F.R. sec. 214.2(b) (temporary visitors) and 8
C.F.R. sec. 214.2(h) (temporary workers). Labor Department regulations on labor
certification are in 20 C.F.R. Parts 621 and 655 (for nonimmigrant aliens) and

Part 656 (for immigrant aliens). The department also prepares *Technical Assistance Guide No. 656* (available from the U.S. Government Printing Office), which contains the departmental operating instructions on labor certifications.

The federal government may exclude certain classes of aliens even though they fit within one of the immigrant or nonimmigrant categories. Section 1182 of Title 8 (8 U.S.C. sec. 1182) establishes the classes of aliens subject to such exclusion; subsections (a)(27), (a)(28), and (a)(32) have particular application to post-secondary education. Section 1182(a)(27) permits exclusion of aliens "who the consular officer or the attorney general knows or has reason to believe seek to enter the United States solely, principally, or incidentally to engage in activities which would be prejudicial to the public interest, or endanger the welfare, safety, or security of the United States." Section 1182(a)(28) permits exclusion of aliens who are anarchists, or members of the Communist party, or "who advocate the economic, international, and governmental doctrines of world communism or the establishment in the United States of a totalitarian dictatorship, or who are members of or affiliated with any organization" that engages in such advocacy. Section 1182(a)(32) permits exclusion of aliens "who are graduates of a medical school not accredited by a body or bodies approved for the purpose" by the U.S. Department of Education, and are coming to the United States "principally to perform services as members of the medical profession." The statute permits an exception only where the graduate alien has passed parts I and II of the National Board of Medical Examiners Examination (or an equivalent approved by the secretary of health and human services) and has demonstrated competency in oral and written English.

The second of these exclusion provisions, 8 U.S.C. sec. 1182(a)(28), was the subject of a major U.S. Supreme Court case involving higher education. *Kleindienst* v. *Mandel,* 408 U.S. 753 (1976), concerned a Belgian citizen (Mandel) who was editor of a Belgian Left Socialist weekly and had authored a two-volume work entitled *Marxist Economic Theory.* In 1969 he applied for a nonimmigrant visa to enter the United States to give an address at Stanford University. When Mandel's planned visit became known, other higher education institutions invited him to address their groups. The theme of one conference was to be "Revolutionary Strategy in Imperialist Countries." The American Consulate in Brussels refused Mandel a visa because, among other reasons, he was inadmissible under 8 U.S.C. sec. 1182(a)(28). Although the State Department subsequently did recommend that Mandel be admitted, the INS, acting on behalf of the attorney general, denied temporary admission. Mandel then brought suit along with eight other plaintiffs, all of whom were United States citizens and university professors in various social science fields. These plaintiffs asserted that their plans to participate with Mandel in various public forums had been disrupted by the visa denial. Thus, the plaintiffs argued, their First Amendment right to receive information had been abridged.

The Court held that Congress had authority to enact legislation excluding aliens with certain political affiliations and beliefs and that the State Department and the attorney general's office had acted properly in excluding Mandel. The Court began by noting that Mandel, as an unadmitted and nonresident alien, had no constitutional right of entry to the United States. The Court then acknowledged that the remaining plaintiffs did possess First Amendment rights to receive information. Nevertheless, Congress's plenary authority to exclude classes of aliens or regulate the terms of their entry overrode the plaintiffs' First Amendment claims:

Plenary congressional power to make policies and rules for exclusion of aliens has long been firmly established. In the case of an alien excludable under Section 1182(a)(28), Congress has delegated conditional exercise of this power to the Executive. We hold that when the Executive exercises this power negatively on the basis of a facially legitimate and bona fide reason, the courts will neither look behind the exercise of that discretion, nor test it by balancing its justification against the First Amendment interests of those who seek personal communication with the applicant. What First Amendment or other grounds may be available for attacking exercise of discretion for which no justification whatsoever is advanced is a question we neither address [nor] decide in this case [408 U.S. at 769–70].

Other more recent controversies confirm the federal government's willingness to use its broad authority to exclude, or condition the entry of, visitors to the United States. In 1982 American philosophy professors invited two Cuban professors to speak at a 1983 meeting of the Society for the Philosophical Study of Marxism. Citing the fact that the two professors were officials of the Cuban Communist party, the State Department denied them visas (see J. Hook, "U.S. Denies Visas to 2 Marxist Cuban Professors Invited to Address Philosophy Meeting," *Chronicle of Higher Education,* Jan. 5, 1983, p. 8, col. 1). When Grinnell College invited Georgi Arbatov, director of the Soviet Union's Institute of United States and Canadian Studies, to speak, the State Department limited his visa to prevent him from meeting with the news media (see D. Oberdorfer, "Gag Order Keeps Soviet Advisor Mum to Press, but Not to Public," *Washington Post,* April 20, 1983). Similarly, the State Department imposed conditions on a visiting Soviet robotics expert that permitted him to review only published data and denied him access to industrial sites; when the University of Wisconsin and Stanford University protested the restrictions, the State Department revoked its permission for the visit (see K. McDonald, "Citing Security Threat, U.S. Bars Visit of Soviet Expert to 4 Universities," *Chronicle of Higher Education,* April 14, 1982, p. 13, col. 2). Read in light of the *Mandel* case, these more recent situations emphasize the practical impact of congressional power and executive discretion to regulate the entry of foreign visitors. Administrators or faculty members who invite foreign scholars to their campuses or to their professional meetings should be sensitive to this power and discretion, under which the federal government may totally exclude certain scholars from visiting the United States or drastically curtail their activities when here.

Similarly, administrators should be aware that the federal government's treatment of visitors, as well as other foreign nationals within or seeking to enter the United States, may depend on current foreign policy considerations. A case arising from the Iranian crisis graphically illustrates that revision of federal immigration regulations is potentially a weapon in the President's foreign policy arsenal. *Narenji* v. *Civiletti,* 617 F.2d 745 (D.C. Cir. 1979), arose as a challenge to presidential actions in the wake of the seizure of the United States embassy in Iran. As part of the Executive's response to the crisis, the attorney general's office published a new regulation, subsequently codified at 8 C.F.R. sec. 214.5, governing nonimmigrant students from Iran residing in the United States. The regulation required all Iranian nonimmigrant postsecondary students to report to a local INS office or campus representative to "provide information as to residence and maintenance of nonimmigrant status" (617 F.2d at 746). Failure to comply with the regulation subjected the student to deportation proceedings. Iranian students challenged this regulation as both beyond the scope of the attorney general's authority and violative of the constitutional guarantee of equal protection. The trial court agreed in a lengthy opinion (481 F. Supp. 1132 (D.D.C. 1979)), but the U.S. Court of Appeals reversed, holding that the attorney general possessed statutory authority to act as he did. It also held that Congress and the Executive have broad discretion to draw distinctions on the basis of nationality when dealing with immigration matters, and courts will sustain these distinctions unless found to be totally irrational. Applying this "rational basis" test to the challenged regulation, the appellate court found it rationally related to the Executive branch's efforts to resolve the crisis generated by the embassy takeover.

As indicated by the foregoing discussion, the immigration laws present a host of thorny problems for postsecondary administrators. Many of the questions that arise will be unforeseeable and dependent on the conduct of foreign affairs. Institutions that have been or expect to be confronted by a substantial number of immigration problems should consider having an administrator or counsel on staff who is knowledgeable about INS and State Department requirements and the paperwork necessary for handling this complex regulatory area.

7.2.7. Laws governing research on human subjects. A newly emerging body of federal law regulates scientific and medical research, especially research on human subjects and genetic engineering. This body of law has been a focal point for the ongoing debate concerning the federal regulatory presence on the campuses. A number of interrelated policy issues have been implicated in the debate: the academic freedom of researchers, the burden and efficiency of federal "paperwork," the standards and methods for protecting safety and privacy of human subjects, and the interplay of legal and ethical standards.

Regulations on human subject and related research are promulgated by various federal agencies. The law is rapidly evolving and in a state of flux. Some existing regulations are being reconsidered, and new regulations are being proposed for sensitive research areas not yet covered by federal law. Thus, only a broad outline of issues and requirements can be sketched at this time.

Among the most significant of the new regulations are those promulgated by the Food and Drug Administration (FDA) and by the Department of Health and Human Services (HHS) to govern the protection of human research subjects. The effective date of both sets of regulations was July 27, 1981.

The FDA regulations apply to clinical investigations regulated by the FDA under the Federal Food, Drug, and Cosmetic Act, 21 U.S.C. sec. 301 *et seq.*, as well as to clinical investigations that support applications for research or marketing permits regulated by the FDA. Failure to comply with the FDA regulations may result in any of a number of sanctions being imposed on the institution. These include "(1) withhold[ing] approval of new studies . . . that are conducted at the institution" or reviewed by its institutional review board (IRB); "(2) direct[ing] that no new subjects be added to ongoing studies subject to [the FDA rules]; (3) terminat[ing] ongoing studies subject to [the FDA rules] where doing so would not endanger the subjects"; and "(4) when the apparent noncompliance creates a significant threat to the rights and welfare of human subjects, notify[ing] the relevant state and federal regulatory agencies and other parties with a direct interest" in the

FDA's actions (21 C.F.R. sec. 56.120). If the institution's "IRB has refused or repeatedly failed to comply with" the FDA regulations and "the noncompliance adversely affects the rights or welfare of the subjects of a clinical investigation," the FDA commissioner may, when he deems it appropriate, disqualify the IRB or the parent institution from participation in FDA-governed research. Further, the FDA "will [refuse to] approve an application for a research permit for a clinical investigation that is to be under the review of a disqualified IRB or that is to be conducted at a disqualified institution, and it may refuse to consider in support of a marketing permit the data from a clinical investigation that was reviewed by a disqualified IRB [or] conducted at a disqualified institution" (21 C.F.R. sec. 56.121(d)). The commissioner may reinstate a disqualified IRB or institution upon its submission of a written plan for corrective action and adequate assurances that it will comply with FDA regulations (21 C.F.R. sec. 56.123).

The HHS regulations, except for specifically enumerated exemptions set out below, apply to all research involving human subjects conducted by HHS or funded in whole or part by an HHS grant, contract, cooperative agreement, or fellowship. Under Section 46.103(b) of the regulations, "the department will conduct or fund research covered by these regulations only if the institution has an assurance approved as provided in this section, and only if the institution has certified to the secretary [of HHS] that the research has been reviewed and approved by an IRB provided for in the assurance, and will be subject to continuing review by the IRB." The HHS regulations do not provide elaborate sanctions for noncompliance, as the FDA regulations do, but only general provisions on fund termination (45 C.F.R. secs. 46.122 and 46.123).

Among the most important issues treated by the FDA and HHS regulations are (1) establishing institutional review boards (IRBs) and (2) ensuring the informed consent of research subjects.

IRBs are fairly recent phenomena; until the early 1960s, only a small minority of research facilities had such committees. "In 1966, the Public Health Service (PHS) initiated the requirement that a committee of the investigator's 'institutional associates' review proposals for research involving human subjects as a condition for the receipt of a PHS grant." Following PHS's lead, other federal agencies began to require IRB monitoring of human subject research. (See B. DuVal, "The Human Subjects Protection Committee: An Experiment in Decentralized Regulation," 1979 *ABA Research J.* 571, especially 573–74 n.1.) As now conceived by the federal agencies, the IRB is designed to ameliorate the tension that exists between institutional autonomy and federal supervision of research. The composition of the IRB as mandated by the FDA regulations is fairly typical of that required under other federal programs. Under these regulations the IRB must have at least five members with backgrounds sufficiently varied to supervise completely the common research activities conducted by the particular institution. Since the IRB must "ascertain the acceptability of proposed research in terms of institutional commitments and regulations, applicable law, and standards of professional conduct and practice," the IRB must include members knowledgeable in these areas. No IRB may consist entirely of members of the same sex or the same profession. The IRB must also include at least one member whose primary expertise is nonscientific, such as an attorney, an ethicist, or a member of the clergy. Each IRB must have "at least one member who is not otherwise affiliated with the institution" and who is not a member of a family immediately affiliated with the institution (21 C.F.R. sec. 56.108(a)-(f)). The HHS regulations set down essentially the same rules on IRB composition (45 C.F.R. sec. 46.107).

The IRB has the duty, under the HHS regulations, "to approve, require modifications in (to secure approval), or to disapprove" all research conducted under the regulations (45 C.F.R. sec. 46.109(a)). The IRB must also monitor the information provided subjects to assure informed consent (45 C.F.R. sec. 46.109(b)). In addition, the IRB must conduct follow-up reviews of research it has approved "at intervals appropriate to the degree of risk, but not less than once per year" (45 C.F.R. sec. 46.109(c)). The institution may also review research already approved by an IRB and may either approve or disapprove such research, but an institution may not approve research disapproved by the IRB (45 C.F.R. sec. 46.112). If research is being conducted in violation of IRB requirements or if subjects have been seriously and unexpectedly harmed, the IRB may suspend or terminate the research (45 C.F.R. sec. 46.113). The FDA regulations governing IRB responsibilities and functions are similar to the HHS regulations on these points (see 21 C.F.R. secs. 56.108-56.112).

Informed consent, a doctrine arising from the law of torts, concerns the amount of information about the research which must be provided to the human subject. The HHS regulations are fairly typical in what they establish as the basic elements of informed consent:

(1) A statement that the study involves research, an explanation of the purposes of the research and the expected duration of the subject's participation, a description of the procedures to be followed, and identification of any procedures which are experimental;

(2) A description of any reasonably foreseeable risks or discomforts to the subject;

(3) A description of any benefits to the subject or to others which may reasonably be expected from the research;

(4) A disclosure of appropriate alternative procedures or courses of treatment, if any, that might be advantageous to the subject;

(5) A statement describing the extent, if any, to which confidentiality of records identifying the subject will be maintained;

(6) For research involving more than minimal risk, an explanation as to whether any compensation and an explanation as to whether any medical treatments are available if injury occurs and, if so, what they consist of, or where further information may be obtained;

(7) An explanation of whom to contact for answers to pertinent questions about the research and research subjects' rights, and whom to contact in the event of a research-related injury to the subject; and

(8) A statement that participation is voluntary, refusal to participate will involve no penalty or loss of benefits to which the subject is otherwise entitled, and the subject may discontinue participation at any time without penalty or loss of benefits to which the subject is otherwise entitled [45 C.F.R. sec. 46.116(a)(1)-(8)].

The HHS regulations also require that, in "appropriate" circumstances (a concept the regulations do not define), additional elements of informed consent be met, as outlined in 45 C.F.R. sec. 46.116(b)(1)-(6).

The FDA regulations contain the same informed consent requirements (21 C.F.R. sec. 50.25(a) and (b)).

The HHS and FDA regulations also contain requirements for documenting informed consent. Unlike their FDA counterparts, the HHS regulations also set out several circumstances in which the IRB may either alter the elements of informed consent or waive the informed consent requirement (see 45 C.F.R. sec. 46.116(c)(1)-(2) and compare 21 C.F.R. sec. 50.25).

The HHS regulations contain several broad exemptions for specific areas of research (45 C.F.R. sec. 46.101(b)(1)-(5)). The secretary of HHS has final authority to determine whether a particular activity is covered by the regulations (45 C.F.R. sec. 46.101(c)). The secretary may also "require that specific research activities . . . conducted by [HHS], but not otherwise covered by these regulations, comply with some or all of these regulations" (45 C.F.R. sec. 46.101(d)). And the secretary may "waive applicability of these regulations to specific research activities otherwise covered by these regulations" (45 C.F.R. sec. 46.101(e)).

In addition to these FDA and HHS regulations, many other sets of regulations governing human subject research have been implemented. The Department of Defense has issued final regulations governing grantees' and contractors' uses of human subjects in "clinical investigations, . . . biomedical research, and behavioral studies"; research on "new drugs, vaccines, biologicals, or investigational medical devices"; and the "testing of military weapon systems" or other technological studies (43 Fed. Reg. 35400 (Aug. 4, 1983), codified at 32 C.F.R. Part 219). The Department of Energy has issued final regulations governing human subject research by all its grantees and contractors (10 C.F.R. sec. 745 *et seq.*). The Department of Education, in its regulations governing grant awards by the National Institute of Handicapped Research (34 C.F.R. Part 350), has explicitly incorporated the HHS regulations on human subject research. HHS has also issued several sets of more narrowly focused regulations. Final HHS regulations on research involving fetuses, pregnant women, and *in vitro* fertilization are codified in 45 C.F.R. sec. 46.201 *et seq.* Final HHS regulations governing the protection of prisoner subjects of biomedical and behavioral research are codified in 45 C.F.R. sec. 46.301 *et seq.* Final HHS regulations governing the use of children as research subjects are codified at 45 C.F.R. sec. 46.401 *et seq.*

HHS/NIH guidelines on recombinant DNA research—a subject of continuing debate—were issued, then revised and repromulgated, several times in the early 1980s. As of early 1985, the guidelines in effect were those published at 49 Fed. Reg. 46266–46301 (November 23, 1984). These guidelines superceded the earlier version published at 48 Fed. Reg. 24556 (June 1, 1983) and its amendments. The legal regulation of recombinant genetics being a volatile area, further amendments and revisions are predictable.

As reflected in the various regulatory actions discussed above, the law of human subject research is complex and rapidly evolving. The impact of this law on individual campuses will vary considerably, depending on their own research programs. Postsecondary administrators responsible for research will want to stay abreast of their institution's research emphases and issues of concern. In consultation with counsel, administrators should also keep abreast of changes in federal regulations and engage in a continuing process of extracting from the various sets of regulations the particular legal requirements applicable to their institution's research programs. Given the recent growth and volatility of legal developments and the sensitivity of some current areas of research emphasis, institutions that do not have a particular office or committee to oversee research may wish to reconsider their organizational structure.

   7.2.8. Copyright laws. The basis for all copyright law is Article I, section 8, clause 8 of the Constitution, which authorizes Congress "to promote the progress of science and useful arts, by securing for limited times to authors and inventors the exclusive right to their respective writings and discoveries." In 1976, after many years of effort inside and outside government, Congress revised the federal copyright law. Effective as of January 1, 1978, the General Revision of the Copyright Law, 17 U.S.C. sec. 101 *et seq.,* has particular relevance to educational institutions because it addresses the question of what kinds of copying of copyrighted materials may be done for teaching and scholarship. This question, previously governed by the judicially created "fair use" doctrine, is now governed by the codification of that doctrine in Section 107 of the new Act. Another section of the new Act particularly important to educational institutions, Section 108, deals with copying by libraries and archives. And a third pertinent section, Section 117 (added in 1980; 94 Stat. 3028), deals with copying of computer programs.

   Section 107 of the Act states that "the fair use of a copyrighted work . . . for purposes such as criticism, comment, news reporting, teaching (including multiple copies for classroom use), scholarship, or research is not an infringement of copyright." The section lists four factors that must be considered in determining whether a particular "use" is "fair": "(1) the purpose and character of the use, including whether such use is of a commercial nature or is for nonprofit educational purposes; (2) the nature of the copyrighted work; (3) the amount and substantiality of the portion used in relation to the copyrighted work as a whole; and (4) the effect of the use upon the potential market for or value of the copyrighted work." Application of these rather vague standards to individual cases is left to the courts. Some guidance on their meaning may be found, however, in a document included in the legislative history of the revised Copyright Act: the "Agreement on Guidelines for Classroom Copying in Not-for-Profit Educational Institutions," in House Report No. 94-1476, 94th Cong., 2d Sess. (1976). A second document in the legislative history, the "Guidelines for the Proviso of Subsection 108(g)(2)," Conference Report No. 94-1733, 94th Cong., 2d Sess. (1976), provides comparable guidance on the provision within Section 108 dealing with copying for purposes of interlibrary loans. The "Guidelines for Classroom Copying" were adopted by thirty-eight educational organizations and the publishing industry to set *minimum* standards of educational fair use under Section 107 of the Act. Guidelines are established for "Single Copying for Teaching" (for example, a chapter from a book may be copied for the individual teacher's use in scholarly research, class preparation, or teaching) as well as for "Multiple Copies for Classroom Use" (for example, one copy per pupil in one course may be made, provided that the copying meets several tests; these tests, set out in the House Report, concern the brevity of the excerpt to be copied, the spontaneity of the use, and the cumulative effect of multiple copying in classes within the institution).

   The guidelines were cited by the U.S. Court of Appeals for the Ninth Circuit in *Marcus* v. *Rowley,* 695 F.2d 1171 (1983). The case involved a public school teacher who reproduced approximately half of a copyrighted booklet and included it in course materials she distributed to her students at no charge. The court ruled that the teacher's use of the copyrighted material did not constitute fair use. The opinion emphasizes that a person need not have sold or profited from copying in order to violate the Copyright Act: "The first factor to be considered in determining the applicability of the doctrine of fair use is the purpose and character of the use, and specifically whether the use is of a commercial nature or is for a nonprofit educational purpose. . . . Nevertheless, a finding of a nonprofit educational purpose does not automatically compel a finding of fair use."

In another copyright case, *Addison-Wesley Publishing Co.* v. *New York University,* filed in December 1982 in federal district court (Civil Action No. 82 Civ. 8333, S.D.N.Y.), the Association of American Publishers coordinated a suit on behalf of nine publishing companies against NYU, nine of its faculty members, and a photocopying shop near the campus. The plaintiffs' complaint listed thirteen instances of alleged unlawful photocopying and sought a permanent injunction against further unlawful copying and an award of damages for the copyright owners. The suit was reportedly the first of its kind involving a university and its faculty members.

In April 1983 the parties reached an out-of-court settlement of the case. In return for the plaintiffs' withdrawal of their claims, NYU agreed to adopt and implement a copyright policy corresponding to the "Guidelines for Classroom Copying," publish its policy in the faculty handbook and publicize it to the faculty periodically by other means, post notices about its copyright policy at all campus copying facilities, and investigate alleged incidents of copyright violation and take appropriate action against faculty members "consistent with remedial and disciplinary actions taken in respect of violations of other university policies." The full texts of the settlement and of the NYU photocopying policy were published in 13 *College Law Digest* 258, printed in *West's Education Law Rptr.,* June 2, 1983 (Special NACUA Pamphlet). The NYU policy was also published in the *Chronicle of Higher Education,* April 20, 1983, p. 23, col. 1. (See also D. Edwards, "University of North Carolina Copyright Guidelines on Photocopying," 14 *College Law Digest* 121, printed in *West's Education Law Rptr.,* Jan. 12, 1984 (Special NACUA Pamphlet), which critiques the NYU settlement and provides guidelines to help faculty and staff comply with the copyright law.)

In light of developments in copyright law, postsecondary institutions should thoroughly review their policies and practices on photocopying and other means of reproducing copyrighted works. An institution that does not have a written policy on reproduction of copyrighted works should develop one. The "Guidelines for Classroom Copying" and the NYU settlement agreement and policy statement may be helpful guides. The institution's copying policy should be published for staff and students as well as faculty members, and a notice apprising users of the policy's existence, and the places where it is published or available for distribution, should be posted at campus photocopying facilities.

7.2.9. Patent laws. The basis for all patent law (as well as copyright law) is Article I, section 8, clause 8 of the Constitution, which authorizes Congress "to promote the progress of science and useful arts, by securing for limited times to authors and inventors the exclusive right to their respective writings and discoveries." The current patent laws passed by Congress are contained in Title 35 of the *United*

States Code. These laws are critical to the research mission of higher education, since they establish the means by which, and the extent to which, institutions or their faculty members, laboratory staffs, and students may protect the products of research.

Protection of research implicates basic patent law questions as well as related contract law questions about institutional arrangements for undertaking and utilizing research: What inventions or discoveries may be patented? Who may hold the patents? What arrangements have been made, or may be made, for licensing patent rights? Behind these legal issues lurk serious questions of policy: What degree and type of protection will allow researchers to share information without fear that their discoveries will be "stolen" by others? As between the institution and its faculty, staff, and students, who *should* hold the patents or license rights for patentable research products? As between the institution and government or industry sponsors of university research, who *should* hold the patents or license rights for patentable research products? Should commercial exploitation of university research be avoided; and if so, how can this be accomplished? The importance of both the legal and the policy questions is underscored by the complexity of new research in fields such as biological engineering and computer sciences, the growing research relationships between industry and academia (see D. Fowler, "University-Industrial Research Relationships: The Research Agreement," 9 *J. of College and University Law* 515 (1982–83)), the presence of substantial government support for university research, and the development of university research consortia.

The core section of the federal patent statutes provides:

> Whoever invents or discovers any new and useful process, machine, manufacture, or composition of matter, or any new and useful improvement thereof, may obtain a patent therefor, subject to the conditions and requirements of this title [35 U.S.C. sec. 101].

Among the other requirements that the invention must meet are those of "novelty" (sec. 102) and "nonobviousness" (sec. 103).

The U.S. Supreme Court has explained 35 U.S.C. sec. 101 as follows:

> In choosing such expansive terms as "manufacture" and "composition of matter," modified by the comprehensive "any," Congress plainly contemplated that the patent laws would be given wide scope. . . .
>
> This is not to suggest that Section 101 has no limits or that it embraces every discovery. The laws of nature, physical phenomena, and abstract ideas have been held not patentable (see *Parker* v. *Flook*, 437 U.S. 584 (1978)). . . . Thus, a new mineral discovered in the earth or a new plant found in the wild is not patentable subject matter. Likewise, Einstein could not patent his celebrated law that $E = mc^2$; nor could Newton have patented the law of gravity. Such discoveries are "manifestations of . . . nature, free to all men and reserved exclusively to none" (*Funk Brothers Seed Co.* v. *Kalo Inoculant Co.*, 333 U.S. 127, 130) [*Diamond* v. *Chakrabarty*, 447 U.S. 303, 309 (1980)].

Two U.S. Supreme Court cases decided in 1980 and 1981 demonstrate the difficulty of determining what products of modern research are "patentable subject matter" under 35 U.S.C. sec. 101. The first of these cases, *Diamond* v. *Chakrabarty* (the source of the above quote), concerned a microbiologist with General Electric who sought to patent a strain of bacteria he had developed by genetic manipulation of a naturally occurring bacterium. The new organism is capable of breaking down multiple components of crude oil, a property possessed by no bacterium in its natural state, and is an important discovery in the control of oil spills. The patent examiner had rejected the application on the grounds that microorganisms are "products of nature" and, as living things, are not patentable subject matter. Chakrabarty, on the other hand, argued that his microorganism constituted a "manufacture" or "composition of matter" within 35 U.S.C. sec. 101.

In a 5-to-4 decision, the Court agreed with Chakrabarty, concluding that his microorganism was patentable because it was not a previously unknown natural phenomenon but a nonnaturally occurring manufacture—a product of human ingenuity. Rejecting the argument that patent law distinguishes between animate and inanimate things and encompasses only the latter, the Court found the relevant distinction to be between products of nature, whether living or not, and man-made inventions.

In the second case, *Diamond* v. *Diehr,* 450 U.S. 175 (1981), the Court also decided in favor of patentability by a narrow 5-to-4 margin. Diehr had sought a patent on a method for molding uncured synthetic rubber into cured products. A computer program developed as part of the process enables a computer to continuously recalculate the cure time and determine when the molding press should be opened to assure a perfect cure. The Court's majority concluded that the invention qualified as a "process" under Section 101 rather than a "mathematical formula" and did not become unpatentable merely because the process involves a computer. The dissenters, in contrast, concluded that the invention made "no contribution to the art that is not entirely dependent upon the utilization of a computer in a familiar process" and was therefore unpatentable under *Gottschalk* v. *Benson,* 409 U.S. 63 (1971), and *Parker* v. *Flook,* 437 U.S. 584 (1978), which held that computer programs for solving mathematical problems are not patentable.

In 1980 Congress added important new amendments (94 Stat. 3015) to the patent and trademark laws. (Federal trademark law is discussed briefly in the introductory pages to Section 7.2 of this volume.) The amendments establish new procedures for the federal Patent and Trademark Office and add a new chapter to the patent laws, entitled "Patent Rights in Inventions Made with Federal Assistance." This chapter, codified in 35 U.S.C. secs. 200–211, contains several provisions directly applicable to colleges and universities (see A. Smith, "Implications of Uniform Patent Legislation to Colleges and Universities," 8 *J. of College and University Law* 82 (1981–82)).

The new chapter's stated goals include "promot[ing] the utilization of inventions arising from federally supported research or development"; "promot[ing] collaboration between commercial concerns and nonprofit organizations, including universities"; and "ensur[ing] that inventions made by nonprofit organizations . . . are used in a manner to promote free competition and enterprise" (35 U.S.C. sec. 200). To achieve these goals, the Act establishes a uniform policy for disposition and licensing of rights to patentable inventions discovered in the course of federally funded research. This policy replaces the prior system, by which each federal agency decided for itself how and when its fund recipients could obtain patent rights to inventions resulting from agency funding. The new policy applies to any "contract, grant, or cooperative agreement" between a federal agency and a "non-profit organization" (defined to include "universities and other institutions of higher education") or a "small business firm" (35 U.S.C. sec. 201).

Under the new system, colleges and universities may elect to retain title to inventions made with the assistance of federal funding (35 U.S.C. sec. 202). There are three situations, however, in which the funding agency may refuse to extend this right to retain title:

> (i) when the funding agreement is for the operation of a government-owned research or production facility, (ii) in exceptional circumstances when it is determined by the agency that restriction or elimination of the right to retain title to any subject invention will better promote the policy and objectives of this chapter, or (iii) when it is determined by a government authority which is authorized by statute or executive order to conduct foreign intelligence or counterintelligence activities that the restriction or elimination of the right to retain title to any subject invention is necessary to protect the security of such activities [35 U.S.C. sec. 202(a)(i)–(iii)].

If the fund recipient elects to retain title, the Act provides that the federal funding agency shall receive a nonexclusive royalty-free license on behalf of the United States (35 U.S.C. sec. 202(c)(4)). In addition, the Act reserves "march-in" rights to federal agencies, similar to those reserved by individual agencies under the prior system, to ensure adequate utilization of inventions where the fund recipient has not fully exercised its right to use the patented invention (35 U.S.C. sec. 203). Other provisions of the Act deal with the assignment and licensing of patent rights by the fund recipient (35 U.S.C. sec. 202(c)(7) and (f)) and the withholding of information about patentable inventions from third parties filing Freedom of Information Act requests (35 U.S.C. secs. 202(e)(5) and 205).

The Office of Federal Procurement Policy (OFPP) within the Office of Management and Budget (OMB) has issued new rules to implement the uniform patent policy in the 1980 patent and trademark law amendments. These rules are published in Circular No. A-124, 47 Fed. Reg. 7556, 7559–7566 (Feb. 19, 1982). Among other matters, the circular requires the use of a standard "patent rights clause" in funding agreements subject to the Act. The clause is contained in Attachment A to the circular. This clause, which may be modified in some respects by individual agencies, includes provisions on such matters as invention disclosure, elections to retain title, application to subcontractors, and march-in rights.

7.2.10. Antitrust laws. There are three primary federal antitrust laws, each focusing on different types of anticompetitive conduct. The Sherman Act, 15 U.S.C. sec. 1 *et seq.*, the basic antitrust statute, prohibits "every contract, combination . . . , or conspiracy, in restraint of trade or commerce." The Clayton Act, as amended by the Robinson-Patman Act, 15 U.S.C. sec. 12 *et seq.*, supplements the Sherman Act with special provisions on price discrimination, exclusive dealing arrangements, and mergers. The Federal Trade Commission Act, 15 U.S.C. sec. 41 *et seq.*, which is discussed separately in Section 7.2.11, prohibits "unfair methods of competition." These three statutes are enforceable by federal agencies: the Sherman and Clayton Acts by the Antitrust Division of the U.S. Department of Justice; the Clayton

Act and the FTC Act by the Federal Trade Commission. The Sherman and Clayton Acts may also be enforced directly by private parties, who may bring "treble damage" suits against alleged violators in federal court; if victorious, such private plaintiffs will be awarded three times the actual damages the violation caused them. Postsecondary institutions could thus find themselves defendants in antitrust suits brought by either government or private parties, as well as plaintiffs bringing their own treble damage actions.

In the recent past, it was thought that the antitrust laws had little, if any, application to colleges and universities. Being institutions whose mission was higher education, they were said to be engaged in the "liberal arts and learned professions" rather than in "trade or commerce" subject to antitrust liability (see generally *Atlantic Cleaners and Dyers* v. *United States,* 286 U.S. 427, 435–36 (1932)). Moreover, as for public institutions, they were considered immune from antitrust liability under the "state action" exemption developed in *Parker* v. *Brown,* 317 U.S. 341 (1943).[4] Postsecondary institutions, however, can no longer rest comfortably with this easy view of the law. Restrictions in the scope of both the "liberal arts and learned professions" exemption and the state action exemption have greatly increased the risk that particular institutions and institutional practices will be subjected to antitrust scrutiny.

The first chink in postsecondary education's armor was made in *Marjorie Webster Junior College* v. *Middle States Association of Colleges and Secondary Schools,* 432 F.2d 650 (D.C. Cir. 1970), discussed in Section 8.2. Although the court in that case affirmed the applicability of the liberal arts/learned professions exemption, it made clear that antitrust laws could nevertheless be applied to the "commercial aspects" of higher education and that educational institutions and associations could be subjected to antitrust liability if they acted with "a commercial motive." Then in 1975 the U.S. Supreme Court went beyond the *Marjorie Webster* reasoning in establishing that "the nature of an occupation, standing alone, does not provide sanctuary from the Sherman Act" (*Goldfarb* v. *Virginia State Bar,* 421 U.S. 773 (1975)). The *Goldfarb* opinion refuted the existence of any blanket learned professions or (apparently) liberal arts exemption. The Court did caution, however, in its often-quoted footnote 17 (421 U.S. at 788–89 n.17) that the "public service aspect" or other unique aspects of particular professional activities may require that they "be treated differently" than typical business activities. Finally, in *National Society of Professional Engineers* v. *United States,* 435 U.S. 679 (1978), the Supreme Court reaffirmed its rejection of a blanket learned professions exemption and emphasized that footnote 17 in *Goldfarb* should not be read as fashioning any broad new defense for professions. According to *Professional Engineers,* the learned professions (and presumably the liberal arts) cannot defend against antitrust claims by relying on an ethical position "that competition itself is unreasonable."

On the heels of these developments, the Supreme Court also decided two cases that refined and limited the state action exemption from antitrust liability. In these cases, *City of Lafayette* v. *Louisiana Power and Light Co.,* 435 U.S. 389 (1978), and *Community Communications Co.* v. *City of Boulder,* 102 S. Ct. 835 (1982), the specific

---

[4]This state action concept is a term of art with its own special meaning under the federal antitrust statutes and has no relation to the state action doctrine used in constitutional interpretation and discussed in Section 1.4.2.

problem was whether this exemption extended to political subdivisions of a state, such as cities. The Court concluded that an anticompetitive "state" action "cannot be exempt from antitrust scrutiny unless it constitutes the action of the [state] . . . itself in its sovereign capacity . . . or unless it constitutes municipal action in furtherance or implementation of clearly articulated and affirmatively expressed state policy" (*Boulder,* 102 S. Ct. at 841).

Under this formulation a public postsecondary institution would qualify for exemption if it is operated by "the state itself," so that its actions are those of "the state itself." Many institutions, however, particularly community colleges and semi-autonomous public corporations, may not fit this characterization (see Sections 2.3.3 and 6.2.2).[5] If an institution does not meet this "state itself" test, it may claim the state action exemption only for actions that further or implement "clearly articulated and affirmatively expressed state policy." It is clear from *Lafayette* and *Boulder* that many acts of state political subdivisions will not meet this requirement. Another requirement—that the party seeking exemption must be subject to "active state supervision" with respect to the actions for which it seeks exemption—apparently has no application to public postsecondary institutions. In *Town of Hallie* v. *City of Eau Claire,* 105 S. Ct. 1713, 1720–21 (1985), the Supreme Court held that this additional requirement applies only to *private* parties claiming a state action exemption.

Another Supreme Court case, decided shortly after *Boulder,* expands postsecondary education's exposure to antitrust liability in yet another way. In *American Society of Mechanical Engineers* v. *Hydrolevel Corp.,* 102 S. Ct. 1935 (1982), the Court held that nonprofit organizations may be held liable under the antitrust laws not only for the actions of their officers and employees but also for the actions of unpaid volunteers with apparent authority (see Section 2.1) to act for the organization. As applied to postsecondary education, this decision could apparently subject institutions to antitrust liability for anticompetitive acts of volunteer groups—such as alumni councils, booster clubs, recruitment committees, and student organizations—if these acts are carried out with apparent authority.

There have also been two legislative developments (both in 1984) that bear on the potential liability of postsecondary institutions under federal antitrust laws. Unlike the case law developments, however, the new statutes narrow rather than expand liability. The first statute, the National Cooperative Research Act of 1984, 98 Stat. 1815, includes several provisions that may be used to limit the antitrust liability of joint research and development ventures. The second statute, the Local Government Antitrust Act of 1984, 98 Stat. 2750, provides partial relief for state political subdivisions that have become subject to antitrust liability as a result of the *Lafayette* and *Boulder* cases. This Act protects such political subdivisions and their

[5]Even if an institution is operated by the "state itself," courts may not consider that all its actions are taken by the state "in its sovereign capacity." A potential distinction between "proprietary enterprises" (nonsovereign) and "traditional governmental functions" (sovereign) has been raised in antitrust litigation but not accepted by a majority of the Supreme Court (see *Boulder,* 102 S. Ct. at 840 n.13 and 842 n.18; see also *Jefferson County Pharmaceutical Association* v. *Abbott Laboratories,* 103 S. Ct. 1011, 1014 (1983), where the Court, in the special context of a Robinson-Patman Act price discrimination claim, held that the Act applies to a state university's purchases "for the purpose of competing against private enterprise in the retail market" but assumed, without deciding, that the Act would not apply to the state university's purchases "for consumption in traditional governmental functions").

officers and employees from paying monetary damages for antitrust violations they commit while acting "in an official capacity." They may still be sued for such violations, however, and subjected to court injunctions.

As a result of these various developments, administrators and counsel should now accord antitrust considerations an important place in their legal planning.[6] Activities most likely to have antitrust implications, and therefore deserving special attention, include broadcasting of college sports events (see *National Collegiate Athletic Association* v. *Board of Regents of University of Oklahoma,* 104 S. Ct. 2948 (1984), involving athletic conference controls over televising intercollegiate football games); purchasing activities (see *Jefferson County Pharmaceutical Association* v. *Abbott Laboratories,* 103 S. Ct. 1011 (1983), involving pharmaceutical purchases by, among others, two pharmacies at the University of Alabama's medical center); retail sales activities (see *Sunshine Books* v. *Temple University,* 697 F.2d 90 (3d Cir. 1982), involving textbook sales by a university bookstore); health care planning and delivery by university medical centers (see generally G. Heitler, "Health Care and Antitrust," 14 *University of Toledo L. Rev.* 577 (1983)); and relationships with accrediting agencies and professional organizations (see H. First, "Competition in the Legal Education Industry (II): An Antitrust Analysis," 54 *New York University L. Rev.* 1049 (1979)).

At the same time they plan to avoid antitrust liability, administrators and counsel should also consider the protections that antitrust law may provide them against the anticompetitive acts of others. In the *University of Oklahoma* case, for instance, two institutions used the antitrust laws to secure the right to negotiate their own deals for television broadcasting of their sports events. Antitrust law, then, has two sides to its coin; while one side may restrain the institution's policy choices, the other side may free it from restraints imposed by others.

7.2.11. Federal Trade Commission Act. The Federal Trade Commission Act, 15 U.S.C. sec. 41 *et seq.,* prohibits covered entities from "using unfair methods of competition in or affecting commerce and unfair or deceptive acts or practices in or affecting commerce" (sec. 45(a)(1)). The Act defines the entities it covers as "any company, trust, . . . or association, incorporated or unincorporated, which is organized to carry on business for its own profit or for that of its members" (15 U.S.C. sec. 44). This language clearly covers proprietary postsecondary institutions, thus subjecting them to the Act's prohibitions. Public institutions, on the other hand, are not covered. Nor, in most situations, could private nonprofit institutions be covered. In a leading precedent regarding nonprofit entities, *Community Blood Bank of Kansas City Area* v. *FTC,* 405 F.2d 1011 (8th Cir. 1969), the court refused to subject a blood bank to FTC jurisdiction, reasoning in part that the organization was "not organized for the profit of members or shareholders [and] [a]ny profit realized in [its] operations is devoted exclusively to the charitable purposes of the corporation."

Some courts have held, however, that the Act's definition of covered entities

---

[6]In one situation nonprofit postsecondary institutions are still, by express statutory provision, excluded from antitrust liability for alleged price discrimination: "Nothing in [the Robinson-Patman Act] shall apply to purchases of their supplies for their own use by schools, colleges, universities, public libraries, churches, hospitals, and charitable institutions not operated for profit" (15 U.S.C. sec. 13(c)). See also Section 7.2.11 regarding the limited application of the FTC Act to postsecondary institutions.

is broad enough to include a nonprofit entity if it is engaging in activities designed to economically benefit other, profit-making, entities. For instance, the courts have allowed the FTC to assert jurisdiction over the American Medical Association because "one of [the AMA's] objectives was to 'safeguard the material interests of the medical profession'" (*American Medical Association* v. *FTC*, 638 F.2d 443 (8th Cir. 1980), affirmed by an equally divided court, 455 U.S. 676 (1982)). In *FTC* v. *National Commission on Egg Nutrition*, 517 F.2d 485 (7th Cir. 1975), the court held that, because the Egg Nutrition Commission was "formed to promote 'the general interests of the egg industry,'" it was subject to the Act. And in the *Community Blood Bank* case, above, the court suggested that "trade associations" organized for the "pecuniary profits" of their members would be a classic example of a nonprofit entity covered by the Act. Although the principles of these cases would usually not apply to private, nonprofit postsecondary institutions, an institution's activities could apparently come within these principles if the institution entered into a business venture with another entity that was profit making. A real estate syndicate, for example, or a research joint venture with industry might fall within the Act's definition, thus subjecting the institution's activities within that relationship to FTC jurisdiction.

The FTC's primary activity regarding proprietary postsecondary institutions has been its attempts to regulate certain practices of proprietary vocational and home-study schools. In late 1978 the FTC issued rules (16 C.F.R. Part 438) covering programs of instruction that "purport to prepare or qualify individuals or improve or upgrade the skills individuals need for employment in any specific occupation" (sec. 438.1). Excluded, however, were programs of public institutions, programs of nonprofit institutions, programs of two years' duration or longer that culminate in a standard college-level degree, and high school equivalency courses. These rules were scheduled to go into effect on January 4, 1980, but the effective date was stayed indefinitely as a result of the decision of the U.S. Court of Appeals for the Second Circuit in *Katherine Gibbs School* v. *Federal Trade Commission*, 612 F.2d 658 (2d Cir. 1979), rehearing *en banc* denied, 628 F.2d 755 (2d Cir. 1979) (three judges dissenting). The court invalidated a number of the FTC rules because they were insufficiently specific and insufficiently justified. The court's opinion provides an extended and controversial analysis of FTC authority over proprietary schools.

After the *Katherine Gibbs* decision, the FTC proposed revisions in its rules and published new "recommended rules" for public discussion (46 Fed. Reg. 35668–35681 (July 10, 1981)). Since some of the original rules were validated by the Second Circuit, these rules are unchanged in the revised version. As of early 1985, no final action had been taken on these revised rules.

Sec. 7.3. Federal Taxation of Postsecondary Education

The federal government also asserts influence over postsecondary institutions through federal tax legislation. This section briefly discusses the tax laws having the most important applications to postsecondary education. These laws are based on Congress's tax power (see Section 7.1.2).

7.3.1. Income tax laws. Most postsecondary institutions, other than proprietary institutions, are eligible to attain tax-exempt status under the Internal Revenue Code. Depending on whether the institution is public or private, one of two different avenues to exemption may be chosen. If the institution is public, it must demonstrate that it is a political subdivision of a state under 26 U.S.C. sec.

115 and related provisions or, alternatively, that it is immune from taxation under the constitutional doctrine of intergovernmental immunities (see G. Burke, "Federal Taxation of State Colleges and Universities: Recent Developments Call for Reconsideration of Theories of Exemption," 4 *J. of College and University Law* 43 (1977)). If the institution is private, it must satisfy the statutory definition established by 26 U.S.C. sec. 501(c)(3) by showing that it is:

> organized and operated exclusively for religious, charitable, . . . or educational purposes, . . . no part of the net earnings of which inures to the benefit of any private shareholder or individual, no substantial part of the activities of which is carrying on propaganda, or otherwise attempting, to influence legislation . . . , and which does not participate in, or intervene in, . . . any political campaign on behalf of any candidate for public office.

Through these requirements for tax exemption, the federal government influences the organizational structures and activities of educational institutions. The express language of the Internal Revenue Code, for example, limits an institution's lobbying efforts and political activities (26 U.S.C. sec. 501(c)(3), above; 26 U.S.C. sec. 501(h)). The U.S. Department of Treasury promulgates regulations on many knotty questions concerning tax exemptions (see 26 C.F.R. sec. 1.501), such as what constitutes an educational purpose or organization within the meaning of Section 501(c)(3). The Treasury Department's Internal Revenue Service (IRS) also issues Revenue Rulings and Revenue Procedures, two devices by which it establishes and publicizes taxing policies and procedures.

The IRS has, for example, used Revenue Rulings and Procedures as a means of combating discrimination on the basis of race, color, and national or ethnic origin in private schools. Revenue Ruling 71-447, 1971–2 C.B. (*Cumulative Bulletin*) 230, announced the basic principle that "a private school that does not have a racially nondiscriminatory policy as to students does not qualify for exemption." The IRS predicated this ruling on its understanding that Congress's intention when devising Section 501(c)(3) was to include only institutions that qualified as "common law charit[ies]," thus precluding exemptions for institutions operating "contrary to public policy" (1971–2 C.B. at 230). Subsequent IRS statements implemented this basic nondiscrimination principle. Revenue Procedure 72-54, 1972–2 C.B. 834, sets out rules requiring private schools to publicize their nondiscriminatory policies; Revenue Ruling 75-231, 1975–1 C.B. 158, provides illustrative examples regarding church-affiliated schools; and Revenue Procedure 75-50, 1975–2 C.B. 587, establishes record-keeping requirements and other guidelines for complying with the nondiscrimination principle.

Clearly, the maintenance of tax-exempt status is a major concern of postsecondary institutions. Its loss can severely affect institutional financial resources. In addition to the obvious imposition of tax liability on institutional income, loss of a 501(c)(3) exemption would prevent donors from deducting their gifts as "charitable contributions" (26 U.S.C. sec. 170) on their own tax returns and might thus inhibit such giving. These financial repercussions create substantial inducement to comply with the standards established for tax exemption.

Other tax provisions can also exert a substantial influence on postsecondary institutions and their staffs and students. Several examples follow.

Section 74 of the Internal Revenue Code excludes from taxable income prizes and awards "made primarily in recognition of religious, charitable, scientific, educational, artistic, literary, or civic achievement," where the recipient did not act "to enter the contest or proceeding" and is not obliged "to render substantial future services" (26 U.S.C. sec. 74(e)(1) and (2)). The Treasury regulations cite the Nobel and Pulitzer Prizes as examples (26 C.F.R. sec. 1.74-1(b)); many other academic awards and prizes may also qualify.

Section 117 of the Code governs the taxability of scholarships, fellowships, assistantship awards, and other forms of financial aid. In general, if the recipient obtains the aid in return for providing services that benefit the institution, the aid is considered to be compensation and is taxable; if no such "strings" are attached, the aid is akin to a gift and the recipient may exclude it from taxable income. The distinction is important not only for the student receiving the aid but also for the institution—which must determine whether to withhold a portion of the student's award for income tax purposes.[7]

The Treasury regulations (26 C.F.R. sec. 1.117-1 *et seq.*) include illustrations of Section 117's application. A number of courts have also ruled on the taxability of various forms of financial aid under Section 117. For example, *Bingler* v. *Johnson,* 394 U.S. 741 (1969), established the basic principle that the "definition of 'scholarship' [does not include] amounts received for services performed"; *Field* v. *Commissioner of Internal Revenue,* 680 F.2d 510 (7th Cir. 1982), held that the plaintiff, a medical resident, had received a stipend for providing services and that this stipend therefore was not exempt from taxation under Section 117; and *Pelz* v. *United States,* 551 F.2d 291 (Ct. Cl. 1977), distinguished a graduate teaching assistant's stipend from a no-strings-attached fellowship and held the former taxable because it was provided as compensation for services. In 1984 Congress amended Section 117 to provide that the tuition remitted to college employees under a college's tuition remission plan is exempt from taxation (Deficit Reduction Act of 1984, sec. 532, 98 Stat. 494 at 887).

Section 119 governs the taxability of meals or lodging furnished to an employee. Generally, if "the meals are furnished on the business premises of the employer" or "the employee is required to accept . . . lodging on the business premises of his employer as a condition of his employment" (26 U.S.C. sec. 119(a)(1)–(2)), the employee may exclude the value of the meals or lodging from income. The lodging portion of Section 119 was at issue in *Winchell* v. *United States,* 725 F.2d 689 (8th Cir. 1984). The plaintiff was a college president who was provided free lodging in a house several miles from campus on land used by the college for athletic and other outdoor activities. The college's board of trustees had originally insisted that the president use the house as his personal residence. He was only "infrequently" required to use the house to carry out job-related duties (such as entertainment or holding meetings); his college office "ordinarily" sufficed to meet most of his administrative needs. To determine whether this lodging was "required . . . as a condition of employment" within the meaning of Section 119, the court considered various tests, one of which was that the taxpayer must "show that the free employer-provided housing is integrally related to the duties of the employee."

[7]For cases on when to withhold in this and other situations, see Annot., "What Constitutes Employer-Employee Relationship for Purpose of Federal Income Tax Withholding," 51 A.L.R. Fed. 59 (1981 and periodic supp.).

Holding that the college president was unable to meet this test, the court determined that he was subject to taxation of the fair market rental value of the house, even though he had occupied it at the trustees' insistence.

Sections 511–513 of the Internal Revenue Code impose a tax on the "unrelated business income" of educational institutions that otherwise are exempt from taxation (26 U.S.C. sec. 511(a)(2)). The tax applies to income generated by "any trade or business the conduct of which is not substantially related . . . to the exercise or performance by such organization of its charitable, educational, or other purpose or function" (26 U.S.C. sec. 513(a)). The trade or business must be "regularly carried on" in order to be subject to the tax (26 U.S.C. sec. 512(a)). Exceptions to the rule of tax liability apply, however, when "substantially all the work in carrying on [the] trade or business is performed for the organization without compensation" (26 U.S.C. sec. 513(a)(1)); when the trade or business is conducted "by the organization primarily for the convenience of its members, students, . . . officers, or employees" (26 U.S.C. sec. 513(a)(2)); and when the trade or business involves the "selling of merchandise substantially all of which has been received by the organization as gifts or contributions" (26 U.S.C. sec. 513(a)(3)). Regulations elaborating the rules and exceptions on the unrelated business tax are in 26 C.F.R. secs. 1.511-1 to 1.513-2.

As can be readily seen, the tax code presents many challenges for postsecondary administrators. In addition to the examples above, numerous other income tax matters may confront the institution from any of a number of directions. Due to the complexity and variety of the potential problems, administrators should have ready access to a specialist who is well versed in the arcana of tax law.

The celebrated case of *Bob Jones University* v. *United States,* 103 S. Ct. 2017 (1983), illustrates the complexities of tax law and the impact it may have on the campus. The IRS had denied Bob Jones University and a second plaintiff, Goldsboro Christian Academy, tax-exempt status under Section 501(c)(3). Each school had racially discriminatory policies, Bob Jones prohibiting its students from interracial dating or marriage, Goldsboro denying admission to most blacks. The schools challenged the basic principle of Revenue Ruling 71-447 (above), arguing (1) that Section 501(c)(3) did not embrace the common law concept of charity; and (2) that, even if it did, the schools' racial policies were mandated by sincerely held religious beliefs and thus protected by the free exercise clause of the First Amendment. When the case reached the U.S. Supreme Court, it became embroiled in political controversy. The Reagan administration announced that Section 501(c)(3) did not give the IRS authority to deny tax-exempt status on the basis of race discrimination and attempted to overturn Revenue Ruling 71-447. Caught in a firestorm of adverse publicity, the administration then introduced legislation to amend Section 501(c)(3). Because the administration had compromised the federal government's position in the case, the Supreme Court took the extraordinary step of appointing special counsel to argue in favor of Revenue Ruling 71-447.

When the Supreme Court finally ruled on the merits, it upheld the long-standing IRS interpretation (and rejected the Reagan administration's reinterpretation) of Section 501(c)(3):

In Revenue Ruling 71-447, the IRS formalized the policy, first announced in 1970, that Section 170 [the provision authorizing individuals to deduct amounts contributed to charity] and Section 501(c)(3) embrace the common law "charity" concept. Under that view, to qualify for a tax exemption pursuant to Section 501(c)(3), an institution must show, first, that it falls within one of the . . . categories expressly set forth in that section and, second, that its activity is not contrary to settled public policy. . . .

Section 501(c)(3) . . . must be analyzed and construed within the framework of the Internal Revenue Code and against the background of the congressional purposes. Such an examination reveals unmistakable evidence that, underlying all relevant parts of the Code, is the intent that entitlement to tax exemption depends on meeting certain common law standards of charity—namely, that an institution seeking tax-exempt status must serve a public purpose and not be contrary to established public policy. . . .

Tax exemptions for certain institutions thought beneficial to the social order of the country as a whole, or to a particular community, are deeply rooted in our history, as in that of England. The origins of such exemptions lie in the special privileges that have long been extended to charitable trusts. . . .

When the government grants exemptions or allows deductions all taxpayers are affected: the very fact of the exemption or deduction for the donor means that other taxpayers can be said to be indirect and vicarious "donors." Charitable exemptions are justified on the basis that the exempt entity confers a public benefit—a benefit which the society or the community may not itself choose or be able to provide, or which supplements and advances the work of public institutions already supported by tax revenues [103 S. Ct. at 2025-28].

The Court then considered whether racial discrimination is so contrary to settled public policy that institutions practicing it cannot be said to be charitable or to confer a public benefit:

Determination of public benefit and public policy are sensitive matters with serious implications for the institutions affected; a declaration that a given institution is not "charitable" should be made only where there can be no doubt that the activity involved is contrary to a fundamental public policy. But there can no longer be any doubt that racial discrimination in education violates deeply and widely accepted views of elementary justice. Prior to 1954, public education in many places still was conducted under the pall of *Plessy* v. *Ferguson,* 163 U.S. 537 (1896); racial segregation in primary and secondary education prevailed in many parts of the country. This Court's decision in *Brown* v. *Board of Education,* 347 U.S. 483 (1954), signaled an end to that era. Over the past quarter of a century, every pronouncement of this Court and myriad Acts of Congress and Executive Orders attest a firm national policy to prohibit racial segregation and discrimination in public education. . . .

There can thus be no question that the interpretation of Section 501(c)(3) announced by the IRS in 1970 was correct. . . . Racially discriminatory educational institutions cannot be viewed as conferring a public benefit within the "charitable" concept discussed earlier, or within the congressional intent underlying . . . Section 501(c)(3) [103 S. Ct. at 2029-31].

Having concluded that Revenue Ruling 71-447 is consistent with Congress's intent concerning Section 501(c)(3) and a correct reading of public policy, the Court lastly considered and rejected the plaintiffs' free exercise of religion claim:

> The free exercise clause provides substantial protection for lawful conduct grounded in religious belief. . . . However, "not all burdens on religion are unconstitutional. . . . The state may justify a limitation on religious liberty by showing that it is essential to accomplish an overriding governmental interest" (*United States* v. *Lee,* 455 U.S. 252, 257–58 (1982)).
>
> On occasion this Court has found certain governmental interests so compelling as to allow even regulations prohibiting religiously based conduct. In *Prince* v. *Massachusetts,* 321 U.S. 158 (1944), for example, the Court held that neutrally cast child labor laws prohibiting sale of printed materials on public streets could be applied to prohibit children from dispensing religious literature. . . .
>
> Denial of tax benefits will inevitably have a substantial impact on the operation of private religious schools, but will not prevent those schools from observing their religious tenets.
>
> The governmental interest at stake here is compelling. As discussed . . . , the government has a fundamental, overriding interest in eradicating racial discrimination in education—discrimination that prevailed, with official approval, for the first 165 years of this nation's history. That governmental interest substantially outweighs whatever burden denial of tax benefits places on petitioners' exercise of their religious beliefs. The interests asserted by petitioners cannot be accommodated with that compelling governmental interest, . . . and no "less restrictive means" . . . are available to achieve the governmental interest [103 S. Ct. at 2034–35].

7.3.2. Social Security taxes. Since the enactment of the Social Security Amendments of 1983, 97 Stat. 65, the postsecondary education community must be more attentive than ever before to the Social Security laws. Passed in an effort to ensure the continued solvency of the Social Security system, the 1983 amendments repeal certain exemptions from tax liability and thus increase the number of postsecondary institutions that must contribute to the system.

The laws establishing the Social Security system are found in two different titles of the *United States Code.* Title 42 (sec. 401 *et seq.*) establishes the "Federal Old Age and Survivors Insurance Trust Fund and Federal Disability Insurance Trust Fund" and sets the requirements on eligibility for benefits. Title 26 (sec. 3101 *et seq.*), the Federal Insurance Contributions Act, defines which employers and employees are subject to taxation and levies the appropriate tax (see J. H. Ditkoff, "Withholding and Employment Taxes: Practices, Penalties, and Questions of Policy," 37 *N.Y.U. Annual Institute on Federal Taxation,* part 2, sec. 30.1 (1979)). The 1983 amendments affect the tax liability of postsecondary institutions in two ways. First, Section 102(b)(1)(C) of the amendments (97 Stat. at 70) deletes the language from 26 U.S.C. sec. 3121(b)(8)(B) that had previously provided an exemption from the system for "service performed in the employ of a religious, charitable, educational, or other organization" as defined in 26 U.S.C. sec. 501(c)(3) (see Section 7.3.1 for discussion of 501(c)(3)). Thus, private institutions formerly claiming exemption under this provision can no longer do so. Second, Section 103(a) of the amendments modifies 42

U.S.C. sec. 418 *et seq.*, which allows states voluntarily to enter into agreements with the secretary of health and human services for the coverage of state and local employees under the Social Security system. As amended, this provision forbids states that have entered such agreements from withdrawing from them. This amendment does not repeal the traditional exemption for states and political subdivisions (26 U.S.C. sec. 3121(b)(7)), but it does "lock" into the system states that are participating under voluntary agreements. Public postsecondary institutions covered by such an agreement thus no longer have the option of dropping out.

Although the 1983 amendments constricted the number of institutions exempt from the Social Security tax, they left intact exemptions for several classes of employees common to postsecondary institutions.[8] Still exempt from coverage are (1) students "enrolled and regularly attending classes" who are also employees of the institution, except for student employees at public institutions that are covered by, and include such students in, voluntary agreements between the state and the secretary of health and human services (26 U.S.C. sec. 3121(b)(10)); (2) students "enrolled and . . . regularly attending classes" who perform domestic services at college clubs, sororities, or fraternities (26 U.S.C. sec. 3121(b)(2)); (3) student nurses "enrolled and . . . regularly attending classes" at a state-approved nurse's training school who are employed at a "hospital or a nurse's training school" (26 U.S.C. sec. 3121(b)(13)); and (4) clergy whose services for the institution are performed in "the exercise of [their] ministry" or members of religious orders whose services for the institution are performed "in the exercise of duties required by such order" (26 U.S.C. sec. 3121(b)(8)).

Another provision of the 1983 amendments of interest to some administrators allows universities that have hospitals affiliated with them to coordinate the Social Security withholding of university faculty members who also hold hospital staff positions. This provision allows affected institutions to avoid what would otherwise be a system of double taxation (see Section 125 of the amendments, according special treatment, under 26 U.S.C. sec. 3121(s), to faculty practice plans).

7.3.3. Unemployment compensation taxes. The Federal Unemployment Tax Act (FUTA), 26 U.S.C. sec. 3301 *et seq.*, was originally passed in 1935 as a response to the unemployment of the Great Depression. Its purpose was and is to provide compensation to qualifying employees who are temporarily out of work. The federal government and the states share the responsibility for the Act's operation. Although ultimate responsibility for the tax rests with the federal government, states are permitted to implement their own unemployment plans. Where a state plan conforms to the requirements set out in the statute (26 U.S.C. secs. 3302–3305) and the corresponding federal regulations (20 C.F.R. Part 601), the U.S. secretary of labor will certify the plan. This system allows the state, rather than the federal government, to become primarily responsible for administration of the compensation program funded by the tax.

---

[8]The issue of who is an "employee" for purposes of Social Security law is often difficult. For relevant cases and authorities, see Annot., "Determination of Employer-Employee Relationship for Social Security Contribution and Unemployment Tax Purposes Under sec. 3121(d)(2) of Federal Insurance Contributions Act (26 U.S.C. sec. 3121(d)(2)), sec. 3306(i) of Federal Unemployment Tax Act (26 U.S.C. sec. 3306(i), and Implementing Regulations," 37 A.L.R. Fed. 95 (1978 and periodic supp.).

At one time FUTA exempted employees of a state or its political subdivisions from the operation of the tax (26 U.S.C. sec. 3306(c)(7)). In 1976, however, Congress added a new section to FUTA; this section overrides Section 3306(c)(7) and brings employees of states and their subdivisions within the statute (26 U.S.C. sec. 3309(a)(1)(B)). Another 1976 amendment gives political subdivisions of a state the option either to reimburse the state for unemployment benefits paid former employees or to make payments in the same manner as private-sector employees (26 U.S.C. secs. 3304(a)(6) and 3309(a)). The constitutionality of these amendments was upheld in *State of New Hampshire Department of Employment Security* v. *Marshall,* 616 F.2d 240 (1st Cir. 1980), where the court rejected the state's argument that the amendments violated the Tenth Amendment of the Constitution as construed in *National League of Cities* v. *Usery,* 426 U.S. 833 (1976) (see Section 7.1.3 of this volume).

Thus, faculty and staff of state colleges and universities and community colleges, formerly exempt, are now covered by the terms of FUTA.

At one time the employees of most private postsecondary institutions, as well as of most private elementary and secondary schools, were also exempt from FUTA. In 1970 and 1976, however, Congress approved a series of amendments that greatly narrowed this exemption. Private nonsectarian schools were clearly subjected to the Act as a result of these amendments; there was some question, however, about church-related institutions.

In *St. Martin's Evangelical Lutheran Church* v. *South Dakota,* 451 U.S. 772, 101 S. Ct. 2142 (1981), the plaintiffs challenged the applicability of FUTA to nonprofit church-related primary and secondary schools. The statutory exemption at issue, as narrowed in 1970 and 1976, provided that:

> This section shall not apply to service performed—
> (1) in the employ of (A) a church or convention or association of churches, or (B) an organization which is operated primarily for religious purposes and which is operated, supervised, controlled, or principally supported by a church or convention or association of churches [26 U.S.C. sec. 3309(b)(1)].

The secretary of labor, relying on the legislative history of Section 3309, had ruled that church-related primary and secondary schools were not included within this language and were therefore subject to FUTA.

The U.S. Supreme Court rejected the Labor Department's interpretation. The Court's own analysis of Section 3309's legislative history provides insight into FUTA's application to both elementary/secondary and postsecondary church-related schools:

> Section 3309 was added to FUTA in 1970. Although the legislative history directly discussing the intended coverage of its subsection (b)(1) is limited, the House Report had the following explanation:
>
> > This paragraph excludes services of persons where the employer is a church or convention or association of churches, but does not exclude certain services performed for an organization which may be religious in

orientation unless it is operated primarily for religious purposes and is operated, supervised, controlled, or principally supported by a church (or convention or association of churches). Thus, the services of the janitor of a church would be excluded, but services of a janitor for a separately incorporated college, although it may be church related, would be covered. A college devoted primarily to preparing students for the ministry would be exempt, as would a novitiate or a house of study training candidates to become members of religious orders. On the other hand, a church-related (separately incorporated) charitable organization (such as, for example, an orphanage or a home for the aged) would not be considered under this paragraph to be operated primarily for religious purposes (H.R. Rep. No. 91-612, p. 44 (1969)).

The Senate Report contained identical language (see S. Rep. No. 91-752, pp. 48-49 (1970)). . . .

The above quotation from the 1969 House Report, and its Senate counterpart, however, are susceptible of a simpler and more reasonable explanation [than the explanation provided to the Court by the South Dakota Supreme Court and the U.S. secretary of labor] that corresponds directly with the language of the subsection. Congress drew a distinction between employees "of a church or convention or association of churches" (sec. 3309(b)(1)(A)), on the one hand, and employees of "separately incorporated" organizations, on the other (see H.R. Rep. No. 91-612 at 44). The former uniformly would be excluded from coverage by sec. 3309(b)(1)(A), while the latter would be eligible for exclusion under sec. 3309(b)(1)(B) only when the organization is "operated, supervised, controlled, or principally supported by a church or convention or association of churches." To hold, as respondent would have us do, that "organization" in subsection (b)(1)(B) also includes a church school that is not separately incorporated would make (b)(1)(A) and (b)(1)(B) redundant [101 S. Ct. at 2147-48].

Apparently, under the *St. Martin's* analysis, elementary/secondary schools are far more likely than postsecondary institutions to be exempt from FUTA. To be exempt under Section 3309(b)(1)(A), a college must be part of—not separately incorporated from—a "church or convention or association of churches." While terms such as "primarily for religious purposes" may be subject to considerable debate, apparently only a small proportion of church-related postsecondary institutions can qualify under these tests. The primary example, as the legislative history reveals, is the seminary.

Under FUTA student employees of postsecondary institutions (public or private) are treated differently from regular faculty and staff employees. If students are employed as part of a financial assistance package (for example, students participating in a work-study program of financial aid), or are employed as part of an educational program that also entails employment experience (for example, student nurses), they are exempt from coverage (26 U.S.C. sec. 3306(c)(10)(B) and (C)).

The FUTA statute also contains a specific provision dealing with the unique aspects of the academic calendar. Under Section 3304(a)(6)(A)(i), states are prohibited from providing unemployment compensation to faculty, researchers, and administrators for gaps in service attributable to customary vacation or recess periods or to periods between academic years or terms.

Since states implement their own unemployment compensation plans under FUTA, college administrators cannot obtain definitive guidance on the issues above or other coverage questions by consulting only the federal law. With the assistance of counsel, administrators must also consult their state's statutes, administrative regulations, and court decisions on unemployment compensation (see this volume, Section 6.5.3).

Sec. 7.4. *Federal Aid to Education Programs*

The federal government's major function regarding postsecondary education is to establish national priorities and objectives for education spending and to provide funds in accordance with those decisions. To implement its priorities and objectives, the federal government attaches a wide and varied range of conditions to the funds it makes available and enforces these conditions against postsecondary institutions and other aid recipients. Some of these conditions are specific to the program for which funds are given. Others, called "cross-cutting" conditions, apply across a range of programs; examples are the civil rights requirements discussed in Section 7.5 and the privacy of student records requirements discussed in Section 4.12. Cumulatively, these conditions exert a most substantial influence on postsecondary institutions, often leading to institutional cries of economic coercion and federal control. In light of such institutional criticism, the federal role in funding postsecondary education has become a major political and policy issue. The particular national goals to be achieved through funding, and the delivery and compliance mechanisms best suited to achieving these goals, are likely to remain subjects of debate for the foreseeable future.

Although some current criticisms of the federal spending role are new, and although the level of federal expenditure has increased vastly since the early 1960s, federal spending for education has a long history. Shortly after the founding of the United States, the federal government began endowing public higher education institutions with public lands. In 1862 Congress passed the first Morrill Act, providing grants of land or land scrip to the states for the support of agricultural and mechanical colleges, and later provided continuing appropriations for these colleges. The second Morrill Act, providing money grants for instruction in various branches of higher education, was passed in 1890. In 1944 Congress enacted the first GI Bill, which was followed in later years by successive programs providing funds to veterans to further their education. The National Defense Education Act, passed in 1958 after Congress was spurred by Russia's launching of *Sputnik,* included a large-scale program of low-interest loans for students in institutions of higher education. The Higher Education Facilities Act of 1963 authorized grants and low-interest loans to public and private nonprofit institutions of higher education for constructing and improving various educational facilities. Then, in 1965, Congress finally jumped broadly into supporting higher education with the passage of the Higher Education Act of 1965 (20 U.S.C. sec. 1001 *et seq.*). The Act's various titles authorized federal support for a range of postsecondary education activities, including community educational services; resources, training, and research for college libraries and

personnel; strengthening developing institutions; and student financial aid programs.
As later amended, the Act now contains most of the student financial aid programs
and provisions discussed in Section 4.3.

   7.4.1. Distinction between federal aid and federal procurement. Funds provided under the Higher Education Act and other aid programs should be sharply
distinguished from funds provided under federal *procurement* programs. Many federal
agencies, such as the U.S. Department of Defense, enter into procurement contracts
with postsecondary institutions or consortia of institutions, the primary purpose
of which is to obtain research or services that meet the government's own needs.
True aid to education programs, in contrast, primarily serve the needs of institutions,
their students and faculty, or the education community in general, rather than the
government's own needs for goods or services. The two systems—assistance and
procurement—operate independently of one another, with different statutory bases
and different regulations, and often with different agency officials in charge.
Guidelines for differentiating the two systems are set out in Chapter 63 of Subtitle
V of 41 U.S.C.: "Using Procurement Contracts and Grant and Cooperative
Agreements."

   The bases of the federal procurement system are Title III of the Federal Property and Administrative Services Act of 1949, 41 U.S.C. sec. 251 *et seq.;* the Office
of Federal Procurement Policy Act of 1974, 41 U.S.C. sec. 401 *et seq.;* and the Federal
Procurement Regulations System, described in 41 C.F.R. Part 1-1, Subpart 1-1.0.
These sources establish uniform policies and procedures which individual agencies
implement and supplement with regulations specific to their own procurement activities. The individual agency regulations are set out in 41 C.F.R. Chapters 3–29.

   Federal procurement law permits federal agencies to exercise more substantial
control over the details of procurement contracts than is typical with grants and
other forms of federal aid; many standard clauses that must be used in procurement contracts are prescribed by federal regulations (41 C.F.R. Chapter 1, Part
1-7). Unlike assistance, moreover, procurement contracts "shall be terminated for
the convenience of the government when it is determined that such action is in
the best interest of the government" (41 C.F.R. Chapter 1, Part 1-8, sec. 1-8.201(a)).
Government contractors found guilty of fraud, embezzlement, antitrust violations,
or other criminal or civil offenses impugning business integrity may be debarred
or suspended for a specified time from obtaining other government contracts. In
1982 the Office of Federal Procurement Policy, a subdivision of the Office of Management and Budget (OMB), in OFPP Policy Letter 82-1 (published at 47 Fed. Reg.
28854 (July 1, 1982)), promulgated new federal policy on debarment. Contractors
may appeal disputes concerning their government contracts to agency Boards of
Contract Appeals, established pursuant to the Contract Disputes Act (41 U.S.C.
sec. 601 *et seq.*), or may bypass this appeals process and bring an action directly
in the U.S. Court of Claims (41 U.S.C. sec. 609(a)(1)).

   Other important federal laws also establish requirements applicable to the
federal procurement system. Executive Orders 11246 and 11375 (Section 3.3.4 of
this volume), for instance, establish affirmative action requirements for federal
government contractors. Similarly, the Davis-Bacon Act (40 U.S.C. sec. 276a *et
seq.*), as implemented by Department of Labor regulations that were substantially
revised in 1982 (29 C.F.R. Part 5), establishes rate-of-pay requirements for employees
working under federal construction contracts. The Service Contract Labor Standards

Act (41 U.S.C. sec. 351 *et seq.*) and its implementing regulations (29 C.F.R. Part 4) establish comparable requirements for employees working under federal service contracts. (A 1983 revision of the regulations for this Act considered and rejected an exemption for research and development contracts; see 48 Fed. Reg. 49736 (Oct. 27, 1983).) Although laws such as these are designed for the procurement rather than the federal aid system, they are often extended to procurement contracts that federal aid recipients enter into as a means of accomplishing part of their work under a federal grant, loan, or cooperative agreement. (See, for example, 20 U.S.C. sec. 1232b (application of Davis-Bacon Act to procurement contracts of ED aid recipients); 34 C.F.R. sec. 74.166 (application of Davis-Bacon Act, Executive Orders 11246 and 11375, and Contract Work Hours and Safety Standards Act, 40 U.S.C. sec. 327 *et seq.*, to procurement contracts of ED aid recipients); 29 C.F.R. sec. 5.2(e) and 41 C.F.R. sec. 60-1.1 (application of Davis-Bacon Act and Executive Orders 11246 and 11375 to procurement contracts of other federal aid recipients).)

    7.4.2. Legal structure of aid programs. Federal aid for postsecondary education is disbursed by a number of federal agencies. The three most important, at least with respect to student aid, are the U.S. Department of Education (formerly U.S. Office of Education), the U.S. Department of Health and Human Services, and the Veterans Administration.

    Until 1980 the Office of Education (OE), created in 1867, was a constituent agency of the U.S. Department of Health, Education and Welfare, headed by the commissioner of education. Under a 1972 statute, 20 U.S.C. sec. 1221a–c, OE, together with the National Institute of Education (NIE), constituted the Education Division of HEW. On October 17, 1979, President Carter signed the Department of Education Organization Act, 93 Stat. 668, 20 U.S.C. sec. 3401 *et seq.* The Act transferred functions of the Office of Education, the National Institute of Education, and several other federal agencies to a new U.S. Department of Education (ED). The Department of Education formally came into existence on May 4, 1980, in accordance with the Act and Executive Order No. 12212 (45 Fed. Reg. 29557 (May 2, 1980)). The House and Senate reports and congressional debates accompanying the legislation are found in 1979 *U.S. Code Congressional and Administrative News,* 96th Cong., 1st Sess., pp. 1514–1644.

    The Department of Education Organization Act also redesignated the remainder of the U.S. Department of Health, Education and Welfare as the new U.S. Department of Health and Human Services (HHS). The Public Health Service, previously a constituent agency of HEW and now of HHS, administers aid programs for students in medical, dental, pharmacy, nursing, and other health education programs (see 42 C.F.R. Part 57).

    The Veterans Administration (VA) administers the veterans' educational benefits programs found in 38 U.S.C. sec. 1651 *et seq.* (See *Max Cleland, Administrator of VA* v. *National College of Business,* 435 U.S. 213 (1978), upholding various federal statutory restrictions (the ''85–15'' rule and the ''two-year'' rule) on veterans' use of VA benefits.) The VA contracts with the State Approving Agencies, which review courses and determine whether to approve them as courses for which veterans can expend veterans' benefits. The State Approving Agencies, and the institutions seeking approval for their courses, must follow criteria and procedures for such approvals that are set out in 38 U.S.C. secs. 1775–1776 (see Section 4.3.2 of this volume).

    Federal aid to postsecondary education is dispensed in a variety of ways.

Depending on the program involved, federal agencies may award grants or make loans directly to individual students; guarantee loans made to individual students by third parties; award grants directly to faculty members; make grants or loans to postsecondary institutions; enter "cooperative agreements" (as opposed to procurement contracts) with postsecondary institutions; or award grants, make loans, or enter agreements with state agencies, which in turn provide aid to institutions or their students or faculty.

Whether an institution is eligible to receive federal aid, either directly from the federal agency or a state agency or indirectly from the student recipient, depends on the requirements of the particular aid program. Typically, however, the institution must be accredited by a recognized accrediting agency or demonstrate compliance with one of the few statutorily prescribed substitutes for accreditation (see Sections 8.1 and 8.3).

The "rules of the game" regarding eligibility, application procedures, the selection of recipients, allowable expenditures, conditions on spending, records and reports requirements, compliance reviews, and other federal aid requirements are set out in a variety of sources. Administrators will want to be familiar with these sources in order to maximize the institution's ability to obtain and effectively utilize federal money. Legal counsel will want to be familiar with these sources in order to protect the institution from challenges to its eligibility or to its compliance with applicable requirements.

The starting point is the statute that authorizes the particular federal aid program, along with the statute's legislative history. Occasionally the appropriations legislation funding the program for a particular fiscal year will also contain requirements applicable to the expenditure of the appropriated funds. The next source, adding specificity to the statutory base, is the regulations for the program. The regulations, which are published in the *Federal Register* (Fed. Reg.) and then codified in the *Code of Federal Regulations* (C.F.R.), are the primary source of the administering agency's program requirements. During 1980 Title 34 of the *Code of Federal Regulations* was reestablished as the Education title, and the Office of Education's program regulations were redesignated as ED regulations and transferred from Title 45 C.F.R. to Title 34 (45 Fed. Reg. 30803 (May 9, 1980); 45 Fed. Reg. 86296–86301 (Dec. 30, 1980)).

Regulations may be backed up by federal program manuals, guidelines, or policy memoranda, which are also sometimes used in lieu of formal regulations. Published regulations have the force of law and bind the government, the aid recipients, and all the outside parties. Manuals, guidelines, and memoranda generally do not have the status of law; although they may sometimes be binding on recipients who had actual notice of them before receiving federal funds, more often they are treated as agency suggestions that do not bind anyone (see 5 U.S.C. sec. 552(a)(1); 20 U.S.C. sec. 1232). Additional requirements or suggestions may be found in the grant award documents or agreements under which the aid is dispensed, in agency manuals on grant and contract policies applicable across a range of programs, or in Office of Management and Budget (OMB) circulars that set government-wide policy on such matters as allowable cost principles and the establishment of indirect cost rates. One of the most important of these circulars, OMB Circular A-21, "Cost Principles for Educational Institutions," was revised in 1982 (47 Fed. Reg. 33658 (Aug. 3, 1982)) to accord institutions more flexibility in documenting the portions of researchers' salaries paid with federal funds and to allow institutions to recover interest costs incurred in purchasing facilities or equipment used for federally supported research.

In addition, the civil rights statutes and regulations (this volume, Section 7.5) establish nondiscrimination requirements applicable to federal aid recipients.

The U.S. Department of Education is subject to federal statutes that place additional restrictions on its rules of the game. The General Education Provisions Act, 20 U.S.C. sec. 1221 *et seq.*, establishes numerous organizational, administrative, and other requirements applicable to ED spending programs. For instance, the Act establishes procedures that ED must follow when proposing program regulations (20 U.S.C. sec. 1232). In addition, ED has promulgated extensive general regulations published at 34 C.F.R. Parts 74–78. These "Education Department General Administrative Regulations" (EDGAR), supplementing the program regulations for each individual grant program, establish uniform policies for all ED grant programs. The applicability of Part 74 of these regulations to higher education institutions is specified at 34 C.F.R. sec. 74.4(c), and Appendix D to Part 74 sets out allowable cost principles devised specifically for higher education institutions. Running to 175 pages in the *Code of Federal Regulations,* EDGAR tells you almost everything you were afraid to ask about the legal requirements for obtaining and administering ED grants.

7.4.3. Enforcing compliance with aid conditions. The federal government has several methods for enforcing compliance with its various aid requirements. The responsible agency may periodically audit the institution's expenditures of federal money and may take an "audit exception" for funds not spent in compliance with program requirements. The institution then owes the federal government the amount specified in the audit exception. In addition to audit exceptions, the agency may suspend or terminate the institution's funding under the program or programs in which noncompliance is found (see 34 C.F.R. secs. 74.113–74.115, and 34 C.F.R. secs. 75.901 and 75.903). Special provisions have been developed for the "limitation, suspension, or termination" of an institution's eligibility to participate in ED's major student aid programs (see 20 U.S.C. sec. 1088f-1(a)(4)).

Federal funding agencies also apparently have the authority to sue institutions in court to obtain compliance with grant and contract conditions, although they seldom exercise this power. In *United States* v. *Frazer,* 297 F. Supp. 319 (M.D. Ala. 1968), a suit against the administrators of the Alabama state welfare system, the court held that the United States had standing to sue to enforce welfare grant conditions requiring that personnel for federally financed programs be hired on a merit basis. And in *United States* v. *Institute of Computer Technology,* 403 F. Supp. 922 (E.D. Mich. 1975), the court permitted the United States to sue a school that had allegedly breached a contract with the Office of Education under which the school disbursed funds for the Basic Educational Opportunity Grant program.

Given the number and complexity of the conditions attached to federal spending programs, and the federal government's substantial enforcement power, postsecondary institutions will want to keep attuned to all the procedural rights, legal arguments, and negotiating leverage they may utilize in case of disputes with federal funding agencies. The institution's legal position and negotiating strength will depend on the provisions of the particular funding program, on the particular facts of the case, and on whether the institution is applying for aid or being threatened with a fund cutoff. Typically, applicants have fewer procedural rights than recipients do.

Under the various statutes and regulations applicable to federal aid programs, fund recipients usually will be given notice and opportunity for a hearing prior to any termination of funding (see, for example, 20 U.S.C. sec. 1234b).[9] Hearings may also be provided before finalization of audit exceptions taken by federal auditors. At the Department of Education, such hearings are held by the Education Appeal Board. This board, established by statute (20 U.S.C. sec. 1234 *et seq.*), has jurisdiction to "conduct withholding or termination hearings," "review final audit determinations," and "conduct cease and desist proceedings" (34 C.F.R. sec. 78.2(a)(1)–(3)). The board may also conduct hearings to review the department's "disapproval of a recipient's written request for permission to incur an expenditure during the term of a grant," or to review the department's "determination . . . with respect to . . . indirect cost rates, computer, fringe benefit, and other special rates negotiated with institutions of postsecondary education," and may "conduct other proceedings as designated by the secretary [of education]" (34 C.F.R. sec. 78.2(a)(4)–(5)). The board's jurisdiction extends to all such disputes arising in ED programs other than the major student aid programs, which are treated separately under 20 U.S.C. sec. 1088f-1 (see 34 C.F.R. sec. 78.3). Final decisions of the board are reviewable in the U.S. Courts of Appeals (20 U.S.C. sec. 1234d).

While such procedural protections can be very important, often the critical issue will concern the substance of what the federal agencies are doing to institutions rather than the procedures by which they do it. In particular, institutions may seek to challenge the substantive validity of particular conditions that federal agencies attach to the expenditure of federal funds. In 1976–77, for instance, a furor arose over a congressional requirement (since repealed) that, as a condition for receiving capitation grants, medical schools had to reserve a number of places for American students transferring from foreign medical schools. But because the federal government's constitutional power to tax and spend is so broad (see Section 7.1), substantive challenges to such spending conditions are difficult and speculative. Arguments that particular conditions violate the principles of academic freedom (First Amendment) or substantive due process (Fifth Amendment) may sometimes be possible (see P. Lacovara, "How Far Can the Federal Camel Slip Under the Academic Tent?" 4 *J. of College and University Law* 223, 229–239 (1977)). When the condition is created by an agency rule or regulation rather than by the funding statute itself, it may be possible to argue that the rule or regulation is *ultra vires,* that is, beyond the authority delegated to the agency under the funding statute. Such substantive legal challenges, even more than procedural challenges, provide an area ripe for creative activity by postsecondary institutions and their legal counsel.

Sec. 7.5. Civil Rights Compliance

7.5.1. General considerations. Postsecondary institutions receiving assistance under federal aid programs are obligated to follow not only the programmatic and

---

[9]If no hearing is provided under the applicable agency statutes and regulations, the federal Administrative Procedure Act, 5 U.S.C. sec. 551 *et seq.,* may provide either a right to a hearing or a right to judicial review of the agency's decision. The due process clause of the Fifth Amendment may also guarantee a right to a hearing regarding fund termination. It is not yet settled whether *state* institutions may assert these Fifth Amendment rights, however, since that amendment protects only "persons"; and state institutions, as government agencies, may not fall into that category.

technical requirements of each program under which aid is received (see Section 7.4) but also various civil rights requirements that apply generally to federal aid programs. These requirements are a major focus of federal spending policy, importing substantial social goals into education policy and making equality of educational opportunity a clear national priority in education. The implementation and enforcement of civil rights have often been steeped in controversy. Some argue that the federal role is too great, and some say that it is too small; some argue that the federal government proceeds too fast, and some insist that it is too slow; others argue that the compliance process is too cumbersome or costly for the affected institutions. Despite the controversy, it is clear that these federal civil rights efforts, over time, have provided a major force for social change in America.

As conditions on spending, the civil rights requirements represent an exercise of Congress's spending power (see Section 7.1.1) implemented through delegating authority to the various federal departments and agencies that administer federal aid programs. As nondiscrimination principles promoting equal opportunity, the civil rights requirements may also be justifiable as exercises of Congress's power to enforce the Fourteenth Amendment's equal protection clause (see Section 7.1.4).

Four different federal statutes prohibit discrimination in educational programs receiving federal financial assistance. Title VI of the Civil Rights Act of 1964 prohibits discrimination on the basis of race, color, or national origin. Title IX of the Education Amendments of 1972 prohibits discrimination on the basis of sex. Section 504 of the Rehabilitation Act of 1973, as amended in 1974, prohibits discrimination against the handicapped. The Age Discrimination Act of 1975 prohibits discrimination on the basis of age. Title IX is specifically limited to educational programs receiving federal financial assistance, while Title VI, Section 504, and the Age Discrimination Act apply to all programs receiving such assistance. Each statute delegates enforcement responsibilities to each of the federal agencies disbursing federal financial assistance. Postsecondary institutions may thus be subject to the civil rights regulations of several federal agencies, the most important one being the Department of Education, created in 1979, which has assumed the functions of the former HEW Office for Civil Rights with respect to all educational programs transferred from HEW's Office of Education. ED has its own Office for Civil Rights under an assistant secretary for civil rights. The HEW civil rights regulations, formerly published in Volume 45 of the *Code of Federal Regulations* (C.F.R.), were redesignated as ED regulations and republished in 34 C.F.R. Parts 100–106.

Although the language of the four statutes is similar, each statute protects a different group of beneficiaries, and an act that constitutes discrimination against one group does not necessarily constitute discrimination if directed against another group. "Separate but equal" treatment of the sexes is sometimes permissible under Title IX, for instance, but such treatment of the races is never permissible under Title VI. Administrative regulations have considerably fleshed out the meaning of the statutes. Since 1978 HEW's (now ED's) Office for Civil Rights has also published policy interpretations of its regulations in the *Federal Register*. Judicial decisions also contribute additional interpretive gloss on major points, but the administrative regulations remain the primary source for understanding the civil rights requirements.

7.5.2. *Title VI*. Title VI of the Civil Rights Act of 1964, 42 U.S.C. sec. 2000d, declares:

> No person in the United States shall, on the ground of race, color, or national origin, be excluded from participation in, be denied the benefits of, or be subjected to discrimination under any program or activity receiving federal financial assistance.

Courts have generally held that Title VI incorporates the same standards for identifying unlawful racial discrimination as have been developed under the Fourteenth Amendment's equal protection clause (see the discussion of the *Bakke* case in Section 4.2.5, and see generally Section 4.2.4.1). But courts have also held that the Department of Education and other federal agencies implementing Title VI may impose nondiscrimination requirements on recipients beyond those developed under the equal protection clause (see *Guardians Association* v. *Civil Service Commission of the City of New York,* 103 S. Ct. 3221 (1983), discussed in Section 7.5.7.2).

Section 100.3(b) of the ED regulations provides the basic, and most specific, reference point for determining what actions are unlawful under Title VI and/or its implementing regulations:

> (b) *Specific discriminatory actions prohibited.*
> (1) A recipient under any program to which this part applies may not directly or through contractual or other arrangements, on ground of race, color, or national origin:
> (i) Deny an individual any service, financial aid, or other benefit provided under the program;
> (ii) Provide any service, financial aid, or other benefit to an individual which is different, or is provided in a different manner, from that provided to others under the program;
> (iii) Subject an individual to segregation or separate treatment in any matter related to his receipt of any service, financial aid, or other benefit under the program;
> (iv) Restrict an individual in any way in the enjoyment of any advantage or privilege enjoyed by others receiving any service, financial aid, or other benefit under the program;
> (v) Treat an individual differently from others in determining whether he satisfies any admission, enrollment, quota, eligibility, membership, or other requirement or condition which individuals must meet in order to be provided any service, financial aid, or other benefit provided under the program;
> (vi) Deny an individual an opportunity to participate in the program through the provision of services or otherwise or afford him an opportunity to do so which is different from that afforded others under the program (including the opportunity to participate in the program as an employee but only to the extent set forth in paragraph (c) of this section).
> (vii) Deny a person the opportunity to participate as a member of a planning or advisory body which is an integral part of the program.
> (2) A recipient, in determining the types of services, financial aid, or other benefits, or facilities which will be provided under any such program, or the class of individuals to whom, or the situations in which, such services, financial aid, other benefits, or facilities will be provided under any

such program, or the class of individuals to be afforded an opportunity to participate in any such program, may not, directly or through contractual or other arrangements, utilize criteria or methods of administration which have the effect of subjecting individuals to discrimination because of their race, color, or national origin, or have the effect of defeating or substantially impairing accomplishment of the objectives of the program as respect individuals of a particular race, color, or national origin.

(3) In determining the site or location of facilities, an applicant or recipient may not make selections with the effect of excluding individuals from, denying them the benefits of, or subjecting them to discrimination under any programs to which this regulation applies, on the ground of race, color, or national origin; or with the purpose or effect of defeating or substantially impairing the accomplishment of the objectives of the Act or this regulation.

To supplement these regulations, ED has also developed criteria, as discussed below, which deal specifically with the problem of desegregating statewide systems of postsecondary education.

The *Adams* litigation, begun in 1970 as *Adams* v. *Richardson* and continuing with various department secretaries as defendant until it became *Adams* v. *Bell* in the 1980s, is the leading case on application of Title VI to postsecondary education. In *Adams* a group of plaintiffs sued the secretary of HEW (now ED), claiming that the department had failed to enforce Title VI in each of ten states. The U.S. District Court ordered HEW to initiate enforcement proceedings against these states (*Adams* v. *Richardson,* 356 F. Supp. 92 (D.D.C. 1973)), and the U.S. Court of Appeals affirmed the decision (480 F.2d 1159 (D.C. Cir. 1973)). (See the further discussion of the case in Section 7.5.8.) In subsequent proceedings in the case, the district judge ordered HEW to revoke its acceptance of desegregation plans submitted by several states after the 1973 court opinions and to devise criteria for reviewing new desegregation plans to be submitted by the states that were the subject of the case (see *Adams* v. *Califano,* 430 F. Supp. 118 (D.D.C. 1977)).

After developing the criteria (42 Fed. Reg. 40780 (Aug. 11, 1977)), HEW revised and republished them (43 Fed. Reg. 6658 (Feb. 15, 1978)) as criteria applicable to all states having a history of *de jure* segregation in public higher education.[10] These "Revised Criteria Specifying the Ingredients of Acceptable Plans to Desegregate State Systems of Public Higher Education" require the affected states to take various affirmative steps, including enhancing the quality of black state-supported colleges and universities, placing new "high demand" programs on traditionally black campuses, eliminating unnecessary program duplication between black and white institutions, increasing the percentage of black academic employees in the system, and increasing the enrollment of blacks at traditionally white public colleges. The revised criteria are analyzed in J. Godard, *Educational Factors Related to Federal Criteria for the Desegregation of Public Postsecondary Education* (Southern Regional Education Board, Atlanta, 1980).

---

[10]Counsel concerned about the legal status of these criteria, and the extent to which they bind ED and the states, should consult *Adams* v. *Bell,* 711 F.2d 161, 165–66 (majority opinion), 206–07 (dissent) (D.C. Cir. 1983).

Since its 1977 order, the *Adams* court has presided over a number of additional proceedings concerning ED's enforcement of the criteria against particular states (see Section 7.5.8 of this volume). As of late 1984, a number of states still had not had plans finally approved by ED or had not fulfilled plans which earlier had been approved.

The application of Title VI and the ED criteria to traditionally black colleges and universities poses a special problem. Black institutions may be charged with Title VI violations or may be included in a statewide remedy for Title VI violations in a state system of postsecondary education. Commentators have suggested, however, that the integration of traditionally black institutions, as long as access for minority students to traditionally white institutions remains limited, will further limit opportunities for minority students. Commentators have also emphasized the intrinsic value of traditionally black institutions as a source of pride in the minority community and a source of role models for minority youths. In its 1973 opinion in *Adams,* the U.S. Court of Appeals recognized the importance of traditionally black institutions in training black professionals:

> The problem of integrating higher education must be dealt with on a statewide rather than a school-by-school basis. Perhaps the most serious problem in this area is the lack of statewide planning to provide more and better-trained minority group doctors, lawyers, engineers, and other professionals. A predicate for minority access to quality postgraduate programs is a viable, coordinated statewide higher education policy that takes into account the special problems of minority students and of black colleges. . . . These black institutions currently fulfill a crucial need and will continue to play an important role in black higher education [480 F.2d at 1164–65].

As the history of the *Adams* litigation makes clear, the desegregation of higher education is very much an unfinished business (see U.S. Commission on Civil Rights, *The Black/White Colleges: Dismantling the Dual System of Higher Education* (1981)). Its completion poses knotty legal, policy, and administrative enforcement problems and requires a sensitive appreciation of the differing missions and histories of traditionally black and traditionally white institutions. The challenge is for lawyers, administrators, government officials, and the judiciary to work together to fashion solutions consonant with the law's requirement to desegregate yet serving to increase rather than limit the opportunities available to minority students and faculty.

7.5.3. Title IX. The central provision of Title IX of the Education Amendments of 1972, 20 U.S.C. sec. 1681 *et seq.,* declares:

> (a) No person in the United States shall, on the basis of sex, be excluded from participation in, be denied the benefits of, or be subjected to discrimination under any education program or activity receiving federal financial assistance, except that:
>
> (1) in regard to admissions to educational institutions, this section shall apply only to institutions of vocational education, professional education, and graduate higher education, and to public institutions of undergraduate higher education;
>
> (2) in regard to admissions to educational institutions, this section shall not apply (A) for one year from June 23, 1972, nor for six years after

June 23, 1972, in the case of an educational institution which has begun
the process of changing from being an institution which admits only students
of one sex to being an institution which admits students of both sexes, but
only if it is carrying out a plan for such a change which is approved by
the secretary of education or (B) for seven years from the date an educational institution begins the process of changing from being an institution
which admits only students of only one sex to being an institution which
admits students of both sexes, but only if it is carrying out a plan for such
a change which is approved by the secretary of education, whichever is
the later;

       (3) this section shall not apply to an educational institution which
is controlled by a religious organization if the application of this subsection would not be consistent with the religious tenets of such organization;

       (4) this section shall not apply to an educational institution whose
primary purpose is the training of individuals for the military services of
the United States, or the merchant marine;

       (5) in regard to admissions, this section shall not apply to any
public institution of undergraduate higher education which is an institution that traditionally and continually from its establishment has had a policy
of admitting only students of one sex.

Title IX also excludes from its coverage the membership practices of tax-exempt
social fraternities and sororities (20 U.S.C. sec. 1681(a)(6)(A)); the membership
practices of the YMCA, YWCA, Girl Scouts, Boy Scouts, Campfire Girls, and
other tax-exempt, traditionally single-sex "youth service organizations" (20 U.S.C.
sec. 1681(a)(6)(B)); American Legion, Boys State, Boys Nation, Girls State, and
Girls Nation activities (20 U.S.C. sec. 1681(a)(7)); and father-son and mother-
daughter activities if provided on a reasonably comparable basis for students of
both sexes (20 U.S.C. sec. 1681(a)(8)).

       ED's regulations implementing Title IX (34 C.F.R. Part 106) include pro-
visions paralleling the language of the previously quoted Title VI regulations (see
34 C.F.R. sec. 106.31). Additional Title IX regulations specify in much greater
detail the acts of discrimination prohibited in programs and activities receiving federal
financial aid. Educational institutions may not discriminate on the basis of sex in
admissions and recruitment (with certain exceptions) (see this volume, Section
4.2.4.2); in awarding financial assistance (Section 4.3.3); in athletics programs (Section 4.11.2); or in the employment of faculty and staff members (Section 3.3.2.3)
or students (see 34 C.F.R. sec. 106.38). Section 106.32 of the regulations prohibits
sex discrimination in housing accommodations with respect to fees, services, or
benefits, but does not prohibit separate housing by sex (see this volume, Section
4.10.1). Section 106.33 requires that separate facilities for toilets, locker rooms,
and shower rooms be comparable. Section 106.34 prohibits sex discrimination in
student access to course offerings. Sections 106.36 and 106.38 require that counseling
services and employment placement services be offered to students in such a way
that there is no discrimination on the basis of sex. Section 106.39 prohibits sex
discrimination in health and insurance benefits and services, including any medical,
hospital, accident, or life insurance policy or plan which the recipient offers to its
students. Under Section 106.40 an institution may not "apply any rule concerning
a student's actual or potential parental, family, or marital status" which would

have the effect of discrimination on the basis of sex, nor may the recipient discriminate against any student on the basis of pregnancy or childbirth.

   7.5.4. Section 504. Section 504 of the Rehabilitation Act of 1973, as amended, 29 U.S.C. sec. 794, states:

> No otherwise qualified handicapped individual in the United States . . . shall, solely by reason of his handicap, be excluded from the participation in, be denied the benefits of, or be subjected to discrimination under any program or activity receiving federal financial assistance.

   The Department of Education's regulations on Section 504 (34 C.F.R. Part 104) contain specific provisions which establish standards for postsecondary institutions to follow with regard to "qualified handicapped" students and applicants, as well as "qualified handicapped" employees, applicants for employment, and members of the public seeking to take advantage of institutional programs and activities open to the public. A "handicapped person" is "any person who (i) has a physical or mental impairment which substantially limits one or more major life activities, (ii) has a record of such an impairment, or (iii) is regarded as having such an impairment" (34 C.F.R. sec. 104.3(j)). In the context of postsecondary and vocational education services, a "qualified" handicapped person is someone who "meets the academic and technical standards requisite to admission or participation in the recipient's education program or activity" (34 C.F.R. sec. 104.3(k)(3)). Whether a handicapped person is "qualified" in other situations depends on different criteria. In the context of employment, a qualified handicapped person is one who, "with reasonable accommodation, can perform the essential functions of the job in question" (34 C.F.R. sec. 104.3(k)(1)). With regard to other services, a qualified handicapped person is someone who "meets the essential eligibility requirements for the receipt of such services" (34 C.F.R. sec. 104.3(k)(4)).

   Although the Section 504 regulations resemble those for Title VI and Title IX in the types of programs and activities considered, they differ in some of the means used for achieving nondiscrimination. These differences exist because "different or special treatment of handicapped persons, because of their handicaps, may be necessary in a number of contexts in order to ensure equal opportunity" (42 Fed. Reg. 22676 (May 4, 1977)). Institutions receiving federal funds may not discriminate on the basis of handicap in admission and recruitment of students (see this volume, Section 4.2.4.3); in providing financial assistance (Section 4.3.3); in athletics programs (Section 4.11.3); in housing accommodations (Section 4.10.1); or in the employment of faculty and staff members (Section 3.3.2.6) or students (see 34 C.F.R. sec. 104.46(c)). The regulations also prohibit discrimination on the basis of handicap in a number of other programs and activities of postsecondary institutions.

   Section 104.43 requires nondiscriminatory "treatment" of students in general. Besides prohibiting discrimination in the institution's own programs and activities, this section requires that, when an institution places students in an educational program or activity not wholly under its control, the institution "must assure itself that the other education program or activity, as a whole, provides opportunity for the participation of qualified handicapped persons." In a student-teaching program, for example, the "as a whole" concept allows the institution to make use of a particular external activity even though it discriminates, provided that the institution's entire student-teaching program, taken as a whole, offers handicapped student teachers "the same range and quality of choice in student-teaching assignments afforded nonhandicapped students" (42 Fed. Reg. at 22692 (comment 30)). Furthermore, the institution must operate its programs and activities in "the most integrated setting appropriate"; that is, by integrating handicapped persons with nonhandicapped persons to the maximum extent appropriate.

The ED regulations recognize that certain academic adjustment may be necessary to protect against discrimination on the basis of handicap:

(a) *Academic requirements.* A recipient to which this subpart applies shall make such modifications to its academic requirements as are necessary to ensure that such requirements do not discriminate or have the effect of discriminating, on the basis of handicap, against a qualified handicapped applicant or student. Academic requirements that the recipient can demonstrate are essential to the program of instruction being pursued by such student or to any directly related licensing requirement will not be regarded as discriminatory within the meaning of this section. Modifications may include changes in the length of time permitted for the completion of degree requirements, substitution of specific courses required for the completion of degree requirements, and adaptation of the manner in which specific courses are conducted.

(b) *Other rules.* A recipient to which this subpart applies may not impose upon handicapped students other rules, such as the prohibition of tape recorders in classrooms or of dog guides in campus buildings, that have the effect of limiting the participation of handicapped students in the recipient's ecucation program or activity.

(c) *Course examination.* In its course examinations or other procedures for evaluating students' academic achievement in its program, a recipient to which this subpart applies shall provide such methods for evaluating the achievement of students who have a handicap that impairs sensory, manual, or speaking skills as will best ensure that the results of the evaluation represent the student's achievement in the course, rather than reflecting the student's impaired sensory, manual, or speaking skills (except where such skills are the factors that the test purports to measure).

(d) *Auxiliary aids.* (1) A recipient to which this subpart applies shall take such steps as are necessary to ensure that no handicapped student is denied the benefits of, excluded from participation in, or otherwise subjected to discrimination under the education program or activity operated by the recipient because of the absence of educational auxiliary aids for students with impaired sensory, manual, or speaking skills. (2) Auxiliary aids may include taped texts, interpreters, or other effective methods of making orally delivered materials available to students with hearing impairments, readers in libraries for students with visual impairments, classroom equipment adapted for use by students with manual impairments, and other similar services and actions. Recipients need not provide attendants, individually prescribed devices, readers for personal use or study, or other devices or services of a personal nature [34 C.F.R. sec. 104.44].

Section 104.47(b) provides that counseling and placement services be offered on the same basis to handicapped and nonhandicapped students. The institution is specifically charged with ensuring that job counseling is not more restrictive for handicapped students. Under Section 104.47(c), an institution that supplies significant assistance to student social organizations must determine that these organizations do not discriminate against handicapped students in their membership practices.

Discrimination on the basis of handicap must not result from the physical inaccessibility of the institution's programs or activities or the unusability of the institution's facilities. The regulations applicable to existing facilities differ from those applied to new construction:

(a) *Program accessibility.* A recipient shall operate each program or activity to which this part applies so that the program or activity, when viewed in its entirety, is readily accessible to handicapped persons. This paragraph does not require a recipient to make each of its existing facilities or every part of a facility accessible to and usable by handicapped persons.

(b) *Methods.* A recipient may comply with the requirements of paragraph (a) of this section through such means as redesign of equipment, reassignment of classes or other services to accessible buildings, assignment of aids to beneficiaries, home visits, delivery of health, welfare, or other services at alternate accessible sites, alteration of existing facilities and construction of new facilities in conformance with the requirements of sec. 104.23, or any other methods that result in making its program or activity accessible to handicapped persons. A recipient is not required to make structural changes in existing facilities where other methods are effective in achieving compliance with paragraph (a) of this section. In choosing among available methods for meeting the requirement of paragraph (a) of this section, a recipient shall give priority to those methods that offer programs and activities to handicapped persons in the most integrated setting appropriate [34 C.F.R. sec. 104.22; see also policy interpretations of this regulation at 43 Fed. Reg. 36034 and 36035 (1978)].

If structural changes in existing facilities—that is, facilities existing in June 1977, when the regulations became effective—were necessary to make a program or an activity accessible, they must have been completed by June 1980. All new construction must be readily accessible when it is completed.[11]

In *Southeastern Community College* v. *Davis,* 442 U.S. 397 (1979), set forth in Section 4.2.4.3 of this volume, the U.S. Supreme Court added some important interpretive gloss to the regulation on academic adjustments and assistance for handi-

[11]Compliance with accessibility requirements may be attained by conforming to the "American National Standard Specifications for Making Buildings and Facilities Accessible to, and Usable by, the Physically Handicapped," American National Standards Institute, Inc., 1430 Broadway, New York, N.Y. 10018 (34 C.F.R. sec. 104.32(c)). "Under Section 2122 of the Tax Reform Act of 1976 [26 U.S.C. sec. 190], recipients that pay federal income tax are eligible to claim a tax deduction of up to $25,000 for architectural and transportation modifications made to improve accessibility for handicapped persons" (42 Fed. Reg. at 22689 (comment 20)). See also 42 U.S.C. sec. 4151 *et seq.* (Architectural Barriers Act of 1968) and 29 U.S.C. sec. 792 (the Act's federal Compliance Board) for further requirements applicable to buildings constructed, altered, or leased with federal aid funds.

capped students (34 C.F.R. sec. 104.44). The Court quoted but did not question the validity of the regulation's requirement that an institution provide "auxiliary aids"—such as interpreters, taped texts, or braille materials—for students with sensory impairments. It made very clear, however, that the law does not require "major" or "substantial" modifications in an institution's curriculum or academic standards to accommodate handicapped students. To require such modifications, the Court said, would be to read into Section 504 an "affirmative action obligation" not warranted by its "language, purpose, [or] history." Moreover, if the regulations were to be interpreted to impose such obligation, they would to that extent be invalid.

The Court acknowledged, however, that the line between discrimination and a lawful refusal to take affirmative action is not always clear. Thus, in some instances programmatic changes may be required where they would not fundamentally alter the program itself. In determining where this line is to be drawn, the Court would apparently extend considerable deference to postsecondary institutions' legitimate educational judgments respecting academic standards and course requirements. Davis had argued that Southeastern's insistence that its students be capable of performing all the functions of a professional nurse was discriminatory, since North Carolina law did not require as much to obtain a license to practice. In a footnote to its opinion, the Court rejected this claim: "Respondent's argument misses the point. Southeastern's program, structured to train persons who will be able to perform all normal roles of a registered nurse, represents a legitimate academic policy, and is accepted by the state. In effect, it seeks to ensure that no graduate will pose a danger to the public in any professional role [that] he or she might be cast [in]. Even if the licensing requirements of North Carolina or some other state are less demanding, nothing in the Act requires an educational institution to lower its standards."

While *Davis* thus limits postsecondary institutions' legal obligation to modify their academic programs to accommodate handicapped students, the opinion does not limit an institution's obligation to make its facilities physically accessible to qualified handicapped students, as required by the ED regulations (34 C.F.R. sec. 104.22)—even when doing so involves major expense. In *Davis* the Court found that, because of her hearing disability, the plaintiff was not "otherwise qualified" for admission to the nursing program. When a handicapped person is qualified and has been admitted, however, Section 104.22 requires that facilities as a whole be "readily accessible" to that person.

7.5.5. Age Discrimination Act. The Age Discrimination Act of 1975, 42 U.S.C. sec. 6101 *et seq.,* contains a general prohibition on age discrimination in federally funded programs and activities. Under the ADA's original statement-of-purpose clause, the prohibition applied only to "unreasonable" discrimination—a limitation not found in the Title VI, Title IX, or Section 504 civil rights statutes (see Sections 7.5.2–7.5.4). Congress postponed the Act's effective date, however, and directed the U.S. Commission on Civil Rights to study age discrimination in federally assisted programs. After considering the commission's report, submitted in January 1978, Congress amended the ADA in October 1978 (Pub. L. No. 95-478) to strike the word *unreasonable* from the statement-of-purpose clause—thus removing a critical restriction on the Act's scope.

In 1979 the U.S. Department of Health, Education and Welfare issued final regulations under the ADA (44 Fed. Reg. 33768 (June 12, 1979)). These regulations, now codified in 45 C.F.R. Part 90, "state general, government-wide rules"

for implementing the ADA (45 C.F.R. sec. 90.2(a)). Every federal agency administering federal aid programs must implement its own specific regulations consistent
with HEW's (now HHS's) general regulations.

The general regulations, together with the extensive explanatory commentary that accompanies them (44 Fed. Reg. 33768–33775, 33780–33787), are very
helpful in understanding the ADA. The regulations are divided into several sub-
parts. Subpart A explains the purpose and coverage of the Act and regulations and
defines some of the regulatory terminology. The core of this subpart is Section 90.3:

> *Section 90.3 What programs and activities does the Age Discrimination Act
> of 1975 cover?*
>
> (a) The Age Discrimination Act of 1975 applies to any program or
> activity receiving federal financial assistance, including programs or activ-
> ities receiving funds under the State and Local Fiscal Assistance Act of 1972
> (31 U.S.C. sec. 1221 *et seq.*).
>
> (b) The Age Discrimination Act of 1975 does not apply to:
>
> (1) An age distinction contained in that part of a federal, state, or
> local statute or ordinance adopted by an elected, general-purpose legislative
> body which:
>
> (i) Provides any benefits or assistance to persons based on age; or
>
> (ii) Establishes criteria for participation in age-related terms; or
>
> (iii) Describes intended beneficiaries or target groups in age-related
> terms.
>
> (2) Any employment practice of any employer, employment agency,
> labor organization, or any labor-management joint apprenticeship train-
> ing program, except for any program or activity receiving federal financial
> assistance for public service employment under the [Job Training Partner-
> ship Act] (29 U.S.C. sec. 1501 *et seq.*).

The commentary to the regulations explains this provision as follows:

> The Act generally covers all programs and activities which receive
> federal financial assistance. However, the Act does not apply to any age
> distinction "established under authority of any law" [the statutory phrase]
> which provides benefits or establishes criteria for participation on the basis
> of age or in age-related terms. Thus, age distinctions which are "established
> under authority of any law" may continue in use. These regulations define
> "any law" to mean federal statutes, state statutes, or local statutes adopted
> by elected, general-purpose legislative bodies.
>
> The Act also excludes from its coverage most employment practices,
> except for programs funded under the public service employment titles of the
> [Job Training Partnership Act]. These regulations do cover any program or ac-
> tivity which is both a program of federal financial assistance and provides
> employment such as the College Work-Study program [44 Fed. Reg. 33769].

Subpart B of the regulations explains the ADA's prohibition against age
discrimination in programs covered by the Act. It also lists the exceptions to this
prohibition. Section 90.12 sets out the prohibition as follows:

(a) *General rule:* No person in the United States shall, on the basis of age, be excluded from participation in, be denied the benefits of, or be subjected to discrimination under, any program or activity receiving federal financial assistance.

(b) *Specific rules:* A recipient may not, in any program or activity receiving federal financial assistance, directly or through contractual, licensing, or other arrangements, use age distinctions or take any other actions which have the effect, on the basis of age, of:

(1) excluding individuals from, denying them the benefits of, or subjecting them to discrimination under, a program or activity receiving federal financial assistance, or

(2) denying or limiting individuals in their opportunity to participate in any program or activity receiving federal financial assistance.

(c) The specific forms of age discrimination listed in paragraph (b) of this section do not necessarily constitute a complete list.

The rest of subpart B sets out the exceptions to Section 90.12:

Section 90.13 Definitions of "normal operation" and "statutory objective."
For purposes of Sections 90.14 and 90.15, the terms "normal operation" and "statutory objective" shall have the following meaning:

(a) "Normal operation" means the operation of a program or activity without significant changes that would impair its ability to meet its objectives.

(b) "Statutory objective" means any purpose of a program or activity expressly stated in any federal statute, state statute, or local statute or ordinance adopted by an elected, general-purpose legislative body.

Section 90.14 Exceptions to the rules against age discrimination. Normal operation or statutory objective of any program or activity.
A recipient is permitted to take an action otherwise prohibited by Section 90.12 if the action reasonably takes into account age as a factor necessary to the normal operation or the achievement of any statutory objective of a program or activity. An action reasonably takes into account age as a factor necessary to the normal operation or the achievement of any statutory objective of a program or activity, if:

(a) Age is used as a measure or approximation of one or more other characteristics; and

(b) The other characteristic(s) must be measured or approximated in order for the normal operation of the program or activity to continue, or to achieve any statutory objective of the program or activity; and

(c) The other characteristic(s) can be reasonably measured or approximated by the use of age; and

(d) The other characteristic(s) are impractical to measure directly on an individual basis.

90.15 Exceptions to the rules against age discrimination. Reasonable factors other than age.
A recipient is permitted to take an action otherwise prohibited by

Section 90.12 which is based on a factor other than age, even though that action may have a disproportionate effect on persons of different ages. An action may be based on a factor other than age only if the factor bears a direct and substantial relationship to the normal operation of the program or activity or to the achievement of a statutory objective.

Section 90.16 Burden of proof.
The burden of proving that an age distinction or other action falls within the exception outlined in Sections 90.14 and 90.15 is on the recipient of federal financial assistance.

The explanatory commentary summarizes these critical regulations as follows:

> The Act contains several exceptions which limit the general prohibition against age discrimination. Section 304(b)(1) of the Act permits the use of age distinctions which are necessary to the normal operation or to the achievement of a statutory objective. It also permits actions which are based on reasonable factors other than age. The regulations provide definitions for two terms which are essential to an understanding of those exceptions: "normal operation" and "statutory objective" (Section 90.13). . . .
> The regulations establish a four-part test, all parts of which must be met for an explicit age distinction to satisfy one of the statutory exceptions and to continue in use in a federally assisted program (Section 90.14). This four-part test will be used to scrutinize age distinctions which are imposed in the administration of federally assisted programs but which are not explicitly authorized by a federal, state, or local statute.

Further explaining the "four-part test" under Section 90.14, the commentary states:

> The test set out in Section 90.14 is designed to require careful scrutiny of age distinctions in programs receiving federal financial assistance. It is not intended to serve as a basis for permitting continued use of age distinctions for the sake of administrative convenience if this results in denial or limitation of services on the basis of age.
> HEW encourages recipients to apply age distinctions flexibly; that is, to permit a person, upon a proper showing of the necessary characteristic, to participate in the activity or program even though he or she would otherwise be barred by the age distinction. Other things being equal, an age distinction is more likely to qualify under one of the statutory exceptions if it does not automatically bar all those who do not meet the age requirements [44 Fed. Reg. 33773].

The comments also make clear that recipients can never justify exceptions to the general prohibition on the basis of cost-benefit considerations alone, but only by meeting the specific tests in Sections 90.14 and 90.15 of the regulations (44 Fed. Reg. 33774, 33783).

Subpart C of the general regulations explains the responsibilities that each federal agency has in implementing the Act, including publication of its own regulations and review of any existing policies that employ age distinctions. Subpart D sets out requirements that each agency must follow in establishing compliance, investigation, conciliation, and enforcement procedures under the ADA; and Subpart E provides for future review of the general regulations by HHS and future review of specific agency regulations by the agencies promulgating them.

Although the regulations and commentary add considerable particularity to the brief provisions of the Act, the full import of the ADA for postsecondary institutions can be ascertained only by studying the specific regulations that agencies have promulgated or will promulgate to fulfill the mandate of the general regulations. The HHS specific regulations, for example, are codified in 45 C.F.R. Part 91. Postsecondary administrators and counsel should thus consult both the specific and the general agency regulations, in conjunction with the Act itself, when reviewing institutional policies or practices that employ explicit or implicit age distinctions.

7.5.6. Affirmative action. Affirmative action poses a special problem under the federal civil rights statutes. The ED Title VI regulations both require and permit affirmative action under certain circumstances:

> (i) In administering a program regarding which the recipient has previously discriminated against persons on the ground of race, color, or national origin, the recipient must take affirmative action to overcome the effects of prior discrimination.
> (ii) Even in the absence of such prior discrimination, a recipient in administering a program may take affirmative action to overcome the effects of conditions which resulted in limiting participation by persons of a particular race, color, or national origin [34 C.F.R. sec. 100.3(b)(6)].

The Title IX regulations also permit affirmative action for voluntary correction of conditions that resulted in limited participation by the members of one sex in the institution's programs and activities (34 C.F.R. sec. 106.3(b)). However, both the Title IX and the Section 504 regulations require a recipient to engage in "remedial action" rather than "affirmative action" to overcome the effects of its own prior discrimination (34 C.F.R. sec. 106.3(a); 34 C.F.R. sec. 104.6(a)). In addition, the Section 504 regulations suggest that the recipient take only "voluntary action" rather than "affirmative action" to correct conditions that resulted in limited participation by the handicapped (34 C.F.R. sec. 104.6(b)). But none of the regulations defines "affirmative action," "remedial action," or "voluntary action," or sets out the limits of permissible action. One federal district court has ruled that in a Title VI case some "affirmative action" may itself constitute a Title VI violation. In *Flanagan* v. *President and Directors of Georgetown College*, 417 F. Supp. 377 (D.D.C. 1976), the issue was that Georgetown Law Center had allocated 60 percent of its scholarship funds to minority students, who constituted only 11 percent of the class. The university claimed that the program was permissible under Section 100.3(b)(6)(ii) of the Title VI regulations. The court disagreed, holding that the scholarship program was not administered on a "racially neutral basis" and was "reverse discrimination on the basis of race, which cannot be justified by a claim of affirmative action." Subsequently, in *Regents of University of California* v. *Bakke*, 438 U.S. 265 (1978) (see Section 4.2.5), the first U.S. Supreme Court case on affirmative action under Title VI, a 5-to-4 majority of the Court agreed that Title VI did not require complete racial neutrality in affirmative action. But no majority of justices could agree on the extent to which Title VI and its regulations permit racial or ethnic preferences to be used as one part of an affirmative action program.

Like the Title VI, Title IX, and Section 504 regulations, the HHS general regulations under the Age Discrimination Act of 1975 (see Section 7.5.5) also include a provision on affirmative action:

> (a) Where a recipient is found to have discriminated on the basis of age, the recipient shall take any remedial action which the agency may require to overcome the effects of the discrimination. If another recipient exercises control over the recipient that has discriminated, both recipients may be required to take remedial action.
>
> (b) Even in the absence of a finding of discrimination, a recipient may take affirmative action to overcome the effects of conditions that resulted in limited participation in the recipient's program or activity on the basis of age.
>
> (c) If a recipient operating a program which serves the elderly or children, in addition to persons of other ages, provides special benefits to the elderly or to children, the provision of those benefits shall be presumed to be voluntary affirmative action provided that it does not have the effect of excluding otherwise eligible persons from participation in the program [45 C.F.R. sec. 90.49].

Paralleling the other civil rights regulations, this ADA regulation distinguishes between required (subsection (a)) and permitted (subsection (b)) actions and, like Title IX and Section 504, uses the term "remedial action" to describe the former. Also like Title IX and Section 504, the government can require, and the recipient can take, "remedial action" only upon a finding that the recipient has discriminated in the past against the class of persons whom the regulations protect. In addition, the ADA regulation contains a unique provision (subsection (c)), which, under certain circumstances, brings the provision of special benefits to two age groups—the elderly and children—under the protective umbrella of "voluntary affirmative action." The ADA regulations do not include explanatory commentary on Section 90.49. Nor, in common with the other civil rights regulations, do they define "remedial action" or "affirmative action" or (except for subsection (c)) the scope of permissible action.

Thus, the federal regulations give postsecondary administrators little guidance concerning the affirmative or remedial actions they must take to maintain compliance, or may take without jeopardizing compliance. Insufficient guidance, however, is not a justification for avoiding affirmative action when it is required by the regulations, nor should it deter administrators from taking voluntary action when it is their institution's policy to do so. Rather, administrators should proceed carefully, seeking the assistance of legal counsel and keeping abreast of the developing case law and agency policy interpretations on affirmative action. (See Sections 3.3.4 and 4.2.5.)

   7.5.7. Scope and coverage problems. In recent years the scope and coverage of the civil rights statutes (this volume, Sections 7.5.2 to 7.5.5) have been the subject of intense debate, considerable litigation, and several congressional bills. The subsections below review the most complex and controversial of the scope and coverage issues.

The administrative regulations implementing the civil rights statutes (particularly the regulations of the Department of Education) provide the initial guidance on the major scope and coverage issues. Courts have sometimes reviewed these regulations to determine whether they are authorized by the statute being implemented. Where there are gaps in the regulations or the statutes, thus leaving scope and coverage issues unresolved, courts have also stepped in to provide answers. And in one instance, after a controversial U.S. Supreme Court decision, Congress has considered bills that would have the effect of overturning a Court decision (see Section 7.5.7.4).

As the volume of litigation has increased, it has become apparent that the similarities of statutory language under the four civil rights statutes give rise to similar scope and coverage issues. Answers to an issue under one statute will thus provide guidance in answering comparable issues under another statute. There are some critical differences, however, in the statutory language and implementing regulations for each statute (for example, as explained in Section 7.5.7.1, Title VI and the Age Discrimination Act have provisions limiting their applicability to employment discrimination, whereas Title IX and Section 504 do not), and each statute has its own unique legislative history. Therefore, to gain a fine-tuned view of further developments, administrators and counsel should approach each statute and each scope and coverage issue separately, taking account of both their similarities to and their differences from the other statutes and other issues.

7.5.7.1. Coverage of employment discrimination. One major scope and coverage issue is whether the civil rights statutes prohibit not only discrimination against students but also discrimination against employees. Both Title VI and the ADA contain provisions that permit coverage of discrimination against employees only when a "primary objective" of the federal aid is "to provide employment" (42 U.S.C. sec. 2000d-3; 42 U.S.C. sec. 6103(c)). Title IX and Section 504 do not contain any such express limitation. Consistent with the apparent open-endedness of the latter two statutes, both the Title IX and the Section 504 regulations have provisions comprehensively covering discrimination against employees (see Sections 3.3.2.3 and 3.3.2.6 of this volume), while the Title VI and the ADA regulations (implementing the command of these statutes) cover employment discrimination only in narrow circumstances (34 C.F.R. secs. 100.2 and 100.3(c); 45 C.F.R. sec. 90.3(b)(2)).

The first major U.S. Supreme Court case on scope and coverage—*North Haven Board of Education* v. *Bell,* 102 S. Ct. 1912 (1982)—concerned the employment issue. *North Haven* was a Title IX case. The plaintiffs, two school boards in Connecticut, challenged the validity of Subpart E of HEW's (now ED's) Title IX regulations, which prohibits recipients from discriminating against employees on the basis of sex. The Supreme Court addressed two issues: (1) whether the Title IX statute applies to the employment practices of educational institutions; and (2) if it does, whether the scope and coverage of the Title IX employment regulations are consistent with the Title IX statute.

Looking to the wording of the statute, the statute's legislative history, and the statute's "postenactment history" in Congress and at HEW, the Court (with three dissenters) gave a clear, affirmative answer to the first question:

Our starting point in determining the scope of Title IX is, of course, the statutory language. . . . Section 901(a)'s broad directive that "no person" may be discriminated against on the basis of gender appears, on its face, to include employees as well as students. Under that provision, employees, like other "persons," may not be "excluded from participation in," "denied the benefits of," or "subjected to discrimination under" education programs receiving federal financial support. . . .

There is no doubt that "if we are to give [Title IX] the scope that its origins dictate, we must accord it a sweep as broad as its language." . . .

Because Section 901(a) neither expressly nor impliedly excludes employees from its reach, we should interpret the provision as covering and protecting these "persons" unless other considerations counsel to the contrary. After all, Congress easily could have substituted "student" or "beneficiary" for the word "person" if it had wished to restrict the scope of Section 901(a). . . .

Although the statutory language thus seems to favor inclusion of employees, nevertheless, because Title IX does not expressly include or exclude employees from its scope, we turn to the Act's legislative history for evidence as to whether Congress meant somehow to limit the expansive language of Section 901. [There follow four pages of legislative history analysis.]

In our view, the legislative history . . . corroborates our reading of the statutory language and verifies the Court of Appeals' conclusion that employment discrimination comes within the prohibition of Title IX.

The postenactment history of Title IX provides additional evidence of the intended scope of the title and confirms Congress's desire to ban employment discrimination in federally financed education programs [102 S. Ct. at 1917–23].

Proceeding to the second question in *North Haven,* the Court then upheld the validity of the Title IX employment regulations. The major issue was whether the regulations are consistent with the statutory language applying Title IX's non-discrimination prohibition to a "program or activity receiving federal financial assistance" and limiting the effect of a fund termination "to the particular program, or part thereof, in which . . . noncompliance has been . . . found." (This issue, which the Court characterized as an issue of the statute's "program specificity," is further discussed in Section 7.5.7.4.) After reviewing the provisions of the employment regulations and HEW's comments accompanying their publication, the Court concluded that the regulations are consistent with the statute's "program" focus and thus valid.

The U.S. Supreme Court has also upheld Section 504's applicability to discrimination against employees. In *Consolidated Rail Corp.* v. *Darrone,* 104 S. Ct. 1248 (1984), a locomotive engineer had been dismissed after having had his left hand and forearm amputated as a result of an accident. When the engineer claimed that he was fit for work and had been discriminated against because of his handicap, the employer argued that Section 504 applies to employment discrimination "only if the primary objective of the federal aid that [the employer] receives is to promote employment." The Court rejected this argument:

It is clear that Section 504 itself contains no such limitation . . . ;
rather, that section prohibits discrimination against the handicapped under
"*any* program or activity receiving federal financial assistance." And it is
unquestionable that the section was intended to reach employment
discrimination. Indeed, enhancing employment of the handicapped was
so much the focus of the 1973 legislation that Congress the next year felt
it necessary to amend the statute to clarify whether Section 504 was intended to prohibit other types of discrimination as well (see sec. 111(a),
Pub. L. 93-516, 88 Stat. 1617, 1619 (1974)). Thus, the language of Section
504 suggests that its bar on employment discrimination should not be limited
to programs that receive federal aid the primary purpose of which is to
promote employment.

The legislative history, executive interpretation, and purpose of the
1973 enactment all are consistent with this construction [104 S. Ct. at 1253–54].

7.5.7.2. Coverage of unintentional discriminatory acts. Another key issue of coverage
is whether the civil rights statutes prohibit actions whose *effects* are discriminatory
(that is, actions that have a disproportionate or disparate *impact* on the class of persons
protected) or whether the statutes prohibit only actions that not only have
discriminatory effects but are also *purposeful* (that is, taken with a discriminatory
intent or motive). None of the four statutes explicitly addresses this question. The
ED regulations for Title VI and the ADA, however, contain provisions that apparently prohibit actions with discriminatory effects even if those actions are not
intentionally discriminatory (34 C.F.R. sec. 100.3(b)(2); 45 C.F.R. sec. 90.12).
The Title IX and Section 504 regulations have no such provision.

The leading U.S. Supreme Court case on the intent issue is *Guardians Association* v. *Civil Service Commission of the City of New York,* 103 S. Ct. 3221 (1983). The
justices issued six opinions in the case, none of which commanded a majority and
which, according to Justice Powell, "further confuse rather than guide." The Court's
basic difficulty was reconciling *Lau* v. *Nichols,* 414 U.S. 563 (1974), which held
that Title VI and HEW's regulations prohibited actions with discriminatory effects,
and *Regents of the University of California* v. *Bakke,* 438 U.S. 265 (1978), which indicated that Title VI reached no further than the Fourteenth Amendment's equal
protection clause, which prohibits only intentional discrimination. Although the
Court could not agree on the import of these two cases, or on the analysis to adopt
in the case before it, it is possible to extract some meaning from *Guardians* by pooling
the views expressed in the various opinions. A majority of the justices did hold that
the intent standard is a necessary component of the Title VI statute. A different
majority, however, held that, even though the statute embodies an intent test, the
ED regulations that adopt an effects test are nevertheless valid. In his opinion Justice
White tallied the differing views of the justices on these points (103 S. Ct. at 3223
n.2, and 3235 n.27). He then rationalized these seemingly contradictory conclusions by explaining that "the language of Title VI on its face is ambiguous; the
word 'discrimination' is inherently so." The statute should therefore be amenable
to a broader construction by ED, "at least to the extent of permitting, if not requiring, regulations that reach" discriminatory effects (103 S. Ct. at 3227; see also
103 S. Ct. at 3253–55 (opinion of Justice Stevens)).

The result of this confusing mélange of opinions is to validate ED's regulations extending Title VI coverage to actions with discriminatory effects. At the same time, however, the *Guardians* opinions suggest that, if ED were to change its regulations so as to adopt an intent test, such a change would also be valid. Any such change, though, would in turn be subject to invalidation by Congress, which could amend the Title VI statute (or other statutes under which the issue arose) to replace its intent standard with an effects test. Such legislation would apparently be constitutional (see this volume, Sections 7.1.1 and 7.1.4; and see *City of Rome* v. *United States*, 446 U.S. 156 (1980)).

In *Alexander* v. *Choate*, 105 S. Ct. 712 (1985), the Court also considered the intent issue under Section 504. After reviewing the various opinions in the *Guardians* case on Title VI, the Court determined that that case does not control the intent issue under Section 504 because Section 504 raises considerations different from those raised by Title VI. In particular:

> Discrimination against the handicapped was perceived by Congress to be most often the product not of invidious animus, but rather of thoughtlessness and indifference—of benign neglect. . . . Federal agencies and commentators on the plight of the handicapped similarly have found that discrimination against the handicapped is primarily the result of apathetic attitudes rather than affirmative animus.
>
> In addition, much of the conduct that Congress sought to alter in passing the Rehabilitation Act would be difficult if not impossible to reach were the Act construed to proscribe only conduct fueled by a discriminatory intent. For example, elimination of architectural barriers was one of the central aims of the Act (see, for example, S. Rep. No. 93-318, p. 4 (1973), U.S. Code Cong. & Admin. News 1973, pp. 2076, 2080), yet such barriers were clearly not erected with the aim or intent of excluding the handicapped [105 S. Ct. at 718-19].

Although these considerations suggest that discriminatory intent need not be a requirement under Section 504, the Court also noted some countervailing considerations:

> At the same time, the position urged by respondents—that we interpret Section 504 to reach all action disparately affecting the handicapped—is also troubling. Because the handicapped typically are not similarly situated to the nonhandicapped, respondents' position would in essence require each recipient of federal funds first to evaluate the effects on the handicapped of every proposed action that might touch the interests of the handicapped, and then to consider alternatives for achieving the same objectives with less severe disadvantage to the handicapped. The formalization and policing of this process could lead to a wholly unwieldy administrative and adjudicative burden [105 S. Ct. at 719].

Faced with these difficulties, the Court declined to hold that one group of considerations would always have priority over the other: "While we reject the boundless notion that all disparate-impact showings constitute prima facie cases under Section

504, we assume without deciding that Section 504 reaches at least some conduct that has an unjustifiable disparate impact upon the handicapped." Thus "splitting the difference," the Court left for another day the specification of what types of Section 504 cases will escape the imposition of a discriminatory intent requirement.

7.5.7.3. Scope of the phrase "receiving federal financial assistance." Each of the four civil rights statutes prohibits only discrimination in (1) "a program or activity" that is (2) "receiving federal financial assistance." Uncertainty about the definitions of these two terms, and their interrelation, has created substantial questions about the scope of the civil rights statutes. The first term is discussed in Section 7.5.7.4; the second is discussed here. The major issue regarding the second term is whether indirect or student-based aid, such as Pell Grants or veterans' education benefits, is "federal financial assistance" triggering the protections of the civil rights statutes.

The statutes do not define the phrase "federal financial assistance." But the ED regulations for each statute contain a broad definition. Under Title IX, for instance:

> "Federal financial assistance" means any of the following, when authorized or extended under a law administered by the department:
> (1) A grant or loan of federal financial assistance, including funds made available for:
> (i) The acquisition, construction, renovation, restoration, or repair of a building or facility or any portion thereof; and
> (ii) Scholarships, loans, grants, wages, or other funds extended to any entity for payment to or on behalf of students admitted to that entity, or extended directly to such students for payment to that entity.
> (2) A grant of federal real or personal property or any interest therein, including surplus property, and the proceeds of the sale or transfer of such property, if the federal share of the fair market value of the property is not, upon such sale or transfer, properly accounted for to the federal government.
> (3) Provision of the services of federal personnel.
> (4) Sale or lease of federal property or any interest therein at nominal consideration, or at consideration reduced for the purpose of assisting the recipient or in recognition of public interest to be served thereby, or permission to use federal property or any interest therein without consideration.
> (5) Any other contract, agreement, or arrangement which has as one of its purposes the provision of assistance to any education program or activity, except a contract of insurance or guaranty [34 C.F.R. sec. 106.2(g)].

The definitions in the Title VI (34 C.F.R. sec. 100.13), Section 504 (34 C.F.R. sec. 104.3(h)–(i)), and ADA (45 C.F.R. sec. 90.4) regulations are similar.

The leading case addressing the definition of federal financial assistance is *Grove City College* v. *Bell,* 104 S. Ct. 1211 (1984). The college, a private liberal arts institution, received no direct federal or state financial assistance. Many of the college's students, however, did receive Basic Educational Opportunity Grants (now Pell Grants), which they used to defray their educational costs at the college. ED determined Grove City to be a recipient of "federal financial assistance" under 34 C.F.R. sec. 106.2(g)(1) and advised the college to execute an Assurance of Compliance (a form certifying that the college will comply with Title IX) as required by 34 C.F.R. sec. 106.4. The college refused, arguing that the indirect aid received by its students did not constitute federal financial assistance to the college.

The U.S. Supreme Court unanimously held that the student aid constituted aid to the college and that, if the college did not execute an Assurance of Compliance, ED could terminate the student aid:

> The language of Section 901(a) [of Title IX] contains no hint that Congress perceived a substantive difference between direct institutional assistance and aid received by a school through its students. The linchpin of Grove City's argument that none of its programs receives any federal assistance is a perceived distinction between direct and indirect aid, a distinction that finds no support in the text of Section 901(a). Nothing in Section 901(a) suggests that Congress elevated form over substance by making the application of the nondiscrimination principle dependent on the manner in which a program or activity receives federal assistance. There is no basis in the statute for the view that only institutions that themselves apply for federal aid or receive checks directly from the federal government are subject to regulation (*Bob Jones University* v. *Johnson,* 396 F. Supp. 597, 601–04 (D.S.C. 1974), affirmed, 529 F.2d 514 (4th Cir. 1975) [reaching a similar conclusion under Title VI regarding veterans' education benefits]). As the Court of Appeals observed, "by its all-inclusive terminology [Section 901(a)] appears to encompass *all* forms of federal aid to education, direct or indirect" (687 F.2d at 691 (emphasis in original)) [104 S. Ct. at 1217].

7.5.7.4. Scope of the phrase "program or activity." The civil rights statutes proscribe only discrimination in a "program or activity" that is "receiving" federal aid. Thus, besides determining that the aid involved fits the definition of "federal financial assistance" (Section 7.5.7.3), schools must also identify the "program(s)" or the "activity(ies)" that receives the aid and is thus subject to the nondiscrimination requirement.

At the time this book went to press, the civil rights statutes did not define this key phrase "program or activity." (As explained later in this section, bills providing such a definition were pending in Congress in the spring of 1985.) The Title VI regulations did contain a comprehensive definition of "program," however, that included within it the concept of "activity" (34 C.F.R. sec. 100.13(g)). The Title IX, Section 504, and ADA regulations had only sketchy references to these terms (34 C.F.R. sec. 106.31(a); 34 C.F.R. sec. 104.43(a); 45 C.F.R. sec. 90.3(a)).

Numerous questions about the program or activity concept have arisen in court litigation. The most controversial has been the question of how to apply this concept to indirect or student-based aid, such as Pell Grants or veterans' education benefits. Do all the institution's programs "receive" this aid, or is the institution itself the "program," thus binding the entire institution to the nondiscrimination requirement? Or is only the institution's financial aid office or some lesser portion of the institution bound? (Compare the majority opinion with the dissents in *Grove City College* v. *Bell,* discussed below.) Another set of questions may apply to both indirect student-based aid and direct (or earmarked) institution-based aid, such as construction grants. If a program or an activity in an institution does not directly receive federal funds but *benefits from* the receipt of funds by other institutional programs or activities, is it subject to nondiscrimination requirements? (See *Haffer* v. *Temple University,* 688 F.2d 14 (3d Cir. 1982), applying the "benefit theory" for extending a civil rights statute's scope.) Or if a program or an activity does not directly receive federal funds but engages in discriminatory practices that "infect" programs or activities which do directly receive funds, is it subject to nondiscrimination requirements? (See *Iron Arrow Honor Society* v. *Heckler,* 702 F.2d 549 (5th Cir. 1983), adopting the "infection theory" for extending a civil rights statute's scope.)

The U.S. Supreme Court first addressed the program or activity concept in *North Haven Board of Education* v. *Bell,* 102 S. Ct. 1912 (1982), discussed in Section 7.5.7.1. In considering the validity of ED's Title IX regulations on employment (Subpart E), the Court noted the " 'program-specific' nature of the [Title IX] statute" and indicated that, to be valid, the regulations must be "consistent with the Act's program specificity." To support this conclusion, the Court cited Section 901(a) of Title IX (20 U.S.C. sec. 1681(a)), prohibiting sex discrimination in a "program or activity" receiving federal funding; Section 902 (20 U.S.C. sec. 1682), authorizing federal agencies to implement regulations regarding any "program or activity" for which it provides funds; and another provision in Section 902—called the "pinpoint" provision—requiring that any fund termination by a federal agency "be limited in its effect to the particular program, or part thereof, in which . . . noncompliance has been . . . found."[12]

Although holding that Title IX is limited in its scope to particular programs and activities, the Court in *North Haven* declined to define "program," the key term giving life to the concept of program specificity. Two years later, however, the Court again confronted this definitional issue in *Grove City College* v. *Bell,* 104 S. Ct. 1211 (1984), discussed in Section 7.5.7.3. Having unanimously agreed that the students' receipt of Basic Educational Opportunity Grants (BEOGs) constituted "federal financial assistance" for the college, the justices then faced the problem of identifying the program or activity that received this assistance and was therefore subject to Title IX. With three of the justices dissenting, the Court held that the program or activity was not the entire institution (as the appellate court had determined) but only the college's financial aid program:

> Although Grove City does not itself disburse students' awards, BEOGs clearly augment the resources that the college itself devotes to financial aid. . . . However, the fact that federal funds eventually reach the college's general operating budget cannot subject Grove City to institution-wide coverage. . . .
>
> To the extent that the Court of Appeals' holding that BEOGs received

[12]Title VI also has a provision requiring the federal agency to "pinpoint" the particular program(s) subject to fund termination (42 U.S.C. sec. 2000d-1). Section 504 incorporates the "remedies, procedures, and rights" available under Title VI, thus apparently including the same pinpoint provision (29 U.S.C. sec. 794(a)(2)). The ADA's pinpoint provision (42 U.S.C. sec. 6104(b)), as developed in the general regulations (45 C.F.R. sec. 90.47(b)), is the most exacting of all, since it appears to prohibit the agency from using the infection theory to expand the scope of the fund cutoff.

by Grove City's students constitute aid to the entire institution rests on the possibility that federal funds received by one program or activity free up the college's own resources for use elsewhere, the Court of Appeals' reasoning is doubly flawed. First, there is no evidence that the federal aid received by Grove City's students results in the diversion of funds from the college's own financial aid program to other areas within the institution. Second, and more important, the Court of Appeals' assumption that Title IX applies to programs receiving a larger share of a school's own limited resources as a result of federal assistance earmarked for use elsewhere within the institution is inconsistent with the program-specific nature of the statute. Most federal educational assistance has economic ripple effects throughout the aided institution, and it would be difficult, if not impossible, to determine which programs or activities derive such indirect benefits. Under the Court of Appeals' theory, an entire school would be subject to Title IX merely because one of its students received a small BEOG or because one of its departments received an earmarked federal grant. This result cannot be squared with Congress's intent.

The Court of Appeals' analogy between student financial aid received by an educational institution and nonearmarked direct grants provides a more plausible justification for its holding, but it too is faulty. Student financial aid programs, we believe, are *sui generis*. In neither purpose nor effect can BEOGs be fairly characterized as unrestricted grants that institutions may use for whatever purpose they desire. The BEOG program was designed not merely to increase the total resources available to educational institutions but to enable them to offer their services to students who had previously been unable to afford higher education. . . .

We conclude that the receipt of BEOGs by some of Grove City's students does not trigger institution-wide coverage under Title IX. In purpose and effect, BEOGs represent federal financial assistance to the college's own financial aid program, and it is that program that may properly be regulated under Title IX [104 S. Ct. at 1221–22].

The *Grove City* analysis of the program or activity issue proved to be highly controversial. Members of Congress criticized the analysis as being inconsistent with congressional intent. Civil rights groups and other interested parties criticized the decision's narrowing effect on federal enforcement of civil rights—not only under Title IX but also under the other three civil rights statutes using the same "program or activity" language, and not only for federal aid to education but for other types of federal assistance as well.

Less than two months after the Court's decision, a bipartisan coalition in Congress introduced a bill to overturn the *Grove City* ruling on the program or activity issue. Known as the Civil Rights Act of 1984 (H.R. 5490 and S. 2568, 98th Cong., 2d Sess.), this bill would have deleted the "program or activity" phrase from Title IX, Title VI, Section 504, and the ADA, substituting for it the term "recipient," broadly defined to include the entire entity receiving the aid. This bill easily passed the House but was narrowly defeated in the Senate amid parliamentary wrangling at the close of the session.

Early in 1985 two new bills were introduced in Congress. One, the proposed

Civil Rights Restoration Act of 1985 (H.R. 700 and S. 431, 99th Cong., 1st Sess.), would add a broad definition of "program or activity" to each of the four civil rights statutes. Although this definition is not limited to educational institutions, it does explicitly include "all of the operations of . . . a university or a system of higher education" (see *Congressional Record,* daily ed., Feb. 7, 1985, pp. S. 1301–1315). The other bill, the proposed Civil Rights Amendments Act of 1985 (S. 272, 99th Cong., 1st Sess.), provides that, when aid is extended to any program of an educational institution, the institution itself will be considered to be the covered program under each of the four statutes.

While the first of these two 1985 bills sweeps more broadly than the second, covering all federal aid recipients rather than just educational institutions, the bills would have a comparable impact on colleges and universities. Under both bills the entire institution would be subject to the prohibitions against discrimination if any part of the institution receives federal aid. (Neither bill, however, would change the civil rights statutes' "pinpoint" provisions limiting fund terminations to the particular programs (within an institution) in which discrimination is found.) Thus, both bills would expand (or restore) the scope of Title IX, Title VI, Section 504, and the ADA, replacing the narrow *Grove City* ruling on "program or activity" with a broad statutory definition. Administrators and counsel should be sure to check for further developments regarding these bills.

7.5.8. Administrative enforcement. Compliance with each of the four civil rights statutes is enforced through a complex system of procedures and mechanisms administered by the federal agencies which provide financial assistance. Postsecondary administrators should develop a sound understanding of this enforcement process so that they can satisfactorily pursue both the rights and the responsibilities of their institutions should compliance problems arise.

The Title VI statute delegates enforcement responsibility to the various federal funding agencies. Under Executive Order 12250, 45 Fed. Reg. 72995 (1980), the U.S. attorney general is responsible for coordinating agency enforcement of efforts. The attorney general has implemented enforcement regulations (28 C.F.R. Part 42) as well as "Guidelines for the Enforcement of Title VI" (28 C.F.R. sec. 50.3) which impose various requirements on agencies responsible for enforcement. Each agency, for instance, must issue guidelines or regulations on Title VI for all programs under which it provides federal financial assistance (28 C.F.R. sec. 42.404). These regulations and guidelines must be available to the public (28 C.F.R. sec. 42.405). The Justice Department's regulations require the agencies to collect sufficient data, on such items as the racial composition of the population eligible for the program and the location of facilities, to determine compliance (28 C.F.R. sec. 42.406). All Title VI compliance decisions must be made by or be subject to the review of the agency's civil rights office. Programs found to be complying must be reviewed periodically to assure continued compliance. A finding of probable noncompliance must be reported to the attorney general (28 C.F.R. sec. 42.407). Each agency must establish complaint procedures and publish them in its guidelines. All Title VI complaints must be logged in the agency records (28 C.F.R. sec. 42.408). If a finding of probable noncompliance is made, enforcement procedures shall be instituted after a "reasonable period" of negotiation. If negotiations continue for more than sixty days after the finding of noncompliance, the agency must notify the attorney general (28 C.F.R. sec. 42.411). If several agencies provide federal financial

assistance to a substantial number of the same recipients for similar or related purposes, the agencies must coordinate Title VI enforcement efforts. The agencies shall
designate one agency as the lead agency for Title VI compliance (28 C.F.R. sec.
42.413). Each agency must develop a written enforcement plan, specifying priorities,
timetables, and procedures, which shall be available to the public (28 C.F.R. sec.
42.415).

Under the Department of Education's Title VI regulations, fund recipients
must file assurances with ED that their programs comply with Title VI (34 C.F.R.
sec. 100.4) and must submit "timely, complete, and accurate compliance reports
at such times, and in such form and containing such information, as the responsible
department official or his designee may determine to be necessary to enable him
to ascertain whether the recipient has complied or is complying" with Title VI (34
C.F.R. sec. 100.6(b)). ED may make periodic compliance reviews and must accept
and respond to individual complaints from persons believing themselves to be victims
of discrimination (34 C.F.R. sec. 100.7). If an investigation reveals a violation that
cannot be resolved by negotiation and voluntary compliance (34 C.F.R. sec.
100.7(d)), ED may refer the case to the Justice Department for prosecution (see
Section 7.5.9) or commence administrative proceedings for fund termination (34
C.F.R. sec. 100.8). Any termination of funds must be "limited in its effect to the
particular program, or part thereof, in which . . . noncompliance has
been . . . found" (42 U.S.C. sec. 2000-1; 34 C.F.R. sec. 100.8(c)). The regulations specify the procedural safeguards that must be observed in the fund termination proceedings: notice, the right to counsel, a written decision, an appeal to a
reviewing authority, and a discretionary appeal to the secretary of education (34
C.F.R. secs. 100.9 and 100.10).

Like Title VI, Title IX enforcement is coordinated by the attorney general
under Executive Order 12250. Title IX also includes the same limit as Title VI
on the scope of fund termination (20 U.S.C. sec. 1682) and utilizes the same procedures for fund termination (34 C.F.R. sec. 106.71). An institution subject to Title
IX must appoint at least one employee to coordinate its compliance efforts and must
establish a grievance procedure for handling discrimination complaints within the
institution (34 C.F.R. sec. 106.8).

Section 504 is also subject to Executive Order 12250, and funding agencies'
enforcement efforts are thus also coordinated by the attorney general. The attorney
general's coordination regulations, setting forth enforcement responsibilities for
federal agencies, are published in 28 C.F.R. Part 41. The Section 504 statute also
establishes an Interagency Coordinating Council for Section 504 enforcement, the
membership of which includes the attorney general and the secretary of ED (29
U.S.C. sec. 794c). ED's Section 504 regulations for its own programs impose compliance responsibilities similar to those under Title IX. However, recipients with
fewer than fifteen employees need not conform to certain requirements: (1) having
a copy of the remedial plan available for inspection (34 C.F.R. sec. 104.6(c)(2));
(2) appointing an agency employee to coordinate the compliance effort (34 C.F.R.
sec. 104.7(a)); and (3) establishing a grievance procedure for handling discrimination complaints (34 C.F.R. sec. 104.7(b)). Most postsecondary educational institutions are not excepted from these requirements, since most have more than the
minimum number of employees. Section 504 also adopts the Title VI procedural
regulations concerning fund terminations.

Under the Age Discrimination Act, federal funding agencies must propose implementing regulations and submit them to the secretary of health and human services for review; all such agency regulations must be consistent with HHS's "general regulations" (42 U.S.C. sec. 6103(b)(4); 45 C.F.R. sec. 90.31). Each agency must hold "compliance reviews" and other investigations to determine adherence to ADA requirements (45 C.F.R. sec. 90.44(a)). Each agency must also follow specified procedures when undertaking to terminate a recipient's funding (45 C.F.R. sec. 90.47). Termination of funds is limited to the "particular program or activity, or part of such program or activity, with respect to which [a] finding [of discrimination] has been made," and may not be based "in whole or in part on any finding with respect to any program or activity which does not receive federal financial assistance" (42 U.S.C. sec. 6104(b)). The ADA contains a number of substantive exceptions to coverage, more expansive than the exceptions to the other civil rights statutes (see this volume, Section 7.5.5).

The federal courts exercise a limited review of federal agencies' enforcement efforts. If a federal agency terminates an institution's funding, the institution may appeal that decision to the courts once it has exhausted administrative review procedures within the agency.[13] If a federal agency abuses its enforcement authority during enforcement proceedings and before a final determination decision, an affected educational institution may also seek injunctive relief from such improper enforcement efforts. On the other hand, if the agency fails to fulfill its enforcement responsibilities, victims of unlawful discrimination may seek judicial enforcement of the agency's affirmative duty to implement the civil rights statute.

In *Mandel* v. *U.S. Department of Health, Education and Welfare,* 411 F. Supp. 542 (D. Md. 1976), HEW commenced fund termination proceedings against the state of Maryland based on alleged Title VI violations in the state's system of higher education. The state sought judicial intervention, claiming that HEW had not in good faith sought voluntary compliance. Maryland complained that HEW delayed review of the state's original desegregation plan, prematurely cut off negotiations, and did not provide guidelines on how to effect desegregation. The state specifically claimed that HEW refused to rule on the importance of statistics in assessing compliance or on the future of traditionally black educational institutions. The court found that HEW did not seek voluntary compliance in good faith. Maryland also complained that HEW failed to "pinpoint" which of the state's programs violated Title VI. The court held that HEW must pinpoint the offending programs before enforcement proceedings are begun:

> It is paradoxical to assume that a recipient of federal funding, such as a state or a large city, could rectify any discriminatory programs within its system without ever being informed which program was considered by HEW to be operating discriminatively. Consequently, a statewide or city-

---

[13]Such judicial review is expressly authorized by the Title VI and Title IX statutes (see 42 U.S.C. sec. 2000d-2; 20 U.S.C. sec. 1683). The Section 504 statute incorporates the remedies available under Title VI, thus apparently authorizing judicial review to the same extent authorized by Title VI (29 U.S.C. sec. 794(a)(c)). The ADA also specifically authorizes judicial review of administrative agency actions, but in terms somewhat different from those in Title VI and Title IX (42 U.S.C. sec. 6105).

wide approach to enforcement of Title VI is, doubtless, not conducive to compliance by voluntary means and, in all likelihood, contrary to congressional nonvindictive intent.

Other reasons come to the fore which, likewise, suggest that plaintiffs' reading of Title VI in this regard is a proper one. In . . . the state system . . . there are multitudinal programs receiving federal financing which, due to the nonprogrammatic approach assumed, are being condemned by defendants en masse. . . . [In the state system] there is federal funding to programs within twenty-eight institutions of higher education ranging from a unique cancer research center to the student work-study program. To compel all of these programs, regardless of whether or not each is discriminatory, to prepare a defense and endure protracted enforcement proceedings is wasteful, counterproductive, and probably inimical to the interests of the very persons Title VI was enacted to protect. It is far more equitable, and more consistent with congressional intent, to require program delineation prior to enforcement hearings than to include all programs in enforcement proceedings [411 F. Supp. at 558].

The U.S. Court of Appeals for the Fourth Circuit subsequently modified the lower court's ruling to allow HEW to take a systematic approach if it first adopted system-wide guidelines and gave Maryland time to comply voluntarily (562 F.2d 914 (4th Cir. 1977)). A rehearing was scheduled, however, because one judge had died before the court's opinion was issued. On rehearing three appellate judges voted to affirm the lower court and three voted to reverse, and the equally divided vote had the effect of automatically affirming the lower court (571 F.2d 1273 (4th Cir. 1978)).

In *Adams* v. *Richardson,* 356 F. Supp. 92 (D.D.C. 1973), affirmed, 480 F.2d 1159 (D.C. Cir. 1973), some victims of unlawful discrimination sought judicial intervention to compel enforcement of Title VI. The plaintiffs accused HEW of failure to enforce Title VI in the southern states. In the part of the case dealing with higher education, HEW had found the higher education systems of ten states out of compliance with Title VI and had requested each state to submit a desegregation plan within four months. Three years later, after the lawsuit had been filed and the court was ready to rule, five states still had not submitted any plan and five had submitted plans that did not remedy the violations. HEW had not commenced administrative enforcement efforts or referred the cases to the Justice Department for prosecution. The district court ordered HEW to commence enforcement proceedings:

The time permitted by Title VI of the Civil Rights Act of 1964 to delay the commencement of enforcement proceedings against the ten states for the purpose of securing voluntary compliance has long since passed. The continuation of HEW financial assistance to the segregated systems of higher education in the ten states violates the rights of plaintiffs and others similarly situated protected by Title VI of the Civil Rights Act of 1964. Having once determined that a state system of higher education is in violation of Title VI, and having failed during a substantial period of time to achieve voluntary compliance, defendants have a duty to commence enforcement proceedings [356 F. Supp. at 94].

The appellate court agreed with the district court's conclusion but expressed more sympathy for HEW's enforcement problems:

> We agree with the district court's conclusion that HEW may not neglect this area of its responsibility. However, we are also mindful that desegregation problems in colleges and universities differ widely from those in elementary and secondary schools, and that HEW admittedly lacks experience in dealing with them. It has not yet formulated guidelines for desegregating statewide systems of higher learning, nor has it commented formally upon the desegregation plans of the five states which have submitted them. As regrettable as these revelations are, the stark truth of the matter is that HEW must carefully assess the significance of a variety of new factors as it moves into an unaccustomed area. None of these factors justifies a failure to comply with a congressional mandate; they may, however, warrant a more deliberate opportunity to identify and accommodate them [480 F.2d at 1164].

On this basis the appellate court modified the terms of the district court's injunction to give HEW more time to initiate enforcement proceedings.

After the appellate court's decision, the district court maintained jurisdiction over the case to supervise compliance with its injunction. The judge has issued a number of other decisions since 1973, some of which have been reviewed by the appellate court. In April 1977 the district court revoked HEW's approval of several states' higher education desegregation plans and ordered HEW to devise criteria by which it would evaluate new plans to be submitted by these states (see Section 7.5.2 of this chapter). In March 1983 the court entered another order requiring HEW (by then ED) to obtain new plans from five states that had defaulted on plans previously accepted by HEW. This order also established time limits by which ED was required to initiate formal enforcement proceedings against these states, and several others whose plans had never been approved, if they had not submitted new acceptable plans; and required ED to report systematically to the plaintiffs on enforcement activities regarding the states subject to the suit.

In between the 1977 and the 1983 orders, HEW rejected North Carolina's plan and initiated formal administrative enforcement proceedings against that state. HEW also indicated that it would defer new federal funding for the state's postsecondary institutions pending completion of the proceedings. North Carolina sued HEW in federal district court, claiming that HEW had no authority (1) to utilize its Revised Criteria in rejecting the plan, (2) to initiate the proceedings, or (3) to defer funding (*North Carolina* v. *Department of HEW*, 480 F. Supp. 929 (E.D.N.C. 1979)). The court upheld HEW's authority to use the Revised Criteria and to initiate enforcement proceedings, but it did enter an injunction prohibiting HEW from deferring funds during the pendency of the proceedings. Subsequently, HEW (by then ED) and the state agreed to settle their dispute. They entered a settlement agreement setting the terms for desegregation of North Carolina's higher education system; ED agreed to terminate its enforcement proceedings; and the *North Carolina* court approved the settlement in the form of a consent decree dismissing the state's lawsuit.

The plaintiffs in the *Adams* litigation then asked the *Adams* court to enjoin ED from implementing the settlement agreement, the terms of which (they argued) were patently inconsistent with the criteria ED was required to apply under the 1977 court order. The district court denied the plaintiffs' request, and in *Adams* v. *Bell,* 711 F.2d 161 (D.C. Cir. 1983) (*en banc*), the appellate court affirmed. Over the perceptive and lengthy dissent of Judge Skelly Wright, the majority determined that:

> The purpose of [the district judge's] 1973 decree was to require the department to initiate appropriate enforcement proceedings under Title VI. It was directed at the department's lassitude, if not recalcitrance, in fulfilling its responsibilities under that Act. However, [the judge's] 1973 decree, as affirmed with modifications by this court and as supplemented by him in 1977, did not purport to supervise or dictate the details of the department's enforcement program, once that program culminated in an administrative proceeding, itself subject to judicial review, against a recipient state [711 F.2d at 165].

Sometime after the original opinions in 1973, the *Adams* litigation was consolidated with other cases to cover enforcement not only of Title VI but also of Title IX, Section 504, and Executive Order 11246. The Women's Equity Action League (WEAL) became an additional named plaintiff in the consolidated cases. The agencies that are now subject to the court's orders are the Department of Education (Office for Civil Rights) and the Department of Labor (Office of Federal Contract Compliance Programs). In addition to its orders on higher education desegregation plans, the district court has also issued broader orders regarding these agencies' enforcement responsibilities under the civil rights acts. In December 1977 the court ordered into effect a settlement agreement establishing timetables for agency compliance reviews and for agency processing of discrimination complaints. Another order, in 1983, established new timetables to supersede those in the December 1977 order. On the government's appeal of this 1983 order, the appellate court remanded the case to the district court for a determination of whether the plaintiffs continue to have the legal "standing" necessary to maintain the lawsuit and justify judicial enforcement of the order (*Women's Equity Action League* v. *Bell* and *Adams* v. *Bell,* 743 F.2d 42 (D.C. Cir. 1984)). No final determination on the future of this part of the *Adams* case had yet been made as this book went to press.

7.5.9. *Other enforcement remedies.* Administrative negotiation and fund termination are not the only means federal agencies have for enforcing the civil rights statutes. In some cases the responsible federal agency may also go to court to enforce the civil rights obligations that educational institutions have assumed by accepting federal funds. Title VI authorizes agencies to enforce compliance not only by fund termination but also by "any other means authorized by law" (42 U.S.C. sec. 2000d-1). ED's Title VI regulations explain that "such other means may include, but are not limited to, (1) a reference to the Department of Justice with a recommendation that appropriate proceedings be brought to enforce any rights of the United States under any law of the United States (including other titles of the Act), or any assurance or other contractual undertaking, and (2) any applicable proceeding under state or local law" (34 C.F.R. sec. 100.9(a)). ED may not pursue these alternatives, however, "until (1) the responsible department official has determined that compliance cannot be secured by voluntary means, (2) the recipient or other person has been notified of its failure to comply and of the action to be taken to effect compliance, and (3) the expiration of at least ten days from the mailing of such notice to the recipient or other person'' (34 C.F.R. sec. 100.9(d)). Similar enforcement alternatives and procedural limitations apply to enforcement of Title IX, Section 504, and the ADA.[14]

Besides administrative agency enforcement by fund termination or court suit, educational institutions may also be subject to private lawsuits brought by individuals who have allegedly been discriminated against in violation of the civil rights statutes or regulations. In legal terminology, the issue is whether the civil rights statutes afford these victims of discrimination a ''private cause of action'' against the institution that is allegedly discriminating.

The basic requisites for a private cause of action are outlined in *Cort* v. *Ash*, 422 U.S. 66 (1975): ''In determining whether a private remedy is implicit in a statute not expressly providing one, several factors are relevant. First, is the plaintiff one of the class for whose *especial* benefit the statute was enacted—that is, does the statute create a federal right in favor of the plaintiff? Second, is there any indication of legislative intent, explicit or implicit, either to create such a remedy or to deny one? Third, is it consistent with the underlying purposes of the legislative scheme to imply such a remedy for the plaintiff? And finally, is the cause of action one traditionally relegated to state law, in an area basically the concern of the states, so that it would be inappropriate to infer a cause of action based solely on federal law?'' (422 U.S. at 78, citations omitted).

If an individual can meet these requirements, two related issues may then arise: whether the individual must ''exhaust'' any available ''administrative remedies'' before bringing a private suit; and whether the individual may obtain monetary damages, in addition to or instead of injunctive relief, if successful in the private suit.

For many years courts and commentators disagreed on whether the civil rights statutes could be enforced by private causes of action. Developments since the late 1970s, however, have established a clear trend toward acceptance of the private cause of action under all four statutes. The 1979 case of *Cannon* v. *University of Chicago*, 441 U.S. 677 (1979), arising under Title IX, is illustrative.

The plaintiff in *Cannon* had been denied admission to the medical schools of the University of Chicago and Northwestern University. She sued both institutions, claiming that they had rejected her applications because of her sex and that such action violated Title IX. The U.S. Court of Appeals for the Seventh Circuit held that individuals cannot institute private suits to enforce Title IX. The U.S. Supreme Court reversed. While acknowledging that the statute does not expressly authorize a private cause of action, the Court held that one can be implied into the statute under the principles of *Cort* v. *Ash*. In applying the four considerations identified in that case, the Court in *Cannon* concluded: ''Not only the words and history of Title IX, but also its subject matter and underlying purposes, counsel application of a cause of action in favor of private victims of discrimination.''

The discussion of the third consideration in *Cort*—whether a private cause of action would frustrate the statute's underlying purposes—is particularly illuminating.

---

[14]ED's Title IX and Section 504 regulations incorporate the enforcement regulations for Title VI (see 34 C.F.R. sec. 106.71; 34 C.F.R. sec. 104.61). The Title IX statute also contains the same ''other means authorized by law'' language found in Title VI (see 20 U.S.C. sec. 1682), and the Section 504 statute incorporates the remedies and procedures available under Title VI (29 U.S.C. sec. 794a(a)). The ADA has its own enforcement scheme set out in the statute (42 U.S.C. sec. 6104) and the general regulations (45 C.F.R. secs. 90.41–90.50).

The Court identified two purposes of Title IX: to avoid the use of federal funds to support sex discrimination and to give individual citizens effective protection against such practices. While the first purpose is served by the statutory procedure for fund termination (see Section 7.5.8 of this chapter), the Court determined that a private remedy would be appropriate to effect a second purpose:

> [Termination] is . . . severe and often may not provide an appropriate means of accomplishing the second purpose if merely an isolated violation has occurred. In that situation, the violation might be remedied more efficiently by an order requiring an institution to accept an applicant who had been improperly excluded. Moreover, in that kind of situation it makes little sense to impose on an individual whose only interest is in obtaining a benefit for herself, or on HEW, the burden of demonstrating that an institution's practices are so pervasively discriminatory that a complete cutoff of federal funding is appropriate. The award of individual relief to a private litigant who has prosecuted her own suit is not only sensible but is also fully consistent with—and in some cases even necessary to—ordinary enforcement of the statute [441 U.S. at 705-06].

In a statement of particular interest to postsecondary administrators, the Court in *Cannon* also addressed and rejected the universities' argument that private suits would unduly interfere with their institutional autonomy:

> Respondents' principal argument against implying a cause of action under Title IX is that it is unwise to subject admissions decisions of universities to judicial scrutiny at the behest of disappointed applicants on a case-by-case basis. They argue that this kind of litigation is burdensome and inevitably will have an adverse effect on the independence of members of university committees.
>
> This argument is not original to this litigation. It was forcefully advanced in both 1964 and 1972 by the congressional opponents of Title VI and Title IX, and squarely rejected by the congressional majorities that passed the two statutes. In short, respondents' principal contention is not a legal argument at all; it addresses a policy issue that Congress has already resolved.
>
> History has borne out the judgment of Congress. Although victims of discrimination on the basis of race, religion, or national origin have had private Title VI remedies available at least since 1965, respondents have not come forward with any demonstration that Title VI litigation has been so costly or voluminous that either the academic community or the courts have been unduly burdened.   Nothing but speculation supports the argument that university administrators will be so concerned about the risk of litigation that they will fail to discharge their important responsibilities in an independent and professional manner [441 U.S. at 709-10].

Subsequently, in the case of *Guardians Association* v. *Civil Service Commission of the City of New York,* 103 S. Ct. 3221 (1983), the Supreme Court determined that private causes of action are also permissible under Title VI. The Court issued no majority opinion, however, so the case's teaching on the issue is limited and can be gleaned only from tallying the views of those justices who accepted private causes of action under Title VI. A year after *Guardians Association,* and relying in part on that case, the Supreme Court also finally held that individuals may bring private lawsuits to enforce Section 504 (*Consolidated Railroad Corp.* v. *Darrone,* 104 S. Ct. 1248 (1984)). Previously the Court had declined to decide this issue in *Southeastern Community College* v. *Davis* (442 U.S. at 404 n.5; see this volume, Section 4.2.4.3) and had bypassed it in *University of Texas* v. *Camenisch* (Section 4.3.7).

Another development, illustrating legislative rather than judicial resolution of the "private cause of action" issue, occurred with passage of the 1978 amendments to the ADA. Congress added a new section to the Act authorizing private suits by "any interested person" in federal district courts "to enjoin a violation of this Act by any program or activity receiving federal financial assistance" (42 U.S.C. sec. 6104(e)).

Courts permitting private enforcement suits under the civil rights statutes usually have not required the complainants to exhaust administrative remedies before filing suit. In its opinion in the *Cannon* case, for instance, the U.S. Supreme Court noted that it had "never withheld a private remedy where the statute explicitly confers a benefit on a class of persons . . . [but] does not assure those persons the ability to activate and participate in the administrative process contemplated by the statute." Title IX not only contains no such mechanism, according to the Court, but even HEW's procedures do not permit the complainant to participate in the administrative proceedings. Moreover, even if HEW finds the institution to be in violation of Title IX, the resulting compliance agreement need not necessarily include relief for the particular complainant. Accordingly, the Court concluded that individuals may institute suits to enforce Title IX without exhausting administrative remedies (see 441 U.S. at 706–08 n.41). Similarly, relying on *Cannon,* U.S. appeals courts have held that exhaustion is not required under Section 504 (see, for example, *Pushkin* v. *Regents of University of Colorado,* 658 F.2d 1372, 1382 (10th Cir. 1981)). Case law under Title VI is more sparse, but there is some authority for not requiring exhaustion there also (see *Yakin* v. *University of Illinois, Chicago Circle,* 508 F. Supp. 848 (N.D. Ill. 1981)). The exception to this trend is the ADA, for which Congress itself has provided an exhaustion requirement. In the 1978 ADA amendments, the provision authorizing private suits also prohibits bringing such suits "if administrative remedies have not been exhausted" (42 U.S.C. sec. 6104(e)(2)(B)). Section 6104(f) of the amendments and the general ADA regulations (45 C.F.R. sec. 90.50) indicate when such exhaustion shall be deemed to have occurred.

Authorization of private causes of action, even when exhaustion is not required or has occurred, does not necessarily mean that a complainant may obtain every kind of relief ordinarily available in civil rights lawsuits. In *Lieberman* v. *University of Chicago,* 660 F.2d 1185 (7th Cir. 1981), for instance, the court ruled that money damages may not be obtained under Title IX. The plaintiff had sued the defendant charging sex discrimination after she was first wait-listed and then denied admission to the university's medical school. Since she had been accepted to and had enrolled at Harvard Medical School at the time of the lawsuit, she argued that the defendant's denial of admission forced her to relocate from her residence in Oak Park, Illinois. She sought money damages to compensate her for moving expenses, emotional pain, and loss of her husband's company. In a 2-to-1 decision, the court held that the private cause of action authorized by *Cannon* should be limited to claims for injunctive relief. The dissenting judge in *Lieberman,* labeling the majority's opinion "an eviseration" of Title IX, reasoned that federal courts should allow any available remedy, including money damages, that is needed to right the wrong done when Title IX is violated.

The as yet unsettled character of the law on this issue is reinforced by the Supreme Court's jumble of opinions in the 1983 *Guardians Association* case. At the same time that it approved private suits to enforce Title VI, the Court limited the remedies available in such suits. Like other issues in the case, resolution of this issue was clouded by the divergency of the views expressed by the justices. But a tally of these views suggests that a majority of the Court would not permit a money damages remedy under Title VI if the plaintiff could not prove that the defendant had discriminated *intentionally* (103 S. Ct. at 3235 n.27) (opinion of Justice White); see also Section 7.5.7.2 of this chapter. In its later *Darrone* opinion on Section 504, the Court briefly explained its *Guardians* decision (104 S. Ct. at 1252–53 n.9) but did not alleviate its uncertainties about private remedies. Moreover, the Court in *Darrone* addressed only equitable remedies (specifically, back-pay awards) for victims of intentional discrimination under Section 504, authorizing such relief but declining to determine "the extent to which money damages are available" even for intentional discrimination.

Remedies under the ADA are also limited; but, again, the statute itself is the controlling authority. Section 6104(e) of the 1978 ADA amendments (quoted previously) provides only for suits "to enjoin a violation of this Act," thus indicating that injunctive relief (and not money damages) is the only permissible remedy.

Whenever private litigation can be brought against the institution under Title VI or Title IX, the institution may be liable for the plaintiff's attorney's fees if the plaintiff wins the suit. Under the Civil Rights Attorney's Fees Awards Act of 1976, 42 U.S.C. sec. 1988, courts have discretion to award "a reasonable attorney's fee" to "the prevailing party" in actions under Title IX, Title VI, and several other civil rights statutes. This Act does not apply to Section 504 suits or ADA suits. The omission is inconsequential, however, since both Section 504 and the ADA have their own comparable provisions authorizing the award of attorneys' fees (29 U.S.C. sec. 794a(b); 42 U.S.C. sec. 6104(e)(1)).

Sec. 7.6. Dealing with the Federal Government

7.6.1. Handling federal regulations. Administrative agencies write regulations either to implement legislation or to formalize their own housekeeping functions. Such rule making "lies along the continuum between legislation and executive decision making. A rule reflects the intent of the statute on which it is based as well as the manner in which the administrator will exercise the discretion that the statute grants. The position on the continuum varies from rule to rule. Where, for example, a rule carries out a statutory direction to define a term by regulation, subject to explicit legislative history regarding the definition, the 'legislation' element may be paramount. Where the rule sets forth funding criteria in order to fill in a gap left by the program statute, the rule reflects a greater degree of executive decision making, the exercise of which is implicit in the enactment of a program statute, leaving details to be supplied by the administrator" (T. Sky, "Rulemaking and the Federal Grant

Process in the United States Office of Education," 62 *Virginia L. Rev.* 1017, 1027 n.26 (1976)). Proposed and final regulations are published in the *Federal Register,* and final regulations are codified in the *Code of Federal Regulations.*

Postsecondary administrators have often complained that the multitude of federal regulations applying to the programs and practices of postsecondary institutions creates financial and administrative burdens for their institutions. These burdens could likely be lessened if postsecondary administrators and legal counsel took more active advisory roles in the process by which the federal government makes and enforces rules. The following suggestions outline a strategy for active involvement that an institution may undertake by itself, or in conjunction with other similarly situated institutions, or through educational associations to which it belongs. (See generally C. Saunders, "Regulating the Regulators," *Chronicle of Higher Education,* March 22, 1976, which discusses some of these suggestions and others.)

1. Appoint someone to be responsible for monitoring the *Federal Register* and other publications for announcements regarding regulations that will affect postsecondary education institutions. The *Federal Register* publishes "Notice(s) of Intent" (NOIs) to publish rules and "Notice(s) of Proposed Rule Making," which are invitations for comments from interested parties. In addition, if advance information on particular regulatory proposals would be useful, ask for an early copy of draft regulations or for information on their content and the issues in dispute. Some agencies may have policies that make draft regulations available for review before the proposed form is published.

2. File comments and deliver testimony in response to NOIs and notices of proposed rule making when the rules would have a substantial effect on institutional operations. Support these comments with specific explanations and data showing how the proposed regulations would have a negative impact on the institution. Have legal counsel review the proposed rules for legal and interpretive problems, and include legal questions or objections with your comments when appropriate. Consider filing comments in conjunction with other institutions that would be similarly affected by the proposed regulations.

3. Keep federal agencies informed of your views on and experiences with particular federal regulations. No regulations should be considered so final that they are beyond comment. Complaints and difficulties with final regulations should be communicated to the responsible agency.

4. When the institution desires guidance concerning ambiguities or gaps in particular regulations, consider submitting questions to the administering agency. Make the questions specific and, if the institution has a particular viewpoint on how the ambiguity or gap should be resolved, forcefully argue that view. Legal counsel should be involved in this process. Once questions are submitted, press the agency for answers.

5. Be concerned not only with the substance of regulations but also with the adequacy of the rule-making and rule-enforcing procedures. Be prepared to object to situations in which institutions are given insufficient notice of an agency's plans to make rules, too few opportunities to participate in rule making, or inadequate opportunities to criticize or receive guidance concerning already implemented regulations.

6. Develop an effective process for institutional self-regulation. With other institutions, develop criteria and data to use in identifying the circumstances in which

self-regulation is more effective than government regulation (see A. Blumrosen, "Six Conditions for Meaningful Self-Regulation," 69 *American Bar Association J.* 1264 (1983)). Use a record of institutional success at self-regulation, combined with developed rationales for self-regulation, to argue in selected situations that government regulation is unnecessary.

Two pieces of legislation enacted in 1980 provide new assistance for postsecondary institutions that do involve themselves in the federal regulatory process. The first statute, the Regulatory Flexibility Act, 5 U.S.C. sec. 601 *et seq.*, adds a new Chapter VI to the federal Administrative Procedure Act (see M. Stewart, "The New Regulatory Flexibility Act," 67 *American Bar Association J.* 66 (1981)). The second statute, the Equal Access to Justice Act, 94 Stat. 2325, amends Chapter V of the Administrative Procedure Act (see D. Stewart, "Beat Big Government and Recover Your Legal Fees," 69 *American Bar Association J.* 913 (1983)).

The Regulatory Flexibility Act benefits three types of "small entities," each of which is defined in Section 601: the "small business," the "small organization," and the "small governmental jurisdiction." The Act's purpose is "to establish as a principle of regulatory issuance that [federal administrative] agencies shall endeavor . . . to fit regulatory and informational requirements to the scale of the businesses, organizations, and governmental jurisdictions subject to regulation" (96 Stat. 1164, sec. 2(b)). This principle is implemented in several ways:

1. In October and April of every year, agencies must publish a "regulatory flexibility agenda." These agendas—which describe and explain any forthcoming regulations that are "likely to have a significant economic impact on a substantial number of small entities"—must be published in the *Federal Register* and in "publications likely to be obtained by" small entities (sec. 602).
2. Agencies proposing new regulations must provide, for public comment, an "initial regulatory flexibility analysis" containing a description of "the impact of the proposed rule on small entities" and a description of "alternatives to the proposed rule" that would lessen its economic impact on small entities (sec. 603).
3. Agencies promulgating final regulations must issue a "final regulatory flexibility analysis" containing a summary of comments on the initial analysis and, where regulatory alternatives were rejected, an explanation of why they were rejected (sec. 604).
4. For any regulation "which will have a significant economic impact on a substantial number of small entities," agencies must "assure that small entities have been given an opportunity to participate in the rule making." The Act requires agencies to use methods such as publishing notice in "publications likely to be obtained by small entities," conducting "open conferences or public hearings . . . for small entities," and adopting or modifying "agency procedural rules to reduce the cost or complexity of participation in the rule making by small entities" (sec. 609).
5. Agencies must periodically review and, where appropriate, revise their regulations with an eye to reducing their economic impact on small entities. Each agency must adopt a plan for accomplishing these reviews and publish it (and any subsequent amendments) in the *Federal Register*. All regulations existing on the effective date of the Act, and all regulations later implemented, are subject to review (sec. 610).

The key issue for postsecondary institutions under the Regulatory Flexibility Act is one of definition: to what extent will postsecondary institutions be considered to be within the definition for one of the three groups of "small entities" protected by the Act? The first definition, for the "small business" (sec. 601(3)), is unlikely to apply, except to some proprietary institutions. The second definition, for the "small organization" (sec. 601(4)), will apply to many, but not necessarily all, private nonprofit institutions. And the third definition, for the "small governmental jurisdiction" (sec. 601(5)), will apparently apply to some, but relatively few, public institutions, most or all of which may be community colleges. Thus, not every postsecondary institution will be within the Act's protected classes.[15]

The second new statute assisting postsecondary institutions, the Equal Access to Justice Act, authorizes the award of attorneys' fees and other expenses to certain parties which prevail over a federal administrative agency in adjudicatory proceedings before that agency. Like the Regulatory Flexibility Act, this Act's application to postsecondary education is limited by its definitions: apparently, to be within the classes of parties eligible for attorneys' fees, a postsecondary institution must have no more than 500 employees and, in some situations, must have a net worth of not more than $5 million. Moreover, an agency may avoid an award of fees if it shows that its position in the proceedings was "substantially justified" (94 Stat. 2325, sec. 203(a)(1)). Individual agencies must publish their own regulations implementing the Act; the Department of Education's regulations, for example, are in 49 Fed. Reg. 31868 (1984). In 1984 Congress passed a bill (S. 919, 98th Cong., 2d Sess.) renewing the Act, but on November 9 of that year the President vetoed the bill. The President indicated, however, that he would support some proposal for renewal in the 99th Congress; interested postsecondary institutions should check for further developments.

7.6.2. Obtaining information. Information will often be an indispensable key to a postsecondary institution's ability to deal effectively with the federal government, in the rule-making process or otherwise. Critical information sometimes will be within the control of the institution—for example, information about its own operations and the effect upon them of federal programs. At other times critical information will be under the government's control—for example, data collected by the government itself or information on competing policy considerations being weighed internally by an agency as it formulates regulatory proposals. When the latter type of information is needed, the following legislation and executive order may help institutional administrators and legal counsel: the Freedom of Information Act (FOIA) Amendments of 1974, the Privacy Act of 1974, the Government in the Sunshine Act of 1976, and Executive Order 12356 (1982).

The Freedom of Information Act Amendments, 5 U.S.C. sec. 552, make available to the public information from federal government files that is not specifically exempted from disclosure by the legislation. Nine categories of information are

---

[15]For institutions falling outside the definitions in the Regulatory Flexibility Act, or for covered institutions seeking additional leverage in the administrative process, a February 1981 Executive Order may help. Part of the Reagan administration's regulatory reform efforts, E.O. 12291 (3 C.F.R.) requires federal agencies to weigh both "the potential benefits to society . . . [and] the potential costs" before engaging in rule making and to prepare a "regulatory impact analysis" for each major regulation to be promulgated.

exempted from disclosure under 5 U.S.C. sec. 552(b), the most relevant to postsecondary institutions being national security information, federal agencies' internal personnel rules and practices, interagency or intra-agency memoranda or letters that would not be available except in litigation, and investigatory files compiled for law enforcement purposes.

The FOIA is useful when an institution believes that the government holds information that would be helpful in a certain situation but informal requests have not yielded the necessary materials. By making an FOIA request, an institution can obtain agency information that may help the institution better understand agency policy initiatives; or document a claim, process a grievance, or prepare a lawsuit against the government or some third party; or determine what information the government has that it could use against the institution—for example, in a fund termination proceeding. Specific procedures to follow in requesting such information are set out in the statute and in each agency's own policies on FOIA requests. Persons or institutions whose requests are denied by the agency may file a suit against the agency in a U.S. District Court. The burden of proof is on the agency to support its reasons for denial. (See A. Adler and A. Profozich, *Using the Freedom of Information Act: A Step-by-Step Guide* (Center for National Security Studies, 1983).)

The Privacy Act, codified in part at 5 U.S.C. sec. 552a, is discussed in Section 4.12.3 of this volume, with regard to student records. The point to be made here is that someone who requests certain information under the FOIA may find an obstacle in the Privacy Act. The FOIA itself exempts "personnel and medical files and similar files the disclosure of which would constitute a clearly unwarranted invasion of personal privacy" (5 U.S.C. sec. 552(b)(6)).

The Privacy Act provides an even broader protection for information whose release would infringe privacy interests. While the Act thus may foil a requester of information, it may also protect a postsecondary institution and its employees and students when the federal government has information concerning them in its files. (For a discussion of the FOIA, the privacy exemption, and the Privacy Act, see Comment, "The Freedom of Information Act's Privacy Exemption and the Privacy Act of 1974," 11 *Harvard Civil Rights–Civil Liberties L. Rev.* 596 (1976); and M. Hulett, "Privacy and the Freedom of Information Act," 27 *Administrative L. Rev.* 275 (1975).) Individual agencies each publish their own regulations implementing the Privacy Act. The Department of Education's regulations are published in 34 C.F.R. Part 5b.

The Government in the Sunshine Act, 5 U.S.C. sec. 552b, assures the public that "meetings of multimember federal agencies shall be open . . . with the exception of discussions of several narrowly defined areas" (H.R. Rep. No. 880, 94th Cong., 2d Sess. p. 2 (1976), reprinted at 3 *U.S. Code Congressional and Administrative News* 2184 (1976)). Institutions can individually or collectively make use of this Act by sending a representative to observe and report on agency decision making that is expected to have a substantial impact on their operations.

Executive Order 12356 (Fed. Reg. 14874 (April 6, 1982)), establishes the necessary procedures and the schedule for classifying and declassifying government documents related to national security. This order, signed by President Reagan in April 1982 and effective as of August 1, 1982, revoked prior Executive Order 12065, which had been signed by President Carter in June 1978. Since Presidents may implement or revoke executive orders at any time—and given the controversial nature of national security questions—there will likely be further changes in future years, particularly as the administration in power changes.

The 1982 executive order has the same function as its predecessor, establishing standards and procedures for classifying and declassifying government documents related to national security. But the 1982 order appears more restrictive than the 1978 order. It adds additional materials to the list of what can be classified; broadens the concept of "national security"; switches, for borderline cases, from a presumption against to a presumption in favor of classification; and deletes procedures for declassification of material after a set number of years.

The 1982 order, like its predecessor, operates in conjunction with the Freedom of Information Act. Section 1.6(d) of E.O. 12356 provides that "Information may be classified or reclassified after an agency has received a request for it under the Freedom of Information Act (5 U.S.C. sec. 552) or the Privacy Act of 1974 (5 U.S.C. sec. 552a)." (For analysis and discussion of when information may be considered to be "agency records" accessible under the Freedom of Information Act, see *Kissinger v. Reporters Committee for Freedom of the Press,* 100 S. Ct. 960 (1980); and *Forsham v. Harris,* 100 S. Ct. 978 (1980).)

Selected Annotated Bibliography

General

1. Gaffney, E. M., and Moots, P. R., *Government and Campus: Federal Regulation of Religiously Affiliated Higher Education* (University of Notre Dame Press, 1982), analyzes various aspects of federal regulation of religiously affiliated colleges and universities. Chapters treat religious preference in employment; student admissions and discipline policies; restrictions on the use of federal funds; accommodation to the needs of handicapped persons, including reformed alcoholics and drug abusers; tax problems; labor law problems; and sexual segregation of on- and off-campus student housing. Each chapter offers recommendations for regulatory changes that would reduce church-state tension. Authors acknowledge some overlap between chapters 2, 3, and 4 of this book, and chapters 4, 6, and 7 of their earlier work, *Church and Campus,* listed in the Chapter One bibliography for this volume (Sec. 1.5, item 2).

Sec. 7.1 (Federal Constitutional Powers over Education)

1. Gaffney, E. M., and Dutile, F. (Eds.), *The Federal Purse and the Rule of Law: Perspectives on Federal Regulation Under the Spending Power* (Notre Dame Press, in preparation), is a series of papers by leading commentators. Papers address the spending power from the perspectives of history, political science, public administration, and law.
2. Nowak, J., Rotunda, R., and Young, J. N., *Constitutional Law,* 2nd ed. (West, 1983), provides, in chapters 3–5, 10, and 17, a comprehensive overview of federal commerce power, taxing and spending powers, civil rights enforcement power, and the doctrine of federal preemption of state authority.

Sec. 7.2 (Federal Regulation of Postsecondary Education)

1. *Advisors Manual of Federal Regulations Affecting Foreign Students and Scholars* (National Association for Foreign Student Affairs, 1982) is a practical guide to

issues postsecondary administrators typically encounter in complying with federal regulations applicable to nonimmigrant foreign students and scholars. Topics covered include types of passports and visas, the handling of extensions of stay, approval of part-time student employment, and various report and record-keeping requirements.

2.   Bell, S., and Majestic, M., "Protection and Enforcement of College and University Trademarks," 10 *J. of College and University Law* 63 (1983-84), reviews issues of trademark law in the higher education setting. Describes and differentiates the trademark protection available under federal statutes, state statutes, and common law; explains the procedures to be followed in registering for state, federal, or international protection; and discusses the licensing of trademarks and the administrative and judicial remedies available for trademark violations.

3.   Cardozo, M., "To Copy or Not to Copy for Teaching and Scholarship: What Shall I Tell My Client?" 4 *J. of College and University Law* 59 (1977), analyzes the 1976 General Revision of the Copyright Law as it applies to the teaching and scholarship functions of postsecondary institutions and provides useful guidance on how to cope with this Act.

4.   DuVal, B., "The Human Subjects Protection Committee: An Experiment in Decentralized Federal Regulation," 1979 *American Bar Foundation Research J.* 571, reviews the past performance of human subjects protection committees and the interaction of composition, structure, and procedure upon performance. Of particular interest to administrators is the section "Six Models of Review," which contains six case studies of human subject committees in six very different institutions.

5.   Gholz, C. L., Laughlin, J. H., Jr., and Urey, D. S. (Eds.), *How to Protect and Benefit from Your Ideas* (American Patent Law Association, 1981 and periodic supp.), is a short, readable guide to patent law concepts designed primarily for inventors and other nonlawyers. Discusses pitfalls that commonly occur, how to protect an idea, how to profit from an idea, and where and how to obtain professional patent law assistance. Other brief sections also deal with copyright, trademark, and trade secret questions.

6.   Gordon, C., and Gordon, E. G., *Immigration and Nationality Law* (Matthew Bender, Desk Edition, 1981 and periodic supp.), is an abridgment, in looseleaf form, of the eight-volume treatise *Immigration Law and Procedure*. Divided into two parts, the first on "Immigration" and the second on "Nationality and Citizenship." Of particular use to postsecondary administrators and counsel are chapter 1, "General Survey"; chapter 2, "What Aliens May Enter the United States"; and chapter 3, "Procedure for Entering the United States."

7.   Kintner, E., and Lahr, J., *An Intellectual Law Primer,* 2nd ed. (Clark Boardman Co., 1982), is "a survey of the law of patents, trade secrets, trademarks, franchises, copyrights, and personality and entertainment rights." Does not focus on higher education but provides a thorough overview, for the nonspecialist, of federal law and its relationship to state law in these technical areas.

8.   Kirby, W., "Federal Antitrust Issues Affecting Institutions of Higher Education: An Overview," 11 *J. of College and University Law* 345 (1984), reviews

general antitrust law principles that apply to colleges and universities; analyzes the potential antitrust liability of undergraduate institutions regarding commercial activities, athletics, accreditation, and joint ventures with private industry; and catalogs the "exemptions" or "immunities" that may be available to protect institutions threatened with antitrust liability. Includes a bibliography of secondary sources on antitrust law's application to higher education.

9. Lachs, P. S., "University Patent Policy," 10 *J. of College and University Law* 263 (1983–84), reviews problems regarding university patents (including conflict of interest problems) and argues that universities should assert patent rights over the results of scientific research by faculty and staff. Article includes an extensive model university patent policy addressing the problems that the author identifies.

10. Latman, A., *The Copyright Law: Howell's Copyright Law Revised and the 1976 Act,* 5th ed. (Bureau of National Affairs, 1979), is a new edition of a standard reference on copyright law. Thoroughly treats provisions of domestic copyright law, analyzing both the 1909 and the 1976 copyright Acts. Includes appendices containing texts of the 1909 and 1976 Acts, Copyright Office regulations, and leading international conventions on copyrights.

11. Maggs, P. B., "New Life for Patents: *Chakrabarty* and *Rohm & Haas Co.,*" 1980 *Supreme Court Review* 57, is a technical review of patent law in the light of two recent Supreme Court decisions—one involving patenting of a new genetically engineered life form; the other involving the patentability of a new herbicidal process. Author concludes that the Court, in these decisions, "has placed the policy of encouraging innovation on an equal footing with that of encouraging competition."

12. President's Commission for the Study of Ethical Problems in Medicine and Biomedical and Behavioral Research, *First Biennial Report,* 47 Fed. Reg. 13272 (March 29, 1982), was prepared in response to two broad congressional mandates: "first, to review the federal rules and policies governing [human subject] research, and second, to determine how well those rules are being implemented or enforced" (47 Fed. Reg. at 13274). Chapter 2, dealing with "The Adequacy and Uniformity of the Regulations," uses the HHS regulations as a framework. Chapter 3, treating "The Adequacy and Uniformity of the Regulations' Implementation," critiques the potential flaws inherent in the HHS and NIH compliance systems and those of other federal agencies. Report also critiques the operation of IRBs and contains a series of recommendations for improving federal regulation of human subject research.

13. Rothstein, M. A., *Occupational Safety and Health Law* (West, 1978 and periodic supp.), is an overview of the federal Occupational Safety and Health Act (OSHA) and its relation to state law. Volume is divided into six parts: "The Scope of the Act," "Duties Under the Act," "Enforcement," "Contested Issues," "Adjudication," and "Extensions of the Act" (which examines the place of state law under OSHA). A table reviewing the "Status of State Plans," the "Commission Rules of Procedure," and the text of the Act are in appendices.

14. Stein, W., "Employee Benefit Reporting After ERISA," 36 *Louisiana L. Rev.* 867 (1976), discusses the reporting requirements in the ERISA statute and regulations as they apply to all types of employee benefit plans. (See also Selected Annotated Bibliography for Chapter Two, entry no. 8 in Sec. 2.2.)

15. Sullivan, L., *Handbook of the Law of Antitrust* (West, 1977), provides a comprehensive general survey of federal antitrust law.
16. Symposium, "Occupational Safety and Health," 38 *Law and Contemporary Problems* 583 (1974), is a collection of articles discussing legal problems arising from the Occupational Safety and Health Act, federal administration and enforcement of the Act, and the role of the states in occupational safety and health.
17. Wang, W., "The Unbundling of Higher Education," 1975 *Duke L.J.* 53, discusses the legal doctrines and policy considerations relevant to the application of federal antitrust laws to private, nonprofit postsecondary institutions; argues for a broad application of antitrust laws.
18. Weistart, J. C., "Antitrust Issues in the Regulation of College Sports," 5 *J. of College and University Law* 77 (1979), is a systematic treatment of antitrust law's particular applications to intercollegiate athletics. Reviews issues facing the NCAA regional conferences and particular schools.
19. See Selected Annotated Bibliography for Chapter Three, Sec. 3.3, for references on federal employment discrimination legislation.

Sec. 7.3 (*Federal Taxation of Postsecondary Education*)

1. Bittker, B., and Rahdert, G. K., "The Exemption of Nonprofit Organizations from Federal Income Taxation," 85 *Yale L.J.* 299 (1976), is an overview of issues regarding the federal tax status of nonprofit entities. Article discusses the unrelated business income tax, the taxation of capital gains and investment income of private foundations, and the tax status of organizations that engage in political activity; also contains sections on the exemption of educational institutions and on appropriate methods by which to measure the income of nonprofit entities.
2. Burke, G., "Federal Taxation of State Colleges and Universities: Recent Developments Call for Reconsideration of Theories of Exemption," 4 *J. of College and University Law* 43 (1977), considers the legal bases on which public institutions may seek federal tax exemption and the differences in the ways such institutions may be treated under each legal basis.
3. Hopkins, B., *The Law of Tax-Exempt Organizations,* 4th ed. (Wiley, 1983 and periodic supp.), is a reference volume that examines the pertinent federal law affecting the different types of nonprofit organizations, including colleges and universities. Contains citations to Internal Revenue Code provisions, Treasury Department revenue rulings, and court decisions.
4. Kaplan, R. L., "Intercollegiate Athletics and the Unrelated Business Income Tax," 80 *Columbia University L. Rev.* 1430 (1980), reviews the unrelated business tax as it affects the postsecondary institution's athletic program. Author argues that many schools' intercollegiate athletic programs have taken on the appearance of business activities unrelated to the institution's educational mission, and thus may be liable to taxation. Article also includes broader discussion of the unrelated business income tax in the higher education context.
5. Symposium, "Federal Taxation and Charitable Organizations," 39 *Law and Contemporary Problems* 1 (1975), is a sophisticated collection of articles on federal tax policy and law concerning charitable organizations. Includes J. H. Levi on "Financing Education and the Effects of the Tax Law," which discusses

the impact of the Internal Revenue Code's charitable deduction provisions on postsecondary institutions; and J. F. Kirkwood and D. S. Mundel on "The Role of Tax Policy in Federal Support for Higher Education," which examines federal tax policy regarding higher education and compares tax programs with spending and regulatory programs.

Sec. 7.4 (Federal Aid to Education Programs)

1. Advisory Commission on Intergovernmental Relations, *The Evolution of a Problematic Partnership: The Feds and Higher Ed* (Advisory Commission on Intergovernmental Relations, 1981), examines the history, growth, and current status of the federal government's involvement in higher education. Chapters in this report include "The Scope of Federal Involvement in Higher Education," "The Evolution of a Federal Role: 1787–1958," "Beginnings of a New Federal Role in Higher Education: The National Defense Education Act," "A Direct Federal Role Established: The Higher Education Acts of 1963 and 1965," "Equal Opportunity Preeminent: The 1972 Higher Education Amendments," and "A Growing Regulatory Presence." Contains various figures, graphs, and tables charting major developments in the federal government–higher education relationship.

2. Cappalli, R., *Rights and Remedies Under Federal Grants* (Bureau of National Affairs, 1979), is a systematic treatment of the federal grants system. Contains sections on "The Theory and Structure of Grants," including analyses of types and purposes of federal grants and constitutional supports for the grant system; "Agency Enforcement of Grant Conditions"; "Expanding Bases of Judicial Intervention"; "Due Process and Federal Grants"; "Grantee Hearing Rights: Withholding of Entitlements"; "Termination of Competitive Grants"; "Grant Suspensions"; "Rights of Applicants for Federal Funds"; "Subgrantees"; "Guideposts for Reform"; and other topics. Author has also published a lengthier treatment of this topic and related topics in a three-volume treatise, *Federal Grants and Cooperative Agreements: Law, Policy, and Practice* (Callaghan & Co., 1982).

3. *Federal Grants and Contracts Weekly* (Capitol), a weekly newsletter, lists new grant application opportunities, contains summaries and detailed explanations of new requests for proposals (RFPs), describes new grant programs, and analyzes the workings of the grant and contract processes.

4. *Federal Grants Management Handbook* (Grants Management Advisory Service, 1979 and periodic supp.) is a guide particularly for administrators. Among the chapters are "Obtaining a Federal Grant"; "How to Organize for Receipt of Grant Funds"; "Financial Administration of Federal Grants"; "Reporting and Recordkeeping"; "How to Comply with 'Strings Attached' to Federal Grants"; and "Disputes, Appeals, and Remedies." Appendices include compilations of Office of Management and Budget and Department of Treasury circulars.

5. Lacovara, P., "How Far Can the Federal Camel Slip Under the Academic Tent?" 4 *J. of College and University Law* 233 (1977), is a constitutional analysis, in the postsecondary education context, of the federal government's spending power and potential First Amendment and due process limitations on that power.

6. Olivas, M., *The Tribally Controlled Community College Assistance Act of 1978: The Failure of Federal Indian Higher Education Policy* (Monograph 82-1, Institute for Higher Education Law and Governance, University of Houston, 1982), is an analysis of the Act's design flaws, the bureaucratic delays in the Act's implementation, and the impoverished condition of the tribal colleges that are the Act's intended beneficiaries. Includes recommendations for improving the Act and its administration. Another version of this paper is published in 9 *American Indian L. Rev.* 219 (1981).

7. O'Neil, R. M., "God and Government at Yale: the Limits of Federal Regulation of Higher Education," 44 *University of Cincinnati L. Rev.* 525 (1975), is an analysis of both constitutional and nonconstitutional issues regarding the extent of federal authority to regulate higher education.

8. Sky, T., "Rulemaking and the Federal Grant Process in the United States Office of Education," 62 *Virginia L. Rev.* 1017 (1976), is a comprehensive, practical review and analysis written by the then HEW assistant general counsel for education. It includes discussion of the General Education Provisions Act and the Administrative Procedure Act.

9. Wallick, R., and Chamblee, D., "Bridling the Trojan Horse: Rights and Remedies of Colleges and Universities Under Federal Grant-Type Assistance Programs," 4 *J. of College and University Law* 241 (1977), describes the legal nature and policy impact of federal assistance to postsecondary institutions, and analyzes steps that legal counsel might take to protect the interests of institutions in grant programs.

Sec. 7.5 (Civil Rights Compliance)

1. Campbell, N. D., and others, *Sex Discrimination in Education: Legal Rights and Remedies* (National Women's Law Center, 1983), is a detailed, two-volume analysis of Title IX. Volume I examines such questions as Title IX's impact on admissions, campus health programs, and sexual harassment, and reviews litigation problems and strategies under Title IX. Volume II is a document sourcebook that includes the legislative history of Title IX, administrative regulations and guidelines, and various court and settlement documents.

2. *Equal Opportunity in Higher Education* (Capitol, biweekly) is a newsletter on recent developments regarding race, sex, age, and handicap discrimination; includes up-to-date information on federal civil rights compliance efforts, especially in the ED Office for Civil Rights.

3. *Handicapped Requirements Handbook* (Federal Programs Advisory Service, 1978 and periodic supp.) provides a comprehensive, practical guide to complying with Section 504 of the Rehabilitation Act of 1973. Includes Section 504 agency regulations and interpretations, summaries of court decisions, a self-evaluation questionnaire, and a glossary of terms.

4. Hunter, H., "Federal Antibias Legislation and Academic Freedom: Some Problems with Enforcement Procedures," 27 *Emory L.J.* 609 (1978), devises an academic freedom perspective on enforcement, against postsecondary institutions, of the statutes prohibiting discrimination by federal fund recipients.

5. Shuck, P. H., "The Graying of Civil Rights Law: The Age Discrimination Act of 1975," 89 *Yale L.J.* 27 (1979), is a theoretical study of the Age Discrimi-

nation Act. Article is divided into four parts: "The ADA and the Analogy to Title VI"; "The Political Context and Legislative History of the ADA"; "Interpreting the ADA: Reading Shadows on Walls" (which presents a detailed explication of the statute's ambiguities and built-in exceptions); and "The Process, Substance, and Form of Age Discrimination Policy." Author is critical of the ADA and furnishes a trenchant analysis of its inherent difficulties.

6. Wegner, J. W., "The Antidiscrimination Model Reconsidered: Ensuring Equal Opportunity Without Respect to Handicap Under Section 504 of the Rehabilitation Act of 1973," 69 *Cornell L. Rev.* 401 (1984), is a comprehensive analysis of the primary federal statute on discrimination against handicapped persons. Author compares Section 504 to other antidiscrimination measures and "discusses the extent to which traditional antidiscrimination principles . . . must be reshaped" to protect against handicap discrimination. Also discusses coverage and enforcement issues and analyzes the elements of the plaintiff's prima facie case and the defendant's defenses in situations where a handicapped individual challenges an exclusion from participation in a program, the denial of benefits of a program, or unequal treatment within a program. Includes a section analyzing the U.S. Supreme Court's decision in *Southeastern Community College* v. *Davis*.

Sec. 7.6 (Dealing with the Federal Government)

1. Bender L., *Federal Regulation and Higher Education* (American Association for Higher Education, ERIC/Higher Education Research Rpt. No. 1, 1977), considers the problem of federal infringement on college and university autonomy, the regulation writing process, the cost to institutions of implementing regulations, and strategies for reform.

2. Bouchard, R. F., and Franklin, J. D. (Eds.), *Guidebook to the Freedom of Information and Privacy Acts* (Clark Boardman Co., 1980), is a compilation of materials that explain the FOIA and the Privacy Act and provide guidance on how to obtain information under them.

3. Clune, W., III, *The Deregulation Critique of the Federal Role in Education* (Project Rpt. No. 82-A11, Institute for Research on Educational Finance and Governance, Stanford University, 1982), analyzes the theoretical basis for deregulation, the criticisms of current federal regulatory efforts, and the benefits and disadvantages of deregulation.

4. El-Khawas, E., "Solving Problems Through Self-Regulation," 59 *Educational Record* 323 (1978), defines self-regulation as "voluntary actions to address problems that broadly affect the academic community." Acknowledges the difficulty of self-regulation and proposes "two kinds of initiatives: efforts to limit further government regulation and efforts to assure that existing regulations adequately come to terms with academic realities."

5. Rosenblum, V., "Dealing with Federal Regulatory Agencies," in D. H. Blumer (Ed.), *Legal Issues for Postsecondary Education II* (American Association of Community and Junior Colleges, 1976), chap. 5, is a concise, practical, "how-to" guide written for administrators of postsecondary institutions.

6. Saunders, C. B., "How to Keep Government from Playing the Featured

Role,'' 59 *Educational Record* 61 (1978), asserts the premise that the federal presence on campus is permanent and proposes a strategy for coping with this presence. Author suggests that both the government and postsecondary administrators adopt a ''test of necessity'' for determining when a new federal regulation may be needed, and that administrators should commit themselves to ''developing a system of self-regulation.''

7. Smith, M. R., ''Protecting the Confidentiality of Faculty Peer Review Records,'' 8 *J. of College and University Law* 20 (1981–82); see item no. 11 in bibliography for Chapter Three, Section 3.3.

8. Steadman, J. M., Schwartz, D., and Jacoby, S. B., *Litigation with the Federal Government,* 2nd ed. (American Law Institute–American Bar Association, 1983), is an overview and analysis of how to sue the federal government and handle the problems encountered in such suits. Includes extensive discussion of the Federal Tort Claims Act, the Tucker Act (for certain claims based on a federal statute or regulation or on an express or implied contract), the Contract Disputes Act of 1978, and the Equal Access to Justice Act. Also discusses the process of settling cases against the federal government and the remnants of the sovereign immunity doctrine that still pose some barriers to suing the federal government.

9. Summerfield, H., *Power and Process: The Formulation and Limits of Federal Educational Policy* (McCutchan, 1974), provides description and analysis of the process by which federal education policy is made; considers the roles of the education lobbying groups, Congress and its education subcommittees, the President and the President's staff, and the federal administrative agencies.

10. See entry no. 8 and entry no. 9 in bibliography for Section 7.4.

✤ VIII ✤

The College
and the Accrediting
Agencies

Sec. 8.1. The Accreditation System

Besides dealing with government agencies at local, state, and federal levels, postsecondary administrators must cope with a substantial external force in the private sector: the educational accrediting agencies. Educational accreditation, conducted by private associations rather than by a ministry of education or other government agency, is a development unique to this country. As the system has evolved, the private accrediting agencies have assumed an important role in the development and maintenance of standards for postsecondary education and have become able to exert considerable influence on individual institutions and programs seeking to obtain and preserve the accreditation that only these agencies can bestow.

There are two types of accreditation: institutional (or general) accreditation and program (or specialized) accreditation. Institutional accreditation applies to the entire institution and all its programs, departments, and schools; program accreditation applies to a particular school, department, or program within the institution, such as a school of medicine or law, a department of chemistry, or a program in medical technology. Program accreditation may also apply to an entire institution if it is a free-standing, specialized institution, such as a business school or technical school, whose curriculum is all in the same program area. Institutional accreditation is granted by six regional agencies—membership associations composed of the accredited institutions in each region. Since each regional agency covers a separate, defined part of the country, each institution is subject to the jurisdiction of only one agency. Program accreditation is granted by a multitude of "specialized" (or "professional" or "occupational") accrediting agencies, which may or may not be membership associations and are often sponsored by the particular profession or occupation whose educational programs are being accredited. The jurisdiction of these specialized agencies is nationwide. Overseeing and speaking for both the regional and the specialized agencies at the national level is the Council on Postsecondary Accreditation (COPA), a private organization created in 1975, with offices at One Dupont Circle, N.W., Washington, D.C., 20036.

Being private, accrediting agencies do not derive their power directly from public law, as do federal, state, and local governments. They owe their existence and legal status basically to state corporation law and to the common law of "voluntary (or private) associations" (see Section 8.2), and they have whatever general powers are set forth in their articles of incorporation or association and the accompanying bylaws and rules. These powers are enforced through private sanctions embodied in the articles, bylaws, and rules, the primary sanctions being the withdrawal and denial of accreditation. The force of these private sanctions is greatly enhanced, however, by the extensive public and private reliance on accrediting agencies' decisions.

The federal government relies in part on these agencies to identify the institutions and programs eligible for a wide range of aid to education programs, particularly those administered by the U.S. Department of Education (see Section 8.3). The states demonstrate their reliance on the agencies' assessments when they exempt accredited institutions or programs from various licensing or other regulatory requirements (see Section 6.3). Some states also use accreditation to determine students' or institutions' eligibility under their own state funding programs, and the state approving agencies operating under contract with the Veterans Administration depend on accreditation in approving courses under veterans' programs (38 U.S.C. sec. 1775(a)(1)). State professional and occupational licensing boards also rely on the accrediting agencies by making graduation from an accredited school or program a prerequisite to obtaining a license to practice in the state. Private professional societies may use professional accreditation in determining who is eligible for membership. Students, parents, and guidance counselors may employ accreditation as one criterion in choosing a school. And postsecondary institutions themselves often rely on accreditation in determining the acceptability of transfer credits.

Because of this extensive public and private reliance on accrediting agencies, accreditation is very important for postsecondary institutions. Administrators usually consider both institutional and program accreditation to be necessary for successful operation. Thus, administrators usually cannot avoid meeting these standards and requirements by forgoing accreditation; needing this "stamp of approval," they must deal with the multitude of accrediting agencies having jurisdiction over their campuses. Consequently, administrators and counsel need to understand the legal limits on the agencies' powers and the legal leverage they might apply if an agency threatens denial or withdrawal of accreditation.

This is not to suggest that institutions should regard accrediting agencies as adversaries. Usually accreditation depends on mutual help and cooperation, and the dynamic between institution and agency can be very positive. Therefore, institutions and programs willing to cooperate and expend the necessary effort usually can obtain and keep accreditation without serious threat of loss. But serious differ-

ences can and do arise, particularly with institutions that are innovating with curricula, the use of resources, or delivery systems. Such institutions may not fit neatly
into accrediting standards or may otherwise be difficult for accrediting agencies
to evaluate. Similarly, institutions that operate in more than one state (see Section
6.4), or contract for the delivery of educational services with nonaccredited outside
organizations, or sponsor off-campus degree programs may pose particular problems
for accrediting agencies.[1] So may institutions organized as proprietary entities, as
illustrated by the *Marjorie Webster* case in Section 8.2. When these or other circumstances involve the institution in accreditation problems, they can be critical because
of accreditation's importance to the institution. Administrators should be prepared
to deal, in an adversary way if necessary, with the difficulties such situations may
create for the institution.

Sec. 8.2. Accreditation and the Courts

There are few reported judicial opinions on the powers of accrediting agencies.
The first case arose in 1938, after the North Central Association of Colleges and
Secondary Schools had threatened to withdraw the accreditation of North Dakota's
State Agricultural College. The state's governor sought an injunction against North
Central. Using traditional legal analysis, the court denied the governor's request,
reasoning that "in the absence of fraud, collusion, arbitrariness, or breach of contract, . . . the decisions of such voluntary associations must be accepted in litigation
before the court as conclusive" (*North Dakota* v. *North Central Association of Colleges
and Secondary Schools,* 23 F. Supp. 694 (E.D. Ill.), affirmed, 99 F.2d 697 (7th Cir.
1938)). Another case did not arise until 1967, when Parsons College sued the North
Central Association.

In 1963 Parsons College was placed on probation by the North Central
Association. This probation was removed in 1965 with the stipulation that the college's accreditation status be reviewed within three years. In 1967 the association
conducted a two-day site visit of the college, after which the visiting team issued
a report noting that "some improvements . . . had not been realized" and that
"other deficiencies persisted." After a meeting at which the college made statements
and answered questions, the association's accrediting committee reported to the
executive board, which recommended that Parsons be dropped from membership.
This recommendation was accepted in a subsequent vote of the association's full
membership. The college then appealed to the board of directors, which sustained
the disaccreditation decision on the basis that the college was not "providing an
adequate educational program for its students, especially those of limited ability."

When the college sought to enjoin the association from implementing its disaccreditation decision, the federal district court denied its request (*Parsons College* v.
North Central Association of Colleges and Secondary Schools, 271 F. Supp. 65 (N.D. Ill.

---

[1]COPA and individual accrediting agencies have prepared policy statements on some
of these problem areas. COPA, for example, has a "Policy Statement on Off-Campus Credit
Programs" that it adopted in 1976 and revised in 1983. See also E. Kuhns and S. V. Martorana,
*Toward Academic Quality Off-Campus: Monitoring Requirements of Institutional Accrediting Bodies and the
States for Off-Campus, Military Base, and Study Abroad Programs* (Council on Postsecondary Accredita-
tion, 1983).

1967)). The court rejected the college's claim that the association must comply with the due process requirements of the federal Constitution, reasoning that "the association stands on the same footing as any private corporation" and is not subject to "the constitutional limits applicable to government" (see Section 1.4). The court then engaged in a much more limited review of the association's procedures and rules. After deciding that the "law applicable to determine the propriety of the expulsion of a member from a private association is the law which he agreed to when he voluntarily chose to join the association—that is, the rules of the association itself," the court found that the college had neither charged nor proved any violation of association rules.

The college further argued, however, that the association's action should be invalidated, even though consistent with its own rules, if the action was "contrary to rudimentary due process or grounded in arbitrariness." Without admitting that such a legal standard applied to accrediting agencies, the court did provide a useful analysis of the association's action under this common law standard. The court defined rudimentary due process to include (1) an adequate opportunity to be heard, (2) a notice of the proceedings, (3) a notice of the specific charges, (4) sufficiently definite standards of evaluation, and (5) substantively adequate reasons for the decision. After reviewing the entire process by which the association reached its disaccreditation decision, the court concluded that "the college has failed to establish a violation of the commands of any of the several rules."

The court found that the college had been afforded the opportunity to speak and be heard at almost every stage of the proceedings and that the opportunity afforded was adequate for the type of proceeding involved:

> The nature of the hearing, if required by rudimentary due process, may properly be adjusted to the nature of the issue to be decided. In this case, the issue was not innocence but excellence. Procedures appropriate to decide whether a specific act of plain misconduct was committed are not suited to an expert evaluation of educational quality. . . .
>
> Here, no trial-type hearing, with confrontation, cross-examination, and assistance of counsel, would have been suited to the resolution of the issues to be decided. The question was not principally a matter of historical fact, but rather of the application of a standard of quality in a field of recognized expertise [271 F. Supp. at 72–73].

The court further found that the college had ample notice of the proceedings because "after a long history of questionable status, the visit of the examining team was adequate notice without more."

The requirement of specific charges was satisfied by the examining team report given to the college. The court found that this report, "supplemented by the evidence produced by the college itself, contained all the information on which all subsequent decisions were made. No fuller disclosure could have been made."

The court also found the evaluative standards of the association to be sufficiently definite to inform the school of what was expected of it. Disagreeing with the college's claim that the standards were "so vague as to be unintelligible to men of ordinary intelligence," the court reasoned as follows:

The standards of accreditation are not guides for the layman but for professionals in the field of education. Definiteness may prove, in another view, to be arbitrariness. The association was entitled to make a conscious choice in favor of flexible standards to accommodate variation in purpose and character among its constituent institutions, and to avoid forcing all into a rigid and uniform mold [271 F. Supp. at 73].

Finally, the court refused its own invitation to explore the substantive adequacy of the reasons for withdrawing accreditation. While courts are well equipped to handle problems of procedural fairness, according to this court, they can hardly claim professional expertise in evaluating educational quality:

In this field, the courts are traditionally even more hesitant to intervene. The public benefits of accreditation, dispensing information and exposing misrepresentation, would not be enhanced by judicial intrusion. Evaluation by the peers of the college, enabled by experience to make comparative judgments, will best serve the paramount interest in the highest practicable standards in higher education. The price for such benefits is inevitably some injury to those who do not meet the measure, and some risk of conservatism produced by appraisals against a standard of what has already proven valuable in education [271 F. Supp. at 74].

In other words, the court assumed that the association had relied on its expertise in making its accreditation decision and deferred to this assumed expression of expertise.

Shortly after *Parsons College,* another federal court tangled with accreditation issues in the *Marjorie Webster* case. In 1966 Marjorie Webster Junior College, a proprietary (for-profit) junior college, applied to the Middle States Association for accreditation. The association refused to consider the application because the college was not a nonprofit organization. The college sued; and, after a lengthy trial, the lower court held that the nonprofit criterion was invalid under the federal antitrust laws, the "developing common law regarding exclusion from membership in private associations," and the federal Constitution's due process clause (*Marjorie Webster Junior College* v. *Middle States Association of Colleges and Secondary Schools,* 302 F. Supp. 459 (D.D.C. 1969)). The lower court ordered the association to consider the college's application and to accredit the college "if it should otherwise qualify for accreditation under Middle States' standards." The appellate court reversed, finding that in the circumstances of the case the association's reason for refusing to consider the application (the proprietary character of the college) was valid (432 F.2d 650 (D.C. Cir. 1970)). Unlike the *Parsons College* opinion, however, the appellate court's opinion (and the lower court's opinion) clearly departs from the traditional judicial reluctance to examine the internal affairs of private organizations.

In relation to the antitrust claims, the appellate court held that the "proscriptions of the Sherman Act were 'tailored for the business world' [*Eastern Railroad Presidents' Conference* v. *Noerr Motor Freight,* 365 U.S. 127, 141 (1961)], not for the noncommercial aspects of the liberal arts and the learned professions," and that, since the "process of accreditation is an activity distinct from the sphere of commerce," going "rather to the heart of the concept of education," an accreditation decision would violate the Act only if undertaken with "an intent or purpose to affect the commercial aspects of the profession." Since no such "commercial motive" had been shown, the association's action did not constitute a combination or conspiracy in restraint of the college's trade.

Regarding the common law claims, the appellate court agreed with the lower court that, under a developing exception to the general rule of judicial nonintervention in private associations' affairs, an association possessing virtual monopolistic control in an area of public concern must exercise its power reasonably, "with an even hand, and not in conflict with the public policy of the jurisdiction." To the appeals court, however, the scope of judicial review under this exception depended on the amount of "deference" that courts should accord to the accrediting agency's action, and deference varied "both with the subject matter at issue and with the degree of harm resulting from the association's action." Since the subject matter was the "substantive standards" of the association, the court accorded more deference to the association than it would if the subject were "the fairness of the procedures by which the challenged determination was reached." With respect to the degree of harm, while "lack of accreditation may be a not insignificant handicap to the college," the court found that "denial of accreditation . . . is not tantamount to exclusion [of the college] from operating successfully as a junior college." Having thus weighed the "subject matter" and the "degree of harm," the court concluded that "substantial deference" should be accorded the association's judgment "regarding the ends that it serves and the means most appropriate to those ends." The appellate court then looked to the basis for the association's nonprofit criterion—that the profit motive is inconsistent with educational quality. The lower court had held that the "assumption that the profit motive is inconsistent with quality is not supported by the evidence and is unwarranted." The appellate court "neither disregard[ed] nor disbelieve[d] the extensive testimony . . . regarding the values and benefits" of proprietary institutions. But in light of the substantial deference it accorded the association in setting its criteria for accreditation, the appellate court held that it had not "been shown to be unreasonable for [the association] to conclude that the desire for personal profit might influence educational goals in subtle ways difficult to detect but destructive, in the long run, of that atmosphere of academic inquiry which . . . [the association's] standards for accreditation seek to foster."

Regarding the due process claims, the appeals court also held that the association's nonprofit criterion was not unreasonable and therefore was valid. The significant point here, however, is that the court in fact engaged in a constitutional due process analysis. The lower court had found that the association's accreditation activities were "quasi-governmental" and thus could be considered "state action" subject to federal constitutional restraints. The appeals court "assume[d] without deciding" that state action did exist. Thus, unlike the court in *Parsons College*, which specifically rejected the state action argument, the lower court in *Marjorie Webster* accepted the argument, and the appellate court left the question unanswered.

A later case, the *Marlboro Corporation* case, concerned the Emery School, a private proprietary business school operated by the Marlboro Corporation. The litigation arose from the school's efforts to have its accreditation renewed by the Accrediting Commission of the Association of Independent Colleges and Schools. During the reapplication process, an inspection team visited the school. The team filed a substantially negative evaluation, to which the school responded in writing. In April 1975 the commission ordered a temporary extension of the school's accreditation through December 1975 and requested the school to submit, by June 30, 1975, evidence of compliance with association criteria in twelve specified areas of weakness. The information requested included an audited financial statement, evidence of adequate library holdings, and a catalogue that met association standards. Rather than complying, the school submitted a progress report that admitted its deficiencies and indicated its plans to correct them. In accordance with its published rule that "a letter of intent will not be accepted" as evidence of the correction of deficiencies, the commission voted in August to deny accreditation. When the school appealed, the commission held a hearing at which the school was given thirty minutes to present its case and respond to questions. After the hearing, the commission reaffirmed its refusal to renew Emery's accreditation.

The lower court denied the school's request for an injunction requiring the association to grant accreditation, and the U.S. Court of Appeals for the First Circuit affirmed (*Marlboro Corporation* v. *Association of Independent Colleges and Schools,* 556 F.2d 78 (1st Cir. 1977)). The school contended that the association had violated its rights to due process under the Constitution and under common law principles and that the denial of accreditation deprived it of rights protected by the rules and regulations of the U.S. commissioner of education (see Section 8.3). The appellate court held that none of the school's procedural rights had been violated, that the commission's decision was not "arbitrary and capricious" because "the irregularities in Emery's financial statement alone . . . justified the commission's decision," and that the rules of the Office of Education were not violated by the association's internal appeal procedure.[2]

First the court considered whether the commission's procedures should be scrutinized under common law due process standards or under the more exacting standards of the U.S. Constitution's due process clause. The lower court had held that the Constitution did not apply because the commission's action was not "state action." The court of appeals, however, found it unnecessary to decide this "close question," since, "even assuming that constitutional due process applies," none of Emery's procedural rights had been violated. To reach this conclusion, the appellate court did review the commission's procedures under the constitutional standard, stating that "under either constitutional or common law standards . . . procedural fairness is a flexible concept" to be considered case by case. The court held that "due process did not . . . require a full-blown adversary hearing in this context." The court noted that the commission's inquiry concerned a routine reapplication for accreditation and was "broadly evaluative" rather than an accusatory inquiry with specific charges. "Emery was given ample opportunity to present its position by written submission and to argue it orally," and more formalized proceedings would have imposed too heavy a burden on the commission.

---

[2]The procedures and standards of this same accrediting commission were also at issue in *Rockland Institute* v. *Association of Independent Colleges and Schools,* 412 F. Supp. 1015 (C.D. Cal. 1976). In relying on both *Parsons College* and *Marjorie Webster* to reject Rockland's challenge to its disaccreditation, the court ruled that the accrediting commission followed its own rules, that the rules provided sufficient procedural due process, and that the commission's evaluative standards were neither vague nor unreasonable.

The court then considered Emery's claim that the decision to deny accreditation was tainted by bias because the chairman of the accrediting commission was the president of a school in direct competition with Emery. While it emphasized that a "decision by an impartial tribunal is an element of due process under any standard," the court found that the chairman took no part in the discussion or vote on Emery's application and in fact did not chair, or participate in, the December hearing. Recognizing the "local realities"—the prolonged evaluation process, the large number of people participating in the decision at various levels, and the commission's general practice of allowing interested commissioners to remain present without participating—the court viewed the question as "troublesome" but concluded that "Emery has [not] shown sufficient actual or apparent impropriety."

Lastly, the court found that the commission's decision was substantively justified by the record and that the Office of Education's rules had not been violated. Although these issues were in the last paragraph of the opinion and only briefly discussed, their mention is significant. In *Parsons College* the court refused to consider the first issue at all, and the second issue raises the novel question whether the Office (now Department) of Education's rules can be enforced by court suits by individual schools. (See Section 8.3.)

The most recent accrediting case, *Avins* v. *White*, involves issues distinct from those litigated in the other accreditation cases. *Avins* is therefore discussed separately, in Section 8.2.4.

The *Parsons College, Marjorie Webster*, and *Marlboro Corporation* cases make clear that the courts will impose some constraints on accrediting agencies in their dealings with postsecondary institutions. Though the accrediting agencies ultimately won all three cases, each court opinion suggests some limits on the authority to deny or withdraw accreditation. It is equally clear, however, that the courts still view accrediting agencies with a cautious eye and do not subject them to the full panoply of controls that state and federal governments impose on their own agencies. Though the law on accreditation is too sparse to permit a precise description of the rights of postsecondary institutions in dealing with accrediting agencies,[3] these cases, supplemented by later developments, do provide valuable guidelines.

8.2.1. Common law requirements. At the very least, it is clear that courts will require an accrediting agency to follow its own rules in withdrawing accreditation (as in *Parsons College*) or refusing to renew accreditation (as in *Marlboro Corporation*). It is less clear whether courts will require an agency to follow its own rules in considering an initial application for accreditation. There is no accreditation case on this point, and some judicial pronouncements in related areas suggest that the right to be judged by the rules accrues only after the applicant has been admitted to membership or otherwise approved by the association. The better view, however, is that an applicant can also require that the agency follow its own rules.

Beyond following its own rules, an accrediting agency apparently must act fairly and reasonably under the particular circumstances of the case. The primary requirement seems to be that the agency must provide institutions with procedural due process before denying, withdrawing, or refusing to renew their accreditation.

---

[3]For an extended analysis of judicial review in a related area of the law, which can be used to predict available rights in accreditation, see W. Kaplin, "Professional Power and Judicial Review: The Health Professions," 44 *George Washington L. Rev.* 710, 716–50 (1976).

The institution appears to have a right to receive notice that its accreditation is being questioned, to know why, and to be heard on the question. *Parsons College* and *Marlboro Corporation* provide useful analyses of the extent of these protections. Apparently, the less broadly evaluative and the more accusatory an action is, the more extensive the due process protections must be. A disaccreditation would thus occasion the highest level of due process protection, perhaps including a formal hearing with the right to counsel, witnesses, and cross-examination.

8.2.2. State action doctrine. It is not clear from the cases whether courts will consider accrediting agency decisions to be ''state action'' subject to the federal Constitution (see Section 1.4.2). The court in *Parsons College* specifically rejected this argument, as did the lower court in the *Marlboro Corporation* case (416 F. Supp. 958, 959 (D. Mass. 1976)). On the other hand, the lower court in *Marjorie Webster* accepted the state action argument; and the appellate courts in *Marjorie Webster* and in *Marlboro Corporation* assumed, without deciding, that the accrediting agency was engaged in state action. Although there is thus room in the precedents for applying the state action label, its general application to accrediting agencies, along with its accompanying constitutional standards, may not serve long-range educational and societal interests as well as application of the common law requirements (see W. Kaplin, ''Accrediting Agencies' Legal Responsibilities: In Pursuit of the Public Interest,'' 12 *J. of Law and Education* 87, 93–104 (1983)).

8.2.3. Antitrust law. Federal or state antitrust law may sometimes also protect postsecondary institutions from certain accrediting actions that interfere with an institution's ability to compete with other institutions. The *Marjorie Webster* appeals court indicated that federal antitrust law could apply when commercial considerations motivate accrediting agency decisions. Subsequently, the antitrust approach was broadened and strengthened by the U.S. Supreme Court's decision in *Goldfarb* v. *Virginia State Bar*, 421 U.S. 773 (1975), the first case in which the Court clearly approved the applicability of federal antitrust law (Section 7.2.10) to professional associations. The application of the antitrust approach to accreditation has been further strengthened by two Supreme Court cases following *Goldfarb*. In *National Society of Professional Engineers* v. *United States*, 435 U.S. 679 (1978), the Court reaffirmed its *Goldfarb* determination that the standard-setting activities of nonprofit professional associations are subject to scrutiny under antitrust laws. The Court then invalidated the society's ethical canon prohibiting members of the society from submitting competitive bids for engineering services. In *American Society of Mechanical Engineers* v. *Hydrolevel Corporation*, 102 S. Ct. 1935 (1982), the Court again subjected a nonprofit professional association to antitrust liability arising from its standard-setting activities. Going beyond *Goldfarb* and *National Society of Professional Engineers*, the Court held that a professional organization can be held liable for the anticompetitive acts of its members and other agents, including unpaid volunteers, if the agents had ''apparent authority'' to act (see this volume, Section 2.1). The characteristics of the society which subjected it to antitrust liability are similar to those which could be attributed to accrediting agencies:

> ASME contends it should not bear the risk of loss for antitrust violations committed by its agents acting with apparent authority because it is a nonprofit organization, not a business seeking profit. But it is beyond debate that nonprofit organizations can be held liable under the antitrust laws.

Although ASME may not operate for profit, it does derive benefits from
its codes, including the fees the society receives for its code-related publications and services, the prestige the codes bring to the society, the influence
they permit ASME to wield, and the aid the standards provide the profession
of mechanical engineering. Since the antitrust violation in this case could
not have occurred without ASME's codes and ASME's method of administering them, it is not unfitting that ASME will be liable for the damages
arising from that violation (see W. Prosser, *Law of Torts* 459 (4th ed. 1971);
W. Seavey, *Law of Agency* sec. 83 (1964)). Furthermore, ASME is in the
best position to take precautions that will prevent future antitrust violations.
Thus, the fact that ASME is a nonprofit organization does not weaken the
force of the antitrust and agency principles that indicate that ASME should
be liable for Hydrolevel's antitrust injuries [102 S. Ct. at 1947-48].

See C. Chambers, "Implications of the *Hydrolevel* decision for Postsecondary Accrediting Associations," *Accreditation* vol. 7, no. 2 (Council on Postsecondary Accreditation, Summer 1982).

As these decisions clearly indicate, federal antitrust law can be a meaningful
source of rights for postsecondary institutions if they are harmed by accrediting
activities that can be characterized as anticompetitive. Such rights may be asserted
not only against decisions to deny, terminate, or condition an institution's accreditation, as in *Marjorie Webster,* but also against other activities undertaken by accrediting
agencies or their agents in the process of fashioning and applying standards.

8.2.4. Defamation law. The first application of defamation law (Sections
2.3.1.2 and 4.9.4) to accrediting agencies and officials is provided by *Avins* v. *White,*
627 F.2d 637 (3d Cir. 1980). *Avins* was a more personalized type of lawsuit than
the other accreditation cases above. The plaintiff was a school official who alleged
that he had been defamed by an accrediting official in the course of a site inspection.
The case arose from the efforts of the Delaware Law School (DLS) to gain provisional
American Bar Association accreditation. ABA accreditation is particularly important
for law schools because most states require that an individual must have graduated
from an ABA-accredited school before he can take the state bar examination.

After a series of accreditation inspections of DLS, the then dean of DLS
(Avins) sued the ABA consultant (White) who had participated in two of the inspections. The dean alleged three counts of defamation. The first two counts were based
on statements in the reports of the inspection team; the third was based on remarks
that the consultant had made to the dean at a luncheon meeting while they were
in the presence of a third party (a Judge DiBona). The dean prevailed at a trial
in federal district court, and the jury awarded him $50,000 in compensatory damages.

On appeal, the U.S. Court of Appeals for the Third Circuit considered each
of the three defamation counts separately. Regarding the first two counts, the court
held that the statements in the inspection team's reports could not be considered
to have defamed the dean. The statements in the first report, according to the court,
were not based on fact but were expressions of "pure opinion." Such expressions
cannot be defamatory, because "ideas themselves," unlike their underlying facts,
"cannot be false." The statements in the second report, according to the court,
referred to the school rather than to the dean personally and therefore could not
have defamed him. Thus, instead of submitting the first two counts to the jury,

the district judge should have ruled the statements nondefamatory as a matter of law. The appellate court therefore reversed the district court's judgment on the first two counts.

The third count presented different problems. The appellate court ruled that the luncheon remarks cited in this count "may have been potentially defamatory." The consultant argued, however, that, because of his role in the accreditation process, he possessed a "qualified privilege" to make the luncheon remarks, which addressed matters regarding the accreditation inspection. Neither the appellate court nor the dean disputed that the consultant could possess such a qualified privilege. The issue, rather, was whether the consultant had abused the privilege by making his remarks in the presence of the third party (Judge DiBona), who was not an official of the law school. The appellate court held that this issue was one for the jury, that the district judge had properly instructed the jury on when it could consider the qualified privilege to be abused, and that "the jury quite properly could have rejected the defense."

The appellate court could not determine whether the jury had actually found the luncheon remarks to be defamatory, however, since the district judge had submitted all three defamation counts to the jury as a package; it was "therefore impossible to determine if the jury based its verdict on all three allegedly defamatory statements or whether the verdict was based on only one or two of the incidents." Because of this technical complexity, the appellate court also reversed the district court's judgment on the third count and remanded the case to the district court for a new trial on that count only.

One critical issue then remained: the "standard of proof" the dean had to meet in order to sustain a defamation claim against the consultant. Although the issue applied to all three counts, the appellate court needed to address it only with respect to the third count, which it was remanding for a new trial. The consultant argued that the dean was a "public figure" for purposes of this lawsuit and therefore had to meet a higher standard of proof than that required for ordinary defamation claims. The district court had rejected this argument.

In a series of cases beginning with *New York Times* v. *Sullivan*, 376 U.S. 254 (1964), the U.S. Supreme Court has formulated the "public figure" doctrine in order to ensure that certain speakers' free speech rights would not be unduly chilled by the fear of defamation suits. To prevail on a defamation claim, a public figure must prove "actual malice" on the part of the defendant—that is, that the defendant had made the statement with a knowledge of its falsity or with a reckless disregard for the truth. The appellate court determined that the dean was a public figure within the meaning of the Supreme Court precedents, thus overruling the district court's determination on the standard of proof to which the dean was subject:

> The [U.S. Supreme] Court in *Gertz* [v. *Robert Welch, Inc.*, 418 U.S. 323 (1974)] gave a description of who may be a public figure:
>
>> For the most part, those who attain [public figure] status have assumed roles of especial prominence in the affairs of society. Some occupy positions of such persuasive power and influence that they are deemed public figures for all purposes. More commonly, those classed as public figures have thrust themselves to the forefront of particular controversies

in order to influence the resolution of the issues involved. In either event, they invite attention and comment.

The *Gertz* test envisions basically two types of public figures: (1) those who are public figures for *all* purposes; and (2) those who are public figures only in the context of a particular public controversy. . . .
    We have no difficulty in concluding that Avins is not a public figure for all purposes, under the first part of the *Gertz* test. Although Avins was apparently well known in legal academic circles, we do not believe he possessed the fame and notoriety in the public eye necessary to make him a public figure for all purposes. This leaves the question whether Avins is a public figure in the limited context of the DLS accreditation struggle. We must accordingly consider whether (1) the DLS accreditation struggle was a public controversy and (2) if so, whether Avins voluntarily injected himself into that controversy.
    Our first task is to determine whether DLS's accreditation struggle may fairly be considered a "public controversy." . . .
    Although DLS was formed and operated as a purely private law school, its success or failure was of importance to the Delaware State Bar as well as to any individual interested in attending an accredited law school in Delaware. It is the only law school in the State of Delaware. Accreditation of DLS would create a new source of attorneys who could qualify to take the Delaware Bar examinations and be admitted to practice in the state. Furthermore, a majority of DLS students were from out of state. Thus, DLS's accreditation would also affect the interests of students from a variety of locales and admission to state bars outside of Delaware.
    Further, there is evidence in the record that mass meetings were held and that individuals from other states concerned about DLS visited the school. The local news media, as well as the Delaware Bar Association, publicized the events surrounding DLS's formation and struggle for accreditation. . . .
    We therefore hold that DLS's accreditation was a legitimate public controversy within the meaning of *Gertz.* . . .
    We have no difficulty in concluding that Avins voluntarily injected himself into the controversy surrounding DLS's accreditation. As creator, chief architect, and the first dean of DLS, Avins spearheaded its drive toward accreditation. Indeed, the first major hurdle which Avins had to surmount in behalf of DLS was accreditation. The record reveals that from the outset Avins, as dean, was actively involved in every facet of the accreditation struggle. He, in fact, invited the first three accreditation teams to inspect DLS, and he personally presented DLS's case before the Council and Accreditation Committee. . . .
    It was Avins who, as dean of DLS, officially requested, invited, and affirmatively invoked the accreditation process of the American Bar Association. We therefore conclude that Avins played an affirmative and aggressive role in the accreditation process and that he was a public figure for that limited purpose [627 F.2d at 646–48].

The court justified this extension of the public figure doctrine to the accreditation context by relying on the nature of the accreditation process itself:

> We believe the importance of the accreditation process underscores the need for extension of the *New York Times* privilege to a private individual criticizing a public figure in the course of commenting on matters germane to accreditation. An accreditation evaluation by its nature is critical; the applicant school invites critical comments in seeking accreditation. In order to succeed, individuals involved in the accreditation process need to be assured that they may frankly and openly discuss accreditation matters. White, in criticizing Avins at the luncheon, was expressing a candid view of Avins' conduct during the accreditation process. To require an individual like White to insure the accuracy of his comments on accreditation matters would undoubtedly lead to self-censorship, which will jeopardize the efficacy and integrity of the accreditation process itself. Since the public is vitally affected by accreditation of educational institutions, we believe that self-censorship in the accreditation process would detrimentally affect an area of significant social importance [627 F.2d at 648–49].

Avins v. *White* thus adds new insight into how courts view the accreditation process. The case affirms the societal importance of the process and underscores the need for courts to provide enough legal running room for accreditation to accomplish its societal purposes. More specifically, the case illustrates the steps to take and issues to be encountered in analyzing defamation claims in the accreditation context. The plaintiff's initial victory at trial suggests that defamation law can be a very real source of legal protection for institutions and their officials, and of legal liability for accrediting agencies and their officials. But the appellate court's reversal provides a mellowing effect: defamation law will not be applied so strictly that it discourages the candid criticism necessary to accreditation's success; and, when the institutional official allegedly defamed is a "public figure," defamation law will provide a remedy against accrediting agencies only in cases of malicious misconduct.

Sec. 8.3. *Accreditation and the U.S. Department of Education*

The Department of Education (ED) plays an important role in the accrediting process. Numerous federal aid to education statutes specify accreditation "by a nationally recognized accrediting agency or association" as a prerequisite to eligibility for aid for the institution or its students (see, for example, the Higher Education Act of 1965, 20 U.S.C. sec. 1141(a)(5)). The statutes authorize or require the secretary of education to "publish a list of nationally recognized accrediting agencies which he determines to be reliable authority as to the quality of education or training offered." Most postsecondary institutions and programs attain eligibility for federal funds by obtaining accreditation from one of the accrediting bodies recognized by the secretary.

Most of the federal aid statutes provide for alternative means to attain eligibility besides accreditation, the primary method. The alternatives available vary with the aid program. Under many aid programs, an unaccredited institution may become eligible if it attains "three-letter certification"—that is, certification by three accredited institutions that they accept the nonaccredited institution's credits on transfer. Another alternative is "preaccreditation status," under which an unaccredited institution or program may be eligible for funds if the secretary of education "has determined that there is satisfactory assurance" that it will meet the accreditation standards of a nationally recognized agency within a reasonable time. Approval by a recognized state agency is an alternative available to public vocational education and nursing education institutions under the student financial aid programs. Thus, for most institutions and programs, accreditation is not invariably necessary in order to be eligible for federal funds. The primary exception appears to be proprietary institutions under the student loan programs; these institutions must be accredited by a nationally recognized accrediting agency in order to be eligible.

Pursuant to his statutory authority, the secretary periodically publishes in the *Federal Register* a list of nationally recognized accrediting agencies and associations. The criteria and procedures for listing are also published in the *Federal Register* and codified in the *Code of Federal Regulations* at 34 C.F.R. Part 149. In addition, the secretary periodically publishes a pamphlet containing a current list of recognized agencies, the criteria and procedures for listing, and background information on accreditation.[4] The listing process and other aspects of institutional eligibility for federal aid are administered within the Department of Education by the Division of Eligibility and Agency Evaluation in the Office of Postsecondary Education.

To be included in the secretary's list of nationally recognized agencies, an agency must apply to the secretary for recognition and must meet the secretary's criteria for recognition. Agencies are reevaluated and their listings renewed or terminated at least once every four years (34 C.F.R. sec. 149.5). The criteria for recognition concern the agency's functional aspects, responsibility, reliability, and autonomy. For each of the four categories, there are specific standards the agency must meet to obtain recognition. The standards cover such matters as the agency's organization, its procedures, and its responsiveness to the public interest. Though these provisions give the secretary of education substantial influence over the accrediting process, he has no direct authority to regulate unwilling accrediting agencies. Agencies must apply for recognition before coming under the secretary's jurisdiction. Moreover, recognition only gives the secretary authority to ensure the agency's continued compliance with the criteria; it does not give him authority to overrule the agency's accrediting decisions on particular institutions or programs.

Postsecondary administrators who deal with accrediting agencies will find it beneficial to understand the relationship between the agency and the Department of Education, because many of the requirements in the secretary's criteria for recognition redound to the benefit of the individual institutions and programs. The criteria require, for example, that an accrediting agency provide specified due process safeguards in its accrediting procedures (34 C.F.R. sec. 149.6(b)(3)) and that an agency's decision-making body be free from conflicts of interest (34 C.F.R. secs. 149.6(b)(2) and 149.6(c)(4)). Because recognition is vitally important to an accrediting agency's influence and credibility in the postsecondary world, agencies will be disinclined to jeopardize their recognition by violating the secretary's criteria in their dealings with individual institutions. Institutional administrators therefore have considerable leverage to insist that accrediting agencies comply with these criteria.

---

[4]U.S. Department of Education, *Nationally Recognized Accrediting Agencies and Associations: Criteria and Procedures for Listing by the U.S. Secretary of Education and Current List* (November 1980 and subsequent editions). The pamphlet may be obtained from the Division of Eligibility and Agency Evaluation, Office of Postsecondary Education, U.S. Department of Education, Washington, D.C. 20202.

Although an institution may complain to the secretary about an agency's violation of the recognition criteria, it is unclear whether the secretary's criteria are enforceable in the courts upon suit by an individual institution. The prevailing judicial view is that government regulations are to be enforced by the government agency that promulgated them, unless a contrary intention appears from the regulations and the statute that authorized the regulations. Since there is no indication that the secretary's criteria are to be privately enforceable, the courts would likely leave problems concerning compliance with the criteria to the secretary. He could require an immediate reevaluation of the agency, withdraw recognition, or do nothing if he believed that no plausible violation existed. Thus, even though the *Marlboro* case (discussed in Section 8.2) suggests that courts may review accrediting agency actions for compliance with the secretary's criteria, institutional administrators should not assume that their institution could go to court and nullify any agency action not in compliance with these criteria.

Even if the criteria are not privately enforceable, that does not mean they would be irrelevant in any suit by an institution against an accrediting agency. Since the judicial standards applying to accrediting agencies are not fully developed (see Section 8.2), courts may look to the secretary's criteria as evidence of accepted practice in accreditation or as a model to consult in formulating a remedy for an agency's violation of legal standards.

When the secretary applies the criteria to grant or deny recognition to a particular agency, a different question about the role of courts arises: On what grounds, and at whose request, may a court review the secretary's recognition decisions? The case of *Sherman College of Straight Chiropractic* v. *U.S. Commissioner of Education,* 493 F. Supp. 976 (D.D.C. 1983), is illustrative. The plaintiffs were two chiropractic schools that were not accredited by the Council on Chiropractic Education (CCE), the recognized professional accrediting agency for chiropractic schools. The plaintiffs espoused a chiropractic philosophy divergent from that represented by CCE and the schools it had accredited: the plaintiffs adhered to a limited view regarding diagnosis, called the "straight doctrine," while CCE took a broader view of diagnosis as an essential part of chiropractic practice. When the commissioner (now secretary) renewed CCE's status as a "nationally recognized" accrediting agency, the plaintiffs challenged his action in court.

Using federal administrative law principles, the court determined that the commissioner's renewal of CCE's recognition was a final agency action subject to judicial review. The court also determined that the plaintiffs, as parties aggrieved by the commissioner's action, had standing to challenge it. On the merits, however, the court rejected the plaintiffs' claim that the commissioner's decision was arbitrary or capricious, or an abuse of discretion:

> For four reasons, this court finds that the commissioner acted well "within the scope of his authority" (*Overton Park* [v. *Volpe,* 401 U.S. 402 (1971)]).
>
> First, *the commissioner correctly found that CCE satisfied the recognition criteria.* . . .
>
> Second, *plaintiffs have ready alternative routes to accreditation available to them.* There is no requirement that a given school be accredited by a particular agency, nor is there any limitation on the number of accrediting bodies that can be recognized in a given field. If dissatisfied with the existing

agency in its field, plaintiffs are free to create and seek recognition for an agency which "represents them and that can coexist with CCE" (oral argument, July 15, 1980). . . .

Third, *the commissioner has a limited statutory role in recognizing accrediting agencies.* Recognition of an agency or association clearly does not bestow monopoly jurisdiction over the field of program specialization as defined by the agency or association in its application for recognition (Boyer deposition, pp. 122–23). . . . Despite the manner in which an accrediting body such as CCE defines its "universe," recognition of that agency or association does not preclude the legitimate interests of those who do not believe they fall within that universe.

Fourth, *the commissioner must not be required to arbitrate educational standards for the nation's professions.* The fundamental question underlying this action is how the commissioner should treat an intraprofessional doctrinal dispute in deciding whether to grant or renew recognition to an accrediting agency that rejects the doctrine of a deviant splinter group. In this case, plaintiffs request the court to instruct the commissioner, among other things, that a chiropractic accrediting agency cannot require clinical diagnostic training. Such a precedent might ultimately require the commissioner to become "a specialist on the matter of educational philosophy" in every field and would make him a "referee in . . . intraprofessional combat" (Boyer deposition, pp. 36, 114). . . . Appropriately, therefore, the statutes do not call for the commissioner to pass upon the substantive standards of an accrediting agency, but only to determine that the agency is "reliable authority as to the quality of training offered." Surely, educational philosophies differ. However, the commissioner acted correctly in deciding the only issue [he] could legitimately determine: that CCE is a "reliable authority" under the statute [493 F. Supp. at 980–81].

Based on the *Sherman College* case, it appears that the secretary of education's decisions to grant or refuse recognition to petitioning accrediting agencies, or to renew or not renew such recognition, are reviewable in the federal courts. A recognition decision may be challenged not only by the accrediting agency itself (as in a case of refusal or nonrenewal) but also by individual institutions that are injured by the decision. Students or faculty members may also be able to challenge recognition decisions whose effects injure them personally. The availability of judicial review, however, does not mean that courts are likely to overturn the secretary's decisions. The *Sherman College* case indicates that courts will accord the secretary considerable latitude in applying the recognition criteria and that courts will not expect the secretary to take sides in disputes over educational philosophies, professional doctrine, or other matters outside the scope of the recognition criteria.

Sec. 8.4. Dealing with Accrediting Agencies

A postsecondary administrator dealing with an accrediting agency should obtain from the agency information concerning its organization and operation. The secretary of education's criteria (Section 8.3) require that an accrediting agency recognized by the Department of Education must have a clear definition of the scope of its activities (34 C.F.R. sec. 149.6(a)(1)(ii)), clear definitions of each level of accreditation status and clearly written procedures for making accreditation decisions (34 C.F.R. sec. 149.6(a)(3)(i)), clearly defined purposes and objectives (34 C.F.R. sec. 149.6(b)(1)(ii)), published evaluative standards (34 C.F.R. sec. 149.6(b)(2)(ii)(A)), and written procedures for reviewing complaints about institutional or program quality (34 C.F.R. sec. 149.6(b)(2)(iv)). The criteria also require that the accrediting agency make available the names and affiliations of the members of its policy and decision-making bodies; the names of its principal administrative personnel; and a description of its ownership, control, and type of legal organization (34 C.F.R. sec. 149.6(b)(2)(ii)(D) and (E)). Administrators may insist on receiving any or all of this information from the accrediting agency. Administrators may also insist, backed up by the court cases (Section 8.2), that the agency scrupulously follow its own rules in dealing with the institution.

Most important, an administrator should have copies of the agency's evaluative standards, procedures for making accrediting decisions, and procedures for appealing adverse decisions. An understanding of the standards and procedures can be critical to an effective presentation of the institution or program to the agency. In particular, the administrator should take advantage of all procedural rights, such as notice and hearing, that agency rules provide in situations where accreditation is in jeopardy. If agency rules do not provide sufficient procedural safeguards to meet the requirements of the court cases and the secretary's criteria, administrators may insist on additional rights. The criteria, which are more specific than the court guidelines, require that the agency (1) provide an opportunity for the institution to comment on the site-visit report of the agency's evaluation team and to file supplemental materials responding to the report, (2) provide the institution with a specific statement of the reasons for any adverse accrediting action and a notice of the right to appeal, (3) provide an opportunity for a hearing before the appeal body, and (4) provide a written decision of the appeal body with a specific statement of the reasons for its action (34 C.F.R. sec. 149.6(b)(3)).

If the institution should be subjected to an adverse accrediting decision that appears to violate the agency's own rules or the requirements of the court cases or the secretary's criteria, or to be otherwise unreasonable or unfair, the first recourse is to exhaust all the accrediting agency's internal appeal processes. Simultaneously, the institution should seek to initiate negotiations with the agency concerning the steps the institution might take to reverse the accreditation decision. Should negotiations and internal appeals fail to achieve a resolution satisfactory to the institution, outside recourse to the courts or to the secretary of education is possible. The developing law on accreditation (Section 8.2) provides significant bases for court challenges to accrediting decisions. The secretary's criteria, while not providing any basis for the secretary to reverse an individual accrediting decision, may provide a basis for the secretary and the Division of Eligibility and Agency Evaluation to use their good offices in disputes regarding compliance with the criteria. But court actions and complaints to the secretary of education should be last resorts, pursued only in exceptional circumstances and only when reasonable prospects for resolution within the accrediting agency have ended.

Thus, the process for resolving accreditation issues parallels the process for most other legal issues in this book. Courts have a presence, and government agencies have a presence—both of which have increased in recent times. But in the end it is usually in the best interests of education for institutions and private educational organizations to develop the capacity for internal resolution of legal disputes. As long as affected parties have meaningful access to the internal process, and the process works fairly, courts and government agencies should allow it ample breathing space to permit educational expertise to operate. It is the challenge of the remainder of this century for courts, agencies, and postsecondary institutions and organizations to work such constructive accommodations in the interests of all participants in the postsecondary community.

Selected Annotated Bibliography

General

1. Kaplin, W., and Hunter, J. P., "The Legal Status of the Educational Accrediting Agency: Problems in Judicial Supervision and Governmental Regulation," 52 *Cornell Law Quarterly* 104 (1966), is a comprehensive legal analysis of accreditation and the authority of courts, the U.S. Office (now Department) of Education, and state legislatures to constrain or channel the operations of accrediting agencies.

2. Young, K. E., Chambers, C. M., Kells, H. R., and Associates, *Understanding Accreditation: Contemporary Perspectives on Issues and Practices in Evaluating Educational Quality* (Jossey-Bass, 1983), is a sourcebook on the history, purposes, problems, current status, and future prospects of postsecondary accreditation. Includes eighteen chapters by fourteen different authors, a substantial prologue and epilogue tying the chapters together, an appendix with various COPA documents, a glossary of terms, and an extensive bibliography.

Sec. 8.1 (The Accreditation System)

1. Selden, W., and Porter, H., *Accreditation: Its Purposes and Uses* (Council on Postsecondary Accreditation, 1977), an "occasional paper" from a series sponsored by the Council on Postsecondary Accreditation, explains the historical derivation of private accreditation, the current purposes and uses of accreditation, and emerging pressures on the accreditation system.

2. Symposium, "Accreditation," 50 *J. of Higher Education*, issue 2 (March/April 1979), provides various perspectives on the accreditation system, its prospects, and its problems. Contains eleven articles, including: M. Conway, "The Commissioner's Authority to List Accrediting Agencies and Associations: Necessity for an Eligibility Issue"; J. Hall, "Regional Accreditation and Nontraditional Colleges: A President's Point of View"; J. Miller and L. Boswell, "Accreditation, Assessment, and the Credentialing of Educational Accomplishment"; J. Proffitt, "The Federal Connection for Accreditation"; W. Trout, "Regional Accreditation, Evaluative Criteria and Quality Assurance"; and K. Young, "New Pressures on Accreditation."

3. Symposium, "Making Accreditation Work for Institutions," 59 *Educational Record,* issue 4 (Fall 1978), is a series of three articles: R. Kirkwood, "Institutional Responsibilities in Accreditation"; D. Peterson, "Accrediting Standards and Guidelines: A Profile"; and R. Tucker and R. Mautz, "Involvement of State-Wide Governing Boards in Accreditation."

Sec. 8.2 (Accreditation and the Courts)

1. Kaplin, W., "Judicial Review of Accreditation: The *Parsons College* Case," 40 *J. of Higher Education* 543 (1969), explores considerations relevant to judicial review of accrediting decisions, analyzes the *Parsons College* case, and evaluates its impact on accreditation.

2. Kaplin, W., "The *Marjorie Webster* Decisions on Accreditation," 52 *Educational Record* 219 (1971), analyzes the antitrust law, common law, and constitutional law aspects of the *Marjorie Webster* case and evaluates its impact on accreditation.

3. Kaplin, W., *Accrediting Agencies' Legal Responsibilities: In Pursuit of the Public Interest* (Council on Postsecondary Accreditation, 1982), another COPA occasional paper, "considers the evolution in the way courts have labeled or categorized accrediting agencies, and the legal and policy consequences of this evolution." Analyzes applicability of four labels to accrediting agencies— "governmental," "quasi-governmental," "quasi-public," and "private"— and selects "quasi-public" as most appropriate. Examines the "public interest" concept, providing a discussion of legal standards, a definition of public interest, and guidance in "promoting the public interest." Reprinted at 12 *J. of Law and Education* 87 (1983).

4. Tayler, C. W., and Hylden, T., "Judicial Review of Accrediting Agency Actions: *Marlboro Corporation d/b/a The Emery School* v. *The Association of Independent Colleges and Schools*," 4 *J. of College and University Law* 199 (1978), analyzes the *Emery School* case in the context of the developing law of educational accreditation; discusses the scope of judicial review and the legal standards courts will apply in accreditation cases.

Sec. 8.3 (Accreditation and the U.S. Department of Education)

1. Finkin, M., "Federal Reliance and Voluntary Accreditation: The Power to Recognize as the Power to Regulate," 2 *J. of Law and Education* 339 (1973), provides an overview of the accreditation process and the role of the federal government in that process; emphasizes the evolution—through the various federal aid to education statutes—of the relationship between private accrediting agencies and the U.S. Office of Education, the present status of the relationship, and the legal basis for the Office (now Department) of Education's recognition function.

2. Finkin, M., *Federal Reliance on Educational Accreditation: The Scope of Administrative Discretion* (Council on Postsecondary Accreditation, 1978), a COPA occasional paper, is a sequel to the author's 1973 article on the same topic (item no. 1 above). Argues that portions of the secretary of education's recognition criteria exceed the scope of statutory authority. Should be read in conjunction with a contrary article by M. Conway listed in item 2 of Section 8.1 bibliography.

3. Kaplin, W., *Respective Roles of Federal Government, State Governments, and Private Accrediting Agencies in the Governance of Postsecondary Education* (Council on Postsecondary Education, 1975), another COPA occasional paper, examines the current and potential future roles of federal and state governments and the accrediting agencies, particularly with regard to determining eligibility for federal funding under U.S. Office (now Department) of Education programs.

Sec. 8.4 (Dealing with Accrediting Agencies)

1. Fisk, R., and Duryea, E. D., *Academic Collective Bargaining and Regional Accreditation* (Council on Postsecondary Accreditation, 1977), another COPA occasional paper, analyzes the potential impact of collective bargaining on regional accreditation and on the relationship between the institution and the agency that accredits it; provides helpful perspective for administrators who must deal with accrediting agencies in circumstances where their faculty is unionized.

2. Heilbron, L., *Confidentiality and Accreditation* (Council on Postsecondary Accreditation, 1976), another COPA occasional paper, examines legal and policy considerations concerning confidentiality of an accrediting agency's records and other information regarding individual institutions; discusses the kinds of information the accrediting agency may collect, the institution's right to obtain disclosure of such information, and the accrediting agency's right to maintain the confidentiality of such information by denying claims of federal or state agencies, courts, or other third parties seeking the disclosure.

3. *Project on Nontraditional Education Final Reports* (Council on Postsecondary Accreditation, 1978), product of a project sponsored by COPA and funded by the W. K. Kellogg Foundation, discusses problems encountered in accrediting innovative or nontraditional programs and institutions. The four-volume set includes a summary report by project director Grover Andrews (vol. 1) and nine individual reports (vols. 2-4), including the following: J. Harris, "Institutional Accreditation and Nontraditional Undergraduate Educational Institutions and Programs" (Rpt. no. 3); P. Dressel, "Problems and Principles in the Recognition or Accreditation of Graduate Education" (Rpt. no. 4); J. Harris, "Critical Characteristics of an Accreditable Institution, Basic Purposes of Accreditation, and Nontraditional Forms of Most Concern" (Rpt. no. 5); K. Anderson, "Regional Accreditation Standards" (Rpt. no. 9).

⚜ Appendix ⚜

Constitution of the United States of America

Provisions of Particular Interest to Postsecondary Education

Article I

Section 1. All legislative Powers herein granted shall be vested in a Congress of the United States, which shall consist of a Senate and House of Representatives.

*   *   *

Section 7. All bills for raising Revenue shall originate in the House of Representatives; but the Senate may propose or concur with Amendments as on other Bills.

Every Bill which shall have passed the House of Representatives and the Senate, shall, before it becomes a Law, be presented to the President of the United States; If he approves he shall sign it, but if not he shall return it, with his Objections to that House in which it shall have originated, who shall enter the Objections at large on their Journal, and proceed to reconsider it. If after such Reconsideration two thirds of that House shall agree to pass the Bill, it shall be sent, together with the Objections, to the other House, by which it shall likewise be reconsidered, and if approved by two thirds of that House, it shall become a Law.

Section 8. The Congress shall have Power To lay and collect Taxes, Duties, Imposts and Excises, to pay the Debts and provide for the common Defence and general Welfare of the United States;

*   *   *

To regulate Commerce with foreign Nations, and among the several states, and with the Indian Tribes;

To establish a uniform Rule of Naturalization, and uniform Laws on the subject of Bankruptcies throughout the United States;

*   *   *

To promote the Progress of Science and useful Arts, by securing for limited Times to Authors and Inventors the exclusive Right to their respecive Writings and Discoveries;

*   *   *

To provide for calling forth the Militia to execute the Laws of the Union, suppress Insurrections and repel Invasions;

To provide for organizing, arming, and disciplining, the Militia, and for governing such Part of them as may be employed in the Service of the United States, reserving to the States respectively, the Appointment of the Officers, and the Authority of training the Militia according to the discipline prescribed by Congress;

*   *   *

To make all Laws which shall be necessary and proper for carrying into Execution the foregoing Powers, and all other Powers vested by this Constitution in the Government of the United States, or in any Department or Officer thereof.

*   *   *

Section 10. No State shall . . . pass any Bill of Attainder, ex post facto Law, or Law impairing the Obligation of Contracts.

*   *   *

Article II

Section 1. The executive Power shall be vested in a President of the United States of America.

*   *   *

Section 3. He shall from time to time give to the Congress Information of the State of the Union, and recommend to their Consideration such Measures as he shall judge necessary and expedient; . . . he shall take Care that the Laws be faithfully executed.

Article III

Section 1. The judicial Power of the United States, shall be vested in one supreme Court, and in such inferior Courts as the Congress may from time to time ordain and establish.

Section 2. The judicial Power shall extend to all Cases, in Law and Equity, arising under this Constitution, the Laws of the United States, and Treaties made, or which shall be made, under their Authority; . . . —to Controversies to which the United States shall be a party;—to Controversies between two or more States;—between a State and Citizens of another State;—between Citizens of different States,— . . . and between a State, or the Citizens thereof, and foreign States, Citizens or Subjects.

*   *   *

Article IV

*   *   *

Section 2. The Citizens of each State shall be entitled to all Privileges and Immunities of Citizens in the several States.

*   *   *

Article VI

*   *   *

This Constitution, and the laws of the United States which shall be made in Pursuance thereof; and all Treaties made, or which shall be made, under the Authority of the United States, shall be the supreme Law of the Land; and the Judges in every State shall be bound thereby, any Thing in the Constitution or Laws of any State to the Contrary notwithstanding.

*   *   *

Amendment I

Congress shall make no law respecting an etablishment of religion, or prohibiting the free exercise thereof; or abridging the freedom of speech, or of the press; or the right of the people peaceably to assemble, and to petition the Government for a redress of grievances.

*   *   *

Amendment IV

The right of the people to be secure in their persons, houses, papers, and effects, against unreasonable searches and seizures, shall not be violated, and no warrants shall issue, but upon probable cause, supported by oath or affirmation, and particularly describing the place to be searched, and the persons or things to be seized.

Amendment V

No person shall be held to answer for a capital, or otherwise infamous crime, unless on a presentment or indictment of a Grand Jury . . . ; nor shall any person be subject for the same offence to be twice put in jeopardy of life or limb; nor shall be compelled in any criminal case to be a witness against himself, nor be deprived of life, liberty, or property, without due process of law; nor shall private property be taken for public use, without just compensation.

Amendment VI

In all criminal prosecutions, the accused shall enjoy the right to a speedy and public trial, by an impartial jury of the State and district wherein the crime shall have been committed, which district shall have been previously ascertained by law, and to be informed of the nature and cause of the accusation; to be confronted with the witnesses against him; to have compulsory process for obtaining witnesses in his favor, and to have the assistance of counsel for his defence.

*   *   *

Amendment X

The powers not delegated to the United States by the Constitution, nor prohibited by it to the States, are reserved to the States respectively, or to the people.

Amendment XI

The Judicial Power of the United States shall not be construed to extend to any suit in law or equity, commenced or prosecuted against one of the United

States by Citizens of another State, or by Citizens or Subjects of any Foreign State.

*   *   *

Amendment XIII

Section 1. Neither slavery nor involuntary servitude, except as a punishment for crime whereof the party shall have been duly convicted, shall exist within the United States, or any place subject to their jurisdiction.

Section 2. Congress shall have power to enforce this article by appropriate legislation.

Amendment XIV

Section 1. All persons born or naturalized in the United States, and subject to the jurisdiction thereof, are citizens of the United States and of the State wherein they reside. No State shall make or enforce any law which shall abridge the privileges or immunities of citizens of the United States; nor shall any State deprive any person of life, liberty, or property, without due process of law; nor deny to any person within its jurisdiction the equal protection of the laws.

*   *   *

Section 5. The Congress shall have power to enforce, by appropriate legislation, the provisions of this article.

*   *   *

Amendment XXVI

Section 1. The right of citizens of the United States, who are eighteen years of age or older, to vote shall not be denied or abridged by the United States or by any State on account of age.

Section 2. The Congress shall have power to enforce this article by appropriate legislation.

Amendment XXVII (Proposed)

Section 1. Equality of rights under the law shall not be denied or abridged by the United States or by any State on account of sex.

Section 2. The Congress shall have the power to enforce, by appropriate legislation, the provisions of this article.

Section 3. This amendment shall take effect two years after the date of ratification.

Case Index

A

Abate v. *Mundt,* and reapportionment, 413

Abington School District v. *Schempp,* and religion, 27

Abood v. *Detroit Board of Education,* and mandatory fees, 325*n*

Adair v. *United States,* and employment at will, 442

Adamian v. *Jacobson,* and tenure termination for cause, 165–166

Adams litigation, and civil rights compliance, 519–520, 542–544

Adams v. *Bell,* and Title VI compliance, xii, 519, 544

Adams v. *Califano,* and Title VI compliance, 519

Adams v. *Richardson:*
and administrative enforcement, 542–544;
and admissions, 377;
and affirmative action, 159, 160;
and Title VI compliance, 519

Addison-Wesley Publishing Co. v. *New York University,* and copyright, 495

Adler v. *Board of Education,* and academic freedom, 183–184

Aiken v. *Lieuallen,* and athletics, 382

Alabama case. *See Dixon* v. *Alabama State Board of Education* . . .

Alabama State Teachers Association v. *Alabama Public School and College Authority,* and admissions discrimination by race, 232- 233

Albach v. *Odle,* and athletics, 350

Albemarle Paper Co. v. *Moody:*
and affirmative action, 151, 156;
and age discrimination, 143;
and Title VII discrimination, 121, 129

Albert Merrill School v. *Godoy,* and contractual rights of students, 228

Alessi v. *Raybestos-Manhattan,* and retirement income, 478

Alexander v. *Choate,* and coverage of unintentional discrimination, 534–535

Alexander v. *Gardner-Denver Co.,* and collective bargaining and antidiscrimination laws, 119

Alexander v. *Yale University,* and grades, credits, and degrees, 301

Alford v. *Emory University,* and property taxes, 402

Allaire v. *Rogers,* and academic freedom, 194–195

Allen case. *See Dow Chemical* v. *Allen*

Allen v. *Regents of the University System of Georgia,* and taxing power, 471

Almodovar case. *See Jimenez* v. *Almodovar*

Ambach v. *Norwick,* and alienage discrimination, 150–151

American Association of University Professors v. *Bloomfield College,* and staff reduction, 201–203, 206, 208, 216

American Can Co., and recognition, 104

American Future Systems v. *Pennsylvania State University:*
case I, 431–434;
case II, 434–436;
case III, 436*n*;
and commercial solicitation, xi, 431–436

American Medical Association v. *FTC,* and nonprofit entities, 502

American Society of Mechanical Engineers v. *Hydrolevel Corp.:*
and accreditation, 569–570;
and antitrust laws, 500

Amherst College v. *Assessors,* and property taxes, 400

Andrews v. *Knowlton,* and judicial systems, 364

Subject Index

A

Academic Collective Bargaining Information Service, 101, 115

Academic custom and usage:
and contract scope and terms, 92–93;
as source of law, 15–16

Academic freedom:
administrative authority over, 192–195;
analysis of legal issues related to, 180–199, 222–223;
in classroom, 186–187;
and confidential information, 195–199;
general principles of, 180–186;
institutional, 429;
in institutional affairs, 187–190;
and liberty or property interest, 192;
and overbreadth and vagueness, 192;
in private life, 190–192

Academic sanctions, in public institutions, 307–312

Accreditation:
analysis of legal issues related to, 561–580;

and antitrust law, 569–570;
bibliography on, 578–580;
and common law requirements, 568–569;
and courts, 563–573, 579;
dealing with, 576–578, 580;
and defamation law, 570–573;
and federal government, 573–576, 579;
institutional and program types of, 561–562;
reliance on, 562;
and state action doctrine, 569;
system of, 561–563, 578

Ad Hoc Committee on Trustee Liability Insurance, 90

Adams, J. F., 84*n*, 85, 86, 89

Adler, A., 552

Administrative adjudications, as source of law, 12

Administrative Procedure Act, 452, 516*n*, 550, 558

Administrative Procedure Act (New York), 302

Administrative procedure laws, and state regulation, 463

Administrative rules and regulations, as source of law, 11–12

Administrators:

analysis of legal issues related to, 40–90;
authority of, 40–44, 50–53, 87–88;
authority over academic freedom by, 192–195;
casebook for, 34;
and employment discrimination laws, 478–479;
and institutional liability, 55–74, 89–90;
and personal liability, 74–84, 90;
sources of authority for, 50–53

Admissions:
to administratively separate unit, 238;
and affirmative action, 252–270;
analysis of legal issues related to, 229–272; 376–377;
and arbitrariness, 229–231;
basic legal requirements for, 229;
constraints on, 229;
and contract theory, 231–232;
nondiscrimination by age in, 250–252;
nondiscrimination by race in, 232–238;
nondiscrimination by sex in, 238–242;

599